15399

W9-ARE-239

THE NEW
CAMBRIDGE MODERN HISTORY

ADVISORY COMMITTEE

G.N.CLARK   J.R.M.BUTLER   J.P.T.BURY

THE LATE E.A.BENIANS

VOLUME II

THE REFORMATION
1520-1559

THE NEW
CAMBRIDGE MODERN
HISTORY

VOLUME II

THE REFORMATION
1520-1559

EDITED BY

G. R. ELTON

CAMBRIDGE
AT THE UNIVERSITY PRESS
1968

Published by the Syndics of the Cambridge University Press
Bentley House, 200 Euston Road, London, N.W. 1
American Branch: 32 East 57th Street, New York, N.Y. 10022

© Cambridge University Press 1958

Standard Book Number: 521 04542 8

First Edition 1958
Reprinted 1962 1965 1968

Printed in Great Britain
at the University Printing House, Cambridge
(Brooke Crutchley, University Printer)

CONTENTS

CONTENTS

CHAPTER III

LUTHER AND THE GERMAN REFORMATION TO 1529

By E. G. RUPP, *Professor of Ecclesiastical History in the University of Manchester*

CHAPTER IV

THE SWISS REFORMERS AND THE SECTS

1. The Reformation in Zürich, Strassburg and Geneva, by E. G. RUPP

2. The Anabaptists, by ERNEST A. PAYNE, *General Secretary of the Baptist Union of Great Britain and Ireland*

I. THE REFORMATION IN ZÜRICH, STRASSBURG AND GENEVA

CONTENTS

CONTENTS

(3) Iceland

(4) Sweden

(5) Finland

(6) The Baltic

CHAPTER VI

THE REFORMATION IN DIFFICULTIES

1. The German Reformation to 1555, by ERNST BIZER, *Professor of Theology in the University of Bonn*

2. Poland, Bohemia and Hungary, by R. R. BETTS, *Masaryk Professor of Central European History in the University of London*

3. France, 1519–59, by F. C. SPOONER, *lately Fellow of Christ's College, Cambridge*

I. THE GERMAN REFORMATION TO 1555

CONTENTS

CONTENTS

CHAPTER VII
THE REFORMATION IN ENGLAND
By G. R. ELTON

CHAPTER VIII
ITALY AND THE PAPACY
By DELIO CANTIMORI, *Professor of History in the University of Florence*

CONTENTS

CHAPTER IX

THE NEW ORDERS

By H. O. EVENNETT, *Fellow of Trinity College and University Lecturer in History
in the University of Cambridge*

CHAPTER X

THE EMPIRE OF CHARLES V IN EUROPE

By H. KOENIGSBERGER, *Senior Lecturer in Economic History in the
University of Manchester*

CONTENTS

CHAPTER XI

THE HABSBURG-VALOIS STRUGGLE

By F. C. Spooner

CHAPTER XII

INTELLECTUAL TENDENCIES

1. Literature: the Printed Book, by Denys Hay, *Professor of Medieval History
in the University of Edinburgh*

2. Science, by A. R. Hall, *Fellow of Christ's College and University Lecturer
in the History of Science in the University of Cambridge*

I. LITERATURE: THE PRINTED BOOK

CONTENTS

CHAPTER XIII

SCHOOLS AND UNIVERSITIES
By DENYS HAY

CONTENTS

CHAPTER XIV

CONSTITUTIONAL DEVELOPMENT AND POLITICAL THOUGHT IN WESTERN EUROPE

By G. R. ELTON

CHAPTER XV

CONSTITUTIONAL DEVELOPMENT AND POLITICAL THOUGHT IN EASTERN EUROPE

By R. R. BETTS

CHAPTER XVI

ARMIES, NAVIES, AND THE ART OF WAR

By J. R. HALE, *Fellow and Tutor in Modern History, Jesus College, Oxford*

CONTENTS

CHAPTER XVII

THE OTTOMAN EMPIRE, 1520-66

By V. J. PARRY, *Lecturer in the History of the Near and Middle East,
University of London*

CHAPTER XVIII

RUSSIA, 1462-1583

By J. L. I. FENNELL, *Lecturer in Russian in the University of Oxford*

CONTENTS

CHAPTER XIX
THE NEW WORLD, 1521–1580
By J. H. PARRY, *Principal of the University College of Ibadan, Nigeria*

CHAPTER XX
EUROPE AND THE EAST
By the late I. A. MACGREGOR, *Senior Lecturer in History in the University College of Achimota, Ghana*

CHAPTER I

INTRODUCTION:
THE AGE OF THE REFORMATION

HE concept of the Reformation as a significant and self-contained period, with characteristics and central events and even perhaps a particular ethos of its own, has had a long life as such historical categories go. Even those who disagree with the traditional interpretation of the early sixteenth century have commonly concentrated their attack on the notion that it marks the beginning of modern times. Some historians of thought trace the Middle Ages right through the sixteenth century and see nothing novel in yet another controversy within the Church; they would put their marker at a point where predominantly religious thinking is replaced by secular (scientific) attitudes of mind. Authors of such re-appraisals do not deny the special character of the years 1520–60 looked at by themselves, but others—partisans of either Catholicism or Protestantism—are willing to do even that. If one is prepared to treat the Reformation as a temporary aberration (a chapter which even after 400 years might still be closed) or as a mere return to the true way—analyses which, though historically invalid, may be denomina tionally necessary—one will rob the period of much of its cohesion by doubting its spiritual and intellectual content. It is also possible to argue that the Counter-Reformation and the religious wars which extended into the next century are properly part of the same story. But historians, so ready as a rule to revise the periods into which for convenience sake they divide the subject-matter of their study, have on the whole allowed the 'age of the Reformation' to survive. It must be the purpose of this chapter to discover how far this acquiescence in an established convention is justified. What is it that gives coherence and meaning to those forty years?

In the first place, the age marked the break-up of western Christendom. The point, which might appear obvious, must be stressed because reason-able doubt has been cast on the once unquestioned uniqueness of the Reformation. It is plain enough that, long before the Lutheran attack demonstrated its unreality, the so-called community of the Latin Church would not have borne investigation. Diversity, sometimes reaching the extreme of heresy, was endemic in the medieval Church, and from the later years of Boniface VIII (d. 1303) onwards the Papacy had been pro-gressively less able to assert a unifying control. The previous volume described the trends of the later fifteenth century towards national Churches and papal weakness, towards the secularisation of Church lands and the ascendancy of temporal rulers.[1] These are the features which, with the addition of the religious and spiritual upheaval associated with Luther, Zwingli and Calvin, make the Reformation; and it is then to be noted that movements like those of Wycliffe and Hus came near to supplying that missing ingredient, while the inclination of the fifteenth century to mystical practices and beliefs anticipated to some degree the denial of universal authority. It is therefore sometimes held that there was nothing novel about the Reformation, nor anything definitive, and that its importance has been overrated.

Now there is truth in these arguments, and they deserve particular attention as against the view, still sometimes encountered, that down to the early sixteenth century a genuine Christian community stood embodied in a united Church under the hegemony of Rome. But the revision would go too far if it supposed that the discovery of trends towards the Reformation robbed this event of its surpassing importance. The addition of the religious controversy—so fundamental and so widely supported—changed the whole character of the ancient troubles. Secularisation, princely ascendancy over the Church, religious diversity, may all have been present before 1517; but thereafter they became effective, general and predominant. The character of European politics, thought, society and religion was made over by that great outburst against the powers of the papal monarchy and the claims of the priesthood, an outburst which should not be regarded as any less revolutionary because it happened to be directed against enfeebled enemies and productive of results neither envisaged nor welcomed by the leaders of the spiritual revolution. All that will hereafter be said in this volume will testify to the overwhelming impact of the Reformation. Uniqueness is properly its hallmark, just because it shared so many features with earlier troubles in the Church and yet produced so different an outcome. Despite earlier movements with similar aims and inspirations, only the Protestant Reformation resulted in a lasting division within the Church that had looked to Rome.

The 'age of the Reformation' should be defined as that period during which the new Churches were on the offensive. It therefore begins properly (and traditionally) with the date of Luther's ninety-five theses (1517) and extends in general to the later 1550's. The third session of the Council of Trent, which began in 1559, terminated the Papacy's retreat; henceforth the Church of Rome was on the attack. Not that the Counter-Reformation had waited for this moment; as the history of the attempt to call a general council for the restoration of unity made plain, the attacker from the first provoked a resistance which grew gradually more confident and vigorous (pp. 170ff.). Resistance was helped by the continued loyalty to the old religion of Europe's premier prince, the Emperor Charles V.

[1] Vol. I, pp. 10ff.

The movement against the new Churches gained experience and some success in preliminary suppressions, especially in Italy and Spain; the latter was to provide not only secular leadership but also the ecclesiastical influence and example of an experienced persecuting Church with a well-trained body of inquisitors. The rise of new orders proved that the old Church was very far from dead (ch. IX). A dress-rehearsal for the counter-attack was staged in the England of Mary Tudor. But despite all this, despite the defeat of the German Protestant princes in 1547, the real dynamic of the age lay with the Reformation. Its German phase ended in 1555 with the Peace of Augsburg; its first English phase with the Elizabethan restoration of Protestantism in 1559. The Scandinavian kings who had established the Lutheran faith died in 1559 (Christian III of Denmark) and 1560 (Gustavus I of Sweden). In France the death of Henry II (1559) marked a period too, but its effect ran oddly counter to general experience: the suppression of Protestantism was well under way until the chaos in government after 1560 gave its chance to militant and military Huguenot power. But if the Counter-Reformation met great difficulties in France, it was none the less a great deal more self-conscious and energetic under the Guises than under Henry II. The older historians had the right of it: the period of some forty years which this volume covers can justly be defined as the age of the Reformation.

In those forty years the Reformation achieved an extraordinary spread, both rapid and wide. No part of western Christendom remained altogether unaffected by it, even though Spain, and Italy to a smaller degree, managed a measure of aloofness. Elsewhere Protestantism in one of its forms grew overnight from the fervour of a few preachers into a wide and popular movement. What gave it so general an appeal remains up to a point uncertain; no one would today be willing to list 'the causes' of the Reformation. So complex a phenomenon sprang from so many things that only a general analysis of some hundred years of history comes near to answering the question. There existed a widespread dislike of the clergy, which played its part; often it went with hostility to Rome and with fervent nationalism. Greed and envy no doubt entered into it, as did policy. But that the reformers' message answered a savage spiritual thirst, which the official Church (not for the first time in its history) was failing to satisfy, cannot be denied; nor can the fact that the stages reached by the Reformation itself did not always content all those who had looked to it for nourishment, so that extremist groups soon began to develop by the side of the more acceptable revolutionaries. The preachers of the Reformation did not need political support to attract followers wherever they went, however necessary such support may have proved in the consolidation which followed the first prophetic onrush. It must never be forgotten that in its beginning and in much of its essence the Reformation was a movement of the spirit with a religious message.

On the other hand—and this should be stressed—the Reformation was not a movement for liberty, except in a very specialised sense. Protestantism in all its forms came to reject one particular authority—that of the Church and the popes—but nearly all its forms substituted some other authority and avoided the thoroughgoing individualism which has at times been associated with the movement. The Bible formed the overriding authority, its interpretation carried out by attention to the text itself without the intervention of the mediating Church. The results were naturally very mixed, ranging from a genuine recovery of the Christian message to all the absurdities associated with a rigorous and uncomprehending fundamentalism. In politics, the leading reformers tended to support the secular arm; though Luther was not the subservient tool of princes and enemy of the people that he is sometimes made out to be (with quotations from his writings against the peasants), he, like most Protestants, had a healthy respect for the magistrate provided he was godly. Perhaps the last liberty to be promoted by the Reformation in the sixteenth century was that of the mind. Movements of missionary passion are not given to tolerance and scepticism, nor do they provoke such reactions in those they attack; among the first victims of this new age of religious controversy were the spirit of free enquiry and the patience extended to the nonconformist. Luther could be highly obscurantist at the expense of intellectuals of Erasmus's type; the fate of the so-called Catholic reformers of Italy (ch. VIII) shows how under the pressure of the great heresies toleration of reasonable diversity changed into fierce hostility; Thomas More developed from the speculative humanist of *Utopia* (1516) into the persecuting lord chancellor of 1530.

The age was passionate, partisan, and narrow. In trying to assess its achievements fairly it does not help that the passions of a time of conflict tend to baffle understanding when the content of the conflict has gone. It is sometimes argued that the twentieth century, familiar with ideological struggles and persecution, should—and does—comprehend the sixteenth century from a fullness of knowledge. It is, however, fatal to overlook the differences between secular ideologies and transcendental religion, concentrating only on their likenesses; the result (seen too often) is to read the twentieth century into the sixteenth. In some ways the Reformation is more remote from the present day than the century or so that had preceded it. The fundamental intellectual attitude of the Reformation involved the doctrine of a decline from an ideal in the past and a devoted attachment to theology and ecclesiology at the expense of other studies; neither of these is a characteristic element in western thought after 1700. Admittedly it will be well to remember that besides the stream directly issuing from the Reformation there flowed a sizeable river of writings concerned with secular things and increasingly 'scientific' in its methods of analysis and interpretation. As one might expect, there are both traces of established modes of thinking and faint hints of great changes to come. Substantially, however, the Reformation was conservative—even backward-looking—in thought: since it was avowedly intent on restoring a lost condition, it could hardly be anything else.

The desire for spiritual nourishment was great in many parts of Europe, and movements of thought which gave intellectual content to what in so many ways was an inchoate search for God have their own dignity. Neither of these, however, comes first in explaining why the Reformation took root here and vanished there—why, in fact, this complex of anti-papal 'heresies' led to a permanent division within the Church that had looked to Rome. This particular place is occupied by politics and the play of secular ambitions. In short, the Reformation maintained itself wherever the lay power (prince or magistrates) favoured it; it could not survive where the authorities decided to suppress it. Scandinavia, the German principalities, Geneva, in its own peculiar way also England, demonstrate the first; Spain, Italy, the Habsburg lands in the east, and also (though not as yet conclusively) France, the second. The famous phrase behind the settlement of 1555—*cuius regio eius religio*—was a practical commonplace long before anyone put it into words. For this was the age of uniformity, an age which held at all times and everywhere that one political unit could not comprehend within itself two forms of belief or worship.

The tenet rested on simple fact: as long as membership of a secular polity involved membership of an ecclesiastical organisation, religious dissent stood equal to political disaffection and even treason. Hence governments enforced uniformity, and hence the religion of the ruler was that of his country. England provided the extreme example of this doctrine in action, with its rapid official switches from Henrician Catholicism without the pope, through Edwardian Protestantism on the Swiss model and Marian papalism, to Elizabethan Protestantism of a more specifically English brand. But other countries fared similarly. Nor need this cause distress or annoyed disbelief. Princes and governments, no more than the governed, do not act from unmixed motives, and to ignore the spiritual factor in the conversion of at least some princes is as false as to see nothing but purity in the desires of the populace. The Reformation was successful beyond the dreams of earlier, potentially similar, movements not so much because (as the phrase goes) the time was ripe for it, but rather because it found favour with the secular arm. Desire for Church lands, resistance to imperial and papal claims, the ambition to create self-contained and independent states, all played their part in this, but so quite often did a genuine attachment to the teachings of the reformers.

There was, however, one aspect of the Reformation which owed nothing to princes and little to the great reformers, a truly popular and very widespread movement to which it became customary to attach the name of Anabaptism (ch. IV, 2). The so-called Anabaptists turn up in many places and guises, a convenient term covering a motley collection of beliefs and behaviour which range from mad millenarianism to pietism, from the reckless use of force to pacifism, from the extremes of personal egotism to humble piety and devotion. All these men and women have one thing in common: they do not fit in with any of the established religions and thus offend the principle of uniformity wherever they go. But the persecution which they so regularly encountered arose from yet another shared quality: the movement spread among the lower orders. It contained strong elements of social protest and (or so it was thought) danger of revolution. The terror of Münster (pp. 128f.) remained a standing warning to governments, as did the *Bundschuh* uprising of the German peasants in 1524–5 in which wild religion joined with economic grievance. We shall not go far wrong if we see in the protean spread of Anabaptist and similar doctrines a sign of an age-old, usually obscure, social antagonism to the powers that be, an antagonism to which the Reformation, by producing an upheaval in the higher reaches of the social order, gave a chance of coming into the open. The fact that Anabaptism drew its following from the unprivileged is significant enough.

One can understand the authorities' reaction. This was an age of inflation and social unrest, expressing itself in riots and risings everywhere—especially in Germany in the 1520's and in England between 1536 and 1558. Even those who accepted the Reformation did not as a rule wish to promote social revolution; there was nothing democratic about the leaders of reform, nor would it have been particularly sensible if there had been. Anabaptism suffered terrible things, but it would be to misunderstand the movement if one were to deny that even among its moderate exponents its social implications were revolutionary. The repression which it provoked did not score anything like a complete success; not only did Anabaptist communities and their descendants survive in places, but the unrest which they represented came out later in other ways. The movement gives a glimpse beneath the usual surface of recorded history; if the manifestations were relatively few and scattered, the underlying body of hatreds and dissatisfactions may reasonably be guessed at as enormous. The repressive governments knew what they were fighting.

The complex of movements which we call the Reformation provides one unifying factor in the period under review; another, equally obvious, appears in the reign of Charles V. The emperor ascended the throne of Spain a year before Luther's first public appearance as a danger to the papal government of the Church; he abdicated his many dominions shortly after the Peace of Augsburg. His empire (ch. x) was the last attempt at something like universal secular rule in the medieval manner; for, 'modern' as many parts of his territories were in their organisation and attitude, Charles himself looked upon his position in something of the spirit of Charlemagne—a Charlemagne whose stature is less manifestly heroic and whose dynastic preoccupations stand out rather more clearly. But the comparison is not totally absurd, for the virtue and ability of this greatest of the Habsburgs are becoming increasingly evident; nor is it unhistorical, because it describes a real element in Charles's own thinking. If Germany and the imperial title defeated him, it is also worth notice that he preserved the ostensible existence of that massive anachronism at a critical time. If he was out of date in regarding himself as the champion of the Church, it must yet be conceded that his championship (readily reconciled with a high-handed attitude to popes as such) prevented the total lapse of central Europe to Protestantism and in Spain and elsewhere prepared for the revival of Roman Catholicism. Charles's reign was by no means all failure. He failed in his chief ambitions because they were extravagant: there was no prospect of making a reality out of those shadows of power and purpose which clung to the title of Holy Roman Emperor. But he gave some coherence to his vast conglomerate of lands and peoples; he assisted the economic heyday of his Burgundian homeland; he saved the Papacy; and if he was the last of the medieval emperors, he was also the first king of Spain's golden age.

As is well enough known, Charles's larger plans for the unity of Christendom were wrecked by the existence and growing strength of the secular national state and its counterpart in the German principalities. The consolidation of the territorial states of western Europe, described in the previous volume,[1] continued energetically in this period (ch. xiv). Indeed, at first sight the phenomenon appears to be universal in Europe. One finds it spreading to Scandinavia, where the Reformation provided Danish and Swedish kings with the means of establishing strong rule (ch. v); even in Russia, Ivan III and Ivan IV seem almost to duplicate the work of England's Henry VII and Henry VIII, of France's Louis XI and Francis I (ch. xviii). The real meaning of these trends is, however, less easily assessed. In the western kingdoms monarchy might look supreme, but it was very far from absolute. Even in France, where autocracy was most nearly achieved, both theory and practice preserved strong traces of the internal diversity of the past and limited kings by the maintenance of 'customary' rights; the destruction of 'liberties' which could always become dangerous to centralised monarchy had barely begun. The rise of Calvinism in the next generation released ancient disruptive forces of an essentially local and anti-monarchical hue. But at least kings of France could tax and legislate at will; no such powers belonged to those of Spain and England. Spain was as yet an alliance of kingdoms with differing

[1] For a summary, cf. vol. I, pp. 5 ff.

constitutions, and although Castile, progressively subjected to more stringent monarchical control, grew more and more dominant, the time of genuine autocratic reorganisation came only with Philip II. England, because of her anciently strong monarchy and by the accident of Henry VIII's quarrel with Rome, provided the tidiest example of a modernised and consolidated monarchy; but England also deliberately rejected autocracy and by making the monarchy rest on the sovereignty of the king in Parliament preserved and adapted inherited constitutionalism in a new era. Scotland had to wait for Knox before drawing a line under its messy medieval politics. In truth, these western monarchies were less autocratic and self-consciously innovatory than is commonly supposed. By comparison with the despotisms of the east, of which Turkey provided an example which western statesmen sometimes regarded with envy, their kings lacked power, and they were as yet a long way from the absolutism of the seventeenth century. Everywhere there survived remnants of past separatism and constitutional rights, asserting themselves at intervals; but only in England, where the Crown achieved a mutually advantageous alliance with the representative institution of Parliament, was autocracy rejected in principle and the way prepared for a formally limited monarchy.

If the consolidation of territorial monarchy even in the west was less complete than appearances suggest, the position farther east is more uncertain still. The fringe of containing kingdoms on Germany's eastern border—Poland, Bohemia, Hungary—was by the early sixteenth century in the hands of one dynasty, the Polish Jagiellons. Constitutionally they were characterised at this time by the weakness of the monarchy, the ascendancy of the nobility which dominated the diets, and the absence of any effective urban or middle-class element. In the period under review the situation changed in some respects (ch. xv). By 1560 Bohemia and such parts of Hungary as were not Turkish had fallen to the Habsburgs, and whatever else may be true of that family it knew how to look after its own. The double impact of the Reformation and the Turks assisted King Ferdinand I in his shrewd and steady, if cautious, policy of consolidation. He established an alliance with the Catholic Church for which there was little precedent in the history of those countries, while the needs of war helped the Crown as the source of military strength. Ferdinand hoped to create a single political unit out of his territories, and it is very interesting to note that he recognised how useful parliamentary institutions could be to a centralising monarchy. But his project of a single diet for the two kingdoms came to nothing, in part because he lacked the material from which to construct a lower house and in part because the particularist traditions of the nobility were too strong: the Bohemian aristocracy tended to be heretical as well. While his advance towards monarchical authority was therefore slow and limited, it is also true that he gave to

Bohemia and Hungary the beginnings of a strong government whose lack was to be so evident in the deplorable history of Poland during the next 200 years.

However, in the eastern kingdoms the increase of monarchy, though it may be traced, did not occupy pride of place. Not only was the west very much more advanced in economic maturity, bureaucratic organisation, settled government and cultural achievement; at a time when the west was improving all these things they tended to get worse in the east. As serfdom and territorial feudalism were vanishing in the west, the great plains of the east—and this includes Germany east of the Elbe—witnessed the gradual destruction of a free peasantry and the creation of vast estates—*latifundia*—with quasi-independent jurisdiction and powers (pp. 35 f.). The growth of this notorious system of *Gutsherrschaft* went a long way to balance the apparent increase in monarchical power, even in Bohemia and Hungary where kings mattered more than in Poland or Lithuania. Prussian autocracy was ultimately to establish itself by destroying the political power of this landed nobility, but especially in the lands of the Habsburg monarchy traces of the great social upheaval of the sixteenth century could be seen as late as 1918. The reasons for a development so contrary to what was happening in the west were partly economic: the opening of the eastern grain-lands brought vast profits to a class of landed lords with great estates and a safe supply of cheap labour. Partly, however, the cause must be looked for in the fact that these territories had once again become marches against an alien foe. The pressure from the Turks, to which that of Russia was later added, drew a frontier down the eastern edge of this eastern fringe which was to last for centuries. The frontier produced its obligatory phenomenon of territorially based marcher lords. Distance from the centre, the needs of defence, the enforcement of serfdom and pride of blood quickly established the semi-independence of these very wealthy men. The wonder is that monarchy maintained itself at all even in the Habsburg territories. It did so by military conquest in Bohemia (1618–20) and by alliance with the nobility in Hungary; these facts gave it a special character, but it was nevertheless self-consciously and bureaucratically monarchical.

In theory, at least, Germany should have been another territorial unit working its way towards a proper consolidation and efficient statehood (pp. 477 ff.). But the German monarchy had for long been so weak that it would have had to start from scratch, a task with which none of its contemporaries were confronted. The weakness resulted in great part from the imperial dignity regularly associated with German kingship, in part from its elective nature, in part from the personal inadequacies of past holders, but mostly from the centrifugal ambitions and policies of the German princes. Charles V tried hard to overcome all these difficulties, but in fact he succeeded only in keeping alive the imperial title and pretence. When he abdicated, the German kingdom had ceased to exist, even though the titles of king and emperor survived as shadows of what had been. The history of Germany from his day to that of Napoleon, or even Bismarck, is that of independent states vaguely held together by a common language and a common past, but rarely by common policy. The 1648 Treaty of Westphalia merely confirmed what Charles V's reign had already decided. The German principalities themselves fitted the general pattern of the age well enough, providing centralised consolidation on the basis of monarchical government and increased bureaucracy. As Italy—that other country to suffer the consequences of the medieval Empire—had gone in the previous 200 years, so Germany went now. Both became, in the famous phrase, geographical expressions. And as the component parts of Italy had produced strong rulers at the heads of reformed political structures, so the German princes tightened their hold on their lands. In Italy itself, this period saw the end of independence for even the particularist rulers and the decline of France; the peninsula became in effect a collection of Spanish satrapies. Venice stood out, but her day was over; Genoa prospered, but accepted Spain. The Papacy came to acknowledge that Borgia, della Rovere, and Medici ambitions to turn the dominions of St Peter into a powerful political unit had failed, and returned to its more appropriate tasks within the Church. However, for the time at least, it could not in consequence escape Spain's dominance.

If princely independence in Germany was one obstacle which made nonsense of Charles V's imperial dreams, the international situation provided another in the prolonged struggle between Habsburg and Valois (ch. XI). This dynastic and national conflict tended to involve most of Europe. Its battlegrounds were first Italy and then the lower Rhine—the two cultural centres of the later Middle Ages—which in consequence yielded pride of place to more favoured regions. England played a part of sorts which in the 1520's looked important because Wolsey's jugglery created the illusion of an independent choice between the combatants. In reality English policy could never get free of the strong trade-links between London and Antwerp which, together with the ancient hostility to France, kept the country essentially imperial (or rather, Spanish) in its sympathies, even after the divorce and the break with Rome had turned Charles V into an enemy. France, on her knees by 1528, restored the balance by allying not only with the Protestants of Germany but also with the Turk. It is easy to mock at these friendships of the Most Christian king, less easy to see how he could otherwise have held off the power of Charles V. Nevertheless, the consequences of these unscrupulous doings were serious. Not only did they materially assist the survival of German Protestantism and the Turkish domination of the Mediterranean (which in turn completed the decline of Italy), but they provoked important questions concerning the principles of international relations and law.

As was pointed out in the previous volume, the essence of international relations lay at this time in the relations of individuals and dynasties.[1] Marriages and blood-relationships determined the alignments of states and nations. Charles V's empire was in itself the greatest triumph ever scored by that principle. But while wars thus assumed something of the virulence of family quarrels, they also took place against the background of family unity—the unity of a far-flung and insecure family still vaguely aware of its common heritage. That heritage was the old notion of united Christendom doing battle with the infidel behind its two leaders, pope and emperor. The notion had never had any practical reality, and even as a pretty theory it had long been put among the lumber of half-conscious memories. It was the irony of this age that it should have seen even the memory destroyed at the very moment when once again an emperor showed signs of taking it seriously. Charles V did believe in his imperial mission. The fight with Protestantism was to him more than a struggle for dynastic ascendancy against disruption; it was a battle for the unity of Catholic Europe. The unity had long ceased to exist—if ever it had existed—and the centre of Charles's physical power, Spain, was the Catholic country least inclined to grant anything to the Papacy; but the emperor still envisaged his task in this grandiose, respectable and impossible light. Of all the many politicians who talked about the Turkish danger and vaguely appealed to Christendom to unite against it, he was the only one willing to translate words into action. Naturally, it may be said that he was also the only one likely to profit by such united action, but this is not altogether true—all Europe would have done well to push the Turk back into Asia—nor does it diminish the element of genuine idealism in Charles's attitude.

However, the days of his ascendancy saw the end of the dream. His imperial title and authority, so far from being an asset, proved an obstacle to the achievement of his more realistic ambitions. Instead of uniting Europe behind himself, he witnessed and in part caused the final disintegration of Germany and maintained a state of almost constant war among the powers. Worst of all, Francis I, by calling in the sultan to assist him, proved the utter emptiness of all that talk of crusades and Christendom. International politics had long (perhaps always) been at heart a matter of power and ambition; now their true character was revealed to the naked eye. But myths have a power to bind, and the myth of Christian unity had exercised a restraining influence which now vanished for good. The assertion of the national state, the rise of national armies, ended the legends of Christendom and chivalry. Wild and horrible as medieval conflicts often were, they took place against a background of

[1] Vol. I, pp. 9f.

common and accepted conventions. Heralds and envoys were protected, safe conducts respected, the rules (odd rules at times) of chivalry observed in the taking of towns and ransoming of prisoners. Of course, exceptions occurred, but traditional opinion was for instance sincerely shocked by the ruthlessness of the Swiss armies, their disregard for prisoners and wounded, their lack of respect for the chivalric conventions. By the middle of the sixteenth century those who observed the rules earned indulgent smiles or contempt: Don Quixote would not have been a figure of fun a hundred years earlier. The point is not whether all these rules and conventions were observed either always, or scrupulously, or from conviction; it is that there existed a set of commonly accepted ideas, vague in parts, on the relations between political communities in peace and war which during the sixteenth century finally lost its hold in European politics.

Its disappearance left a gap which had to be filled. The very fact that such totally and admittedly anachronistic practices as the delivery of defiances by heralds still continued shows that new conventions about the way to do these things were needed. Out of this need there ultimately grew an accepted body of international law, a law, that is, governing the relations between nations (or sovereign states).[1] The situation itself was new inasmuch as this law was to operate among sovereign and independent polities: it had and has no sanctions. Significantly, the practice of referring disputes to the arbitration of some recognised third party—a superior or an impartial authority—which had been common enough in the Middle Ages, declined now that dealings were between parties which recognised no superior and trusted to no one's impartiality. Direct negotiations or ultimately war were the only ways in which sovereign states could deal with each other. Both methods received attention and elaboration, in practice and in law.

In the history of diplomacy this is the period when the methods worked out on the small stage of Renaissance Italy were extended to at least the western and southern parts of Europe.[2] All the greater powers began to exchange resident ambassadors, and although special embassies continued to travel into foreign parts, foreign policy came to rely more and more on the regular contact of a resident representative with the statesmen of the monarch to whom he was accredited and on his equally regular despatches. To the familiar figures of Venetian, Milanese and Florentine 'orators' there were now added French, imperial and English

---

[1] Professor S. E. Thorne of Harvard University, who was to have written a chapter on International Law, had unhappily to cancel his contribution for reasons of ill health and on doctor's orders. A chapter from that hand would have been illumination indeed; the editor very much regrets the necessity which compels his prentice hand to obscure the subject instead.

[2] The subject is discussed and admirably summarised in G. Mattingly, *Renaissance Diplomacy* (1955).

ambassadors. Before the period was out, some of these men had done important work and given some lustre to what had begun as a subordinate and little-regarded office. The significance of the special embassy grew increasingly more formal, despite the often exalted standing of its leaders. The outlines of modern diplomatic organisation are clearly visible. The existence of residents raised problems of law, especially of immunity. Here the early sixteenth century did not advance very far. The sanctity of an ambassador's person was recognised in theory, though there was a feeling that it operated only in the country to which he was accredited. Little respect, however, was as yet accorded to the protection of a diplomatic bag: in 1529 Wolsey even searched the papers of his fellow cardinal Campeggio before allowing him to leave the country. Houses occupied by foreign embassies enjoyed a certain amount of freedom from interference, for reasons of prudence and mutual advantage rather than because anyone accepted a principle of extra-territoriality. The rights of an ambassador's suite caused a great deal of trouble because clashes between his servants and the natives were common enough; this issue was immensely complicated by the existence of residents. All these points received discussion and consideration: the problems inherent in the new practice were beginning to be recognised. Mutual necessity and common sense established some degree of established custom long before it came to be embodied in the formal rules of international law.

War was an older problem, and one which had always had the knack of escaping any rules or conventions imposed upon it. In this period it grew in a sense more 'serious', less the personal concern of professionals who knew the rules and more the political preoccupation of great powers. It may be that the Habsburg-Valois conflict of 1520–59 merely enlarged the scale of the Franco-Spanish wars in Italy between 1494 and 1516; but the enlargement was such that it profoundly affected the place of war in the life of society (ch. XVII). Growing expenses—*pecunia nervus belli* was one of the favourite tags of the day—were driving the lesser practitioners out of business; even Henry VIII, technically the head of a wealthy nation, found himself near bankruptcy when he engaged in war in the 1540's. As for that great potentate, the Emperor Charles V, he was always in financial difficulties, living off irredeemable loans and forced, in his extremity in 1552, to call piteously for help to Anton Fugger. There was much progress in military science, in equipment, in siege-craft and fortifications, in naval practice; but the most noticeable thing about warfare in this period was the readiness of princes to engage in it who could not, in the simplest sense, afford it. The most formidable army remained that of the Sultan, but even the great Sulaimān found that the technical resources of the age set a tight limit to wars of conquest (pp. 514f.).

Legal thought about war was at this time pretty well confined to the problem of the just war. No one seems to have paid much attention to such questions as the rights (if any) of prisoners, the duty of a commander to the countryside through which he passed, and the like. No one talked of humanising war. In part this was no doubt because the old rules concerning quarter or the surrender of a town still obtained at least lip-service, and in fact the wars of the period do not appear unduly marked by atrocities. Even the civilian population suffered little compared with what was to happen in the next century. The worst outrages, such as the sack of Rome in 1527, were always the work of mutineers, and the mutinies were always caused by lack of pay. A paid army—an unusual thing—was a contented army and apparently willing, within limits, to obey orders.

If the surviving body of medieval conventions explains the lack of interest shown in devising rules for conduct under arms—of regulations within armies, which are of course another matter, there were plenty—the attention lavished on the problem of just and unjust wars was also inherited from an earlier age. Oddly enough, it was not war in Europe which produced the most important treatise. The lectures, later published, which Francisco de Vitoria gave in the 1530's at the university of Salamanca were provoked by Spain's conquest of the Indies and the problem whether wars against heathens were invariably just or not. Vitoria applied common standards of justice to all wars, explicitly condemned much that had been done in America, and asserted that an unjust war—in essence one fought for purely selfish ends—should be resisted by the inhabitants of the guilty country and punished by the common action of (one supposes) Christendom. Of course, this was on the one hand an impracticable notion and on the other justified the many hypocritical leagues against one power or more in which the age abounded. More interesting in the context are Vitoria's striking high-mindedness and freedom from nationalist prejudice, as well as his knowledge of American conditions; more significant is the barrenness of the moral approach to international law. It had tradition and respectability, but it served no practical purpose. The real content of such rules as states observed in their dealings with each other will rather be found in the decisions of maritime and mercantile courts, in the treaties of the day, and in the dynastic arrangements often resembling purely private settlements of property which really determined the fates of nations. However, it appears that the work has not yet been done which would interpret the law embodied in these highly technical documents.

The years 1520–60 thus form an unusually well-defined period. The great revolution in religion and the Church, the rule of the last emperor who attempted to realise the universal claims of his title—these with their by-products in thought and learning, in constitutional changes and legal revision, in national and international affairs, give the period its unmistakable unity. But it may be said that the criteria so far used look markedly old-fashioned. Some leading opinion today no longer regards politics in Church and State as the historian's main concern. The prevalent passion of our day is for social history—the history, as it has been defined, of man in society—which in practice involves a concentration on economic, social and cultural factors. Changes in political and institutional structure are held to be less significant than the ways in which people earned their living, habitually thought, or adjusted themselves in the stratifications of society. These are indeed profound questions; one would not wish to doubt their relevance, even though one may wonder whether they really merit primacy in the study of the past. At any rate, they must be considered. Is there anything in the economic and social developments of those years which might be specifically ascribed to the 'age of the Reformation'? And further, does such knowledge as we possess of the thought and attitude of the age enable us to reconstruct and describe that elusive concept, its mental climate?

Economics and society undergo their changes, but only rarely do these happen so rapidly that any half-century can claim a specific position with relation to them. Time and again, what were regarded as characteristic developments of some age have turned out to be fully apparent at a much earlier period; few weapons of analysis have proved more destructive of traditional categories than research into the realities of society. Up to a point, this is also true of the Reformation period. If one takes a longer view, it becomes apparent that the 200 years after the middle of the fifteenth century witnessed, for instance, important changes in agrarian practice and society: in the west from predominantly subsistence-farming to predominantly capitalist farming, and in the east from a free peasant community to an era of *latifundia* and serfdom (ch. II, 1). Social changes include the full assertion of the English gentry, at the expense of the strata above and below them, if one may be permitted so to summarise a problem which is now bogged down in controversy and will require much research before the full story is known. They include the increasing power of the nobility of office (*de la robe*) in France, the decline of an independent bourgeoisie in Germany and Italy, as well as the increasing strength of this element in northern Burgundy, in Holland and Zeeland. They include the growing importance of the greater nobility and the decline of the lesser in central and eastern Europe, and the decline of all elements independent of the monarchy in Spain. But these phenomena, highly significant as they are, cannot be expected to accommodate themselves to the historical contours of a couple of generations. As it is, the period of the Reformation played a vital enough part in some of these trends. The Reformation produced a great movement in the land market, most strikingly in England where the dissolution of the monasteries conveyed something like one-fifth of the nation's landed income to new hands, but also in those areas of Germany and Scandinavia where Reformation meant secularisation of land. The Turkish threat and the decline of imperial power had much to do with the social developments in eastern Europe. The consolidation of monarchy had social effects wherever it made itself felt.[1]

In the history of trade and industry, too, this period is simply part of a story which extends in both directions without clear termini, a story of major trade-routes shifting to the sea-lanes and of new commercial centres gradually replacing the traditional marts of medieval Europe.[2] The full effects of new markets and new commodities were not to be felt till later, though an interesting but as yet tentative expansion of industrial enterprise (the refining of sugar, processing of tobacco, new draperies in Flanders and England, advances—partly demanded by war—in the metal industries) can be discerned here and there before the middle of the century. One particular phenomenon, the rise and fall of Antwerp as Europe's foremost commercial centre (rivalled in the south by Lyons, the centre of Mediterranean finance), falls with some neatness into the age of the Reformation (ch. II, 2). It is also worth notice that this was the last age before the nineteenth century during which the machinations of great international financiers independent of territorial governments played a major part in affairs: the age of the Fuggers has much in common with the age of the Rothschilds, but little with what came between.[3] This is no accident. Two things destroyed the world of those great German and Italian families. One was the unreliability of princely finances which led to the failure or very serious decline of all the great houses and the growing development, especially in France, England and the Netherlands, of native financial resources. The other was the great inflation which increased the needs of government to a point where their demands became impossible to satisfy except by increased taxation. The price-rise of the century has already been discussed;[4] here it will be enough to point out that its most serious and general manifestations came only after 1560 when the influx of American specie had made itself properly felt. England provides an exception: its worst difficulties, with prices doubling within five years, occurred in the years 1546–51 and were directly due to government policy—expensive war financed by ruinous debasement. On the whole it is clear that these economic developments, vital as they are to an understanding of the period, do not give it any special character. Agrarian change, trading developments and inflation stretch beyond it at both ends,

[1] No space can naturally be found within the framework of a general history for a full discussion of these economic and social changes. In any case, it is hoped that they will receive more adequate treatment in the appropriate sections of the *Cambridge Economic History*.

[2] Cf. esp. vol. I, ch. XVI; but also vol. I, ch. XV, and chs. XIX and XX in the present volume.

[3] The most comprehensive account is still to be found in R. Ehrenberg, *Das Zeitalter der Fugger* (1896; English translation 1928).

[4] Vol. I, pp. 450 ff.

as indeed one would expect them to do; the period of the Reformation has its particular significance in these larger phenomena, but it is not easily to be defined in terms of them.

Touching the problem of men's minds—of 'mental climate'—one thing stands out: there was a great revival in the discussion of theological questions. The Reformation saw to that. Since this was an age of controversy, and since printing had by now got established, it was also an age of copious pamphleteering. If only the scale was new, scale matters when the difference becomes so pronounced. Luther might have been only another Wycliffe—admittedly an unlikely supposition for many reasons—if the printing press had not given him the chance of appealing to favourable sentiments far and wide; Henry VIII would almost certainly have encountered greater difficulties in his Church policy if he had not been able to employ official propaganda to good purpose; both Reformation and Counter-Reformation owed much to the spread of books. But overwhelming concern with theology did not kill writing on other topics (ch. XII, 1), and there remained traces of the earlier, more secular humanism in unexpected places. The 'new learning' provided many weapons in the armoury of anti-papal and anti-clerical writers, from Erasmus's edition of the New Testament, through the part played by the German (and later other) universities in the training of reformers, to the historical arguments (sounder than is commonly admitted) of Thomas Cromwell's propagandists. Science made some strides, though it continued to suffer from the attention of humanism with its predilection for finding things in the classical world (ch. XII, 2). The secular, often vernacular, writing of the period is of greater interest than writings on the Church (the few great men always excepted): its value often endures while the ephemeral controversies are only too likely to bore and repel. But to concentrate on the non-theological output, legitimate as this is in a discussion of literature, is to run the danger of forgetting what it was that most engaged the age itself.

At first glance these forty or so years seem to lack the attraction of great intellects, fine writers, artists of the first rank. There are indeed many important and some pleasing writings in many European languages, but, with all respect to their other qualities, men like More, Calvin, Bucer or Loyola cannot be rated in the first flight of literary art. There is a gap in the history of political theory between Machiavelli and Bodin, though some interesting second-rank stuff came from the pens of men like Cujas and Budé in France or Starkey and Ponet in England. There is even something of a break in the history of poetry between the Renaissance in Italy and its consequences in France and England (Ronsard and Shakespeare must be relinquished to another volume) and in that of art between Michelangelo and Velásquez. The fact that the leading intellects of the period concentrated on religious matters has allowed them to be classified in another category, and rightly so; though it ought to be mentioned that

Luther had a great hand in shaping the German language, that Cranmer's liturgy reveals poetic gifts of a high order, that the English pamphleteers helped their language to gain in flexibility and power,[1] that the northern vernaculars grew to adulthood in the hands of the reformers, and that altogether a concentration on theology and religion was nowhere necessarily divorced from considerations of literature. But an age whose most distinctive output consists of Protestant hymns is not primarily one of artistic distinction, and the absence of vital happenings in the field of culture must justify the omission of chapters on art and poetry. Such things as can be said about them are better said in dealing with the greater periods that came before and after.

Everything allowed for, it therefore remains reasonable to think of this age as one in which the graces of life and learning found it hard to survive among the battles into which the learned themselves rushed rather than were drawn. The revival of religious fervour worked contrary not only to tolerance but also to intellectual advance; Luther's huge awareness of the grace of God left little room for Erasmus's faith in human reason. As has already been pointed out, this goes counter to the theory that we ought to date the beginning of modern times from the first half of the sixteenth century. One must agree that the search for antecedents and straight lines of development is here quite as misplaced as usual, but it is just worth notice that one of the less obvious interests of the age lay in a field which later became very important, the study of history. The treatment which French civilians meted out to the Roman law may fairly be regarded as a striking early instance of the historical method.[2] Since the growth of a genuinely historical method is quite as significant of modern thought as science itself, it may be held that despite the 'medievalism' of its science this period has unsuspected affinities with the mental attitudes of later times and may yet be thought of once again as a seminal age of thought, a place at present occupied by the seventeenth century. But frankly these speculations, like all speculations about ancestry in thought, are intellectual games rather than historical investigation, and dangerous games at that, because they always tend to single out in a period things that became significant in later and distant ages at the expense of the things that mattered at the time.

But can we discover a formula to describe what did matter at the time? Is it safe to think of this period under any particular heading? The fate suffered by this 'age of faith' or that 'age of reason' should warn us that even the Reformation may have been insufficiently simple to accommodate itself to the (often prejudiced) straitjackets we like to put on it. Most people will agree that because it was, among other things, a spiritual and

---

[1] Compare, for instance, the sermons of Hugh Latimer with the devotional or controversial writings of Thomas More.

[2] Cf. J. G. A. Pocock, *The Ancient Constitution and the Feudal Law* (1957), ch. I.

moral upheaval of formidable proportions, it put a stamp upon the mentality of the age. But what the stamp was, and whether a single one will do, is another matter altogether in a field of problems where all answers tend to be vague and unsatisfactory at best, plainly insufficient and misleading at worst. Is 'mental climate' to be judged from the writings of the day? They may be all we have, but surely they leave out a lot—among other things, most of the people then alive. Is it to be described in terms of social conventions? Though these may have varied less from country to country than they do today, they varied so much more among the social strata that generalisation becomes very unsafe. Nor, as a matter of fact, has anything like enough work yet been done to give reality to the concept.

Take Europe's governing classes alone.[1] It would be fair to say that two highly intricate series of relationships governed their behaviour, and that neither of them has as yet been studied sufficiently to justify general statements about 'mental climate'. One was anchored in connection by blood, in the consequences of dynastic marriage at all levels. The other derived from a system of mutual obligations and favours which would seem to have done more to determine a man's action or inaction than loyalty, plain duty or plain self-interest. Much of the real powers and obligations, dependence and independence, prejudices and privileges of those who really mattered can never be discovered from a calculation of manorial possessions or an analysis of legal rights. The nobility and gentry adapted a quasi-feudal attitude to the realities of a far from feudal age, substituting for the duty of service and the right to protection a system of doing services in the justified expectation of suitable recompense from the princely bounty. An important book, as yet unwritten, would investigate the part played in holding together the social and administrative structures of western Europe by the relationship between master and man, by the bestowal of gifts and rewards, by the possession of patronage and the search for it.[2] At the same time, signs have occasionally been found, especially among the French and Spanish bureaucracies, of a 'civil-service' attitude to office as no longer a piece of property bought

---

[1] One problem which has received some attention is that of the Christian gentleman—the ideal of old-fashioned Christian chivalry combined with Renaissance virtue—which is found here and there in the pages of Castiglione's *Courtier* (cf. vol. 1, p. 74), Thomas Elyot's *Boke of the Governour* (1531), etc. For this cf. F. Caspari, *Humanism and the Social Order in Tudor England* (1954).

[2] When the estates of Holland complained to their governor, the count of Hooghstraeten, that he was not doing enough to represent their interests at court, he replied: 'If anyone does me a favour up to here' (and he pointed to his wrist) 'I shall do him a favour up to here' (pointing to his elbow); 'but', he added, 'if anyone does me so much disfavour I shall do the same to him.' I owe this story, which so ingenuously illustrates accepted notions, to Dr H. Koenigsberger who had to omit it from ch. x for lack of space but hoped that I should find room for it. He in turn wishes to record his thanks to Dr P. A. Meilink of The Hague, for enabling him to see a transcript by E. van Bienna (ii, fos. 309 f.) in the Amsterdam Stadsarchief.

or bestowed by grace, but a place of work owing duty to an impersonal state and in turn providing a living for him who fulfilled his duties well.

None of this, of course, applied below the level of the political nation—among peasants, artisans, small traders—the bulk of the people. Even the greater merchants had different conventions of their own. Concentration on their particular notions has before this led historians to see in this age something peculiarly modern, a phenomenon described as 'the rise of capitalism'. There is perhaps no need to enter once more upon that hoary topic: 'capitalist' attitudes, however defined for the purpose, are found long before the sixteenth century and were far from clear-cut even among the more obvious capitalists of that age. But in such high and low variety, and where so little sorting has yet been done, who shall say what 'people' thought about the world in which they lived or what their significant attitudes were? Guesses are justified and some sound more convincing than others; every historian of the period has in him an impalpable yard-stick for deciding what is and what is not 'right' for the age. But that does not mean that he can describe its 'mental climate'. Perhaps the present writer had better confess his distrust of the whole concept and leave it at that.

The attraction of the sweeping and enlightening generalisation, however dangerous, is legitimate; what distinguishes the historian from the collector of historical facts is generalisation—preferably successful generalisation. In the larger stretches of history in which it is set the age of the Reformation played its part. Sometimes it stimulated existing trends, sometimes it diverted them, sometimes—it may be—it dammed them up for ever or for a time. Side by side, a revival of religion and the secularisation of society gained momentum. The political history of central Europe in particular took a turning that, for all the earlier indications of decay in Germany, was yet new. Signs of humanism and tolerance, which had made their appearance, went underground. These may be vague statements, but the time has not yet come for precision, the more so because older traditional convictions are in process of dissolution. Exactly what place we assign to the period in the stream of history remains after all a matter of personal judgment. The present writer feels that it is idle to credit the age with the beginning of modern times (in itself a sufficiently uncertain term) if only because its intellectual leaders looked determinedly back rather than forward. But the beginning of something else is certainly to be found here—of what one should call the ascendancy of Europe, an ascendancy which the future may well decide came to an end in 1914. We are often today exhorted by various historians and publicists to resist the parochialism of European history, to remember that compared with the empires of the east even the larger European powers were insignificant, to treat history 'globally'. Persuasive as such views can be, and doubtless relevant to the present day, they do nothing but distort if they lead one to overlook the dominant role of Europe from the sixteenth to the early twentieth centuries. In that period concentration on Europe is not parochial: it marks rather a proper appreciation of the true balance of history. European political superiority, European customs, European law and science and culture spread outwards over the globe from the early discoveries onwards, until the world was to all intents Europeanized. Of all conquests, this, which has virtually substituted the inheritance of classical antiquity for even more ancient native traditions in such time-honoured civilisations as those of India and China, has been the most penetrative. It got under way in the era of the Reformation when Spain conquered and settled the Americas (ch. xix) and Portugal opened up the Far East (ch. xx). In a sense it is astonishing that Europe—riven internally by new faiths, violent wars and private ambitions, and pressed hard by the last of the great Mongol attacks from Asia—should have had the strength for these beginnings of an explosive expansion. But then nothing so much astonishes in the history of European expansion as the prodigal waste of forces at home and the prodigious achievements of small forces overseas. European superiority in technical equipment, certainly part of the explanation, made itself felt also in these early stages.

The expansive activity shown by Europe—or rather by some individuals in parts of western Europe—is curiously contrasted with what was happening to Europe itself. Here one notes contraction, loss of territory, and a realignment of forces internally which restricted the effective potential of European energies to a narrower area, but one which happily lay open to the oceans. The Europe of the sixteenth century was smaller than that of the fourteenth. The Turkish conquest of the Balkans and the Russian conquest of the Ukraine drove back the frontiers of medieval Europe with lasting effect. Both Turkey and Russia might pretend to be building upon the ruins of the Byzantine empire, but both were essentially less European than their alleged precursor. Furthermore, the existence of these aggressive forces on Europe's landward border concentrated vast energies upon defence and produced a degree of acclimatisation along this broad strip from Poland to Croatia which robbed central Europe of some of its European quality. The effect upon tenurial arrangements and constitutional developments has already been observed. The immediate outcome of this 'frontier-situation' was the rise of two new powers, Austria and Brandenburg-Prussia, whose beginnings one may trace to this period: Charles V virtually founded the Austrian empire when he bestowed the eastern Habsburg lands upon his brother Ferdinand, and the Reformation not only accorded the margrave of Brandenburg some handsome promotion but also so altered the balance of power in the area between Lübeck and Riga that the rise of Prussia may be foreseen a century before the Great Elector. On the seaward side, the increasing importance of the Atlantic nations needs no further stressing.

Europe, in fact, opened out; its centre dropped and its margins rose. The great line of the high Middle Ages had run through Germany and Italy, through the Holy Roman Empire. Subsidiary centres of significance lay elsewhere—in the region of the lower Rhine, in the axis through France reaching up to England which had been visible in the Angevin empire of the twelfth century, in the massive block of Lithuania stretching nearly to the lower Volga. But despite the early decay of the Empire, Europe's centre of gravity rested in the middle; even France, whose achievements in politics and civilisation stood high, remained turned to her east, to Burgundy. Now both Italy and Germany stepped down. For some centuries the essential Europe—the expanding and conquering Europe—was to be found not in the centre, the south or the east, but exclusively in the west. This was a development to which much in the past led up and which must never be stressed to the exclusion of the continued significance and interest of other areas; but it came into the open during the early sixteenth century when the Reformation, and the collapse of Charles V's imperial ambitions, confirmed the decline of central Europe and furthered the rise of Spain, France and England.

CHAPTER II

ECONOMIC CHANGE

I. AGRICULTURE[1]

IF no branch of economic history may ignore the fact that economic matters cannot on principle be understood in isolation but only with reference to a larger framework, this is particularly true of agrarian history. Agrarian economy is interconnected with other branches of economic activity: one might perhaps enlarge the economists' 'law of the interdependency of prices' into a 'law' governing the interdependency of all economic phenomena and therefore also of all branches of economic life. Furthermore, the manifold links with other fields of life must be given full weight. In the field of agrarian economy—to mention the essentials only—these are characterised by the fact that the soil (the right, that is, to dispose of it) carries great social and political importance. After all, the soil is not only an economic medium, a factor of production; it is also man's living space. Thus dominion over the soil always involves in some way dominion over the people who live on it. At every turn we meet the social and political significance attached to control over the soil: in the military conquest, for instance, by which a superior race overlays the indigenous population (a point which some sociologists have of late almost overstressed as a factor in the origin of states), or in the growth of social stratification. In the centuries commonly called the 'age of feudalism', this social and political significance was particularly marked. During them there grew up that form of a social and especially agrarian constitution which Max Weber has called 'lordly possession on the soil', that is, lordship over the people who live on the soil and work it (more particularly over peasants) achieved indirectly by way of rights derived from the soil. In contrast to true personal serfdom, this sort of lordship subjected the peasant not directly in his person but indirectly through the interposition of an intermediate stage.

Sociologically this meant that the governing classes—those groups which were concerned with political, cultural, military, social, and possibly also economic leadership—sought their material foundation in landed property, the degree to which the lands were directly exploited by these lords being of secondary importance. The rents and labour services of a tenurial peasantry formed the income of the governing classes, in kind or in money; and this determined the agrarian structure of the age.

[1] In view of the fact that nothing on this subject appeared in vol. I, it was thought advisable to make this chapter a general introductory survey of changes in agrarian structure.

23

As far as we are here concerned, the behaviour of feudal society (lords as well as peasants) towards matters economic was marked by two characteristics. For one thing, they existed in a condition of moral reciprocity. The peasant's duty to render certain payments or services must be seen as a product of his allegiance to the lord. As a product of the loyalty which he owed in his turn, the lord had a moral duty to protect and assist, to provide peace and care—moral duties which could manifest themselves in concrete economic counter-services (supply of food, a share in the harvest, help in straitened circumstances, etc.). In other words, an essential part of economic life was determined by such moral considerations. The rendering and exchange of economic services and values rested therefore primarily on such personal ties and not on the demands of the law of property or debt. Secondly, typical economic behaviour was not in the first place determined by the market and by prices but by the demands of subsistence economy. The peasants' labour was intended to meet their lords' needs as well as their own, the lords expecting to have theirs covered by the work of their peasants. In the purest realisation of this principle, changes not in price levels but in the needs of peasants and lords led to changes in production.

If, however, in historical fact the tightening-up of economic interrelations produced the realities of market and prices (however rudimentarily), the result was a situation of conflict. The problem then arises whether and how far traditional behaviour altered with an eye to these facts. All sorts of transitional states occurred, from the complete ignoring of such economic data with the economically important result that changing price levels caused no changes at all in production and did not by means of a 'market mechanism' lead to a levelling off, to the opposite situation in which the economic data of prices determined production and a rational economic organisation replaced a traditional one.

Such rational organisation was particularly promoted by the intrusion of money and with it of the price mechanism into the agrarian sector of the economy. This is by no means a simple causal relationship but rather a functional interaction, inasmuch as the rise of rational economic thinking in its turn attracted the rational medium of money; it did not confine itself to purely agricultural problems. The question which arises from this re-orientation of economic thinking towards money prices and markets is twofold. In the first place one must discover the changes which it produced in the structure of the agrarian economy. Secondly one must ask how these changes in the field of economics affected the social field—whether there were corresponding changes in agrarian society. Elsewhere social changes may have taken the lead and worked themselves out in corresponding economic changes. These are questions to be investigated.

They all came to a particular point in the transition from the so-called Middle Ages to so-called modern times, in the centuries from the fourteenth to the sixteenth. The time was full of fundamental changes both in agrarian society and in agrarian economy. Historical conditions were in part responsible for the fact that the changes assumed very different forms in the various countries of Europe, with the result that since then differences throughout Europe have become extraordinarily great; this makes it necessary to devote careful attention to developments in the preceding historical era. This is further essential because by the sixteenth century Europe had produced a number of profoundly different national economies together with an international exchange of goods and services which makes it possible to speak of a world economy. This means that the agrarian economy of any given country, and often enough its social structure too, were frequently influenced by the economic facts of a totally different country to which it was bound by well-defined ties of imports and exports.

If the changes of the fifteenth and sixteenth centuries must be understood from their historical background, it is equally true that this period affected the succeeding centuries. This compels one to direct one's attention also to these later ages, because in the last resort the meaning of events can only be judged from their effects on a subsequent period. It will therefore be proper first to sketch the general tendencies implicit in the development, and then briefly to describe separate developments in the most important European countries.

One of the decisive lines of development, which ran through all these centuries and in a way culminated in the fifteenth, was the winning of personal freedom even by those peasants who had not originally possessed it. It is important to be clear about the meaning which the age ascribed to freedom and servitude.

Originally freedom meant that the freeman was a full member of his kinship or his people and could thus play his part in the popular assembly, as a member of the host, and as a juror in court. Opposed to him was the unfree man who stood outside the folk and had no backing in kinship. This sort of personal unfreedom began to disappear as early as Carolingian times. Christianity, introducing a totally new ethos, here played the decisive part. Of secondary importance was the fact that the Germanic nations did not as a rule employ their unfree men as slaves but gave them a plot of land to which a duty of rendering specific services and payments was attached. On the other side, men originally free gradually and in a variety of ways dropped into tenurial relationships. Thus, there grew up between the eighth and twelfth centuries a uniform peasantry, uniform in the sense that personal status, which had once determined the position, had lost all importance as compared with the facts of the relations between lord and tenant. Since this development was not complete, particular importance attaches to those measures by which ancient dependent status on personal grounds came to be abolished. The best-known example occurred in north-west Germany where in the twelfth century the lords began to dissolve the great estates. From the fourteenth and fifteenth centuries onwards this involved an emancipation of the peasantry, to a point where the earlier villeins were replaced by peasants personally free and only bound to render tenurial payments. At the same time bond status disappeared among the West German peasants, though the *ungesessene Laten*—members of peasant families without lands of their own—did not achieve their freedom until the fifteenth century, after a temporary accentuation of their dependent status; all that remained here, too, were certain rent duties. In south-west Germany, too, the great estates were fractionalised as early as the high Middle Ages, and the peasants' duties in the framework of the new smaller estates settled down to simple rent burdens. At the same time the old personal ties disappeared in central Germany. Even more radical was the development in Italy where the old *servus* turned into the *colonus*, and where personal dependence continued into the fifteenth century only in such marginal areas as Friuli and Sardinia. In France, the process began in the thirteenth century and with few exceptions was complete by the fifteenth. From at least the thirteenth century onwards, the same applied in England, even if the causes were different.

To seize upon a basic tendency in this emancipation: the great depopulation of the fourteenth century played everywhere its part, together with the subsequent change of a feudal society into one that may be called bourgeois, itself up to a point a result of that depopulation.

All this reinforced the tendencies which were already at work—especially in Italy and the Low Countries—to draw the agrarian economy, and with it those who lived by the land, more and more into the nexus of a money economy and into the effects of markets and prices. It is unnecessary to stress further that an increasing money economy had great importance for the development of the agrarian economy by adding to the complications produced by market conditions. As early as Carolingian times we find throughout Europe that agrarian burdens were defined in money terms, which does not necessarily mean that they were rendered in cash; often they were in kind, the cash terms only defining their size. A money economy began in Italy and Flanders but spread increasingly from the twelfth century onwards, to be generally predominant by the fifteenth to sixteenth centuries at the latest. The lords needed money to obtain the imported goods demanded by their rising standard of living, goods for which they could rarely exchange natural products. It was for this reason also that it seemed good sense to get the peasants' payments in money, leaving it to them to sell their produce in the market.

For the lords this great advantage had—or at least might have had—a great drawback, while the peasants in their turn enjoyed a benefit. A change in the purchasing power of money influenced the real value of the rents received, and since this change as a rule and consistently throughout the centuries amounted to a decline the lords, even if their normal needs did not alter, found their real revenues declining and their position weakening. This trend could be met only if it was possible to change things in the lords' favour by changes in payments, possessory rights, and methods of farming—matters which will frequently engage our attention. Insofar as this was not possible—and we shall have to show again and again that often it was not—the landed lords declined economically and therefore as a rule also in their social and political standing. The peasants reaped the advantages, either in the windfalls which a current diminution of their burdens implied, or at times even in the chance of buying off all or part of these with a single payment. The spread of money thus had far-reaching consequences.

The same is true of the effects of changing price levels. Sometimes these occurred because of the changing (declining) value of money which has already been mentioned; but sometimes prices changed relative to each other. That is to say, there were alterations in specific price levels either among individual groups of products or among individual national economies. Changes in the price ratio of groups of goods could mean changes affecting separate products of agriculture: thus the relative rise in the price of wool and the relative backwardness in the price of grain had great importance for the economy of England and Flanders. Much the same was true of wine in southern and western Europe, or of commercial agrarian produce in the Low Countries and Thuringia and elsewhere. Wages, representing costs to the farmer, are a special kind of price: rising wages after the Black Death so affected production costs in agriculture— insofar as it depended on wage labour—that all countries experienced structural alterations.

Thus the problem of the agrarian cycle with its depressive culmination in agrarian crisis began to assume importance in this period. Ignoring specific deviations, a straightforward rise from the eighth to the fourteenth century was followed in the middle of that century by the first general decline, which in turn towards 1500 made way for a new rise lasting for something over a century. In this respect also the sixteenth century was therefore of special significance. The beginning of the seventeenth witnessed a general and sudden collapse. The 'fièvre agricole', in d'Avenel's phrase, had led to ever more colonisation and intensified agriculture; overproduction—marked after several exceptionally good harvests— depressed prices both for agrarian produce and for land. In Germany the Thirty Years War produced a distinct development—a collapse caused from outside the economic sphere—while western Europe experienced a new rise which by about 1660 gave way to a new decline. All these ups and downs had effects of greater or lesser intensity on agrarian economy and society.

The whole complex of problems was affected by another point of great importance—the process of clearing the waste which for several centuries was enlarging the cultivated area in all European countries, even though there was occasional retrogression. Additions to this area may be accompanied by the maintenance of existing complementary relations between all the relevant factors of production, in which case production does not tend to increase. If the price of agrarian produce rises under such conditions, it is on the one hand possible to bring additional and less productive soil into cultivation (and this happened everywhere); on the other hand, however, the better soil will command constantly rising ground rents. This raises the question whether the benefits accrued to the peasant or the lord. By and large, developments down to the middle of the fourteenth century enabled the peasant to enjoy the increment; only thereafter, and because of a rapidly changing situation, did the matter become a subject for strife whose outcome differed according to the relative distribution of strength.

An improvement in the peasants' condition meant a worsening in the lords'. At the same time, the lords' position could grow worse if the peasants got into difficulties and lost some measure of their productivity. The lords were therefore in a double danger. Occasionally there could be a complete collapse, as happened for instance most notably in France. The question then arose whether and in what way the lords could arrest this decline in their position: as by an increase in direct exploitation, by additions to rights and rents, or by the channelling of mercantile wealth into the agrarian sphere. These expedients at times enabled members of the old nobility who had survived the crisis to display even a tendency to improvement. Special importance attached to the degree of concern which kings and princes evinced towards their nobility. A ruler possessed of a strong centralised power, like the king of England, did not need to defer to his nobles and did not allow them any particular position in politics. Thus in England the social fact of lordship carried less weight than the economic fact of ownership. In other countries, as for instance in many parts of Germany, the sixteenth century witnessed a close alliance between territorial prince and nobility, with the result that the burgher element in the towns lost power as compared with the nobility; feudalism experienced a revival. Only when mercantilist princes as well as noble lords began to ascribe greater force to economic factors, thus accepting 'bourgeois ideals', did landed lords change here, too, into landlords, a development which ended with the liberal emancipation of the peasants round about 1800.

A separate question concerns the suppliers of capital, that is the identity of those who led the way towards an entrepreneurial attitude. In England it was the leasehold tenants rather than the landlords who occupied this position at the height of the development. The latter took an indirect part because the institution of primogeniture secured a concentration of economic power which the strong monarchy never allowed to develop into political power, let alone territorial independence. The landlords were thus frequently able to supply capital to agriculture. In France, and also in Italy, capital for farming was mostly supplied by wealthy townsmen. In Germany the situation varied a great deal. In most German territories townsmen were not allowed to acquire noble estates; in such cases, town capital—if one ignores loans—came in only by way of intermarriage with citizens' daughters. Other sources existed: accumulated ground rents, or the salaries, loot, dowries, etc. of military and civil officials and their like who, of course, were as a rule also landed lords. On the princely demesnes, which especially in Prussia played an important role, the princes themselves acted as pioneers in agrarian enterprise.

Thus we may discern quite a series of general trends, all of which culminate more or less plainly in the fifteenth and sixteenth centuries, and which in accordance with historical, political, economic and geographical conditions produced different effects in the different countries.

Well past the middle of the fifteenth century, Germany[1] continued to suffer the after-effects of the loss in population caused by the Black Death and the subsequent agrarian crisis. The considerable depopulation of the country, much devastation, a decline in landed rents and the position of the nobility, the rise of the towns and the burgher element, rising prices for commercial products and the consequent growth of a price situation unfavourable to agriculture—all these implied a violent break after the preceding centuries.

A change began in the last quarter of the fifteenth century and continued throughout the sixteenth. It originated in the enormous population increase which as early as the first half of the fifteenth century appeared as a problem to contemporaries and led to many (and occasionally surprising) proposals. Ulrich von Hutten suggested the renewal of war with Turkey to deal with overpopulation, while other writers said frankly that plague and similar diseases were necessary to cope with the human surplus. By 1500, the losses of the great plague were made good; the population of the Empire without the Netherlands is estimated to have stood then at roughly twelve millions or something like double the numbers of the eleventh century. This growth continued throughout the sixteenth century, at the end of which twenty millions is a reasonable estimate.

All this growth implied the deployment of powerful forces which also affected economic life. Their effect on agriculture was reinforced by the fact that thanks to the rise of the towns the previous period had witnessed

---

[1] This account of Germany also includes developments in Switzerland and the Low Countries which at this time were only beginning to move away from the old Empire.

a great intensification in money economy. Prices of agrarian produce rose steeply and consistently—those of grain even more than those of meat and dairy produce—and acted as a stimulant to farming. And indeed, from about 1500 the process of colonisation was resumed which, expressing itself in a revival of the German expansion eastward, continued throughout the sixteenth and subsequent centuries. This renewed activity not only led to the recultivation of land that had returned to the waste since the middle of the fourteenth century; in addition, moorland and waste were broken up, forests were cleared, pasture came under the plough, and new land was won by dyking along the North Sea coast. Something over 110,000 acres of land was drained in the Netherlands between 1565 and 1615, and similar efforts were made on the North Sea shores of Germany.

Furthermore, improvements took place in methods of farming; a slowly growing agricultural literature was carrying knowledge of new discoveries into wider circles. Starting in Italy in the thirteenth century, a wave of scientific writings on the subject spread outwards, reaching Germany and France in the sixteenth century. While these in the main discussed improvements within the old system of farming, the Low Countries were experimenting in the sixteenth century with the cultivation of new crops like clover and turnips and other feeding stuffs or commercially useful products. As a result new methods of cultivation came into being. England adopted them from the Netherlands, and from the seventeenth century onwards they penetrated into Germany, France and other countries under the name of 'English agriculture'.

Thus it can be said of Germany, too, that the fifteenth and particularly the sixteenth centuries marked a watershed in agrarian history, just as they did in England, the Low Countries and France, and, after delays, in Denmark and Sweden—in effect all over Europe. In Germany these changes linked up with the separate developments observable for centuries in the individual German lands. These will have to be mentioned briefly below, particularly since the absolutist state of the seventeenth and eighteenth centuries inherited these separate tendencies and developed them further.

Before this happened there occurred an event which, though itself outside economic factors, decisively affected the future, especially in agrarian matters: the Thirty Years War. In areas relatively untouched by the war the population increase was simply used up, so that at its conclusion population stood where it had been at its beginning; in those areas, however, where the fury raged most fully, it destroyed some sixty or seventy per cent (sometimes more) of the population. All told, the total losses of the German nation must be reckoned at about fifty per cent. In addition there were the enormous losses in money and every kind of property. In consequence, even though agrarian prices stood very high on account of underproduction, agriculture collapsed. Many years of re-construction were needed to overcome the consequences of this catas-trophe. Only slowly did the gaps in the population fill up and the wasted fields come under the plough again. Not until a century or a century and a half after the conclusion of peace did the population once more reach its old size of some twenty millions. It was only because France, thanks to the policy pursued by Louis XIV, experienced a marked decline in population from the middle of the seventeenth century onwards (calcu-lated by François Quesnay with some exaggeration to have amounted to a reduction from twenty-four down to sixteen millions) that she failed to gain a permanent numerical ascendancy over Germany.

The catastrophes just described were naturally of considerable impor-tance for the history of agrarian society after about 1500. In the main they accelerated tendencies which had been present for some time, such as the growth of a money economy and the formation of distinct types of landed lordship in the various parts of Germany. A separate phenomenon is the growth of the great estates in the east, which carries a peculiar significance.

German agriculture, too, experienced the invasion of money economy and the growing importance of price levels, especially from the middle of the fourteenth century onwards. This development, which began in Italy, happened at varying rates of speed and with varying intensity in the different parts of Germany. It was quickest and most intensive in the Rhineland (including the Low Countries) and in the neighbourhood of the larger towns, while its speed and intensity were less in the more distant regions. But the tendency is unmistakable. The consequences were, on the one hand, a greater degree of farming for the market, on the other a decline in the revenue derived from rents by lords of all kinds which was also conditioned by the decline in the purchasing power of money, itself a result of frequent debasements. In many parts of Germany, especially the south-west and north-west, this led to a dissolution of the great landed estates.

These tendencies received a marked impetus with the catastrophe of the mid-fourteenth century, the Black Death. As already pointed out, many holdings were left empty, there was much reversion to waste, peasants ceased to render their dues, and, relying on their scarcity, the survivors secured not only improvements in their rights but also reductions in their rents. The nobility decayed rapidly: the feudal age of chivalry was at an end. The nobility were so heavily in debt that in 1390 King Wenceslas found it necessary to decree a general *Judenschuldenerlass* (an indemnity for debts owed to Jews), but the measure came too late for many and brought only temporary relief to others. The greatest of all landed lords, the Teutonic Order (to take a striking example), got into such difficulties that it suffered a total financial collapse from which it never recovered.

At first it took up a heavy burden of debt by mortgaging its lands; but since it proved impossible to redeem them, the Council and the High Master tried hard and in vain throughout the first half of the fifteenth century to save the order by selling its possessions. Princes, gentry, and towns all refused to touch them. Everywhere things were much the same. It was rare for mercantile wealth to enter into these landed estates or into any part of agriculture. Italian practices, especially the burghers' desire to buy land, were not copied, if only because prospects of profit were better within the towns' own economy and also because there seemed no chance of arresting the decline. A typical instance occurred when the citizens of Metz, offered land by the Council, replied that they would not have it as a gift because the costs of cultivation and especially of wages were too high—because, that is, landed property did not pay.

A few towns only, as for example Leipzig, entered as early as this on the systematic purchase of landed estates and whole villages. Only as prices rose and the population recovered (from the last quarter of the fifteenth century and throughout the sixteenth) did wealthy citizens here and there begin to buy land, the best-known example being the acquisition in 1507 of the lordships of Kirchberg and Weissenhorn by Jacob Fugger. But in Germany there was no question of a large-scale intrusion into landed ownership by burgher elements, such as occurred in France, in England, and (earlier) in Italy. The powerful and growing ascendancy of the territorial princes, the revival of the nobility from the middle of the sixteenth century when it allied itself with the princes and so at times managed to augment its landed revenues from official salaries, and the burghers' concentration on other sources of income, were responsible for this.

The second great catastrophe, the Thirty Years War (1618–48), once more revived all these points. Once again the lords lost a great part of their revenue; such rents in kind as might yet be payable were often so small that they were useless for the market and thus brought in no money. With even greater need than before, the lesser nobility, unable to live on their rents, sought and found additional sources of income in the pay of the officer or in the salary of the court and state official. The agrarian depression, which persisted into the middle of the eighteenth century, so far from arresting this tendency added to it.

The question necessarily arises whether the lords could not have found a way out of their difficulties by increasing their revenues in other ways. Essentially, this could be done either by raising rents (if necessary by effecting a change in the land law) or by an increased direct exploitation of the lands. After all, the pursuit of both these possibilities was characteristic of agrarian changes in England. Lords either developed direct farming or else altered or even removed the lord-tenant relationship by substituting leaseholds, in particular short-term leases which offered a chance of adjusting revenue to the condition of the market. Except very occasionally, this last possibility did not arise in Germany. Leasehold, a purely contractual relationship, was hardly able to establish itself there; the tenurial rights of the peasantry, a matter of *Personalrecht* (the law of persons), remained in possession. These rights were commonly so defined that they could not be changed unilaterally, and the peasants took good care not to agree to any changes. Only such legal customs as *Leibrecht* (personal serfdom), which existed particularly in Bavaria and the neighbouring Austrian provinces, made possible a revision of rents after a tenant's death. A similar principle applied to the *Freistift*, a form of tenancy which under certain conditions could be cancelled by the lord; but since customary law prevented this being done except in a few definite cases, the possibilities of exploiting it were few.

By and large, therefore, German lords could not increase their income by raising their rents, even supposing that this rise had only been designed to compensate for the fall in the value of money. Where, as in north-west Germany, attempts at fundamental reforms of this kind were made, the princes soon interfered by promulgating agrarian measures favourable to the peasants and thus prohibiting the policy. As has already been said, the general tendency was rather for the peasants to be able to exploit their scarcity value in diminishing their burdens, most markedly after the great catastrophes of the plague and the Thirty Years War, but naturally also after other and lesser devastations by war and disease. It is well known that the various German peasants' risings down to the great Peasants War of 1524–5 were not caused by an increase in their burdens. Apart from struggling against the growing power of the princes, the peasants were rather resisting legally just and materially insignificant demands by the lords which the latter, in trying to arrest their decline, were exacting more completely and intensively than in the preceding era. Such behaviour the peasantry, economically strong and full of a new assurance, rejected outright. Even after the peasants' defeat the lords did not try to increase their rents and other rights because they were fully aware of the hopelessness of such measures. Exceptions are found only where the princes supported such endeavours or even perhaps led the way, as for instance in Bavaria where fines for renewal were increased in the sixteenth century, at a time of rising prices when it was possible to argue that an improvement in lords' rights represented a kind of *quid pro quo*. On the whole, therefore, there remained only the possibility of more intensive direct demesne farming.

In this respect, too, the situation varied to an extraordinary degree in the different parts of Germany and the regions to the east. For one thing, the legal position naturally differed widely, according as the existing state of the law provided varying chances for this kind of exploitation. If, as was usually the case, the peasant's rights were so secure that the lord could not expropriate him legally, this road was blocked as long as justice got done and the princes did not alter the legal position to the peasant's disadvantage. Much, therefore, depended on the forces available to work for a change in the law, and it is of course true that political and economic interests must be reckoned among them.

Not surprisingly, the material and social decline of the nobility from the middle of the fourteenth century onwards led to a desire to arrest this collapse. In many cases the great Death brought about an almost automatic enlargement of the lord's demesne because many peasants' holdings had fallen waste and vacant. But this could have only temporary significance; in fact, it was bound to have no more, especially where direct exploitation did not pay because the costs of cultivation and of wages were too high, a point which applied for something like a century. It was therefore more usual to seek new tenants for vacant holdings, even if reduced burdens had often to be offered to the peasant. In the sixteenth century, as the gaps in the population gradually closed and grain prices rose, the problem essentially continued to be one of economic returns. Side by side with this another question acquired importance: could the nobility, by acquiring official positions in the manner already mentioned, secure other kinds of income (salaries) and so reduce the relative importance of rents from land; or would they find themselves more or less driven from official places by middle-class officials (jurists) trained at the universities, and so would have to fall back on their agrarian incomes? Such trends appeared widely in the fifteenth century, but they were arrested in the sixteenth in some German lands, though they continued in others (for instance in Saxony). A last factor affecting the nobility could be the financial troubles of territorial rulers which caused them to sell political privileges, as happened in eastern Germany; later on, as they did in Prussia, they might in turn use this re-established nobility as officers in their armies. The basis of any increased direct exploitation, involving larger estates, lay in a suitable complex of economic interests, together with the degree to which the problem of labour supply could be overcome.

Thus round about 1500 and after, lords in several parts of Germany were deliberately increasing direct farming. In some parts, as in Bavaria, these attempts failed. There, transport costs rendered it impossible to take the produce to the markets of western Germany, Flanders and England, and the early beginnings soon petered out. In north-west Germany— especially in Lower Saxony, in the lands north of the Harz mountains, and elsewhere—a certain degree of increased exploitation took place, though mostly not until the seventeenth and eighteenth centuries. Similar endeavours can be seen in Electoral Saxony, where, however, from the sixteenth century onwards a strong and financially sound government followed a consistent policy of protecting the peasant. This prevented lords from destroying their peasantry, so that only a small part of peasants' holdings were lost and added to the demesne.

It is possible that a certain enlargement of demesne occurred also in Thuringia.

East of the Elbe, however, the augmentation of estates took place in much greater measure. It was not confined to Germany, but reached well into Poland, Bohemia-Moravia, the Baltic countries, White Russia, etc. At first—anyhow, in the German lands including Bohemia—the process did not involve a deliberate destruction of the peasantry; waste or vacant holdings only were added to the demesne, instead of being re-let to peasants. In the east conditions favoured this development because the colonising knights had as a rule obtained estates comprehending several manors which they farmed with the help of household servants and forced peasant labour. From the beginning of the colonisation there thus existed middle-sized estates scattered over the whole country, which could now be exploited in the manner described. The Thirty Years War (which raged most destructively in eastern Germany—particularly in Pomerania, Brandenburg, Mecklenburg, and Bohemia) produced, often against the lords' desires, further accessions of vacated holdings and consequent increases in the demesne. Because needy princes had often granted judicial and other rights, and because new tenants often held their lands on the unfavourable terms known as *Lassrecht* (a terminable right to the use of the land) and were therefore ill-protected and exposed to the lords' demands, it proved possible to increase the labour services by which the larger estates were now farmed. The necessary labour force was further augmented by exercising an advance hiring right over peasants' children who opted for domestic service, a claim which was occasionally enlarged into bond service for a term of years.

The peasants thus became bound to the soil (*glebae adscripti*) and could leave the estate only with their lord's permission; peasants' sons might be forced to take over a given vacant holding; and so on. The servile relationship which developed in this manner is commonly described as hereditary or 'real' service—real because in his person the peasant was free, and the burden of bondage rested on the holding or on the tenant for the time being.

The economic foundation of all this lay in the easy marketability of agrarian produce, especially grain, in the west European and west German markets, together with the fact that the lake and river systems of east Germany with the Baltic and the North Sea provided cheap transport. From this arose a determined production for the market, not (as in England) of wool, but of corn.

Towards the end of the seventeenth century the development branched into two. In the Hohenzollern lands (Brandenburg-Prussia) the rulers legislated vigorously for the protection of the peasant. They began to do this as soon as the lords started systematically to wipe out peasants' holdings by driving out tenants and adding the land to the demesne. This was resisted for political and economic reasons, and since protection was enforced energetically the peasantry in these areas by and large maintained their existence. Only the emancipation of the nineteenth century, which did not pass off without serious errors of policy, resulted here, too, in a great loss of peasant land. Elsewhere, as for instance in Mecklenburg, the Swedish part of Pomerania, Bohemia, etc., and in the Slavonic countries to the east, the peasants were not protected and lost most of their lands.

Both these regions have in common a transformation of landed lordship into the special form called *Gutsherrschaft*. In this system the lord has rights of lordship in his whole territory or estate. The estate is therefore something like a small political unit within the State: its inhabitants are only indirectly subjects of the territorial prince. At the same time, the estate under the rule of its lord is the basic administrative unit in the total structure of the State, occupying the same position as corresponding official organs directly responsible to the ruler. *Gutsherrschaft* is therefore a political and social complex, whereas *Gutswirtschaft* (estate farming) represents a purely economic complex. Its development from the sixteenth century onwards fundamentally distinguished the region east of the Elbe (excepting Electoral Saxony) from the middle and west both of Europe and Germany.

In this respect, too, the sixteenth century therefore marks a profound break in German agrarian history. This applies not only to society—the rights and duties of lords and peasants, possessory rights and the linking of judiciary power with territorial ownership, and so forth—but also to agriculture. The princely demesnes and the estates of the nobility introduced the new rational methods of arable and cattle farming, while peasant farming remained backward.

The centuries which followed upon the Norman conquest of England were characterised economically by a steady progress interrupted by several setbacks. The twelfth century was a time of relative stagnation; but the greatest break came with the Black Death in the middle of the fourteenth century, even though scholars are not yet agreed as to the extent of the structural changes produced by the crisis. The history of social structure is much more even, consisting as it does of the creation of a feudal order in the course of the Conquest and its gradual replacement by one of more bourgeois character. It was of notable importance for the specifically English version of feudalism—as contrasted with the form it took in, say, Germany or France—that English feudal law prohibited the creation of vassal tenants by the bestowal of lands received from the king or some other great lord; since most tenants were therefore Crown tenants, the king could exercise a tighter control over his vassals than was possible (especially) in Germany.[1] The group of feudal lords established in the eleventh century at first undertook their given tasks with much energy. Systematically, and with royal permission, they went about the clearing and settling of uncolonised areas, so that with the means at their disposal they succeeded in providing accommodation for the growing population (it doubled between the eleventh and fifteenth centuries). In this respect their achievements were the same and as great as those of landed lords in other countries, especially Germany. Clearances by the lords were accompanied by similar activities on the part of peasants, such as have recently been investigated in detail for some localities (e.g. Devon and Lincolnshire). Rising agricultural prices resulting from steadily rising demand conditioned the line of development. The benefit of those prices was reaped to some extent by the peasants themselves; the lords enjoyed them only if they practised direct farming or received rents in kind. In most parts of England—Northumberland formed a striking exception—the feudal lords personally farmed large demesnes and therefore participated in the benefits of the market. The same applied where the demesne was let to farm for a short period, as for instance for one life as happened frequently even before the Black Death: such leases made it possible to bring the rent periodically into line with the general economic situation. Where rents were paid in cash the decline in the purchasing power of money led to a decline in lords' incomes. Whether the results were made good by more intensive farming or other measures like participation in trade—the result in either case was a growing money economy.

These changes went hand in hand with the dissolution of this medieval and feudal agrarian society. For one thing, from the twelfth century onwards rents in kind were consistently commuted for money rents, used by the lords to farm their lands with paid labour which was cheaper and worked better. This measure was supplemented by the transformation of villein holdings into free tenancies (the services being commuted) and after that into virtual leases; thus the ancient relations between manorial lord and villein tenant were replaced by purely contractual relationships. These measures, which took some four hundred years to accomplish, were among the really important events of the period.

The other decisive factor, closely connected with the points just described, was enclosing. The word describes various practices which in fact often existed together: rationalisation of the division of the field, changing arable into pasture, the acquisition of neighbouring holdings (engrossing), and at times even simple clearance and colonisation. The

[1] The practice of subinfeudation had been limited by the provision of Magna Carta (1215) that the remainder must be large enough to enable the enfeoffing tenant to fulfil his duties to his lord. The statute *Quia emptores* replaced subinfeudation by the practice of selling parcels of land and provided that the purchaser should owe the services and dues attaching to that parcel not to the vendor but to the vendor's lord—commonly the king.

practice which had real influence for the future was the transformation of arable into pasture, going hand in hand with the rounding out of estates both by enlargement and by consolidation, especially where fields were cultivated in individual strips. Enclosing began in the early thirteenth century but did not properly develop for another two hundred years. The thirteenth century supplies the first governmental measures against it, particularly the statutes of Merton (1235) and Westminster (1285). In these early instances lords were beginning to enclose parts of the waste (assarts) which, though it had hitherto at best been used for pasture, began to attract the land hunger of the growing population. Since the peasants enjoyed rights of pasture in the waste, such enclosures undermined one of the foundations of peasant economy. The statutes prescribed that in enclosing care must be taken to leave enough pasture for peasants, an attempt on the part of the Crown to protect peasant interests against the lords which shows clearly that the lords were disinclined to take such care of their own accord. The State was thus pursuing a policy favouring the peasantry. But the policy also favoured economic progress, for it did not prohibit enclosures but merely tried to keep them within bounds. In enclosing the lords were endeavouring to increase their revenue and to guard against a social or economic decline. This was done either by farming the enclosed land or more commonly by letting it out at money rents—in larger pieces to peasants (farmers) and in smaller ones to cottagers, village artisans, etc. Connected with this was an important change in social structure. All these people thus received their personal freedom: the peasants (now farmers), and also the cottagers and the rest, abandoned bond status and became free in the new meaning of the word; that is, their relations with their lords ceased to be governed by personal ties and became subject to a legal contract. In a way these were the beginnings of peasant emancipation in England, for in a process lasting about a century, without legal compulsion and by voluntary agreements, the old tenurial relationships were abolished.

The distribution of new land to cottagers, artisans, and their like assisted the numerical growth of a class below peasant level which was available as free agricultural labour outside the framework of compulsory labour services. This led to a change in methods of working. With the tenurial tie gone, the lords in their turn no longer depended on such services. This is significant because, on account of perquisites owing to the villeins, serfs in some extreme cases even established a profitable right to do this labour and enjoy the benefits connected with it. In this sense of the word, therefore, the lords also became free. They used their freedom either to farm the demesne with free labour or to go over to an economy based purely on rents derived from what were in effect leases. In the latter case they accepted the tasks of the landlord; in the former, they became the heads of great landed estates. This change in working methods involved a further point whose full effects were only seen later. Linked closely with the growing money economy, the industrial labour force increased steadily. The cottagers and others, once they were equipped with land, soon ceased to find all their living in agriculture—as agricultural labour—but drifted more and more into industry and especially the manufacture of cloth. This again enlarged and strengthened those parts of the nation which were no longer tied to landed lordship and confronted economic problems with a greater degree of rationality.

As in the whole of Europe, so also in England the effects of the Black Death acted as stimuli to far-reaching further developments. It is generally agreed today that not far short of half the population of England died in the years 1348-9. As a result, the existing relations among lords, peasants and labourers became fluid. Peasants could exploit their scarcity by extorting improvements in their condition, while labourers could similarly increase their wages. Thorold Rogers, and W. J. Ashley following him, spoke of wage increases of fifty per cent; W. Abel, calculating harvesters' wages against the price of wheat from 1300 to 1380-90, concluded that wages rose twofold; the wages of other labour groups appear similarly to have nearly doubled.

Emergency measures like the Statute of Labourers failed in the sense that they provided no lasting solution; attempts to fix wages were defeated despite temporary success by the competition for labour among landlords and larger peasants. It is small wonder that all concerned should have looked for new answers. The situation confronting the entire national economy as well as the individual lord was this: labour was scarce and dear, while land was plentiful. The lord often found himself in the possession of waste holdings without tenants which somehow he had to exploit. He could then either farm himself or let out afresh. It was neither really possible nor particularly useful to attempt the latter by bestowing land on the traditional feudal terms. Not possible, because tenants were hard to find on those terms or demanded impossible conditions; not useful, because land could have been bestowed in the old way only in return for heavily reduced revenues. Thus the practice of leasing, introduced earlier, spread rapidly. While in earlier days the lords had been the exponents of a rational market economy, their place was essentially taken by the peasant farmers. The tenant of a small farm used the labour of his family, thus achieving more and saving bailiffs and overseers. If he farmed on a larger scale he might, by a grant from the lord, command the services of the villein labour which he was in a position to use more completely and rationally and without the interposition of an administrative machine. If the lord decided on direct farming—disposing as he did of more land and less labour—he had to change the method of cultivation and farm more extensively. This suggested the adoption of pasture farming, sheep-rearing being the obvious step. 'In these circumstances', says Trevelyan, 'the increase in pasture was pure gain in the general disaster'—because of the excellent market for wool at home and abroad. This can only be understood from the larger economic standpoint: the rising demand for cloth at home and abroad, even when prices rose, produced a growing demand for wool at a time when prices for this raw material were good. The export of wool, of great and growing importance from the thirteenth century onwards, was accompanied from the early fifteenth by the export of cloth.

It is therefore impossible to understand these changes in English agriculture unless the wool trade and cloth industry are taken into account. In no other country were agrarian developments influenced so powerfully by urban economic interests.

The clothing industry had been growing for centuries in England (and in other countries). Its centre was at first the open country where wool was spun and woven at home by peasants and their servants, by widows, the poor, and others. Merchants (middlemen) bought up the cloth and sold it. There is evidence of cloth exports to the Frankish empire, as early as the eighth century. However, because of its inferior quality English cloth suffered in international trade as compared with that of other countries, especially the Netherlands. The notable export of English cloth, mainly from Stamford, began in the thirteenth century. Gradually and with royal encouragement the urban cloth industry developed. In many towns, especially in London, clothiers (mercers and drapers) achieved outstanding importance. Since the trade brought great profits, the stimulus for expanding the industry was constantly present. The Crown, too, was eminently interested in the trade because the wool customs, especially those collected by the Calais Staple, formed an important source of revenue. The fourteenth century witnessed a significant and in part planned expansion of the cloth industry, marked both by its spread in the countryside and the admission of foreign (mainly Flemish) weavers. The consequent changes in the existing economic structure attracted both absolutely and relatively a large share of the labour market; this being mainly drawn from agriculture, farming was forced to do with a smaller labour force. However, becoming a cloth-worker did not necessarily involve urbanisation. On the contrary, the invention of water-driven fulling mills, erected in hill valleys, led to a move from town to country, despite the resistance of the town gilds; this happened not only because the town weavers, too, sent their cloth to be fulled in the country, but more particularly because the entrepreneurs came to employ rural labour in the neighbourhood of the mills. This relative decline of urban industry characterised developments from as early as the fourteenth century. None the less, a certain general spread of industry based on native wool did occur. When employment and wages declined late in the fifteenth and throughout the sixteenth century, there resulted no corresponding return of men into agriculture; this killed all chance (supposing one to have ever existed) of a revival of peasant farming with a stress on grain production, even though wheat prices rose in the second half of the fifteenth century and more sharply still in the sixteenth. In a way, the sixteenth century—and especially its first half—was characterised by a coincidence of high prices for both wheat and wool, with results reflected in agricultural production.

The high price of wool reinforced the earlier tendency towards an expansion of sheep-farming. Enclosures led to the setting up of sheep farms, mostly of middling size, though there were also big farms and more small-scale sheep-rearing on the part of peasants. Rational economic thinking took charge. Increased sheep-farming depends on an increase in the area of pasture. But then wheat prices rose as well, and so these 'modern' farmers attempted to utilise this further potential line of profit and went in for corn-growing side by side with sheep-rearing. This produced in the first half of the sixteenth century the development of a method of cultivation which G. Hanssen has described as 'intensive arable-and-grass economy' and Cunningham as 'convertible husbandry'—a method which combines pasture and arable with each other in a long-term rotation.

These changing methods of cultivation were accompanied by a further dissolution of the feudal system which also, of course, stood in the way of a rational economy. Admittedly, one has to be careful to avoid the generalisations and exaggerations often met with in the older literature, for only parts of England—especially the Midlands—were affected by these changes, while other parts (the north and up to a point also the south) remained untouched. None the less, these changes are highly characteristic for the age, and one is entitled to stress them. Their effects on agrarian structure were, thus, a further wearing away of the feudal order and with it of peasant serfdom. The old relationships disappeared without ever being formally abolished, because the lords lost interest in labour services: where they practised direct farming they found servile labour too expensive on account of its inefficiency, and where they leased out the demesne as a whole or in part they would have had to secure the services in the manorial court on behalf of the tenant who had leased them. The old legal basis for possession disappeared and was mostly replaced by customary tenure recorded in the manor roll (*per copiam rotuli curiae*): here lies the origin of the copyholder, a free peasant. The facts that copyhold took various forms—in particular with regard to right of possession which might be for a term of years, for one or more lives, or hereditary—and that other legal forms like true leasehold also occurred, are of less importance than the shift in the peasant's standing. From the fifteenth century onwards, and especially from the sixteenth, he began to lose ground to the sheep-farmer, until by the end of the sixteenth he ceased to determine the structure of English rural society. The numbers of those below peasant level also declined, for the great sheep-farms needed only a few shepherds and no peasants. As Max Weber has put it, perhaps too epigrammatically but yet in essentials correctly: 'The peasants were freed from the land and the land from the peasants.' This may be asserted even though the change took place in various parts of England to very different degrees, and even though it happened in stages of varying intensity. The declining fifteenth and early sixteenth centuries marked the first culmination in this process; a second spanned the turn of the eighteenth, or more precisely lasted from 1760 to 1830. The extent of enclosures made in this latter period compels one not to overestimate the upheavals of the sixteenth century. Nevertheless, from that time England ceased to be a land of peasants. The dominating figure, though not everywhere to the same degree, is not however the landlord who supplies the 'dépenses foncières' of the physiocrats, nor is it the peasant; it is the farmer or leaseholder who farms on a basis of entrepreneurial profit-making, who utilises the market as well as all agricultural techniques, and from whom this attitude radiates outwards to other groups. The decisive characteristic is found in the dissolution of the ancient feudal and traditional order and methods and their replacement by an attitude governed by entrepreneurial and profit-making activities. In short, agriculture was acclimatised to a system and to production methods determined by market conditions.

This decisive change, which was of great weight for the whole future development of English agriculture, did not take place at the same time in all parts of England or among the various categories of landlords. Ashley already pointed out—and the more recent researches of Hoskins, Hallam, Beresford, Finberg, Rawson, Chapman and others have developed the theme more firmly—that it happened with different intensity in different counties: markedly so in Kent, Essex, Suffolk, Worcestershire as well as in Shropshire, Leicestershire, Northamptonshire, the Isle of Wight, etc., while such counties as Yorkshire, Lincolnshire, Gloucestershire, Oxfordshire were hardly affected. The Midlands dominated the story. Here enclosure brought the greatest upheavals because population was concentrated and land was scarce, so that enclosing cut deep into rural life. There were also differences in the behaviour of lay and ecclesiastical landlords. The latter in particular—but some lay lords as well—resisted the development right into the sixteenth century and occasionally even continued to collect their rents in kind. On the other hand, as Elton for instance has pointed out, the Reformation was unlikely to have any marked effect on agrarian economy and structure: monasteries and other ecclesiastical lords had already leased out much of their land, and the farmers often simply bought up their leasehold after the Dissolution. Legal relationships might change, but not the social and economic order. The importance of this lies in the fact that Church lands covered something like a quarter of England's arable. Bond status, too, disappeared only in the course of the sixteenth century, by manumission and other means. Neither in the sixteenth nor in the two following centuries did situations or forces arise in England which favoured a revival or even perhaps intensification of the old feudal order—as was so successfully attempted in the eastern parts of Germany and more particularly in Bohemia, Poland, White Russia and other countries to the east.

The reason is not to be found only in the fact that the new farming was so profitable that it satisfied for a long time the growing economic self-consciousness and the farmers' increasing search for profits. More weighty still was the complete harmony which existed between the developments in agriculture and those in other branches of the economy, such as trade, industry, and shipping. Here, too, new forms embodying the principle of the new economic freedom—replacing the old commitments by free contract (contracts of labour, of sale, etc.) and the traditional attitude by a rational one—were adopted at the same time. These branches of the economy needed labourers, seamen, clerks, soldiers, and so forth, in order to develop the new economic system at home and more particularly to introduce it into the newly acquired colonies. They obtained this labour from agriculture, not so much because the new order reduced livelihoods on the land and forced a migration away from it, but rather because agriculture was being reorganised on a basis of rational economic considerations and threw up a labour surplus. This seems to me to be the element of truth in G. Brodnitz' paradoxical statement that by a peculiarity of English development capitalist ideas penetrated earlier and more quickly into agriculture than into industry.

The development was further assisted by merchants, shipowners, and industrialists with new wealth who were eager to invest their capital in land. Because of the social standing attached to land, they would no doubt have done so even if estates had been farmed on a less profitable and rational system. Since, however, members of old noble families considered it perfectly honourable to practise such modern rational farming on their own estates, wealthy townsmen saw no reason why they should not follow suit. On the contrary, they thought their own new economic attitude endorsed and might, by scoring particularly striking successes, even hope to elevate themselves still further in the social scale. Here there began and grew, in a manner highly significant for future centuries, a close connection between the aristocracy and 'bourgeois' economic practice—so much closer than in many continental countries— as well as that constant recruitment of the aristocracy from successful merchants and industrialists. Even as in the time of the Norman Conquest the feudal system received exceptionally sharp definition in England, so its dissolution and the turning over to a 'bourgeois' attitude happened here to a degree which can only perhaps be paralleled in Italy. All other countries experienced these changes only later, in part not until the nineteenth century. The fact that England—if one may so express it— stood for a long time in the van of the development had fundamental importance both for England herself and naturally also for those other countries.

The English development was moreover peculiar in the extensive use of entail on great estates, going back to the statute *De donis conditionalibus* of 1285. The immobility of property which resulted meant that, despite all the supply of capital from the owner, the real advantages accrued to the beneficial occupier, that is the farmer who really represented the link with the world of money and credit and therefore also the entrepreneurial attitude.

Compared with England, events in France were markedly more conservative. Such changes as are to be found here cut much less deeply.

In a sense the 110 years from about 1450 to 1560 form a period which best explains both preceding and later events, and in which one can also trace the beginnings of a new development. In those years France at long last enjoyed a prolonged period of peace and with it increased prosperity. The preceding age, from 1339 onwards, was dominated by the so-called Hundred Years War whose devastating effects were at times reinforced by the plague (which hit France also in 1348), with the result that one can hardly distinguish these two causes in the general misery. In 1562 there began the wars of religion which once more destroyed much of France's prosperity and arrested or even turned back economic growth. The reign of Louis XIV (1643–1715), marked as it was by great wars, had similar effects.

The dreadful conditions of the Hundred Years War and the plague meant that there is little documentary material from which to judge growth or arrest of growth, except for constantly repeated statements about the general distress and the extent of devastation, looting, and murder. It is thus only possible to judge the trends of the sixteenth century and after by going back to an earlier time, which has also been relatively well investigated.

In the ninth and tenth centuries monarchy decayed and the feudal system and landed lordship grew up. Even then differences existed in the several parts of France which were to remain operative down to the eighteenth century. Thus the feudal system developed most completely in Burgundy and Champagne, but less so in Brittany, Normandy, Provence, and the other territories of the south. As elsewhere in Europe, demesne farming and peasant farming existed side by side. The legal position of the peasantry displayed a number of variations, from serfs through villeins (who composed the majority) to old and new freemen. Soon, however, France also witnessed a process of simplification: personal dependent status and personal burdens became attached to the soil, and rights of usufruct virtually consolidated into property rights.

As in England, Germany, and the rest of continental Europe, the thirteenth century introduced a strengthening money economy. Rents in kind were largely replaced by money rents, though Brittany, where rents in kind maintained themselves until the eighteenth century, formed a notable exception. At the same time, lords' demesne farming, which as late as the eleventh century covered between one-quarter and one-half of France's cultivated land, declined. The land was let to peasants, often on definitely favourable terms. The thirteenth century was also characterised by a commutation of most or part of the peasants' service for money payments; in this there was a measure of emancipation. The lords were forced to do this by their need for money and by the necessity to combat the attraction of the towns. Moreover, the old conditions of serfdom began to disappear in this time, without, however, totally vanishing, as they did in Flanders and Brabant. The process of dissolution continued in most parts of France until the sixteenth century, when it came to a stop. Finally the thirteenth century witnessed the end of a colonising process lasting several centuries which did not, as in Germany, consist in the clearing of aboriginal forest but in the removal of scrub which had grown on territory once cultivated. It was only in this century that cultivation was resumed on all the land which had been used in Roman times. In connection with this process, peasants acquired common ownership of woods and pastures, or at the least firmly defined rights in such common land.

On this basis there began a development which could take place only piecemeal during the Hundred Years War and became fully apparent thereafter. The troubles of the war augmented by the effects of plague admittedly led to general distress and to new devastations, but one can also see that the old relationships were dissolving further. Because the purchasing power of rents declined the nobility grew so poor that they could not prevent the further disappearance of traditional serfdom. Characteristically, serfdom survived most easily in parts like Lorraine, Burgundy and Franche Comté which were not affected by the war. Elsewhere the lord, by now no longer equipped with most or even any of his servile labour and unable to pay the increased wages of day labourers, saw himself compelled to surrender even the farming of the demesne to peasants; leasehold (mostly part and short-term leases) increasingly replaced the old tenants' rights of the peasantry. This contractual settlement of economic relationships may have been assisted by the fact that wealthy townsmen, mostly merchants, began to acquire landed estates, especially in the neighbourhood of towns. In the second half of the fifteenth century, when peace had been restored, the same development— decay of landed lordship and especially of demesne farming, the growing practice of renting out—continued unchecked.

The decisive contrast with English developments appears in the fact that no impulse to pursue a different line came from the industrial and merchant class, in the manner in which wool export, cloth production, and cloth trade affected things in England. French industry was very undeveloped in this period; mostly it produced for the local market, and goods were of low quality. It is true that burghers, merchants, financiers, speculators, jurists, and occasionally also prosperous peasants penetrated into the territorial aristocracy, while the old landed families grew poor and looked for places at court and in the army; but this new nobility adopted the fashions and usages of the old. Indeed the new lords, often members of the *parlements* and in control of the judicial process, applied all their influence to a consolidation of a landed lordship which, though at one time they had fought against it, now gave them social standing and income in rents. Admittedly, the great clothiers of Poitou and Picardy organised an extensive domestic industry and export trade, but unlike their English counterparts they had no thought of systematically promoting wool production and thus adapting agriculture to sheep-farming. Neither were they concerned to revive and develop direct exploitation which had virtually disappeared—as happened, up to a point, in England and more still in eastern Europe. Attempts made in the seventeenth and eighteenth centuries to restrict peasants' rights in wood and pasture, or by way of a radical solution altogether to abolish common lands, were motivated only by a desire to increase the revenue from rents—or rather, to counteract their steady decline. These attempts did not involve changes in farming methods or in capital equipment, nor were they so intended. The peasants, on the other hand (even supposing that they had realised the economic possibilities), could not introduce innovations because they were entirely without the necessary capital. The lack of capital in agriculture was never cured until the nineteenth century. This arrested development was caused not by the pressure of tenurial dues or rents, which were generally quite low, but by the small size of holdings, which limited productivity, and by the pressure of public burdens such as taxes. The majority of French peasants owned farms so small that they could barely maintain a man and his family; in many cases they were insufficient even for this purpose, so that peasant families were forced to find additional work outside agriculture. Where in such a situation could capital have accumulated? Such capital as was available in France came from sources other than agriculture and did not go into it, but into trade, speculation, industry, or even mining. An inadequate internal transport system—bad roads and, more important still, manifold interior tolls and the like—resulted from this arrested development and in turn perpetuated it.

France thus experienced almost none of that marked outburst of rational economic thinking and action in agriculture. The changes of the thirteenth century and their continuation in the sixteenth did produce the replacement of rents and services in kind by money rents and an end to personal serfdom, a consolidation of possessory rights, and an increase in the practice of renting; but things stopped at this stage. France remained a land of peasants overlaid by a class of rentier lords; she remained a poor and poorly developed country relying on traditional economic methods. The trends which began in the period of peace before the outbreak of the religious wars did not mature, whereas in England they underwent a straightforward development. Only the ideas and policy of the physiocrats (Quesnay, Turgot, etc.), and of course the great Revolution, produced a tempestuous eruption of new economic forces.

Among the countries of southern Europe, Spain and Italy occupy a special position. Both underwent the economic reforms of the late West-Roman empire and then encountered, under the sway of conquering peoples, novel forms of social and agrarian organisation alien to their previous development. In both cases the conquerors were at first Germanic, bringing with them their way of life and merging it with the existing late-Roman culture. In 415 the Visigoths founded an empire, with its capital at Toledo, which at first included southern France and Spain but was then limited by the Frankish king Clovis to Spain only. In Italy, after a brief triumphal procession of Visigoths and Vandals, the Ostrogoths under Theodoric the Great founded a kingdom in 493 which lasted only until 533 and was replaced in the north as early as 568 by the Lombard kingdom. In both cases the Germanic concept of the 'following' and the feudal system arising from it determined the agrarian structure through the personal relationships between lord and follower. In 711 all Spain except the north fell before the Arab conquest. In Italy the Germanic element was reinforced by the incorporation of the Lombard kingdom in Charlemagne's empire (774) and the later domination of the German emperors who frequently settled their vassals there. In Spain, the Reconquest began after some centuries of Arab rule during which the political structure had undergone further development. Independent forms of rural organisation began to grow in Italy in the tenth century; in the eleventh, in the course of a struggle with the Germanic feudal system, they acquired momentum. Ultimately the city and urban mentality triumphed over feudal lordship. As Alfred Doren has put it: 'Nearly everywhere in Italy, the polity of ancient Greece and Rome overcame the Germanic feudalism of the north.' Free self-governing communes established themselves—city states which even politically subjugated the surrounding countryside.

Thus the critical period in the development of Italy and her agrarian structure lasted from the eleventh to the thirteenth century. Thereafter the story runs without interruption down to the present day. The formative period is characterised by a coalescence of classes once strictly separate in law into one uniform class which enjoyed personal freedom independent of any contractual agreement or commitment. The old *servus* became the *colonus*, and the *livellarius* (personally free but tied as to duties) and *arimanus* (Germanic and personally free) combined with the *colonus* into a uniform stratum of peasant tenants. The decisive factor now was not status at birth but only the fact that burdens were owed. In marginal territories like Sardinia and Friuli, however, personal unfreedom continued to exist as late as the fifteenth century. The first step was immediately followed by the second: even this factual form of tenurial dependency declined and was replaced by services expressed in rents (commonly money payments). In the event, tenurial possessory rights changed into the legal form of the free lease. All this was accompanied by the abandonment of demesne farming. Its role had never been comparable in Italy to that which it played on the great estates north of the Alps; but there had been estates on which labour services had to be rendered and payments made, estates which came under a different law from peasant law. The demesne was now largely distributed on lease; what remained— mostly used for gardens, parks, orchards, and vineyards—no longer occupied a separate legal position. In other words, there was now only a uniform 'bourgeois' land law, no longer a feudal and manorial land law.

In purely material respects these changes did not as a rule improve the peasants' lot; here and there leasehold rents or shares owed amounted to more than the tenurial rents had done. But the peasants were entirely free as to the manner in which they practised farming. In consequence, landowners and landworkers of all kinds were forced into an economy dominated by the towns. In the same way, the nobility turned more and more from a rural to an urban aristocracy, invested most of its wealth in moveables instead of real estate, and shared in the profits made by trade. This process of urbanisation was assisted also by the other side, the towns themselves, when wealthy citizens bought landed property on which they raised part of their own needs in fruit or poultry, but which they also used as summer residences and rural retreats. In assessing the mutual approach of town and country and the levelling off of the original differential legal concepts, one must ascribe very considerable importance to these 'villas'.

In most parts of Italy—especially in Tuscany—the process was complete by the thirteenth century. The sixteenth, which produced such new developments in nearly all Europe, had no significance for Italy. While it is true that throughout the centuries and even to the present day great estates remained in the hands of leading aristocratic families and the Church, there was no large-scale farming but only smallholding. The Church, too, found it necessary to let out and sell the better part of its great possessions because the large contributions demanded by the Papacy for the crusades had resulted in an intolerable burden of debt. Neither in lay nor in ecclesiastical hands were there therefore any great economic units which might have supported an ideal of self-sufficiency and a turning away from involvement in the general economy.

Developments in Spain were totally different. This was due not only to considerable differences in climate in the several parts of the peninsula, but also to differing political fortunes. While most of it remained for centuries under Moorish rule, Catalonia belonged to the Carolingian empire and witnessed the growth of a strict feudal system as a basis for the military class engaged in the struggle with the Moors. Other parts of the north-west developed similarly, though special features soon began to show in the Basque provinces. Here the influence of trade and shipping—the influence of towns—opposed the feudal system which in these parts had grown from the rule of clan chiefs and not from the commendation of vassals. In a measure as Basque agriculture accommodated itself to the market economy of neighbouring towns, a development very similar to that of Italy became apparent. In the territories which were gradually reconquered from the Moors things also did not develop uniformly. In Aragon the high nobility took the place of the Moorish lords and, in alliance with the towns, so forcefully restrained royal power that the peasants remained in extreme dependence from which they were not freed until the eighteenth century. The central parts of Castile and Leon retained the settlements developed by the Celt-Iberians—fortified towns surrounded by a circle of unfortified villages. As the Reconquest proceeded, these towns became the seats of lords from hidalgo ranks who dominated the plain around it, a feature which may also be met with in Italy. The south did not know this kind of urban settlement; here lordship rested either with the territorial nobility or with the military orders, and sheep-farming dominated agriculture. The territories bordering on the Mediterranean fell under the sway of great landed lords who maintained the necessary irrigation systems. The hinterland of Seville, on the other hand, was characterised by small estates. In the fifteenth and sixteenth centuries these were bought up by Seville merchants trying in this manner to climb into the aristocracy.

Neither the upper nor the lower nobility displayed any economic initiative. They left the administration of their estates to officials. A great part of the nobility lived in quite humble conditions. Mostly they handed their lands over to lessees who on occasion formed a hierarchy of first and second lessees; at times, as in Andalusia, they farmed directly from the centre. From the high Middle Ages onwards the peasants enjoyed freedom in their persons, and in the land either a hereditary right of exploitation or a right based on rents. In addition there were day labourers. The burdens were generally high, especially where they could be raised; this could not be done in Valencia and Murcia where the peasants could rely on an unchanging incidence of burdens.

All told, Spain presents a special picture which matches the general development of Europe only in those parts where the great harbours and trading towns could exercise their influence.

2. THE GREATNESS OF ANTWERP

The 'golden age' of Antwerp is by common consent one of the most notable chapters in the history of Renaissance Europe. To the men of the time Antwerp was, as the English diplomat Sampson put it, 'one of the flowers of the world'. Some scores of these men, princes, diplomats, artists, poets, travellers and merchants, have left on record their astonished admiration at this queen of commercial capitals. Growing in volume and rising in pitch towards the middle of the sixteenth century, this crescendo of praise reaches its climax in the Florentine Guicciardini's description of 1565, one of the most splendid epitaphs—for when Guicciardini wrote Antwerp had already passed its zenith—ever written by a foreigner on the city of his adoption. If contemporaries accounted the city unique, the historian's endorsement of their verdict is still weightier testimony, for unlike them he can measure its stature against that of its gigantic successors and yet conclude that 'never since has there been a market which concentrated to such a degree the trade of all the important commercial nations of the world'. A similar claim might be made, although in less sweeping terms, for the Antwerp money-market: and it is certain that the city's discharge of both functions was an unrepeatable achievement. To borrow Unwin's analogy with Victorian England, Antwerp was not only the London of the sixteenth century, it was the Manchester as well; and we should hardly be wrong in adding the name of Bolton or Oldham, for Antwerp boasted an industrial life whose importance, neglected by the city's earlier historians, it has been left to recent writers to demonstrate.

Among the immediate causes of this florescence no single event deserves greater prominence or has a stronger claim to mark its beginning than the choice of Antwerp as the Portuguese spice-staple in 1499. It was at Bruges that the Portuguese had begun, from about 1460, to market the produce of their oceanic enterprises: but it was not until the Portuguese royal factor established himself at Antwerp that the spice-trade leapt into importance. He had already transferred himself there temporarily during the Flemish revolt of 1488–93, but this sojourn had been at the behest of the Emperor Maximilian, whereas the return in 1499 was made on his own initiative: moreover, this time he came to stay. His decision, coinciding with the success of Vasco da Gama in penetrating to the source of East Indian spices, ensured that for half a century to come Antwerp was to be the main channel of Portuguese spices into Europe. For the Portuguese colonial trade was a royal monopoly and the disposal of its products the chief duty of the royal factor. The first consignment of pepper and other goods from Lisbon reached Antwerp in August 1501. Two years later the factor concluded his first contract with an Antwerp merchant, with the result that in July 1504 a thousand tons of spices were brought up the Scheldt.

The yield of the consignment of 1504 the factor spent partly on grain, of which Portugal was then in urgent need. But normally what he wanted in exchange were metals, especially copper, metal goods, cloth and silver, which could be shipped to Africa and the Far East to pay for more spices. It was because these things were brought to Antwerp in growing quantity by two other 'national' merchant groups already trading there, the metals by the South or High Germans, and the cloth (with some lead and tin) by the English, that for fifty years the Portuguese factor kept his residence there: and his withdrawal in 1549 was at once a consequence and a symbol of a change in conditions to Antwerp's disadvantage. But spices were a magnet which attracted other things besides metals and cloth. Unlike those goods, which travelled along short and fairly safe routes, the spices which came to meet them did so by a long sea-voyage from regions remote and insecure and in consequence underwent great fluctuations in their supply. Thus, from the outset, nothing could have prevented dealing in spices from being a gamble. But the dealers did not try to prevent this; on the contrary, they were quick to exploit the speculative element in the trade. The risks were great, but so were the rewards: and it was no accident that the same South Germans who traded copper and quick-silver for spices also threw up some of the greatest financiers of the age.

It was no accident either which had brought the Portuguese, the English or the South Germans to Antwerp, and with them the assurance, for good or ill, of unprecedented commercial and financial power; their coming was a natural culmination of the developments of the preceding period. From the eleventh century to the seventeenth the Netherlands, the low alluvial region forming and embracing the great delta of the Rhine, Maas and Scheldt, were one of the nodal points of European trade; the fact itself is well known to the point of triteness, the reasons for it are almost self-evident, and neither calls for elaboration. But just as this region as a whole constituted an economic centre of gravity, so at any given time it contained within itself a point of maximum commercial intensity: among the towns with which it abounded one enjoyed the status and power of a metropolis. From the twelfth to the fifteenth century that town was Bruges in Flanders. Then, in the course of the fifteenth century, Bruges was overtaken by Antwerp, and for upwards of fifty years Antwerp wielded a supremacy greater than that of Bruges in its heyday. Antwerp in turn went down under the combined assault of economic change and political upheaval, and this time the leadership passed to the northern fringe of the delta, where Amsterdam awaited its coming. Never so complete as

Antwerp's had been, Amsterdam's supremacy lasted considerably longer and was only to pass away when the region as a whole relinquished for a time its long-held primacy.

The rise of Antwerp is thus the obverse of the simultaneous decline of Bruges. It was in the early fourteenth century that Antwerp had made its first challenge: in 1338, for example, the town had its first foretaste of its great future by becoming a centre of English trade. But in 1357 Antwerp had become an appendage of Flanders, and for half a century its economic interests were sacrificed to those of that county. Only with the advent of the house of Burgundy was this constraint removed and the forces working in Antwerp's favour again given free play. What those forces were was the subject of a famous passage in the sketch of sixteenth-century Antwerp given by Pirenne in his *Histoire de Belgique*:[1] the deepening of the waterway from the sea, the amenities of its harbour, the rise of the English cloth trade and the advent of the High Germans, and above all the liberalism which characterised the town's approach to business problems—these were, for Pirenne, the main reasons why Antwerp forged ahead of its neighbours. To review these points briefly will be a convenient way of glancing at the results of some of the work done since his day.

Ease of access is a prime requisite of a great seaport, and since Antwerp's ascendancy coincided with the final natural improvement of its waterway to and from the sea, it is tempting to place this high among the changes operating in the town's favour. The amelioration of the western Scheldt certainly encouraged sea-going ships to make its passage instead of mooring at its mouth, in the 'road of Walcheren', and there trans-shipping their cargoes. In the 1520's the number of ships which paid the 'anchorage money' due from this direct traffic varied between six and thirty-six a year: in the 1530's the corresponding figures are 88 and 319, and thereafter the number settled down to between 200 and 300. The years which saw Antwerp at the height of its prosperity thus also saw the maritime navigation of the western Scheldt in full swing. But the system of trans-shipment was still far from superseded even as late as the mid-sixteenth century: and it is not difficult to understand why. Not only was the passage of the river by 'great ships' still a somewhat risky business, but the port facilities at Antwerp were so limited that a ship passing directly upstream might be seriously delayed on arrival. In this respect the facilitation of direct access from the sea had created, rather than solved, a problem, and in general we may conclude that its benefits, although substantial, were less decisive than has sometimes been claimed. What is clear is that these benefits were only an addition to the advantages which the town already enjoyed in its communications with a wide hinterland to the south and east. The network of waterways radiating

[1] *Ed.* 1923, III, iii, 271.

southwards was one of the two physical features which from early times made Antwerp a natural focal point for movement from the landward side: the other was the town's location at the terminus of one of the land-routes running westwards from the Rhine towards the North Sea and the Channel. The great medieval road from Cologne to Bruges ran through Ghent and Mechlin, but a branch road left this highway after its crossing of the Maas and ran north-west across the Campine towards the Scheldt estuary. This was the South German's way to Antwerp, as the western Scheldt was the Englishman's way there. It was an inexpensive route, passing through a poor countryside where provisions were to be had cheap, and was notably free from tolls and other exactions. In the villages of the Campine one may yet meet with inn-names like 'The Cologne Wagon' which preserve the memory of this vanished highway.

Before the arrival of the Portuguese, the South Germans were one of the two leading 'nations', as such groups were called, who came to do business at Antwerp. There was a time when the name 'Hanse' was written large across this page of the town's history. But it is now clear that the importance once ascribed to the Hanse corresponded more to that league's high degree of organization, and its resulting prominence in the documents of the period, than to economic realities. By contrast, the South Germans used to be overlooked, with the exception of a few leading firms, chiefly because, as a loosely-knit group, they left little trace in the archives. Based upon Nuremberg, Augsburg and Frankfurt, and linked with such places as Berlin, Breslau and Leipzig, they traded in the metals yielded by the mines of central Europe and in the fustians woven in the rural industry of the South German uplands, for both of which there was a brisk demand from all Mediterranean countries. Their big firms, the Fugger, Höchstätter, Welser and Tucher, had all begun with a combined metal and cloth trade, but in their upward progress they tended to shed cloth and to specialize in metals, above all copper and silver. Of the Mediterranean 'nations' at Antwerp, Italians took the leading place. They were important not only for their trade in costly wares, including fine cloth and the expensive Levantine spices which the cheaper Portuguese product never drove off the market, but for their commercial and financial *expertise*: the first generation of bankers at Antwerp were all Italians, successors of the firms which had until then clustered at Bruges, and later they threw up many business leaders and officials as well as, in Ludovico Guicciardini, the town's greatest publicist.

But it is undoubtedly the English who hold pride of place among the Antwerp 'nations' of this time, and the choice of Antwerp as the 'mart town' for English cloth ranks second only to the establishment of the spice-staple as the reason why merchants were drawn there from all over Europe. It was in the face of many discouragements that the English cloth trade had struggled to acquire an entrepôt in the Netherlands during the fifteenth century. The persistence which it displayed, and which was to be so amply rewarded, was a virtue born of necessity, for it was their failure to maintain themselves elsewhere along the coast of Europe which drove so many English merchants to try their fortunes in the Netherlands; there is much to be said for the view that the rise of the English cloth-trade to Antwerp, like the rise of the Merchant Adventurers' Company which came to dominate it, was a function not of the growth but of the contraction of English overseas trade as a whole. It might be supposed that this situation would have tied the Englishmen's hands when it came to bargaining about the terms of their admission. Had the Netherlands then formed a unitary state, this might well have been the case. But the union of those territories by the dukes of Burgundy was a personal one which, after the collapse of its central power on the death of Charles the Bold, waited for half a century before seriously resuming the task of state-building. Thus well into the period under review—and in some respects throughout it—the various territories, and within them their powerful urban communities, continued to enjoy a measure of autonomy, and to display a degree of particularism, which belonged wholly to the Middle Ages. From the English point of view this was the saving grace, for it turned their weakness into strength. One of the secrets of the privileged position which the Merchant Adventurers came to enjoy in the Netherlands was their calculated avoidance of any commitment to the sole use of one of the towns—Antwerp, Middelburg and Bergen-op-Zoom were the three chiefly concerned—which were available to them. In defence of this tactical principle they had to resist not only the blandishments of the towns themselves but also the pressure of the dukes of Burgundy, who would have preferred in their own interests to see the cloth trade organised under a compulsory staple. When in 1497, for instance, Philip the Fair sought Henry VII's approval for the erection of such a staple at Antwerp and Bergen-op-Zoom, the Merchant Adventurers set their face against it and insisted on the freedom of choice which enabled them to 'drive the townships, by fear of their withdrawing and absenting, to reform their wrongs'. The mere threat of withdrawal was not always enough, and from time to time the Englishmen transferred themselves to a rival town for a period of one or more fairs.

But it was Antwerp which was to be the English mart town *par excellence*, and it was there that they were to be joined by almost all the other trading 'nations'. Was this because these merchants found better and more enlightened treatment there, fewer restraints and greater tolerance —in other words, was it because Antwerp was more 'liberal', more 'modern', than her neighbours? Four main conditions governed the conduct of international trade at Antwerp: the technique of the trade itself; the conditions upon which the various 'nations' were admitted; the special régime which obtained during the town's two fairs; and the policy of the Netherlands government. Of these, the first is the least important. The technique of trade was, generally speaking, common to the whole of Europe, with advances—like the double-entry bookkeeping which quickly reached Antwerp—being usually made first in the south and brought north by their originators: but in the fifteenth century goods were bought and sold, delivered and paid for, according to much the same rules in all trading towns. It is true that after 1500 the growing volume and complexity of business at Antwerp were accompanied by some refinements of business practice: but in so far as these helped to make the town a freer and more modern business centre the credit belongs less to the town than to the merchants who devised and perfected them.

Of greater importance are the terms upon which the 'nations' came to Antwerp, for here, if anywhere, we should expect to find specific evidence of the town's liberality: and since of all the nations it was the English who secured the best terms, they are the example most calculated to bear out the argument. It is undeniable that among the privileges accorded to the English merchants by Antwerp in the half-century after 1446, the year of the first 'statute' defining their position, were several of a 'liberal' and 'modern' kind: thus in place of the old *gastenrecht*, the code of rules regulating the foreigner's sojourn, Englishmen at Antwerp came to enjoy almost complete freedom in this respect, and if they were still required to employ native brokers in their dealings with other foreigners, the scope of these go-betweens' activities, both legitimate and otherwise, was increasingly limited. But all the evidence goes to show that it was not only Antwerp which was thus relaxing the rigid aliens' code: even Bruges, which is generally represented as lagging far behind, was making perceptible progress in the same direction. Moreover, it seems certain that, far from being spontaneously bestowed by the towns, these privileges were extorted under that threat of withdrawal of which we have already heard the Merchant Adventurers boasting. The towns themselves were under no illusion as to the way in which they were being played off against one another, and on occasion they could draw together in self-defence, as Antwerp and Bergen-op-Zoom did in 1488 'against the injustices which the merchants of the kingdom of England, more than those of any other nation, commit against them'.

We are on firmer ground when we come to the Brabant fairs, the 'four markets' so famous in the history of the delta region. As instituted, or perhaps only regularized, by Duke John II at the opening of the fourteenth century, each fair was to last for two weeks only, but these had soon lengthened to six (of which in theory the first two covered the journey to, and the last two the departure from, the fair itself), so that during the fifteenth century the four fairs covered, with an overlap of two weeks, a minimum of twenty-two weeks, not much less than half the year. They were not evenly spaced, but fell into two groups. The *Paasmarkt* or Easter

Fair at Bergen-op-Zoom, which opened on Maundy Thursday, was followed immediately by the *Pinxten* or *Sinxtenmarkt*, the Pentecost Fair, at Antwerp: similarly the Antwerp *Bamismarkt* or St Bavo's Fair, which opened towards the end of August, was followed with scarcely a break by the Bergen *Koudmarkt* or Winter Fair, beginning in the last week of October. The proximity of the two towns (they were only thirty miles apart) made it easy for merchants to visit both in the course of their spring or autumn round, and this helps to explain why the two Bergen fairs, after they had lost their commercial significance (as they had largely done before 1540), could still fulfil the more modest but useful purpose of providing two of the 'settlement periods' in the financial year. Of the value of these fairs to the two Brabant towns during the fifteenth century there can be little question. Their régimes, it is true, did not differ significantly either from one another or from those of other towns: the freedom of persons and goods from legal process save in criminal causes, and their special protection against violence, robbery and similar misdeeds—these were the essential features. But the jealousy with which the towns guarded their fair-rights, and their eagerness to extend their duration, are proof sufficient of the importance attaching to them.

When we move into the sixteenth century, however, the picture changes. While the fairs remain outwardly unaltered in both towns, their real significance begins to differ. Bergen-op-Zoom continues as a 'fair town', its foreign trade concentrated within the few weeks of its two fairs and almost non-existent outside them; moreover, its fairs themselves are soon in full decline, with the number of merchants visiting them dropping steadily from some 400 in the 1520's to 100 or less in the early 1540's. Indeed, it is hardly too much to say that the Bergen fairs were kept alive only by the determination of the English cloth merchants to use them as a foil to Antwerp. At Antwerp, on the contrary, not only do the fairs themselves flourish, but they do so increasingly as the peaks of a commercial year which is becoming more or less continuous: here again, English influence was important, or even decisive, for the control exercised by the Merchant Adventurers' Company was in favour of periodicity rather than of continuity in trading, and the cloth fleets were timed to arrive during the fairs, especially the *Sinxtenmarkt*. While it appears, on the one hand, therefore, that Antwerp's trade was bursting out of its medieval fair-limits, on the other it remains true that, even when trade had attained its maximum volume, the fairs still provided the framework of the commercial year, as well as being the basis, as we shall see, of the financial calendar.

There remains the attitude of the Burgundian rulers of the Netherlands towards the rising metropolis on the banks of the Scheldt. The medieval constitution of those territories, that cumbrous mass of privileges, customs and institutions which it was the fatal mission of the houses of

Burgundy and Habsburg to attempt to suppress and supplant, for long obstructed their freedom of action and hindered the pursuit of any consistent policy, economic or otherwise. It is therefore only in those few fields of economic policy, such as the administration of the toll and currency systems or the negotiation of commercial treaties, in which the central government had a freer hand that we must seek, at least during the earlier period, traces of partiality towards Antwerp. It was Flanders which had given the house of Burgundy its first footing in the Netherlands, and this fact continued to be reflected in its measures until, under Charles the Bold and still more under Maximilian, the persisting decline of Flemish industry and trade, and the political unruliness which accompanied it, broke that original tie. What Flanders lost, Brabant, and above all Antwerp, gained. It was the town's support of Maximilian during his ten years' struggle with the Flemish towns which forged the bond between Antwerp and the dynasty which was to last unimpaired until the advent of Philip II seventy years later. The alliance was inaugurated by Maximilian's charters of 1488 calling upon the 'nations' resident at Bruges to transfer themselves to Antwerp. These brought, among others, the Portuguese factor to the town for the first time.

If, therefore, Antwerp owed something to political good fortune during the formative years which closed the fifteenth century, it continued to enjoy the legacy of those years throughout its half-century of maturity and grandeur during the sixteenth. In the state which, for good or ill, its Habsburg rulers began to bring progressively under their direct control, Antwerp was able to boast a degree of political, religious and fiscal autonomy remarkable even in its own country. But it did so on two conditions. The first was its ability and willingness to 'support the prince in his necessities', the second its acceptance of the policy which the prince pursued with the resources thus provided. For the first fifty years of the century, which were all but coterminous with the rule of Charles V, these conditions were substantially fulfilled. The magistracy was invariably ready with the money required to confirm an old privilege or acquire a new one, to redeem a toll or farm a tax, while its wealthiest strangers made the loans which an imperial foreign policy called for increasingly. In the same way, the town accepted, with no more than an occasional complaint, a policy which it could either approve or, so far as its own interests were concerned, neutralise. This was notably true of religion. In an age of rising intolerance the magistrates used the town's privileges to protect its business community. They were not interested in small fry, who furnished the great majority of the Antwerp martyrs, many of them under the generic term of 'Anabaptists'. But anyone who mattered in the business world, whether one of the 'New Christians' who flocked to Antwerp from Portugal or an errant member of one of the Catholic 'nations', would be given the manifold protections of municipal law and custom.

It was the growing rift between this attitude and the government's policy which more than anything else estranged them, especially after 1555. Had the government not been so financially dependent upon the town and its money-market, it might have struck earlier against this privileged obstructionism. As it was, Granvelle could counsel Philip II to foster the trade of Ghent as a counterpoise to Antwerp—Ghent, which had given no trouble since its overthrow in 1540 and which would be easier to manage than the 'overmighty subject' on the Scheldt. It was an idea far removed from that of 1488.

Until a generation ago the only figures relating to Antwerp's trade at or near its peak were those of Guicciardini. Writing of the years about 1560, when decline had perhaps already set in, Guicciardini gave a series of round sums of the value of the various commodities imported into the town each year. Out of a total value of nearly sixteen million gold crowns, English cloth accounted for five millions, or nearly one-third; next came Italian wares, especially fine cloth, amounting to three millions, Baltic wheat at nearly one and three-quarters and German wines at one and a half millions, and French wines and Portuguese spices each at one million. Spanish wines and wool, German cloth, French *pastel*, English wool and French salt, representing progressively smaller sums, made up the total. These traditional figures may now be compared, thanks to the work of Belgian historians, with total figures of Antwerp's exports for certain years obtained by multiplying the yield of taxes levied by the Netherlands government upon the country's export trade to help to pay for the French wars. Chief among these taxes were that of one per cent laid upon all exports in 1543–5 and that of two per cent levied upon goods exported to southern Europe in 1552–4. The totals thus derived include one of about 1,100.000 pounds Flemish[1] for all exports, both by land and water, from Antwerp for the twelve months February 1543 to February 1544, and one of more than 1,200.000 for the twelve months following, while the yield of the one-half per cent tax of November 1551–January 1552 represents an annual total of two and a quarter millions. Since the government was, in a fiscal sense, less interested in the import than in the export trade, we are less well informed about it: but there is an import figure corresponding to that for exports in 1551–2 of roughly 1,600.000 pounds.

Wide as may be their margin of error, these and similar figures bear out what can be inferred from non-statistical evidence, that the volume of

---

[1] Here, as elsewhere in this section, the term 'pounds Flemish' means the pound of 240 groschen, not the pound of 40 groschen, or Carolusgulden, in which the accounts in question were made up. The totals given here thus equal one-sixth of those taken from the accounts themselves, plus an estimated addition for the exports of the Merchant Adventurers which, as De Smedt has shown (*De Engelse Natie te Antwerpen*, II, 437, 441), are not represented in them.

trade passing through Antwerp varied considerably at different periods of the town's 'golden age'. A broad indication of this pattern of commercial activity is furnished by the figures, published in 1939, of the yield of the toll of Iersekeroord, or toll of Zeeland. This was the principal toll levied upon traffic using the waterways of the Scheldt delta, including the western Scheldt between Antwerp and the sea, a route which probably accounted for one-half of the town's trade. Since the toll was usually farmed, most of the figures are those of the annual rents paid by lessees, but from time to time the actual yield is recorded. Taken together, these figures point to the conclusion that the 'golden age', the years between 1500 and 1560, was made up of three fairly well-defined phases: an opening phase of intensely rapid expansion during the first twenty years of the century, followed, after a recession during the next ten years, by some twelve to fifteen years of stability at about the maximum so far achieved, and then, from the late 1540's, by a dozen years of violent fluctuation, during which new high records alternated rapidly with deep troughs of depression.

The trade totals of the 1540's and 1550's can be made the basis of some instructive comparisons. Used to measure the trade of Antwerp against that of other Netherlands ports, they show that the town was handling between seventy and eighty per cent of the country's foreign trade, eloquent testimony to the extent to which the whole region had become, in Pirenne's phrase, only a suburb of the metropolis. Again, the export totals of the years 1543–5, the equivalent of about £900,000 sterling, are nearly three times as great as the corresponding figure for London and about half as much again as that of all English ports put together. One notable feature is that Antwerp appears to have enjoyed a 'favourable' balance of trade. In view of the large loans raised by foreigners in Antwerp, we might have expected an import surplus representing the service of these loans. That the reverse seems to have been the case is a tribute to the importance of the town's industrial effort in converting its imports of raw materials and semi-manufactures into finished products of greater value.

It is generally believed that the trade of sixteenth-century Antwerp was predominantly 'transit' in character, that the town was little more than a great entrepôt for goods produced elsewhere than in the Netherlands and passing through it to more or less distant destinations. In fact Antwerp did a good deal more than act as a conduit for a stream of trade set in motion elsewhere. For not only was the town itself an important final market for many goods, but the industrial life which it shared with the surrounding region was an integral part of its commercial activity. The 'special trade', to use a convenient modern term, thus generated or quickened consisted, on the import side, of foodstuffs, raw materials and semi-manufactured goods, and on the export side of goods produced or processed within the town or in the surrounding region. Antwerp was the largest town of the most densely populated part of northern Europe. A mid-sixteenth century estimate of 3,000,000 for the population of the Netherlands is probably something of an exaggeration—a modern authority would reduce it to less than two—but density was certainly greatest in Flanders and Brabant, with the latter accounting for more than half a million. Antwerp's own resident population increased from less than 50,000 at the opening to about 100,000 by the middle of the century, when the town ranked, in point of size, next after the six greatest cities in Europe; and there was the large floating element of visiting merchants, shippers and travellers. The victualling of this urban concentration required a continual flow of trade. The produce of local agriculture and fisheries, together with great quantities of fuel in the form of peat, arrived week by week for the town's sustenance and warmth; while its possession of the three staples of grain, fish and oats meant that it also handled much of the food imported from abroad for the whole of Brabant. A number of these imports underwent processing at Antwerp which brought them within the scope of industrial activity: fish-curing, sugar-refining and soap-making were early prominent there.

By far the most important branch of the special import trade was that concerned with textiles. By the sixteenth century there was little spinning or weaving done at Antwerp, but cloth-finishing had developed into a major industry: in 1564 the cloth dressers' gild alone counted 1600 masters and apprentices. The bulk of the cloth dressed at Antwerp came from England, for those who bought English cloth usually had it finished in the town before carrying it to its destination. In 1565 the Antwerp magistracy estimated the annual importation of English cloth at upwards of 700,000 pounds Flemish, of which more than 400,000 pounds' worth were for re-export; since the cost of the finishing processes averaged one-third of the wholesale price, the town's earnings from this branch of its trade may have reached 100,000 pounds Flemish. Besides the cloth itself, the finishing industries needed various other imports. First in rank was alum, the indispensable mordant for fixing colours (it was also used in making copper). After the discovery of the deposits at Tolfa in the Papal States, Charles the Bold had forbidden the import of alum from any other source, and in 1491 Philip the Fair and Maximilian had strengthened the monopoly by making Antwerp the staple for alum. The trade itself was in the hands of contractors, generally Italians, but the town assumed responsibility for the payment of a duty of 25 shillings a last: as the trade grew the sum involved became very large, until in 1555 it was redeemed by a capital payment of 240,000 pounds Flemish. Next come the dyes which the alum was used to set. The Antwerp dyeing industry had three stock colours, black, blue and tan. Not until after the middle of the century did the Antwerpers find an alternative to woad as the source of their blue dye, and this woad (the French *pastel*) formed a principal import from southern France, Spain and Portugal, while some was re-exported to neighbouring countries. The opening up of the world brought new dye-stuffs. Indigo was known at Antwerp from soon after 1550, but was not used in dyeing until somewhat later, and the redwood from which Brazil took its name, although among the earliest items of the Portuguese trade, only slowly replaced the traditional madder. Cochineal came in from about 1550.

A marked feature of the other new industries which developed at or near Antwerp was their growing consumption of metal. The armaments industry rose and flourished under the stimulus of the French wars; while the weapons and armour sold at Antwerp partly came in ready-made from Germany or from the valley of the Maas, some of them were made at Antwerp or at near-by Mechlin from imported metal. An impression of the abundance of artillery can be gathered from the fact that at the ceremonial entry of Prince Philip in September 1549 about a thousand guns were ranged outside the gate through which he entered the town. Another flourishing industry was bell-founding, for which the in-numerable steeples which soared above that flat landscape kept up a brisk demand.

It is clear that out of the total volume of Antwerp's imports no small proportion was moving into rather than merely through the town, either to be consumed there or to leave it again only after fashioning at the hands of local craftsmen. The corresponding export trade included, besides the major items already mentioned, a host of things which contributed to that rising standard of material comfort and cultural progress which characterised the age: furniture of all descriptions, floor- and wall-coverings, tapestries, paintings and statuettes, ornaments and jewellery, glassware, books, papers and maps, and the musical instruments for which the Netherlands were renowned. The list is lengthened and diversi-fied by the wide range of goods produced elsewhere in the Netherlands and brought to the town for disposal, like the 'new draperies' turned out by the rural cloth industry of Flanders or the cloth towns of the northern provinces, great quantities of which were carried from Antwerp by the Spaniards and Portuguese.

It is a commonplace that Antwerp's trade was handled almost ex-clusively by foreigners and that natives played a subordinate, even a negligible, part in it: this was Guicciardini's view and, like most of his *dicta*, it was long accepted without question. So far as the main branches of overseas trade are concerned it is indeed substantially correct: from the outset it was Englishmen, Germans, Portuguese and Spaniards who brought their wares to Antwerp and carried one another's away, not Antwerpers who went in search of these things. In this respect sixteenth-century Antwerp occupied a position markedly different from that soon to be taken by Amsterdam, whose overseas trade was largely the creation of the Hollanders themselves. But it would be wrong to conclude either that the Antwerpers had from the beginning tamely acquiesced in this state of affairs or that it left them with nothing to do but 'stand and wait'. At least during the earlier phase of the town's ascendancy, the Antwerp merchant fleet had not been wholly negligible. In European waters we hear of Antwerpers who trade actively with their near neighbours and even penetrate the Baltic, and outside Europe of their sporadic efforts to emulate the great voyages. It was between 1510 and 1520 that the enterprising Dirk van Paesschen was organising his luxury trips for pilgrims and traders to Italy and the Levant, and in 1521 that three Antwerp ships made the voyage to the Far East from which only one returned. But in measure as the town's trade grew, its own part certainly became more passive. This was, to no small extent, a result of the hostility which the earlier efforts had provoked. In the Baltic the Antwerpers had fallen foul of the Hanse; in England they struggled against mounting discrimination; above all, their essay in breaking the spice monopoly incensed the Portuguese and might, if persisted in, have jeopardised that golden trade. There was, of course, nothing exceptional in all this; merchants were everywhere called upon to face jealous rivals as well as natural hazards. If the Antwerpers showed less fortitude than, say, the Hollanders, it was because they already had so much more to lose by trade-wars and so much more to gain by accepting the role assigned to them. There was still plenty for them to do. Trade called into being a whole range of 'commercial services', and while some of these, notably the financial ones, also passed into foreign hands, others retained a more 'national' character: thus the notaries public, who flourished on commercial documentation, were usually natives, as were those more numerous, but less respectable, intermediaries, the brokers, although these became more cosmopolitan as time went on. One form of business which made great strides and yet remained largely in native hands was the commission agency; one of these firms, Van de Molen Brothers, has left a unique record of its dealings in the form of more than a thousand letters dating from 1538 to 1544.

A simple division of the Antwerp trading world into foreign and native elements ignores that intermediate group of strangers who became domiciled in the town and assimilated to its life. Of these foreign colonies the largest was the Spanish. The political connection put Spaniards on a different footing from other strangers and swelled their numbers with non-commercial figures, chiefly officials and soldiers. In the 1540's about fifty Spanish merchants were ordinarily resident, and by 1560 the total had risen to 100, with perhaps an equal number of servants and factors. The Portuguese seem to have been numerically about half as strong, while the English colony probably amounted, towards the middle of the century, to fifty or sixty individuals or families, and the Italian 'nations'—Genoese, Florentines and Luccese predominating—to about the same number combined. Frenchmen were numerous, but there are no figures for them, and the Germans also remain indeterminate. All told, by about 1550 there were probably some four hundred to five hundred merchant strangers domiciled at Antwerp, with an equal number of foreign dependents.

Not all of these foreigners settled there for life, and they included individuals at every stage of assimilation. The factor of a foreign firm spending some years in the town and then returning home might be counted a foreigner still, but a merchant establishing himself there, marrying into a native family and rearing children to whom it would be home, would have moved in the direction of 'naturalisation'. But few strangers took the final step of becoming citizens. Between 1533 and 1582 only 179 individuals of Mediterranean origin, Spaniards, Portuguese and Italians, were admitted to the freedom of the town, and in only two of those years did the number exceed ten: during the same period no more than twenty-three Englishmen became citizens. Clearly, only a small minority of foreign-born residents decided, for whatever reason, to throw in their lot with the town's. Yet it is among this small group of Antwerpers 'by adoption' that we find some of the leading figures of the business world. Erasmus Schetz, who inherited copper, married into spice, and transmuted both into one of Antwerp's largest personal fortunes, belonged to it, as did Gillis Hooftman, the sugar king. These men were as influential as any undiluted foreigner in shaping the town's destiny.

There was very little wholesale buying or selling for cash at Antwerp: cash purchasers were hard to come by and could exact a discount of up to thirty per cent. Of the various forms of credit payment in use the most regular was the division of the sum involved into parts and the fixing of separate days of payment for these parts: the customary division was into three parts, the first payable at the forthcoming fair and the others at the two succeeding fairs. One circumstance which helped to make this arrangement, long established in all European trading countries, all but universal at Antwerp was the convenient intervals which separated the fairs. By the sixteenth century the 'settlement periods', which had originally fallen within the fairs, had come to follow immediately after them: ten days were normally allotted but these could be extended, and with a little adjustment the four 'settlement periods' could be made the basis of quarterly payments. By an ordinance of 1521 the four periods were timed to begin early in February, May, August and November, the first two being the settlements of the two Bergen-op-Zoom fairs and the others those of the Antwerp fairs.

It was on the dual foundation of credit-purchases and bill-payments that the trade of Antwerp was borne. To contemporary merchants it was self-evident that without these facilities trade upon the scale to which they had become accustomed would have been impossible. 'Merchants', declared Sir Richard Gresham in 1538, 'can no more be without exchanges than ships at sea without water.' The provision of the necessary credit was the chief function of the sixteenth-century banker. Although the mutual dealings between merchants which had characterised exchange operations in the later Middle Ages lasted on into the sixteenth century, by that time, especially in great trading centres, the buying of bills, and other forms of advancing money, were increasingly taken over by bankers. The indiscriminate use of the word 'merchants' to denote both traders and bankers shows that there was as yet no clear differentiation. The universal tendency of traders, once possessed of some capital, to forsake trading for banking was everywhere noticed and deplored. Clement Armstrong's denunciation of the 'rich old merchants' who 'occupy their money by exchange' was echoed a generation later by Guicciardini, who spoke of both gentlemen and merchants employing 'all their available capital in dealing in money, the large and sure profits of which are a great bait'. But in so far as these merchants-turned-bankers took over and improved the enormous business in commercial bills, they represented a necessary stage in specialization and helped to eliminate some of the disadvantages attaching to the older practice. They relieved the trader of the necessity to find his opposite number and they supplied a much-needed element of confidence. There was much defaulting on bills: payers continually refused to honour them, often alleging that they had never heard of the drawers. A merchant who dealt with a well-known firm which had agents or correspondents in all the chief centres was less likely to encounter this difficulty and consequently found it easier to persuade creditors to accept bills in payment.

In the sixteenth century there was no regular discounting of bills; they were bought and sold outright and redeemed on maturity. Interest normally ran at three per cent per fair, or twelve per cent per annum, and brokerage at one-half per cent. Thus if a London banker bought a 'usance' or one-month bill at 26s. 8d. Flemish to the pound sterling, about 4d. of this rate represented the profit from interest and brokerage, leaving a 'net' exchange rate of 26s. 4d. If, simultaneously, an Antwerp banker was buying a similar bill on London, he would deliver for every pound he was due to receive there this 'net' figure of 26s. 4d. minus the 4d. due for interest and brokerage, that is, 26s. Thus an identical exchange rate was normally represented on the Bourse and in Lombard Street by two figures differing by 8d., and it was always the Antwerp rate which was the lower. For bills at longer terms, or at times when money was 'tight', interest was higher and the gap between the two figures proportionately greater. A banker buying a bill and arranging for its collection abroad thus derived from the transaction a profit which could be calculated beforehand. But if he wished to bring his money home again he had to repeat the process in reverse: in the language of the time, he had to 'rechange'. It was this 'change and rechange' (Latin *cambium et recambium*, Italian *ricorsa*) which constituted the simplest and most widespread form of exchange speculation. The element of uncertainty arose from the fact that the banker could not tell in advance the rate at which he would be able to rechange. He could, however, insure against an unfavourable movement by the various devices which went under the name of 'agio', and these could be used to make profits as well as to avoid losses. Exchange fluctuations, and the variations in interest rates with which they were closely connected, provided the sixteenth-century financier with one of his two major fields of speculation. (The other was the movement of commodity-prices, and in particular the prices of wares which, like spices, were irregular in supply and could be 'cornered'.) The conditions of success were then, as now, adequate funds and the ability to move them rapidly in pursuit of marginal advantages. The chief markets involved were Antwerp itself, the South German towns, especially Augsburg, the cradle of German high finance, Lyons, Genoa and the Italian cities. The axis Antwerp–Augsburg was the monopoly of the big German firms, the triangle Antwerp–Lyons–Italy that of the Italians.

Among other branches of speculative business at Antwerp one of the safest and most lucrative was real estate; since the demand for accommodation of all kinds in the town was always ahead of the supply, the buying of land or buildings for a 'rise' was an attractive proposition in which foreigners took an active share. (It was, however, a native, Gilbert van Schoonbeke, who pioneered the greatest of these undertakings, the development of Antwerp's New Town, to the north of the original site, in 1548.) Then there were various forms of insurance. Merchants undertaking long or dangerous voyages were in the habit of insuring their lives during their absence, and out of this practice there developed something resembling modern life insurance: this was, however, frowned upon owing to its many abuses—for one thing, it led to an increase in homicide —and was forbidden in 1571. Marine insurance was in hardly better case. Considering its importance to the commercial world, its unsystematic character is something to wonder at; entrusted for the most part to notaries and brokers, it developed during the first half of the century with a minimum of control and was riddled with abuse and fraud. The first ordinance against these appeared in 1550, and in 1559 the Piedmontese J. B. Ferufini was appointed controller; ten years later Alva issued his important ordinance on the subject. With so much that was akin to gambling as part of the daily round at Antwerp, it is only to be expected that gambling proper would be rife there. The lotteries which were soon to become the vogue all over Europe took their rise at Antwerp, but another popular form of gambling until its prohibition in 1544, wagers on the sex of children, seems to have been brought there from Spain.

If Antwerp had remained in the sixteenth century simply what it had become in the course of the fifteenth, the commercial and financial centre of the Burgundian Netherlands, it would have played a considerable but limited role in European finance. What transformed the town's role in this respect was the dynastic tie which linked the Netherlands, first with the Empire, and then with Spain. Thus drawn into the web of Habsburg dominion, the Low Countries were laid under contribution to Habsburg power; fighting men, weapons of war, shipping, all these entered into the account, but as time went on it was the financial resources concentrated at Antwerp which came to outweigh all else. Since Lyons played a similar part in French government finance, the long-drawn-out struggle between Habsburg and Valois involved a contest in stamina between these two money-markets in the course of which both were stimulated into important advances in technique. It was the French war of 1511 which first led the Netherlands government to use Antwerp for loan operations, and from that date until 1542, the year which marked the dividing-line between growth and maturity in the money-market, public borrowing, while remaining spasmodic, became more frequent. The Netherlands government—and the same is true of other borrowers, save that the Portuguese transactions, being bound up with the spice trade, had a character of their own—raised loans to meet particular needs as they arose; there was no attempt at systematisation and the terms were short. Ehrenberg dates from 1516, a year in which the government borrowed the then large total of 50,000 pounds Flemish, the adoption of the fair-calendar for the timing of loans. Sums were then borrowed for periods varying from one to four fairs, that is, from three months to a year, and if necessary they were 'prolonged' on the same basis. Charles V's ordinance on the dating of the 'settlement periods' was probably not unconnected with his own interest in these dates.

In negotiating these loans the governments concerned relied almost exclusively upon a small group of leading financiers. Besides the Fugger, Höchstätter, Welser, and other South German houses, whose chief transactions with the emperor originated elsewhere, but who are found doing an increasing amount of government business at Antwerp, the principal names were, at the outset, those of the Frescobaldi and Gualterotti, the last two great Florentine houses in the Netherlands, and later those of the Spaniards De Vaille and Moxica and of Lazarus Tucher, the first of the Antwerp 'money kings'. The restricted nature of the market, combined with irregularity of demand, meant that interest rates were high and erratic; in the course of the single year 1516, for example, the Netherlands government raised loans at between 11 and 31 per cent per annum, and in the two years 1520–1 at between 15½ and 27½ per cent.

During the 1530's the rate fell steadily to between 12 and 15 per cent, and although between 1539 and 1542 it tended to rise again, partly owing to the government's clumsy meddling with the financial system, by the end of this period the lowering of the rate and the smallness of its fluctuations bespeak considerable progress in the management of the business.

The fifteen years between 1542 and 1557 saw financial operations of unprecedented magnitude at Antwerp. With the outbreak of the new French war the Netherlands government itself greatly increased the size and frequency of its borrowings; in 1543 alone it raised over a quarter of a million pounds Flemish, a figure several times greater than that for any previous year. Moreover, Charles V now began to borrow heavily on Spanish account through the Spanish royal factor. Even so, the combined Habsburg demand was at first outstripped by that of the emperor's English ally. During the last four years of his reign Henry VIII borrowed at Antwerp not far short of a million sterling, or about a million and a half Flemish, to finance his share in the war. Meanwhile, the third royal borrower, the king of Portugal, continued to raise money on a big scale against the delivery of spices and is said to have owed half a million Flemish there in 1543. Notwithstanding the size of these totals, there were few occasions during these years when money was really scarce, and the shortages did not last long. Nor did interest rates rise. In general they ranged between 12 and 15 per cent, the level to which they had fallen during the 1530's. Moreover, they were now much steadier than ever before. Clearly, the supply of money was adequate to the demand. For the capital accumulation which enabled Antwerp to shoulder these great new burdens the money-market had to thank the forty years of commercial pre-eminence enjoyed since 1499. But for the machinery by which this capital was mobilised into these huge credits the governments concerned had to thank the financial experts upon whom they had come increasingly to rely.

The greatest of these experts in the Antwerp of the 1540's was the Italian Gaspar Ducci. His career is an epitome of most of the financial developments of the age. Beginning as a commodity broker and commission agent, in which capacities he made big deals in several of the staples of Antwerp trade, he gravitated in the accustomed manner into finance. Operating mainly between Antwerp and Lyons, he quickly became the greatest exchange speculator of the time. Ducci was not content to profit by the normal discrepancies in interest rates and exchange rates; he used his own resources to create plenty and scarcity of money alternately at each end of his line of operations, driving up the rates to his own profit and to the undoing of his competitors, especially the Florentines. To the violent hostility which his methods aroused on commercial grounds there was added the suspicion provoked by their political implications. For Antwerp and Lyons were the financial strongholds of rival and often warring governments, and Ducci's activities cut across this alignment. Yet it was to this king of the financial jungle, who was moved by nothing save the spur of his own unbounded avarice and ambition, that the Habsburg monarchy was chiefly indebted for that mobilisation of the financial power of Antwerp which carried it through the 1540's and early 1550's. The chief instrument which Ducci employed for this purpose were the *Rentmeestersbrieven*, the bonds which the receivers-general of the Netherlands issued in their own name but which were secured upon the revenues coming into their hands. They were 'bearer bonds', redeemable by whoever came into their possession, and were thus readily negotiable, being in this respect the counterpart of commercial acknowledgements of indebtedness whose widespread use as negotiable instruments had been given legal recognition by an ordinance of 1536. What Ducci grasped was that the regular issue of such bonds would both serve the government directly by attracting small-scale capital and also indirectly by linking its borrowing more closely with commercial borrowing. At Lyons the same object was to be achieved by the 'King's Letters' issued by the French Government.

It was the Antwerp world of high finance which was smitten by the first of the catastrophes of the third quarter of the century. In 1557 Spain and France declared themselves bankrupt, and three years later Portugal did the same. For the bankers who had lent the two Iberian governments such great sums these were heavy blows: they saw their loans compulsorily converted into five-per-cent annuities, which meant not merely a drastic reduction of interest but a large-scale amortisation of funds. But they were not the only ones to suffer. The state bankruptcies were followed by those of public authorities in the Netherlands, among them the receiver-general and a number of towns, and these by a host of private ones: the recent mobilisation of small-scale capital by the money market and the investment boom now spread the effects of the failures far and wide.

The financial crisis was in itself a shock from which recovery would not be rapid or easy; but it had been heralded and accompanied by disturbances, less sensational yet more ominous, in the world of trade. First in point of time, and perhaps in significance, had been the discontinuance, as a permanent institution, of the Portuguese royal factory in 1549. Whatever the reasons for this step, or its immediate consequences, it symbolised the passing of an age. Half a century of relative stability in the pattern of the spice trade, with Antwerp as its centre, was to be followed by twenty years of dislocation and scarcity in the course of which a different pattern would emerge, a pattern in which Europe would draw its spices direct from Lisbon or from the reviving Levant route and

Antwerp would sink from pre-eminence to parity with other towns, especially the ports of the Mediterranean, in its handling of this trade. One of the changes which may have weakened the Portuguese dependence upon Antwerp was the ease with which, from soon after 1545, silver needed for the East Indies could be scooped up out of the great stream which then began to flow into Spain from the New World and thus the supply of European silver, which the Portuguese had previously obtained from the South Germans at Antwerp, be the more readily foregone: perhaps another was the willingness of those same purveyors to deliver their other metals elsewhere than on the banks of the Scheldt. The huge list of copper goods covered by a three-year contract between the Fugger and the royal factor in 1548 was to be delivered at Lisbon.

For the English cloth trade these were also years of strain. The steady expansion of that trade since the beginning of the century—London exports rose from some 50,000 pieces a year in 1500 to twice that figure by the early 1540's—was quickened by the currency debasement from 1544 to reach its peak in 1550, when the London total was over 130,000. But then the simultaneous effect of temporary saturation in the market, of rising English prices, and of the devaluation of 1551 intended to bring these down, was to deal the trade a severe blow and to leave it unsettled for more than a decade. In this situation English efforts to find new markets and to reach old ones directly, and the sharpening of measures against foreign (including Antwerp's own) competition, induced a worsening of relations which, within a dozen years, was to provoke a complete stoppage of trade and the first removal of the 'mart' outside the Netherlands.

It was this weakening of the pillars of Antwerp's trade, more than the damage to the financial superstructure, which brought the 'golden age' to its close about 1560. The great upheavals, which would cast those pillars down, were yet to come—in 1566, 1576 and 1584–5: and even after those disasters the town would be far from prostrate. Indeed, with the dwindling and departure of the strangers who had so largely created and so richly profited from the golden years, native energies would to some extent reassert themselves: thus the years 1562–5 saw the erection of a number of Antwerp companies for trade to the Baltic and the Mediterranean. But Antwerp's role henceforward was to be, in more than this sense, a 'national' one, a reversion to what it had been before the great currents of European politics and trade had made this town the centre of the economic world.

CHAPTER III

LUTHER AND THE GERMAN
REFORMATION TO 1529

Q UIDAM, nomine Martin Luther'—the casual reference, in a letter
from Adrian of Utrecht to the Emperor Charles V, recalls the
moment when the affair of Martin Luther was but a small cloud,
the size of a man's clenched fist, above the horizon of Christendom, when
it seemed incredible that it could be more than a marginal gloss upon the
main chronicle of European history. There is an authentic element of
remoteness. Martin Luther was born on 10 November 1483 in the Saxon
town of Eisleben, and he died in the same city on 18 February 1546.
Most of the interval he lived in Wittenberg, a little town 'perched on the
edge of beyond'. Unlike Erasmus, who moved back and forth, always
close to the pressure points, the great arterial highways, between Oxford,
Louvain, Paris, Basle, Venice and Rome, Luther came but thrice, and
then for a few days, to the pulse of things in Rome, Augsburg and
Worms.

Thus, more than most, he took history as it came to him. 'Let us see
what God will do' is a line from his last letter which is a clue to his
existence. Yet the impression of remoteness, isolation, passivity is quite
misleading. In the world of thought and of ideas there is movement,
energetic, drastic, vehement. When Martin Bucer reproached the theologians of Wittenberg for not being sufficiently mindful of the precept, 'Go
ye into all the world...', Luther's reply touched nearly all the truth:
'We do that with our writings.' From this little space, Luther launched
vast armies of ideas, outpacing his opponents, swiftly moving to the
corners of the Christian world, taking the ears of cottagers and kings.
Men came to hear him, and caught the infection of the Word. The
16,000 students who attended lectures in Wittenberg between 1520 and
1560 represent a missionary influence which helps to account for the deep
root, the persistence of the Lutheran reformation in Germany, its spread
to northern Europe and the New World.

Behind the swiftly developing, ever more complicated patterns of
Protestantism, his was the simple primary design. What happened within
his soul affected the whole Reformation movement, giving it a thrust and
a direction, disconcerting to the student of the late medieval scene,
familiar enough with anti-clericalism, moralism and mysticism, and not
unprepared for a Hutten, a Carlstadt, a Münzer, or even for Zwingli and
the Anabaptists. In the unchartable realms of the mind, then, Luther was
an apostle, as a voyager and pioneer not behind a Wesley or a Livingstone.

We are here concerned with his great first works, which in a deeper sense than is generally realised precede the emergence of 'Protestantism'.

There seems to have been little remarkable about Luther's home or Luther's schooling. Between them his parents and his ushers knocked a good deal of sense into him, and nonsense out of him. Hans and Margaret Luther regarded their offspring with gruff pride, and he repaid them with something more than a customary filial piety. A certain directness, shrewdness and obstinacy mark his peasant background, and that fondness for proverbial wisdom with which his writings are drenched. His home may have been superstitious and sombre, but his humour was bred there too. Hans Luther had come the hard way to moderate affluence and influence in the mining community at Mansfeld, and, with the exaggerated deference towards learning of the self-made man, made willing sacrifices for the education of his gifted son. Luther's schools, at Mansfeld, Magdeburg and Eisenach, had given him the tools of learning, a grounding in that rhetorical education which the medieval world had inherited from the classical past. When, in 1501, 'Martinus Ludher ex Mansfelt' was enrolled in the university of Erfurt, he was at least skilled and competent in two life-long enthusiasms, good music and great argument.

Erfurt was a fine city, prosperous and fair with its towers and gardens, and its university, and particularly its school of law, was renowned. It was a citadel of the 'via moderna'—the Nominalist antidote to Thomism, and two eminent teachers, Trutvetter and Arnoldi, gave him his training in Aristotle, within the perspective of Occamism reflected through Gabriel Biel. If Luther came to repudiate their teaching, he kept affectionate gratitude for his teachers, and indeed owed more than he ever realised to the intricate mental discipline of his syllogistic and philosophic training. In 1505, aged twenty-two, Luther was placed second out of seventeen successful candidates for the M.A. degree and turned towards the study of law and the fulfilment of parental ambition. Then, suddenly, his father was outraged to learn that his son had decided to enter religion and had been admitted to the Erfurt house of the Austin Friars. If some mental conflict preceded the decision, his family had no intimation of it, and the evaluation of the confused evidence is perhaps better confined to Luther's certain words: 'not freely or desirously did I become a monk... but walled around with the terror and agony of sudden death (*terrore et agone mortis subitae circumvallatus*) I vowed a constrained and necessary vow'. Probably Luther would have made an uncommonly bad lawyer and was perfectly gifted to become a divine.

In joining the Reformed Congregation of the Eremitical Order of St Augustine Luther had joined a mendicant order which, in Erfurt, had important connections with the university. The new world was engaging and engrossing and the novitiate passed smoothly and swiftly in learning the etiquette and discipline of conventual life, the technique of devotion in cell and choir. He made his profession with its irrevocable vows in September 1506 and was then prepared for ordination. He became priest in April 1507 and his first mass a month later was for him a solemn and tremendous ordeal.

He was selected as apt for further study, which he resumed at the university under Occamist directors. When in 1508 he was sent to the new university of Wittenberg, to lecture in the arts faculty, he found the enforced preoccupation with Aristotle uncongenial and sighed to get back to theology. This he did, when, having taken the degree of *Baccalaureus Biblicus*, he returned to Erfurt where as *Sententiarius* he lectured on the *Sentences* of Peter Lombard. A proposal to unite the Conventual and Observant Augustinian houses in Germany provoked a dispute in which Erfurt was involved, and Luther was sent to Rome to assist the presentation of an appeal from seven dissident houses. It was an interesting holiday and devout pilgrimage, and it is a fable that he found in Rome a premonition of justification by faith. He returned home with an earnest Teutonic distaste for what he had seen of Italian clerical professionalism, and mixed memories of a city in which there was a good deal to shock innocent susceptibilities. On 12 October 1512 he became a doctor in theology and almost immediately succeeded his friend, patron and vicar general, John von Staupitz, in the chair of biblical theology at Wittenberg.

Town and monastery in the city were involved in an ambitious building programme, and Luther had begun his momentous preaching career in a ridiculous temporary shack which he was glad to exchange in 1514 for the pulpit of the parish church. He became involved in an ascending series of ecclesiastical chores which culminated in 1515 when he was made district overseer of eleven monasteries. But his lectures were the main thing. It has been a major achievement of modern scholarship to edit and publish the collections of Luther's lecture material in these years: the *Sentences* of Peter Lombard (1509); Psalms (1513–15); the Epistles to the Romans (1515–16), Galatians (1516–17) and Hebrews (1517–18). The examination of these documents, in some cases Luther's own copy, its wide margins crammed with minute, tidy annotations, has revealed that in many essentials Luther's theology ante-dates the indulgence controversy and may no longer be thought of as a rationalisation or improvisation of the Church struggle.

Reputable historians no longer question the integrity of Luther's own account of his monastic life. He kept the rule and entered with characteristic whole-heartedness upon the path to evangelical perfection. For a time all went well, but thereafter he found himself caught in deep spiritual currents which brought him to the edge of disaster. The Church had many safeguards against such ills: conventual discipline could be modified; moral theology could be read; there were at hand the sacraments, the advice of skilled confessors, the reassurance of the scriptures;

from all of these Luther found a measure of comfort but no permanent relief. Nor was all his instruction best calculated to support a trembling spirit. Teaching about penance had come to stress unduly the outward act of satisfaction, so that it was a salutary counterpoise when Staupitz pointed Luther to the 'Wounds of Jesus' as the true direction of inward repentance. The Occamist concern to safeguard the liberties of God and man, within the doctrines of free will and merit, had come to throw much upon the will. A man might make an act of love to God from his own moral resources; to him who did what lay within him, God would not deny grace—a strenuous optimism infinitely removed from Luther's experience of temptation (*Anfechtung*)[1]—the desperate, guilty isolation of one trapped, condemned, alone beneath the Wrath of God. The Occamists admitted a baffling point of uncertainty, the distinction between a true and a feigned love of God. Yet here was the root of Luther's unease, his conviction that love to God must be free, joyful, unconstrained, and the bitter knowledge that in his own case, 'however irreproachable my life as a monk, I felt myself in the presence of God (*coram Deo*) to be a sinner with a most unquiet conscience, nor would I believe him to be pleased with my satisfaction. I did not love, rather I hated this just God who punished sinners.'

Here his Biblical studies intensified his distress. The declaration in the opening of the Epistle to the Romans, that the righteousness of God (*justitia Dei*) is revealed in the gospel, seemed the last straw. That there was an exposition of this divine justice from the time of Augustine, in terms of salvation bestowed upon sinners, is a fact of which Luther seems to have been effectively unaware. The later schoolmen had evolved a dialectic of the divine attributes, so that Gabriel Biel invariably reserves 'misericordia' for the divine clemency, and reserves 'justitia' for the active, punishing justice of God envisaged in Aristotelian rather than biblical terms. That this, according to St Paul, is revealed not only by the law but by the very gospel itself drove Luther to final despair, to wish he had never been born, and to the verge of the dreadful sin of open blasphemy.

Then, marvellously, he found relief as he pondered in exegetical study the connection of the scriptural words in Romans i. 17 and understood that the justice of God must be interpreted 'passively...as that whereby the merciful God justified us by faith...at this I felt myself to be born anew, and to enter through open gates into Paradise itself'. We need not discuss the originality of what was in any case embedded in the biblical material before him. As Lortz has said, 'it was new for him'. If the evidence had not survived, we should have to invent something like it, to account for the importance of the doctrine of justification by faith for Luther and its consequent high place on the agenda of subsequent Protestantism.

[1] P. Bühler, *Anfechtung bei Martin Luther* (1942), p. 4.

Recent study has sought to identify the place where this conception emerges in Luther's early lecture material. It has been suggested that the many-sided Biblical hermeneutic, which Luther inherited, may have helped him. For through the interpretation of 'justitia Dei' first in terms of the 'literal prophetic' sense (i.e. Christologically) and then tropologically, in terms of the work of God within the soul, there was ready to hand a combination which interpreted the 'justitia Dei' through the work of Christ, apprehended by faith. We may foreshorten an unfinished discussion by suggesting that it seems likely that Luther resolved his personal crisis before his lectures on Romans (1515–16).[1] Certainly Luther's lecture material between 1509 and 1518 shows his thought in movement. If the dogmatic comments in the lectures on Peter Lombard are in the main traditional, there is evident an active hostility towards the intrusion of philosophy into theology, and especially of Aristotle, 'that rancid philosopher'. There is the vigorous attempt to disentangle the patristic fundament from what Vignaux calls the 'philosophic envelope' of later scholasticism. The most important single voice in the sixteenth century was not that of any reformer or counter-reformer, but St Augustine's, and Luther's enthusiasm for him, while never uncritical, may be traced in these early lectures. The present fluid state of Occamist studies prohibits more than tentative reference to Luther's relation to Occamism, the one kind of scholasticism which Luther knew intimately. Three points may be made. First, like Gabriel Biel, Luther was no debtor to Occam's anti-papal writings. Second, Luther's doctrine of justification by faith, his use of the conceptions of 'imputation' and 'non-imputation' is within a Christocentric frame quite dissimilar from the late medieval discussion of these notions within the dialectics of the 'absolute' and 'ordained' power of God. Third, Luther's nominalist training, despite his sharp reaction against it, must have influenced the undertones of his ways of thinking, stimulating problems and suggesting the direction of much of his thought.

Luther's first lectures on the Psalms are an unwieldy mass of material, in which scholastic elements jostle side by side with a renovated Augustinianism. More important is the evidence of his growing biblical concentration, for no exposition of Luther can be just which fails to reckon with the extent to which the whole biblical material, and not some selected doctrines or favourite epistles, came to form the normative element in his theology. More compact, much more impressive are the succeeding lectures on the Epistle to the Romans. Here the Pauline theme evokes a delineation of the plight of man, in whom sin is a restless inward ferment involving the whole person, an egocentricity which disguises itself in splendid idolatries, but which is exposed 'coram Deo' when the living God confronts men in judgment against their rebellion and their

[1] For another view see E. Bizer, *Fides ex auditu* (Neukirchen, 1958).

pride. Within this awful context no human, intrinsic righteousness can stand, but God has prepared instead another righteousness, the salvation through his Son, the mercy and forgiveness which he apprehends through faith. And faith is no mere act of intellect, emotion, or habit of the will, but the response of the whole man to personal confrontation by the living God. In this relation, which on God's side is of sheer, unconstrained, free mercy, man finds the spring and motive of his new life, of love of God and neighbour, and of true Christian liberty. This justification is not over and done with at some initial stage, or in some unique experience, but the standing term of reference for that movement of the Christian man from sin to perfection which Luther summarises in the great formula *Semper peccator, semper penitens, semper justus.*

In 1516 Luther read the writings of Tauler, and the 'Theologia Germanica'. They deepened in him the emphasis upon the egocentric character of sin and the need for the Christian to conform to the humiliation and sufferings of Christ. This 'theology of the Cross' with its antagonism to scholastic speculation, 'the theology of glory', is a notable stress in his next courses of lectures, on Galatians and on the Epistle to the Hebrews. More important in these years is his awareness of the importance of the dialectic of law and gospel, wherein sinners are brought through 'Christ's strange work', the condemnation of the law, into the sphere of God's own work (*Opus proprium Dei*), to be saved through divine mercy. By the middle of 1517 Luther had made Wittenberg a centre of redirected theological studies, and could speak of 'our theology'. He could even contemplate carrying the campaign to other universities and sent a copy of ninety-seven theses against the late schoolmen to Erfurt and Nuremberg in an adventurous challenge which was not regarded. Trouble came swiftly from an unlooked-for quarter.

Christian repentance involves an ancient and difficult theological problem. Much depends on the right balance between inward motive and outward act, between theory and practice, between the teaching Church and the instruction of the laity. By the beginning of the sixteenth century these delicate adjustments had been upset in relation to the system of indulgences. The indulgence was originally the commutation of the act of satisfaction which belonged to the sacrament of penance. In the early Middle Ages, the Celtic and Germanic penitentials had introduced secular notions which exaggerated the possibilities of commuting moral offences by monetary payments. There were extensions of indulgences during the crusades, and by those popes whose financial difficulties were most acute. The jubilee indulgence of Pope Boniface VIII in 1300 was a success which later popes could not ignore. The system found its rationale in the communion of the saints, in the thought of a treasure of merits. It had been expounded by Alexander of Hales, while the bull *Unigenitus* of Pope Clement VI (1343) affirmed that 'Christ acquired a treasure for the

Church militant'. In 1476 Pope Sixtus IV extended the scope of indulgences to the souls in purgatory, a doctrine demanding nice theological discrimination and opening ominous possibilities of misrepresentation and abuse. There was a good deal of uncertainty about many undefined points, and many Catholic moralists had expressed doubts about them, while some Catholic rulers distrusted the whole business. By the beginning of the sixteenth century indulgences had become an important part of papal finances, under the care of the great banking house of Fugger, and involving so many middlemen at varying ecclesiastical levels that the possibility of unsavoury scandal was never remote.

In 1513 Prince Albert of Brandenburg became archbishop of Magdeburg and administrator of the see of Halberstadt at the age of 23, and in the following years archbishop of Mainz and primate of Germany. The huge fees due upon this accumulation involved a debt to the house of Fugger and a financial crisis which was resolved when Albert undertook the promulgation in his lands of the new indulgence which was to rebuild St Peter's, Rome. It is true that this secret arrangement between Albert of Mainz and the curia was not known until after the Church struggle had well begun. The immediate cause of the indulgence controversy was a simple affair, the preaching in the neighbourhood of Wittenberg of the Dominican commissary, John Tetzel. But it was no accident that this matter which touched the human conscience and involved the hope of salvation, and which had now become the tool of financial commodity, should set off the chain reaction which dissolved European and Christian unity. That Frederick the Wise of Saxony had forbidden the sale of the things in his territories is not to be accounted to him for righteous indignation. Rather the contrary. In the last years he had lavished money on building schemes in Wittenberg. The castle and its church, under the most eminent German architects and artists, including Dürer and Cranach, had attained a flamboyant Gothic magnificence. The castle church was a collegiate foundation, closely related to the university on the one hand and the surrounding parishes on the other. But the spectacular feature which determined its very shape was the vast collection of holy relics which Frederick had gathered, which in 1518 amounted to 17,443 particles housed in twelve galleries along its great nave. It was much more than a pious museum, for there were granted to penitent sightseers indulgences amounting to over a hundred thousand years. In forbidding Tetzel access to his lands, Frederick's motive was a blunt determination to keep Saxon money at home and to cut out competition with his local shrine.

The instructions to the commissaries and the indulgence letters seem invariably to have been carefully worded. But there is no doubt that Tetzel's preaching was scandalous and should have been offensive to pious ears. Of these things the best proof is his later repudiation by his friends. Luther himself had long been exercised about indulgences, and was now exasperated when some of his parishioners returned from Zerbst and Juterbög, a few miles off, with pardons which they brandished in his face, the real meaning of which they had entirely misconceived. Tetzel's expositions would have shocked a good many contemporary moralists, but Luther they affronted to the depth of his being, for they touched on convictions about which he was hypersensitive—the awful cost of redemption and the catastrophic inward character of true repentance. That he chose the eve of All Saints' Day to make his protest, when Wittenberg was thronged with prospective pilgrims, shows that he was not afraid to point the moral home. Momentously, he wrote out ninety-five theses for disputation 'in the desire and with the purpose of elucidating truth'. They were in Latin, apparently no more striking than his theses against the scholastic theologians. Yet because they touched Church politics he sent a covering letter with a copy of them to Albert of Mainz and prostrated himself in prayer, asking God to be with him in this adventure. About midday on 31 October 1517 he walked the length of the town and fixed the large placard to the door of the castle church. In the main, they were not revolutionary and at points expressed, in the manner of disputations, what were only tentative opinions. Yet there are echoes in them of what Luther had called 'our theology', notably in the first thesis, 'Our Lord wished the entire life of believers to be one of penitence', and in the sixty-second, 'the true treasure of the Church is the holy gospel of the glory and the grace of God'.

And now the invention of printing was fateful. Luther's theses, to his consternation, were turned into German, printed, and soon circulating everywhere. He began to write a long, careful apologia for them, and sent one copy to his ordinary, the bishop of Brandenburg, with a most submissive covering letter. But Albert of Mainz had forwarded the documents to Rome, with the request that Luther be inhibited, and in February 1518 the pro-magistrate of the Augustinian Order, Gabriel della Volta, sent instructions to Staupitz to that effect. More overt danger threatened from the Dominicans. Momentarily, their blustering closed the Augustinian ranks, so that the Heidelberg Chapter of 1518 became a personal triumph for Luther. In the next months, however, Luther's situation became perilous. He owed his survival perhaps to the firm friendship of Spalatin (1484–1548), librarian, secretary and chaplain of the Elector Frederick. It is one of the unpredictabilities of history that Frederick, whose convictions, loyalties and interests must surely have been offended by Luther's protest, should have refrained from the very simple step of abandoning a single professor whom he never met.

In October 1518 Luther was summoned to Augsburg, to a memorable interview with the cardinal legate and general of the Dominicans, Cajetan. He was an eminent Thomist whose unbending orthodoxy betrayed no premonition that his opinions would, at his latter end, undergo an Erasmian landslide. As instructed, he demanded from Luther present and instant revocation, and future silence. The attempt to settle the matter out of hand broke down when the two theologians, one of the ancient and the other of the modern way, became involved in a heated wrangle about the meaning of the word 'treasure' in the bull *Unigenitus*. That Luther had found a loophole is suggested by the fact that immediately afterwards Cajetan sought and obtained from Rome a less ambiguous statement about indulgences, the decretal *Cum Postquam* (9 November 1518). But Luther was beyond the help of debating points, and perhaps for the first time somebody in authority realised that this monk, with his deep eyes and teeming eloquence, was more than an obstinate moralist. The interviews terminated angrily, and there followed a lull so ominous that Luther's friends hustled him out of the city; he fled home, pursued by an angry and contemptuous demand from Cajetan that this *fraterculus* be surrendered.

Luther's loyalties were by now strained and affronted, and though conciliar theories were to be but a very transitory halting place for his opinions, he had at Augsburg stressed the superior authority of a general council, and on 28 November 1518 drew up a formal appeal to a future council of the Church. He now awaited arrest or exile, and the crisis came on 1 December, when two messages arrived during a farewell meal, the first speeding the parting scholar, the second bidding him tarry. That he did in fact stay for another twenty-eight years was due to the intervention of high politics. On 8 December Frederick sent Cajetan a firm reply: he did not intend to send Luther for trial to Rome or let him be put away without at least some sort of hearing. This was the very moment when Frederick's goodwill was courted both by pope and emperor. For Frederick was one of seven imperial electors and himself a possible candidate for the imperial crown. The emperor wanted to secure the succession for his grandson Charles, while the other European powers were appalled at the prospect of a prince whose sovereignties would be unparalleled since the time of Charles the Great. The interval between the death of Maximilian, 12 January 1519, and the election of Charles V at Frankfurt at the end of June, was a time when the pope needed the support of Frederick badly enough to allow his envoy, Charles von Miltitz, to employ a new tactic of conciliation which achieved nothing from the papal point of view beyond a fatal waste of time. For thus these precious weeks slipped by, the last point in history at which the *affaire Luther* might have been hushed up, halted on the edge of revolution. Now such forces were in motion that, when pope and emperor would be ready to act in concert they would no longer be faced with a single cleric but with an ugly, swelling tide of national grievance against Rome.

While the Augustinians, including Staupitz, began to draw aloof, the university moved solidly behind him. The study of the sacred languages had received powerful reinforcement in the accession of Philip Melanchthon (1497–1560), a young layman who was great-nephew to Reuchlin and something of a prodigy in his own right.

Andrew Bodenstein von Carlstadt (1477–1541) was Luther's academic senior, professor in the 'via antiqua', a secular priest elbowing his way energetically up the hierarchy of the castle church. At first suspicious, then patronising, he had characteristically become of a sudden more wholeheartedly Augustinian than Luther himself. Thus when John von Eck (1489–1543), the redoubtable theologian of Ingolstadt, circulated some animadversions against Luther, the so-called 'Obelisks', Carlstadt plunged enthusiastically into the defence of his absent colleague, with 380 theses, adding 26 more as an afterthought. As a result both theologians became entangled in a dispute which led to the famous Leipzig disputation of July 1519. The primary debate was still between Eck and Carlstadt upon the theme of grace and free will; but Luther had all along been the real target and at last obtained permission to participate. Preliminary skirmishing had again raised the question of the papal power, and Luther had recently turned to an intensive reading of canon law and Church history which soon pressed him beyond the conciliar position. The Leipzig disputation was a personal success for Eck; the younger man, who had tackled both Carlstadt and Luther single-handed, had made Carlstadt appear a figure of fun and had dangerously manœuvred Luther into appearing to attack the great German Council of Constance and into a suspicion of Hussite sympathies. The disputation had drawn attention to wider issues than indulgences and had accelerated the pamphlet war. It also forced Luther himself to examine the implications of what he had said and done. Yet even now the actions of the curia were hesitant and protracted. The case against Luther was muddled. The universities of Cologne and Louvain had examined the one-volume edition of Luther's writings of which Frobenius had published an edition in Basle, and from their theological pickings and from earlier documents forty-one articles were collated against Luther and embodied in the bull *Exsurge Domine* of 15 June 1520. Its garbled citations were soon to be out-dated by Luther's utterances in the next months.

For Luther had now embarked on an immense literary activity. A new fact entered the situation: the proscribed theologian was also a literary genius with unexampled fluency in the vernacular, displayed in a flood of tracts and pamphlets, now shocking in polemical virulence, now shot through with the comic spirit, but also expressed in works of edification which combined profound intuitions, tender beauty and a limpid simplicity. Thus in an inaccessible corner of the Christian world, protected by a powerful prince, his university enthusiastically behind him, the more learned opinion in Germany sympathetic, with powerful allies articulate on his side among princes, knights, merchants and peasants, Luther was no longer alone, but fast becoming a symbol of national anti-clerical resentment against Rome.

The German humanists were at first cordial towards Luther. As the excitement of the Leipzig debate died and Luther's impeachment proceeded, they became more reticent, and in 1520 the papal bull and Luther's violent replies divided the ranks and caused many to draw back from him. The changing temperature is discernible in the writings of Erasmus. Yet at this time he did not cease to hope to act as mediator, nor did he conceal his view that Luther had said many urgent and salutary things. In a famous interview with Frederick the Wise at Cologne in November 1520 he fobbed off the request for a plain verdict with an epigram, but it counted for much that he did not fling his great prestige against the reformer and strengthened the elector's determination that Luther should get a hearing.

Luther replied to formal condemnation with open defiance. In the summer of 1520 he composed three revolutionary manifestoes. The first, *An Appeal to the Christian Nobility of the German Nation,* is the document which had most effect upon public opinion, so well was it suited to the national ferment. Defective in form, for it tails off into a recitation of widely aired grievances and remedies, it more than compensated for its defects by simple intensity and forthright boldness. Papal tyranny was entrenched behind three buttressing walls of paper claims: the claim that spiritual power is superior to temporal power; the claim to have the sole authority to interpret scripture; the claim that only the pope may call a general council. Against an overweening and arrogant clericalism, Luther turns to the fundamental Christian estate of which all Christians are members. It is in virtue of this priesthood of all believers that he appeals to the Christian magistrates of Germany. For in this crisis, when the spiritual power has so long and obstinately refused self-amendment, the magistrate may fittingly intervene on behalf of all the faithful, by virtue of his God-given office.

The second tract, *A Prelude concerning the Babylonish Captivity of the Church,* was written in Latin, addressed to the clergy and the learned world. Here was a direct attack on the liturgical and sacramental sources of the authority and prestige of the clergy. Luther reduced the sacraments from seven to three, to penance, baptism and the eucharist. He denounced the withdrawal of the cup from the laity, the doctrine of transubstantiation, and the sacrificial work of the mass. These were daring strokes and did more than anything Luther had written to shock timid or conservative opinion. The third writing, *Of the Liberty of a Christian Man,* is entirely different, a work of edification. In some ways complementary to his fine sermon 'Of Good Works', it traces the religious and ethical implications of justification by faith. But the main stress, as the title suggests, is on the free, joyful, creative character of Christian liberty, expressed through loving obedience to God and service to one's neighbour. Good works are not technical ecclesiastical performances, but the fruit of faith, from which they spring. *The Liberty of a Christian Man* belongs to the first two manifestoes, not only by the date of its composition but as testifying to the wholeness of Luther's programme—to the fact that it is more than indignant moralism or anti-clericalism. The doctrines which Luther had worked out in lecture room, cell, pulpit, which with a Cellini-like intensity he had forged in the fire of his own *Anfechtungen*, are not something apart from what we might call the practical writings of improvisation of 1518–20 but form the ground bass of them all. These were the great events of 1520. The solemn burning in December by the Elster Gate in Wittenberg of the works of canon law, and the adding to the flames by Luther of the papal bull, were gestures symbolizing defiance more potently expressed already in the printed word. The pope published the final bull of excommunication, *Decet*, on 3 January 1521.

Intricate constitutional and financial problems faced Charles V at the first imperial diet of his reign. He must walk delicately, and this was why the papal nuncio Jerome Aleander failed to prevent the appearance of Luther at the Diet of Worms. Aleander (1480–1542) was himself a humanist turned diplomat, a former companion of Erasmus in Venice. He at least was under no illusions about the gravity of the situation, and his agitated despatches to Rome sought to shake the curia into recognition that here was a crisis not only for Germany but for Christendom. To allow Luther to appear before the diet might be a calamitous advertisement and would in any case imply the insufficiency of the papal condemnation. Yet Aleander's bribes, entreaties, oratory failed, though it is true that, as the time drew near, the imperial advisers became apprehensive and did a little to scare Luther off. Luther's friends tried to do the same though, as usual, their sedative intentions worked on him with opposite effect, so that as they grew more doleful he grew more cheerful and answered their fears with a serene confidence and unshaken determination. When on the morning of 16 April 1521 he entered the streets of Worms, his cavalcade swollen to the dimensions of a procession, they were not devils innumerable who peered down at him from the roof tops, but a German crowd of whose vociferous sympathies for Luther Aleander bitterly complained.

Luther appeared before a crowded assembly late on the following afternoon. It may well be that he had no information as to what would happen and was disconcerted by what did take place. Almost before he had got his bearings, the sharp voice of Ulrich von Pappenheim, Master of the Imperial Knights, ordered him to keep silence until ordered to speak. Heaped before him on a table was a pile of volumes, the collected works, to date, of Dr Martin Luther. He was asked two simple questions. Did he acknowledge the works as his own? Would he revoke them? Whether

Aleander had contrived to get Luther's 'hearing' reduced to this thorny ultimatum cannot be known, but Luther sensed his peril. In a moment it might have been all over, and he could have been bundled out of the diet, all drama avoided, with some sort of colour that the promise to his elector had been kept. His voice sounded faint and abashed as he asked for time to consider, and, fatefully, an adjournment was granted him.

The next evening came the scene which was to linger, beyond Aleander's worst fears, in the memory of Europe. In a larger, yet more crowded hall, with the audience restless after many hours in the stuffy air, Luther stood under the flaring torches, before the majesty of the empire embodied in the pale, grim, forbidding countenance of the young Emperor Charles V; face to face, too, with the Christian nobility of the German empire to whom he had but recently so poignantly appealed. There seems to have been an exchange of argument between Luther and the imperial official, John von Eck. Luther then gave his answer. He must distinguish between his writings. Those of edification he ought not and need not retract. The writings against the papal tyranny he must not revoke. His controversial writings against individuals contained things unseemly in temper and expression, and for these he would apologise. Yet in those, too, was a core of Christian doctrine which he could not withdraw. But, and here he cleverly threw the case at his opponents, let them convince him of error, reasonably and on scriptural grounds, and he would gladly retract and burn his books. He had done rather too well: bidden to make answer, he had succeeded in making a speech, and for many had clouded the issue by an offer to retract, the irony of which might escape them. Very sharply, the imperial official demanded a straight answer, 'without horns or teeth', and swiftly Luther flung back at him the iron defiance. He would not recant, 'for it is neither safe nor right to act against one's conscience. God help me. Amen.'[1] Amid some confusion, the emperor dismissed him, and he emerged through a threatening press of Spaniards to the safe company of his German friends.

Luther had made an appearance. He could hardly be said to have had a hearing. The problem 'What next?' could not be discussed by the authorities on strictly legal merits, while squadrons of armed knights loomed menacingly in the vicinity, and when overnight appeared the peasant warcry of the *Bundschuh*. Luther was granted what he had vainly sought for a long time, a genuine discussion with friendly interrogators, who now included the archbishop of Trier. It may be that there were those who toyed with the idea that Luther might be politically useful, as the mouthpiece of a national movement for a German council, and there may have been more than sweet reasonableness in the attempt in the next days to pin him back to the conciliar theories. At any rate, the discussions

[1] The celebrated words 'Here I stand; I can do no other' are absent from the primary document.

broke down on this point, the fallibility of councils, and on Luther's refusal, by compromise at this stage, to go back upon his resolute defiance.

The emperor would respect the safe conduct; no doubt he would keep his word. In any case, the national rising which had followed the execution of John Hus was a cautionary tale which the German princes kept much in mind in these months. Luther was told to get off home while the twenty days' limit remained unexpired. He withdrew accordingly, with his companions, and travelled quietly homeward through his native lands. Then, suddenly, he disappeared and the wildest rumours began to circulate. Not until much later did it become known that Luther had been kidnapped with the connivance of his prince, that friendly hands had plucked him from the little convoy, to convey him through the forests to a safe stronghold.

Luther had now been outlawed by the temporal and spiritual powers, and Aleander may have composed the strong terms of the imperial edict passed by a rump diet after Luther had been dismissed. The Edict of Worms was to become a rallying point for the Catholic princes, though its immediate effect was diminished by the political events which took Charles away from Germany in the next decade. Its shadow was to hang over Luther all his days. Yet he had defied pope and emperor and he lived to tell the tale in eighty folio volumes. 'The Word did it all', said Luther; 'had I desired to foment trouble, I could have brought great bloodshed upon Germany. Yes, I could have started such a little game at Worms that the emperor himself would not have been safe. But what would it have been? A mug's game. I left it to the Word.' None the less, the kidnapping of Luther was itself an intervention of political power. In the next months Luther was able to induce Albert of Mainz to cry off an indulgence scheme in Halle, by exercising a superior kind of spiritual blackmail. The problem of handling power, moral, spiritual, political, legal, had only just begun.

Luther got a badly needed rest in the castle of the Wartburg. But the sudden relaxation, an unwontedly rich diet, and the loneliness brought a crop of physical and spiritual ills, a whole series of *Anfechtungen*. But he was soon writing again—an exposition of the 68th Psalm, the writing out of his 'Postills', those expositions of the liturgical portions of scripture at which he excelled, and most important of all, the first steps towards his translation of the Bible, beginning with the New Testament. (The first edition of his New Testament, revised in collaboration with Melanchthon, was to appear in September 1522.) He spent most of his remaining years in its constant revision, and enlisted many collaborators, for he never believed that translation could be a one-man job. But his genius was upon it: his intuitive sense of common speech, his own inrooted simplicity and his capacity to think within the biblical world, so that the translation won its way by superior excellence. And although he was away from his books, at this very time he produced in his *Contra Latomum* his ablest contro-versial writing, his most striking elucidation of justifying faith.

Against these positive achievements in exile must be set the situation in Wittenberg, with Luther absent but the momentum of reform still under way. For Luther's followers there were a number of practical problems. What was to be done about the abuses in the Church? What of the religious vocation? What of votive masses, shrines and images? Of fasting? Of communion in both kinds? Of clerical celibacy? Carlstadt had been invited to Denmark in 1521 to assist in the planning of its reformation, but the movement had been abortive and he had returned home frustrated and with a programme. He now took the initiative in Wittenberg. He expounded his radical prospectus in thousands of theses, in dozens of tracts ('printed in the Christian city of Wittenberg'), and in scores of sermons, first in the castle church of which he was archdeacon, and then in the parish church, Luther's pulpit, where he had no right at all.

To a certain extent the moderate and radical programmes overlapped, and the differences were of method and timing. Luther himself began in the autumn of 1521 to compose his *On Monastic Vows* and a tract in Latin and in German on *The Misuse of the Mass,* and was very angry when Spalatin held up their publication. A university commission began to study reform in October, but Philip Melanchthon and Justus Jonas, the dean of the castle church, had little gift for leadership. Melanchthon had recently composed in his *Loci Communes* a manual of pure doctrine of ominous clarity which Luther ecstatically praised, but his talent was for learning; he had no great passion for affairs and tended to panic in a crisis. Carlstadt dominated the town council. Early in December there were iconoclastic riots, and for thirty-six hours the students had the town in an uproar. They seriously alarmed the court, not least because they gave Duke George an excuse for pressing that the Edict of Worms be enforced in Saxon lands. On 19 December Carlstadt announced that on New Year's Day he intended to celebrate the eucharist, communicating the faithful in both kinds, but he deemed it expedient to advance the date of the innovation, and on Christmas Day, without vestments and with a Latin service from which the canon was omitted, he gave the cup to the laity. At this season he announced his betrothal to a young lady of sixteen, Anna von Mochau. Then there arrived the Zwickau prophets, bearded patriarchal figures of simple mien, from the borders of Bohemia. They spoke impressively of divine colloquies and of heavenly visions vouchsafed to them, greatly impressing Melanchthon and Jonas, while Carlstadt, enraptured, began to lecture on Malachi and Zechariah and was soon boasting that nobody on the faculty had said as much about dreams and visions as himself.

The worthy Ordinance for the Princely City of Wittenberg which now appeared was a joint act of town and gown. It attempted a moderate programme for the removal of images. More important, and a valuable precedent, was the beginning of poor-law regulation, measures for the handling of sturdy beggars, the establishment of a common chest from which cheap loans might be available for artisans. On 6 January the Augustinian chapter met in Wittenberg, after contact with Luther, and it was decreed that those who felt constrained to do so might leave their monasteries.

In the next months Carlstadt developed a highly idiosyncratic theology and ethics, a compound of Bible, ultra-Augustinianism and mysticism. Where Luther put the biblical notion of 'faith', Carlstadt placed the supreme virtue of *Gelassenheit*, a dedication of the soul in complete renunciation. Where Luther had used the dialectic of law and gospel, Carlstadt retained the Augustinian dichotomy of letter and spirit. Where Luther had allowed large room for things indifferent, and for Christian liberty, Carlstadt turned to a puritan and Old Testament legalism, which insisted that there must be communion in both kinds and that there must be a vernacular liturgy, which denounced all images and pictures and even choirs and church music. He soon renounced all academic distinctions on behalf of the simple gospel, and in the interests of what might be called 'the laity of all the priesthood', describing himself as a 'new layman', walked abroad bare-footed, wearing a peasant sombrero, as 'Brother Andrew'.

Two things brought his campaign in Wittenberg to an end. First, the hostility of the university authorities. Then, in March 1522, the momentous return of Luther. Luther broke his hiding, announcing his intention to the elector in the most famous of all his letters. He got back safely, and the heavens refrained from raining Duke Georges for his discomfiture. Now he put away the secular dress in which in the last months he had masqueraded as 'Junker Georg' and deliberately attired as an Augustinian monk (there is the whole method of his Reformation in the touch) he preached in the parish church a decisive series of sermons. He won back the townsfolk from lay puritanism to conservative reformation, and he did this by preaching, for it is not true that he triumphed over Carlstadt merely because the elector upheld his party line. Once again he laid before his hearers the inwardness of true religion, the victorious power of the Word, which by gaining the consent of the heart wins the whole man, the need to respect the conscience of the weaker brethren, to handle them in love.

Luther had refused to become entangled in the plans of the German knights for anti-clerical war and rejected the proffered help of their leaders, Ulrich von Hutten and Franz von Sickingen. He thought that to make war on priests was to levy war on women and children. But the knights found nothing womanish or infantile about the archbishop of Trier, and after the disaster at the Landstuhl, the death of von Sickingen and the exile of Hutten, there was an end of the political power of the knights, of what might under happier circumstances have been a stabilising element amid German constitutional chaos. In 1523 the emperor began the active persecution of reformers in his hereditary lands, and the protomartyrs were the two Dutch Augustinians, Henry Voes and John van Esch.

In Wittenberg the advent of Bugenhagen (Pomeranus) more than offset the defection of Carlstadt, and his great abilities were employed first in Wittenberg and then in organising the Churches of northern Europe. For by 1523–4 the Reformation had spread to many cities of Germany by the agency of Luther's friends and disciples: Lang in Erfurt, Link in Altenburg, Brenz in Schwäbisch Hall, Myconius in Gotha, Amsdorf in Magdeburg, Osiander in Nuremberg. Others were more independent of Wittenberg: Bucer and Capito in Strassburg, Blaurer in Constance, Oecolampadius in Basle, Zwingli in Zürich. Nor did the radicals lack disciples, and Carlstadt's pupils Reinhard and Westerburg were active in Cologne and Jena. The correspondence and writings of Luther in this period are preoccupied with practical questions of the emerging evangelical Churches. His short essay *Von Ordnung Gottes Dienstes in der Gemeinde* (1523) makes suggestions for public worship in which the regular reading of scripture and frequent preaching restore to its due place the proclamation of the Word. His *Formula Missae et Communionis* (1523) is a Latin rite, conservative save for the excision of the canon. Not until 1525 was a German mass celebrated in Wittenberg and Luther's German rite (*Deutsche Messe*) was published in 1526. By this time there existed vernacular liturgies in many cities, notably from Münzer in Allstedt and Zwingli in Zürich, while after the appearance of the rite of Theobald Schwarz in Strassburg in 1524 there was a whole spate of liturgical experiment in that city under the direction of Martin Bucer. Luther wrote his first hymn to honour the Dutch martyrs in 1523: he proved a superb hymn-writer and, among many fine compositions, his 'Eyn' feste Burg' became itself an event in European history.

Social unrest aggravated the tension in Saxony between reformers and radicals. There was nothing in Germany comparable with the English knights of the shire, gentlemen and burgesses, justices of the peace, who could take the strain at the middle levels of the social pyramid. Between the princes and the peasants were great inequalities and festering wrongs, while the machinery of amendment, cumbrous and often arbitrary, could ill keep pace with economic revolution. The Reformation itself had its undeniable effect on common men, with the stress upon a fundamental Christian equality before God, the assertion of a common Christian priesthood. That Storch the weaver should also be among the prophets might be as disconcerting to the Elector Frederick the Wise as the translation of his fellow craftsman, Bully Bottom, was to the duke of Athens. But it was a sign of the times. Luther's German Bible was important, for unlike earlier vernacular versions, which were the preserve of the educated devout, it became itself a vehicle of proletarian education, a means whereby hitherto silent and submerged social levels became religiously articulate and theologically competent.

But the German Bible put the new problem. It emanated from a university: it was a work of scholarship; a product, in new guise, of the teaching Church. But the radical appeal was to a simple gospel, hidden from the wisdom of scribes and pharisees, revealed to the believing layman. The tension is most apparent in the writings of Münzer.

Thomas Münzer (1491–1525) was, like Luther, a Saxon, a secular priest of sufficient learning who had deeply imbibed mystical and apocalyptic writings, including the commentaries falsely ascribed to the Calabrian seer, Joachim da Fiore. From being an admirer of Luther he became his bitter enemy. Oecolampadius, who in 1524 entertained Luther's archdevil unawares, recognised the identity of his visitor by his vitriolic depreciation of Luther. He accused Luther and the papists of teaching a false doctrine of faith (*Von dem gedichteten Glauben*, 1524), attacked the carnality of Luther ('Brother Soft Life'), the pharisaism of 'Dr Liar'. Luther, in his *Of Earthly authority* (1523), had comforted the conscience of the Christian magistrate with the assurance that government had its due place in the providential order. Münzer was much more suspicious of authorities, truculent towards them, and played strongly to the gallery of 'the poor common man' and the 'elect friends of God'. After a stormy ministry at Zwickau he published a manifesto in the city of Prague, and when the Czech nation failed to rally to his summons he went to the little town of Allstedt which he dominated and where his liturgical experiments attracted thousands of visitors. They included some fine vernacular renderings of medieval hymns, vernacular forms of matins and vespers, and a rite for the mass, fully choral, of which the only eccentricity is the provision that the consecration should be repeated by the whole congregation. It was one of the sad consequences of 1525 that later Lutheran visitations erased all trace of what is one of the most interesting liturgical experiments in the first 'age of the Reformation'.

The evidence for his communism rests on the doubtful evidence of 'confession' under torture. What is certain is that, wherever he went, he enlisted followers among the mining and weaving populations, pledged by secret covenant to take up arms in an apocalyptic struggle. It particularly enraged Luther that these goings on could only take place under the protecting liberty of his own Reformation and dared not infiltrate into Catholic territory. 'Is it not a brave thing', he said of Münzer, 'that he sits in our shadow, and shares in our victory, without bearing any of our warfare, sits on our dungheap and yells at us.'

The crisis in Allstedt came in July 1524 when Duke John, his son John Frederick, and senior Saxon officials came to a trial sermon to test

Münzer's fitness as the preacher of Allstedt. Münzer preached before them, and his sermon, an exposition of the second chapter of Daniel, has some claim to be considered the most remarkable oration of the century. With daring impudence, Romans xiii, the *locus classicus* of the doctrine of civil obedience, is turned into a tool of revolution, for the rulers of Saxony are incited to prove themselves the ministers of God by using their sword to wipe out the ungodly. The sermon made the worst possible impression on the court. Münzer was forthwith summoned to an audience, from which he was seen to emerge silent and yellow with fear, and he fled the city. After some months of wandering to Nuremberg and Basle, and some correspondence with other radical preachers, he alighted on Mühlhausen, though he never had there his former ascendancy over Allstedt.

There were now two centres of 'Schwärmertum' in Saxony. At Orlamünde, where Carlstadt had become his own vicar, he added to his former doctrines a denial of infant baptism and a symbolic doctrine of the eucharist. Luther, in his *Against the Heavenly Prophets* (1524), had profoundly diagnosed the theological differences between himself and the extremists, mocking the obscure jargon of these religious Bunthornes and angering Carlstadt by lumping together his quietism with Münzer's programme of anti-clerical revolt. He now undertook a preaching tour of the valley of the Saale and confronted Carlstadt in an inn at Jena where, as they glared at one another across the table, one drew a guilder from his purse and tossed it to his adversary, an ancient token of open feud. By now the elector had decided that Carlstadt was incorrigible, and he was sent into exile. The problem of what to do with such a person would have exercised any authority in any age (ten years later Bullinger and Myconius would be saying the same hard things about him as Luther and Melanchthon now). But perhaps the Saxon authorities might have pondered the parable of the tares a little longer, for Carlstadt, wandering pathetically from city to city, not hiding his misfortunes under a bushel ('Andrew Carlstadt, unheard and unconvinced, driven out by Dr Martin Luther'), leaking venomous tracts by the thousand, was able to work harm untold to their reputation and their cause.

The Peasants' War broke out at Stühlingen in the Black Forest in June 1524, and the revolts spread rapidly into the Rhineland, Swabia, Franconia and Thuringia. In the main they were concerned with a medieval programme, specific liberties and the redress of particular ills: with the abolition of serfdom, the alleviation of feudal dues, with clerical exactions, with tithes. The lettered men among them drew up their manifestoes, of which the most notable was the 'Twelve Articles' of the men of Memmingen. The movement soon got out of hand. The rebel bands were swollen with those they had intimidated into their ranks. Lacking adequate commissariat, they had to live off the land and were drawn inevitably towards the easy prey of relatively undefended religious houses. Actions of extremists, like the Weinsberg massacre, damaged the reputation of the whole. Carlstadt became caught in the movement when the rebels encircled Rothenburg ob der Tauber, but he had no sympathy with violence of this kind and escaped according to local legend in apostolic fashion in a basket let down from the walls, though with the unapostolic inclusion of his family. But his former doings in the town put him in such jeopardy in the next days that only a piteous appeal to Luther and an abject recantation saved him. Münzer had no qualms at all and in a state of endemic mental intoxication was issuing bloodcurdling orders of the day, signed 'The Sword of the Lord and of Gideon'. At the beginning of May the rebels had got control of most of Franconia and seemed to be carrying all before them. Suddenly, signs of dissolution and collapse multiplied. Münzer and his comrades were encircled at Frankenhausen on 15 May, when the evangelical Philip of Hesse held the rebels in check until the Catholic Duke George arrived with the artillery. In the slaughter which followed, Münzer headed the rout from the field, was taken in hiding in the town, tortured and executed. But he died decently, as Philip of Hesse testified, and for all his fanaticism, we touch in him an appeal for justice which would be trodden underfoot in the terrible reprisals which now followed.

The moderate rebels had turned eagerly toward the leading reformers. Luther's attitude was firm and consistent. For three years, in a series of writings, more clearly than any person in Germany, he had foretold that religious incendiarism must end in social revolt and political doom. He had expounded the Christian duty of civil obedience, and asserted the evil of rebellion which must always stir up more ills than it could cure. He knew that civil disturbance (as in Wittenberg in 1522) would be laid at his door: 'For I see well that the devil, who has not been able to destroy me by means of the pope, now seeks to abolish me and swallow me up by means of the bloodthirsty prophets of murder and spirits of turbulence.' Yet his *Admonition to Peace* (May 1525) was a mild enough commentary on the 'Twelve Articles' which laid blame on both sides and assented to the justice of many of the peasant claims. What he did utterly condemn was the sin of rebellion and the fanaticism which could parade violence and murder as 'Christian revolution'. He concludes by blaming both sides: 'You are both wrong, and your fighting is wrong.'

By the time this tract appeared, the peasants were in the heyday of their power, and arson, robbery and violence, magnified by rumour, were the order of the day. Luther, who had risked his life by preaching in the disaffected areas of Thuringia, now wrote his leaflet *Against the murdering, thieving Hordes of Peasants*. He wrote at a time when it seemed that the peasants might win ('even though it happen that the peasants get the upper hand, for with God all things are possible, and we do not yet know whether it may be His will through the devil to destroy all order and rule'), and Luther turned to the Christian princes who desired to obey the will of God, assuring them that they might do the office of a magistrate and wield the sword for the punishment of evil-doers. The tract is violent, but in its context not as bad as it is sometimes made to appear. But once again events outran Luther's pen, for when this tract appeared, printed as an appendix to his earlier 'Admonition', what he had said when the rebels were in triumph read differently over their cold blood.

Many among his friends and followers were offended by Luther's words, for they seemed to give sanction to the unmeasured ferocity of the reprisals. He had proved his consistency, but gained a point of divinity at the price of his humanity. With that obstinacy which was no doubt a defect in him, he now wrote an *Open Letter concerning the Hard Book against the Peasants*, and perhaps it is this writing and not the little broadsheet which contains the brutal, cruel and indefensible things. None the less, this too concludes with strong words against the younger princes: 'I had two fears: if the peasants became lords, the devil would become abbot: but if these tyrannical princes became lords, the devil's mother would become abbess.'

At this time, when he believed the world's sands to be running out and his own days numbered, Luther, to spite the devil, had got married to Katherine von Bora, the last of a group of escaped nuns. It turned out marvellously well for its unromantic beginning. Certainly Luther, whose bed had not been made for years, needed looking after. He found deep joy and refreshment in his family, and as the children came, and some of them died, his home became a more effective apologetic for marriage of the clergy than any writing and the prototype of a pattern of a Christian minister's household which has greatly enriched European history.

The year 1525 drew from him his *De Servo Arbitrio* in which he replied to the attack of Erasmus. Erasmus had to cope with his own difficulties after 1521. There was a growing band of Catholic divines, in Louvain, Italy and Spain, headed by his old enemy Aleander, who were out for his blood. His friends and patrons, including King Henry VIII and Pope Adrian VI, had long urged him to enter the controversial lists against Luther. This reluctantly he agreed to do, for he was more and more alienated by the violence of the reformers, and as a type Luther was the kind of dogmatic mendicant theologian he most detested. But Erasmus's *Diatribe Concerning Free Will* (1524) was not a great success. It did not excite his Catholic friends or satisfy his Catholic enemies. Sensitive to criticism, he was exasperated beyond measure by the reply made by Luther who retorted to ironical pinpricks with resounding clouts on the ear. Moreover Luther had a theological equipment which touched heights of argument beyond the greater scholar, so that Luther's treatise, one-sided and wrong-headed and extreme, abounds in memorable epigrams and is still an object of fruitful theological attention. Erasmus wrote in reply two very long-winded disquisitions, the *Hyperaspistes*, while Luther confined himself to an open letter, bitterly unfair, and to caustic comments at the supper table.

The eucharistic controversy which broke out among the reformers in 1524 is the most intricate theological debate of the first period of the Reformation, and it is not to be despised. All the reformers agreed in attacking the doctrine of the mass, in rejecting transubstantiation and the scholastic philosophy which expounded the orthodox doctrine of the real presence. But the reformers could not leave it at that. There had inevitably to be a debate, an examination of the doctrine in terms of scripture (with the new philological tools), of patristic evidence (with the newly available printed texts), and the attempt to expound Christian truth in biblical rather than scholastic categories. But it is sadly true that here is much heat and sound and little light. And the eucharist became the focus of Christian dissension. Carlstadt had put forward a symbolical doctrine in 1524 (with the fantastic exegesis that 'touto' in 'this is my body' referred to the physical body of Christ, and not to the elements). But the real controversy was precipitated when Zwingli received a letter from the Dutch scholar Cornelius Hoen, which encouraged him to believe that the word *is* in the sentence of institution should be expounded as a trope: as though the *est* were *significat*. Oecolampadius gathered together citations from the Fathers and his *De Genuina Verborum Domini*... (1525), in which he stressed Tertullian's use of *figura corporis*, became a handbook for the symbolical view. A reply to Oecolampadius by his fellow Swabians, the Lutheran Brenz and his colleagues, the *Syngramma*, caused great offence and growing excitement.

In his early writings, Luther had in mind his Catholic opponents and had stressed the need for faith and the fact that the eucharistic presence is given 'in the use of the sacrament'. At the same time, in 1520 he had rejected scholastic categories and so modified the notion of substance that it is misleading to describe his own view as being that of 'consubstantiation', or, in a phrase ironically coined by Oecolampadius, 'impanation'. Luther expounded his doctrine most clearly in an important writing, the *Confession concerning the Lord's Supper* (1528). His unshakeable belief in a real presence is there shown to rest upon the view that all communion with God must be mediated for sinful men through a sensible vehicle, apprehended by faith: that Christ as God-Man is the mediator of salvation, and that by reason of the indissoluble unity of his person he is present in the eucharist not only in his divine but in his human nature even though the mode of his real presence is not to be defined in terms of space.

Bucer was at first won over by Zwingli and Oecolampadius, but in 1529 became convinced by Luther's *Confession* that he had misunderstood him, and that Luther did not intend a localised presence. He himself favoured formulae which employed the realistic language of the Fathers to convey a spiritual interpretation of a true presence, and believed that there was here a genuine basis for evangelical unity. Luther, who continued to see all who differed from him as fellows to Carlstadt and Münzer, was deeply sceptical and suspicious of the whole business, and entirely unwilling to do now what he had refused to do at Worms in 1521—to compromise his convictions for the sake of ecclesiastical unity. The Marburg Colloquy of 1529 was brought about by Philip of Hesse's conviction that evangelical unity was an over-riding political necessity. It began with the positive achievement that the most eminent reformers of Germany and Switzerland came together under one roof in the last days of September. The debates were frank and earnest, and only occasionally flared up, as when Zwingli said (of John vi), 'This will break your necks', and Luther retorted, 'Not so fast! Necks don't break so easily here. You are in Hesse, not Switzerland.' A great field of misunderstanding was cleared up and not again would the sharp and extreme reproaches be woundingly exchanged. The famous remark of Luther to Bucer—'You are of another spirit from us'—reveals the deep distinction between the Wittenberg, Zürich and Strassburg patterns of reform. None the less, important agreements were signed in the fifteen Marburg Articles, in which fundamental disagreement had to be registered only about the eucharist. But the point of failure was deep. No doubt, as Christian theologians the Lutherans were right to refuse to compromise conviction in the interests of a popular front. But in the end it was political events which prevented the Marburg Articles from becoming an important concordat. Zwingli departed, deeply chagrined, to face a dangerous political situation bereft of hoped-for allies. Melanchthon even more than Luther was moved by a loyalty to emperor and empire which the Swiss could not understand, but which made them hope for some accommodation between Catholics and reformers in Germany. The years 1524–9 had seen the hardening division of Germany into Catholic and evangelical princes. The Edict of Worms had been the rallying point of Catholic pressure, but, with the formation of the league of Dessau in 1525, the reforming princes banded in the league of Torgau under the leadership of Duke John of Saxony (Frederick the Wise had died during the Peasants' War) and Philip of Hesse. With the dukes of Brunswick and Mecklenburg, the prince of Anhalt and the counts of Mansfeld, they formed a coherent group when at the Diet of Speyer in 1526 the recess was enacted which laid down that in relation to the Edict of Worms each prince 'is to live, govern, and bear himself as he hopes and trusts to answer to God and his imperial majesty'.

In Saxony the important Church visitations were planned and carried out in 1527–8, Melanchthon writing the *Instructions* to which Luther contributed a preface. Five regions were visited by mixed commissions of theologians, lay representatives from the court, and preachers. The visitations became a model for reform in other parts of Germany. Their immediate effect was to reveal the appalling ignorance of clergy and people, the prime need for Christian education. In 1529 Luther accordingly produced two notable documents. The first, the *Large Catechism*, was a manual for Christian pastors and teachers. The second, the *Small Catechism*, was perhaps Luther's finest work, in its simple beauty unique among the documents of Protestantism, a vehicle of prayer which a child might use, and from which, characteristically, Luther made his devotions for the rest of his days.

Philip of Hesse was obsessed by the military and political danger and became a prey to the forged documents with which the adventurer Pack persuaded him in 1528 that an attack by Catholic powers was imminent, so that he began to angle for an alliance outside the empire with France and with Hungary. The exposure of the deception resulted in a weakening of the evangelical cause. Divided in counsel, they had to face a determined and truculent Catholic majority at the Diet of Speyer in 1529. The recess of 1526 was declared to be abolished, the evangelicals forbidden to inaugurate any innovations or to secularise more Church property. This evoked the *Protestation* of the evangelical princes, signed by the Elector John of Saxony, Margrave George of Brandenburg, Landgrave Philip of Hesse, Dukes Ernest and Francis of Brunswick-Lüneburg, Prince Wolfgang of Anhalt and fourteen cities of the empire. The conclusion is famous, that 'in matters which concern God's honour and salvation and the eternal life of our souls, every one must stand and give account before God for himself'. Thus Protestantism found a local habitation and a name, and its beginning as a political force. Things would no longer be left to the Word, and what Luther had once denounced as a 'mug's game' was now afoot, with all the ominous presentiment of bloody ploys.

The next year, 1530, brought matters to a head. Since 1521 the emperor's purpose had never changed: he adhered to the Edict of Worms with its condemnation of the new doctrines. But his policy, dependent as it was on his circumstances, had been less straighforward. Late in 1529, after the Ladies' Peace of Cambrai and with Italy firmly under his hand,[1] he was for the first time free to turn to the settlement of Germany, and he called the diet to assemble at Augsburg in the following summer. The Diet of Speyer in 1526 had adjourned the Lutheran problem till a general council should meet; now at last Charles had a promise from the pope to call one if only the Lutherans could be brought to terms. He himself would for once be present in person and could hope that a combination of the Turkish danger and an appeal to loyalty within the empire—strong among the Lutheran princes—would lead to a reconciliation. The imperial summons asked the dissenters to prepare statements of faith as a basis for discussion, and it did so in no inflexible spirit. Nearly all the parties

[1] Below, p. 345.

approached the Diet of Augsburg with the best intentions to see peace restored.

But matters had gone too far. Not only was the new religion too well entrenched by this time; not only was the emperor too orthodox himself to bear hardly upon papal stubbornness; there was also the problem of secularised Church lands (the chief cause of the 1529 *Protestation*) to keep the Lutheran princes up to the mark. Doctrines more extreme than those of Wittenberg were by now widespread in Switzerland and the South German towns, as the confessions prepared by Constance and Strassburg proved only too clearly. The tussle at Augsburg was three-cornered, with Catholics, Lutherans and 'Oberdeutsche' all pulling in different directions. In the outcome, the Confession of Augsburg, produced as a statement of Lutheran tenets after weeks of waiting for Charles V's arrival, was moderate. Its authors—Melanchthon had the assistance especially of the humanist George Spalatin, lately secretary to Frederick the Wise—laboured under criticism not only from Zwingli but even from Luther himself. The reformer, still under the imperial ban, could come no nearer Augsburg than the castle of the Coburg, from where he watched with anxiety lest his views be misrepresented. He need not have feared: the Confession embodied the essentials of the new creed. Its language was conciliatory; it took anxious care to dissociate the Lutherans from Anabaptist and subversive doctrines; it was so moderate on the Lord's Supper that the Catholic confutation, produced at the emperor's request, could find little wrong with that article. Yet reconciliation was shown to be a mirage. On the one hand, Melanchthon's mildness confirmed the eucharistic conflict with the Swiss whose deliberations were not affected by the feeling of loyalty to the empire which made the Lutherans approach the diet in the genuine hope of peace in Germany and united action against the Turk; on the other, and more seriously still, there was the duplicity of papal policy in the hands of Cardinal Campeggio who was under orders to avoid the Council and insist on the Edict of Worms. Prolonged negotiations between him and Melanchthon showed that Rome was not looking for mutual concessions, only for surrender.

Thus the Augsburg Confession, rightly today regarded as the product of a particular situation, became—despite its mild longwindedness and explanatory, almost apologetic, tone—the firm and lasting basis of a separate Lutheran Church. So far from healing the breach, it confirmed the schism. Moreover, it was followed by a rash of confessions, and therefore Churches, which now spread over Europe. For another thirty years Christendom would talk in terms of reconciliation, the general council, and the restoration of unity; yet the striking fact that, come what might, the Papacy would yield nothing on the essential points at issue was here demonstrated by Clement VII at the time of his greatest weakness. From Worms to Trent, Rome stood firm on the papal supremacy, the sacrifice of the mass, the orthodox doctrines of the sacraments, good works and prayers to saints. With the best will in the world—and at times they showed good will—the other side could not accept any of this without abandoning their inmost convictions. When Bucer set the Tetrapolitan Confession, the South German reaction to Melanchthon's eucharistic doctrine,[1] by the side of that of Augsburg, the facts were plain. The diet ended the Erasmian dream: the Church would not return to unity, reformed from within in a spirit of reason and peace. Equally it ended the hopes of Charles V. From now on he would have to fight in Germany as well.

[1] Below, p. 111.

CHAPTER IV

THE SWISS REFORMERS AND THE SECTS

I. THE REFORMATION IN ZÜRICH, STRASSBURG AND GENEVA

THE Reformation in the cities of the Rhineland and of Switzerland has its own character. Here a whole set of circumstances, geographical, political, cultural, gives a different pace and direction to the impulses of change which worked out differently in the landed principalities of Germany or the unified kingdoms of France and England.

By the end of the Middle Ages, many of the European cities had achieved independence of their temporal or spiritual overlords, and had come to exercise rights of intervention in ecclesiastical affairs which the Reformation extended and accelerated. It counted for much in Switzerland that the diocesan framework bore no relation to the all-important cantonal structure. The balance of internal forces varied from city to city. In Berne there was a persistence of aristocracy, in Strassburg a cathedral chapter and collegiate churches, in Basle a resident bishop, while in Basle also the craft gilds became an instrument of reforming pressure and the presence of a university offered facilities for propaganda which in Zürich and Strassburg devolved upon the parochial clergy. In Switzerland military prowess, prosperity, independence gave stimulus to alertness and self-confidence. 'My lords of the council' in Zürich were accustomed to regulate important affairs and to control events after a different manner from the small town politicians of the Saxon cities. Wackernagel's fine picture of Basle at the beginning of the Reformation, with its great houses, its famous publishers, its artists and scholars, gives due place to the merchants, rich men furnished with ability, who could throng the lectures of Oecolampadius with an intelligent and devout awareness of great issues.

In these cities there is continuity between humanism and reform. The great Swiss and Rhineland sodalities made possible the transition, not only from 'good letters' to 'sacred letters'—the study of the sacred languages and of the Fathers, with the new tools and texts—but beyond that to what we may call evangelical letters, to the biblical humanism of which in the 1520's Zürich, Basle and Strassburg afford impressive evidence. These cities, still small enough for all those of account to know one another by name, were naturally attracted by the concept of a Christian commonwealth. Luther had established the two great dimensions of the Church, Word and Sacrament, and had powerfully recalled the Church to the centre of its existence, the present rule of Christ. Now a third dimension emerged, 'the discipline of Christ' and with it a whole set of problems concerning the Christian circumference. Notable among these was the relation between the *jus reformandi* of the godly magistrates and the pastoral discipline of the Church. In the first years of the Reformation, when all the older ecclesiastical machinery was hindered, blocked and in the hands of vested interest, the evangelical pastors, themselves with no powers of jurisdiction, found the godly magistrate to be literally a godsend, an effective, competent instrument for getting things done. Only later did second thoughts suggest some of the dangers which lay before the Reformed Churches in tapping ancient sources of moral and political power. By this time the magistrates themselves were reluctant to yield anything of their authority, the more so as they were sensitive and suspicious of a new clericalism. The revolt of the Anabaptists in the cities came sharply up against this Christian office of the magistrate, though in their ways they, too, often upheld the doctrine, in a more apocalyptic setting, of a Christian commonwealth.

But impersonal considerations alone do not explain the Reformation. They were men who made it, and when we think of it, surprisingly few in relation to the creative work which they achieved. These groups of scholars, preachers and pastors are of surprisingly impressive calibre. Most of them were good men, many of them great men. The cities of Zürich, Strassburg and Geneva stand out in the story because Zwingli, Bucer, Calvin were giants.

(a) Zürich

Of all the reformers, Ulrich Zwingli (1484–1531) was most at home in his environment. Not for nothing did an enemy murmur over his dead body, 'A rotten heretic, but a good confederate'. Born on 1 January 1484 in the village of Wildhaus, high in the Toggenburg valley, the sights and sounds of the mountain sides lived again in the imagery of his speech and writing.

Taught Latin by his uncle Bartholomew, the dean of Weesen, he went to schools in Basle and in Berne, and in 1498 to the university of Vienna. Here he met a group of Swiss scholars, including the polymath Vadianus and the obstreperous Glareanus, who combined devotion to the classics with enthusiasm for the newer disciplines of geography, mathematics, medicine. Zwingli was sent down, and we need not seek with the pious biographers for some highly spiritual and creditable reason, since these young Swiss threw their weight about, and there is a field of undergraduate indiscretion which stops well short of the disgraceful. But he was allowed to come back and finish his course, and went on to the university of Basle where he took his M.A. in 1506 and made contact with Thomas Wyttenbach, a teacher of the 'via antiqua'. In after years Zwingli paid repeated tribute to him. In 1506 he went to Glarus as priest, and in the next years combined study and pastoral care as best he could. He made at least two trips with the Swiss troops into Italy. He also joined a circle of humanists, and though the precious classical allusions of this mutual admiration society must be discounted, he was eminent among them and attracted in 1516 the favourable notice of his hero Erasmus, whose Greek New Testament was of great moment for him.

In 1516 he accepted the benefice of Einsiedeln and there effectually withstood the indulgence seller, Bernardino Samson, without any rebuke from the pope, whose pensioner he became and remained until 1520. In 1518 his friend Oswald Myconius nominated him for the post of 'people's priest' in the Great Münster in Zürich. Despite a facility for playing musical instruments which shocked the more staid, and the more serious blemish of a sordid affair with a barber's daughter in 1516, he was appointed to an office which in itself might have counted for little, but which in fact became the key to the Reformation in Zürich.

The older historians stressed his humanism and thought of him as an intellectual concerned with practical abuses at a superficial religious and theological level. The learned studies of modern Swiss scholars have demolished this facile view and, though they have not closed their own case, have decisively re-opened a number of questions. It seems that Zwingli was trained in the 'via antiqua' and read a good deal of Scotus (though how much simpler would be the explanation of his eucharistic doctrine were there evidence that he had been a nominalist!). He had some evident contact with the Platonism of the Florentine Academy, though the paucity of his references forbids us, again, to press this too tempting source of his sacramental 'spiritualism'. His debt to Erasmus is beyond question. It stimulated his enthusiastic study of Greek and his Erasmian preference for Jerome and Origen among the Fathers, for it was only later that he became increasingly indebted to Augustine. Unlike Erasmus, however, he valued the Old Testament highly and for its sake was prepared to work away at Hebrew. It has been suggested (by Cristiani) that the year 1516 was critical in his development, as the year of the New Testament of Erasmus, the year when the concordat between the pope and the king of France hardened his mind against the Papacy, and the year of his moral crisis, which it is thought might have driven him to the help and comfort of the Scriptures. Another important date is 1519 when the plague brought him to death's door. The fine hymn which he composed after his recovery suggests the deepening of his religion by this intimation of mortality, though we ought not to read too much into the famous lines:

in Haf bin ich
mach gantz ald brich
('Thy vessel am I, to make or break')

It is certain that Zwingli's religion became more and more centred on the Bible, to which the key was not philology alone, but faith.

At last I came to the conclusion, 'You must leave all the rest, and learn God's meaning out of his simple Word.' Then I asked God for light, and light came.

This, after all, is the man who put the evangelical invitation, 'Come unto me, all ye that are weary and heavy-laden' upon the frontispiece of his writings and at the heart of his liturgy. Wernle's saying that 'Providence takes in Zwingli's thought the place of Grace in Luther's' is worthy of discussion but does not perhaps do justice to the Christocentric element and the extent to which the doctrine of Providence (even in the famous exposition of the *Summum Bonum* in his great sermon of 1529) has been thought through in biblical terms. There is, of course, a persistent humanist fundament, and to the end his writings abound, a little self-consciously, in classical allusions. Though he had reasons for stressing his independence of Luther, it may well be a fact that he shared the general enthusiasm of the humanists in 1518 for the 'German Hercules'.

When the new preacher took up his duties on 1 January 1519 and announced that he would depart from precedent by preaching right through St Matthew's Gospel, the Zürich Reformation had begun. 'O Blessed are those princes, cities, peoples among whom the Lord speaks freely through his servants the prophets' (*Complanationis Isaiae Prophetae*, 1529). Zwingli exalted the conception of a Christian community, a prophetic commonwealth, a city under the Word. His Reformation was begun, continued and ended through the agency of prophetic preaching. Short-sighted and with a weak voice, he lacked the gifts of the popular orator, but his preaching is the secret of his dominance of the great city, and not all his actions in the small or great council can match it in importance. It is something with few parallels (Calvin, Knox, Latimer?)—this continuous biblical exposition, adjusted to the practical needs of each changing day, in a community small enough for everybody to be known, and where all the effective leadership in the city sat under the Word. The historicity of the mandate of 1520 whereby the council authorised evangelical preaching has been questioned, but of the fact there is no doubt; this scriptural preaching went on here, first of all the cities of Switzerland.

One of its first-fruits related to the traffic in mercenary soldiers. It is anachronistic to speak of Zwingli's pacifism, for he lacked entirely the controlled meekness, the doctrinaire belligerence of the modern opponent of war. The tension in his mind, which was real, reflects a division in Swiss sentiment generally. On the one hand was pride in Swiss arms, renowned and courted throughout Christendom, which partly evoked and partly reflected interest in the military art. Zwingli, who covered his copy of Josephus' *Jewish Wars* with topical remarks, was recognised by his friends as more than an armchair strategist. There is a revealing remark by Vadianus, 'We love the use of weapons, as Zwingli loved it, not for the purpose of revenge, but to maintain and protect the truth'. His sketch of a campaign (1524) is an extraordinary document, treating of strategy and tactics and commissariat, with rules for chaplains and music for the trumpeters, but it was seriously intended and received. On the other hand, most of the Swiss had a conscience about mercenary war. With the trade in arms an ugly element of venality had entered into Swiss politics, aggravated by bribes and pensions. And the Swiss did not always win. Zwingli witnessed the bloody fray of Marignano, and the defeat at Bicocca (1522) swung opinion when the news came to bereft villages and to widows and orphans, and the cripples limped home. Zwingli saw war at first hand, from the battlefield to the village memorial. His *Eine Göttliche Ermahnung* (1522), despite its Erasmianism, its rhetoric, is a genuine revulsion. His early hostility towards the entanglement of his country in the great game of power politics, which finds sharp expression in his political poem, 'The Labyrinth' (1516), with its cry 'Is this what Christ taught us?' became a burning conviction. He urged it from the pulpit until it bore fruit, first when, alone among the cantons, Zürich refused to bargain with the king of France, then against the formidable Cardinal Schinner and the pope himself, until in 1522 the council decided to have done with mercenary war.

Oscar Farner has shown how in 1525, once the initial crisis was over, Zwingli's daily preaching took a more and more practical turn, examining urgent affairs within the orbit of the Word. Zwingli's biblicism was more radical than Luther's, leaving a much narrower field for liberty in things indifferent. He put forward a Carlstadt-like programme with a Melanchthon-like caution. He could make the startling admission that there was little biblical support for tithes or the baptism of infants. He made scripture the basis for the demand that images and pictures be removed and choirs and church music abolished. But in 1522 he walked circumspectly, always careful to keep behind the pace of events. On Ash Wednesday a group of reformers deliberately broke the Lenten fast in the house of the printer, Froschauer, but Zwingli characteristically refrained from touching the two smoked sausages which were the emblem of revolt, though he defended the principles of the innovators in his bold sermon *On the Choice and Free Use of Foods*. In July Zwingli and his friends petitioned the bishop of Constance to permit clerical marriage and were ignored. (Zwingli himself married in that year, though he did not publicly announce the fact until 1524.) In July there arrived the Franciscan Francis Lambert of Avignon, tall and gaunt, stooping over his donkey, who rides through the story of the Reformation from one city to another, like a Don Quixote after El Greco. He lost in spectacular fashion a debate with Zwingli about the intercession of the saints. A few days later the burgomaster issued an order in favour of evangelical preaching, 'from scripture, to the exclusion of Scotus and Thomas and the like'. At the end of the year, Zwingli wrote in his *Archeteles* a crushing retort to the protests of the bishop of Constance and foreshadowed a whole programme of reform.

This he now embodied in sixty-seven articles (19 January 1523) which began with a summary of the gospel, and went on to attack the authority of the pope, transubstantiation, intercession of saints, fasts and pilgrimages. There followed, by command of the council, a public disputation on 29 January 1523. Johann Faber, the capable vicar-general of the bishop of Constance, was badly outmanœuvred. What he had taken to be a disputation on the usual lines, which could be put out for arbitrament to some distant theological faculty, he found to be a great public demonstration at which decisive action was to be taken.

He found an audience of 600, which included the council, while the evangelical preachers formed a group, great Bibles open before them in the three sacred languages, ready for an argument in German which all the audience would understand. Fatally, he tried to carry it off with silence, and then decided too late to argue. When he cried, 'There must be a judge', Zwingli retorted, 'The Spirit of God out of Holy Scripture itself is the judge'—begging some questions, but carrying the audience fervently with him. In fact, the day had already been decided by the announcement of the burgomaster that in default of an answer Zwingli should continue to preach. After iconoclastic riots in the autumn, a second disputation followed in October in which Zwingli's colleague Leo Jüd attacked the use of images and Zwingli the mass. By the end of the year the break with diocesan authority was complete, and in the following summer organs, relics and images were officially removed from the churches and the religious houses in the city were dissolved. In 1525 there was a renewed attack by Zwingli on the mass, which was abolished on 12 April. It was followed by the appearance of Zwingli's communion service, in which he presided over a table laid with beakers and wooden vessels, at which the seated faithful communicated first, the ministers after, in a commemorative rite of great simplicity. There appeared also a new order for baptism. Zwingli's liturgical reforms of 1525 were the conclusion of his half-way measures of 1523. He instituted a preaching service with prayers, which some have thought to be the descendant of the medieval service of prone (and so different from the rite of Strassburg, with its eucharistic pedigree). More original was the office of 'prophesying' which replaced the early morning choir service. Zwingli began this in 1525 when the Anabaptist movement was afoot, and the name does not indicate a preference for spontaneity and subjectivism but, as a study of 1 Corinthians xiv reveals, control and regulation in a service of biblical exposition where in turn the preachers add their comment to what has gone before. In the 'prophesyings' the Old Testament was expounded; there was a New Testament exposition in the afternoon. The great Zürich Bible was in part the result of these services, the fruit of the collaboration of a group of distinguished scholars who seconded Zwingli, Leo Jüd, Pellicanus, Bibliander. The Zürich version of the Psalms penetrated into the Netherlands and England in translation with an influence which has not been fully detected and explored. In May 1525 a court was set up to regularise and control marriage, and in 1526 regulations were issued for the general overseeing of public morals, these being extended in 1530.

Zwingli cordially accepted the *jus reformandi* of the godly magistrate. His concern for Christian discipline is evident in the sixty-seven theses, though his conception, as Ley suggests, may have been more prophylactic than remedial, too much influenced by Old Testament considerations. Yet though in 1526 the council took over the power of excommunication 'in the name of the whole Church', they worked in collaboration with the pastors and until 1531 under a dominant influence from Zwingli. In 1528, in an important letter to Ambrose Blaurer in Constance, Zwingli stressed that the Kingdom of God has to do with external things, and called upon the senators there to do their duty of reform. In his exposition of the Christian faith in the last year of his life, there is the famous phrase: 'A Church without the magistrate is mutilated and incomplete.' To a growing emphasis upon the godly magistrate he had been impelled by the contradiction of the Anabaptists, whose prominent leaders in Zürich, Conrad Grebel and Felix Manz, came from his own pupils and disciples. Whatever its origins elsewhere, the movement in Zürich could put up a specious appearance of being consistent, thoroughgoing Zwinglianism. Zwingli's own hesitations about infant baptism, his doctrine of original sin (the thought of it as a disease—*Morbus, Präst*—even if the disease be plague-like, lacks the intensity of an Augustinian or Lutheran doctrine of guilt), his liturgical simplifications, his eucharistic views, the Anabaptists could claim to have carried to their logical end. But the sharp contradiction came at the heart of Zwingli's doctrine, the Christian commonwealth and the office of the magistrate. In a fiery interview, when Zwingli told the rebels that the time when the mass should be abolished was for the council to determine, Manz shouted, 'No, the Spirit of God is the one who must decide'. Zwingli fully endorsed the savage sanctions which the Swiss cities now applied against the Anabaptists and which sharply reduced what had been a fast-growing movement. He himself became more and more involved in theological controversy about the eucharist, and we could have spared some of these polemic tracts for more positive works like his fine *Commentary on True and False Religion* (1525). His own theology was deeply spiritualist, imbued with the dichotomy between letter and spirit. For him a great text was 'The flesh profiteth nothing'. He abhorred the notion that sensible things could convey spiritual grace. Thus for him the sacraments are not the means whereby the invisible God meets fallen man, but rather pledges and symbols, marks of the covenant between God and the elect. Once convinced of a symbolical explanation of the Words of Institution in the eucharist, he stressed more and more that Christ's body is in heaven, and that he is present in the eucharist only in the unity of the Godhead. The most striking of his eucharistic tracts is his *Amica Exegesis* (1527).

Zwingli strongly felt the political weakness of Zürich against the Catholic cantons and the power of Austria. He dreamed to see his city at the head of a great evangelical confederation and in 1528 succeeded in building the Christian Civic League which by 1529 included Berne and Basle, Constance, Biel, Mühlhausen, Schaffhausen, St Gall, and in 1530, Strassburg. He thought it might stretch out to join hands with the German princes of the League of Torgau, and if need be was prepared to make alliance with France or Venice. He became more and more tempted to the thought of a spoiling and preventive war and by 1529 had created a formidable military force. But perhaps his leaders had heeded his sermons too well in earlier years, for while the troops fraternised the politicians parleyed, and the result was the first Peace of Cappel, an appeasement ot which Zwingli cried in disgust, 'The peace you want means war: the war I want means peace'. Certainly in the next months the strength of his alliance melted away, so that at the Colloquy at Marburg it was Zwingli who had tears in his eyes at the breakdown of the projected evangelical coalition. In 1531 he desperately engineered economic sanctions against the Catholic cantons (oddly announced from the pulpit on Whitsunday) and provoked a fatal military retort in October. On the eve of battle, Zwingli met the young Bullinger and in tears said farewell—'Dear Henry, God keep you. Keep faith with our Lord Christ and his Church'—and disappeared into the night. The day of battle was full of muddle, disaster and, it may be, treachery. There were thirteen preachers among the Zürich troops, including the abbot of Cappel. Zwingli's broken body was found upon the field, treated with contumely and burned. How he died will never be known, but, as Köhler has said, he did not wear a steel helmet, a great sword and an axe for purely ornamental purposes.

The second Peace of Cappel, though it put an end to the adventurous foreign policy of Zürich, was not as disastrous as it might have been, and Henry Bullinger carried on the Zwinglian tradition with pious modification. The statue of Zwingli, with Bible and sword in his arms, would have seemed to Luther an evil mingling of two kingdoms which invited and merited the doom it had received. But it is easy for our judgment of Zwingli's politics to be too much affected by the military disaster which befell them, and we ought not to undervalue the boldness and vision of his hope of an evangelical Swiss Confederation, with Zürich at the head. For Zwingli's was no ignoble dream, a commonwealth in which God might speak freely through his servants the prophets in every part of the public and private life of a Christian community.

Within a few weeks of the death of Zwingli, there came a second blow in the death of the Basle reformer, Johannes Oecolampadius (1484–1531). A scholarly, introverted spirit, Oecolampadius is among the most attractive of the reformers. Bearded, with pendulous nose, sallow of complexion, peering through his spectacles at some codex, he could have sat for Rembrandt's 'Philosopher'. 'Such a man', sighed Luther of his defection to the sacramentaries, and he saw in him Icarus, beguiled by the Daedalus of Zwingli. Born in Weinsberg in Swabia, Oecolampadius came in contact as a student with the 'sodalitas litteraria Rhenana' which included the great names of Reuchlin and Wimpheling among the older men, and among the younger generation Brenz, Bucer and Melanchthon. He studied in Heidelberg, Bologna and Tübingen, took his D.D. and acquired an amazing mastery of Latin, Greek and Hebrew. When his friend Wolfgang Capito went to Basle in 1515 as professor and preacher in the Münster, Oecolampadius went in the more modest role of proof-corrector in the great house of Frobenius and helped launch the great New Testament of Erasmus, writing many of the philological notes. He was next employed on the Erasmian edition of Jerome and introduced into the world of the Fathers of the fourth and fifth centuries whose scholarship, asceticism and piety fascinated him, so that the study of the Fathers became an engrossing occupation. Thus in Oecolampadius we touch an authentic and important element in the Reformation, one which has more in common with the Oxford Movement than the Evangelical Revival, finding in the 'Old Fathers' new tracts for later times.

He produced one after another a series of translations and printed texts of the Greek Fathers, beginning with Chrysostom. He came into friendly contact with the humanists of Augsburg and Nuremberg, Pirckheimer and the brothers Adelmann, who secured him the appointment of preacher in the cathedral of Augsburg. He found the pressure of ecclesiastical work rather a 'treadmill' and suddenly disgusted his friends by entering the Briggitine Order in its Bavarian house at Altomünster ('Thoroughly scruffy, and as you know, run by women!' wrote Adelmann in disgust), an order of men and women which specialised in scholarly and late vocations. But he was soon disillusioned and in 1522 left the monastery, leaving his precious library behind and taking refuge with Bucer in the castle of the Ebernburg. In November he arrived with Hutten in Basle, where he saw his latest translations through the press and exercised his right as a doctor to lecture in the schools. He was soon appointed a professor and began there a work of amazing concentration, for apart from Simon Grynaeus he had not the band of distinguished evangelical colleagues who supported Zwingli in Zürich, or who formed such an impressive team in Strassburg. Soon he was lecturing in three languages on book after book of the Old Testament as well as in German to a burgher audience of several hundreds. He began to preach first in St Martin's and then in the Münster. In 1522 he formed a close friendship with Zwingli and began a correspondence which leaned heavily on the Zürich reformer. In 1524 the eucharistic controversy began, and Oecolampadius brought his knowledge of the Fathers to the help of his friends. His *De genuina verborum Domini...* (1525) became the handbook and arsenal of the sacramentarians and the object of attack from Catholics like Fisher and Cochlaeus, as well as from the Lutheran Brenz.

In May 1526 there was a public disputation in the town of Baden; the Catholics had profited by the lesson of the Zürich disputations to pack the conference and to invite a doughty protagonist in the famous John Eck. With typical circumspection, Zwingli would not go, pleading the refusal of the council to allow the visit, even under a safe-conduct, and contenting himself with sending little helpful notes to Oecolampadius who found himself outnumbered, outvoted, and bearing almost alone the burden of the evangelical cause. He did well, for while Eck roared and rampaged in his most impressive manner, Oecolampadius held his ground with quiet dignity, and with a strength which showed how much he had grown from the scholarly dilettantism of a few months before. The next disputation in Berne, in 1528, was an evangelical field day. Zwingli, Bucer, Capito and others preached about the city, Oecolampadius characteristically choosing as his theme, 'Of the love of Christ for his Church'. Reform followed swiftly in the city of Berne, but in Basle there was a strong Catholic element in the council and a coherent group of Catholic preachers. The crisis came at the end of 1528. That Christmastide armed bands of Catholics and evangelicals walked through the streets at night. But at a meeting on 4 January it was seen that the evangelicals were in their thousands, the Catholics in hundreds. After a few hours of not very wild iconoclasm had shaken the city, the council announced on 8 February that the mass would be abolished and all images removed in Basle and the surrounding countryside. (Erasmus, Glareanus and their friends packed their bags, for quieter pastures.) On 1 April 1529 came the great reforming ordinance, with its new frame for parochial organisation, education and public worship. In the next months Oecolampadius exercised a genuinely episcopal oversight over the Church, which on the Zürich model began to organise a system of synods. From the time when as a young man he had held in Basle the office of penitentiary he had been concerned about Christian discipline, which his study of the moralist Greek Fathers had encouraged. He became more and more concerned to safeguard the spiritual discipline of the Church and to differentiate it from the police action of the Christian magistracy. This important distinction he expounded in a great oration in 1530 (*Oratio de reducenda Excommunicatione*), which Staehelin justly claims to be of first-class importance in Church history. Oecolampadius distinguished between the pastoral discipline of the Church, which is remedial and which seeks to restore the penitent, and the sanctions of the magistrate. He put forward a plan for the establishment of lay elders who should exercise this discipline and would represent the preachers, the congregations and the council. He hoped that his plan might be adopted by other cities in Switzerland, but found them reluctant to abandon the powers already exercised by the magistracy and highly suspicious of a new evangelical clericalism. Bucer shrewdly suggested that Oecolampadius's scheme smacked more of 'patristic severity' than 'Pauline lenity' though he was considerably impressed by the plea for spiritual autonomy, and through him, the distinction between the two powers, dangerously blurred, was re-introduced into evangelical discipline in the Strassburg system which Calvin would later stabilise and trim into a method of permanent importance.

The news of the battle of Cappel threw Oecolampadius into deep grief which brought on physical illness, a carbuncle which became fatal in its venom. On 22 November he said goodbye to his family and his pastors. At one point, when asked whether the strong light was painful, he smote his breast and smiling faintly, punning on his own name, he said 'Abunde lucis est'.

In Basle, Oecolampadius was followed by Oswald Myconius in the office of chief preacher or *antistes*. He was a fine pedagogue, but lacked academic distinctions and left this side of things very much to Simon Grynaeus. In 1534 there arrived Andrew Carlstadt who was appointed professor in the university and within a few months had conjured up a characteristic and most ugly rumpus. Myconius had always been a little sensitive about his lack of academic standing. Carlstadt now began to pitch over and against one another the authority of the ministry (the parochial clergy under Myconius) and of the teaching Church (the university). He, who a few years before had derided all academic dignities, now insisted that none should teach in the city below the rank of doctor and that all must take the degree and so become liable to academic university discipline, a situation not eased by the patronising concession that the examinations might be waived in the case of Myconius and Grynaeus! It was an unhappy affair which broke the heart of Grynaeus and roused Myconius to an unwonted ire. The death by plague in 1541 of Carlstadt brought the affair to an end, and he departed this life leaving behind a crop of poltergeist phenomena and a bitter pathetic widow in her forties, crippled from the endless pains of trapesing behind her husband on his incessant wanderings.

In Henry Bullinger Zürich had found a gifted leader. Lacking Zwingli's genius and his capacity for political adventure, from which in any case the second Peace of Cappel had finally excluded the city, he was content to be an exemplary pastor and teacher, one whose vast correspondence with all the leading reformers of Europe made him into a figure of eirenical importance second only to the more diffuse energies of Bucer. It is Bullinger's Zürich rather than Zwingli's which made the Swiss contribution to the English Reformation in the reigns of Edward VI, Mary and Elizabeth.

Myconius had produced a confession of faith in Basle in 1534. Zürich and Basle collaborated in producing in 1536 the second confession of Basle or the first Helvetic Confession, a work of distinction and authority. In 1549 the important *Consensus Tigurinus* between Bullinger and Calvin opened the way for the reconciliation of all the Swiss Reformed Churches. In 1566 Bullinger's second Helvetic Confession followed, which was adopted by most of the Swiss reformers. Bullinger's sermons and polemical chronicles, while lacking the stamp of profundity or originality, made possible the transition of reformed Christianity from the work of Zwingli to the achievement of John Calvin.

(b) Strassburg

The Imperial Free City of Strassburg occupies a distinctive role in the story of the Reformation. In the Rhineland plain, strategically more vulnerable than the cities of the Swiss Confederation, it was fatefully within the orbit of imperial authority. From its position at a great European crossroad, it drew a thriving, energetic prosperity, and it is no accident that it was a Strassburg reformer who (in Bucer's *De Regno Christi*) gave Protestantism its first rationale of what has been called 'the gospel of hard work'. From the time of the *Schwörbrief* (1482) its constitution involved an intricate welding of oligarchic and democratic balances which worked reasonably well, while frequent elections ensured that the opinions of the craft gilds would be well ventilated. More than in most cities, the magistrates could hold a watching brief, while it is important that the city found, in this period, a great statesman in Jacob Sturm.

There was a flourishing book trade, and the city was early involved in circulating the works of Luther and Melanchthon. The pioneer of the Strassburg Reformation was Matthew Zell (b. 1477) who in 1521 as priest and penitentiary began to preach in a side chapel in the cathedral. His eloquence and his attacks on abuses swelled the congregation, and when the authorities forbade him the use of the stone pulpit in the great nave, which had been built for Geiler of Keysersberg, the gild of carpenters made him a wooden pulpit from which he preached to congregations which numbered over 3000. In May 1523 Wolfgang Capito arrived in the city. Capito (1478–1541) was a doctor in three faculties, law, medicine and theology. He had been professor in Basle and cathedral preacher. As a Hebraist of eminence, he had been a respected collaborator of Erasmus. He had then been chancellor and chaplain to Albert, archbishop of Mainz. Perhaps a more granite-like character might have made the office momentous in the story of the Reformation. But he could ill bear on the one hand the attacks of Catholics, and on the other the reproaches of Wittenberg, and left for what he hoped would be a more placid existence as provost of the collegiate church of St Thomas in Strassburg. One interview with Zell, however, persuaded him to whole-hearted participation in the strenuous war for reform. Somehow Capito seems to have belonged to that class of 'coming men' who never emerge after all, for his stature seems gradually to diminish, and the verdict of history has been to put him high up but in the second class among the reformers.

Capito came to Strassburg as a person of recognised academic and ecclesiastical eminence. Very different was the case of Bucer, who arrived in the same month, poor, unemployed, unknown, and who yet within a year had become 'the soul of the Church in Strassburg'. Martin Bucer (1491–1551) was educated in the fine Latin school at Schlettstadt and entered the Dominican order so young that he had little difficulty later on in getting release from his vows. His friend Beatus Rhenanus introduced him to the works of Erasmus, of whom he became a devotee. Then, in 1518 he heard Luther speak at the Heidelberg chapter of the Augustinians, and that day was won to the cause of reform and to an enthusiasm for Luther which no amount of rebuffs could ever quench. He became chaplain to von Sickingen in 1521, and after the Knights *sic* War went to Wissemburg and thence to Strassburg. Zell was immensely impressed and soon had the newcomer expounding the Bible, until the gild of gardeners asked him to be their priest in the church of St Aurelia. In October there came Caspar Hedio, a D.D. of Mainz and a scholar of versatility. They were joined by Lambert of Avignon. The result was an impressive co-operation in the biblical theology which was a supreme need of the reformers in the 1520's. Capito lectured on the Old Testament and Bucer on the New. Hedio lectured on Greek, then turned to Church history and to the Latin Fathers, and began a German translation of Augustine. Commentary followed commentary, and in them an exact philological exegesis became the basis of theological exposition. Lambert on Hosea, 1525, Capito on Habbakuk in the following year. Bucer poured out a flood of almost illegible writings, including commentaries on the gospels and on Ephesians, while in 1529 he produced a commentary on the Psalms which ran into five editions and was hailed by Calvin as one of the magisterial works of the age.

At the end of 1523 the council published (on the Zürich model) a mandate authorising evangelical preaching. This was followed by a demand from the preachers for a public disputation. But the reformers were not the only ones with memories, and the bishop of Strassburg, seconded by the chapters of the collegiate churches, evaded an open conflict. At the end of 1523 Matthew Zell was married, openly, in the cathedral. The excommunication, in the next months, of seven eminent married priests served only to show the weakness of episcopal authority in the city. In 1523 the preachers had produced a reasoned statement why images should be abolished, and this came about without much of the violence which occurred elsewhere. In 1524 came the great reorganisation of parishes under evangelical preachers, new measures of discipline, and the beginning of educational reforms which were to culminate in the famous academy under John Sturm.

It was of the essence of the Reformation according to Bucer that public measures must go hand in hand with explanation and the instruction of public conscience. None knew better the worthlessness of reformation by public law alone. Thus in 1523 he produced the striking little tract *That nobody should live for himself alone, but for his neighbour*. In 1524 the liturgical reform was heralded by a lucid rationale (*Grund und Ursach...*). In 1538 when the new civic order was fully established there came the impressive document, *Of the Pastoral Care* (*Von der wahren Seelsorge*). Bucer acceded to the *jus reformandi* of the magistrates. But from 1530 onwards he was impressed by the plea of Oecolampadius for an autonomous Church discipline. The appointment by the authorities in 1530 of churchwardens, the *Kirchenpfleger*, involved a certain tension between their and Bucer's interpretations of the office. These lay officials found criticism of the preachers a congenial duty, and it was with alacrity that they reported to the council that Hedio was longwinded and that Bucer preached above the heads of most of the congregation. But Bucer did succeed in 1534 in getting some recognition that these lay officers represented a scriptural office, and were in fact elders of the Church. His concern for Church discipline turned in another direction. Perhaps taking a hint from Luther's *Deutsche Messe* (1526) or from the conventicles of the sectaries, he proposed to form *Gemeinschaften*, small Christian cells, in which groups of laymen exercised a mutual cure of souls. Though not favourably regarded by the magistrates, these met until 1550. On 20 February 1529 there came the formal abolition of the mass, by 184 votes to 1, 94 voting for delay, and 21 being absent from the council. In 1534, following a synod in which the magistrates presided, there came a definitive settlement on the basis of sixteen articles of faith presented by the preachers, followed by an ordinance of discipline in 1535, the influence of which persisted until 1789.

Partly by reason of its situation, but more because of the eirenical temper of its rulers, Strassburg became the great city of refuge of the Reformation. The city achieved a noble record for the relief of suffering. When the peasant armies swarmed across Alsace in 1525, Zell, Capito and Bucer met the leaders at Altdorf. Their severe rebukes were treated by the rebels with respect. But in the dreadful aftermath the citizens of Strassburg, under the leadership of the pastors, more especially of Mrs Zell, the founding mother of all vicars' wives, produced food, clothing and shelter for the homeless multitudes. In 1529 the good work was repeated under the impact of a great famine, and many thousands were succoured. Not for nothing had Bucer added 'love' to the three dimensions of the Protestant Church (Word, Sacrament, Discipline).

Almost all the great exiles of the period came to Strassburg. What a list it is! Lefèvre, Farel, Lambert, Calvin; Carlstadt, the Zwickau prophets, Denck, Hetzer; Sattler, Kautz, Rothmann, Hübmaier, Hoffmann, Joris, Servetus, Schwenckfeld, Franck. There were many groups of humbler sectaries who found refuge. Zell and Capito especially were impressed by many of these visitors, knowing they were not all fanatics. They agreed with them about the inwardness of true religion, the importance of a godly life. Yet there were enough obstinate and truculent fanatics to drive the authorities to take action in an edict (27 June 1527) banning the sectaries and threatening all who gave them refuge, though the repetition of this enactment in following years suggests the difficulty of its enforcement. Capito seems more than once to have been carried away by their doctrines, most notably by Schwenckfeld. In 1529 he was seriously ill, and the death of a beloved wife drained him of his energies. Bucer, who had a great way of marrying off his friends, made, in an incredible 'open letter' to Margaret Blaurer, a vicarious proposal which that formidable bluestocking turned down, enabling Bucer's second thoughts to succeed by the winning for his friend of the merrier widow Wibrandis Oecolampadius ('sancta, hilaritatis facilitatisque incredibilis') who would one day become the second Mrs Bucer. But Capito never quite got over his melancholy and died of plague in 1541.

On 16 February 1524 Theobald Schwarz introduced a German mass in the cathedral. It was the beginning of creative experiment which produced twenty-four interesting liturgies in the next ten years. The dominant influence was Bucer's. Brightman has criticised the extent to which the didactic element protrudes in Bucer's liturgies, but we must remember that for him this was only one aspect of a general reformation in which at each point explanation and instruction must accompany change. First in importance came the restoration of the primacy of the Word in preaching and the exposition of the scripture. There is the story of how Bucer erased from the cathedral service books the ascriptions of the divine Name which late scholasticism had pitched against one another in subtle dialectic, inscribing in their place the words 'Our Father'. Like Oecolampadius he made provision in his eucharist for silent prayer. He gave to congregational hymn-singing so important a place that it has been claimed that for Bucer 'the Church is built round the hymn', and of the many collections issued during these years the most beautiful is the hymn book of 1541. With Münzer in Allstedt, Strassburg led the way in services of vernacular matins and vespers for the congregation. Roussel described the worship in the city in 1526:

At five in the morning there is a sermon and common prayer, and again at seven o'clock in each church. Next, at eight the people are called together, but this time in the cathedral alone, and there a sermon is preached to them. Preceding and following the Word of God are songs, translated from the Hebrew psalter into the language of the people... Again at four hours after breakfast a meeting of the people is held in the same church and in like manner the work of Christ is performed.

Bucer's order of baptism attempted to avoid Roman and Zwinglian extremes, while his concern for Christian education led him to stress, more than any other reformer, the importance of confirmation.

His two characteristic themes are the pastoral care and the doctrine of the Church. Following Luther and Oecolampadius he expounds the thought of the Church as the communion of saints. He begins with predestination, with the elect who are chosen in Christ. But it is of great practical importance for Bucer that, by an act of charity, Christians may assume that those who live godly lives and share in the worship and sacraments of the Church are in fact members of the elect, and that therefore the exercise of Christian discipline, including the fencing of the Lord's table, becomes possible. His expositions of the epistle to the Ephesians, and especially of the fourth chapter, stress the importance of the scriptural ministry which he thinks of as four-fold—pastors and teachers, elders and deacons. Of all the reformers he is the most missionary-minded, and as Margaret Blaurer teasingly called him, 'a fanatic for unity'. Bucer and Capito believed, and this is an important trait of the Strassburg Reformation, that while unity was essential in primary matters, there were other issues about which Christians might agree to differ. So Bucer could write: 'Flee formulae, bear with the weak. While all faith is placed in Christ, the thing is safe. It is not given for all to see the same thing at the same time.'

In the eucharistic controversy he badly queered his pitch as a mediator by two inexcusable gaffes, inserting his own views without advertisement into what were intended to be official translations of works by Bugenhagen and Luther, so that when they met at Marburg we can understand why Luther wagged a finger at him and said 'You rogue!' But when he read Luther's eucharistic confession in 1528, he realised that he had misunderstood him to mean a localised and circumscribed presence, and he became convinced that agreement was possible, persisting after the failure of the Marburg Colloquy. For himself, he could use the realistic language of the Fathers to convey a spiritual doctrine of the true presence, and would say that the body and blood of Christ are really delivered (*exhibentur*) to the faithful, that the impenitent receive the body and blood of Christ to their judgment, but that the godless receive only bread and wine. Though he would not accept the eucharistic article of the Augsburg Confession in 1530, and with a Baxter-like alacrity produced the *Confessio Tetrapolitana* (of Strassburg, Constance, Memmingen, Lindau), he pressed on at Schweinfurt (1532) and Kassel (1535) until he brought off the Wittenberg Concord of 1536 with Melanchthon, though he continued to seek agreement with the Swiss at Basle (1536) and Zürich (1539). With Calvin and Melanchthon he attended conferences with Catholics at

Worms, Hagenau and Regensburg (1539–41 and again in 1546), and although these broke down, a genuine understanding was reached between them and the mediating theologians, Gropper, Pighius, Contarini, in important matters concerning justification and the work of the Holy Spirit.

In 1546 came the military disasters of the Schmalkaldic war, and Jacob Sturm, on bended knee, had to sue for pardon for his proud city at the feet of the victorious Emperor Charles V. The emperor would have nothing to do with a new confession of faith proffered by Bucer and insisted that Strassburg must sign his Interim. This Martin Bucer altogether refused. In his growing age, amid much physical weakness, he picked out the most laborious among his many invitations and adventured with his family towards the distant, uncouth, backward land across the sea. In England he lived, and taught in Cambridge as Regius Professor of Divinity, until his death. King Edward VI gave him the royal gift of a stove, which gave off nostalgic continental blasts of brimstone to offset the dank mists of the fens. In gratitude he gave back a princely offering, the treatise *De Regno Christi*. This noble document sums up all the dreams and plans (most of them now shattered) of the twenty-five years of the Strassburg Reformation. It is in part a practical retrospect, but at another level reads like a wonderful premonition of seventeenth-century puritanism. Above all it attempts the accommodation of the reign of Christ to human history in terms statesman-like and prophetic enough to be treated with respect.

The Interim bore its fruit. When better days came for the Strassburg Protestants, Bucer's work was overlaid by a triumphant and intransigent Lutheranism under Marbach and Pappus. Bucer's Strassburg, therefore, never became comparable with Luther's Wittenberg, Zwingli's Zürich or Calvin's Geneva. He himself in reputation has not attained to the first three. A heavy earnestness, a lack of humour, an incurable verbosity limited the range and influence of his writings. In a well-meaning way he got across so many people that we suspect a defect of temperament. But he was greatly admired and really loved, as a truly great man and as a 'character', not least in the England of his latest exile. He had, says M. Strohl, a 'charisma for assimilation' and was hospitably aware, beyond most of his contemporaries, of the many-sidedness of truth. That is why, of all the fierce voices of that contending age, he hails those today who labour, as he laboured, for the Peace of Jerusalem.

(c) Geneva

In John Calvin, France added a new and vital quality to a Protestantism too deeply imbued with a teutonic spirit. It is as though the Spirit of the Pities, foreseeing what the grim Furies would do with the Reformed Church of France in coming days, snatched from them its beginnings, and made possible this great offering, decisive, superb, lasting, to the Churches of the Reformation.

The Reformation in Geneva takes its rise in close connection with reform in the city of Berne. Berne, thriving, ambitious, aggressive, with its eyes on the Pays de Vaud, was the one city strong enough to withstand the duke of Savoy and the Catholic bishop of Geneva, and it encouraged the city of Geneva to seek an independence from temporal and spiritual suzerainty, which by 1536 it had almost attained. In Berne itself a strong patrician element acted as a brake on change. But the activities of Berthold Haller (1492–1536) and Sebastian Mayer resulted in the great disputation of 1528 to which all the leading Swiss reformers came and in which Capito and Bucer took prominent part. The result was the formal abolition of the mass, on 7 February 1528 and the adoption of the Reformation, with its rapid extension into the adjacent commanderies. In this work the leaders were William Farel (1489–1565), a pupil of Lefèvre, of moderate learning, little practical sense, but fiery and fearless eloquence, Antoine Froment (1510–84)—these two Frenchmen—and Peter Viret (1511–71), a native of French Switzerland and soon to be the reformer of Lausanne. Farel, after evangelising Aigle and Neuchâtel, came to Geneva on 4 October 1532 but had to leave at once. Froment remained, disguising reformed propaganda under the cover of a modern language school. The conflict in Geneva was violent and bitter on both sides. The Catholic party behaved with incredible indiscretion, fanning the flames of an already powerful anti-clericalism, while the agitation of the Dominican Furbiti only brought the intervention of the council of Berne on behalf of the reformers. Farel re-entered the city on 20 December 1533. A disputation in January 1534 routed the opposition, and in March Farel was allowed the use of a Franciscan chapel. The attempt of the bishop to subdue the city by force enabled the reformers to show their solidarity with the cause of civic freedom, which they were able to sustain. An attempt to poison the reformers won them still more sympathy. In May and June 1535 there was a public disputation at which the Catholics made a lamentable showing. In August the councils of the city ordered the mass to be suspended. In the following February ordinances were passed regulating public morals and church attendance. On 21 May 1536 the general council met in the cathedral and swore solemnly, with uplifted hands, to live according to the Word of God. The victory of the reformers had been swift, but the leaders knew only too well that it was superficial and precarious. As Calvin said later: 'They had preached. They had burned images. But there was no real reformation. It was all in the melting pot' (tout était en tumulte). This was the situation when, two months later, John Calvin passed through the city, and was memorably intercepted by Farel.

John Calvin (1509–64) was born at Noyon on 10 July 1509, the son of a notary of sufficient influence to secure for his son, at the age of twelve, a cathedral benefice to support his education. In 1523 he went to the university of Paris, to the Collège de la Marche. There he learned Latin from the great Mathurin Cordier and developed a style of Ciceronian delicacy. He then studied theology, perhaps under John Major, a famous exponent of the 'modern way'. He took his M.A. degree in 1528 and went next to Orleans where he studied law under the eminent Pierre de l'Étoile. It may be that at this time he began to learn Greek under the Lutheran Melchior Wolmar. But he soon moved to Bourges, where there was a group of humanists, and became whole-heartedly devoted to the study of good letters. His father died in May 1531, and, free to go his own road, Calvin returned to Paris and the study of the sacred languages, taking his doctor's degree in law at Orleans. In Paris he wrote his first book, an edition of Seneca's *De Clementia* which appeared on 4 April 1532. It is very much a young man's book, a little too bedecked with learning, coruscating too showily with classical and patristic allusions. It did not sell. But it is evidence of his thoroughgoing humanism, and as M. Wendel says, 'Calvin always remained more or less the humanist he was in 1532'. But at some time in the next months he underwent a change of mind which was more than the intellectual transition from good to sacred letters. God 'subdued my heart to docility by a sudden conversion' (*subita conversione ad docilitatem subtegit*) runs the famous enigmatic testimony of his later preface to the Psalms. He now became an associate of dangerous friends. One of them, Nicholas Cop, the rector of the university of Paris, delivered an official address on 1 November 1533 which roused a storm. It now seems unlikely that Calvin had any hand in the making of this oration, which was in the main an unimpressive patchwork of Erasmian and Lutheran citations, made inflammatory mainly by its protest against persecution. But as a result of it many reformers, including Calvin, went into hiding. He made his way to Poitiers and Angoulême, and again to Orleans where he wrote his first theological tract, the *Psychopannychia*,[1] a disquisition on the state of the departed which suggests that in his mind classical and biblical ideas were not fully integrated. The fury about the 'placards' (October 1534) induced Calvin to leave the country, and to seek the city of scholars, the city of books and Erasmus, Basle. There he printed a little book. He did not take it to one of the great publishers of the city, but to the rather amateurish establishment of Thomas Platter. With a bold, elegant epistle to the king of France, it appeared to be just another rather lengthy primer, an octavo of 532 pages, simply entitled *Christianae Religionis Institutio*. Neither publisher nor author could have dreamed that they had given to the world one of its normative religious documents. He went on to Italy to the court of Margaret of Navarre and the company of compatriot poet exiles. He seems to have made a trip to Paris on urgent family business, and to have made a wide detour on his return, around the embattled

[1] In part, this tract was an attack on Anabaptism (below, p. 129).

armies of Francis I and Charles V, which brought him by chance through the city of Geneva. He, whose hopes and plans lay all in the world of letters, was now rudely summoned into the rough world of practical reform. Only the awful conjuring of Farel at his most prophetic saved him from the great Erasmian refusal. But once he had accepted this call he never again faltered.

Calvin began quietly in Geneva, as reader in holy scripture in the church. At the beginning of October 1536 he attended a disputation in Lausanne. At the tired end of a wearying debate, the audience woke sharply to attention when the lean, fastidious stranger rose and rattled off from memory a phenomenal chain of citations from the Fathers, references and all, with a casual ease which told them that, that day, a portent had appeared.

The council of Geneva, like those of Basle, Berne and Zürich, was in no wise minded to admit a new Protestant clericalism. But Calvin believed with Oecolampadius and Bucer that it was vital for the Church to control its pastoral discipline. In January 1537 he submitted articles for the reorganisation of the Church, and a confession of faith in which explicit mention was made of discipline. Farel and Calvin then became involved in a long and angry wrangle with the scholar Pierre Caroli who charged them with dabbling in Arianism and a suspicious reluctance to endorse the Athanasian creed. The debate was carried into the synods of Berne and Lausanne, to the eventual discomfiture of Caroli. None the less, suspicions were aroused in Berne which came to a head when Farel and Calvin refused to accept the Bernese liturgy which the council of Geneva had accepted over the heads of the preachers. At the same time the council denied the pastoral right of excommunication. Calvin and Farel were then dismissed the city.

Calvin's stay in Strassburg (1538–41) was fruitful. It has been said that he went there a younger theologian and returned an ecclesiastical statesman. As pastor of the French congregation he had cure of souls over a compact society. He learned much from practical collaboration and theological discussion with the Alsatian reformers and above all from Bucer. Bucer's emphasis on the doctrine of the Church and upon pastoral care found congenial echo in his own mind. Bucer had stressed the doctrine of predestination and as early as 1536 had treated this in a Christocentric setting. Bucer it was who insisted on a scriptural ministry, and thought of it in terms of pastors, teachers, elders and deacons. The Strassburg liturgy was a model for Calvin's simpler rite, while both agreed on the value and importance of congregational psalm singing. As M. Strohl has said, we must not confuse influence with imitation, and Calvin transmuted what he learned into his own idiom, his own superb clarity.

He wrote important tracts. The *Letter to Sadoleto* is a fine piece of apologetic. In 1539 he published a revision of the *Institutes* enlarged by two chapters. In 1541 he produced the French translation, which was seen to be a literary masterpiece and a landmark in the history of the French language. His *Little Treatise of the Holy Supper of our Lord* (1540) was a notable exposition of an eirenical nature, between the Lutheran and Zwinglian extremes. In August 1540 he married Idelette de Bure. A few weeks before, the council at Geneva had decided to ask him to return. 'I would submit to death a thousand times rather than to that Cross on which I had daily to suffer a thousand deaths' he complained to Farel. But he went, and that strange relationship with Geneva, which de la Tour has likened to a marriage of convenience, persisted to his death. The magistrates were eager to please. They allotted him a house, the famous No. 11 Rue des Chanoines, and a sufficient stipend. Characteristically, he went immediately to the council on arrival with a plan of reform and demanded that a commission be set up forthwith to deal with it.

The *Ordonnances Ecclésiastiques* (20 November 1541) show that Calvin, unlike many of his followers, was no doctrinaire but a statesman willing to accept concessions and limitations. The scriptural doctrine of the Church and ministry is expounded in the fourfold frame of pastors, teachers, elders and deacons. The bone of contention was still discipline and the right of excommunication. The lay elders were nominated by the magistrates. The consistory was a Church court, but the preachers and elders met under the presidency of one of the four syndics of the city. The elders could exercise a general moral oversight, but had no power to impose sanctions or to excommunicate, apart from the consent and co-operation of the magistrates. Not until 1555 did Calvin get his way. By this time there had developed an important controversy among the Swiss Churches and two ideologies struggled for mastery in the Pays de Vaud: Calvin's with the clear distinction between civil and ecclesiastical discipline, and that of Zürich, whose doctrine of the godly magistrate was expounded at Berne by Wolfgang Musculus, the precursor of Erastus.

Calvin had to accept other modifications: a eucharist quarterly rather than monthly, the imposition of hands in ordination to be discontinued, the meeting of preachers for 'fraternal admonition' (to be held weekly in Calvin's intention) to be quarterly. The council kept firm hold on its prerogatives in regard to the appointment of teachers, marriage regulation and civil crime. Calvin published his *Forme des prières et chants ecclésiastiques*, a revision of his earlier services in Strassburg. He issued a revised catechism in French and Latin in 1542. He was a great preacher, and the regular biblical preaching of the reformers in Geneva became here as elsewhere a prime agency of reform. But he cared much for education, and invited the best teachers he could get, Mathurin Cordier and then Sebastian Castellio. Deeply impressed by the academy of Strassburg under John Sturm, he did not rest until in 1559 Geneva had erected its own fine academy under the rectorship of Théodore Béza. One by one, in successive edicts, Calvin attempted to win the great, profligate multitude to habits of right virtue by a network of measures which touched every part of life and whose sanctions spared neither high nor low. Naturally he had many enemies, and the old pressure groups used religious devices for political ends. The affair with Caroli left him sensitive to the charge of unorthodoxy. The expulsion of Castellio in 1544 came after a sharp theological quarrel, of which the question of the authorship of the *Song of Songs* was the occasion rather than the cause. More serious was the burning of Servetus. Michael Servetus (1511–53) was a Spanish scholar of versatile gifts. The bent for novelty which enabled him to make at least one important medical discovery was dangerously turned to the critical investigation of the doctrine of the Trinity and his *On the Errors of the Trinity* (1531) horrified most contemporaries and brought him in danger from the Inquisition. Denial of the divine Name was not only heresy but open blasphemy and had been inscribed as such in the law of the Christian empire for a thousand years. He had also written a vitriolic attack on Calvin's *Institutes* and Calvin had given fair warning that if he ever showed up in Geneva he would get short shrift. This was in fact meted out to him when he had the folly and effrontery to appear in a Genevan congregation in 1553. He was arrested and condemned. That Calvin attempted to get the sentence commuted from burning to execution is a concession which only a Gilbertian casuistry could make impressive, and the death of Servetus, though endorsed by most public opinion of the age, has seemed to posterity the gravest blemish on the record of Calvin's Geneva.

In the last years of his life Calvin dominated the city, an honoured and respected leader, one whose shy nature hid an attractive friendliness which the multitude never saw. Geneva had become the great city of refuge and a centre of evangelical instruction and propaganda. If it seemed to be to some, as to John Knox, 'the most perfect school of Christ', its catechumenate, like that of Origen, never forgot the horizon of martyrdom. From Geneva there went out a ministry, trained, disciplined, committed, the nearest Protestant counterpart to the Society of Jesus. Within a few years 161 pastors went into the Reformed Church in France, already a 'Church under the Cross'.

Calvin's *Institutes* have been called the Protestant *Summa Theologica*. But it was much more than a theological compendium for the learned. This exposition of the economy of redemption was also a prospectus of the Church militant on earth, a handbook for Christian warriors. In 1543 the new Latin edition had grown to twenty-one chapters. In 1550 the work was divided into sections and paragraphs, now of thirty-three chapters. Finally, in 1559 came the great definitive edition, enlarged by more than a fourth, in eighty chapters. Some of it is ephemeral, and the controversies with Osiander, Westphal and Servetus spoil the shape. But here, at last fully deployed, are all Calvin's majestic intellectual resources, the full stretch of biblical and patristic knowledge (there are 341 quotations from Augustine).

Calvin was one of the greatest patristic scholars of the age, and the greatest biblical theologian of his generation. The Bible was the important thing. We who strain with all our historical imagination, who swoop on every precious gleam among the evidence, to come close to these men and women of four hundred years ago must never forget that they did precisely this, with even greater intensity, and with much more at stake, to comprehend the holy prophets and apostles, to hear the Word of the Lord. Calvin lectured twice a week for many years on the Bible, and published commentaries on all the books of the New Testament save Revelation, and on many books of the Old Testament, including a great commentary on the Psalms. Into his writings he took up all that was profitable in the reformers before him. He has imbibed Luther much as St Thomas is saturated in Augustine, even though he differs from him about the relation of gospel and law and the doctrine of the eucharist. He learned much, too, from Bucer and from his friend Melanchthon.

The older view that his dominating conception is the sovereignty of God, even when this is interpreted in terms of sovereign grace, has been modified by theological research which in recent years has brought to the fore its Christocentric reference. He joins together what twenty years of Protestant controversy had begun to part asunder, the doctrines of Word and Spirit: the great watchwords, 'Sola fide: sola gratia'; 'Sola Scriptura'; 'Soli Deo Gloria'. The doctrine of predestination has to be seen in the context of the late medieval exposition of the subject, and Calvin can hardly be blamed for all that later Protestants have made of it. And if we think his doctrine perverse as well as wrong, we must remember that for Calvin what is inscrutable in the divine will is but the darkness of excessive light. Calvin treats with impressive reverence of the ineffable goodness, the infinite condescension of God in passages which achieve a solemn and moving beauty, even though he lacks something of Luther's tenderness and joy. His austerity, real as it is, lacks something of the hardness of the Zwinglian *Hartseligkeit*.

In the sacramental controversy he was fortunate in coming at a time when the initial bitterness was past, and when Bucer had kept alive the hope of mediation. He insisted on a true, spiritual presence in which the faithful, ascending by faith into the heavenly places, receive the strength and virtue of the body and of the blood of Christ. He shared in the conferences with the Catholic theologians in 1539–41 and never ceased to hold the brave hope of a free, Christian council which might join all the divided Churches. His great correspondence with reformers in many lands shows remarkable freedom from insularity, a rare gift for imaginative understanding of conditions and temperaments very different from his own.

Calvin, as has been often said, is the reformer of the second generation, the giant among the epigoni. Protestantism had been slowing down, its initial impetus spent, divided, tired, disheartened. After Calvin it is once more on the move, singing on the march, ready to strike new blows for liberty. He restored the exhilaration of Christian comradeship. He renewed the brave vision of the Word going forth conquering and to conquer.

2. THE ANABAPTISTS

The great reformers, Luther, Zwingli and Calvin, as well as their chief supporters—men like Melanchthon, Bullinger and Bucer—found themselves involved in controversy not only with Rome but also with those of more radical views than their own. They had to fight on two flanks at once. While they were still struggling with the Roman authorities, there appeared on the left wing of the Reformation movement a series of independent thinkers. Carlstadt, Denck, Franck and Schwenckfeld come to mind. There were also a number of sizeable groups, 'not a single sect, but a congeries of sects', as Mackinnon put it. Many of these widely scattered groups had in common a rejection of the baptism of infants. The rite should be administered, they believed, only on profession of faith. Their reading of the New Testament led them to regard the sprinkling of children as no real baptism, and they therefore did not hesitate to submit to the rite themselves, and to administer it to others, as a sign of personal repentance and faith, whatever else might have happened to them in infancy. To Catholic and Protestant alike, this seemed monstrous. The rite had always been regarded as unrepeatable. Re-baptism was a grievous offence. When there were added to it other views and tendencies which seemed erroneous and dangerous, both the major religious parties felt justified in exacting the most severe penalties. The very name 'Anabaptist', to which Zwingli gave early currency, became a term of general abuse, charged with an emotional content in which fear played a considerable part.

The term was so widely and loosely applied in the sixteenth century, and even a hundred years later, that it is not easy even today to decide which individuals and groups should be included in a study of the movement. The Reformation was so profound an upheaval, involving such great changes in men's outlook and habits, that it would in any case have led to extravagance and antinomianism in some quarters. The savagery with which 'Anabaptists' were treated, particularly from 1529 onwards, increased the tendencies towards fanaticism and abnormality among those who were attacked. Only now is it becoming possible to attempt a more just and balanced appraisal of the course of the movement and the principles for which its best representatives stood.

Where should one begin the story? In Wittenberg in 1521 with the

Zwickau 'prophets' and Thomas Münzer, or in Zürich in 1523 with Conrad Grebel, Balthasar Hübmaier and the Swiss Brethren? The historians of the past have differed sharply. Those who have treated the attack on the baptism of infants in Wittenberg as the opening scene of the Anabaptist drama have this justification, that the Zwickau prophets seem to have advocated a Church of the near separatist type, though they probably never practised believers' baptism. Münzer began as a religious revolutionary in controversy with Luther on questions of scripture, faith and baptism. In 1524, if not earlier, he certainly had some contact with the Swiss radicals, though they rejected his violent methods. His fiery leadership of the peasants' revolt stirred up widespread unrest and questioning in places where afterwards many Anabaptist sympathisers were found.[1] One of Münzer's lieutenants, Hans Hut, who escaped the massacre which followed the defeat of the peasants at Frankenhausen in 1525, later became a well-known Anabaptist propagandist. But all this was only one contributory stream to the Anabaptist movement and not the most important one. Those historians who concentrate attention on events in Zürich are almost certainly right in finding there the real source from which the movement effectively spread.

Zwingli established his position in Zürich in January 1523 after a public disputation with Roman Catholic representatives.[2] Within a few months he was engaged in argument with some of his supporters as to how far they should go in regard to tithes and interest, images in churches and changes in the mass. Hübmaier claimed that in May of that year Zwingli admitted that it was doubtful if children, who had not been instructed in the faith, should be baptised. But at the 'Second Disputation' held in the following October, those who stood for a more radical reformation and a Church order which tried closely to reproduce that of the New Testament failed to win the day, though they were led by Conrad Grebel, whom Zwingli himself called 'a noble and learned young man', and by Simon Stumpf, an ex-Franciscan. During 1524, however, the question of baptism increasingly agitated these men and their friends, their concern perhaps being deepened by contact with Carlstadt, who had been banished from Saxony, with Martin Cellarius, and with Münzer, either in person or by way of his writings. A number of persons in and around Zürich refused to have their children baptised, although ordered to do so by the city council. In January 1525 Grebel, Felix Manz, an ex-priest who had supported Zwingli since 1519, and Wilhelm Reublin, another ex-priest, discussed this and kindred matters with Zwingli and Bullinger in the presence of the council, but could secure no satisfaction. Those who had unbaptised children were ordered to have them baptised within a week, the penalty for disobedience to be banishment.

[1] Above, p. 89.
[2] Above, p. 101.

A few days later, probably on 21 January 1525, at one of the meetings the little group of friends were regularly holding for Bible study, two decisive steps were taken. George Blaurock, yet another ex-priest, was baptised by affusion on profession of his faith, by Conrad Grebel. He then himself baptised the rest of the company, who numbered about fifteen. Shortly afterwards they celebrated the Lord's Supper together in simple fashion, regarding it as a memorial of the sufferings and death of Jesus, a fellowship meal in which only believers should share. The mass was still being celebrated in Zürich. The little group had decided that they could no longer remain subject to Zwingli and the council.

Within a few days, baptisings also took place at Zollikon, a village some five miles down the eastern shore of the lake. The council tried to assert its authority by arrests and imprisonments, but a popular revival movement had been touched off. The details are difficult to disentangle, but it is clear that the leaders of the group travelled widely in the surrounding countryside. By Easter time, in St Gall and Waldshut, scores and possibly hundreds had been baptised, Grebel and Blaurock apparently immersing men and women in rivers and streams. Church buildings were deserted and services held in private houses and fields. In the preaching of the brethren an apocalyptic note may occasionally have been sounded, though it was not characteristic of the movement as a whole. The popular excitement cannot have been entirely unconnected with the revolt of the peasants in Germany. May 1525 saw the publication of Luther's notorious pamphlet against the peasants and Zwingli's booklet, *Vom Touf, Widertouf und Kindertouf*. During the second half of 1525, Grebel, Blaurock and Manz all suffered periods of imprisonment. Young Michael Sattler, formerly a monk, was banished from the canton. Hübmaier, driven from Waldshut, was arrested in Zürich, recanted his baptist views under torture, then withdrew his recantation, recanted once more and was finally allowed to leave the city. But the movement was not checked. In March 1526 the council decided that sterner measures were necessary. The drowning of Anabaptists 'without mercy' was ordered, and about the same time parish registers of births were instituted to try to ensure that all infants were baptised. The drowning edict was re-enacted in November 1526 and those who listened to the preachers were threatened with death. The ardent Grebel had died a few months earlier, either in prison or of the plague. Manz and Blaurock were captured again in December. In January 1527, with Zwingli's knowledge and approval, Manz, brave to the last, was tied to a hurdle and thrown into the river Limmat to drown. Because the fiery Blaurock, who was perhaps chiefly responsible for the spread of the movement in and around Zollikon, was not a citizen of the canton, the death penalty was not inflicted on him. After being beaten through the streets, he was banished. For a time Anabaptism continued to spread in the neighbouring valleys, but those of its leaders who survived fled elsewhere. Though the movement continued in Switzerland in scattered, underground fashion till early in the seventeenth century, it no longer presented a serious problem to the authorities.

Grebel and his associates had had few opportunities of working out any complete Church order. They had, however, made clear the main principles which appeared subsequently in other places. They stood for what Köhler calls 'an inward, apostolic Biblicism', claiming that they were but carrying to its logical conclusion Zwingli's own principle of reliance on scripture. The main characteristics of the Swiss movement were the practice of believers' baptism, a 'voluntary' Church, emphasis on the precepts of the Sermon on the Mount, the rejection of the oath, war and resort to legal proceedings, and insistence on far-reaching mutual material help. It seems doubtful whether the brethren practised community of goods, though undoubtedly they moved in that direction.

The action of the Zürich magistrates aided the spread of the movement elsewhere, in spite of the wide circulation of the violent denunciations of Anabaptism which came from Zwingli and Bullinger. Driven from Zürich, Anabaptist missionaries passed through the Grisons territory into northern Italy where their teaching was accepted by many of the interesting group of intellectual rebels from Catholicism who ultimately became associated with Socinianism.[1] Blaurock made his way into the Tyrol, proving himself a most successful evangelist and baptising many hundreds of persons before his capture and burning in 1529. The Tyrol remained to the end of the century both the classic mission field of Anabaptism and the reservoir in which the forces were collected which, from the time of Jakob Huter (Blaurock's successor), were directed to Moravia.

Hübmaier, who had in 1524 addressed to his former friend, John Eck, a notable plea for toleration entitled *Concerning Heretics and Those that Burn Them*, and who had been baptised as a believer by Wilhelm Reublin, made his way after his banishment from Zürich to Augsburg. In June 1526 he was present at an important gathering of Anabaptist sympathisers in that city and administered baptism to Hans Denck who had witnessed some of the baptisms in St Gall and had also been impressed by the writings of Thomas Münzer. Denck was described by one of his contemporaries as 'the Apollo of Anabaptism', but his association with the central stream of the movement was probably brief, though close and definite enough for him to have been the one who baptised Hans Hut. A young man of lofty character, spirituality of mind, considerable learning and great personal charm, Denck moved to a more individualistic and mystical view of religion and, shortly before his death at the early age of thirty-two, expressed regret that he had compromised his spiritual mission by his baptism. Meantime, Hübmaier had journeyed 300 miles farther east to Nikolsburg in Moravia.

[1] Below, p. 269.

Moravia proved one of the chief areas of Anabaptist success. The majority of the inhabitants of the south were of German extraction. The writings of Hus and Jerome of Prague were still treasured. The general principles and practices of the Lutheran Reformation were already established there. Hübmaier quickly became the leader of a popular radical movement, winning over to his views the chief evangelical preacher in the city and the two barons of Lichtenstein, Leonard and John, as well as other local nobles. Within a year, at least 6000 persons were adherents of the movement, though there was probably little instruction given prior to their baptism. The arrival of the printer, Froschauer, from Zürich gave new opportunities for the spread of Anabaptist tracts. The period of unbroken success was, however, short. Hans Hut, who had developed into a powerful personality, made his way to Nikolsburg. He had not abandoned views he had imbibed from Thomas Münzer. There were already in the neighbourhood some who were trying to practise community of goods, who rejected the magistracy and refused to pay taxes for war, in spite of the nearby threat from the Turks. Hut joined forces with their leader, Jakob Widemann—'one-eyed Jakob'—and before long there developed an apocalyptic, millenarian movement, which split the Anabaptist forces. Hübmaier stood firmly against all fanaticism, but many who had been his followers were swept away by Hut's wild enthusiasm. When the lords of Lichtenstein imprisoned Hut, Hübmaier approved their action, setting out his views in a booklet, *On the Sword*, which argues clearly and temperately from scripture for the support of the magistracy. But the imperial authorities were seeking Hübmaier and, within a few weeks, he and his wife were on their way to Vienna as prisoners. As a man of learning and eloquence, who had held important positions, including that of cathedral preacher in Regensburg, Hübmaier was regarded by Johann Faber as 'the patron and first beginner of the Anabaptists.' He was their best-known protagonist. On 10 March 1528 he was burnt as a heretic and three days later his wife, with a great stone tied round her neck, was thrown into the Danube. Through his writings, however, to many of which he had appended the phrase: 'Veritas est immortalis: Die Wahrheit ist untödlich', Hübmaier remained a considerable influence.

Escaping from prison, Hans Hut made his way back to Augsburg, but was shortly afterwards again arrested and died in mysterious circumstances. In Moravia acute controversy continued between the *Schwertler*, the men of the sword, who were ready to adopt Hübmaier's attitude towards the magistracy, and the *Stäbler*, the men of the staff, who followed Widemann. Leonard Lichtenstein encouraged the latter to leave his territory. They moved to the neighbourhood of Austerlitz and were soon joined by Jakob Huter and considerable numbers of Anabaptists from the Tyrol. Huter was a wise leader of considerable organising ability and by 1536, when, during a new wave of persecution, he was taken to Innsbruck and burnt to death, there were no fewer than eighty-six Anabaptist settlements, most numbering several hundred persons each, one having as many as two thousand members. They proved themselves sober and industrious colonists and craftsmen, practising community of goods and a strict religious discipline. The attacks upon them in 1536, which were largely the result of the happenings in Münster, gradually died down, but were renewed a decade later. The period from 1547 to 1564 is spoken of in the Hutterite chronicles as 'the time of the great persecution'. The occupants of the *Bruderhöfe* were driven backwards and forwards between Moravia and Hungary for a generation or more.

The story of these Anabaptist communities of Moravia, though in many ways a tragic one, is yet shot through with the romance and glory that come from the steadfast devotion of men and women ready to suffer great hardships for their convictions. During the middle decades of the sixteenth century the Hutterites were in touch with other Anabaptist groups in Poland and south-eastern Europe. They were joined by refugees from North Italy. They were visited by men of liberal theological views like Laelius Socinus and Peter Gonesius. They were known to the little group of Anabaptist refugees who established themselves in Salonica between 1540 and 1560. It was among the Hutterites that Bernardino Ochino died in 1567. They were also in fairly constant touch with Anabaptists in central and western Europe.

In the late 1520's, while Blaurock made his way into the Tyrol and Hübmaier journeyed down the valley of the Danube, others of the Swiss Brethren followed the course of the Rhine. Strassburg became for many refugees the 'city of hope', 'the refuge of righteousness'.[1] Capito, in particular, had considerable initial sympathy with radical views and was deeply shocked when he heard of the drowning of Felix Manz. Bucer himself appears at one time to have questioned whether it would not be better to baptise adults. For six or seven years Strassburg was the scene of vigorous debates on the theological and practical issues raised by the reformers. During that period at one time or another one might have found there Wilhelm Reublin, Michael Sattler, Ludwig Hetzer, Hans Denck, Pilgram Marbeck and Melchior Hoffmann, as well as men less closely connected with the main stream of Anabaptism such as Carlstadt, Franck, Schwenckfeld and Servetus. All were aware of the challenge presented by the Swiss movement. 'There already are in our times', said Franck, writing in 1530, 'three distinct faiths which have a large following, the Lutheran, the Zwinglian and the Anabaptist.' By 1533 Bucer and Capito were agreed in their opposition to the separatist tendencies of the Swiss Brethren, and in the following year the Protestant Church of Strassburg was formally established on the basis of the Augsburg Con-

[1] See also above, pp. 109 f.

fession, which enjoins the baptism of children and in five of its clauses specifically condemns Anabaptists. But there were at the time some 2000 Anabaptists in Strassburg, in a population of not much more than 20,000.

Sattler, Marbeck and Hoffmann call for further mention. Michael Sattler, who had been driven from Zürich in 1525, appears to have been one of the few men who gave thought to some kind of organisation to bring together the little church fellowships that were springing up in so many places. After a short stay in Strassburg as the guest of Capito, he settled in the valley of the Neckar, combining a personal puritanism with an ardent evangelistic zeal and a consistent pacifism. 'If the Turk should come, no resistance should be offered to him; for it is written, Thou shalt not kill.' Early in 1527 a gathering of Anabaptists took place at Schlatt, near Schaffhausen, and approved a document which they described as the 'Brotherly Union of a number of Children of God concerning Seven Articles', now more usually known as the 'Schleitheim Confession'. Whether or not Sattler drafted this document, there seems little doubt that it represented his views. The seven Articles agreed on at Schlatt were:

1. Baptism, which is to be given only to 'those who have learned repentance and amendment of life...and who walk in the resurrection of Jesus Christ'.

2. Excommunication from the Church (i.e. the ban), which is to be employed against those who 'slip sometimes and fall into error and sin', but only after two private admonitions and a third public one. It should take place prior to the breaking of bread, so that a pure and united Church may sit down together.

3. The Lord's Supper, which is to be partaken of only by those who have been baptised, and is primarily of a memorial character.

4. Separation from the world, by which is meant 'all popish and anti-popish works and Church services, meetings and church attendance, drinking-houses, civic affairs, the commitments made in unbelief and other things of that kind'. 'Therefore there will also unquestionably fall from us the unchristian, devilish weapons of force—such as sword, armour and the like and all their use.'

5. Pastors in the Church of God, who must be men recognised for their integrity by those 'outside the faith'; whose office is 'to read [the scriptures], to admonish and teach, to warn, to discipline, to ban in the church, to lead out in prayer...to lift up the bread when it is to be broken, and in all things to see to the care of the body of Christ; and who are to be supported by the Church'. If a pastor suffers banishment or martyrdom, 'another shall be ordained in his place in the same hour so that God's little flock and people may not be destroyed'.

6. The Sword, which is ordained to be used by the worldly magistrates for the punishment of the wicked, but must not be used by Christians even in self-defence. Neither should Christians go to law, or undertake magisterial duties.

7. Oaths, which are forbidden in accordance with Matthew v. 34 and James v. 12.

The Schleitheim Confession circulated widely in the sixteenth century. Copies reached Zwingli within a few months of its adoption, and he incorporated the articles in his *In Catabaptistarum Strophas Elenchus* (July 1527). Calvin seems to have had a printed French version before him when, in 1544, he issued his *Brière Instruction pour armer tous bons fidèles contre des erreurs de la secte commune des Anabaptistes.* German, Latin and Dutch versions appeared. The Articles represented the views of probably the majority of Anabaptists in all parts of Europe. Soon after the Schleitheim gathering Sattler and a number of his associates were arrested and cruelly done to death.

Pilgram Marbeck was a well-educated man, born in the Tyrol, and a mining engineer. His spiritual pilgrimage took him from Catholicism to Lutheranism and thence to Anabaptism. During the three years he spent in Strassburg, he became a leading figure in the city, honoured for his professional skill. In 1532, however, he was banished for his speeches and writings against the baptism of infants and for the rest of his life was the leader of the Anabaptist communities between the Neckar and the city of Ulm. He was engaged for some years in literary controversy with Schwenckfeld, who had lost faith in the outward ordinances of the Church and advocated an individualistic Christ-mysticism. Marbeck's *Vermanung* provides instruction for candidates for baptism and the Lord's Supper. It invites comparison with the *Rechenschaft unserer Religion, Lehr und Glaubens* prepared about the same time by Peter Riedemann, who had been 'head pastor' in Moravia from 1542 to 1556. Both works show a loyalty to the Apostles' Creed, an emphasis on a strictly disciplined life of personal piety and an attitude to baptism and the Lord's Supper essentially similar to that of the Swiss Brethren and the Schleitheim Confession.

With Melchior Hoffmann we come to one who has been described as 'the evil genius of Anabaptism'. He is first heard of as a furrier in the neighbourhood of Waldshut, swept early into the Reformation movement, but, ever an individualist, was soon in conflict with Zwingli. 'The good-for-nothing fellow who prepares skins', wrote Zwingli to Vadian in 1523, 'has begun to play the evangelist in this place and questions me.' Hoffmann was never happy unless he was propagating his views. He made his way to Wittenberg and was encouraged by Luther to journey on to the Baltic regions and Scandinavia.[1] By 1529 he was in Denmark, arguing with Bugenhagen that Luther was but 'the apostle of the beginnings', the herald of the more radical changes that were to usher in the final age of the Church. From Denmark he made his way to Strassburg and there joined the Anabaptists. Ordered by the council to give up preaching and mind his own business, Hoffmann engaged in extensive and successful missionary work in north-west Germany and the Low Countries. Banished from one city, he appeared in another, a prophet proclaiming the speedy approach of the Day of the Lord, organising and shepherding the increasing number of Anabaptist congregations and teaching an unorthodox Christology, which he seems to have derived directly or by misunderstanding from Schwenckfeld. Christ was born,

[1] And see below, p. 157.

said Hoffmann, 'out of' the Virgin Mary, but not 'of' Mary. 'As the heavenly dew falls into the shell of a mussel and changes there into a pearl without taking over anything from the shell, so the Holy Ghost, the Word of God, fell into Mary's womb and there of itself became the spiritual pearl, Jesus Christ.' The civil and religious authorities of Flanders were still loyal to Rome. They burned and executed a number of Ana-baptists as a warning. As persecution increased, so did Hoffmann's confidence in his mission and its approaching climax. The 'Melchiorites' increased in numbers, and their leader announced that Strassburg had been chosen as the New Jerusalem from which the true Gospel and true baptism would be spread by the 144,000 righteous over the whole earth. The great fulfilment would begin in 1533. With an assurance not unlike that of Münzer and Hans Hut, Hoffmann cast himself for the role of Elijah *redivivus* and made his way back to Strassburg, arriving there just as Bucer and Capito had finally secured the condemnation of Anabaptism. He was at once clapped into prison. Schwenckfeld bravely befriended him, but the Strassburg authorities were adamant. Hoffmann was kept in close confinement until his death ten years later.

Would the tragic sequel have been avoided had Hoffmann remained free, or would it have been even more tragic? Who can say? His imprison-ment did not stay the excited expectations he had created. Persecution fanned the flames of fanaticism. Jan Matthys, a baker of Haarlem, became the leader in the Netherlands. Around Amsterdam and in Kampen, Zwolle and Deventer, hundreds of converts were made. When the penalties inflicted by the authorities were increased, the harried victims—many of them simple and devout believers—decided to seek refuge in some more hospitable place. The city of Münster seemed to offer hope of freedom. Thirty ships were chartered with the intention of sailing round the coast to the mouth of the river Ems. They were inter-cepted and either sunk or forced back. A number of families who had set out overland with all their goods were cut down by the soldiery. Driven to desperation, the Anabaptists remaining in Deventer tried, in December 1534, to seize control of the town; they failed. Similar attempts were made in Leyden and Amsterdam, but without success. Early in 1535 an incident occurred which was often subsequently reported to the dis-credit of the Anabaptist movement as a whole. Seven men and five women stripped off their clothes, as a sign, they said, that they spoke the naked truth, and ran through the streets of Amsterdam crying 'Woe! woe! woe! the Wrath of God'. They were set upon and killed, and persecution rose to a new crescendo of intensity. An imperial edict declared that the re-baptisers of others were to be burnt; those who were re-baptised or who harboured such persons were to be executed; women guilty of these things were to be buried alive. Several thousands suffered these penalties.

These tragic events cannot be separated from what had been happening in the same months in Münster. The town council, supported by the gilds of artisans, had appointed an evangelical preacher, Bernhard Rothmann, who had already shown strong social sympathies. Bernhard Knipperdolling, a wealthy cloth merchant, had been with Hoffmann when the latter was in Sweden. When Rothmann began to question the baptism of infants and to favour some kind of community of goods among Christians, the general populace supported him against the local magistrates. At about the same time Jan Bockelson, a close associate of Jan Matthys, managed to reach Münster from Holland, followed a few months later by Jan Matthys himself. The Anabaptist party secured control of the council, Knipperdolling becoming one of the burgomasters. Matthys was soon the controlling figure in the city. He ordered that no unbelievers, that is, no unbaptised adults, should remain there. To leave meant to risk falling into the hands of the troops which were being brought up by the Roman bishop in an effort to capture the city. Wholesale baptisings took place in the market-place. These were followed by a number of steps towards an enforced community of goods. Lindsay's careful words are to be noted: 'What existed at first was simply an abundant Christian charity enforced by public opinion, and latterly a requisitioning of everything that could be used to support the whole population of a besieged city.'[1]

But in April 1533 Matthys and twenty companions sallied out to attack the besiegers and were overwhelmed and killed. Leadership passed to young Jan Bockelson (John of Leyden). He abolished the council, appointed twelve elders to rule the city and proclaimed himself king. He is described as an able and eloquent man who had travelled widely as a journeyman tailor and over whom Münzer's pamphlets exercised a considerable influence. The situation inside the city became increasingly difficult, but it was successfully defended. In July 1534 Bockelson took the step which not only brought his own name and that of the Münster Anabaptists into enduring disrepute, but gave the opponents of the radicals everywhere a new weapon of abuse and a fresh excuse for repressive measures. There were in Münster at the time only some 1700 men. There were four times as many women and several thousand children. Bockelson proposed that the men be allowed to take several wives each, justifying the action from the pages of the Old Testament. The preachers and elders hesitated for eight days, but in the end gave their approval. Bockelson himself took sixteen wives, including the widow of his friend, Matthys. There were protests from within the city. The besiegers were growing stronger. In the summer of 1535 a deserter helped to betray his comrades. The defenders, led by Knipperdolling and Rothmann, gathered for a final desperate stand in the market-place, but were overwhelmed. The city was given over to pillage and slaughter. Bockelson, Knipper-

[1] *History of the Reformation*, ii, 462.

dolling, the widow of Matthys and a few others were kept for public execution after torture, their heads being hung on the tower of the parish church.

For many generations the accounts which circulated regarding what took place in Münster were greatly exaggerated and distorted. But what had occurred could not but cause a wave of horror throughout Europe. 'God opened the eyes of the governments by the revolt at Münster,' said Bullinger, 'and, thereafter, no one would trust even those Anabaptists who claimed to be innocent.' In the Swiss cantons, in Moravia and Hungary, in Germany and the Low Countries, the attempts by both Roman Catholics and Protestants to stamp out Anabaptism were redoubled. Lutheranism was effectively freed from Anabaptist rivalry, though it became thereby even more positively than before a party of princely and middle-class sympathies. It has been estimated that in the ten years after the fall of Münster no fewer than 30,000 Anabaptists were put to death in Holland and Friesland alone. 'No other movement for spiritual freedom in the history of the Church has such an enormous martyrology.'[1]

Münster was still besieged when, in 1534, young John Calvin, then a fugitive in Orleans, wrote the preface to his first theological treatise, *Psychopannychia*, a refutation of the ancient heresy that the soul after death remains unconscious till the Day of Judgment, a view which had been, he said, revived by 'some dregs of Anabaptists'. It was certainly prevalent among many of the radicals of the period and had exponents in England a century later. In the *Institutes*, Calvin gave the Anabaptists no quarter whatsoever. They were, according to him, 'frenzied', 'reprobate spirits', 'devils', and he attacks not only their view of baptism, but their attitude to oaths and the magistracy. Those who relied on the 'inner light' were equally abhorrent to him. In 1544, provoked by a tract of Hübmaier's which was circulating in a French translation, Calvin issued his *Brière Instruction*. The arrest, trial and burning of Servetus took place in Geneva in 1553. Servetus was not associated with any of the main groups of Anabaptists, but in his *Christianismi Restitutio* he had said: 'I call infant baptism a detestable abomination, a quenching of the Holy Spirit, a laying waste of the Church of God, a confounding of the whole Christian profession, an annulling of the renewal made by Christ and a trampling under foot of His whole Kingdom.' It was, perhaps, but natural that the references to the Anabaptists in the definitive edition of the *Institutes* of 1559 are among the most violent.

Between 1548 and 1551 at least four pamphlets against the Anabaptists were published in England. Three of them were the work of John Véron, a Frenchman, who had settled at Cambridge in 1536 and in 1551 was ordained in the English Church. They were based on Leo Jüd's enlarged

[1] Rufus Jones, *Studies in Mystical Religion*, p. 392.

edition of Bullinger's denunciations of the radical movement. The fourth pamphlet was the translation of Calvin's *Briève Instruction*, which had appeared only five years earlier; it also may have been prepared by Véron. In addition, John Hooper in his *Lesson of the Incarnation of Christ* criticised Hoffmannite Christology. Edward VI was on the throne and the English Reformation had entered a critical phase.[1] Peter Martyr and John à Lasco visited England in those years, and Bucer died while in Cambridge in 1551. Bernardino Ochino was also in the country for a time, and probably Hendrik Nicklaes, the leader of the Familists. There was much debate on issues similar to those which had arisen on the continent. Cranmer's Forty-two Articles of Religion, which were first drafted in 1549, contain at least three—Of the Civil Magistrates, Of Christian Men's Goods, which are not common, and Of a Christian Man's Oath—directly aimed against the views of certain of the Anabaptists and no less than seventeen can be similarly construed.

To what extent had Anabaptism already secured a foothold in England? The question is difficult to answer. There were certainly many groups holding radical views in the eastern and south-eastern counties. In 1550 young John Knox was offered the bishopric of Rochester, in the hope, as Northumberland wrote to Cecil, that he would 'not only be a whetstone to quicken and sharpen the bishop of Canterbury, whereof he hath need, but also he would be a great confounder of the Anabaptists lately springing up in Kent'. John Hooper had already written to Bullinger about Anabaptist troublers in Kent and Essex, and about disturbers of his 'lectures' in London. A certain Robert Cooche appears to have been the first Englishman to venture into print in defence of Anabaptism and he was replied to by both William Turner and Knox. In May 1550 Joan Boucher, a remarkable woman who had worked in Kent and Essex for a decade or more, was burnt, after interrogation by Cranmer, Ridley and other English reformers. A few months later, George Van Parc, a member of the Strangers' Church in London, suffered a similar fate. Both had links with the continent.

It was in the colonies of Dutch refugees that Anabaptism had first appeared. How far their views had spread among the English is uncertain. Twenty years earlier Archbishop Warham had warned his countrymen against extreme views of this type and Henry VIII had issued proclamations directly mentioning Anabaptists. In 1535 or 1536, at the time of the fall of Münster, fourteen Dutchmen had been burned, two at Smithfield and the others at various towns in the home counties. They were charged with views similar to those of Melchior Hoffmann. There had been further burnings in 1538. When Mary succeeded Edward, the searching out and burning of Anabaptists continued. With the accession of Elizabeth, there was a new wave of immigration from the Low Countries. A fresh chapter

[1] Below, p. 243.

in the English Reformation began in which radical views regarding the Church and baptism were later to play an important part.

It would hardly have been surprising if, in the dark decades after the Münster revolt, the Anabaptist movement on the continent had completely disappeared. As has already been shown, however, the Hutterite communities, though sadly reduced in numbers, survived the period of intense persecution. In the Low Countries the situation remained extremely confused. Anabaptism was there the only serious challenge to the Roman Church; Calvinism came later. Tens of thousands of Dutch Anabaptists were put to death in the middle decades of the century, but out of this blood bath there slowly emerged the communities now known as Mennonites, groups which drew their inspiration primarily from the Swiss Brethren. Luther regarded the heroism of the Anabaptists in the face of death as evidence of diabolic possession. Not all who witnessed it felt as he did. In January 1536—within a week or ten days of the execution of Bockelson and Knipperdolling in Münster—Menno Simons, the parish priest of Witmarsum, a village near the western coast of Dutch Friesland, renounced his remaining connections with the Roman Church and was baptised on profession of his faith by Obbe Philips, a barber and surgeon by profession. Philips was leader of one of the groups of pacifist Anabaptists. Simons was already forty years old. By his action he became a homeless man. Those who sheltered him were liable to imprisonment and death. For the next quarter of a century, however, he journeyed about shepherding the little groups of harried believers. By 1539 he had prepared the first edition of his most important work, *Dat Fundament des Christelycken leers*, still basic for an understanding of Anabaptism in general and its Mennonite wing in particular.

Within a few years, Obbe Philips withdrew to Rostock and left the leadership in the hands of Menno Simons. Traces of the latter's activity are to be found not only in Amsterdam and the Low Countries, but in Cologne, in Emden (where in 1544 he held a public disputation with John à Lasco), in Lübeck, and as far east as Prussia. A remarkable organiser, mild in disposition, though an advocate of a rigid Church discipline, Menno Simons had, before his death in 1561, rescued the remnants of the Anabaptist communities of north-west Europe and had added to them. He was an outspoken opponent of the 'Münsterites', though his Christology had some similarities with that of Hoffmann and Schwenckfeld. It was by way of his communities that much Anabaptist teaching passed over into the seventeenth century. Not all the Dutch Anabaptists, however, accepted his leadership. There were, for example, the 'Jorists', followers of David Joris, a glass-painter, who had visited England. Joris believed that the age of the Spirit had begun and, under the influence of visionary experiences, came to regard himself as 'the Third David'. For eight years he travelled about in much the same way as Menno Simons, inculcating a strict discipline among his congregations. Then, in 1544, with a number of his followers, he made his way from the constant dangers in the Low Countries to Basle, establishing himself there as a noble foreign gentleman of exemplary piety, waiting, as he seems to have believed, for the coming of the kingdom of which he was the prophet, secretly in touch with those he had left behind. He became the friend of Castellio and was brave enough to protest against the burning of Servetus. His identity was not discovered until 1558, two years after his death. The scandalised authorities at once disinterred his body and burnt it, together with as many of his writings as they could collect.

Adam Pastor, a former Catholic priest, who had joined the Anabaptists in 1533, co-operated for a time with Menno Simons but by 1547 professed anti-Trinitarian views and became the leader of a group in the area of the lower Rhine, small in numbers but continuing for several generations and not without influence on later Mennonitism in Holland. Yet another leader, who gathered up some of the scattered fragments of the earlier Anabaptist communities was Hendrick Nicklaes, a successful merchant, influenced by David Joris. Nicklaes came to regard himself as the prophet of the third and last era in religious history and, working from Emden between 1540 and 1560, established the *Familia Caritatis*, a perfectionist brotherhood, which had representatives in England, probably as a result of a visit by Nicklaes himself.

It is, however, the followers of Menno Simons who chiefly deserve attention. They became the heirs of the best traditions of the Anabaptist movement as a whole. They treasured those traditions. In 1562 there appeared in Holland a collection of biographies and testimonies entitled *Het Offer des Heeren*, perhaps based on an earlier work. To it there were added a number of hymns. Two generations later, Hans de Ries, the pastor of the Mennonite church in Amsterdam, used this material in his *Historie der Martelaren*, afterwards expanded by T. J. van Bright into the work now known as the *Martyrs' Mirror*. This remains one of the most moving and important works for an understanding of the outlook and spirit of the sixteenth-century Anabaptists. Here are to be found the stories of how Manz, Sattler and many another Swiss and Dutch believer bore their last testimonies. Van Bright is more than an annalist. He attempts an interpretation of Christian history, tracing the story of martyrs from apostolic times to his own day, and concluding that the true Church has always been the Church 'under the Cross'. This was the faith which sustained the simple believers who made up the Anabaptist congregations. It is to be found in the manuscript history books of the Hutterites and in the *Ausbund*, the earliest Anabaptist hymn-book, which has as its nucleus some fifty hymns said to have been composed by a group of Swiss Brethren imprisoned in Bavaria in 1535.

The Anabaptists have sometimes been portrayed as essentially medieval in spirit and directly linked with earlier schismatic groups and in particular with the Waldensians. They have been described as 'the step-children of the Reformation'. The attempt to establish direct connection with the Waldensians has now been abandoned. A link with medieval mysticism there certainly was. Several of the Anabaptist leaders knew and treasured the writings of John Tauler and Thomas à Kempis. They were influenced by the *Theologia Germanica*. But this was true also of Luther. Like him, many of them had had a Catholic upbringing and training. It would perhaps be more accurate to speak of 'the fourth Reformation' or—to borrow a phrase from P. T. Forsyth—'the co-Reformation'.[1] What is important is to note those main features which give some unity to its variety and which later became influential in the Free Churches of the modern world. If the Swiss Brethren, the Hutterites and the Mennonites be regarded as the most significant representatives of the movement, then H. S. Bender is right in saying: 'The Anabaptist vision included three major points of emphasis: first, a new conception of the essence of Christianity as discipleship; second, a new conception of the Church as a brotherhood; and third, a new ethic of love and non-resistance.'[2] Following Christ involved for them treading the way of the Cross and they did not flinch from this. They were resolved 'to make the world fit the vision, with no shade of levelling down and with no hairsbreadth of compromise'.[3] They were *Schwärmer*, enthusiasts. Many of them were fanatics or were driven into fanaticism. Most of them showed a deep moral earnestness. Their appeal, like that of the great reformers, was to scripture. Some of them became extremely literal biblicists, but it is to be noted that it was among the Anabaptists that some of the most spiritual and profound views of scriptural authority appeared. All were agreed that the baptism of infants is not true New Testament baptism and that the Church is by its very nature separate and different from the State. In their attitude to the magistracy they were not all of one mind, some rejecting it altogether, others recognising its rights within its own sphere. The personal use of force was almost universally rejected by the Anabaptists, save in the quite exceptional circumstances leading up to the Münster episode. In the long run one of their greatest contributions to the modern world lay in their pleas for religious freedom. Hübmaier's tract *Concerning Heretics and Those that Burn Them* antedates the pleas for toleration and freedom of conscience of both Franck and Castellio. But more important than their pleas was the witness they bore in the face of adversity. What P. J. Spener once said is still true: 'There is much to be learned from the Anabaptists.'

---

[1] *The Church and the Sacraments*, p. 213.
[2] *Mennonite Quart. Rev.* XVIII (1944), 78.
[3] Jones, *op. cit.* p. 31.

CHAPTER V

THE REFORMATION IN SCANDINAVIA AND THE BALTIC

(1) *Denmark*

IN the early 1520's the Reformation took root in Denmark and quickly spread over a wide area. As in Germany, the ground had been prepared beforehand. There were many signs in the later Middle Ages of an increasing need for religion among the people, as well as numerous complaints that the Church was on the decline and willing to abuse its power. With few exceptions the bishops were inadequate to their tasks—noble landowners without any real sense of the religious needs of the age. Bishoprics and greater benefices were reserved for the aristocracy, which meant that the higher clerics were closely bound to the nobility and the gap between them and the parish priests was wide. Humanism was widespread among the clergy, many of whom had studied at foreign universities.

One of the most important representatives of this biblically based humanism and of the movement for Catholic reform was the Carmelite friar Paulus Helie who in 1520 became the head of the order's new foundation in Copenhagen, while at the same time lecturing on the Bible at the university. His ideas rested on the Bible which he interpreted according to the Fathers of the Church. He violently attacked the worldliness of the clergy and the customs and superstitions fostered by the Church, but although he had originally hailed Luther as a welcome ally, he completely rejected him when he realised that the Lutheran movement was leading to a break with the Church, for 'abuse does not abolish use'. Though consistent, Helie's standpoint was untenable. His biblical humanism was, however, of considerable historical importance because it eased the transition from the religious life of the later Middle Ages to evangelical Christianity. The accomplishment of the Reformation in 1536 did not mean any violent break; practically speaking all the clergy remained in office.

Apart from Helie, Christian Pedersen must be mentioned as a leading representative of biblical humanism. He was a canon in Lund and had studied for several years in Paris where he had published a number of devotional, liturgical and historical works. Later he gave his support to the Reformation and published in Antwerp Danish translations of the New Testament (1529), the Psalms of David and a number of Lutheran pamphlets. After this he lived as a printer in Malmö for a number of years. The idea of Catholic reform was also supported by the king,

Christian II (1513–23), and is apparent from his laws and Church reforms. Christian II wished to advance the interests of the Crown, the burghers and the peasants at the expense of the nobility and clergy. The Church keenly felt the effects of his wilfulness: he appointed and dismissed bishops as he thought fit, and the recklessness of his rule actually caused a rebellion in 1523 which forced him to flee the country. Until 1531 he lived in the Netherlands, engaged in plans for reconquering his kingdom. After a visit to Wittenberg in 1524 he was converted to Lutheranism and had the New Testament translated into Danish. This, the first Danish translation of the New Testament, was sent to Denmark and had much to do with the quick spread of the Reformation.

After Christian II's flight from Denmark, the council elected his uncle, Duke Frederick of Schleswig-Holstein, to the throne. In his coronation charter Frederick I promised to uphold the rights and privileges of the Church and to persecute those who preached Lutheranism. Soon, however, he adopted another attitude: as far as possible, he would uphold the remaining rights of the Church, but at the same time, and until a general council should arrive at a final settlement, he would allow any doctrine which was in agreement with the Bible.

At the same time a popular evangelical movement was gaining ground. Its first known centre was the market town of Husum in Schleswig, where Herman Tast preached Lutheranism perhaps as early as 1522. Schleswig became an important point of entry for the Reformation. Here, where Frederick was not bound by the Danish charter, a Lutheran party was formed by some of the nobility who also became the king's leading advisers in the kingdom proper. At the Diets of Rendsburg (1525) and Kiel (1526) the clergy failed to persuade Frederick I to suppress heresy. His eldest son, Christian duke of North Schleswig, eagerly supported the Reformation: he had been present at the Diet of Worms where Luther had made a lasting impression on him. In 1528 Haderslev and Torning provinces were reformed in accordance with a Lutheran Church ordinance, the Haderslev Ordinance, which affected some sixty parishes. Celibacy was abolished; if a priest did not wish to marry, he had to provide the duke with a reason. Liturgically the ordinance was conservative. Priests were ordered diligently to teach their congregations the Word of God and the catechism, to inculcate obedience to authority (among other things, in connection with the payment of taxes), and also to persecute the Anabaptists who were gaining some influence in the duchies.

In Jutland the evangelical movement came into the open at Viborg in 1526. It was here that Hans Tausen, the most important of the Danish reformers, was active. He was a monk of the Order of St John from the monastery of Antvorskov in Zealand who in the course of several years' university studies had acquired a solid humanist education. In 1519 he took his master's degree at Rostock and thereafter studied in Copenhagen under Paulus Helie, at Louvain, whence his uncommon command of Hebrew presumably derived, and from May 1523 for about eighteen months at Wittenberg. After his return to Denmark in 1525 he was moved to the monastery in Viborg where the prior allowed him to teach and to preach in public. After he had preached for several months amidst great acclamation from the burghers his support for the Reformation became so pronounced that he was expelled from the order in the spring of 1526. In October of the same year the citizens of Viborg obtained a royal letter of protection which appointed him chaplain to the king and so withdrew him from the bishop's jurisdiction. A strong evangelical movement developed. A printing press was established from which a number of pamphlets in support of the Reformation were distributed. Before long Tausen found a helper in Jørgen Jensen Sadolin, who (also in 1526) was granted permission by the king to found an ecclesiastical college in the town. By ordaining Sadolin and marrying his sister, Tausen plainly indicated his break with the Catholic Church. Soon the Reformation had carried the day in Viborg. Tausen and Sadolin became parish priests at the churches in the two mendicant monasteries, while twelve superfluous churches and monasteries were pulled down. At the same time evangelical preachers were sent to several of the towns of eastern Jutland, and Lutheranism also spread far and wide in the country districts. In Funen we hear of Lutheran influence at Assens where Peder Laurentsen, a former follower of Helie, worked zealously for the Reformation.

In eastern Denmark the important trading centre of Malmö became the heart of the evangelical movement. Its connections with the great North German towns were of great importance, as ships bringing merchandise also carried evangelical preachers and pamphlets to Denmark. The movement began in 1527 under the leadership of the priest Claus Mortensen Tondebinder and the monk Hans Olufsen Spandemager. In 1529 an evangelical seminary was founded which counted among its teachers men like Peder Laurentsen and the Carmelite Frans Vormordsen, a learned humanist. The reformers in Malmö also had a printing press at their disposal, and a number of their polemical, devotional and liturgical works survive. The first Danish hymn-book, containing translations of Luther's hymns, was published in 1528 and was followed by new and enlarged editions. In the same year a new Danish order of service, the Malmö Mass, was published, based on Döber's *Nürnbergmesse* and Luther's *Deutsche Messe*. In 1529 the council decided to carry out an evangelical reform. In Copenhagen the evangelical movement came into the open in 1529 with the appointment of Tausen to St Nicholas's Church, and by the following year there were four Lutheran preachers in the city.

The diets held at Odense in 1526 and 1527 and at Copenhagen in 1530 were responsible for decisive ecclesiastical legislation.

In 1526 the Odense diet decreed that in future bishops should apply to the archbishop and not to the pope for consecration and that the fee should be paid into the treasury. As members of the royal council, the bishops had some measure of responsibility for this decision which broke the link between the Danish Church and Rome, but they succeeded none the less in persuading the king to take steps against the evangelical movement. They promised changes along the lines of Catholic reform, but demanded that letters of protection, which encroached on their sphere of jurisdiction, should be withdrawn, and that in future no one should be allowed to preach without a bishop's licence. The king merely replied that his letters protected no injustice and that he had not commanded anyone to preach anything but the Word of God. The decisions on future Church policy made at the Odense diet were to a great extent influenced by social conditions at home and political developments abroad. Christian II, popular among the burghers and peasantry, constituted a considerable threat; it was expected that his brother-in-law, the Emperor Charles V, who had just been victorious against France, would give him military assistance against Denmark. At the same time there were peasant rebellions in Jutland and Scania, the rebels refusing to pay tithes and other dues on the ground that the churches were neglected and the Word of God was not being preached.

At the 1527 diet the bishops demanded that the peasant leaders should be punished, the ancient privileges of the Church upheld, the letters of protection revoked, and also that priests should be forbidden to marry and monks to leave their monasteries. The king certainly promised the prelates that he would uphold the privileges of the Church, as he also confirmed the duty of the common people to pay tithes, but he would not support the legal authority of the bishops. He replied in famous words:

> The Christian faith is free. None of you desires to be forced to renounce his faith, but you must also understand that those who are devoted to the Holy Scriptures, or to the Lutheran doctrine as it is called, will no more be forced to renounce their faith. Both parties believe that they are in the right, but as yet there is none to judge. His majesty is king and judge and has power over life and property in this kingdom, but not over souls.... Therefore shall every man conduct himself in a way which he can justify before Almighty God on the Day of Judgement, until a final decision is made for all Christendom.

The king promised to grant no more letters of protection, but at the same time he took everyone under his protection who preached a doctrine which could be defended by the Bible. Frederick I thus adopted the attitude familiar from the German diets of that day, the latest of which had been that of Speyer in 1526: until a general council had decided in the struggle between the conflicting faiths, toleration must prevail. The Word of God in the Bible is the Church's sole foundation; but its interpretation, whether Catholic or evangelical, is a matter of personal choice.

On the basis of this decision the king felt obliged to refuse the demand that he should oppose the evangelical preachers and communities; priests were allowed to marry and monks to leave their monasteries 'on their own responsibility'.

A legal basis for a tolerant organisation of the Church was thus created. The Church in Denmark was now divided into the official Catholic Church and an independent evangelical Church. But this legal arrangement could not be maintained in practice. Many parishes received Lutheran priests from the patronage of the king and of sections of the nobility with Lutheran leanings, and when, in 1529, after paying the king 3000 guilders for his election, Joachim Rønnow was acknowledged as bishop of Roskilde, he had to promise not to prevent anyone from preaching the gospel. Both sides were eager to reach a final decision, asserting that the rival party was heretical, unbiblical and therefore illegal. In addition the prelates referred to the king's promise in his coronation charter that he would persecute the Lutherans.

In July 1530 the diet met at Copenhagen. A new feature was that evangelical preachers, twenty-one in all, were summoned to answer for their teachings. The prelates had the assistance of the most important Danish theologians, including Paulus Helie, together with a number they had summoned from Germany. It may have been the king's intention to hold a disputation between the parties in the German manner to solve the religious problem, but he is unlikely to have desired a final accomplishment of the Reformation, as the Lutherans believed. He had to assure himself of the support of the bishops and of the Church for the large military expenditure which the political situation demanded. The danger from Christian II, who had once more gone over to Catholicism, was now imminent. In Denmark it was considered that with the support of the emperor he was now in a position to gather an invasion fleet. In view of this the Danish bishops had to make great concessions to the king's financial demands, but in return they asked that he for his part should also oppose the Lutheran movement. While these negotiations were taking place the evangelicals prepared a confession of faith, the Copenhagen Confession, as a basis for the expected disputation and preached on its articles to great crowds bitterly opposed to the prelates and their supporters. The disputation, however, never took place. A number of theses were exchanged by the two parties, but they could not agree who should judge the outcome. The Catholics demanded a learned theologian as judge, while the Lutherans thought the diet sufficiently competent to decide whether their simple faith was in agreement with the Bible. Similarly there was disagreement over language: the Reformers would only argue in Danish, whereas the prelates demanded the Latin tongue which would have kept the matter from the people. Finally the negotiations broke down, which presumably suited the king best. In its ecclesiastical section the diet's decree merely confirmed the *status quo*, and both parties left in disappointment.

The Copenhagen Confession (*Confessio Hafniensis*), which was probably composed by Peder Laurentsen, was, then, of no historical importance, but it is of great interest as an expression of the Reformation in Denmark as distinct from elsewhere. It differs from the Augsburg Confession—of which it is entirely independent—by its pronouncedly polemical, popular and untheological form. The Danish reformers had sprung from biblical humanism and had not experienced Luther's struggles in the cloister. Their humanism and insistence on biblical truth was related to an earlier, humanistic Lutheranism of the sort that existed in the early 1520's in the large cities of southern and northern Germany which provided the inspiration for the movement in Denmark. The Lutheran doctrine of justification had a less fundamental importance among the Danish reformers than for the theologians of Wittenberg. The central feature is a simple, undifferentiated, biblical Christianity which especially stressed demands for reform and was partly based on a non-Lutheran interpretation of the Bible: in the medieval manner it thought of the scriptures as a book of laws, 'the law of God'. The Confession is reminiscent of the writings of the Malmö Reformation, which on the whole were more radical than those of Tausen and Sadolin.

The years until the death of Frederick I (1533) witnessed a progressive dissolution in the Catholic Church. The mendicant friars suffered particularly; they were driven from the towns, often by violence. Before long the secularisation of Church lands was in full swing. In 1530 all landowning monasteries in Zealand were granted away in fief. In Funen, which so far had been more or less untouched by the Reformation, Bishop Gyldenstjerne, who favoured reforms, took Sadolin as his assistant. In 1532, when Gyldenstjerne was sent to Norway to oppose Christian II who had at last landed there, Sadolin planned a visitation of the diocese by means of which the clergy were to be reformed according to Luther's Shorter Catechism and the Augsburg Confession, which he now translated into Danish. In 1537 Sadolin became the first evangelical bishop of Funen.

After the death of Frederick I the prelates sought to regain their lost command. At the Diet of Copenhagen in 1533 they opposed the choice of Duke Christian and tried instead to elect a brother of his, as yet a minor, whom they hoped to bring up in the Catholic faith. The interregnum brought great misfortunes to the country, and civil war followed. The archbishop's excommunication of the Scanian preachers caused a riot in Malmö in 1534. Copenhagen and Malmö made an alliance with Lübeck which sent an army to Zealand under the leadership of Count Christopher of Oldenburg. A peasant rising broke out in north Jutland. Then, in the summer of 1534, the nobility of Jutland elected Christian III as king, and thanks to a well-equipped mercenary force he soon succeeded in reconquering the kingdom, entering starving Copenhagen in August 1536. Victory left the king with an enormous debt. In vain he asked the Church for help. Encouraged by his German advisers, he therefore decided on a *coup d'état* which led to the dismissal of the bishops and the secularisation of Church property. In future the kingdom was to be governed by the temporal authorities alone; bishoprics would be purely spiritual posts. The bishops were made responsible for the misfortunes of the war because they had delayed the election of a king. Their lands and tithes were seized by the Crown which thus trebled its income. In return the king was to pay the new evangelical bishops (at first called superintendents) and to support schools and hospitals. In October 1536 the estates accepted the new order. The bishops, too, with the exception of Rønnow, soon resigned themselves to the situation and continued their lives as nobles and landowners.

The king immediately took the initiative in drafting a new evangelical Church order. Even before the estates met he had tried without success to persuade Bugenhagen and later Melanchthon to come to Denmark. In January 1537 a commission consisting of Lutheran preachers and members of the chapters was set up to frame a new ecclesiastical constitution. By April the final draft was ready to be sent to Wittenberg for Luther's approval. After a final revision by Bugenhagen, who went to Copenhagen in the summer of 1537, and by some of the king's advisers, Christian III proclaimed the new (Latin) Church Ordinance on 2 September 1537, the day on which Bugenhagen ordained the seven evangelical bishops in Copenhagen cathedral. The difficulty of carrying out the decrees of the ordinance, however, made it desirable that it should be proclaimed as a general law by king and council, and in 1539 a diet in Odense accepted a Danish translation with certain amendments and additions as the 'true' ordinance. The Church Ordinance of 1539 (printed in 1542) remained the constitution of the Danish Church until Christian V's Danish Law (1683) and Church Ritual (1685), and it was partly incorporated into these. Although it was actually intended to be valid for the entire kingdom—Denmark, Norway and Schleswig-Holstein—it finally applied only to Denmark (with Norway) as conditions in the duchies necessitated a special Low German ordinance which was adopted by the Diet of Rendsburg in 1542.

The ordinance is founded on the conception of the Christian state. Supreme authority in Church matters belongs to the king as the Christian leader, but ecclesiastical affairs are to be in the hands of the Church's own representatives. A sharp distinction is made between Jesus Christ's unchangeable ordinance (the preaching of the Word, the administration of the sacraments, the Christian upbringing of children, support for the servants of the Church and the schools, and care of the poor), and the king's decree which is to serve that of Christ and in which alterations can, if necessary, be made. Divine service is dealt with at great length, as are sermons and ritual, schools, status of bishops and priests, and so on. Subject to royal confirmation, bishops are to be chosen by the clergy in the towns of the diocese. In the towns the clergy are to be chosen by the mayor and council, and in the rural districts by respected men of the parish together with the dean. The aristocracy's right of patronage is preserved. The type of Christianity contained in the ordinance is Lutheranism, as formulated by Melanchthon. Once the Reformation was established, the direct influence from Wittenberg also became much more powerful. The preachers' simple belief in the Bible gradually gave way to a Christianity dictated by Luther's catechism. The evangelical awakening of the years of strife before 1536 lost heart; the congregations became passive, and growing emphasis was laid on the Church as an institution and on the dignity of the clergy.

Of the seven new bishops who on 2 September 1537 were consecrated by Bugenhagen—without the apostolic succession, as Bugenhagen was only a priest—the most important was Peder Palladius who became bishop of Zealand. He had not taken part in the Reformation struggle in Denmark, but had studied for six years at Wittenberg where he became a doctor of theology in June 1537. Highly recommended by Bugenhagen, Luther and Melanchthon, Palladius did not disappoint the confidence which Christian III showed in appointing a man of only thirty-four as the premier bishop in the land. His famous *Visitation Book*, which shows his rare ability as an ecclesiastical administrator and popular speaker, is a cultural document of supreme importance, typically Danish in its combination of seriousness and warm humour. By 1543 Palladius had managed to visit the 390 parishes in his diocese, but his influence stretched far beyond. He was the king's adviser in all ecclesiastical affairs; he counselled his colleagues and presided over the meetings of the bishops. He also occupied himself with Church matters in Norway and Iceland. As a professor at the university, which had been re-founded after a period of decline, Palladius gave frequent lectures and was an influence on the students. His theological writings were read throughout the Protestant world. Most famous was his introduction to the biblical writings, *Isagoge*, of which sixteen Latin editions were published as well as translations into German, English, Polish and Danish. In addition he published a large number of treatises in Danish. From a theological point of view Palladius was a disciple of Melanchthon, but he did not follow Melanchthon's subsequent deviations from the teachings of Luther.

Hans Tausen, 'the Danish Luther', was not one of the new bishops in 1537. He became a lecturer in Hebrew at the university and in 1538 also began to give lectures in theology and to act as a priest in Roskilde Cathedral, where Catholicism was still strong. Only in 1541 was he made bishop of Ribe. As such he laboured to found schools and hospitals and sought to improve the training and financial position of the clergy. He had many difficulties to combat: the ignorance and superstition which were widespread among the laity, Anabaptism, recalcitrant members of the nobility, and so on. Of Tausen's important works mention should be made of his translation of the Pentateuch (1533), a *Book of Sermons* (1539), an important guide for the clergy, and a hymnal of which several editions are known.

The first evangelical bishops wore themselves out in their work for the establishment of the Reformation and died about 1560. This marks the end of the first generation of the Reformation. Christian III also died in 1559 after leading the Reformation both as king and by his personal example. The time was full of difficulties, poverty, ignorance, the survival of Catholic custom, and numerous complaints of a decline in the people's moral standards such as always follows in the wake of great spiritual upheavals. None the less there was a spirit of optimism about this generation. They knew that they had left the darkness of popery for 'the bright day of the Gospels' (Palladius). The most important and permanent heritage which the Reformation left for posterity was the simple Danish service and the uncomplicated Christianity of the catechism on which the coming generations were raised. For its most significant monument we have the great *Christian III's Bible* of 1550, the first Danish translation of the Bible in its entirety.

(2) *Norway*

After Christian III's victory in Denmark, the Reformation and the Church Ordinance were also introduced into Norway. Politically, culturally and religiously, the land was at this time passing through a depression. Even though there were here and there faint traces of Catholic reform and biblical humanism, the Reformation came to Norway on the whole without preparation, and it never produced a popular movement as in Denmark.

The first Lutheran preacher in Norway was a German monk, Antonius, who was active among the Germans in Bergen in 1526. His teaching caused considerable unrest in the town and made the Germans more defiant in their attitude towards the Church and the local population. In 1529 Frederick I issued letters of protection to two evangelical preachers in Bergen, one of whom, Jens Viborg, was later to become parish priest there. In Stavanger, too, and also in Finmark faint Lutheran influences are discernible. Some of the nobility were at the same time beginning to break fasts and to adopt evangelical customs, but they were especially eager to take possession of the Church's property. In 1528 a number of monasteries were seized, and soon the secularisation of Church property was in full swing.

The most important defender of the Catholic Church and of Norwegian independence was Archbishop Olav Engelbrektsson, an able and learned man, but politically unstable. During his journey to Rome in 1523 to obtain the papal bulls of confirmation he had sworn fidelity to the exiled Christian II. After his return home in 1524 he took part in the royal council's denunciation of Christian II and the election of Frederick I as king of Norway. However, Frederick I was obliged to sign a strict charter, which, like the Danish one, contained a clause on the persecution of Luther's disciples. Meanwhile there was soon a distinct cooling off in relations with the king, among other things because Frederick supported the preachers in Bergen. When in 1531 Christian II landed near Oslo in an effort to win back his lost kingdom by way of Norway, the archbishop and the highest-ranking clergy supported him. After his imprisonment Trondhjem was visited by a Danish fleet, and Olav was obliged to humiliate himself and come to terms with Frederick I. After the death of the king in 1533 the archbishop endeavoured with the help of the emperor to get Christian II's son-in-law, a German count, installed as king, but with Christian III's victory in Denmark in 1536 Norwegian independence and the rule there of the Church of Rome were soon at an end. Before a Danish fleet reached Trondhjem in 1537 Olav Engelbrektsson had fled to the Netherlands where he died the following year.

Norway was now subjected to Denmark; its council ceased to exist, and Norwegian independence was greatly reduced. By order of Christian III the Reformation was to be carried out in Norway as in Denmark. In 1539 the diets in Oslo and Bergen accepted the Danish Church Ordinance. The bishops' possessions were seized by the Crown. A large part of the Church's treasures was taken to Denmark to be melted down. On the other hand, the Danes proceeded cautiously in introducing liturgical and doctrinal reforms so as not to provoke unnecessary opposition. It was also some time before new bishops were installed. The bishops of Stavanger, Hamar and Oslo were imprisoned. The last of these was reinstated in 1541, and the dioceses of Hamar and Oslo were combined. The diocese of Trondhjem remained without a bishop until 1546. Only Bergen received a new bishop immediately. In 1536 the chapter there had chosen its archdeacon, Geble Pederssøn, as bishop. He was a Catholic and a humanist with a master's degree from Louvain, but he soon joined Christian III, so that he not only avoided the fate of the other bishops but was even taken up by the king as an evangelical bishop and ordained by Bugenhagen in 1537 together with the Danish bishops. He retained part of the see's former income which among other things was used in the work of reconstruction carried out by the Church. Geble Pederssøn was the friend of Bishop Palladius whose Latin *Interpretation of the Catechism for Norwegian Parish Priests* (1541) was published in several editions.

The introduction of the Reformation into Norway did, however, meet with considerable difficulties. In general the priests were untouched by

Lutheranism, and consequently many parishes were for a period without an incumbent. The population clung to its traditions, and Catholic customs continued to be observed for a very long time. Many complaints were heard of widespread poverty and low moral standards among both priests and laymen. A special difficulty was created by the fact that Danish was the official language. The Bible, the catechism and the hymnal were not translated into Norwegian. The Reformation was thus preached in a partly incomprehensible language and in every way used to further Danish culture in Norway. It never became a popular movement, and it took decades to educate the people in the Lutheran faith. The most important of the bishops of the Reformation was Jørgen Erikssøn of Stavanger (1571–1604), a powerful figure filled with the spirit of the Reformation who brought order into Church affairs. As a guide to priests he published a collection of sermons which are considered to be the most important literary monument from the Norwegian Reformation. A Norwegian Church Ordinance was proclaimed in 1607.

(3) *Iceland*

Iceland, too, was completely unprepared for the Reformation. Its last two Catholic bishops, Øgmundur Pállson of Skálholt and Jón Arason of Hólar, were both men of note who ruled their sees with a firm hand. Their theological training was presumably slight, but Jón Arason was a poet of some importance. As was usual among the clergy in Iceland, he was married and had several children. At one time there was a threat of open conflict between the two bishops. However, at the *althing* of 1526, where both arrived accompanied by large armed contingents, they came to terms, and after this, fear of their common enemy, advancing Lutheranism, bound them closer together.

Nothing is known of the beginnings of Lutheran influence in Iceland. Regular trading communications with Germany, and especially with Hamburg, must have introduced Reformation pamphlets into the country. In 1533 the *althing* adopted a resolution that 'all shall continue in the Holy Faith and the Law of God, which God has given to us, and which the Holy Fathers have confirmed'. At the same time, Oddur Gottskálksson, who had adopted the evangelical doctrine after a stay abroad lasting several years, returned to Iceland where he became secretary to the bishop of Skálholt. Here he translated the New Testament into Icelandic, but did not otherwise publicly appear as a champion of Lutheranism. He was not ordained, but lived as a farmer on his own farm.

The first real representative of the Reformation in Iceland was Gissur Einarsson, who during a period of study in Germany had become acquainted with Lutheranism and became assistant to the bishop of Skálholt in 1536. For the time being, however, he did not express his Lutheran sympathies.

After the victory of the Reformation in Denmark Christian III attempted to introduce it into Iceland. In 1538 the Church Ordinance was put before the two bishops at the *althing* and promptly rejected. The Danes proceeded in a high-handed fashion, among other things dissolving the monasteries. The aged Bishop Øgmundur, who was almost blind, now resigned his position and recommended Gissur Einarsson as his successor. The latter was sent to Copenhagen to be examined by the theologians there, and in March 1540 the king appointed him superintendent of Skálholt.

It proved, however, difficult for this bishop of twenty-five to maintain his position. Both the old bishop and the clergy turned against him. In 1541 a royal emissary went to Iceland to promote the acceptance of the ordinance. Bishop Øgmundur was arrested in a revolting manner and died on the difficult journey to Denmark. The envoy succeeded in getting the ordinance accepted by the diocese of Skálholt, while it was still rejected in Hólar, largely because of the influence of Jón Arason. Bishop Gissur, who was ordained by Palladius, made energetic attempts to organise the Church in his large diocese according to Lutheran principles, despite unfavourable circumstances. In the course of frequent visitations he opposed Catholic ceremonies and superstition, exhorted the clergy to marry, and improved their financial situation. He persuaded Oddur Gottskálksson to translate a German collection of evangelical sermons and commanded the priests to obtain this together with the translation of the New Testament which was published in 1540. He himself translated parts of the Old Testament together with the Church Ordinance.

Gissur Einarsson died as early as 1548, and despite opposition from the clergy Jón Arason now also took possession of Skálholt diocese. He took Gissur's successor prisoner, upon which he was outlawed by the king. Soon after this he and two of his sons were arrested and handed over to the Danes. As the Danes dared not keep them in Iceland throughout the winter and could not get them transported to Denmark, the prisoners were executed in November 1550. In 1552 Hólar diocese also submitted to Christian III and accepted the Church Ordinance. With this the external opposition to the Reformation was broken. Church property was secularised and the systematic plundering of churches and monasteries began.

The new bishops now had the difficult task of promoting the observance of Lutheran principles and community life, but they did not make much progress. In both dioceses Church manuals and small hymn-books with Danish hymns in bad translations were published. In the cathedral towns schools were established to train the clergy. Bishop Palladius showed a special interest in Icelandic conditions and acted as a sort of chief inspector for the Church in Iceland. Only several decades later was the Reformation so firmly established that a growing religious life can be observed. Of special importance was the able and energetic Gudbrandur

Thorláksson, bishop of Hólar from 1571 to 1627, who devoted his energies to the Christian education of the communities and an improved training for the clergy, and also published some ninety pamphlets. In 1584 the first Icelandic translation of the Bible in its entirety was published. However, Bishop Gudbrandur, who was one of Iceland's greatest bishops, belongs properly to the period following the Reformation.

(4) Sweden

In Sweden the Reformation, introduced under Gustavus Vasa (1523–60), took a course very different from that in Denmark. Episcopal traditions and the independence of the Church were far stronger, and the period of transition lasted for a greater number of years, approximating to an organic development rather than a sudden break. Outside Stockholm the Reformation depended little on a popular awakening. The attitude of the king was of first importance.

Gustavus Vasa became the leader of the national uprising against Christian II of Denmark in 1521 and was elected king in 1523. His objective was a strong Crown in an independent nation. The position of the Church as a state within a state had therefore to be destroyed and its superfluous properties confiscated by the Crown. The king's most important adviser on Church affairs was Laurentius Andreæ, the chancellor and archdeacon of Strängnäs, a man of great political ability who after studying abroad was well acquainted with the ecclesiastical problems of the later Middle Ages and favoured Catholic reform. Accordingly he formulated a programme for a national Church. He argued that, since the Church was the community of the faithful, the Christian people, its property belonged to the people whose king administers it. The Bible and not the pope's decree was the supreme authority, and Luther's writings must therefore be read and tested in the light of God's Word.

The archbishopric was vacant during the first tempestuous years, as Gustav Trolle, who had remained faithful to Christian II, had fled to Denmark. As the pope still supported him another archbishop could not be elected for the time being. Little by little the king filled vacant bishoprics with reliable men who favoured Catholic reform. In 1524 direct contact with the pope ceased when the king sought in vain to be allowed to retain the annates. The most important of the Swedish bishops and the most energetic opponent of Lutheranism was old Hans Brask of Linköping, who as early as 1522 threatened to excommunicate those who bought and read Luther's writings. Through the numerous German merchants in Stockholm Lutheranism began to gain a footing.

Sweden's great reformer was Olavus Petri. He was born at Örebro in 1493, the son of a blacksmith. From 1516 to 1518 he studied at the university of Wittenberg, the centre of humanism, where he took his master's degree in 1518. There he gained his broad humanistic education and his knowledge of Greek and Hebrew. Presumably he watched Luther developing into a reformer during those years. In the autumn of 1518 Olavus became secretary to the bishop of Strängnäs, and in 1520 he was ordained deacon and became a teacher at the cathedral school. His move over to the Reformation was a harmonious development; only gradually did he grow aware of the extent of Luther's thought. Though he always felt himself to be the disciple of Luther, his authority was the Bible. Nevertheless, from 1523 his message was quite clearly Lutheran. At the Diet of Strängnäs in that year, Gustavus Vasa's attention was drawn to Olavus, probably by Laurentius Andreæ who, like the king, soon realised the importance of the new religious ideas in the field of ecclesiastical policy.

In 1524 Olavus Petri became clerk to the city and began to preach in Stockholm, gaining a considerable influence. The city was half German, and a German Lutheran, Nicolaus Stecker, became parish priest. In 1525 Olavus married. Bishop Brask now delivered violent attacks against him and the Lutheranism he was preaching. In a letter to the king he described Olavus's marriage as a mark of shame not only for the Swedish Church, but for the whole of Christendom. Gustavus Vasa replied that with his limited knowledge he found it strange that the clergy should be excommunicated for marrying, which was not forbidden by God, but not for fornication, which was. This sort of marriage was accepted abroad, and he therefore suggested that they should await the decision of a general council.

Positive attempts were also made to uphold the ancient faith. The printing press of Uppsala Cathedral published a number of important devotional works. Upon the king's instigation, however, the press was removed to Stockholm, where as a counter-measure Olavus Petri published an evangelical devotional book, *Useful Instruction* (1526), the first publication of the Swedish Reformation. The treatise, which began Olavus's comprehensive and momentous production, is based on Luther's *Betbüchlein*, but is otherwise more marked by South German humanistic evangelicalism than by Wittenberg. Reformation pamphlets from Nuremberg and Franconia had reached Sweden by way of Königsberg and were studied by Olavus. The first Swedish translation of the New Testament, which appeared in 1526, was probably his work, done in co-operation with Laurentius Andreæ. In the main it follows Luther's German version, but it is based on the Strassburg edition of 1523, the first literary proof of Olavus's connection with south-western Germany. He also made use of Erasmus's Greek edition and Latin translation. The Swedish New Testament was of great significance, both from a religious and a cultural point of view.

Developments in Sweden were accelerated by the progress of the Reformation in Germany, the Baltic and Denmark in 1525–7. Of special importance was the connection with Duke Albrecht of Prussia who concluded a treaty with Gustavus Vasa in 1526 and had Reformation pamphlets sent to Sweden. Prussian envoys stayed with the king while he was making preparations for the Diet of Västeras in 1527. In 1526 Gustavus Vasa attempted to arrange a religious disputation between the learned Thomist, Peder Galle of Uppsala, and Olavus Petri. In Switzerland, southern Germany and northern Germany disputations had been adopted to decide the ecclesiastical struggle. However, Peder Galle would give only a written answer to the questions put by the king. Olavus composed a detailed reply to this, *Answers to Twelve Questions*, which he published in 1527 together with Galle's statements. This pamphlet, in which Olavus, using the Bible as his basis, gave a clear and simple presentation of the evangelical doctrine, stressing the preaching of the Word of God as the Church's sole duty, was of decisive importance in ecclesiastical politics and a direct preparation for the Diet of Västeras.

In the summer of 1527 the king summoned this momentous diet. There he reviewed the miserable political and economic situation in the realm: revolt in Dalecarlia, Lübeck's demand for repayment of the war debt, and so on. In such conditions he said he could not reign, but he made no proposals himself, asked the diet to find a way out of the difficulties, and put the blame on the rich prelates. He denied the rumours that he was to introduce a new religion and offered to have a disputation take place before the assembly. It was quickly decided to support the king in his struggle against the peasant revolt in Dalecarlia which could also have repercussions for the nobility and clergy. In order to reach a decision in the ecclesiastical struggle, the reformers now sought to arrange the disputation. On behalf of the bishops, however, Brask rejected the idea as unnecessary: the Church had already decided what the true faith was, and he would not argue with heretics. He certainly promised the king financial help, but demanded that the Church's privileges should be maintained and that the pope's sanction should be obtained for all ecclesiastical changes. In this the nobility supported him. In a fury the king renounced the throne and withdrew. By dint of separate negotiations with the various estates, the reformers, who had been in mortal danger, succeeded during the stormy days that followed in obtaining a hearing for the king's demands. One of the Catholic reform bishops offered to give way on political and economic matters, but held fast to the Catholic doctrine and liturgy. This put an end to the solidarity of the bishops. The king's abdication was in fact a clever political move. The assembly now voted for a considerable reduction in Church property; the bishops' palaces together with their 'superfluous' property and that of the cathedral chapters and monasteries were confiscated by the Crown. The nobility recovered all the property given to the Church since 1454. Even the disputation took place, and the estates noted that the reformers justified themselves well and that they only preached the Word of God. It was decided that the pure Word of God should be preached in the entire kingdom—the principle of toleration familiar from Denmark and Germany. The Diet of Västeras destroyed the Church's privileged position in political and legal matters, while the ecclesiastical organisation and the authority of the bishops in all internal matters was retained. The problem of Sweden's relations with the Holy See was passed over in silence. After the meeting of the diet, Bishop Brask fled the country.

Formally the Diet of Västeras only decreed that both parties should enjoy religious freedom as long as they could justify themselves by the gospels, the pure Word of God which both Catholics and Protestants acknowledged as the supreme test. In fact, the decision of the diet involved not only a change in Church politics but also a religious upheaval, since it legalised the preaching of Lutheranism. The way was now open for the reformers' propaganda.

The following years were difficult ones. The king's harshness in reducing the wealth of the Church—he even confiscated church bells and fixtures—and the people's dislike of the Lutheran movement caused constant revolts which Gustavus Vasa put down with a firm hand. The changing fortunes of the Reformation abroad influenced his attitude towards the Swedish movement. However, after the formation of the Schmalkaldic League, which gave greater security to Protestantism in Germany, he adopted a patently anti-Catholic position.

In his important sermon on the occasion of Gustavus's coronation in 1528, Olavus presented the reformers' view of the relationship between Church and State. He based his arguments on the idea of a popular Church and described the positions of bishop and priest as identical; their sole purpose was to preach the Word and to rule people's consciences with its help. Temporal authority was ordained by God and must therefore be obeyed by all; but the king was also subject to the laws for which all the people together were responsible. The authorities' duty towards the Church was to defend it so that it could freely preach the Word. In 1528 Olavus Petri translated Luther's *Book of Sermons* and published a number of polemical writings opposing Catholic ceremonies and customs, the sacraments, confession, celibacy, monastic life, etc. His production dominated the entire book-market. In the next few years his numerous writings assisted in a gradual transformation of the Swedish liturgy and the acceptance of services in the vernacular. In 1531 he published the Swedish Mass.

In the same year, his brother Laurentius, thirty-two years old, was appointed archbishop. The immediate occasion for this was the king's desire to celebrate his marriage and the crowning of the queen in as splendid a fashion as possible. As the pope supported the exiled Gustav Trolle, none of the Catholic bishops could accept the archbishopric.

Therefore Gustavus Vasa had to choose an evangelical bishop, and he considered Olavus's younger brother to be a suitable candidate. The consecration took place according to Catholic ritual, that is to say with the retention of the apostolic succession, although those who officiated at the consecration made a secret declaration that they were acting under pressure.

Laurentius had studied at Wittenberg where Melanchthon especially had influenced him. He had had a broad theological and humanistic training, was possessed of qualities both as an organiser and as a teacher, and in addition had a fine ear for the divine service and liturgical language. His ability to adapt himself to the demands of the situation, which did not mean that he lacked firmness, enabled him throughout all the ensuing changes to retain the confidence of a restless and despotic king. During his more than forty years as archbishop he had a great influence on the Swedish Reformed Church.

In 1536 the archbishop held a synod at Uppsala. There it was decided that priests everywhere should preach the pure Word of God, and that Olavus Petri's Swedish Mass and manual should be introduced throughout the country. Celibacy was abolished. When the king gave his silent consent to the resolutions of the synod, the break with Catholicism was complete and the Swedish Church had now officially become an evangelical Swedish national Church. New editions of Olavus Petri's book of sermons, hymnal and mass were published. Luther's Shorter Catechism also appeared in Swedish for the first time, and the honour for this seems to be due to Olavus. The Church's great task now was to educate the people in the evangelical faith. The reformers therefore laid special stress on teaching the catechism and on family prayers, which were just beginning to become customary.

To give some idea of Olavus's incredible capacity for work during these years, mention must also be made not only of his Swedish-Latin dictionary, but also of his *Judge's Rules*, which still form the introduction to the Swedish book of laws, and his *Swedish Chronicle*. Thanks to these two works he has had an enormous influence on Swedish life and culture.

The years immediately following the synod brought considerable progress to the Reformation in every way. But soon new difficulties arose in its relation with Gustavus Vasa whose policy towards the Church was always fluctuating. Round about 1538, a change of mind led him away from the reformers' idea of the Church. The king's pride and suspicion were growing. Influenced by conditions in the German Lutheran Churches, he now began to lay increasing emphasis on the idea that the magistrate was appointed by God and that all subjects had a duty to obey him. He wished to promote the victory of Lutheranism, but the Church was to be completely subjected to the king. This policy led to a quarrel with the reformers who maintained the old Swedish policy of the equality of all before the law; their ideal was a Swedish popular Church under the leadership of the bishops and with independence in all internal matters. The three reformers were in agreement on this point. The people do not belong to the ruler but to God and are therefore free citizens. As one preaching the Word of God, Olavus boldly stressed the responsibilities of the authorities and violently attacked their misdeeds.

The apparent cause of the break was a sermon preached by Olavus Petri. In Sweden as elsewhere the period of religious strife had led to a serious moral decay. Catholic discipline had gone, and the new evangelical message had not yet penetrated the nation's life. In a sermon at Stockholm, Olavus violently attacked the increasing tendency to swear and curse, and he made it plain that the king did not present the people with a good example. About the same time as this sermon was preached—and it was printed at the beginning of 1539—Laurentius Petri incurred the king's wrath by complaining that he was not putting sufficient funds at the disposal of the schools. Gustavus Vasa, who always went in suspicion of the bishops, accused the archbishop of wanting to regain the ancient episcopal powers. He was allowed to keep his position but was forced into the background, and as the king's representative a German Lutheran, George Norman, became in fact the leader of the Church. Legal proceedings were instituted against Olavus Petri and Laurentius Andreæ who were condemned to death on 2 January 1540 after a biased trial. Both were, however, pardoned in exchange for heavy fines. The intention had merely been to compromise them so that they should not stand in the way of the king's new Church policy, and they soon recovered the king's confidence. In 1542 Olavus became parish priest in Stockholm, while Laurentius lived in retirement in Strängnäs until his death in 1552.

George Norman now became 'superintendent' of the Swedish Church. He was a typical disciple of Melanchthon and prepared the way for Melanchthon's theology and conception of the Church in Sweden. The Reformation was to be carried out according to the German pattern and with German thoroughness, both in doctrine and in ceremonies. The independence of the Church and the bishops disappeared, and new diocesan leaders had to be found. This so-called German period lasted only for a comparatively short time, from 1539 to 1544. Norman carried out extensive visitations, ruthlessly enforcing the Reformation in the parishes and plundering the churches of their silver and valuables. In 1542 the most serious of all the revolts against Gustavus Vasa broke out in southern Sweden. It was caused chiefly by social and economic discontent and was directed against the king's trade regulations which were ruining the border population in Smaland and Blekinge who traded with Denmark. But Catholic priests fanned the flames, and their objective was to reintroduce the Catholic faith. The emperor and other foreign rulers were also interested in the revolt which Gustavus Vasa succeeded in putting down in 1543 after it had spread far up into Sweden; but before he could succeed he had had to rescind the 'German' Church edicts and reintroduce the older Swedish system. Norman still retained the confidence of the king, but now became his political adviser.

The revolt had shown the king the need for a complete break with Catholicism and the firm establishment of the hereditary national monarchy. The important Diet of Västeras of 1544 therefore officially pronounced Sweden to be an evangelical kingdom, the entire diet engaging 'never to renounce the faith which has now arisen'. The worship of saints, requiem masses, pilgrimages and other Catholic customs were forbidden. The monarchy was made hereditary in the house of Vasa.

In the course of the following years a change took place in the popular attitude to religion. Negatively this was the result of the suppression of Catholic customs and old heathen superstition; wayside crucifixes were removed and the fraternities were dissolved. Positively it was the result of evangelic preaching and the teaching of the catechism. In 1541 the brothers Petri published the magnificent Vasa Bible, the first Swedish translation of the Bible in its entirety, which proved to be of great importance for Swedish Christianity, language and culture.

After 1544 Laurentius and Olavus Petri together with the bishops once more held leading positions. Relations with the king were in the main good. Yet Gustavus Vasa's suspicions of the bishops and therefore of the Church's independence remained. He would have no 'government by priests'. New bishops were no longer given the title, but were called *ordinarii* or superintendents, their position being reduced to that of royal inspectors in the Church after the fashion of the German superintendents. In order to reduce the power of the bishops, several dioceses were divided and 'superintendents' put in the new dioceses which were left without chapters. The old chapters almost disappeared. The churches, and now even the presbyteries, were subjected to further confiscations of property and fittings, so that the economy of the parishes was seriously threatened. One point of light was the educational system which now began to take a definite shape; it was to play a decisive part in bringing the people up in the Christian faith.

Until his death Olavus Petri remained the king's adviser in several important concerns. His last years were darkened by personal sorrows. After his death in 1552 and that of Norman in 1553, Laurentius Petri stood unchallenged as the leading figure in the Church. Like his brother before him, he almost completely dominated the book-market. Apart from his work on the translation of the Bible and such books as were necessary for conducting services, his literary production included a large number of polemical writings and works of a practical religious nature. The archbishop's great period came especially after the death of Gustavus Vasa in 1560. His capacity for work and his initiative in all the spheres of

Church life were outstanding. In the theological struggles of the day he maintained the middle way of the old Swedish Lutheranism.

Throughout his life the archbishop showed a special interest in the drafting of an evangelical ordinance for the Swedish Church. A final draft was put before the king in 1547, but it was not accepted because Laurentius continued to uphold the reformers' ideal of an independent Church under the protection of the State with freedom in all internal matters. During the following years the archbishop sought to regulate Church affairs by provisional decrees covering separate spheres. These statutes were included in the final draft of the Church ordinances which were published in 1571 and accepted by a synod at Uppsala in 1572. Formally the Church ordinances adopted the standpoint of the 1527 Diet of Västeras. The Word of God, the Bible, is the confession of the Swedish Church and the test of its laws. Any dependence on German Lutheran confessional writings is rejected. Luther and Melanchthon are given equal weight. Similarly, in deliberate contrast to the manner in which the German Churches were ruled by their princes, stress was laid on the relative independence of the Swedish Church whose representatives were the bishops. They were to be chosen by clergy and laity, the final decision resting with the king. Priests were ordinarily to be appointed by the congregations. The order of service and liturgical practice were dealt with at length. An elaborate form of worship showed great respect for medieval tradition. The schools were put into the hands of the Church: the ordinances bear the stamp of Melanchthon's pedagogy and humanism. To help in the Church's task of educating the people, Lutheran Church discipline and private confession were introduced. These ordinances of 1571 formed the basis of subsequent developments and had the same significance for the Church of Sweden as the Church Ordinance of 1539 had for Denmark.

In 1560 Gustavus Vasa died soon after signing his will in which he expressed his simple Lutheran faith, the faith of a layman. In 1573 the archbishop followed him. Therewith all the main figures in the tempestuous Swedish Reformation had passed away, and the first chapter in the history of Swedish Lutheranism was closed.

(5) *Finland*

At the time of the Reformation Finland was under Swedish rule, so that it largely followed Swedish developments in Church affairs. However, the actual work of reform was carried out by some young Finns who had become acquainted with the new movement during their studies in Germany. The Finnish Reformation has its own special character. The transition from the Middle Ages to the Reformation took place there without the disturbances which otherwise characterised this period.

At the end of the Middle Ages the Catholic Church in Finland still retained its full glory. Its bishops and prelates were able men who through studies abroad had acquired a considerable theological training. The lower-ranking clergy were certainly less well equipped, but the usual complaints of abuses within the Church play no part worth mentioning in the Finnish Church at this time. Developments had not been so rapid nor the demand for reforms so forceful as elsewhere. The Reformation was here an affair of bishops and clergy; it was conservative and traditionalist and did not result in any popular movement, as it did in Denmark and Germany. With Latin predominating in its ritual, the medieval Church had not been able to fill the people with a true Christian faith, but when the Roman superstructure of sacramental magic, justification by works and the worship of saints was done away with, the reformers were able to touch hands with the true religious life of the later Middle Ages, with its reverence for Christ, the mystery of the Passion and penance which in evangelical form provided the transition to the new age. The writings of Agricola show this clearly. The reformers were aiming at a personal faith, and in their efforts they gave Finland a liturgy and a religious literature in the vernacular. Finland's reformer, Mikael Agricola, became the founder of the written Finnish language.

From the ecclesiastical point of view Finland consisted of one diocese, with Åbo as its seat. In 1528 the pious 70-year-old Dominican Martin Skytte became bishop. He was a biblical humanist and a Catholic reformer, had studied abroad, at Rostock among other places, and was not entirely averse to the ideas of the Reformation. He supported young Finns in their studies at Wittenberg, and later these same men became the pioneers of the Reformation in Finland through their activities as teachers at the cathedral school, Finland's clerical seminary in fact if not in name. On his appointment Bishop Skytte had had to promise Gustavus Vasa to take care that the priests preached the Word of God in accordance with the decision of the 1527 Diet of Västeras. Because of opposition from the members of his chapter he appears to have adopted a cautious attitude, with the result that a royal letter of 1528 ordered him to follow the evangelical doctrine and to take less notice of his canons. The reduction in Church property which was also decreed at Västeras had its effect during his period as bishop: the bishop's palace of Kustö was pulled down, Church property confiscated, tithes seized by the Crown, and churches and monasteries robbed of their treasures.

In the 1520's Lutheran influence made its entry into Finland. The first 'Lutheran' was Peder Särkilaks. Born of a noble family, the son of a mayor of Åbo, he returned to Åbo in 1523, after several years of foreign study in Rostock, Louvain and perhaps also Wittenberg among other places, there to become canon and later archdeacon. Särkilaks preached against the Roman worship of saints and images, celibacy and monastic life. His words aroused some opposition among the members of the chapter, but as a teacher at the cathedral school he exerted a great influence on the young people who listened enthusiastically to these new and liberating ideas. He died early in 1529.

Towards the east, Viborg and the school there became the centre of the Reformation movement. The town's links with the neighbouring city of Reval and the Baltic states, among the German population of which the Reformation spread quickly in the 1520's, were of considerable importance. By 1529, and perhaps as early as 1526, Viborg had a parish priest, Peder Soroi, with Lutheran tendencies. Mikael Agricola, the real reformer of Finland, also started from Viborg. He was born about 1510 in the parish of Perna in southern Finland. After studying at the school in Viborg he went to Åbo in 1528 where he became the bishop's scrivener and later his secretary. In Åbo Särkilaks's message made a profound impression on him. He preached evangelism in the cathedral and during the bishop's visitations also in the rural parishes. Agricola was one of the young people whom the bishop decided to send abroad to study, and in 1536 he went to Wittenberg. He returned in 1539 and began a literary production which soon gave the Finnish Lutheran Church both the New Testament and other parts of the Bible, together with Church manuals in the vernacular. After nine years as principal of the cathedral school in Åbo he became assistant to Bishop Skytte, in which capacity he undertook extensive tours of inspection throughout the country. After the bishop's death in 1550 Agricola succeeded to the post, but as the king was at the time considering a reorganisation of the dioceses he was not appointed bishop until 1554. The diocese was then divided and a new one created at Viborg, presumably to reduce the bishop's power. Agricola proved zealous and worked hard for his clergy and flock, but he was not to occupy the position for long. In 1557 he was sent to Moscow with other representatives to negotiate peace between Russia and Sweden. On his way home he fell ill and died on the Karelian Isthmus in 1557.

Agricola's importance rests on his literary output which has justly earned him the name of 'the father of written Finnish'. His translation of the New Testament was finished by 1543, though not published until 1548; based on the Greek Testament, it used Luther's German translation as well as Erasmus's Latin version and Olavus's translation. In addition it incorporated most of Luther's introductions and marginal notes, including the important introduction to the Epistle to the Romans. Agricola's most interesting work was *A Biblical Prayer Book* (1544), a manual for priests in the fashion of the day with varied and complex contents, filling 875 pages of small size. He translated not only Reformation writers (Luther, Melanchthon) but also humanists (Erasmus) and mystics (Schwenckfeld). A large number of liturgical prayers were taken from the Åbo Missal. After the synod at Uppsala in 1536 the publication of liturgical books in Finnish became an urgent necessity, but only with

Agricola's book of ritual and *Order of the Mass*, both of which (based on Olavus Petri's corresponding works) appeared in 1549, did Finnish religious life take on a definite shape. Agricola also published a book on the story of the Passion as well as some of the prophets and the Psalms of David (1551). In his introduction to the translation of the New Testament and the Psalms he included some information on the conversion of Finland to Christianity, the Swedish colonisation of Finland, Finnish topography, families and dialects, the gods of the heathen Finns, and so forth, all of which bears witness to his humanist interests.

Characteristic of Agricola's reforming activities was his reverent attitude towards tradition. He accepted the essential elements of the evangelical faith—justification by faith, the new life in God, and the profound reverence for the Word of God—but otherwise he often held fast to a vague and traditionalist point of view, as for example on the doctrines of purgatory and Mariology. The mysticism of the Passion and late medieval piety in general always retained an important place in his religious thinking. His prayer book contains a collection of prayers for Passiontide. Similarly he retained the feast of Corpus Christi, the most popular feast of the later Middle Ages and the mainstay of the medieval mysticism centred in the sacraments. Agricola's conservative attitude is also apparent in the practical work of reform. He wished the Reformation to be introduced with caution. Like Luther he wanted enlightenment to go before reforms, but unlike him he generally avoided polemical attacks on the institutions of the Catholic Church. His was a profoundly religious nature. The strength of his writings does not lie so much in theology and theory as in the reverence and practical Christianity which they reflect. He laid great stress on prayer. Several of the introductions to his writings bear witness to his considerable pastoral abilities. He addressed himself to the clergy, censuring ignorance and carelessness and encouraging them to carry out their tasks faithfully in a chaotic period of change. As the reformer of Finland Agricola made possible the transition from medieval piety to a Lutheran form of Christianity; thanks to his tolerant attitude towards various forms of religious life and doctrines, and his stress on practical Christian life, he stands as the typical exponent of Finnish religiosity.

The Lutheran Reformation won a more complete victory in the Nordic lands than in any other country. Varied political and national conditions produced two main types, one Danish-Norwegian-Icelandic and the other Swedish-Finnish. The Nordic Churches are still national Lutheran Churches to which to all intents the entire population belongs.

(6) *The Baltic*

The evangelical movement reached the Baltic states round about 1520; its progress was speedy, especially among the German population in the towns. The unhindered progress of the Reformation was favoured by the struggle for power among the bishops, the city councils of the three most important cities (Riga, Reval and Dorpat), and the Order of the Teutonic Knights to whom the greater part of the region belonged. The grand master, Walther von Plettenberg, sought at first to maintain a balance of power between the three political powers in the area in order to prevent interference from outside. This policy failed, because the burghers and the knights, both of whom had Lutheran leanings, soon joined forces against the bishops, and when the latter sought help abroad, even from Russia, the country disintegrated and its various parts were subjected to neighbouring states.

At the Diet of Wolmar in 1522 the representatives of the towns and the knights joined forces to oppose the domination of the bishops. Protests were lodged against the publication of the Edict of Worms and the bull of excommunication against Luther, asserting that a land which was conquered by the sword should not be ruled by the bishops' power of excommunication. No side was taken in the actual religious struggle, but it was decided to await the decision of a general council some time in the future. When the diet met again in Reval in 1524 the estates decided 'to maintain the Holy Word of God and His gospels, without the teachings of man or any additions whatsoever', and to defend this to the death. Now the Reformation could make rapid progress. Though a powerful evangelical movement already existed in the larger towns, the history of the Baltic Reformation is a stormy one containing several instances of churches and statues being pillaged and destroyed, as in Riga and Reval in 1524 and in Dorpat in 1525 where a riot was caused by the German fanatic Melchior Hoffmann.

Riga provides the most interesting chapter. Its reformer was a person of note, Andreas Knopken. A native of Pomerania, he became a curate in Riga in 1517. Knopken was influenced by the ideals of humanism and even corresponded with Erasmus. After a few years' stay in Riga he went to the school at Treptow in Pomerania of which Bugenhagen was the principal. Knopken had studied there previously and under the guidance of Bugenhagen he continued his humanistic studies, occupying himself especially with the study of the Bible and the Fathers of the Church. After 1520 the ideas of the Reformation reached Bugenhagen and his disciples through Luther's main writings. A powerful movement resulted which caused the bishop to intervene. While Bugenhagen joined Luther in Wittenberg, where he was to carry on his activities, Knopken together with a number of pupils from Livonia went back to Riga in 1521. Now an evangelical, he resumed his clerical duties at St Peter's Church and soon collected a considerable following by his teaching. In his polemical writings against the prevailing order he was moderate. Apart from his sermons he lectured to the citizens on the Epistle to the Romans. After copies had circulated in manuscript, Knopken's commentary was published in 1524 in Wittenberg with a preface by Bugenhagen, and several editions followed. In the form of practical homilies, and polemically directed against what Knopken called the perverted doctrine and the abuses of the Church of Rome, the author here gave a summary of evangelical teaching, especially of the doctrine of justification as it was evolved by Luther and Melanchthon in the 1520's.

The evangelical movement in Riga soon took on considerable proportions and had the support of the mayor, Conrad Durkop, and the city clerk, John Lohmüller. Archbishop Linde then requested the grand master to intervene. But Plettenberg would not resort to repressive measures, suggesting instead a public disputation, like those arranged in other countries, to solve the religious problem. On 12 June 1522 a disputation accordingly took place in the choir of St Peter's between Knopken and some of his Catholic opponents on the basis of fifteen theses from his commentary on the Epistle to the Romans. Knopken refuted the attacks of his opponents and proved that his doctrine agreed with scripture. The result of the disputation, which was attended by several members of the city council (including Durkop) and a large number of the congregation, was that the council decided to introduce the Reformation. As the archbishop had rejected a request for reforms and the appointment of evangelical preachers, the council together with the older of the city's two fraternities appointed Knopken archdeacon at St Peter's Church.

While Knopken was a conservative Lutheran theologian, moderate in his demands for reforms, Sylvester Tegetmeier, appointed pastor at St James's Church, was a passionate man whose radical demands for reforms soon resulted in destructive iconoclastic attacks on the churches and monasteries of the city. In March 1524 the two parish churches of Riga, St Peter's and St James's, were pillaged. The altars were destroyed, the relics removed, and statues and pictures of the saints dragged out and burnt in a great bonfire outside the city. At this time St Peter's Church had more than thirty-two chapels and altars. Later the cathedral itself was stormed and desecrated under the leadership of Tegetmeier. With the threat of bloodshed about, the city council early one morning had the hated Franciscans move outside the city. In May the Catholic priests were driven out. At the same time the council seized the treasures of the cathedral, but in August the interior was once more subjected to desecration. Even the magnificent statue of Our Lady was dragged from the high altar to the river Dvina to undergo the ordeal by water and be burnt.

At the same time relations between the burghers and the archbishop grew steadily more strained. When the archbishop died in 1524 and Bishop Blankenberg of Dorpat-Reval was chosen as his successor, the council declared that in future they would not acknowledge any bishop as a temporal lord. In an important pamphlet, *That the Pope, Bishops and Clerical Estates Shall Not Possess or Rule over Land or People*, Lohmüller presented the citizens' point of view. At the same time a request for protection was made to Plettenberg. After some hesitation he took over the temporal government of the city and in a declaration of 21 September 1525 assured the Lutheran Church of extensive liberties. During the subsequent developments the interests of the citizens, the nobility, and the grand master were bound closely together. At the Diet of Wolmar in 1526 the estates suggested that Plettenberg should establish his rule over the whole of Livonia as an evangelical prince, as Duke Albrecht had done in Prussia, but Plettenberg refused. Meanwhile he was soon obliged to take steps against the archbishop. When the latter sought help both from the emperor and the pope, indeed even from the Russians, he was proclaimed traitor and imprisoned. After ostensibly submitting to Plettenberg he was released, but in August 1526 he left Livonia only to prefer accusations against the grand master to the emperor and the pope. However, he died abroad the following year. His successor Thomas Schöning was only interested in regaining the bishops' privileges and wealth; in return he confirmed the rights and liberties of the Lutherans.

At the end of the 1520's the organisation of the Church and the order of service took on definite shape. In 1527 Dr Johannes Briesmann from Königsberg, a conservative Lutheran theologian who played a considerable part in the Reformation in Königsberg and East Prussia, was called in. Together with Knopken he evolved an order of service for Riga which was published in Rostock in 1530 and introduced the same year. The ordinances committed decisions on Church matters to the council, two members of which were delegated for the purpose. While these 'superintendents' and the mayor were to attend to the Church's outward affairs, the internal administration was the business of the 'chief priest', later called the clerical superintendent. In 1532 it was decided that Knopken and Tegetmeier should alternate as chairman in the clerical council for periods of six months each. Through their elders the congregations also took part in the administration of the Church, as in the choice of priests, the care of the poor, and Church discipline.

At the beginning of the Reformation the Church's position in the other Baltic cities was roughly like that in Riga. Next to Riga the most important city was Reval whose Church Ordinance of 19 May 1525 is one of the oldest Lutheran ordinances. There the new doctrine was preached by Johannes Lange, Hermann Marsow and Zacharias Hasse. As in Riga, the movement quickly gained a foothold in the city gilds and led to violent clashes with the Dominicans who were particularly hated by the people.

When the preachers vainly offered the monks a disputation on the true faith, the council decided to organise reform and decreed that for three consecutive Sundays evangelical priests should preach in the abbey church to enlighten the monks. At last things came to such a pass that a furious mob broke into the abbey church on 14 September 1524 and destroyed the 'idols', altars and other articles of value. Soon afterwards the churches of the Holy Spirit and St Olaf were razed to the ground, while St Nicholas's Church only escaped the same fate because the churchwardens had barred the doors and filled the keyholes with lead. The council, however, soon gained control of the situation and decided on the day after the riots that those who had robbed the churches of their valuables should deliver them to the town hall, as otherwise proceedings for theft would be started against them. But at the same time it was decreed that people who owned altars, statues of the saints, and the like in St Nicholas's Church should take them down and remove them, or they would be confiscated. In January 1525 the monks were turned out of the city.

A few days after the storming of the churches the three evangelical preachers submitted proposals for a Church ordinance, which, as stated above, was accepted by the council in May next year. The characteristic aspect of this Church ordinance, as in that of Riga, is a differentiation between the Church's spiritual mission and its temporal administration, the latter being committed in its entirety to the council and the congregation; at the same time the chief priest (*oberste Pastor*) was made independent of the council in the carrying out of his duties, responsible only to God and his conscience. Johannes Lange was chosen for this exacting task; he wore himself out in his work for the accomplishment of the Reformation and died young in 1531.

Officially, the Reformation had won the day throughout the whole country when in 1554 the Diet of Wolmar proclaimed freedom to preach the gospel and general religious toleration. The continual struggles between the grand masters and the bishops who, in order to retain their power, made alliances with neighbouring states, led, however, to the speedy dissolution of the country. In 1558 Ivan the Terrible broke into Livonia and ravaged it in such a fearful manner that the country completely disintegrated.[1] The separate parts sought protection from the neighbouring states and were soon incorporated into them. The division was completed between 1559 and 1561. The greater part of Estonia came under Sweden. The bishopric of Øsel fell to Prince Magnus of Denmark who, however, was not capable of deriving any advantage from the situation. Livonia, together with Riga and Dorpat, was incorporated into Poland-Lithuania, while the Livonian grand master kept Courland as an hereditary duchy. Despite the political dissolution, Lutheran Christianity and the Church ordinances continued to flourish.

[1] Below, p. 559.

CHAPTER VI

THE REFORMATION IN DIFFICULTIES

I. THE GERMAN REFORMATION TO 1555

IN the sixteenth century, to reform the Church meant to reform the world, for the Church was the world. The enterprise could therefore only succeed if the authorities who governed this universe could be won for it. The Papacy had from the beginning denied support. In 1530, at the Diet of Augsburg, the emperor and Empire proffered similar denials. The concluding act of this diet—returning to the Edict of Worms —declared open war on the reformers. What were they to do now? Men to whom this was the bread of life could not stop preaching the gospel. They could only rely on the strength of their good cause and establish the new order in their own restricted spheres: unless the general council, the last court of appeal, came over to them, the Reformation would fall into the hands of particularist powers.

The diet threatened force, and force could be met only with force. Naturally enough, the project of a Protestant alliance came once again to the fore. But it was a project complicated by grave theological problems. Was it possible to defend the cause of the gospel by force? Was it permissible to do so even against the emperor? And who were the true adherents of the gospel? The quarrel over the eucharist had led to divisions among the followers of the new faith until mutual recognition had ceased to be possible. In forming an alliance men ran the danger that in defending the gospel they might find themselves defending that which they thought to be death to the gospel. These two problems would have to be solved first.

Thus the theologians had the first word. While the Augsburg Diet was still sitting, Martin Bucer—who had only recently drafted the Tetrapolitan Confession in opposition to that of Augsburg[1]—met Luther at the Coburg, in order to arrive at an agreement on the eucharist. Luther was at first hostile: though he understood that Bucer did not intend to explain the sacrament as a mere 'symbol' but found in it a personal, spiritual encounter with Christ, he yet wanted more. The meeting must be outward as well; it must take place in the elements, independently of the receiver's faith but as a reinforcement for faith—*manducatio oralis* and *manducatio impiorum*. Both men, however, felt new hope. Even though unity remained to seek, hope of unity had been achieved; by making possible the alliance, it acted at once as a factor in politics.

The other question, whether it was permissible to defend the new

[1] Above, p. 111.

Church by force of arms and even against the emperor's legitimate authority, proved no less difficult. Did not this view contradict everything that Luther and the Lutherans had so far written on suffering for the faith's sake? What was wanted was not only an alliance but also a sound conscience in the alliance, and this involved the search for a theologically convincing justification of the right to resist. But Luther had forbidden resistance and had contented himself with warning princes and some individuals against taking part in the suppression of the gospel. He wished to rely on the power of prayer:

> I cannot and will not fear those miserable enemies of God; their fury is my pride, their rage my laughter. They cannot take from me anything but a sackful of sick flesh. But they shall shortly learn what it is that I can take from them.

He had only given way to the extent of seeing no rebellion in self-defence. But the lawyers found a way out. The law of the Empire itself permitted resistance to the emperor in cases of manifest injustice, and Luther compromised sufficiently to concede the lawyers their law, on the grounds that the gospel did not overthrow secular laws. But on no account would he counsel resistance. It was possible to work on this basis. Nuremberg alone remained firmly in the earlier position, and Luther had much difficulty to explain to them that he had not suggested the alliance and the policy of resistance. To him the main thing was that all action should rest on faith: the result might then be good, 'even though it were an error and a sin'. The landgrave of Hesse, on the other hand, maintained not only the right but the duty of resistance. The politicians simply interpreted Luther's written opinion to suit their desire for an alliance—by mutilating it, as Melanchthon said—and ignored his reservations.

In the meantime, Bucer utilised his negotiations in a tract on the Lord's Supper which was meant to combine the various points of view. It satisfied no one, but the hope for unity remained. Thus, in December 1530, princes and cities concluded the preliminaries of alliance, and in the course of 1531 the cities ratified the agreement.[1] It was to be a defensive alliance, 'solely for the maintenance of Christian truth and peace in the Holy Empire' against unjust force. Luther's advice was no longer sought. From this point the Protestants were a political power, and from this point too the validity of the gospel became a question of power. The Swiss stood aside. Bucer had found it impossible to come to an agreement with Zwingli whose followers withdrew their earlier consent when the problem of a formulary of faith came up. They demanded either recognition of their own Confession or an alliance in which the Confession played no part; the Saxon representatives refused to accept either, although the other princes, led by Hesse, were ready to agree. All this was a sad disappointment to the South German towns: their political and

[1] Cf. below, pp. 350.

theological ties with the Swiss were close, and they placed greater reliance on military support from Switzerland than from distant and slow-moving Saxony. However, these considerations were soon cancelled by the defeat of Zürich and death of Zwingli.

The history of this collapse must here be mentioned, not only because of its political consequences but also because it serves to demonstrate the 'other spirit' of the Zürich Reformation. Zwingli was from the start both politician and Church reformer, while Luther had always dreaded the political possibilities in his work. To Zwingli, the law and the gospel were one, not opposed. Significantly enough, the Reformation began in Zürich with a breach of the Lent fast, a matter of no importance at all to Luther. In effect, Zwingli conducted the policy of Zürich, developing it—unhindered by religious or confessional scruples—into a general policy of alliances directed against the Habsburgs and reaching from the North Sea to the Adriatic. Early in 1531 he sent the king of France a description of his faith (*Expositio Fidei*) which was meant to demonstrate that Zürich by no means condemned authority and religion. The little tract (not printed until 1536) is of special interest because it so forcefully illumines the differences between Zwingli and Luther. While for Luther the Word of God equals the Grace of God, for Zwingli the Word, too, is but a symbol —or else the word 'ape' were itself an ape. Word and sacrament are not the consolation of God but a pointer to Christ, a memory of Christ, not the miracle of meeting God in person. Zwingli's death, which Luther thought a well-deserved fate, ended the Christian polity in Zürich, though the town, under Henry Bullinger's pastoral guidance, remained evangelical.

The German Protestants, however, were now united in the League of Schmalkalden, so named after the little town on the border between Saxony and Hesse where the League's assemblies often took place. Although the League was as yet far from solid both inwardly and outwardly, it registered a major success at this time. During a meeting at Frankfurt—otherwise pretty insupportable to the towns because of Saxony's intransigence—members learned that the electors of Mainz and of the Palatinate had offered to act as intermediaries between the emperor and the Protestants. The emperor was no less interested in maintaining internal peace; he needed all his strength for his external enemies, in particular the Turks. At a further meeting of the League at Schweinfurt, held after the catastrophe of Cappel, the real negotiations began. Once again there was acute danger that the towns, being Zwinglian, would separate themselves from the Lutherans. To prevent this, the Strassburg theologians were ordered to investigate whether a move towards the Confession of Augsburg were not possible; and when they replied that there was nothing in that document with which they could not agree in sense and content, the town council declared that Strassburg would accept the Augsburg Confession side by side with that of the four cities.

These negotiations had taken a long time. The first task at Schweinfurt concerned the organisation of the League itself; material and personal difficulties produced a complicated and ponderous machinery. In the negotiations for a religious peace the Protestants at first put their sights very high. Since a peace could in any case only endure until the council met, the Protestants had reason to define precisely their conception of such a body—a general, free, Christian council which would have to meet in Germany. They wished the peace to extend to all evangelicals; the towns would not have the Zwinglians excluded and demanded the protection of the law also for newly won co-religionists. The Imperial Chamber, the highest court of the realm, was to have no competence in questions of religion. Naturally enough, the emperor was not prepared to make such concessions. The negotiations were interrupted for a month before being resumed at Nuremberg; during that time the theologians reported their views. The representatives of Strassburg and Hesse thought it a matter of conscience that future adherents of the Augsburg Confession should be included in the peace, since they too were entitled to the gospel. Luther energetically contested this: it was every man's duty to accept the gospel at his own risk, and the emperor's offer of peace was an act of grace which one could not force him to extend to others. The negotiations were resumed on the Hessian basis, and it took several weeks before the League contented itself with the 'external' peace whose acceptance Luther had strongly urged on 29 June 1532. 'For God sends us his greetings and it is time for us to thank him.'

In the outcome the emperor again proclaimed the imperial peace, extending it to matters religious 'until the council', and ordered the cessation of processes before the chamber. At the same time he promised to make fresh efforts towards a council which was to be announced within six months and held within the year. The peace was put into operation by an imperial rescript. The diet, then meeting at Regensburg, did not give its consent. Charles's agreement with respect to the chamber is not even in the rescript but was only communicated to the mediating electors. The emperor's difficult situation must be considered: the head of the state was being asked nothing less than that his justice should cease to apply to one of the vital problems of the nation. It seems that in fact he promised rather a continuous series of pardons than a general suspension of the court. The Protestants on their side agreed to assist against the Turks. During the final discussions there were again violent disputes between Hesse and Saxony: the emissaries of Hesse gave their consent only on condition that their prince should later approve it, as indeed he did.

Nonetheless, a legal foundation had been created on which the Protestants could exist until the council should meet. The question of lawsuits remained difficult, if only because religious matters never appeared purely in that guise but always involved politics and property, so that a wide margin was left for the discretion of judges and emperor. As far as the Empire was concerned, the peace at least made possible common action against the Turks. Charles V himself visited Vienna (where he was received with great enthusiasm) and then moved on to Italy and his Spanish lands, revolving the problem of the council which seemed necessary for Germany and yet would only come about if Italy could be kept at peace, if the pope would subordinate the interests of his dynasty to those of the Church, and if France kept the treaties. All this was uncertain; it required quite as much skill on the emperor's part as good will on that of the other parties.

For the Reformation the time of peace—as its enemies had feared—meant a period of further expansion. The forming of the League of Schmalkalden had caused a number of towns to adopt the Reformation officially. Others followed at intervals, a process in which democratic and reforming endeavours often met. Among others, Pomerania and Mecklenburg in the north-east, and the Silesian principalities of Liegnitz and Brieg in the east, were added to the fold.

The most important gain was the duchy of Württemberg which was at the time under Austrian administration, since the Swabian League had driven out Duke Ulrich. At the Augsburg Diet Charles V had formally bestowed the fief on his brother Ferdinand, thus adding it to the Habsburg possessions but also stirring up anew all the friends of the exiled duke and the enemies of his own house. The duke meanwhile lived in his county of Mömpelgard where he established contact with the Swiss and adopted the Reformation; later he appeared at the court of Hesse to whose landgrave he was related. However unpleasant this passionate and violent man may have been, his exile remained an act of force and his deprivation had no legal basis. Even among the strictly Catholic but anti-Habsburg dukes of Bavaria the plan to restore him found favour. Duke Christopher, Ulrich's son and a nephew to the Bavarians, had been educated at the court of Vienna but escaped with Bavarian assistance.

The issue united Hesse and Bavaria, since both were working against the Archduke Ferdinand's election as king of the Romans. France was approached and offered support. The situation seemed favourable when the Swabian League, containing Ulrich's old enemies, began to dissolve under the pressure of religious dissension and not without the assistance of Hesse. In January 1534 Philip of Hesse met Francis I at Bar le Duc and obtained the necessary supplies from him; it is not clear whether the pope even may not have known of the project. Francis hoped to unleash a general war against the Habsburgs; the landgrave was only interested in the duke's restoration. This was achieved in a short campaign. The Peace of Kadan in Bohemia settled the political problems arising from it, thanks to the services of the elector of Saxony and in spite of Ulrich's vigorous resistance. Württemberg was to be held as a fief from Austria, but Ulrich's right to introduce the Reformation was recognised (though of course with the reservation that the land must not turn Zwinglian) and the Reformation was in fact carried through at once. A great deal of Church property thus fell into the duke's hands, very necessary to him for the payment of his debts. The theological problem consisted in this: the towns of Swabia, with which the duke had to remain on good terms, leant towards Zwingli, and the duke himself had learned about the Reformation from the Swiss; yet the peace treaty excluded a Zwinglian Reformation which the League of Schmalkalden and Hesse would in any case not have permitted. The duke compromised by committing the Reformation in the northern half of his dominions to a Lutheran, Erhard Schnepf, and that of the southern half together with the university of Tübingen to Ambrosius Blaurer, a friend of Bucer's from Constance. The two theologians agreed at Stuttgart on a common formula regarding the Lord's Supper, using the formula suggested by the Lutherans to the Swiss at the Marburg Colloquy where it had been turned down. What was at first regarded as a great step towards unity soon proved to be a new difficulty: the Swiss thought the formula too Lutheran, while the Lutherans mistrusted Ambrosius Blaurer and cast doubts upon the preachers he appointed. Following the advice of Jacob Sturm of Strassburg, the pastors took their oaths not on the agreed formula but on the Augsburg Confession. Once again the problem of agreement on the eucharist had raised its head in the Protestant ranks, and once again an attempt was made to overcome it by means of a meeting. Towards the end of 1534 Melanchthon and Bucer met at Kassel, at the court of Philip of Hesse, and arrived at a formula which for the moment satisfied Luther. By the manner of its achievement the Reformation in Württemberg was miles away from all the principles which Luther had once put forward: it was purely an act of authority, carried through from above by order of the prince. But these blemishes could not alter the result: there was now in the south also a great Protestant region which could act as a bridge between Hesse and Switzerland and as a prop for the scattered towns, and which moreover formed a wedge between Austria and the Habsburg family lands. Under the leadership of Johannes Brenz from Schwäbisch Hall, the country soon became the pattern of a Protestant state of strongly Lutheran character; the university of Tübingen, which at first proved obstreperous, turned into an important centre of evangelical studies.

At nearly the same time, events in the town of Münster demonstrated the dangerous forces which the Reformation might release and the passions which it had to tame. Like other episcopal towns, Münster was engaged in a struggle with its bishop over municipal liberties. And as in other towns, the lower orders—the gilds—were opposed to a wealthy and conservative town aristocracy and intent upon developing municipal self-government into a democracy. In this uncertain setting, the preacher Bernhard Rothmann began to preach evangelism in an episcopal church outside the town. When the bishop, under imperial orders, expelled him, he obeyed the command by moving into the town and preaching in the house of the merchant gild. Within two months his followers won him a municipal church; five months later, in August 1532, all the town churches were filled with evangelical preachers. Rothmann's activities had turned Münster Protestant in the space of a few months. Though the victory had not been won without acts of violence, it remained to begin with in the hands of the evangelical cause. But as early as December 1532, letters from Luther and Melanchthon warned of the dangers of mystic enthusiasm: 'the devil is a knave who can mislead even fine and pious and learned preachers.' The dangers lay in the existence of the fanatics. Mysticism had long been at home around the Lower Rhine; here was a centre of the Brethren of the Common Life who practised the thought of the *Imitatio Christi* and had produced in Wessel Gansfort a mystic pre-reformer whose writings Luther himself had edited in earlier days. Here, too, the Anabaptist movement had found followers, though—since secrecy was essential to their survival—we know little enough of them. Their triumph and defeat at Münster have already been described.[1] For a second time it had been shown that reliance on inspiration only led to an overthrow of all good order. Events themselves seemed to prove the necessity of extreme treatment: only Philip of Hesse acted more mildly and tried to use Bucer to bring the Anabaptists back into the Church. The Catholics, of course, tried to explain the revolution in Münster as a consequence of the Reformation; but Luther had long been the most energetic opponent of baptists and their ideas, and the Lutherans could point out that Anabaptism was strongest where the gospel was not free and where there existed no control of the mind. It is, in truth, significant enough that the driving spirit should have come from the Netherlands where under imperial rule the Reformation was kept down by force.

As has been said, the case of Württemberg led to a renewal of efforts to find agreement on the sacrament of the altar. Luther had no objection to Bucer's Kassel formula, but he did not want to build on a formula which had been agreed to by only two men, however eminent. A valid concord must be arrived at by all the Churches. It is, in fact, far from certain whether Bucer could speak for all those whom ostensibly he represented: the Wittenberg suspicions had some substance. On the other hand, Bucer was for ever moving nearer to the Lutheran position. In Augsburg—the 'German Corinth'—where the situation was particularly difficult, he admitted in the pulpit that he had so far misunderstood the matter. The Augsburg pastors then composed a new Confession which they sent to Luther; at the same time they asked him for a Lutheran preacher.

[1] See above, pp. 127 ff.

Admittedly, they were driven not purely by theological passion but rather by force of necessity—by the need to prepare the reception in the League of Schmalkalden of a town whose position was so exposed. In Switzerland, too, the problem was discussed by leading men; Bullinger could not follow Bucer any more than Zwingli had done, though he also saw more in the Lord's Supper than a 'symbol' of Christ's presence. Early in 1536 the Swiss, too, by order of their magistrates composed a Confession—the first Helvetic Confession which originated in a meeting in Basle. The authors were not thinking of agreement with the Lutherans but of the need to defend their faith before a general council. Of the Supper they said that it was not only a symbol but contained 'essentials', that in it God offered something and 'forthrightly achieved' it; but in so far as explanations were offered, they continued to hold that symbols interpret a thing which must be got outside the sacrament. Capito and Bucer admittedly reported to Luther as though all Switzerland had now turned Lutheran. The Swiss themselves hoped that Luther might be content with their Confession; only Constance had learned from the experiences of Ambrosius Blaurer in Württemberg and saw the differences. In their view it was not right to say 'in coena exhibetur remissio peccatorum', for thus the sacrament would cease to be *remissionis memoria* and be *remissionis opus*. But this was precisely the core of Luther's position. The Swiss continued to make their views plainer in a series of publications: it was now that Zwingli's *Expositio* appeared, in which Zwinglianism assumes an especially uncompromising form.

The conclusion of the concord was to take place in a congress of theologians. Bucer invited the South Germans, though not those who were known Lutherans. The Swiss did no more than hand him their Confession for transmission. Melanchthon faced the prospect of the meeting with much perturbation, greatly fearing lest the attempt at unity should only make certain of the breach. Eisenach had first been picked as a meeting place; but because of Luther's illness the southerners moved farther north to Wittenberg where they arrived on 21 May 1536.

The negotiations opened under great difficulties because Luther had taken the recent Swiss publications to show that there had been no change of views. Bucer was hard put to it to excuse himself and his friends. Luther then demanded the recognition of Christ's presence not only by faith or for the faith, but by virtue of Christ's intercession, with no regard to the subjective qualities of the receiver. Faith or lack of it did not affect Christ's intercession. In technical theological terms: he demanded recognition of *manducatio impiorum*. This was a hard nut for Bucer: for him it was essential that a pneumatic, spiritual reality should be received in the Supper which only he could receive who possessed the necessary organ, the spirit. Bugenhagen, pastor of Wittenberg, proposed the solution: that the unworthy received the body of Christ. This meant a distinction between the 'godless' who cannot receive anything, and the 'unworthy' who are Christians and so possess the spirit as the receiving organ, but who cannot make proper use of it and so receive the gift without the fruit. The distinction is no doubt highly artificial; it has been much argued, but Luther surprisingly was content with it. Using this formula, Melanchthon drafted the articles of the so-called 'Wittenberg Concord' which is not an agreement in which both parties had made concessions but a Confession of the southerners which those of Wittenberg had recognised. They thus acceded to the Wittenberg position, while Luther left no doubt that he had not altered his views.

It is certain that important differences remained and that Luther recognised them. Bucer did not surrender the symbolical views which he had held for so long; he modified them so far that they were no longer totally inacceptable to Luther. Bucer recognised that it is not *contemplatio fidei* which produces grace, but that in the sacrament Christ comes to man by virtue of his promise. He also admitted the connection between Christ's deeds and those of the priest. But he continued to hold that the spiritual reality can only be received by the spirit. It surprises to find that Luther was content with this. He clearly was so only because he saw his religious interests satisfied. For when he defended the taking of the sacrament by the godless he was not concerned with Turks and Jews (for whom the sacrament is not appointed) but with the need of convincing all communicants that they were truly receiving the whole of Christ's grace; and if he rejected spiritual communion, he did so not because he wished to interpret the reality of Christ's body in a materialist sense, but because he did not wish to rest the certainty of grace on a certainty depending on the receiver's subjective faith. Grace does not depend on faith, but faith on grace. The Christian man's assurance does not depend on himself but on that which he receives in the sacrament. Since these points seemed to him now accepted, he no longer resisted agreement with the southerners. But in fact ambiguities remained. They appeared in Bucer's attitude: not only was he not prepared to draw the line against the Swiss, but he acted towards them also as though there were no need to change their views. He sacrificed the lucidity of the theologian to the hopes of the politician. But if one stresses, however slightly, the conditions applying to the unworthy, then Bucer's views change into something quite different. On this ambiguity rests the ambiguity of Calvin's teaching on the eucharist; as a Strassburg pastor, he accepted the concord. In any case, as far as Luther was concerned, this agreement, too, was to be provisional only and would have to be solemnly confirmed later on by all the Churches. Bucer therefore endeavoured to get the Swiss to agree, but Zwinglianism rejected both the directness and the ambiguity of the statement. The split continued. While the southerners used Bucer's bridge to cross over to Lutheranism, and while in the South German towns the Wittenberg agreement for long had confessional force, Switzerland retained a special interpretation of the Lord's Supper with which Calvin was later to establish contact.

The spread and internal development of Protestantism in those years had only been made possible by the postponement of the general council. The German princes—including the Catholics—thought a council absolutely indispensable; since the Diet of Augsburg the emperor had struggled for it; the Protestants had long demanded it and had used the preface to the Augsburg Confession to record their demand. But the pope held back, for reasons connected not only with theology and Church policy but also with general politics. And indeed, the demand for a council involved a large number of unsolved problems. As early as the Leipzig Disputation of 1519, Luther had maintained that even general councils could err. Would the Protestants submit to one? Could they even be admitted, proclaimed heretics that they were? What were the relations between pope and council—who stood above whom? Was there, on the other hand, any other way of carrying out the necessary reforms and restoring the unity of the Church? At first the pope saw in the council nothing but 'a deadly physic' for the sick Church; the emperor, however, could see no other way if violence was to be avoided. There was also the position of France whose king treated the whole matter as one of politics and might at any moment go the way of the king of England.

At the Diet of Regensburg (1532) the Catholics proposed that the emperor should himself summon the council. Charles would not think of this: he respected the papal office. But he tried at Bologna to move the pope to action. Clement VII wished first to consult the other powers, but France sabotaged the plan for political reasons and the pope was not ill content. Nevertheless, a nuncio was sent to Germany in order to make a preliminary announcement of the pope's intentions. He was received joyfully by the Catholics, but the Protestant League replied that a council announced to be 'after the accustomed usage of the Church' was not the council wanted by the Protestants and promised by the imperial diets because it was not 'Christian'—it would not determine by Holy Writ—and because it was not 'free'—it would be dependent on the pope. Luther delivered a written opinion in which he forcefully pointed out these shortcomings; yet he also advised participation in the assembly if it should ever materialise. Following him, the League declared that it could not admit the papal conditions but reserved the right to attend if it should seem useful to the gospel. They did not wish to prevent the synod, but would urge the emperor to see that it was a proper Christian synod. It thus appeared that the demands put forward hitherto by both Protestants and Catholics really meant quite different things on the two sides. However, at this time the council was not wrecked by Protestant resistance but by the negative attitude of France which Francis I finally confirmed in a meeting with the pope at Marseille (October–November 1533). This was the meeting at which Dr Bonner appealed before the pope to a future general council of the Church against the papal judgment condemning Henry VIII's marriage to Anne Boleyn. Before that Henry VIII had not even replied to the pope's enquiry. To the Catholics the postponement was 'a terrible annoyance'; even the Catholic world ceased now to think the pope serious in his endeavours.

However, the new pope, Paul III Farnese, was quite serious about it. Early in 1535 nuncios again went out into the various countries to inform the princes of the pope's firm determination and hear their views. The man sent to Germany was Pietro Paolo Vergerio: he was received like the bearer of gospel tidings. Yet he was less successful than he had expected. He met Luther in Wittenberg: the latter refused to believe the pope in earnest but promised to come 'even if I knew that you would burn me'. The legate thought that this meant also the elector's agreement, but was told to consult the allies. They replied at a diet of the League held at Schmalkalden in 1535, neither agreeing nor declining but elaborating at length what they expected of a council. It was on this occasion that the English envoy, Edward Foxe bishop of Hereford, by order of his king delivered an impassioned address against the pope, who, he said, was only out to maintain his rule, and associated England with the demand for a free and Christian council. Negotiations followed for an alliance between the League and England, but the Protestants wanted first to be assured about the teaching of the English Church. This was discussed afterwards at Wittenberg and resulted in the 'Wittenberg Articles' which, however, were quickly forgotten as the plans for a council once again came to nothing. Again France stood in the way. At the time Francis I had hopes of himself restoring the unity of the Church by means of negotiations with Melanchthon—hopes which were blocked by the Saxon elector who barred Melanchthon from travelling to France. Belatedly and after many efforts, King Francis too gave his consent to a council. During a visit by Charles V to Rome it was decided to call it at Mantua; the bull was published on 4 June 1536 and the date of assembly was 23 May 1537. Its tasks were defined: removal of errors and heresies, reform of morals, restoration of peace in Christendom and the preparation of a great war against the infidel. Once more nuncios went out, though now they were only charged with transmitting the invitations in the proper form.

The Protestants now faced a time of decision. The elector of Saxony at once ordered his theologians to consider whether he could accept the invitation without 'tacitly committing himself' to attend the council and recognise it in whatever form it might take place. The consultations, interrupted by a journey of Melanchthon's to the south, took a long time. Everyone was agreed that the council would be papal and fail to accord with the demands of the Protestants. Nevertheless, the theologians thought that it was both possible and necessary to attend it, so as to bear witness for the faith. The elector and his lawyers arrived at the opposite conclusion: they thought he could not even accept the invitation without recognising the council and its decisions and thus denying his faith. In a memorandum of his own the elector contemplated the calling of a Protestant anti-council. In the course of these deliberations, he asked Luther to compose a new evangelical Confession which might serve as a basis for negotiations at the council or even at the anti-council. This was the document later known as Luther's 'Schmalkalden Articles'. Naturally the problem of resistance re-appeared: it was generally thought certain that the council would condemn the Protestants and that the emperor would then carry out his duty by proceeding against them. Even Luther now declared that in such a case defence was permissible: more, he would 'do his part in prayer and even (if it so be) with his fists'. The theologians of Hesse also demanded that the papal proceedings be answered publicly with a new Confession.

The League was now called to a meeting at Schmalkalden, attended by the theologians, where the emissaries were to produce detailed statements on the question of the council. In all the Protestant centres discussions materialised in memoranda. All were agreed in their opinion of the papal encyclical and the coming council; but views differed as to the action to be taken. Hesse demanded immediate and energetic preparation for war; others still hoped that with the emperor's assistance they might turn the council into one answerable to Protestant desires; Melanchthon hoped for a new, clear and unambiguous formulation of doctrine; the Wittenberg theologians stuck to their vigorous condemnation of the council but continued to think it advisable to attend to bear witness for the faith. In this they plainly opposed the intentions of their elector.

Before he departed for Schmalkalden, Luther with great earnestness called his Wittenberg congregation to prayer; the bell which 'is to be cast will ring through all the world and through posterity'. But at Schmalkalden it was the princes who decided. On the grounds that to attend the council meant to submit to its decisions, they at once agreed to decline the invitation. A reply to this effect was made to the imperial envoy, the vice-chancellor Held; the towns and Melanchthon gave way. The envoy thought that the Protestants might fight for the proper form and procedure at the council itself, but the Protestants thought this impossible. Only afterwards the papal nuncio appeared at Schmalkalden in order to present the invitation to the elector and the landgrave. Though the elector received him, he had Melanchthon reply that the nuncio should address the allies and take his letters with him. The nuncio refused, saying that the elector had already accepted the invitation tacitly. The elector was not trying to humiliate the legate. He refused the invitation because it would have bound him to go to the council and accept its decisions: the handing over of a summons was a juristic act which committed the man summoned and was therefore commonly carried out in the presence of a notary. Philip of Hesse simply would not receive the nuncio. As for the emperor's concomitant demand for an extraordinary aid against the Turks, the League would only assist if a secure peace was granted to them; the rejection of the council thus had immediate political consequences.

In these circumstances the theologians had little to do at Schmalkalden; Luther's articles had been rendered superfluous by the turning down of the council. The towns were in any case afraid that discussions of doctrine would only lead to a new split; Melanchthon seems to have badly misunderstood the ideas behind Luther's draft and tried to prevent its consideration. All that happened was that the Augsburg Confession was looked over and a paragraph 'De potestate papae' added which Melanchthon had written. A nascent quarrel over the eucharist was arrested at once. When Luther's articles were submitted to a number of theologians, they at least expressed their agreement by signing them. Bucer and Luther met at Gotha to discuss the concord; Luther, very ill and near to death, warned against ambiguities but was peaceable and hopeful of complete unity in the future.

The official outcome of the League's assembly was the rejection of the council. Melanchthon had to write an official apology which was to be published in the name of the League. Although he himself was of the other opinion and dreaded the possibility of war, he briefly summarised the grounds for rejection. It would be said that the Protestants would recognise no court of law if they rejected the highest court in Christendom. But to agree to this council would mean recognising the pope as the judge in matters of faith, and since this would mean judgment not by the Word of God but by the existing canon law, this would amount to a denial of the faith.

Before the assembly dispersed they received a letter from the king of France informing them that he, too, would not consent to the council. Once again it was not Protestant refusal but the attitude of France which prevented the calling of the council. Admittedly, the French did not rest their refusal on such fundamental grounds as did the Protestants. Francis only maintained that he could not come to Mantua while he was at war with the emperor and would not, for that reason, permit French bishops to be invited. In addition, the duke of Mantua was alleged to have made the reception of the council depend on impossible conditions. Thus the council was twice prorogued and no one really believed that it would ever assemble. Luther published a whole series of pamphlets against the pope, following them up in 1539 with his great work *Of Councils and Churches*, a general discussion of the Catholic ideas on these subjects. His chief argument was that a general council could not rest on the consensus of the Fathers who were themselves not at one: if the truth was wanted, there was no certainty outside scripture. A council could not find new truths but only defend old truth, as was done daily in school and church. If a solemn council became necessary it must judge by scripture, for here alone lay the 'law' of the Church. It was true that the decay of doctrine and living necessitated such a council—the emperor and princes must even compel the pope to call it; but if a proper council could not be obtained it was better to be silent and to hold none at all. In the last part of his book Luther gave a coherent account of his conception of the Church. The pope looks to externals, to law and order; but the Church is only made by God's holy Word—by preaching—and the offices necessary for it— prayer and faith. Because it did not take these things seriously, the Roman Church had become the devil's chapel which he had built for himself beside the Church. The whole thing is a fundamental justification for rejecting the council; it makes plain how far the Protestants had moved from the old order despite all their demands for a general council.

On 25 April 1538 the pope prorogued the council indefinitely. There followed a meeting of pope, emperor and king of France at Nice which resulted in a ten years' truce, though not in full peace. The council could now have taken place in an atmosphere of relative peace; instead it was adjourned in 1539 *ad beneplacitum*, at the pope's pleasure. More than ever the world was convinced that the pope did not want it. Even the emperor was complaining of the pope's cooling zeal. Indeed, the pope's behaviour in this matter is one of the strangest features of the Reformation period. One can enumerate a large number of political reasons; it is true that the pope feared the ascendancy which a council would grant to the over-powerful emperor. But are such reasons anything but a condemnation of a pope who could so badly neglect the needs of the Church?[1]

What was to happen—what could happen—if there was no council? What means remained to be tried? The emperor would have nothing to do with a council of the German nation which would result in open schism. Force he was in no position to use, even if he had contemplated it, for while his resources were immensely great they were not liquid and remained tied up by the needs of foreign policy. What was he to do?

A way out had seemed to appear even before the last prorogation of the council: soon after Nice, the new elector of Brandenburg (Joachim II) offered his services in peaceful negotiations for the healing of the schism. Ferdinand favoured the attempt which he hoped would produce Protestant aid against the Turks; even the pope did not seem disinclined, since in this manner he might escape the council. The background to this proposal was not, however, only the good will of the new elector but lay rather in a widespread state of opinion. Neither Wittenberg nor Rome so completely dominated the minds of their followers as may appear to the backward-looking glance. There were many who did not see or would not

[1] For the Papacy and the council, cf. also below, pp. 270ff.

admit how radical the conflict was, many who while they recognised the need for Church reform thought it possible to remain Catholic. The great Erasmus had published such views in his *De sarcienda ecclesiae concordia* (1533); though in dogma he could talk virtual Lutheranism, he yet meant by faith the *fides formata* and adhered firmly to the interpretation of the Church as the superior order. As to justification, he spoke of two kinds of justness—the justness of faith and the justness of love; would not one complement the other? To many the formula appeared to be the proverbial egg of Columbus. It seemed to satisfy Protestant interests and yet prevent the dangers inherent in a neglect of good works. Did it not enable one to be evangelical and Catholic at the same time? Erasmus had many disciples of whom numbers occupied leading positions. Leading Catholics like Julius Pflug, Georg Witzel, Johannes Gropper listened to him. Konrad von Heresbach was chancellor to the duke of Cleves who in 1532 had introduced an almost reformed Church order without turning Protestant. Carlowitz, councillor to the duke of Saxony, was accessible to such ideas and had just (or so it seemed) opened a promising road in the course of a religious colloquy with Bucer. Even in Italy there was a party of reform which included the best of the cardinals and which responded to Erasmus's views.[1]

But before the road could be trod, it was once again necessary to create a political foundation. After their rejection of the council the Protestants reckoned upon war. Vice-chancellor Held, after his failure at Schmalkalden, had formed the Catholic League of Nuremberg and had thus added fresh material to the explosive danger of war. The Protestants were also concerned with the legal position of those allies who had joined their League only after the Peace of Nuremberg and were thus not protected by the religious truce. A number of processes were pending against them; Minden, an imperial city, lay under an interdict. These doubts would first have to be removed.

The emperor took his time with his preparations. When the Protestants assembled in a diet in February 1539, it looked as though the assembly would serve the preparation of war rather than peace. However, an imperial plenipotentiary appeared in the person of John of Weza, the exiled archbishop of Lund, and the emperor agreed to treat without a papal representative. The negotiations took much the same course as those of Schweinfurt and Nuremberg seven years earlier. The Protestants put forward very high demands and had to be told by Lund that he could not agree to demands whose acceptance would destroy the order of the Church, the decrees of imperial diets, and the proper administration of justice. He suggested a temporary truce for the strengthening of the peace and proposed a disputation in which the religious differences might be cleared up. Both sides had to display much patience before agreement became

[1] Below, p. 258.

possible; once again the Protestant demand that the peace should extend also to future members of the League caused the greatest difficulties. All the efforts finally resulted in the 'Frankfurt Interim' of 19 April 1539 which promised the Protestants security from attack for fifteen months from 1 May. The Peace of Nuremberg was to remain in force—for the existing followers of the Augsburg Confession even after the stated term and until the next diet. Processes pending were to be held over for the duration of the peace. On the other hand, the Protestants were not to accept new members into the League for fifteen months and were to stop secularisation. The date of 1 August was provisionally fixed for the disputation, to be held at Nuremberg; the Protestants refused to allow papal participation in it. They declared themselves ready to take part in negotiations for an aid against the Turks and to submit to the decisions of a general assembly on this point. The demands that the peace extend to all Protestants and that the League of Nuremberg should also abstain from recruiting during the peace were to be put before the emperor; should he reject them, the present treaty was to last only six months and should then again be replaced by the Peace of Nuremberg.

This was one of those treaties of which it matters more that they should have been concluded at all than what particulars they contain. The Protestants could count it a success that after their rejection of the council the emperor should have been prepared to deal with them at all. For the moment the danger of war had been removed. In this atmosphere it was possible to contemplate also negotiations over religion. There was, admittedly, sharp criticism from both sides. Bucer considered it treason to the gospel that the League had accepted the moratorium on expansion. The Catholics were angry; Aleander, then legate with Ferdinand, accused Lund of having taken Protestant bribes and interpreted the coming disputation, at which the pope was not to be represented, as the threat of a German national council. Rome attempted to prevent it and was soon demanding that the emperor should break off his policy of agreement. Though Charles, in fact, did not confirm the treaty, he adhered to its principles; not even the fact that the duchy of Saxony, hitherto faithfully Catholic, went over to Protestantism after the death of the duke on 17 April 1539 could affect him. In spite of all endeavours to the contrary, and in spite of some wobbling, he issued on 18 April 1540 his invitation to a disputation to be held at Speyer on 6 June.

Rome did its best to arrest the whole of this policy and did succeed in making sure that the pope was not excluded from the occasion, as the Protestants had demanded. The pope could hardly be expected to consent to the religious question being settled without him, and the Catholics could hardly desire this to happen. The Protestants, on the other hand, might well take part in a discussion, but they could not sacrifice their whole doctrine by submitting to a papal primacy. They felt entirely sure of their cause; the Wittenberg theologians, for instance, said that 'such a split pleased God, as far as they were concerned'. They were afraid of the search for a 'middle way', for there could be no change in a doctrine which was the true teaching of Christ, even if the 'worldly wise' failed to understand this. They could see only the hope of a 'worldly, passable peace' of the kind which might be maintained with people of an alien faith. The Church's unity could not be obtained because the Protestants would not recognise the pope's spiritual power while the other side would not abandon this recognition. Wittenberg at least was from the beginning clear-sighted about the hopelessness of the new way.

Because of the plague, the disputation was transferred from Speyer to Hagenau. The pope sent a nuncio, Morone, who was to take no part in the disputation but was to advise the Catholic disputants. Matters did not get beyond the preliminaries, and the disputation proper was adjourned to a new meeting at Worms for which at least the procedural details were fixed. The Protestants now agreed that a papal legate might take part, as long as this was not interpreted as recognition of the papal headship. The situation had thus altered to this extent that these disputations could no longer look like a national council.

At Worms a papal legate did in fact appear. He was under orders to guard the authority of the Church and reserve papal sanction with respect to all proposals of settlement. The Protestants were under orders to make no concessions and not to recognise the papal power under any circumstances. The preliminaries again took much time: the Catholics were determined to see that voting methods should not work to their disadvantage and wished to have strict limits placed on freedom of speech. Their whole behaviour demonstrates clearly a lack of interest in the whole business. Granvelle, who as the emperor's minister conducted the negotiations, lost all hope and asked Charles for another adjournment. There were only three days of genuine disputation during which both sides agreed on an acceptable formula concerning original sin. The real successes, however, remained a secret of the participants. Johannes Gropper, of Cologne, and the imperial secretary Veltwyk held secret discussions on doctrine with Bucer and Capito, and the two sides came together in the doctrine of double justification outlined above. Bucer did not, of course, intend to sacrifice evangelical doctrine, but he thought himself bound to agree so as to preserve some hope of unity and avoid a religious war. The outcome of these negotiations was put on paper and could now serve as a basis for the further negotiations which were to be resumed at the Diet of Regensburg in 1541.

In the meanwhile Granvelle was making propaganda for the Worms agreement. Luther received a copy from the elector of Brandenburg and came to the conclusion that the authors had meant well but had made impossible proposals to which neither the pope nor the Protestants could agree. The Saxon elector realised that the other side would first demand recognition of the pope and might be able to give way on details for the sake of this prize. At best one could hope for no more than an outward and stable peace.

The emperor himself was present at Regensburg. On his motion, the diet entrusted a committee of theologians with the theological negotiations for union: Melanchthon, Bucer, and the Hessian Pistorius among the Protestants, and Pflug, Eck, and Gropper among the Catholics. The pope had sent a legate, Cardinal Contarini, to whom the Catholic participants reported daily before and after meetings and whose discretion kept Eck within bounds. The basis was not, as the Protestants had wished, the Augsburg Confession but the Worms Agreement whose text was read out to the parties section by section, though few changes were made in it. Yet at first progress was relatively swift; on 2 May the battle seemed won since, contrary to all expectations, the two sides had found a common formula on justification, even Eck and Calvin, who had come from Strassburg, agreeing with it; the emperor saw God's hand in this. But the negotiations over the mass quickly ended the unity; views on confession, absolution and satisfaction, Church and Church government, remained irreconcilable. In the end, all that could be produced was a set of articles on which agreement had been reached and a long list of points on which it had proved impossible. What was to happen now? Since some people thought Luther more likely to see sense, the elector of Brandenburg sent him an embassy to ask whether he would not admit or at least tolerate for a time the articles put forward by the Catholics. His answer was disappointing: he stood by Melanchthon's articles and would suffer the other views only in so far as they left evangelical teaching 'in its purity'. Even Philip of Hesse, of all the Protestants the man most concerned to secure agreement, came out against further concessions. On the other side the Catholics criticised the emperor's book and maintained that unity was not to be obtained. The estates could offer nothing better than further discussions and, should these remain without result, once again the general council. The emperor decided to hand the whole business over to the legate and to treat with him. But Contarini, as was to be expected, referred him to a decision of the Apostolic See which would do, either in a prospective general council or in other ways, what was best for the Church and the German nation. At the same time he addressed an urgent warning to the German bishops and called them to a reform of morals in the Catholic spirit.

This exhausted the possibilities; even the emperor could see no way now except to refer things to a council. If this latter were to be further delayed, a general imperial assembly would have to take things in hand. The Protestants immediately reminded him of their earlier objections to a council which they had already once refused to attend. The final decree of the diet did indeed once again appeal to the council which, it was said, the legate had promised for the near future and for which the emperor was to continue to strive. If this hope should fail, there would remain nothing but a national council or another imperial diet. In the meantime the prelates were 'to take order and reform' so as to bring about 'a good and healthful administration, as well as ultimate concord'. As was to be expected, the legate at once protested against the national council which had thus been shown to be still possible. The Peace of Nuremberg was confirmed till the end of the general council, and lawsuits remained suspended for the same time, despite Catholic protests. The official decree had to be supplemented by two imperial declarations. Agreed decisions had become impossible. Was it even possible still to govern the empire whose machinery, clumsy enough at the best of times, had been virtually brought to a standstill by the religious schism?

The great glory of the diet—agreement on the doctrine of justification—soon proved a sham. The elector of Saxony smelled treason because *sola fide* had not been mentioned. Luther and Bugenhagen called the Regensburg article 'a thing of vagaries and patches'. Contarini could not even obtain the consent of his Italian friends. Carafa would only admit that the declaration could be read in a Catholic sense. The consistory of 27 May held that it would be better to leave the Germans in error than to make concessions to them contrary to the dignity of religion. The official reply sent to the cardinal only remarked that, since the negotiations had come to no positive end, it was not opportune to speak of these matters. Contarini was soon defending himself against charges of heresy. Later, the Council of Trent most sharply rejected the doctrine of two kinds of justness and thus abolished even this last small basis for unity.

Unquestionably the emperor was serious about his attempts to mediate. He spared no effort at Regensburg to secure success. That he failed must have been deeply disappointing to him. It is to be supposed that from that moment he began to doubt whether Germany could be brought together by peaceful means, though admittedly there is no word of his on record on this point. But to what conclusions would further thought bring him? From the treaties with Philip of Hesse (to be dealt with in a moment) and Joachim II of Brandenburg, it may be deduced that he was getting ready for the use of force which the dukes of Bavaria and Brunswick and the Roman curia had long held to be the only possible and promising way. The idea of an external peace and mutual toleration, which appears repeatedly in writings from Wittenberg at this time, could find no response in a man of Charles V's stamp.

One success the emperor could register without doing anything towards it—the treaty with Hesse just referred to. The business is one of the least pleasant to be recorded in that wild age. The landgrave, the most active leader of the Protestants, was also possessed of quite irresistible sexual passions. As a result of his excesses he suffered an illness which in 1539 led to a physical collapse. Unable to believe himself capable of marital loyalty, he desired a second lasting liaison. The lady of his choice, a lady-in-waiting with his sister, stood under the protection of a very formidable mother who did not intend that her daughter should become a prince's concubine but would, if necessary, be content with a bigamous marriage if learned opinion thought this permissible. Bucer, in any case Philip's confidential adviser, was ordered to collect the necessary opinions. Luther was left with the impression that the prince's troubled conscience was seeking a way out; furthermore, Philip quoted the Old Testament and occasional remarks of Luther's which seemed to leave this particular way open. He would have liked Luther to come out publicly for this solution, but in any case he wanted something in writing. Luther refused to be impressed by some gentle hints of political threats, but he was the more impressed by Philip's conscientious troubles. In the event, he gave him something like an episcopal dispensation, but demanded that it be kept secret so as to avoid offence. Luther had no intention of introducing a new order after the Anabaptist fashion; he only wished to offer a sort of absolution in an exceptional case. With the consent of the true princess the marriage was celebrated, Melanchthon being one of the guests. Of course, the affair could not be kept secret. The prince now feared the emperor's wrath, for the imperial criminal code of Charles V, which Philip had himself proclaimed, punished bigamy very severely; he therefore demanded that Luther should defend him in public. This Luther refused to do, not because he would not stand by his opinion—there were, he frankly told his elector, cases known to every confessor in which appeal to the general order was of no avail—but because such publication would not help Philip. A confessor's dispensation could not make public law. The confessor could only say what was right in the eyes of God, but public law nevertheless remained law, and a man who followed his confessor's advice must be ready to suffer the consequences in the world. In addition Luther had to hear from the prince's political friends that they did not believe in the troubles of the princely conscience: if he had appealed to his conscientious scruples he would presumably have excited only general ridicule. I cannot agree that Luther here stained his good name or acted wrongly as a theologian. The landgrave, however, now sought security from the emperor. Negotiations were proceeding even during the Worms colloquy, and they concluded at Regensburg in the treaty already mentioned. This made the landgrave in effect the emperor's ally: he gave up all alliances with non-German powers and prevented the admission to the Schmalkaldic League of the duke of Cleves, the emperor's enemy. In return he received an imperial pardon for everything he had so far done against the realm and its constitution, 'excepting always if for religion's sake a general war were to be moved against all Protestants'.

The landgrave kept his promise, thus still further impeding the allies' power to act; nevertheless he was far from giving up either his Protestant faith or the Reformation in Hesse.

In the electorate of Cologne, on the other hand, the Regensburg Diet led to a new attempt at Reformation. Hermann von Wied, archbishop and elector, had already judged from the Münster affair that only a serious reformation could prevent similar happenings in the future. His first attempt, supported theologically by Gropper, did not succeed. Now, relying on the diet's decree, the elector called Bucer to preach in his capital Bonn: Cologne was an imperial city and in any case, as was customary, opposed to the episcopal ruler. Melanchthon came as well to assist in reorganising the Church. However, the bishop now found himself energetically opposed by Gropper, hitherto his adviser, and the clergy of Cologne. The writings which were exchanged demonstrated a new method in polemics. The Cologne clergy would have nothing to do with the disputation demanded by Bucer but refused to allow any doubts as to fundamental teaching of the Catholic Church on the pope and the hierarchy. Bucer, being an enemy to the hierarchy who had offended against their order, they considered a heretic who was to be dealt with not by disputation but by expulsion. Although the elector had the support of his estates, the opposition obtained their ends. The emperor stood behind them, and when the pope excommunicated the archbishop, who could get no active assistance from the Schmalkaldic League, Hermann had to leave his lands and died a few years later as a private person in the little principality of Wied. This was the first great defeat suffered by the evangelical cause in the Empire; many things now began to press for a violent solution.

However, few things in this age of the Reformation are more difficult to disentangle than the road which finally led Charles V to war. After Regensburg the emperor had gone to Italy and met the pope at Lucca. The results were encouraging: the pope promised to hold the council but was as doubtful as ever about the practical possibilities. The Turkish war in Hungary and an expedition against the infidel in Algiers failed miserably. Thereafter the emperor was busy in Spain; for two years problems of his Iberian kingdoms delayed his return to Germany. A diet held at Speyer in the spring of 1542 only served once more to reveal the difficulties of the situation: once again, all that could be obtained was a general decree accompanied by two additional declarations. In the same year the war with France reopened; the Netherlands were attacked through Guelders, occupied since the death of its last duke by Cleves. But when Charles returned to Germany in the spring of 1543 he came with troops, and Duke William of Cleves was overcome in one brief campaign. This victory ended all attempts at a reformation in Cleves; the duke was bound firmly to the Catholic party and Guelders became part of the Netherlands. The emperor seems to have been somewhat surprised to find force so effective as a political weapon. He then had to turn to the problem of France. The campaign was interrupted by a second diet at Speyer at which he secured aid against France and the Turks even from the Protestant estates. His relations with the pope, who supported France, were so bad that it was agreed to put before the next diet 'a Christian Reformation'—that is to say, the German national council was assuming reality. The emperor entirely abandoned his earlier attitude on this point; both Luther and Calvin at this time defended him against the pope's attacks. In the ensuing campaign he penetrated deep into France; the Peace of Crespy acknowledged him victor and gave him not only a French promise to attend the council but a secret undertaking on the part of France to assist him against the German Protestants.

At last, then, the general council could really take place; the pope summoned it to Trent for 15 March 1545. Before then, however, the German diet had to meet again, and by the promise of Speyer it was supposed to turn into a German national council. However, since the general council had now been called, the emperor seemed free of that promise, provided the Protestants recognised the papal council. Not only were they not prepared to do so; they even made all their concessions at the diet depend on a guarantee of peace without the council. The imperial machine had virtually stopped because the Protestants proved immovable. In this situation, conversations between the emperor and the papal legate seem to have given birth to the idea of war; the legate not only promised papal aid but immediately returned to Rome to secure firm promises. Armies were at once raised in Italy.

Yet once again Charles hesitated: he did not want war that year. The Diet of Worms ended with the prospect of another religious disputation and the decision postponed to the next diet. The negotiations with the pope took their time, and the council at Trent (where the assembled prelates were beginning to show signs of impatience) could not be opened while the final decision was awaited. At the next diet, again at Regensburg, the disputation once more came to nothing; thereafter the imperial formalities were but a cover for the real events. The pope came to terms; the Bavarians overcame dynastic enmities in favour of religious sympathies; and at last it proved possible to bind some Protestant princes by treaties to the emperor—Duke Maurice of Saxony, the son-in-law of Philip of Hesse, and the Margrave Alcibiades of Brandenburg-Culmbach. These young princes no longer thought the religious point of view all-important. The emperor tried to present the coming war in the light of purely political issues, but he deceived no one and is unlikely to have expected belief. Although the Schmalkaldic League was rotten with internal difficulties, it yet proved its worth in the hour of need: its leaders managed to raise an army of their own in much less time than had been thought possible. The decision rested with the weapons of war.

Luther died at Eisleben in the night of 17–18 February 1546, before the outbreak of war. He was there to arbitrate in a quarrel of his territorial rulers, the counts of Mansfeld; till his last hours his mind was busy with the Council of Trent which appeared to him as the real danger to the faith.

The history of the Schmalkaldic War is described elsewhere.[1] Like, apparently, the history of most wars, it is a story of unbelievable mistakes on both sides. It left the emperor the uncontested victor: the two leaders of the League, the elector of Saxony and the landgrave of Hesse, were prisoners in his hands. The elector was tried by an imperial court and sentenced to death, but even so he would not recognise the council; in the end the emperor contented himself with a promise that in future he would obey imperial decrees.

But victory in war did not provide the solution to the problem and the Council of Trent was no congress of peace. On the contrary, it called forth a series of new difficulties. In the middle of the war, the pope had deserted the emperor. Against Charles's desires, the council first turned its attention to dogma instead of Church reform, thus destroying from the start all hope of reunion. It was soon held among the emperor's men that this council under the tyrannic rule of papal legates was doing more harm than Luther had done: it seemed hard to believe that this mean-spirited assembly met under the guidance of the Holy Ghost. In the spring of 1547, against all the emperor's protests, the council was adjourned to Bologna and then provisionally suspended. Thus at the Diet of Augsburg (September 1547 to June 1548) it proved impossible simply to refer the Protestants to the council; the unity of faith was after all attempted by an imperial act, the 'Interim', which met the Protestant demands in minor matters, produced cautiously Catholic definitions on dogmatically difficult points, but was to serve as a bridge for the return to the fold and therefore stressed inessentials. Difficulties arose at once. The Catholics would not recognise it, nor would the Protestant Duke Maurice whose territory now included Wittenberg; supported by Melanchthon, he produced a modified form, the 'Leipzig Interim' which Melanchthon thought tolerable because it did not touch doctrine but only demanded a return to Catholic cere- monies held to be *adiaphora*. In the whole of North Germany, where the emperor's military power did not extend, resistance remained strong. The theological opponents assembled in Magdeburg—'the chancellery of our Lord'—and Maurice was ordered to carry out the imperial ban against the town; thus he kept his army in the field. In the south, too, it proved easier to proclaim the Interim than to enforce it. The preachers had to give way; Bucer went to England, Brenz into hiding, others were arrested. But the congregations had no love for the Catholic priests; naturally

[1] Below, pp. 355f.

enough, it was not the best spirits that pressed forward now, and the authorities did nothing to help them. The rules were evaded in every possible way. In this crisis it became clear that even where the Reformation had been imposed from above the gospel had been received and taken root among the people; it could no longer be torn out by a mere command and by acts of force.

On the other hand, the theological controversies among the successors of Luther revealed a deep flaw. Melanchthon became the target of violent attacks, at first because he had agreed to the Leipzig Interim and later for other reasons, too. The trouble was his doctrine of the relation between faith and works and his doctrine of free will. Soon, violent troubles started round the person and the theology of Andreas Osiander from Nuremberg who had taken refuge in the duchy of Prussia where he preached differently from colleagues trained under Melanchthon; here the problem concerned the presence of Christ in or among the faithful. More bitter than the strife between Luther and the Swiss was this new struggle between the school of Melanchthon and the 'Gnesiolutherans' led by the learned Flacius. Necessarily, they would soon touch again on the problem of the eucharist. More, however, was involved than an argument among theologians. It was true that Melanchthon, working side by side with Luther and endeavouring to provide a firm doctrine for the Reformation, had entered upon a road which imperceptibly but with growing certainty was leaving Luther's teaching. Trying to found God's grace as objectively as possible in the acts of God, he restored room for the subjective acquisition of an objective grace. Thus he made possible an understanding not only with Erasmus's teaching, which he had defended in Wittenberg as early as 1535, but also with the Swiss; but in the process he lost Luther's original starting point. While Luther lived, his authority protected Melanchthon, even though the latter—as he related, rather unpleasantly, in a letter written to Carlowitz after Mühlberg—suffered from the pressure of the greater man. In the point that mattered the Gnesiolutherans were admittedly as much Melanchthon's pupils as his opponents; they felt the problem but had neither the strength nor the insight to seize the root of the trouble and protested only on details. For this reason the controversies of those troublesome years create an impression of *rabies theologorum*: even where the right lines were seen, the ability to make the difference plain was lacking, so that the causes of disagreement never became understood.

On 1 May 1551 the emperor's urging succeeded in getting the council reopened. The Protestants could not now escape their duty of attendance. Melanchthon in Saxony and Johannes Brenz in Württemberg composed Confessions for the purpose; others joined either. But the appearance of Protestant envoys at Trent showed up the impossibility of the emperor's policy of councils: the council could not admit long-condemned heretics as negotiating participants, nor could it suspend its earlier decisions. Prolonged efforts by the imperial representatives obtained only permission for them to hand over their Confessions. There were no discussions among the theologians, even though Brenz was in Trent as his duke's ambassador. The Saxon theologians were stopped at Nuremberg. The council proved to be but an instrument of the Catholic Church, not an instrument for the composing of differences. It was the end of the emperor's policy of relying on councils—the end, in fact, of all attempts at unity.

The decision came in a different and violent manner, through the uprising of the Protestant princes, prepared by Duke Maurice of Saxony with cunning and lack of scruple. Their motives were not in the main religious; the rebels were concerned with preserving German liberties— the princes' liberties against the emperor—rather than with religion. Their manner of proceeding, in particular, was not hampered by Lutheran scruples but by political considerations. French support was bought by the surrender of imperial territory—the bishoprics of Metz, Toul and Verdun. Not surprisingly, therefore, not only the emperor's sister, the regent of the Netherlands, but also that good Lutheran, Duke Christopher of Württemberg, warned the emperor of what was coming. But the rebellion succeeded, at first in the Treaty of Passau, concluded on 2 August 1552 after difficult negotiations.[1] Since neither the council nor the diet had been able to solve the religious question, Maurice demanded an outward and enduring peace, though the emperor, on grounds of conscience, would only grant it till the next diet. The danger over, he tried in vain to recover Metz which the French had occupied. The disappointment of defeat, the hopelessness of the situation, inclined even him to peace, though he would not make it himself. Thus he handed over the rule of the Empire to Ferdinand who at the next diet in Augsburg agreed to the so-called Religious Peace of Augsburg. The decree of this diet, delivered on 25 September 1555, for the time being granted recognition in imperial law to the Augsburg Confession, side by side with the Catholic faith; explicit provision was, however, made for further endeavours to restore unity. Since no better solution was ever found, this peace became in fact the basis of the new age. Not the council nor the emperor had ended the struggle, but the diet; the decision was neither religious nor theological but political. There began a period of peace, while the religious wars reached their climax in France, the Netherlands and England; but it was also a time when politics dominated religion, a time that testified to resignation rather than to faith.

[1] Cf. also below, p. 357.

2. POLAND, HUNGARY AND BOHEMIA

NOT the least notable successes of the Protestant Reformation of the sixteenth century were scored in the three kingdoms which constituted the eastern frontier-land of the Latin Church: Poland, Hungary and Bohemia. The historical interest of the fortunes of the Reformation in these lands is due largely to the peculiar form given to its manifestation east of Germany by those political, social and economic characteristics which distinguished this area from western Europe. For whereas in Germany, the Netherlands, France and Britain we can observe the impact of reformative ideas on societies which were already enjoying the benefits of strong monarchy, where aristocratic separatism had already been largely defeated, where commerce and the towns were increasingly potent, and where society was no longer based on an adscript, service-rendering peasantry, in the countries east of the Elbe, the Böhmerwald and the Leitha we can watch the impact of the Reformation on a society where kings were weak and noble landlords strong, where medieval parliaments were still dominant, where the towns were relatively few, small and impotent, and where serfdom was being ever more widely and severely established and legalised. The western Slavs and the Magyars had ever since their admission into Christendom constantly been stimulated by the importation of techniques, art forms, institutions, ideas and persons from the earlier developed societies of Germany, Italy and France, and had given to them a character that was peculiarly Polish or Czech or Magyar. That process of importation and modification was in the sixteenth century applied to the principles and practices of the religious reformers of Wittenberg and Geneva.

The Church in Poland was at the beginning of the sixteenth century as ripe for reformation as any in Europe. The good relations between Poland and the Papacy which had subsisted from the eleventh to the fourteenth century had become strained by the consistent support given by the Papacy to Poland's rival, the Teutonic Knights. Not till 1505, when Julius II counselled the grand master to take the oath of allegiance to Alexander, king of Poland, was this feeling of tension relaxed. The Polish kings, too, had been engaged in a struggle with the Papacy over the higher patronage in the Polish Church, the outcome of which was that, though the primate, the archbishop of Gniezno, was provided by the curia, the bishops and the greater abbots were elected on royal recommendation, usually to the damage of the reputation of the Church for piety and virtue.

During the conciliar period Polish churchmen had been among the leading exponents of the theory and practice of conciliar sovereignty, had been almost the sole supporters of Hus at Constance, had remained faithful to the Council of Basle to the end, and had learned the habit of criticising the government and practice of the Papacy. Reformist sentiment, particularly in the theological faculty of the university of Cracow, continued throughout the fifteenth century and survived to provide a seed plot for Erasmian ideas in the sixteenth. The prescription by Martin V and the Council of Basle for regular provincial and diocesan synods had borne fruit in Poland: Polish canon law and capitular statutes had been codified and clerical abuses such as drunkenness, concubinage, dancing, dicing, taverning, absenteeism, and the forcing of ill-paid vicars to supplement their pittances by engaging in such unsuitable occupations as inn-keeping, had all been revealed and condemned, but not eradicated, by frequent synods. As elsewhere in Europe, the Polish prelates of the early sixteenth century were as likely to be saints and scholars as worldly cynics. The prelates, regular as well as secular, were of noble birth: in 1515 Leo X accepted a request of the Polish parliament that no one should be admitted as canon or prebendary who was not *ex utroque parente nobilis*, a principle which the parliament confirmed in 1538, adding abbots and priors to the list. Religious houses, which had greatly increased in number and wealth in the fifteenth century, were infected by the epidemic diseases of worldliness, concern for property, failure of religious enthusiasm, love of ease, and obscurantism. Humanism passed the Polish cloister by. The parish clergy, most of them nominees of the local landlord or town council, were often but indifferent shepherds of souls, ignorant, negligent, poor, and socially inferior. Since 1406 the episcopal courts had secured the recognition by the State of their exclusive jurisdiction over the delicts of clerics and offences against clerics, as well as in all matters of marriage, dower, probate, contract, if confirmed by oath, and heresy. This wide and indiscriminate ecclesiastical jurisdiction was particularly galling to the nobles and gentry who, even though the prelates were their brothers and cousins by birth, found the Church courts an obstacle to their acquisition of Church property, a constant interference with their freedom of conduct and belief, and an insult to their aristocratic independence.

The ecclesiastical position of Poland on the eve of the Reformation differed fundamentally from that of the states of western Christendom in that Poland harboured schism within its borders before ever the New Religion arrived. Not only was the Ruthenian population of Galicia still predominantly Orthodox, but the Russian inhabitants of the grand principality of Lithuania even more firmly still maintained their Orthodox faith and Slavonic liturgy. The efforts of the Jagiellon rulers of Poland and Lithuania to establish and support the Greek Catholic Church which had been born of the Union of Florence in 1439 had ultimately failed. Thus during the great struggles of Protestant and Catholic the majority of the people of Lithuania acknowledged the Orthodox metropolitan of Kiev as their head and the majority of the Ruthenes the Orthodox bishops of

Galicia. The Roman Catholic archbishop of Lvov exercised authority over a minority of immigrant mendicants, landlords and burgesses.

The state of religion and the Church in Hungary at the beginning of the sixteenth century was similar to that in Poland, though the greater feebleness of the Jagiellon kings of Hungary, Vladislav (Ulászló) and his successor Lewis (Lajos) II, and the consequent greater power of the Hungarian magnates and prelates made the Hungarian Church more worldly and political even than the Polish Church. Its Angevin kings, Charles Robert and Lewis I, and more recently its native rulers, John Hunyadi and his son Matthias Corvinus, though they had failed to destroy the political and economic power of the nobles, had reduced the Hungarian Church to the condition of a department of state, a condition which continued even when Corvinus was succeeded as king by Vladislav 'Very Well' in 1490 and he by his young son Lewis II in 1516. The wearer of the crown of St Stephen claimed to have inherited those apostolic and legatine rights which tradition said had been conferred on the first Hungarian king by Sylvester II in the year 1000. The strong kings of Hungary of their own motion, and the weaker kings at the behest of their all-powerful magnate councillors, therefore nominated archbishops, bishops, capitular clergy and the abbots and priors of royal foundations, and the pope was content merely, and often belatedly, to confirm the royal appointments. The possession of this royal patronage at a time when the Hungarian monarchy was as weak as it was at the beginning of the sixteenth century meant that the Hungarian prelacy was the private property of the few great families which controlled the Crown and monopolised the Church. Few humbly-born Wolseys or Cranmers occupied the rich sees of Hungary when they were assailed by Turks and Lutherans. The same families which provided the prelates in person also, together with the other nobles and gentry, nominated as patrons the main body of the secular clergy. Only in the towns, where patronage was owned by the town council, was any part of the Hungarian clergy not the nominees of the nobility. In these circumstances it is not surprising that the Church in Hungary showed little of that activating piety, virtue and learning which might have made it able to survive intact the simultaneous impact of Turkish invasion, Protestant incursion and civil war.

Like Sigismund of Poland, King Lewis II had many subjects of the Orthodox faith: in Transylvania, the Vlach shepherds preserved with their Romance language their Orthodox faith and institutions and the Slavonic rite; in the Bánát and in the Bácska lived a growing number of South Slavs, chiefly Serbian in speech, but all Orthodox in faith and practice.

The position of Bohemia on the eve of the Reformation was unique. Most of its inhabitants accepted a faith and practised a religion which the Church condemned as heretical; they were members of the Hussite national

Church which was undoubtedly schismatical. During the century of its existence Hussitism had established itself as the religion of most of the peasants, farmers, gentry and townsfolk of Bohemia; the Catholic minority was composed largely of magnates and their dependants and of the German-speaking inhabitants of the towns and villages of the frontier districts. The Hussites did not differ from the Church profoundly in doctrine or practice. There was in fact only one serious obstacle to reunion: the Hussite claim that the chalice should be given to laymen at the eucharist. Even this they believed was not a doctrinal matter, but merely one of use; they were merely asking the Church to forego a custom which had been only comparatively recently introduced and to permit a return to a practice which, as pope and councils had admitted, had been that of Christ and his apostles and of the early Church. But the councils of Constance and Basle (the latter after some havering) and, in 1462, Pope Pius II had pronounced communion of the laity *sub utraque specie* an heretical practice, for the Church, as well as the more realistic Utraquists, knew well that something more than liturgical use was in question. The Hussites maintained that the cup for the laity was not merely beneficial and preferable, but *de precepto divino* and therefore necessary for salvation; that is why they gave it to infants immediately after baptism. Therefore what made Utraquism the basis of a schism which lasted from 1415 to 1620 was that the Utraquists denied that the authority of the Church as expressed in papal or conciliar decrees could override the authority of the scriptures. Thus the Czechs had raised the fundamental issue of authority long before Luther challenged the Church's right to sell indulgences. The services in the Hussite churches had been greatly simplified; vestments were less ornate, and few sacred pictures and images had survived the iconoclasm of the earlier, more enthusiastic years; the vernacular was largely employed in the pulpit and at the altar; Hus and his fellow martyr Jerome of Prague were commemorated as saints; the scriptures had been translated and were widely read, and there was a great wealth of hymns in the vernacular which were sung at public and private worship. But while it is true that the pre-Reformation Hussite Church had a 'Protestant' appearance, it is also true that doctrinally it was conservative. Despite some radical aberrations in the earlier 'Taborite' period, the Utraquists had continued to accept the teaching of the Church about transubstantiation and all the seven sacraments. Though they had destroyed many crucifixes and many pictures of the Virgin, they did not deny honour to her or to the saints. They did not deny the efficacy of good works; their christology and soteriology were perfectly orthodox; and they maintained the celibacy of the clergy. The Hussites were divided about one fundamental question: there was a conservative right wing which sought for speedy reunion with the Church on the sole condition of the concession of the privilege of communion in both kinds for the laity; but the majority, both of the clergy and laity, proud of what had been achieved, believing that they were chosen by God to lead the world back to the acceptance of a scriptural, uncorrupted, moral and popular Christianity, proved amid the storms of the sixteenth century fundamentally unwilling to surrender the ecclesiastical and political independence of what had become in fact a national Church.

The Hussite Church comprised nearly all those subjects of the Bohemian king who received the communion in both kinds; its clergy were those who so administered it. Most of the parish churches were occupied by Utraquist priests, who were provided with modest salaries but who received no fees. In the countryside the incumbents were usually the nominees of the local landlord; in Prague and the other royal towns they were either elected by their parishioners or nominated by the magistrates. The ordination of priests still proved a difficult problem; the Hussites were anxious to maintain the principle of episcopal ordination; they wanted a canonically consecrated archbishop of their own, but the Church had refused to give them one. The Hussites therefore had to get their candidates ordained where they could and had had recourse to the compliance of the archbishops of Venice or other Catholic prelates who were not over-careful to conform to papal policy in this matter. In default of an archbishop of Prague (the see remained vacant from 1431 to 1561) the government of the Hussite Church was in the hands of two administrators and a consistory, both nominated by the estates. Ultimately sovereignty in the Utraquist Church resided in the lay and not exclusively Utraquist estates, though important questions of faith and morals were usually discussed and often decided in occasional assemblies of the clergy and university masters.

The secular head of this schismatic Church was, since 1471, a Catholic king who had sworn at his election to maintain the 'Compactata' of 1436 which enshrined the liberties of the Hussite community. The Catholic Jagiellon kings, Vladislav and Lewis, were not zealous to coerce the Hussites, but they permitted some recovery of the Catholic Church; in particular many of the magnates, who in fact governed the country between 1471 and 1526, were Catholics or had reverted to Catholicism. The other strongly Catholic element was the German population of the border areas and of towns with a predominantly German population. In the first generation of Hussitism the Church had been robbed of nearly all its landed property; the estates of the bishoprics and of the monasteries had been seized not only by Hussite lords and gentry and the Hussite towns, but also by King Sigismund who had used them to purchase the support of those nobles and towns which remained faithful to him and the Church. During the years 1419 to 1434, all monastic houses had been despoiled of their property, most of them had been demolished or burnt to the ground; the monks and nuns had been expelled; many of them had been killed. But during the short period, 1436 to 1439, when the Catholic kings Sigismund and Albert had reigned, and during the long period of Jagiellon rule, something had been done to restore the Catholic Church in the country. The chapter of the archiepiscopal see of St Vitus and its administrator were recognised by king and pope as the supreme Catholic authority in the kingdom, though the Catholic administrator was often absent in Catholic Plzeň (Pilsen) or at the king's other court in Buda. A miserable fragment of their former property was restored to cathedral chapters, and half a score monasteries were reconstituted, but the number of the monks and nuns in them was small and they, like the chapters, were kept poor by the unwillingness of the new owners of Church lands, Catholic almost as much as Hussite, to surrender their loot.

It is notorious that schism breeds schism. In its earlier years the Hussite movement had been fecund of sects within itself: Taborites, Horebites, 'Orphans', Adamites and 'Pikharti'. But the more conservative, middle-class faction of the 'Praguers' or 'Calixtines' had destroyed or absorbed most of these sectarian groups, except for the last, the 'Unitas Fratrum', which had survived persecution by Catholic and Hussite rulers alike and in the early sixteenth century was, though a small minority of the nation, a vigorous and important element in the national religious life. The Church of the Brethren preserved the most radical and democratic elements in earlier Hussitism: its scriptural theology, its puritanical and evangelical practice, its democratic government by autonomous congregations occasionally collected in general assemblies of the whole communion, where the faith was defined, policy determined, and the 'bishops' or 'seniors', the priests, deacons and deaconesses, and the executive or 'narrow council' were elected. A movement which had been at first one of artisans and small farmers had been steadily broadening its social basis and now counted a number of the well-to-do and influential lords among its members. This development had only become possible because in the last decade of the fifteenth century the Brethren had by a large majority discarded the pacifism, the condemnation of war, capital punishment and service on juries and as magistrates, which they had learnt from Peter Chelčický at their first formation. Under the statesmanlike leadership of their 'senior', Brother Lukáš, the Church of the Brethren was well prepared to play a vigorous part in the Reformation not only of Bohemia, but of Poland also.

Any student of the beginnings of the Reformation in central Europe must ask the question of how far the ground had been prepared by the advent of Hussites and Hussite ideas to the neighbours of Bohemia. It is fashionable today, particularly among Czech Marxist historians, to ascribe great influence to Hussitism, particularly in Poland, Hungary and Roumania. It was certainly considerable in Germany and northern Hungary, and appreciable in Poland and Moldavia. But when every scrap of evidence has been assembled there seems hardly enough to make it possible to say with assurance that either Poland or Hungary had been so much affected with Hussitism as to make them much more susceptible to Protestant ideas than they would have been had there been no Hussite schism. There is virtually no evidence at all of Hussite influence abroad during the fifty years before the coming of the Reformation.

A more influential factor than the dissemination of Hussitism in facilitating the reception of the Reformation in Poland and Hungary was humanism. It had come to Bohemia as well, but there it was a matter of a few individual men of letters, usually of noble birth, for the Charles University of Prague did not provide a centre for the new learning as did the university of Cracow; nor did the royal court in Prague, for since the union of the Bohemian and Hungarian Crowns in 1490 the king usually kept his court in Buda. This court of Vladislav and Lewis II in Hungary not only had preserved some of the Renaissance culture that had been imported by Matthias Corvinus, but it was in lively contact with Germany, especially after the marriage of Lewis to Mary of Habsburg. Some of the enquiring spirit of German humanists was communicated to Hungary by the visits or residence of German lords, knights and men of letters. Hungarians were already in correspondence with Erasmus. It was much the same in Poland, where the university of Cracow and the court of Sigismund I, and even the cathedral chapter, welcomed and fostered the new learning. German, Swiss and Italian humanists (for example, Buonacorsi) visited Cracow. There were humanist Polish prelates such as Grzegorz of Sanok, archbishop of Lvov, and humanist Polish nobles like Jan Ostroróg. Queen Bona's chaplain, the Italian Franciscan Lismanini, conducted a circle of enquirers in Jan Trzecieski's household; Jakub Uchański, later to be archbishop of Gniezno, was a member of it. Many Polish nobles and many of the German merchants of the Polish towns sent their sons to be educated in German and Italian universities.

Visiting Germans and returning natives early brought news of Luther's doings to Poland and Hungary. Merchants, students, ambassadors, courtiers and travelling booksellers began to spread the exciting news from Wittenberg and Worms in the districts nearest to Germany and Austria, and by the time Luther was safely ensconced in the Wartburg Lutheran arguments and practices were being repeated from Danzig and Cracow, from Sopron (Ödenburg) and Buda, from mining towns in Slovakia and the German towns of Transylvania. Here and there, particularly in the towns, a parish priest would begin to preach in the vernacular doctrines which smacked of reform. Every such expression of criticism or demand for reform was named 'Lutheran' by the scared and offended prelates and princes, but that does not mean that these reformers of the first decade either deemed themselves or were thought by their hearers to be avowed disciples of Luther. Many preachers and congregations slipped into reformist opinions and practices without realising that they were drifting away from the Church and with no conscious desire to identify themselves with the Wittenberg heretic. It was the authorities of State and Church who branded every critic with the opprobrious name and thereby made the progress of Lutheranism appear more rapid and widespread than it was, and in so doing probably drove many who would have been content to try to reform the Church from within into a schism which they at first abhorred. Certainly for many years in both Hungary and Poland there were many laymen, like the Palatine Tamás Nádasdy and the Polish royal secretary Frycz Modrzewski, and many prelates and parsons, who remained champions of reform in an Erasmian sense without ever leaving the Church; and many parishes also, particularly in northern Hungary, which, though openly Lutheran in faith and practice, long paid tithe to and recognised the ecclesiastical authority of the Catholic prelates. There was no catastrophic and deliberate mass secession from the Church in either country. What we observe is that here and there a parish priest will begin to use the pulpit more and more for expounding current concepts about the necessity for repentance as well as penance, about venerating rather than worshipping the Virgin and her image, about duty to the living being more important than devotion to dead saints, about fasting not being an end in itself. Such casual and uncoordinated reformist preaching was increasingly accompanied by such innovations in practice as the simplification of vestments, the use of vernacular hymns and the deliberate breach of Friday and Lenten fasts. Typical of this early stage was the situation at Nagyszeben (Hermannstadt) in 1526 as described in a letter written by the chapter of that town to Archbishop László Szalkai of Esztergom:

In the city of Szeben...a certain schoolmaster has set up a school where the Nicene creed is sung in German as are other cantilenae related to the mass and the divine office....Ecclesiastical jurisdiction is almost completely destroyed, for almost all spurn the courts, saying that they have secular judges and will not come before priests....They insult the most holy blessed Virgin Mary, neglect the exequies of the dead, declare the saying of Hours to be foolish, and want to persuade nuns and other religious women to quit God's service.

The German-inhabited towns of northern and eastern Hungary were natural points of infection with the new *lues teutonica*; their links with Germany were close; they treasured their Germanity for which they found welcome expression in the Germanisation of their religious life. Their citizens, returning from visits to Germany, brought back the products of the Lutheran presses, and the flood of Reformation literature was swelled by the wares of colporteurs, despite the fate of one of them who was burned in 1524. This first martyr of the New Religion in Hungary was the servant of a brother of the reformer Conrad Cordatus who had been a favourite preacher at the Buda court of King Lewis and Queen

Mary. Indeed, so little did people at first associate reforming zeal with Lutheran heresy that not only Cordatus, but other German reformers such as Johann Henckel, were high in favour there. Of Henckel the humanist Cracovian physician, John Antony of Košice, wrote in 1526:

When I was in Hungary I saw no one who was more welcome to the queen, the king and the other optimates of the kingdom, nor anyone who was more ready to express in his sermons at home and abroad on every occasion sheer admiration for the great Erasmus.

Nevertheless, the youthful king was easily induced to give his name to an effort to root out the Lutheran weeds. The legate Borgio persuaded him to order the burning of Lutheran books in 1524, and seems to have been instrumental in inducing the Hungarian parliament in 1523 to ask the king 'as a Catholic prince, to proceed against all Lutherans and their supporters by capital punishment and forfeiture of all their goods as public heretics and enemies of the most holy Virgin Mary'. Only when the reformers seemed to be provoking social revolt did the State take effective measures, as happened in the mining districts of Slovakia. Queen Mary's favourite preacher, Conrad Cordatus, and Johann Kressling, a parish priest of Buda, were arrested in 1525 for having disseminated Lutheran ideas among the miners of Banská Bystrica (Besztercebánya) and Kremnica (Körmöcbánya), and the next year Borgio reported to the pope that 'the *villani* who work in the copper mines, which the Fuggers operated, have risen in arms. Four thousand of them have attacked the town church and have incited the *villani* of the neighbourhood, chiefly those who are German.' A commission under the famous jurist Verböczi was sent to enquire into the cause of the rising and its leaders were executed as rebels and Lutherans.

In Poland also it needed the coincidence of religious with social and political revolt to induce king and parliament to vigorous action. Here too it was in the most Germanised part of the kingdom that the clash occurred. By the Treaty of Thorn (Toruń) of 1466, West Prussia had been ceded by the Teutonic knights to Poland. Its towns—Danzig, Thorn, and Elbing (Elbląg)—were thoroughly German. From 1518 students and merchants brought back Lutheran writings which influenced some of the German clergy of Danzig to champion reform in the parish pulpits. The leaders were a trio of friars: the Dominican, Jakub Knade, the Franciscan, Alexander Svenicken and the Carmelite, Matthias Binewald. They were left undisturbed until 1523 when the number of their adherents had grown so large that the local bishop, Maciej Drzewicki, had one of the Lutheran preachers arrested. Such strong pressure was exercised by his adherents that the bishop was forced to release him after six months. This success seems to have gone to the heads of the Danzigers who, at the end of 1524, attacked and destroyed those Danzig churches and monasteries which they regarded as the centres of opposition to reform. The patrician town

council acted vigorously and arrested the ringleaders. The religious conflict was by now involved with a social struggle of the craftsmen, journey-
men and urban proletariat against the patrician government of the
merchants and financiers. The excited people demanded the abolition of
taxes and the publication of the financial proceedings of the town council.
On 22 January 1525 the insurgents invaded a meeting of the town
assembly and forced it to enact certain measures of reform. When they
were not immediately enforced the insurgents expelled the council and
installed a new one which at once began to legislate in a Lutheran sense:
Catholic usages were stopped, Church property was seized for the city, all
religious houses but two were abolished, reformed pastors were appointed
to the parish churches. The displaced patrician magistrates appealed to
King Sigismund. The king and his council were obviously disturbed by the
social revolt and the danger that Danzig and all West Prussia might be
lost to Germany, and the Polish parliament urged the king to go in person
to restore the old political and religious order; the West Prussian *Landtag*
at Marienburg (Malborg) concurred. In April of 1526 Sigismund,
supported by an army of Polish nobles, entered Danzig and at once set
up a special court to deal with the heretic rebels. The revolutionary town
council was dismissed; the old ecclesiastical order was re-established; the
Lutheran leaders were arrested and fifteen of them were executed; the
former magistrates were reinstated. In July of the same year Sigismund
published a decree which made death the penalty for apostasy from the
Church.

The coming of the Reformation to central Europe down to 1526 had
been gradual and limited; it had begun to affect primarily the German
communities, but had hardly yet greatly influenced the native Czechs,
Poles and Magyars, or the nobility of those nations who were later to be
its most effective patrons and supporters. The ensuing rapid development
of central-European Protestantism was given impetus by a series of
political events, the first of which was the revolution in the relations of
those hitherto inveterate enemies, Prussia and Poland. Since the conversion of Lithuania at the end of the fourteenth century the Teutonic
Order had ceased to have any legitimate function; it had steadily lost
ground to Poland and had surrendered West (Royal) Prussia to Casimir IV
in 1466. The last grand master, Albrecht of Hohenzollern-Ansbach, had
already in 1512 begun preparations for the conversion of East (Ducal)
Prussia into a secular duchy. In April 1525 he did fealty to Sigismund I
who enfeoffed him as duke; as such Albrecht became a member of the
senate, the upper house of the Polish parliament. Three months later, in
July 1525, Albrecht acknowledged himself a Lutheran and renounced his
semi-clerical character so that he could marry and make his duchy
hereditary in the Hohenzollern family (it was inherited by the elder
Brandenburg branch a hundred years later); by the first post-Reformation

application of the principle of *cuius regio, eius religio*, Albrecht made Lutheranism the state religion of his Prussian duchy. These events were very important for Polish Protestantism, for not only did Albrecht henceforth (he lived until 1568) protect and foster Protestant interests in the Polish senate, but he contributed greatly to the spread of Lutheranism in Poland, by giving hospitality to religious refugees from Poland, and by encouraging the printers of his capital, Königsberg, to provide evangelical literature, not only in German, but also in Polish, in the first instance for his own Polish-speaking subjects in Masuria. A Polish version of Luther's *Shorter Catechism* was published there in 1530; Polish hymn-books and confessions followed; in 1544 he founded a Protestant university at Königsberg.

The political event which profoundly affected the religious history of Hungary and Bohemia was the battle of Mohács, where, on 29 August 1526, Sultan Sulaimān's guns wiped out the Christian army which had tried to obstruct his victorious progress from Belgrade to Buda.[1] Mohács set in train a series of events which profoundly affected the history of King Lewis's two realms. Lewis was himself killed as he fled from the stricken field. His brother-in-law, Ferdinand of Habsburg, became king of Hussite Bohemia; he was also elected by a minority of Hungarian lords and prelates king of Hungary, but not before the majority had elected the *voivode* of Transylvania, the richest of the native magnates, John Zápolyai, rival king. For twenty years Hungary was distracted and devastated by bitter civil war which Ferdinand waged from his base in north-western Hungary and King John and his successor from their stronghold in Transylvania. At the same time Hungary was subjected to a succession of Turkish invasions: the siege of Vienna in 1529 was only the high-water mark of a succession of destructive incursions; almost every important town in Hungary, including the archiepiscopal see of Esztergom, was at some time besieged and occupied by the Turks. From 1541 they remained permanently in the land, establishing the pashalik of Buda, and occupying a great triangle of territory, its base on the Sava-Danube line and its apex in southern Slovakia. From that time Hungary was virtually three separate states: Habsburg Hungary in the north-west, the principality of Transylvania in the east, and the pashalik of Buda; the civil war and the war with the Turks continued with only brief intermissions until 1606.

The primary importance of the civil and the Turkish wars in the history of religion in Hungary is that they were a catastrophe for the Hungarian hierarchy. Of the sixteen prelates of the kingdom, seven were killed at Mohács: the two archbishops, László Szalkai of Esztergom and Pál Tomori of Kalocsa, and the bishops of Györ (Raab), Pécs (Fünfkirchen), Csanád, Nagyvárad (Grosswardein) and the titular bishop of Bosnia. The Church in Hungary never recovered throughout the sixteenth century.

[1] See below, pp. 512.

There were long vacancies in many of the sees, partly because the popes were unwilling to alienate the rival kings by confirming the nominations of either of them. There was no archbishop of Esztergom at all from 1573 to 1596, and even before that the primate usually had to reside at Trnava (Nagyszombat) in western Slovakia, because Esztergom was for long periods in the hands of the Turks. The other archbishopric, that of Kalocsa, was almost perpetually in Turkish hands and there was no archbishop confirmed to it between 1528 and 1572. The sees of Csanád, Gyulafehérvár (Karlsburg), and Szerém (Sirmium) were left pastorless for long periods while they suffered occupation by the infidels. No Catholic bishops resided in the pashalik of Buda, where Protestant preachers, tolerated by the Turks as fellow iconoclasts, met with little Catholic opposition. If sees were not left vacant they often suffered from the almost equally debilitating evil of having two rival claimants appointed by the rival kings, each seeking to attract the revenues while they absented themselves at one or other of the rival courts. Some bishops apostatised to Lutheranism, like Ferenc Thurzó, bishop of Nitra, who in 1534 became a Lutheran and twice married, and András Sbardellati, bishop of Pécs, who in 1568 married a wife and was deprived of his see; Márton Kecseti, nephew of the primate and bishop of Veszprém, and Simon of Erdöd, titular bishop of Zagreb, also became Protestants. Other bishoprics were sometimes made impotent by the conversion of their revenues to help pay for the expense of the holy war, or even completely secularised. In 1528 Ferdinand I pawned the revenues of the see of Györ for 15,000 florins to his treasurer, Johann Hoffmann, from whom they passed into the hands of the lay lord, Pál Bakics, a great sequestrator of Church lands though he was totally indifferent in matters of religion. In 1534 King John Zápolyai sought to retain the support of the rich (Lutheran) magnate, Péter Perényi, by giving him the episcopal revenues of Eger (Erlau). This did not prevent him from going over to Ferdinand five years later.

Mohács not only crippled the Roman Church in Hungary, it also gravely hamstrung the monarchy. As Ferdinand I showed in his Bohemian kingdom, he was a patient, shrewd, realistic defender of the Catholic unity of Christendom. But in Hungary he was powerless to save it. The strength of his position there depended on his ability to win or purchase the support of the Magyar nobles whose castles were the key to the military problem. Therefore neither he nor King John could afford to be too nice about the religious proclivities of any potential adherent. They were both Catholics, but neither dared insist on the conformity of his supporters; both were prodigal of the incomes of bishoprics and monasteries, and both were therefore the chief agents in the process of secularisation of ecclesiastical property which was at the same time the ruin of the Church and the best guarantee of the survival of Protestantism. Neither Ferdinand nor John made any serious attempt to arrest the spread of Protestantism in Hungary; it is true that Ferdinand summoned a parliament to Pressburg (Bratislava; Pozsony) in 1535 which decreed that all the property of ecclesiastics and seculars unlawfully occupied since 1526 should be restored, and when at Nagyvárad in 1538 a temporary peace was made, one of its clauses decreed a general restitution of Church property. The expropriators paid not the slightest attention to either of these decrees.

Between 1526 and the establishment of the Turks permanently in central Hungary in 1541 Lutheranism spread with great rapidity, not merely in the German areas of Slovakia and Transylvania, but also in the more purely Magyar areas, for now the Magyar magnates had seen its spiritual and material attractions and became the active agents of its propagation. Much of the groundwork was prepared by lords who never left the Church, but who supported Erasmian scholars, hymn-writers, and translators of the scriptures whose printed works gave an impetus to Protestantism which neither their authors nor their patrons intended. János Sylvester, whose translation and publication of the New Testament in Magyar was of basic importance to Hungarian Protestantism, was the protégé of the Catholic magnate, Tamás Nádasdy, and apparently himself never broke from the Church. But many, in this period perhaps most, of the magnates openly embraced Protestantism. As they exercised un-restricted powers of ecclesiastical patronage in their estates they were able to fill the village churches with Lutheran clergy whose parishioners had no choice but to submit to Protestant doctrine and practices. Protestant magnates thus brought whole counties over to Protestantism. The process throughout the kingdom was accelerated by the growing number of avowed Lutheran pastors, some of them native Germans, Silesians or Germans from Bohemia, most of them Hungarian Germans, who had often been to Wittenberg for part of their education; some of the most active Lutheran preachers were apostate monks or friars; some were Slovaks. During the period of the civil war the Lutheranisation of the German towns of Slovakia and Siebenbürgen (Transylvania) continued. The town councils of Košice (Kassa; Kaschau) Banská Šťavnica (Schem-nitz), Banská Bystrica (Neusohl), Kremnica, Prešov (Eperiesch; Eperjes) and Levoča (Löcse; Leutschau) appointed German Lutheran 'predicants' and school masters; nor did they neglect their Slovak fellow townsmen, for at Šťavnica and at Bystrica there were appointed 'Wendish' preachers, Polish Protestants from Silesia.

Lutheranism also rapidly spread in Transylvania during the reign of John Zápolyai, especially in the 'Saxon' towns. The Transylvanian 'Sachsen' were a privileged and chartered community, and it was their chief magistrate or 'count', the influential Mark Pemfflinger, who from the first encouraged Lutheran preaching. Nagyszeben, Brassó (Kronstadt) and Nagyvárad (Grosswardein) were the earliest Lutheran centres;

Johann Honter, who came to Nagyvárad in 1533, became the leader of the Transylvanian Lutherans.

In the purely Magyar part of Hungary Lutheranism was spread by the preachers, many of them Magyars, whom the magnates favoured and maintained in their courts and castles. The most eminent of them was Mátyás Dévai Bíró. Bíró was originally a Catholic priest; but he is recorded as a student at Wittenberg in 1529 and 1530, where he became the friend of Luther and Melanchthon; on his return he was patronised first by Tamás Nádasdy and Ferenc Batthyány, and then by Péter Perényi; he established Lutheranism on the estates of all three lords. A feeble attempt to check his activities was made in 1533; he was arrested and sent to Vienna to be examined by the bishops there, but he escaped to continue his labours henceforward without check. Bíró's reply to the charges made against him at Vienna provides a valuable illustration of Lutheran teaching in Hungary at the time: he admitted to a belief in communion in both kinds for the laity, the doctrine of the remanence of the substance of the bread and wine in the Host after its consecration, in salvation *sola fide*, and in the priesthood of all believers, and he disavowed the doctrine of purgatory, complete freedom of man's will, and the practice of extreme unction. Bíró's work amongst the Magyars of the Tisza valley was ably assisted by such fellow missionaries as István Magyari Kiss of Szeged who laboured here and in central Hungary even after the Turkish occupation. Kiss was exceptional in that he seems to have worked independently of the patronage of the lords and to have approached the peasants directly. By 1547 the centre of Magyar Lutheranism was the chief town of the upper Tisza, Debrecen.

The disaster of Mohács profoundly affected the course of the religious history of the kingdom of Bohemia as well as that of Hungary. The Bohemian parliament was scared and bribed into electing Lewis's brother-in-law, Ferdinand of Habsburg, as his successor. Though it was one of the conditions of his election that he promised to give equal consideration to the Catholic and Hussite confessions, the Czechs had got for themselves a king very different from his predecessors. Ferdinand shared the monarchical policy of his contemporaries and kinsmen on the thrones of western Europe. He set a high value on religious uniformity and made it his policy to reconcile his Utraquist subjects with the Church of Rome and to prevent the establishment of the new sectarians in the kingdom. Ferdinand indeed was no zealot; he was prepared to urge the popes and later the Council of Trent to concede things which were not essential to the faith, such as the cup for the laity, the marriage of the clergy, and the appointment of a Bohemian archbishop, for he realized that Utraquism was for the moment too strongly established to be eliminated by the limited powers at his disposal; moreover, Ferdinand was too dependent on the support of the Czech nobles, most of them Utraquists and the possessors of church lands, for him to be able to proceed to immediate and open war with the schismatic Bohemian Church. But his policy in respect of the other non-catholic sects was different, for here he believed he could rely on the support of the Utraquists. He tentatively tried to get the Bohemian and Moravian parliaments to support a campaign against the well-established and growing sect of the Bohemian Brethren; but the Brethren now had sufficient influence amongst the lords, and the executive force at the disposal of the king and the parliaments was too small for him to be able to restrict the growth of the Brethren's community before 1547. Nor was Ferdinand able to arrest the progress of Lutheranism in Bohemia and Moravia. This danger was not in itself as serious as it was in Hungary and Poland, for the Czech subjects of Ferdinand had already achieved their own reformation of religion. It was therefore predominantly among the German-speaking Bohemians that Lutheran views and practices spread. As early as 1520 Lutheran ideas had begun to percolate into the Teutonic fringe of Bohemia and into those towns which still had a considerable German-speaking population. During the first twenty years of Ferdinand's reign we find German Lutheran preachers being inducted by town councils to parishes in towns in western and northern Bohemia, such as Pilsen (Plzeň), Asch (Aš), Joachimsthal (Jáchymov), Kaaden (Kadaň), Aussig (Ústí nad Labem), Elbogen (Loket), and Olmütz (Olomouc) in Moravia. Though the Czech Utraquists would not accept Lutheran views about salvation by faith alone or about clerical marriage, good relations between Hussites and Lutherans were furthered by Luther's acknowledgement of his own debt to the pioneer work of John Hus, a debt which he amply repaid by the encouragement he gave to the publication of Hus's writings and of Hussite hymn-books, vernacular Bibles and treatises in Germany. Even closer were the friendly relations of the Bohemian Brethren with Luther; after the death of Brother Lukáš in 1528 the succeeding 'seniors' of the Brethren, in particular the courageous and masterful Brother Augusta, expected some sort of union of the two communions. Yet another link between the German and Czech reformations was made by the arrival of German Anabaptists in the Czech lands. By 1526 there were more than a thousand of them settled in southern Moravia. Though Ferdinand made repeated efforts to induce the Moravian parliament to expel them, these Anabaptist refugees from southern Germany, Switzerland and the Tyrol were too valuable to the Moravian lords as craftsmen, for there were skilled millers, weavers, locksmiths, potters, and even physicians amongst them, for the diet to execute decrees against them. There was some savage but spasmodic persecution. After the execution of its first leader, Balthasar Hübmaier, in 1528, the Anabaptist colony in southern Moravia was given new life by the arrival of the radical Jakob Huter from the Tyrol in 1529. From then onwards, though Ferdinand continued to urge the diet to the enforcement of persecuting measures which achieved occasional and partial success, the Anabaptist community survived, diminished but persistent, under the protection of the local landlords.[1]

In the kingdom of Poland the progress of the Reformation was not disturbed by any great crisis like that of Mohács nor complicated by the existence of a schismatic Church such as existed in Bohemia. Under the powerful protection of Duke Albrecht of Prussia, the Lutheranism of the German towns of Royal Prussia, Danzig, Elbing, Thorn and Braunsberg (Braniewo) survived the crusades of 1526. He was the protector of the former Dominican Andrzej Samuel and the preacher Jan Seklucjan, who were spreading the new religion in Poznań (Posen); when criminal proceedings were successfully taken against them in 1542 Duke Albrecht gave them refuge in his capital of Königsberg, where Seklucjan published his Polish-Lutheran Confession and his Polish translation of the four gospels. The province of Great Poland, next door neighbour to Brandenburg, was the first to suffer the impact of Lutheranism. There some of the great landlords patronised the heretical preachers. In Little Poland too and in Lithuania the new doctrines began to be heard. In Cracow as early as 1528, burgesses and nobles began to listen to and applaud the Reformation sermons of Jakub of Iza. But much of the activity in Cracow was still as Erasmian as Lutheran. The king's secretary, the Alsatian Jost Dietz (Decius) and the castellan of Cracow, Seweryn Boner, maintained a lively correspondence with the humanists of Germany.

King Sigismund I, like Ferdinand I, was anxious to conserve his realm in united fidelity to Rome. But though he detested and feared apostasy he was not blind to the faults of the Church or to the justice of much that was alleged by its critics. He roundly rejected the suggestion made to him by John Eck that he should treat the Lutherans as vigorously as Henry VIII was doing in England. Sigismund's young and domineering second wife, Bona of Sforza, gave free play to the radical and dangerous activities of her favourite preacher, Francis Lismanini. But Sigismund could not altogether resist ecclesiastical pressure and therefore reinforced the measures enacted by provincial and diocesan synods against the Lutherans by a series of edicts and statutes. In 1523 he raised the penalty for the importation of heretical books to that of death by burning; in 1534 he ordered all his subjects in heretical universities to return; the death penalty was decreed for disobedience in 1540, but in 1543 it was removed; it is clear that all such edicts were widely disregarded. Only the prelates showed any great zeal against Protestantism and even they were not unanimous: Leonard Słonczewski, bishop of Kamieniec, and Jan Drohojowski, bishop of Kujawia, were at least sympathetic to Lutheranism. On the other hand, the provincial synod of Piotrków in 1542 decreed the

[1] Cf. above, pp. 122ff.

strongest inquisitorial measures against heresy. The Church courts spasmodically punished such offences as neglect of fasts, the distribution of heretical literature and heretical pronouncements against the doctrines of purgatory, transubstantiation and auricular confession. But, after the suppression of the Danzig revolt, there were no burnings at the behest of the Church courts, with the exception that the sixty-year-old Katherina Weigel was burned in 1539, but whether as a Lutheran, Arian or Judaiser is not clear. Thus until Sigismund I's death in 1548 the Reformation in its Lutheran form made steady if unspectacular progress in Poland; it had seduced only a small fraction of the people: some of the magnates favoured it, and reformist ideas were popular amongst the intellectuals and had planted themselves in the towns. The most powerful element in the State, the lesser nobles and gentry, were not yet profoundly influenced by this German and Erastian form of the new religion. But already before 1548 another body of religious thought which would have for them a greater appeal was becoming known in central Europe, the doctrines of John Calvin.

Calvin's name and fame were known in Bohemia from 1536, but his theology and system of Church government never secured a great hold in that country, for the majority of the Czechs were well satisfied with Hussitism and the Bohemian Germans with Lutheranism. There was however a mid-century crisis in the history of the Bohemian Reformation. When the Schmalkaldic War began in Germany in 1546 the Bohemian parliament, in defiance of Ferdinand, prepared to assist John Frederick of Saxony; his defeat at Mühlberg on 24 April 1547 left the Czech rebels at the mercy of Ferdinand who characteristically used his strong position to weaken the constitutional position of the diet and the towns, but was careful not to offend the lords on whose support he still had to rely. He did take tentative measures to subordinate the Utraquist Church by seeking to control the appointment of its clerical administrators and lay 'defensores'; but he soon prudently returned to his policy of seeking the restoration of religious unity by the incorporation of the Hussites in the Roman Church. He also sought to use the opportunity afforded by the abortive rebellion of 1547 to make an effort to get rid of the Unity of Brethren for good. With the support of the parliament and the conservative Utraquist leaders the edict of 1508 against the 'Pikharti' was renewed in 1547 and the next year a royal edict ordered all Brethren to conform or go into exile. Many of them were driven out and sought refuge in hundreds in Prussia and Moravia. Under the leadership of one of their 'seniors', Jiří Izrael, many found a refuge in western Poland, under the protection of Andrzej Górka, Jakub Ostroróg and other Polish lords. By 1551 the Bohemian Brethren were well established; in their centres at Toruń, Poznań, and Leszno they attracted adherents from the Polish *szlachta* and townsfolk. Not all the Brethren left Ferdinand's dominions, for Bohemian magnates, such as the lord of Pernštejn, had no desire to lose valuable serfs and craftsmen and therefore protected the Brethren on their estates from persecution. Nor could the royal edict be enforced in Moravia, whither many of the exiles fled and where the Unity continued to flourish. Ferdinand had further sought to weaken the Unity by arresting its senior bishop, Jan Augusta; he was kept in prison from 1547 to 1564 and at first subjected to savage torture, but despite his absence the Unity survived the years of persecution and after Ferdinand's death flourished again under the leadership of Jan Blahoslav, who as historian, theologian and above all as a translator of the Bible from the original tongues, proved himself to be the greatest leader of the Unity before Comenius.

Ferdinand seized with great skill the opportunities afforded by the Counter-Reformation to solve the religious problem of Bohemia. He brought Peter Canisius from Vienna to establish a Jesuit community in Prague in 1556; he endowed a Jesuit university there in the Clementinum and schools in both Prague and Olomouc. In 1561 Ferdinand also at last persuaded the curia to restore the Catholic archbishopric of Prague in the person of Antonín Prus. Prus laboured hard to complete the reconciliation of the Hussites, even going so far as to ordain some of their clergy. He and Ferdinand seemed nearest to success when, on 16 April 1564, they persuaded Pius IV, in defiance of the decrees of the Council of Trent, to issue a *breve* permitting the giving of the communion in both kinds to the laity within Ferdinand's dominions. But it was too late. All but the most conservative of the Hussites rejected the opportunity of ending the schism; indeed, in 1567 they got Ferdinand's successor Maximilian II and the Bohemian parliament to concur in the formal abolition of the *Compactata* and to recognise an independent Utraquist Church governing itself 'according to the scriptures'. Ferdinand's policy had failed. Despite all his efforts, Catholicism in Bohemia and Moravia continued to decline; the Jesuits had little success; the religious houses, with the exception of those of the Premonstratensians, withered away, and everywhere not only the Utraquists but even more the Lutherans continued to win towns and villages from the old faith. By the end of Maximilian's reign Protestantism was so well established in Bohemia and Moravia that it needed a disaster of the magnitude of that of 1620 to uproot it.

Though there was little room for Calvinism in Bohemia, in Poland and Hungary there was a large and powerful class for which it had a strong attraction, the native middle and lower nobility. They were already jealous of the wealth of the Roman Church and hostile to the wide jurisdiction of its courts; on the other hand the German character of Lutheranism made it unwelcome to Polish and Magyar gentlemen; nor was its doctrinal conservatism and its subservience to the authority of the secular sovereign attractive. Calvinism, however, seemed to the landlords to suffer from none of these defects. It was not German, not even predominantly French. It was radical, uncompromising, logical, and above all republican. Its denial of any authority, papal or monarchical, over religion had a powerful appeal to a class which was fighting and winning, in both countries, a war for the sovereignty of the landholders. But it was above all the presbyterian government of Calvinistic churches that won the adherence of the Polish, Lithuanian and Magyar nobles and gentry. A Church in which at every level from the local presbytery to the national synod the pastors were elected or nominated by the laity, and where the lay elders were the dominant element, was the precise ecclesiastical counterpart of what the landlords were in the course of achieving in the secular government of their county, provincial, and national assemblies.[1]

The conversion to Calvinistic Presbyterianism of many of the Polish lords and gentry was not so much the work of foreign missionaries as an internal development. The writings of Calvin, Béza, and Bullinger began to exert their influence in the decade in which Sigismund II Augustus became king in 1548. Polish laymen and clergy, some of them hitherto only vaguely Erasmian, others already Lutherans, drifted into acceptance of the Genevan theology and ecclesiastical practice. Three men were particularly influential: first, the immensely rich Mikołaj Radziwiłł 'the Black', who brought all his vast estates and innumerable dependants over to Calvinism. The second was Jan Łaski (Johannes à Lasco), perhaps the noblest figure produced by the Polish Reformation. He was of noble birth, the nephew of a former primate. He had gone first to Ducal Prussia where he had organised the Protestant Church; but his doubts about the validity of Lutheran theology had compelled his departure. For three years Łaski was in London, in the latter part of Edward VI's reign; there he formed and led a congregation of foreign Protestants. The accession of Mary compelled the resumption of his travels, but his refusal to accept the Augsburg doctrine of the eucharist caused him to be driven out of Copenhagen, Rostock, Wismar, Lübeck, and Hamburg. A meeting with Calvin in Frankfurt seems to have completed his conversion. In 1557 he returned to Poland. For the remaining three years of his life he worked with the support of Lismanini and Radziwiłł for the establishment of a national Polish evangelical Church; but neither the Polish Lutherans nor the Bohemian Brethren's Church in Poland would accept his theology or his organisation. The third builder of the Polish Calvinistic community was Feliks Krzyżak or Cruciger. He was first a Lutheran priest in Secemin and in 1554 the Lutherans of Little Poland elected him superintendent of the Lutheran churches of that province. But the clerical character of this Church government was so little pleasing to the lords that in the same year at a synod in Pińczów it was decided that a number of

---

[1] Below, pp. 466 ff.

nobles, distinguished by their virtue and wisdom as the *Praecipua Membra Ecclesiae*, should be elected to support and defend the clerical 'seniors', who were instructed to employ the advice of the nobles in their decisions. By 1557 this Evangelical Church of Little Poland had acquired a fully developed system of presbyterianism. Though in theory burgesses and peasants were eligible for the presbytery, in fact the *szlachta* dominated the Church as elders and patrons. Calvinism became the dominant element in the Polish province of Little Poland and in Lithuania; in Great Poland and Prussia Lutheranism and the Bohemian Brethren retained their supremacy.

Until the middle of the sixteenth century the Lutherans had had almost a clear field in Hungary. We do indeed hear of Zwinglians or 'Sacramentarians' in Nagyszeben in 1530 and at Debrecen after 1540; but it seems probable that they were in fact Anabaptists expelled from Zwinglian Zürich. In 1533 the chief magistrates and judges of the thirteen Spiš (Zips) towns were ordered to take measures against certain Anabaptists there; in 1535 they were refused a settlement in Péter Perényi's town of Sárospatak. But they were no considerable element in Hungarian Protestantism. Calvinism, on the other hand, achieved a success as rapid and striking in Hungary as it was doing in Poland. As in Poland it was welcomed by the native lords, who had little sympathy with the German burgesses and their German religion and who welcomed the possibility of lay domination which presbyterianism afforded. In Hungary, too, Calvinism was propagated not by missionaries but by native converts. Mátyás Bíró, as a good Magyar, drifted from Lutheranism into Calvinism and took the largely Magyar town of Debrecen with him; after 1560 it was the 'Hungarian Geneva'. Bíró was helped in his calvinisation of the Magyar lords and lands of the Tisza valley and Upper Hungary by the priest Lénárt Heckel and his patron Péter Petrovics. The apostle and organiser of the Calvinist community in north-eastern Hungary was Péter Melius Juhász, for twenty-five years bishop in Debrecen. He was a mighty polemist, and it was largely due to him that the confession of faith of 1561, the *Confessio Catholica* of the Magyar Calvinists, was strictly Genevan in its doctrines of the Lord's Supper and predestination. In Transylvania the progress of the Reformation was arrested as long as the powerful and notorious Fráter György, bishop of Nagyvárad, was master of King John Zápolyai's widow Isabella and infant son John Sigismund. But with Fráter György's murder in 1551 the floodgates were opened again, and among the Magyar lords of Transylvania Calvinism spread rapidly. In 1563 the Transylvanian Calvinists produced their Confession at Kolozsvár (Klausenburg, Cluj). The Reformation in Transylvania from 1551 to 1571 was in no way hindered by the rulers of that country. John Zápolyai's widow Isabella lived on the revenues of the secularised bishoprics of Nagyvárad and Gyulafehérvár; the secularisation of Church property was completed by the Transylvanian diet in 1557; the monasteries and the monks disappeared. Indeed, had it not been for the election of a Catholic prince, Stephen Báthory, in 1571, the Roman Church in Transylvania might have disappeared. Meantime during the principate of his predecessor John Sigismund (1559–71) the Protestants had a free hand; the Diet of 1564 in its fifth article declared:

> The Kolozsvár Magyar believers (i.e. the Calvinists) and the Szeben Saxons (i.e. the Lutherans) having fallen into disputes, for the peace of the realm it is permitted to both factions to practise their religion, and the preacher in any town or village shall not compel its inhabitants to conform to his religion, but the town or village is free, whatever the religion of its preacher, if he does not please them, to expel him.

This local religious autonomy probably meant in practice that the will of the local landlord prevailed.

This famous 'Transylvanian toleration' was in fact not due to the victory of a principle quite alien to the sixteenth century, but merely the result of the weakness of the monarchy and the equality of power of the Lutheran-German towns and the Magyar-Calvinist lords. But this peculiar tolerance in Poland and Transylvania provided a refuge and a sphere of activity to that form of Protestantism which theologically and socially was its logical ultimate form, namely Socinianism.

There had been occasional accusations of Anti-Trinitarian error in the welter of theological speculation in Bohemia during the fourth and fifth decades of the sixteenth century, but no persistent body of such heresy appeared anywhere until the arrival of a number of expatriate Italian theologians who found in Poland and Transylvania a final refuge after Calvin had made even Geneva too hot for them. It is one of the most curious phenomena of the Reformation that its most extreme theological and social manifestation should have originated in the two countries, Spain and Italy, where otherwise it was least successful. But it is not really surprising that the native country of humanism and rationalism, of Lorenzo Valla and Savonarola, should have given birth to and expelled a score or so of extreme eccentrics who did not stop in their examination of the bases of the faith before they came to a criticism of its fundamental doctrines of the Atonement and the Trinity. These men, Giovanni Gentile, Lelio Sozzini and his nephew Fausto Sozzini, Francesco Stancaro, Giovanni Alciati, Bernado Ochino and Giorgio Blandrata, all of them moved by the potent combination of piety and learning, had come under the influence successively of Erasmus's disturbing textual criticism of the New Testament, of Calvin's theological radicalism and of the revived knowledge of Neoplatonic philosophy and of patristic Christological controversy. Like Arius and Nestorius they had been convinced that Athanasius had misled the Church into constructing an unnecessary, irrational and erroneous mystery of the Trinity. Erasmus's deliberate omission of the 'comma of John' from his first two editions of the New Testament had led them to question the scriptural authority for the orthodox doctrine.

The Anti-Trinitarian movement in Poland may be said to have begun with the appointment of Stancaro to the chair of Hebrew in Cracow in 1549. During the next twenty-five years his fellow countrymen, the elder Sozzini, Gentile, Alciati, Pauli, Ochino, Blandrata, and finally Fausto Sozzini all found a refuge, more or less permanent, in Poland. They were welcomed by the more theologically adventurous leaders, lay or clerical, of the Calvinist communities in Little Poland and Lithuania. But the publication of Stancaro's Nestorian treatise *De Trinitate et Mediatore Nostro Jesu Christo* in 1559, and a little later of Ochino's *Dialogus* and Gentile's *Antidota*, alarmed the more conservative majority of the Polish Calvinists so far that a breach was inevitable. In 1562 the Anti-Trinitarians broke with the Calvinistic Church of Little Poland and set up their own 'Lesser Community'. To it adhered a growing number of native Poles: Calvinistic clergy, many of them originally weavers, spinners, or artisans of other crafts, such as Piotr of Goniądz, Grzegorz Paweł of Brzeziny, Walenty Krawiec and Marcin Czechowic. It seems that the dominance of the *szlachta* in the Reformed Church was often the occasion for the secession of its ministers to the Arians. The new sect attracted many and retained the loyalty of a few of the great lords and gentry, but its basis was, like that of the Anabaptists, the craftsmen and shop-keepers who saw in it the only hope of realizing those dreams of freedom from social oppression of which they had been disappointed by Lutherans and Calvinists alike. The Polish Anti-Trinitarians consciously shared many of the social and moral ideals of Anabaptists to whom they sent a mission of enquiry in Moravia; in their synods from 1562 onwards they repeatedly discussed the lawfulness of bearing arms or of taking life and of serving as magistrates or jurymen. Individual clergymen amongst them from time to time condemned the lordship of man over man, of the ownership of hereditary property, and preached that all men, noble and cleric as well as peasant and artisan, should live by the labour of their own hands.

Sigismund Augustus, together with the largely Protestant diet and the Catholic hierarchy, made half-hearted efforts to rid Poland of these latest heretics. In 1564 some of the Italian heresiarchs were compelled for a time to leave the country. The only other country where the authority of the State was so weak that they might expect to find some freedom was Transylvania. Stancaro and Blandrata had already visited it and sown the seeds of Anti-Trinitarianism amongst the Calvinists of eastern Hungary. In 1563 Blandrata became body-surgeon and privy councillor to the prince of Transylvania, Zápolyai's son John Sigismund. He and others from Poland worked so persuasively amongst the Transylvanian Magyars and Szekels that they converted many to their heresies, including John

Sigismund himself and some of his court and clergy. But the most important convert was the 'bishop' of the 'Kolozsvár', or Calvinistic Transylvanian community, Ferenc Dávid. The publication of his *De Falsa et vera Unius Dei Patris, Filii et Sancti Spiritus Cognitione* in 1567 marked Dávid's full secession to Anti-Trinitarianism. In the same year the Transylvanian diet at Torda allowed free preaching to all sects. In 1568, when the prince openly adhered, the Great Church at Kolozsvár became Dávid's seat as 'bishop' of the Transylvanian Arian Church. As in Poland, there was also in Transylvania much bitter controversy among the Anti-Trinitarians; in 1579 both Blandrata and Fausto Sozzini condemned Dávid for his extreme Unitarianism, and Dávid spent the last months of his life in prison. Nevertheless the Transylvanian Anti-Trinitarian Church survived these storms to endure as a living community to our own day.

The half-century which followed the appearance of Luther's Reformation treatises saw an almost continual growth of Protestantism in central Europe. Thereafter the tide began to turn. Tolerant rulers died and gave place to champions of the Catholic Church: in 1571 the Arian John Sigismund was succeeded as prince of Transylvania by the Catholic Stephen Báthory who four years later was elected king of Poland; in 1576 the tolerant Maximilian II was succeeded as ruler of Austria, Bohemia and Hungary by the Spanish-educated Rudolf II. The new generation of rulers found their realms divided between the two faiths. In Poland the great majority of the people was still Catholic, but there were four organised dissident Churches: the Lutherans, now based on the acceptance of the Revised Augsburg Confession of 1551; the Calvinists, united in the Helvetic Confession of 1568; the Bohemian Brethren in Great Poland; and the Unitarian community, still not agreed on its theology or permanently organised. In that fraction of Hungary which the Habsburg king ruled, the Catholic Church was in 1576 still prostrate despite the efforts of Archbishops Oláh (1553–68) and Verancsics (1569–73) to revive it by the introduction of the Tridentine programme and an unsuccessful attempt to establish the Jesuits in Trnava. The Lutherans of the mining towns, German and Slovak, had developed their own organisation out of the *Confessio Pentapolitana* of 1549. In Transylvania and the adjacent counties, ruled, usually under Turkish suzerainty, by the princes of the Zápolyai and Báthory families, the three Protestant Churches, Lutheran, Calvinist and Unitarian, were organised and dominant; the Catholic Church in Transylvania seemed to be perishing of neglect until Báthory interfered to preserve the remnant from extinction. The Calvinists and Unitarians each also had an organisation in Turkish Hungary, where Catholicism was barely preserved by the devoted labours of the Franciscans in the sixteenth century and of the Jesuits in the seventeenth. In Bohemia and Moravia during the reign of Maximilian II the sects had consolidated their supremacy, not only the majority Church of the Utraquists and the growing Lutheran community, but even the still harassed Unity of Brethren who, especially in Moravia, were increasing in numbers and influence.

The achievements of the forces of the Counter-Reformation in central Europe had not been great before 1576. Besides archbishops Oláh and Verancsics in Esztergom, the archbishop of Prague, Antonín Prus, and his colleague in Olomouc, Bishop Vilém Prusinovský, and in Poland Archbishop Uchański and his much abler and more effective colleague, Cardinal Hosius, bishop of Warmia (Ermland), had all embarked on the Augean task of reforming their own Church; Jesuit settlements, seminaries and schools had been established in Slovakia, at Prague and Olomouc, and in Poland and Lithuania. Though, except in Poland, their success had hitherto been small, yet the Protestants were sufficiently alarmed to try to resolve their sectarian differences. In Bohemia in 1575 the Utraquists, Lutherans and Brethren agreed on a common confession of faith, the famous *Confessio Bohemica*, which, though it did not create a united Bohemian Protestant Church, did help them to present a united front to Rudolf II and his Counter-Reformation. In Poland the Calvinists and the Bohemian Brethren had made an agreement of mutual recognition at Koźminek in 1555, but it was not until 1570 that the imminent demise of the sonless Sigismund II compelled the Polish Protestants to take precautions against the accession of a more militantly Catholic king. At Sandomierz the Calvinists, Lutherans and Polish Bohemian Brethren made a *Consensus Mutuus*, having with the greatest difficulty agreed on a eucharistic formula whose involved vagueness alone made it generally acceptable. The Sandomierz agreement provided for occasional general synods of the three sects, but it fell far short of being an organic union. When, in January 1573, it seemed certain that Henry of Anjou would become king of Poland, the Polish Protestants, in collaboration with some of the Catholics, drew up at Warsaw a 'Confederation', a charter of religious liberty. Andrzej Firlej is said to have presented it to Anjou in Paris with the words, 'Si non jurabis, non regnabis'. In the event neither the Sandomierz *Consensus* nor the Warsaw 'Confederation' proved effective to save Polish Protestantism from the full flood of the Catholic counter-attack. It was never in Poland, as it was in Bohemia, so strongly based on broad national support that it needed military disaster to destroy it, nor did Polish Protestantism, unlike Hungarian Protestantism, have the advantage of a continually weak and divided monarchy. It is ironical, but nevertheless in the logic of history, that the only part of central Europe in which Protestantism survived the Counter-Reformation was in the shattered kingdom of Hungary.

3. FRANCE, 1519–59

To understand the many long vicissitudes of the Reformation in France, we must put ourselves at a point of time well after the drama itself, at the conclusion, at the moment of disillusionment. At the close of the century, indeed, France remained Catholic. Henry IV was obliged to recognise this fundamental reality and abjure his Protestantism before entering into full possession of his inheritance. In its hour of greatest success and stoutest resistance, French Protestantism was unable to escape from being the creed of a minority. Its very mentality was the mentality of a minority. The way in which it forced itself into the structure, or rather into the inner structures, of the diverse life of France is one of the great dramas of history. When considered together, the host of crises of conscience which made up the beginnings of the Reformation in France (and we must think of the Catholic as well as the Protestant movements for reform) creates a problem which is, without doubt, fundamental to French history in the first half of the sixteenth century.

In the second place, it is important to remember that the group which remained a minority in France was able to impose the Edict of Nantes (1598) and so protect its spiritual life by a barricade of political rights, and even of fortified positions. Thus the Protestants created their own structures.

The religions, moreover, which at this time began to grow into opposition, very often had a complementary character. It is too often customary to see (and so to explain) these religions by their conflicts. Yet they admit of interdependences and similarities. Thus, the Reformation in France, won over to Calvinism, that extreme form of thought and action, can be appreciated only when seen against, even in the terms of, the Counter-Reformation, that other voluntary excess. This reality, this movement of counterpoint, deepens and contrasts our knowledge of these opposing and therefore associated forces, both established during the first half of the sixteenth century.

Another observation supports this point of view: religion must always be reset in its social context. Thus, the liberty of the reformed faith, in a society like that of Catholic France at the time, could express itself, or attempt to express itself, only in the company of other liberties, friendly or hostile, complementary and even interdependent; the latter then existed in the terms of the former. In the absence of an organic, authoritarian system, both general and effective—in sixteenth-century France everything or nearly everything expressed its social disparity—disorder and anarchy were avoided, or in reverse provoked, by a host of separate authorities. In this, the monarchy saw its authority always in danger.[1] Yet, in this diversity, liberties were relative. It was not, and could not be,

[1] Cf. below, p. 440.

a question of societies without religion, for they were all embraced in the structural and constraining unity of a single religion.

During the whole of the first period, until about 1530, the spiritual and intellectual life, in relative peace, are found to be closely linked. As a result, conditions were at first complex, full of nuances, somewhat ill-defined; they appear in the following separate heads: the Church and the monarchy, the diffusion of Lutheran influences, humanism and the Reformation, the response, finally, of traditional forms.

The Church in France, under Francis I, had a character of its own, derived from the Pragmatic Sanction named after Bourges (1438) and born in the age of the great councils. It found itself independent, and therefore protected from the great blows suffered by Rome or issuing from Rome. On the morrow of his victory at Marignano (1515), the young Francis I had opened negotiations with Pope Leo X. The Concordat of 18 August 1516 was the result. By the first article of the agreement, the king received the substantial right to nominate archbishops, bishops and abbés in his kingdom, in all some 620 preferments. With this arrangement the earlier gallicanism, or rather independence, of the Church of France, which derived from its conciliar character, gave way to a royal gallicanism. At a stroke, the monarchy imposed its solution of the problem of *regnum et sacerdotium*. At a stroke, also, Francis I and his successors were faced with a problem—that of seeing in all the mounting pressure of ultramontanism a real threat to their authority.

It is easy to understand the great increase in royal authority which came from control of the higher clergy in the Church of France. The Concordat reinforced the absolute power of the monarchy, by denying, at the same time, the notion of free elections, the role of councils, the principle of consent in ecclesiastical matters. Royal competence took over the ground won from these ancient practices. This conquest of the Church by the king opened wide the road to theories of Divine Right. Thus, there appeared in 1538 the *Regalium Franciae, libri duo*, by Charles de Grassaille, which supported the right of the king to raise taxes and to nominate the high Church dignitaries; Du Moulin, in 1539, in his *Premier commentaire sur la coutume de Paris*, asserted that the king had jurisdiction over the clergy. A century had passed since the Pragmatic of Bourges! At the same time, the rise in studies of Roman law facilitated the royal cause. Schools of law and lawyers—Bourges was a notable example—led the attack both on local rights and on the principle of necessary consent in the affairs of government. At Bourges, as elsewhere, a relentless progress was shown towards absolutist ideas.

In this struggle at the beginning of his reign, Francis I, deliberately and spontaneously furthered the increase of his authority, by taking care not to trust the designs and intrigues of the members of the *parlements*, those opponents of every development in royal power. The Concordat was held up for almost two years before being registered by the *parlement* of Paris (22 March 1518). Yet the court had to give way.

Another fundamental characteristic of the problem lay in the fact that the early Reformation in France found support, both willing and un-willing, in the distractions and efforts of the king's foreign policy. These adventures, these long and murderous campaigns in Italy, drew from France many men, who, in the words of Commynes, 'pour toutes en-seignes n'y est memoir d'eux que pour les sépultures de leurs prédeces-seurs'. The mad desire to cross the Alps at the head of an army and march down into the plains sprinkled with opulent, magnificent cities, did not spring from a real inclination to aid the pope and ultramontanism. Indeed, on the contrary. For a brief instant, however, when the balance of power in Europe was upset by the defeat of France at Pavia (February 1525), Clement VII was driven into the League of Cognac with France in order to curtail the too great victory of Charles V. The recovery was almost immediate: the sack of Rome came in 1527. From then on, the policy of the Holy Father remained almost continually until 1559 in bondage to Spanish and imperial policies. The master of Italy mastered the pope. In losing Italy, France put Rome against her policy.

Moreover, in fighting beyond the Alps, France neglected her north-eastern frontier, the great avenue of Franco-German intercourse. She found herself obliged to follow an oblique policy which was ultimately favourable to the Protestants. The frenzied appeal, without pang of conscience, to the Sultan Sulaimān on the morrow of Pavia, the great battle of Mohács (1526) and the subsequent unleashing of the Turkish marauders across Hungary even to the very gates of Vienna—these were so many indirect blows against the body of Germany. This policy on the part of the Very Christian King to incapacitate the empire demanded *rapprochements* and *ententes*—very often secret, on occasion open (as with the restitution of Württemberg to Duke Ulrich in 1534; and again with the seizure of the three bishoprics in 1552)—with the Protestant princes, those protectors of Luther and his successors.

Freedom of thought, condoned and encouraged about the year 1520, opened the whole country to the gusts and flurries of the German Reformation. Indeed, extensive exchanges between France and Germany went on under cover of a vigorous commercial life, of which there is ample evidence, if need be, in the merchants and merchandise at the famous fairs of Lyons, that great dispersion-centre for the Reformation. No one will doubt the influence of Luther in France.[1] The direct, real, warm and human style of the great German populariser had an immediate appeal of which traces reappear in the style of such French works as those of Farel and of De Maigret, or even in the *Miroir de l'âme pécheresse* of

[1] For this see W. G. Moore, *La Réforme allemande et la littérature française* (Strassburg, 1930).

Margaret of Navarre. This influence was increased by the growing impact of printing and the work of numerous translaters. The books, which were hurried from the presses of Germany and then of France, gave to the ideas of the German Reformation a large diffusion and even a revolutionary force. Thus, at the fairs of Frankfurt and of Antwerp, where the books were printed in French; at Basle, where the brilliant printing of Froben was sustained by Erasmus, Lefèvre, Farel; at Strassburg, which turned Protestant and welcomed refugees from France (and on occasion Lefèvre and Roussel); at Neuchâtel and Geneva—to cite the more important sources—from all these towns in constant relation with the great international centre, Lyons, the books crossed the frontiers and circulated in France. Here, also, the secret presses, particularly in Lyons, Meaux, Alençon and Paris, turned out books which were to pass quickly along the great highways. In 1519 Luther was informed by Froben that 600 books were *en route* for France and Spain: 'they are sold at Paris, they are read even at the Sorbonne', he added. In 1520, 1400 copies were sold at the Frankfurt fair. Thus, there was a massive invasion of France. At this happy period, Luther's books were eagerly awaited, 'acceuillis par toute la cohorte des savants'; in April 1524 Lefèvre (then at Meaux) wrote to Farel, 'Omnia quae a te veniunt et Germania mihi maxime placent'. They arrived in casks, secreted among merchandise, in the pedlar's knapsack, concealed in bales of hides. For one instance in this clandestine traffic brought to the light of justice, and so of history, there were hundreds of similar cases throughout France, as throughout Spain, which was more difficult to reach.

This rapid and stealthy propagation was a force which escapes exact measurement. A striking example will show that this circulation of books was not confined only to Protestant groups. It is taken from the will (about 1559) of a member of a Norman family, the Miffants. Belonging to the gentry, Catholic to all appearances if we may judge from his list of small images of the Virgin and the saints, he left a library of greater interest. Among the 149 volumes, we note the *Courtier* of Castiglione, the *Odes* and *Amours* of Ronsard, Machiavelli, Pliny and Plato, a series of volumes of Erasmus, but also the *De Anima* of Melanchthon, whose works had been condemned by the Sorbonne in 1522.

In addition, it must not be forgotten that all these ideas drawn from the thought of Luther, and of other German and Swiss reformers, had an even greater impact when translated into French. The Reformation in France was well served by translaters, such as François Lambert, a cordelier who took refuge in Germany after 1522, to become in 1526 the guest of the landgrave of Hesse; or Guillaume Dumolin, living at Wittenberg in 1525, and later at Strassburg; not to mention the names of Louis Berquin, Papillon, Lempereur, Dubois. Before 1535 a dozen German writings appeared in French translation. Thus, *La Summe de l'escripture saincte, et l'ordinaire des Chrestiens, enseignant la vraye foy Chrestienne* (Basle, 1523; second edition in 1544); *La Manière de lire l'évangile...* (Antwerp, 1528); *La Prophétie de Jésaie* (1527); *Le livre de vraye et parfaicte oraison* (Paris, 1529); *La Consolation Chrestienne contre les afflictions de ce monde et scrupules de conscience* (Paris, 1528); *Le Pater noster faict en translation et en dyalogue par la Royne de Navarre* (undated; the original of 1519); *Le Sermon de la manière de prier Dieu et comment on doibt faire processions et rogations* (undated). It is worth considering the activity of a man like Robert Estienne who took part in the printing of excerpts from the Bible in 1522, 1541, 1542, 1543 and 1545, and of full editions in 1528, 1535, 1540, 1545 and 1546. As a result of all these activities of translaters, printers and pedlars, a new spirit was at work throughout France, shaking ideas and traditions to the very roots.

The first period of the Reformation in France remains ill-defined, for, along with these shades of ideas and uncertainties of beliefs, it was aided and abetted by humanistic studies. This humanism was a vigorous, robust, national tradition, fed and encouraged by ceaseless contacts with scholars from abroad, and rooted—it must not be forgotten—in a spontaneous, almost traditional, anti-clericalism. Already before Luther, Jean Bouchet in *La Déploration de l'Église militante* of 1512 wrote:

> Cessez, cessez me donner ornemens
> Calices, croix et beaux accoutrements...

The same remark applies to Jacques Lefevre of Étaples in his *Commentaire sur les Épîtres de St Paul*, in which, some years before Luther, he asserted justification by faith. It was the bishop of Autun in 1534 who declared that 'we have come to the point when only, or almost only, the most cowardly and most unworthy aspire to such an honorable profession...'; and Mathieu Malingre sang in 1533:

> Rien ne m'y sert: François ne sa grant mance
> Estre vestu de noir, de blanc ou gris:
> Je laisse aussi Dominicque et sa panse
> Je viens a toy car tout bien est compris
> En toy mon Dieu.

The movement found its first organised expression at Meaux, in the group which surrounded the bishop, Guillaume Briçonnet. Briçonnet (1470–1534) came from a family of lawyers, merchants and financiers. He was the son of Guillaume Briçonnet, the all-powerful minister, almost the prime minister, of Charles VIII. He himself, given a canonry at an early age, took part in the Council of Pisa and in the negotiations leading up to the Concordat. Elevated to the bishopric of Lodève, he was afterwards made bishop of Meaux on 31 December 1515. Once established in his diocese, he energetically set about reforming his clergy. About him, a group of friends and scholars was soon established, active, humanist, and bold in thought. His palace was a meeting-place for learning. Jacques Lefèvre of Étaples (1455–1536), leaving St-Germain-des-Prés, arrived there about the end of 1520 and, appointed to administer the hospital (11 August 1521), was made vicar-general on 1 May 1527; the eloquent Gerard Roussel (1480–1550) was soon made treasurer of the chapter; the scholars Vatable and de Quincey; the theologians Martial and Mazurier (appointed to the benefice of St Martin of Meaux); Pierre Caroli, so versatile as it turned out; the disturbing Guillaume Farel; and there were others besides. In 1523 Lefèvre published his translation of the Four Gospels; then, in 1527, his translation of the Old Testament. Thus, with the preachers and the direct appeal to congregations, the centre of Meaux with its leaning to Pauline doctrines was well placed to echo the thought and examples of Germany. As a centre of dissemination, it was the most influential in France and was to have an even more remarkable destiny. Behind the actions of the leaders, we must keep in mind the host of smaller people, serried in ranks—fullers, wool-carders, cloth-workers, a world of craftsmen—who were stirring after 1523, as two years later were the peasants in Germany. Such was the little 'flock' of Meaux. Beyond this, Briçonnet certainly envisaged a more general reform, and the salvation of a distinguished soul, that of Margaret of Navarre, to whom he was friend, confidant and confessor, and who also put her faith in the sole merits of Christ.

In his diocesan work Briçonnet tried to re-establish discipline, after the manner of the Oratory of Rome. On 15 October 1519 a decree ordered that priests should reside in their parishes, but the order had to be re-issued on 7 January and again on 27 October 1520, thus showing that resistance was stubborn. This attempt at reform, even though moderate, roused the passions of obscurantists and conservatives who desired neither principles nor opinions that were new. In 1520, however, his friend Josse van Clichtove (d. 1543) declared himself against dangerous innovations, and the growing opposition drew Briçonnet without difficulty to defend tradition. When called to Paris in 1522 he agreed with measures taken against Luther's books. The following year, on returning to Meaux, he issued a decree (15 October) against selling or concealing these books; on 13 December he forbade parish priests to receive preachers suspected of advanced ideas. In March and April 1524 he opened an attack on doctrines which questioned fundamental dogma—the mass, the saints, purgatory—at the same time trying to revive the spiritual forms and restore their spontaneity. Clichtove is a good example of the cross-currents in these troubled waters of the early Reformation—so troubled, indeed, that contemporaries were often confused. Guillaume Farel (1489–1565), who was later won over to the Reformation, could write to Cormalle Scheffer on 2 April 1524 that 'notre France reçoit déjà avec la plus grande joie la parole de Dieu'. This was a questionable assertion, in all truth. How, then, are we to classify this collection of men of ideas, of devotion so shaded, at heart so different one from another: Briçonnet, Lefèvre, Roussel, Farel, Clichtove?

About and especially after the year 1530 remarkable changes affected the intellectual and emotional climate of France. They could only aggravate a situation which was by no means simple. The Church was keenly aware that its unity and authority were seriously threatened. It attempted, by strengthening traditions, to oppose ideas which it considered schismatic. Two forces at Paris helped to control the spread of new doctrines: the *parlement* of Paris and the faculty of theology at the Sorbonne. The former was the adversary of any increase in royal power, and, needless to say, new ideas in religious matters; the latter was aware of its high reputation for intellectual judgment both in Paris and throughout Europe. Thus in 1530 Henry VIII asked the advice of its theologians on the question of his divorce. Thus in 1532 the merchants of Antwerp submitted their scruples on the subject of usury. It was Paris which Ignatius Loyola considered worthy, after Rome, to shelter a new college of his disciples. A well-merited reputation, and hence the proverbial compliment to argue 'like a doctor of the Sorbonne'.

After the papal condemnation of Luther's works, the faculty of theology issued a similar condemnation on 15 April 1521. In August the same year the *parlement* of Paris ordered 'a son de trompe' that books by Luther were to be given up within a week, and it then instituted a search for persons. In June 1523 Louis Berquin was arrested at Paris, the only person of quality among the small fry questioned at this time. He was saved by the direct intervention of the king, not to mention the private pleadings of his sister Margaret of Navarre. In August, Jean Vallière was condemned and burnt in Paris, the first victim, although it should be noted that he was not condemned for Lutheranism. Heretical books were found everywhere: in 1523, the Sorbonne was still finding them in Paris. The same news came from Bordeaux and from Grenoble; in 1524 from Bourges; in 1525 from Normandy.

The hardening of positions corresponded to the first and dramatic war of Francis I against the Emperor Charles V. In its need to pursue the conduct of the war, the government perhaps condoned the initiative of the *parlement* and the Sorbonne. Already in 1523 Farel took flight to Basle. About 1524, just as Lefèvre was publishing his New Testament in French, the group at Meaux was seriously threatened. In January and February Caroli and Mazurier reaffirmed their adherence to the Catholic Church; in December Maigret was imprisoned. In February 1525 came the defeat of Pavia when Francis I was captured and taken from Italy to Madrid. About 1525 we can speak of the end of the group of Meaux. Briçonnet, under the judgment of the *parlement*, reopened the search for forbidden books. A little later he was denounced by the Cordeliers of

Meaux whose preachings he had hindered. In October and December, he was called to Paris to answer these accusations before the *parlement*. He was accused of having had distributed in his diocese 'des livres en françois qui étaient tous erreur et hérésie'. In October, Lefèvre and Roussel fled to Strassburg.

In May 1525, at the request of the regent, the pope gave cognisance of heresy to four judges of the *parlement*, two ecclesiastical and two lay. This extraordinary tribunal lasted only until 1527. The situation was such that Francis I, from his prison in Madrid, wrote to the *parlement* to suspend the trials. In February 1526 the king was freed. In April, thanks once more to the interposition of Margaret, Lefèvre and Roussel returned to France. But the *parlement* did not follow counsels of moderation. On 12 March 1526 it again condemned the works of Louis Berquin, who remained at liberty only through the insistence of the king. On 8 October he once more had to write to the *parlement*: 'Nous vous mandons... délivrer ledit Berquin.' Once again, the king, aware of the threat to his authority, had supported the cause of free thought. Yet was he by himself of sufficient stature to dominate these hostile circumstances? In reality, his authority was seriously impaired by the defeat of Pavia, by the Treaty of Madrid (1526) and by the Ladies' Peace of Cambrai (1529). By this last treaty, the king was obliged to pay a ransom for his two sons, then hostages in Spain, of two million *écus*, of which 1,200,000 were to be in gold at one payment. This was a heavy burden for the royal finances, already stretched by the extraordinary levies for the war. At the Assembly of Notables in 1527, the cardinal of Bourbon had remarked on the spiritual condition of the realm and on the king's conduct in this matter. This assembly was followed by important provincial Church councils, in particular those of Sens and of Bourges.

The Council of Sens, convened in Paris under the presidency of Antoine Duprat, chancellor of France, cardinal, bishop of Albi, archbishop of Sens, held its meetings from 3 February to 9 October 1528. Josse van Clichtove was called to attend. The council was to concern itself with raising the money required by the king, as well as with the problems of religious and ecclesiastical life. The decrees on dogma aimed at the vigorous restoration of the authority of the Church: it alone had the right to distinguish in the texts between heretical ideas and those which were orthodox; it alone was to decide or define matters concerning the mass, the sacraments, images, the doctrine of grace. And even more, the Council of Sens strengthened parish discipline, leaving to the regular orders the control of preaching. At Bourges, the council, which was under the active presidency of the cardinal of Tournon, produced a whole series of measures designed to control heretical sermons and books. 'The book and the word,' writes Michel François, '[were] instruments *par excellence* of the new doctrines.' The Church of France thus strove to defend itself, and then reconstitute its spiritual force. Yet, is it possible, even so, to speak of a Church of France, when, in order to restore its discipline and authority, it had recourse to provincial councils rather than to a national council? Without insisting on this, the fundamental character of France in the sixteenth century must once more be recognised. It certainly had unity, if we consider the monarchy; but it was a huge country, in which the provinces in the widest meaning of the word played, with interruptions, a powerful part.

These provincial councils coincided with the energetic pursuit of Lutherans, followed by executions at Paris in October 1527 and December 1528, and at Rouen in June 1528—where Pierre Bar, in truth, was not a Lutheran and was condemned for having denied the divinity of Christ. There was also a new attack on Berquin: in 1528 his third captivity was to end tragically, and he was executed after trial on 17 April 1529. Numerous arrests and some executions of suspects must be noted: at Langres in 1529; at Dijon in 1531, 1534, 1536, 1538, 1539; at Beaune in 1534; at Montpellier in 1532, 1533, 1535, 1536 (where already in 1527 it was reported that 'the greater part of the town are Lutherans'); at Toulouse in 1530, 1532, 1538; at Tours in 1526, 1530; at Bordeaux in 1530, 1534, 1535; throughout the south, for example at Cahors, Castres, Mende, Rodez, Montauban, Carcassone; in Normandy, in several towns; and not least at Lyons. These were so many red tokens of a bloodstained future. Under these circumstances, the first phase of the Reformation drew to a close.

From this point, trends of different colours and consequences were to form. Thus, mysticism and humanism, as noted above, drew apart. Thus also the material well-being of the period seemed to become corrupted, for up to that time it had been sustained by gains easily won, by a certain happy humour. A France new in body and spirit emerged. Its countenance changed fairly rapidly in the course of these critical years.

The end of the agreement between humanists and reformers was an event of outstanding importance. It is not possible to speak here of a clean break, but in fact there was a fairly complex change in attitude. The intellectuals had lived under various protections. Clement Marot, although a prisoner, had enjoyed a well-disposed *laisser-aller*, thanks to the bishop of Chartres; Étienne Dolet had been in the service of the bishop of Limoges; Roussel had had the constant sympathy and encouragement of Margaret of Navarre; Maigret had lived in the clientele of the Du Bellay family. Hence, the cloak of Maecenas, of intellectual patronage, of protection. More precisely these supports were, little by little and on occasion abruptly, taken from the intellectual. There was a lassitude, a sort of treason, more or less open, by the sons of Maecenas, and at the top of society by the reorientation of royal policy. This was a great drama of repeated themes and consequences. It was no longer the hour for men of moderation who were clear-minded and aware of the arguments for and against. Circumstances betrayed these men—men like Guillaume du Bellay who tried in vain to repair the open breaches in the unity of the Church by a movement similar to that epitomised in Germany in the conduct of Melanchthon. Was there not also, in the shadow of these changes, the passing of an older generation—Briçonnet died in 1534, Lefèvre in 1536, the year when Erasmus also disappeared from the scene? Younger men now had their say. Bubbles were rising in the new wine.

The cleavage between literary production and religious enthusiasm was soon complete. Was there not, with the growing severity of persecution, a sort of down-grading of the former elite? Persecutions, moments of truth and manly resolution—in all this a whole reality of action and popular violence was established. The popular song summed up the situation: thus, against the detested Sorbonne—

> Là où la clarté se porte
> L'obscurité sortira
> L'Évangile qu'on rapporte
> Le Papisme chassera
> > La Sorbonne la bigotte
> > La Sorbonne se taira.

But it did not keep quiet. With ruthless persistence, it hunted down innovations and new ideas. About 1530, with the initiation of royal *lecteurs*, the nucleus of the Collège de France was established. Without hesitation, the Sorbonne protested through the words of Noel Beda against

les livres grecs ou hébrieux en la Saincte Escriture viennent la pluspart des Allemaignes où peuvent avoir esté les livres changez. Et quant à l'hébrieu, plusieurs juifs qui font imprimer leurs livres hébraiques sont luthériens....

Violent words, persecutions and heresy-hunting became increasingly severe. The hour of the sword was close at hand. The deaths of Berquin in 1528 and of Jean de Caturce at Toulouse in 1532 must have been exceptions. They ought not, however, to hide a list of more humble victims. Indeed, right in the very heart of the intellectual movement of the Renaissance, a whole anti-popular tradition asserted itself. Did Luther act differently five years earlier in 1525 in the face of the peasants' revolt in Germany? More than in the past, the rift between humanism and the Reformation was to show the many aspects of the popular character of the Reformation. Witness the great and revealing success of preaching, even more noticeable later, on the wave of Calvinism; or the popularity of the Huguenot song and the Protestant psalter. An edition of psalms was printed in German in 1524, in French in 1539; but the greatest influence was reserved for the later editions by Clément Marot (1496–1542). Begun in 1532, completed at Geneva, they were not published by Étienne Dolet (fifty psalms in French) until August 1543. Between 1543 and 1560, there followed some twenty-eight editions; the complete translation, finished by Théodore Béza in 1562, had twenty-five editions in a year. Along with the *Institution Chrétienne*, the French psalter was a great force in the popular Reformation in France. No document is more revealing than the *Chronique de Rouen* which records in the city in March 1560 'plusieurs gens du popullaire...chantans et submurmurans les pseaulmes et cantiques de David traduictz en langaige vulgaire et rithme comme par Clément Marot'.

All these considerations allow us more easily to place the critical years of 1533–4. At Easter 1533 Gerard Roussel preached in the Louvre before Margaret of Navarre. Nothing could excite more keenly the anger and animosity of the Sorbonnists who had just condemned a new edition of the *Miroir* (first edition, 1531), printed this time with the addition of a translation in French of the Sixth Psalm by Clément Marot. For Francis I, intent upon supporting his sister, it was a trial of strength. A commission of enquiry, directed by Duprat and the bishop of Paris, decided on 18 May 1533 that Roussel should remain but that Beda be banished from Paris. It was a hard but indirect blow, and on 8 November the Sorbonne withdrew its earlier condemnation. And so all was restored to harmony. On the surface, the king was successful and the moderates triumphed, and through them, it should be noted, the very cause of the Reformation. In this calm there exploded, like a clap of thunder, the serious incident of the *placards*. In the night of 17–18 October 1534 printed posters were put up everywhere. Their title was: 'Articles véritables sur les horribles, grands et importables abus de la mess papale inventée directement contre la Saincte Cène de notre Seigneur, seul médiateur et seul sauveur Jésus-christ.' These *placards* were posted in Paris, and also at the same time in Orleans, Rouen, Blois, Tours, Amboise. The king was staying at Amboise, and a poster was nailed to the very door of his bedchamber. His first reaction was a terrible anger. Repression followed. On 16 November some 200 persons were arrested of whom twenty-four were later consigned to the flames. The greater part of the victims were humble people, some of them ribbon-makers returned from Germany with proscribed books. There was soon afterwards a return to a policy of moderation: by the Declaration of Coucy (16 July 1535), the king offered an amnesty to fugitives who abjured within six months. An important turning-point, however, had been reached.

At the same time, the death of the last Sforza opened the succession to much-coveted Milan. The war lasted from 1536 until 1538 and was patched up in the truce of Nice (18 June). In fact, the adversaries were reconciled so that they could unite against heresy, as was planned in August, in the negotiations between the king and the emperor at Aigues Mortes. Thus the king took charge of the repression in France, and for many years that policy aroused feelings which inspired in 1546 the song of the anti-royalist, E. de Beaulieu:

> Je ne croy point qu'un tel Prince ne sente
> Quelque malheur et que Dieu ne l'absente
> De plus regner, veu ses ferocitez
> Tant qu'il perdra ses villes et citez,
> Et sera mis dehors par main puissante.

Such was the direction of royal policy until the last days of Francis I. There lies the tragedy of the reign which is fairly difficult to explain, although the acts are clear enough. The edict of 16 December 1538 ordered the sovereign courts to give 'tel ordre soing et regard pour tout leur ressort, sur ceulx qui sont entachez desdictes hérésies'; the edict of 24 June 1539 and that of Fontainebleau (1 June 1540) entrusted the repression to lay judges, that is to the *parlements*. In the same line of action is an excerpt from the Edict of Villers Cotterets (31 August 1539) at the time of the strike of printers in Lyons and Paris:

sur l'humble supplication [declared the king] de nos bien amés les maîtres imprimeurs des livres de notre bonne ville et cité de Paris, contenant que pour acquérir science à l'honneur et louange de Dieu notre créateur, maintention soutènement et dilation de la saincte foi catholique et sainte chrétienté par l'universel monde et décoration de notre royaume....

Perhaps it is tedious to show how the meshes were formed. Suffice it that in 1542 the Sorbonne established a list of proscribed books; in 1543 it formulated twenty-four articles of Catholic faith which Francis I accepted; in 1544 it published a new index of forbidden books.

All these attacks against the Protestants were again confirmed by the Peace of Crespy (18 September 1544) when Francis I renewed his promise to fight heresy. The last years of his reign were clouded by the execution of the Fourteen of Meaux (1546) and the destruction of the Vaudois in 1545, already decided by the decree of 18 November 1540, named after Merindol.

The death of Francis I in March 1547 carried his son Henry II to the throne. The new reign, a decisive phase in the history of Protestant groups in France, followed the same path as the last years of his father's government. From father to son, there was only a tragic emphasis and aggravation of the drama. Calvinism, in cause and effect, had a part and responsibility. According to traditional explanations, it is customary to link the active beginnings of Calvinism with the appearance in French in 1541 of Calvin's *Institution Chrétienne*. This assertion is reasonably precise and is followed here with particular reference to the growth of Calvinism in France, above all at the end of the new reign, from 1557. Here was the depth and catastrophe of the drama.

The reign of Henry II was in many respects a water-shed, a point of departure for the long-term trends which characterised the second half of the sixteenth century in France and perhaps beyond France. It seems, at this juncture, that there was a set-back and stagnation in economic life. At the same time, after 1540 and even more after 1550, the mosaic of the provinces of France again changed colour. In this change, the very future of the towns along the great highways was in question. Now, in speaking of towns, we speak of heresy. In the history of the early Reformation and of humanism, the rôle of the great continental centres in France is clearly evident: for example, Meaux, Tours, Bourges, Troyes, Montpellier, Lyons. Precisely during the second half of the century, these towns were to find themselves apart from the great new currents sustaining the material life. Of this long crisis of stagnation, Lyons was a good example. Stricken to the heart after the bankruptcies of 1557, it had subsequently found life far less easy than in the past. To emphasise this hypothesis, France during the years 1540–60 turned towards the maritime zones, which were to become the most active regions invigorated by the young blood of commerce. In contrast, the continental provinces tended to harden: once open to the Lutheran Reformation, Champagne and Burgundy became indifferent, even hostile to Calvinistic ideas. They fell without resistance under the influence of the great feudal family, the Guises, and became with the adjacent Lorraine a part of the great corridor of the Counter-Reformation which passed from Italy across to the Spanish Low Countries. Without doubt, these general views are to be put forward with the greatest caution. Nevertheless, the tilting of France towards the Atlantic could not but add to the complexity of the Reformation in France on the eve of its last act—the Wars of Religion. In a recent book, I have tried to show this see-saw movement in the light of monetary and economic history.[1] It is necessary here only to indicate that this profound movement had its beginning in the reign of Henry II. The point adds to the usual discussion of the Reformation a stress on the great torsion of the economy and life of France.

That country was once again seized in the coils of European history, to which it was wide open and from which it could not escape. Indeed, the crisis in the last years of the reign of Henry II is not clear except in the light of the great events of Europe. The year 1555, with the Peace of Augsburg, saw both in appearance and fact the stagnation and putting-to-sleep of the great religious disputes in Germany. Happiness and calm on one side; in France, misfortune, awakening to acts of decision, and mounting tension. The foreign wars tested the endurance of France. All its structure was put in question during this exhausting struggle. It was out of all proportion, scarcely interrupted by the truce of Vaucelles (1555), and finally brought to a close by the collapse of the two adver-

[1] *L'Économie mondiale et les frappes monétaires en France 1493–1680* (Paris, 1956).

saries, the France of Henry II and the colossal Spain of Philip II. The Peace of Cateau-Cambrésis (April 1559) followed the bankruptcy of the two enemies. Imperial Spain regained breath. France did not have the same good fortune, but opened and offered herself as a battlefield for the intrusions of her neighbours. This conflict, which was also spiritual, was defined, however, by two armies, two leaders of purpose, two great fighters, who carried on a long and unending quarrel which was eventually passed on to their successors: Jean Calvin (1509–1554) and Don Iñigo López de Recalde, St Ignatius de Loyola (1491–1556).

It is rewarding to compare them for a moment. Characteristically, both well knew the France of their time; it is even possible that during their studies in Paris they may have met in the Collège Montaigu. A strange and important encounter indeed! Characteristically, both were also opposed to those territorial, or rather national, traditions, so dear to the gallican Church or to the negotiators of the Peace of Augsburg. Calvinists and 'soldiers' of the Society of Jesus knew no frontiers. Another curious trait was that the first Jesuits considered themselves apostles and refused to dress and conduct themselves as monks. Cells and action groups, not to mention their active and pugnacious corps—these comparisons could be pressed endlessly.

The destiny of the Society of Jesus in France is of outstanding importance. On 27 September 1540 the bull *Regimini militantis ecclesiae* brought confirmation of their Society. Loyola had the idea to concentrate the effort on two colleges, one in Rome, the other in Paris. In France, the Jesuits had the powerful support of the cardinal of Lorraine. Their efforts led to the issue, in January 1551, of the letters patent of Henry II to 'construire, des biens qui leur sont aumônés, une maison ou collège en la ville de Paris'. Was the royal sympathy sufficient? A real gallican crisis was produced in August 1551, for, with the *entente* engendered by the king's policy towards the Protestant princes of Germany, the occasion was hostile to the society. The relentless opposition of the *parlement* of Paris and of the Sorbonne to recognition of the society drew to a head the stern efforts to defend the ancient Church. But, then, the Jesuits were not of the ancient Church. On 10 January 1553 new letters patent and *lettres de jussion* convinced the *parlement* by a show of strength; again on 1 December 1554 the Sorbonne passed a decree against the society. In face of this opposition, the society was obliged to wait until 15 September 1561 for registration and official recognition—a significant date, on the very eve of the Wars of Religion. Meanwhile, the Jesuits had begun their mission of teaching in Auvergne where the Collège of Billom was founded by Duprat in 1555.

The rôle of the Calvinists was to be more spectacular and most revolutionary, though this is not to say that in the end it was the more effective. Geneva, the capital of the new religion, overlooked the frontiers of France from a point of vantage; by another stroke of fortune, Calvin was French by birth, upbringing and mind. Few will doubt that he exercised an enormous intellectual influence on his country. His *Institution Chrétienne* of 1541, his Bible of 1551, passed without difficulty from the Genevan printers into France. Then there were his numerous letters to groups and militants in France, his repeated advice, his directives and his orders. Thus, a force from beyond the frontiers gave to the groups of Calvinists in France a supranational character, a position of *imperium in imperio*. The same thing can be said of the Society of Jesus.

A whole discipline, indeed, was made by persecution and repression. The list of Henry II's measures compares with that of the preceding reign. On 20 July 1546 the condemned bibles of Robert Estienne were put on the index. On 11 December 1547, by the Edict of Fontainebleau, books, above all those coming from Germany and Geneva, were no longer to circulate without the formal permission of the Sorbonne. On 3 December 1547 Henry II ordered the *parlement* to administer 'bonne justice et principalement sur le faict des Luthériens'. The name is already behind the times. In truth, now was the time for blows, and hard blows at that. On 2 May 1548 a special court was created in the *parlement*—the famous *Chambre Ardente*. It had jurisdiction in Champagne, Brie, Île-de-France, Picardy, Maine, Anjou, Touraine, Poitou, Aunis, Angoumois, Beauce, Orléannais, Sologne, Berry, Nivernais, Lyonnais, Forez, Auvergne, Bourbonnais, Morvan, Maconnais. Finally, the Edict of Châteaubriant (27 June 1551) entrusted the punishment of heretics to the new *juges des présidiaux*.

This methodical fury of repression stayed abreast of the rapid diffusion of Calvinism in France, a diffusion which was largely popular (as is shown by the list of cases before the *Chambre Ardente*); in this was concentrated the essence of the history of the Reformation on the eve of the Wars of Religion. In this respect, the arrival after 1553 of preachers trained in Geneva was of great importance. In 1553 Philibert Hamelin reached Saintonge; in 1555 de Launay and François de Morel arrived in Paris and established a church. Groups of Calvinists announced their existence: in 1553 at Poitiers and Angers; in 1556 in Bourges; in 1557 in Blois, Rouen, Caen, La Rochelle, Lyons, Aix, Bordeaux, Issoudun, Anduze; in 1558 in Dieppe, Le Havre, Tours, Saintes, Montargis, St Jean d'Angély, Marseilles, Bergerac, Sainte Foy, Montoire; in 1559 in Nantes, Tarascon, Gap, Valence, Gien, Villefranche, Châteauroux, Thouars, Nerac. In 1558 an estimate listed at least thirty-four churches with ministers: in 1561 the Admiral Coligny claimed, according to Catherine de Médicis, that there were 2150. On 25 May 1559 the first national synod assembled in Paris. Thus was established a Protestant Church, at once national and supranational. The rapidity of its diffusion astonished contemporaries, even Calvin himself. In 1560, he wrote to the Calvinists of Montélimar:

nous vous prions de vous tenir restreints...nous ne voyons pourquoi vous le pensez nécessaire d'aller si vite. Il sera suffisant, si vous essayez de faire croître la congrégation et entretemps vous gardez tranquils....

This was astonishingly wise advice, but not at all unusual for the inflexible old man of Geneva. Events, however, were not to be favoured by the prudence either of men or of nations.

War had broken out once more, a vast and demanding conflagration from the moment of the march on the Rhine in 1552. Everywhere the flames spread. The war abroad could scarcely end, they thought at Geneva and among the Protestants, without opening the sluice-gates of civil war. 'Si le Roi', wrote Macar to Calvin on 17 August 1558, 'obtient la paix, il engagera, comme il l'affirme, toute son âme et tous ses biens dans une guerre contre les *luthériens* pour détruire jusqu'à la racine et leur race et leur nom.' On 3 April 1559 the Treaty of Cateau-Cambrésis was signed. The peace concluded by the Catholic powers was to open the opportunity to disorders within. On 2 June 1559 war was declared on Protestantism by the Edict of Ecouen which declared 'nous ne voullons aulcunement estre troublés par les damnés entreprises des hérecticques ennemys de nostre dicte foy et religion'.

Then, on 10 July 1559, in an accident at tilting, Henry II met his death.

Events, however, were to follow their course and war would erupt in the kingdom. These long and complicated struggles form another chapter in French history. When marked on a map, they show that the Protestants had not taken root over the whole country. After the third war in 1569 we see Protestantism shifted towards the Atlantic, finding its capital in La Rochelle. It is worth remark that the events in the dramatic reign of Henry II had long in advance prepared the geography and destiny of Protestantism in France, prepared at the same time its lines of strength and its lines of weakness. There is a coincidence, clumsy to be sure, but a coincidence between economic activity and the war and, as well as the infiltration of the Reformation, the resistance and revival of the old religion, restored by what can be called the Catholic Reformation, so strongly installed elsewhere with the momentum of tradition that Protestantism lost its grip and entity, and in spite of its heroic exploits did not carry the day.

CHAPTER VII

THE REFORMATION IN ENGLAND

ENGLAND, as is notorious, wore her Reformation with a difference. While elsewhere a religious upheaval carried in its wake political and constitutional reconstruction, England's march away from Rome was led by the government for reasons which had little to do with religion or faith. Yet there are factors—circumstances, feelings and passions, as well as indifferences—which explain the English Reformation. The dislike of priests and the pretensions of the Church, which appeared all over western Europe, had not left England untouched. A whole folklore of the disreputable cleric testifies to a common opinion whose significance is quite independent of its accuracy. The abuses of the Church—simony, nepotism, pluralism, ostentatious wealth, corruption, worldliness—gave pause to good orthodox Christians like Thomas More who only started to deny them when denunciation had become linked with heresy. Since 1515, Thomas Wolsey, the great cardinal,[1] had governed Church and State and had given a concrete and comprehensive example of all that was wrong with the former. Like his master, the pope, he had done the work of this world and paid merely formal attention to the work of the next. The extenuating circumstances which later ages may discover—his buildings, his patronage of the arts and learning, his tolerance—seemed to his own age only to aggravate his unashamed worldliness. There were truer Christians among the English clergy than Wolsey, but both in high places and in low, among the bishops and in the parishes, the not-so-spiritual greatly outnumbered the rest. A bench of bishops, promotion to which had for two centuries lain through royal service, through the careers of the lawyer, the diplomat, and the civil servant, could indeed be (as it was) a model of efficiency, hard work, even rectitude; but it was unlikely to offer much spiritual guidance or even undertake the reform of undoubted abuses. Bred in the system, the rulers of the Church necessarily perpetuated it.

To this general dislike of priests—this refusal to be any longer ruled by them—the laity added other more obvious desires. The Church excited hatred by the wealth it had and the wealth it sought. About one-third of England's lands was in ecclesiastical hands: great lords like the abbot of St Albans or the bishop of Winchester (both of which benefices Wolsey

---

[1] Thomas Wolsey (c. 1475–1530), son of an Ipswich grazier, fellow and bursar of Magdalen College (Oxford), king's almoner 1509, bishop of Lincoln and archbishop of York 1514, chancellor 1515, papal legate 1516, etc., etc. He derived his eminence from offices granted by both king and pope, but though he pursued a foreign policy designed to support the latter it was really on the former that his power depended.

added to his archbishopric of York) controlled larger revenues than any temporal nobleman. The gentry, who had obtained the use of much monastic land on lease, now wished to convert their rights into true tenure; schemes of expropriation had a long history. The current exactions of the Church, in particular the tithe, caused constant resentment. The fees taken by the clergy in the performance of their office and especially for burials (mortuary fees), and the revenues collected by the ecclesiastical courts, had come under attack on many occasions in the previous centuries. The courts, once so useful, were by this time only hated. Notoriously corrupt, dilatory and incomprehensible, they also represented a degree of interference in private lives that could not be paralleled on the secular side. Moreover, they stood for that fatal thing: the Church as a separate organisation, a State within the realm.

All these feelings, ancient but none the less vigorous and in fact increasing in strength, are commonly summed up under the title of anti-clericalism. Assuredly England was anti-clerical: it had little respect, much dislike, and often virulent hatred for all the institutions of the Church. The feeling was particularly marked in the populous south, especially in London, where a famous case of 1514–15 demonstrated its strength. A London merchant, Richard Hunne, arrested on suspicion of heresy, was found hanged in the bishop's prison. The bishop swore it was suicide; a coroner's jury accused the jailer and the bishop's chancellor of murder. There ensued uproar and rioting in the city and in parliament, and though the chancellor escaped with a fine the Church came ill out of the affair. Hunne's real crime was that he had appealed to secular jurisdiction against an excessive mortuary fee, and the unpleasing attempt to rig the record by burning his dead body for heresy is a sad reflection on the state of mind of the clergy. Hunne was not forgotten when parliament at last got its chance of attacking the Church.

It is, however, important to remember that all this anti-clericalism did not mean that heresy was rampant in England. On the whole, the nation, in any case more formally than profoundly pious, adhered to orthodoxy. Lollardy, the last decline of Wycliffe's scholastic attack 150 years earlier, played no part in the Reformation. More formidable was the newer heresy of Lutheranism which was beginning to spread at the universities. In 1524 William Tyndale fled the country, to publish an English translation of the Bible and lead the stirrings of English Protestantism from abroad. (In 1536 he was caught and burned by the imperial authorities.) In Cambridge, a discussion group dubbed 'Little Germany' began the academic response to Luther's teaching; when Wolsey transferred some Cambridge divines to staff his new college at Oxford, he inadvertently infected the other university. The bishops tried to do their duty, and the martyrology of the Church of England begins in these years with men like Thomas Bilney and John Frith. Wolsey's secular temper kept the persecution in check; after his fall in 1529, Thomas More, the layman who succeeded him as chancellor, encouraged the bishops to act. But all in all, while the Church of England may rightly look back to Tyndale, Tyndale would have remained a lost voice in the wilderness but for the king who hated him and whose beliefs were set down in his book against Luther (*Assertio Septem Sacramentorum*, 1521), for which pious and moderately learned work a grateful pope had given him the title of Defender of the Faith. English anti-clericalism was secular, not evangelical. Nor should we look to intellectual movements for a cause of the Reformation. England had heard of the 'new learning', of the humanist revolution in the schools, as much as any country; had she not harboured Erasmus, and had not Erasmus and his friends looked to the young Henry VIII as to their great patron? But the English humanists remained true to the Church; in More and Fisher they supplied two of the very few martyrs of the papal cause. If the English Reformation began as a movement neither of the spirit nor of the mind, it was none the less devastating, enduring, and deserving of respect.

The real mainspring of the Reformation was political. All the anti-clericalism of the people, supported by such nationalist objections to a foreign pope's interference in England as might be found, would not have led to a break with Rome if the Crown had not thought it necessary to deal with the papal control of the Church. For the Church represented a franchise, a liberty in the medieval sense, independent in its laws, its courts, and its sway over the spiritual life of Englishmen. English kings always had means of interfering in ecclesiastical affairs: they taxed the clergy and by agreement shared in the appointment of the hierarchy. But, as Henry VIII was to discover with an unconvincing air of surprise, the clergy owed allegiance to two masters. The English Church did not in strict accuracy exist at all; there were only the two provinces of Canterbury and York, parts of the universal Latin Church subject to the monarchical rule of Rome. The court of Rome drew a very large number of cases each year from England by appeal or revocation; the canon law of England was the canon law of Rome; the English clergy paid sizable revenues to Rome. In the fourteenth century, when kings and lords in England had found their rights of patronage threatened by the growing papal habit of 'providing' incumbents for benefices all over Europe, legislation was passed to protect the 'regality' of the Crown against such invasion—the acts of provisors and praemunire about whose restricted intention so much uncertainty prevailed that the sixteenth century was able to use them in a novel and sweeping manner. But throughout the fifteenth century and later, the English Crown maintained the friendliest relations with Rome, and England was the most papalist of countries. Henry VIII's effort against Luther and the pope's bestowal of the famous title only continued a well-established tradition of co-operation, at that time visibly embodied in Wolsey's position as Henry's chancellor and the pope's legate. If anyone suffered from this bland agreement it was the English Church, polled and harried by both its masters.

It is, of course, true that there were occasional difficulties in the relationship, especially over those liberties of the Church which went contrary to the energetic royal policy of consolidation. The clerical privileges of benefit of clergy and sanctuary endangered the restoration of order, the first by allowing every criminal who could claim to be even in minor orders his first crime free, and the second by offering refuges to escaping criminals in general. Legislation to limit the evil effects of these rights was passed both under Henry VII and in the early years of Henry VIII, and a law of 1512, which deprived those in minor orders of their clergy, served to provoke a conflict which revealed the latent troubles. In 1515 Robert Winchcombe, abbot of Kidderminster, preached a sermon against it, to find himself answered by Henry Standish, a friar and later bishop of St Asaph. Convocation tried to proceed against Standish who sought the king's protection, and in the course of the ensuing debate Henry had occasion to remark ominously that kings of England had never had superiors on earth. Patently he had neither doubts nor surprise in the matter: it had never occurred to him that any power outside England could possibly thwart him.

It is not too much to say that the Reformation got under way when he found that in this he was wrong. The gentry and nobility might resent clerical wealth, the people might despise priests and hate the tithe and fear the summoner who called them to the incomprehensible and annoying processes of the archdeacon's court, but while the king stood by the pope the Church was safe—safe from both reform and Reformation. The importance of Henry's desire to divorce Catherine of Aragon is just this: it turned the king from the pope's protector into the pope's foremost enemy. Thus it released the feelings against Church and pope which had hitherto been impotent to break down the defences behind which this 'foreign potentate' sheltered. Without the divorce there would therefore have been no Reformation, which is not at all the same thing as to say that there was nothing to the Reformation but the divorce. The strength and rapid spread of the flood indicate the amount of genuine and spontaneous feeling that underlay the Reformation. Moreover, as the sequel was to show, once England had broken with Rome the purely political beginning of the Reformation very quickly acquired a truly religious and even a truly spiritual companion force.

A word must be said about the attitude of the Church itself. Its collapse was neither so sudden nor so uncontested as is commonly supposed, but it was still on the rapid side. Before 1529 no cleric in England (except a few heretics) doubted the papal claim to be, under Christ, supreme head of the Church, even as none could assert this claim after 1534 without jeopardy of his life. The Church in England may have been Catholic before and after the Reformation, but Anglican it was certainly only after it. At first it had no reason to defend itself, for it was not so much subjected to attack as made to remember that the king had his rights and that it owed some allegiance to the Crown. The battle was lost before ever the pope came under attack. Furthermore, Wolsey had inadvertently prepared the Church for its doom. By means of his autocratic legatine administration he had for the first time established some sort of lasting unity in the two provinces; he had weakened the viability of the Church by concentrating all power in his hands and turning the bishops into mere agents of his greatness; he had lessened ecclesiastical influence by driving all bishops but himself from the royal counsels;[1] by his enormous unpopularity he had convinced the Church itself of the dangers inherent in papal power; finally, in his fall he was to provide the enemy with a useful tactical weapon for reducing the Church to subjection. When Wolsey's baleful influence is properly studied, the really surprising thing is not that the Church gave in to Henry VIII but that after fifteen years of the cardinal's vigorous, selfish and quite disastrous rule it had sufficient strength to resist as much as it did.

Some time in 1527 Henry VIII came to the conclusion that in marrying his brother's widow he had sinned against the divine law. God's wrath, he thought, was manifest in the fate of his offspring. Stillbirths, miscarriages, and deaths in infancy had left him with only one legitimate heir, Mary, now eleven years old. There has been much doubt whether Henry was really concerned with the problem of the succession or merely used it to cover his improper desire for Anne Boleyn and his discreditable disgust with the ageing Catherine. The doubtful and insecure succession certainly troubled him. Neither he nor his nation had yet forgotten the difficulties of the preceding century; if the dynasty, and peace with it, were to be assured, it seemed very necessary for the king to add to his legitimate heirs. At the same time, he unquestionably was in love with Anne. But his own mind did not analyse matters in so rational a fashion, for with all his strong will, quick intelligence and learned interests the king was essentially a man of little depth. He had the egoist's supreme gift, the superb conviction that right is always on his side. Hypocrisy did not enter into it: his conscience invariably, and quite sincerely, amalgamated the demands of reason and desire into an assurance of righteousness. He did not think that he wanted to exchange wives or secure the succession, and had better find a respectable cloak for such desires; he thought that he was

---

[1] One curious immediate effect of the Reformation was to strengthen the clerical element in the king's council. Stephen Gardiner, appointed secretary in 1528 and a bishop in 1530, was the first bishop to hold office since Wolsey became chancellor in 1515, and there were on an average four bishops on the council in the 1530's.

sinfully living with Catherine and had better have the matter cleared up. Thus all these points of policy and personality became a question of canon law.

The steps for dissolving an awkward dynastic marriage were clear enough: the pope could declare it null on one of the many grounds provided by canon law, and ordinarily the pope was quite ready to oblige crowned heads of Henry VIII's proven devotion to the Holy See. But in this instance two obstacles appeared. One arose from the circumstances of the marriage: the problem of Catherine's earlier contract to Henry's brother had then, of course, been realised and had been solved by a papal dispensation. Clement VII was therefore being asked to deny his own powers to dispense with the law of scripture. More important still, soon after Henry first opened negotiations in the matter, the sack of Rome and capture of the pope by imperial troops put Clement in the power of the one man who would force him to refuse Henry's request. Charles V was Catherine's nephew, and both his strong family sense and his belief in dynastic prestige drove him irrevocably to oppose the dissolution of his aunt's marriage.[1] Spanish influence and Clement's timidity were too much for Wolsey. Repeated embassies and two years' negotiations resulted only in the granting of a commission to him and to Cardinal Campeggio to try the case in England, with a secret commission to Campeggio to let the business come to no conclusion. However, apart from showing up Catherine's innate dignity and goodness, the unsavoury proceedings brought no progress. Skilful delays protracted action, till Wolsey was driven desperate by the growing danger that Clement would give in to Spanish pressure, annul the commission, and revoke the case to Rome. The cardinal knew his king well enough to prophesy that such action would bring about his own downfall and with it the fall of the Church's independence in England. In July 1529 Wolsey's world collapsed around him. Pressed by Charles V, Clement revoked the case; Campeggio prorogued the legatine court till October, or rather till doomsday; and the Peace of Cambrai between France and Spain ended Wolsey's last hope of yet once again reversing the Italian situation.

Thus ended the attempt to settle the divorce by peaceful co-operation with Rome. Its obvious protagonist, the pope's legate, was quickly disposed of: by October Wolsey had full experience of the readiness of princes to discard the unsuccessful councillor. Deserted by all, deprived of the chancellorship, accused of praemunire and threatened with permanent imprisonment, the cardinal threw himself on Henry's mercy. This at least saved him from the vindictiveness of personal enemies and left him with the archbishopric of York, but his political life was at an end. After fifteen years of ruling England and manipulating Europe, he could not believe it. Though he went north to devote himself to his ecclesiastical

---

[1] It is sometimes argued that Charles V cannot have cared all that much for a middle-aged aunt, but that is to forget that family feelings were to him the case of policy (cf. p. 303).

duties, he never reached York and kept in touch with affairs at London. Within a year his enemies had evidence of burrowings behind the scenes; arrested for conveyance before the council, the old man died on his way south at Leicester Abbey (November 1530). His fall and death mark the end of an order of things. They also graphically describe the essential barrenness and wasted purpose of his years of power.

Having failed to get Rome's co-operation by persuasion and request, Henry now cast about for an alternative policy. Sir Thomas More took the vacant chancellorship, under pressure and in return for a promise that he would not have to involve himself in the business of the divorce. Even though he thus cut himself off from the only political issue that mattered in those years, he had put himself into a disastrously equivocal position from which only martyrdom was to release him. The other ministers inspired little confidence. Among them Stephen Gardiner, principal secretary since 1528, was the ablest; but throughout a career spanning the next twenty-five years, Gardiner could never quite reconcile his sincere devotion to the Tudor Crown with an equally sincere attachment to the pretensions of a political priesthood. For nearly three years Henry virtually devised such policy as there was. His aims remained fixed: a new wife and a safe, legitimate succession; nor could he rid himself of the conviction that both could only be achieved by papal sanction. But since the pope would not please him of his own free will, it was now necessary to force compliance upon him by threats, appeals and hostile demonstrations. The calling of parliament naturally suggested itself. Like all kings of the western kingdoms, Henry VIII called parliament when he thought it might be of use to him, and the awed admiration commonly bestowed on his alleged political genius misses the mark. It would have been surprising if at such a moment of crisis the estates had not been summoned. This is not to say that Henry did not display considerable skill in using parliament. He wanted from it ready co-operation and could not, therefore, ask for subsidies; moreover, memories of 1523, when Wolsey's financial demands had led to a most disturbed and unsatisfactory session, counselled caution. But parliament eased the difficulties of the Crown (another of Wolsey's legacies) by cancelling the king's debts, and it helped to bring the Church of England to a more compliant frame of mind. The Commons at least remembered not only Richard Hunne but all the many cases in which ecclesiastical abuses of exactions had troubled the laity. The king gave them a chance of freely airing their grievances, and the priests soon felt the terrible alarms which a French envoy had prophesied for them. Committees of lawyers drafted bills limiting mortuary and probate fees and attacking such evils as non-residence, pluralism and the gainful employment of the clergy in secular pursuits. The whole system of Church courts came under attack, though for the moment this produced only a passionate remonstrance from John Fisher, bishop of Rochester.

However, this spontaneous outburst of popular resentment did not directly help the king: the divorce made no progress. It now turned on the question whether Clement VII would permit a solution in England or insist on trying the case in Rome (which Henry resolutely refused to contemplate), and nearly three more years were filled with pointless negotiations and recriminations. Henry talked darkly of using parliament to settle matters, but when his legal advisers declared such spiritual matters outside its competence (December 1530) this single promising line of attack was abandoned. Instead there remained nothing but a bluster which declined in vigour as time passed, attempts to use France as a mediator, and the typical and typically futile enterprise in 1530 to convince the pope by means of the opinions of selected universities that Henry's case was just. This had been suggested by an obscure Cambridge divine, Thomas Cranmer, who was rewarded with an archdeaconry.

In January 1531, when parliament and the Convocations met again after a prorogation lasting since December 1529, a step of greater purpose was taken: the whole clergy in their Convocations surrendered to an indictment of praemunire—for exercising their spiritual jurisdiction in despite of the king's rights!—and bought a pardon for £118,000. At the same time they acknowledged Henry as 'their only and supreme lord and, as far as the law of Christ allows, even supreme head'. In this surrender lay the germ of a revolution, but for the moment Henry showed no signs of understanding its implications. According to his own interpretation, the title gave him only temporal and no spiritual rights of headship. The reservation which Fisher and Archbishop Warham had inserted made plain that the king had not yet replaced the pope as supreme head of the English Church, for the law of Christ, however defined, clearly traversed this. Loudly though Henry might thunder, fearful though the clergy and Catherine's supporters might be, Rome would not yield to this shadow-boxing, and even over his own clergy the king had not yet achieved that degree of control which Francis I, for instance, enjoyed by means of the Concordat of 1516. Late in 1531 Henry's evident bankruptcy in ideas produced a crop of rumours that he had decided to abandon the quest.

At this critical moment, however, he found the man who could resolve his difficulties. Thomas Cromwell, late a servant of Wolsey's, who had entered parliament in 1529 and been working his way up in the king's councils ever since, was a man of low birth and powerful intelligence; he had travelled widely and read widely; one way and another, as a merchant, a solicitor, and Wolsey's general agent, he had acquired a penetrating understanding of the political scene both at home and abroad. Secular in his temper and unusually free from preconceived notions, he was capable of taking the most radical decisions and executing them brilliantly; since, in addition, he understood the value of tradition and was devoted to parliament and the common law, he always built on firm foundations.

He simply offered to give reality to all the vague threats and claims that had been floating about for years. Once Henry was persuaded that the lawyers (and he himself) had been wrong—that the divorce did not need papal sanction and that parliament could act in the matter—the way was clear. Cromwell's intention was to create a self-contained and self-sufficient realm: a sovereign national State which, using the civilian concept of *imperium* existing in any polity whose ruler did not recognise a superior on earth, he called the empire of England. His own most important contribution to the structure of this State was his understanding that this 'empire' could in England be expressed in the sovereign legislative action of the king in parliament, embodied in statute. Freeing statute of that older limitation which wished to test it by reference to some external law—the law of nature, the law of Christendom (Thomas More's test)—he held that it was omnicompetent and must be obeyed.

The work was done in four sessions of parliament. In 1532 Cromwell utilised some of those Commons' grievances of 1529 to force the clergy into surrendering authority over its laws to the Crown (the Submission of the Clergy) and promoted a measure which deprived the pope of the annates or first-fruits from England, though Henry's reluctance to go to extremes led to the inclusion of a clause which postponed the effect of the act at the king's pleasure. Thus at last the real attack on the Papacy had begun, with the undermining of its legislative and financial powers over the Church in England. In 1533 the great Act in Restraint of Appeals to Rome destroyed the most important weapon of papal interference in English affairs by prohibiting appeals from courts inside the realm to courts outside it. Its famous preamble outlined Cromwell's theory of the State by describing the empire of England. The two sessions of 1534 completed the work by transferring to the Crown all other papal powers in the Church, such as the granting of dispensations, the appointment of bishops, and the right to tax freely. The Act of Supremacy (1534) merely declared that the king was supreme head of the Church of England and must be regarded as such. A treasons act of the same year added the penal sanctions to the claim. In the meantime the divorce, having ceased to be the real issue, had resolved itself. Once Cromwell's policy had gained the king's ear, the resistance of Anne Boleyn was quickly overcome. By January 1533 she was pregnant and a secret marriage was celebrated. In that month Thomas Cranmer found himself giddily promoted to Canterbury; Warham, ready for martyrdom and about to stand fast, had died in 1532, and Gardiner, who was angling for the place, had fallen out of favour during the negotiations over the Submission of the Clergy. In May Cranmer used the powers conferred by the Act of Appeals to declare Henry's first marriage void, and in June Anne was publicly married and crowned queen. The expected reaction from Rome (declaring these proceedings invalid and summoning Henry to return to Catherine), the king's appeal in October to a general council—these were but formalities. The Act of Appeals had declared war, and though for years to come there was to be talk of negotiations and pretence that the unity of Christendom had not been broken, the schism was plain.

The king's position was straightforward. He derived his supremacy from God: by virtue of his kingship he was also God's vicar on earth as far as his temporal dominions extended. The notion could claim an ancestry going back to Constantine. It is not true to say (though it has been said) that his supremacy was in any sense parliamentary. No one supposed that such an office could rest on an act of parliament: the statutes all took the fact for granted. Nor was the supremacy at this time exercised in or through parliament: it was personal, monarchical, even despotic, as had been the pope's from which it derived. This appeared most plainly when in 1536 Henry by commission transferred all his ecclesiastical powers—the whole royal supremacy—to Thomas Cromwell as vicegerent in spirituals, a transfer which rested solely on the supreme head's own authority. Nevertheless, parliament occupied an essential place in the revolution. For practical reasons, and since the sanctions available to spiritual jurisdiction could not guarantee a revolution, the supremacy had to be enforced through the ordinary courts of the realm. That meant that penal legislation, establishing new treasons, had to be added to the body of the law, an addition which only statute—only parliament—was competent to make. This basic necessity, together with Cromwell's devotion to the certainty and definition of statute, accounts quite sufficiently for the surprisingly parliamentary air of the revolution. When in due course the English Church needed a definition of doctrine, the true faith was similarly decreed by the supreme head but on occasion given enforceability by parliament.

However, the first exercise of the supremacy did not concern itself with the establishment of religious truth. The dissolution of the monasteries has at times been allowed to usurp the first place in the story, and though in fact it is of less importance than the establishment of the supremacy it remains a striking event. In one sense, the attack on the monasteries proclaimed as essential a break with the ecclesiastical past as did the emancipation from Rome, and it is possible that Cromwell thought the religious orders dangerously papalist, though in fact there is no evidence that they were any less English than the secular clergy. But in the main the attack must be seen as the one result of all that hatred of clerical wealth: the Crown needed money and the gentry needed lands. No one now takes very seriously the charges of corruption which Cromwell's agents collected in their general visitation of all monasteries late in 1535; while everybody pays careful attention to the *Valor Ecclesiasticus*, compiled a few months earlier on the basis of a general fiscal enquiry, which recorded with surprising accuracy the total wealth of the Church. The *Valor* not only provided a basis for the assessment of first fruits (one year's income due from all newly beneficed clergy) and tenths (an annual levy of one-tenth of all clerical income), but it also supplied the necessary stimulus for the dissolution. In 1535 all houses with less than £200 a year were declared dissolved; in the years 1536-9 the greater monasteries accepted voluntary or forced surrender; in 1540 the whole expropriation was rounded off with an act vesting all such property in the Crown.

All orders of regulars and friars thus vanished from England in four years. The dissolution was carried out in an orderly and efficient manner, with a surprising degree of consideration for the dispossessed, provided they did not resist dispossession. Adequate pensions—abundant in the case of abbots and priors—were allotted and paid; there was astonishingly little physical suffering. The Crown gained an additional income of well over £100,000 a year which roughly doubled the ordinary revenue. From the first, however, some of the lands were passed on. Leading ministers and courtiers benefited from the few free gifts made; others had to pay fair value for what they got or be content with leases. After 1542 a decline in administrative efficiency and a revival of wasteful war led to wholesale alienation, and by the end of Edward VI's reign the Crown retained little of the new lands. The royal coffers had enjoyed a great capital influx which in turn had been wasted. If the dissolution was undertaken to secure the financial independence of the Crown, it failed; on the other hand, the landed gentry old and new, established shire families as well as younger sons, rising yeomen and merchants all buying land, had succeeded in spreading the interest in retaining the monastic estates throughout the politically influential part of the nation.

All this vast upheaval did not pass off without opposition, though what strikes one most forcibly about the opposition is its small size and lack of real purpose. From the first many men both high and low had stood by in wonderment at doings which it was quite widely thought would lead to disaster, but success brought its reward in quieting such fears. More serious were the objections of those who stood by the papal supremacy. In 1534 a poor distracted servant girl, Elizabeth Barton, who had acquired the name of the Nun of Kent by wild preaching against the divorce and stage-managed pronouncements for the pope, was executed together with her clerical sponsors. Later in the same year, the first succession act demanded an oath to the new state of affairs which was refused by few to whom it was tendered; but Thomas More, John Fisher, and the monks of the London Charterhouse were among them. These provided the martyrs of the old faith: executed in 1535 after dubious trials and, in the monks' case, torture in prison, they stood alone for conscience against conformity. (Of course, there were some who supported Henry for conscience' sake.) More's case was the hardest. Trained as a royal servant and a politician, he had wrestled long with himself before deciding on his steadfast course, but so careful was he during his imprisonment to save his private conscience privately that only Henry's vengefulness and perjured evidence at his trial led to his end. When next year Queen Anne was added to the tally (for treasonable adultery, but really for having ceased to please the king) Henry's reputation as a sanguinary monster was established. While one must admit the king's intelligence and political skill, one really cannot deny that there is much truth in this verdict of contemporaries and others.

Whatever Europe's horror, England took the revolution quietly enough, until the dissolution brought matters to a head in the north, the least settled part of the realm. Here disaffection, never altogether absent, had been gathering since Henry first showed signs of breaking with the pope. Resentment of control from the centre, dislike of a policy (pursued since Edward IV) which tried to break down the ancient but disruptive loyalties of the border region, anger over the spread of sheep-farming and enclosure, annoyance at the Statute of Uses (1535) and its attack on the gentry's illegal but well-established practices in devising lands by will, all these combined with a growing fury over the religious changes to produce a rising whose membership was quite as mixed as its motives. Trouble, which first broke out in Lincolnshire (October 1536), spread quickly to Yorkshire. Here the movement found its leader in Robert Aske, a lawyer of York who popularised its banner with the five wounds of Christ and thought of the rising as a pilgrimage, the pilgrimage of grace. The rebels' demands centred round religious conservatism: they wanted the heretical bishops and statesmen punished and asked that the monasteries be restored. But in addition they displayed the particularism of the north and the selfishness of the gentry as well as of the common people. For a time the rising looked dangerous, especially because the government had no forces to suppress it; but neither Henry nor Cromwell ever hesitated in their course. Negotiations and their own dissensions kept the rebels north of the Humber; the rest of the realm remained absolutely loyal; the king's lieutenant, the duke of Norfolk, collected a sort of army; and after a promise of pardon Aske told his followers to disperse (December 1536). Lesser troubles in the next few months enabled Henry to break his word: his vengeance was terrible, and Aske himself died on the scaffold. The movement has attracted much sympathy as the last manifestation of medieval England and the common people's resistance to the Reformation; in fact—if one excepts Aske and a few sincere men—it only proved the backwardness and waywardness of those notoriously restless parts. Its chief result was to induce Cromwell to reorganise the Council of the North which proceeded energetically with the important task of destroying the line of the Trent which had divided England in two since the Norman Conquest. What must really strike the unbiased observer is not that the north revolted against Tudor rule and the break with Rome, but that the larger and vastly more populous south showed itself thoroughly content with both.

The suppression of the pilgrimage of grace and the progressive destruction of the remaining monasteries ended the first phase of the English Reformation—the political phase marked by the reconstruction of the body politic and the triumph of the national State. The years 1536–59 were to see the working out of the problems raised by that revolutionary change: the nature of the royal supremacy and the faith of the Church of England. These internal difficulties, both political and doctrinal, suffered further complication from the shifts of the European scene and the needs of England's foreign policy, not to mention the troubles caused by a major economic crisis. If Cromwell dominated the first and critical phase, it is not too much to say that Cranmer stood in the middle of things in the second. A slow and honest scholar, firm in his convictions while he held them but progressing through inner changes throughout those years, the archbishop of Canterbury presented a very different figure from the ruthless, statesmanlike and forthrightly secular vicegerent. Cromwell's was undoubtedly the more powerful personality and more certain purpose, but Cranmer's gentleness and relative tolerance are more attractive qualities. They were very good friends.

Henry VIII seems to have thought that the break with Rome could be carried through without altering the doctrine and worship of the English Church. He, if no one else, apparently credited the persistent pretence that there had been no revolution, only a restoration of the proper and ancient organisation. But elsewhere the political Reformation was beginning to stir up religious turmoil. The small yet vocal group of divines who had embraced the doctrines of Luther and Tyndale thought their time come, and Cranmer, pursuing the studies which had first turned him from orthodoxy in his Cambridge days, felt inclined to support them. Cromwell tended the same way: eager to find allies against the potential dangers of a Franco-Spanish alliance, he sought them among the Lutheran princes of Germany who at least had a similar interest in keeping the pope down and the emperor occupied. The signs were clear but by no means bright: there was to be some cautious drifting away from existing practices and beliefs, especially those which, depending on the doctrine of purgatory, were particularly obnoxious to the reformers. The Ten Articles of 1536, enforced by the vicegerent's Injunctions on clergy and laity, embodied this compromise: they 'lost' all sacraments except the three accepted also by the Lutherans (baptism, holy communion and penance) and cautiously adumbrated a growing hostility against the practice of praying to the saints and for the dead. The Injunctions deserve notice because they ordered every parish to possess and exhibit a Bible in the native tongue.

In 1539 the appearance of an official translation ('Matthew's Bible', based on the work of Tyndale and Miles Coverdale) enabled the Church to obey. The characteristic instrument of English Protestantism thus appeared at an early stage in the battle.

However, 1536 was also the year in which Catherine of Aragon died and Anne Boleyn was executed, the year in which France and Spain renewed their endemic wars. Henry thus saw no further need for these manœuvres in the direction of Lutheranism; as soon as external pressure ceased, he always arrested Cromwell's attempts to create an anti-papal block in northern Europe. In 1537, therefore, as the king (remarried to Jane Seymour) gained a son and lost a wife, he authorised the publication of a primer, *The Institution of a Christian Man,* which withdrew even from the cautious advance of the Ten Articles. But in the summer of 1538 the continental powers concluded the Peace of Nice; for a time it looked as though they would at last turn upon England and exploit such disaffection as they could find there. Cromwell temporarily got a free hand. He busied himself with strengthening the neglected defences of the country; he satisfied his own desire for security and Henry's dynastic fears by wiping out the Pole and Courtenay remnants of the Yorkist line who had mingled family ambition with treasonable activities on behalf of the old faith and the pope; and he pursued his reformist policy with renewed vigour in the Injunctions of September 1538 in which he attacked 'superstitious practices', shrines and pilgrimages. He also made a fresh attempt to form a Lutheran alliance. But he was beginning to raise doubts in the king's mind; the danger against which he was planning seemed never to be coming. Cardinal Reginald Pole's mission early in 1539 showed up the unwillingness of the great powers to do more than call Henry names, while at home, on the other hand, the trumpet calls of the reformers and the attacks on such ancient centres of devotion as St Thomas Becket's shrine at Canterbury were exciting trouble. The people of England had accepted the substitution of Henry for the pope with marked equanimity, even though many in the north had resisted the assault on their familiar monasteries. Real uneasiness came only when a generation of little spiritual zeal, used to the formal devotions and propitiatory devices which was all that by this time the Christian religion meant to a large number, heard some of their clergy call these comforts in doubt, deny the efficacy of prayers to saints and masses for the dead, and denounce as superstitious the wonderworking intercession of images and shrines. The religious Reformation certainly began in the 1530's, as the immediate result of the political upheaval which removed an ancient barrier against dissent; in its turn it immediately began to breed that religious passion, that *furor theologicus,* so characteristic of the next 150 years and so very different both from the formalism of the order overthrown and the cold lucidity of Cromwell's secular mind.

By 1539 the country was stirring in a swelling murmur in which one may discern the signs of a crisis of faith and conscience. The king and his government saw in it the signs of trouble: the country was being torn in two by the upstart arrogance of the new religion and the boorish stubbornness of the old. However, a word from on high would settle all questions and still debate. Thus parliament and the convocations were summoned to meet in April 1539, an unusual time—being near summer and the season of sickness—which points to the urgency of the problem. Prolonged debates both in the ecclesiastical assemblies and in the House of Lords produced at last a definition of dogma, the famous Six Articles which decreed Catholic orthodoxy. They marked a triumph for the conservative bishops, led by Gardiner, over Cranmer and Cromwell; the king accepted them when he saw them supported by majority opinion. However, though they continued to mark the official standard of orthodoxy, they remained virtually dormant: there was no wholesale persecution of Protestants while Henry lived, though a few were to suffer.

The act did, however, end Cromwell's policy of a gradual advance towards Protestantism. The minister himself survived a difficult session still in the saddle, but he was sufficiently disturbed to make the fatal mistake of forcing Henry into a distasteful marriage. The projected alliance with the League of Schmalkalden was abandoned in May 1539; instead, Cromwell found a new wife for his master in Anne, daughter of the duke of Cleves, whose territories commanded the imperial route from Italy to Burgundy. From first seeing her, Henry hated Anne of Cleves. The marriage in itself was not the occasion of Cromwell's fall, but it predisposed the king to listen to his minister's enemies. For some five months early in 1540 the bitter battle was waged behind the scenes. Personal hatreds and international considerations played their part; but ostensibly, and up to a point actually, the struggle was between the conservatives and reformers in religion. Henry continued to trust, or at least to support, Cromwell to the very end; at last persuaded by specious lies that his vicegerent was a heretic, he had him arrested on 10 June and executed, after attainder without trial, on 23 July. In the meantime, Cranmer and parliament had obediently freed the king from Anne of Cleves.

Cromwell's fall was a disaster for England, for despite Henry's smug assumption of statesmanlike qualities there was no one left who could direct affairs with his skill, perspicacity and assiduity. To the Protestant cause it proved much less disastrous. Cranmer retained the king's confidence: a strange relationship between men totally unlike yet held together by mutual admiration and even devotion. Furthermore, powerful as he was, the king could not single-handed stem a tide which, almost single-handed, he had let loose; all his querulous complaints about disunion and brawling over religion availed him nothing. At the head of the Church itself the clear purpose was lacking, for until Henry died matters were in the charge of one who only excelled in opportunism. But if his qualities prevented the king from giving the storm direction, they also saved him from the rash and doctrinaire measures of the next reign. As it was, he held for six years a quivering kind of balance between the parties.

The immediate ascendancy of the conservatives after Cromwell's fall ended when their nominee for the royal bed, Queen Katharine Howard, was executed for treasonable unchastity (1542). A year later, alliance with Spain and the excesses of the reformist zealots tilted the balance a trifle the other way. The English bible was reserved by statute to wealthier men; a new primer (*The Necessary Doctrine and Erudition for Any Christian Man*) removed all traces of Lutheranism from that of 1537; the Catholic bishops attempted several times to be rid of Cranmer as they had been rid of Cromwell. But before long events once more advanced the Protestants. At court the younger generation, led by Prince Edward's uncle, the earl of Hertford, and by John Dudley, Viscount Lisle, was turning towards the new ideas and Henry recognised the shape of the future when he committed his heir to the tuition of so good a Protestant as Sir John Cheke. Late in 1546 the Howards, secular mainstay of the Catholic faction ever since Cromwell's rise to power, at last took a wrong step. The old duke of Norfolk was not to blame: he had proved his skill by surviving two nieces both of whom had married and offended the king. But his son, Henry earl of Surrey, not only showed traces of an irresponsible and immature leaning towards reform but also talked of his descent from Edward I. The Howards had plenty of enemies, and when Henry VIII died, on 27 January 1547, Surrey was dead on the scaffold and his father a prisoner in the Tower under sentence of death (which was never carried out).

Certainly, the last years of Henry VIII did not see any formal advance in the direction of the religious Reformation. The Act of Six Articles remained to protect orthodoxy, and occasional burnings of Protestants underlined the fact. Cranmer, busy translating the litany, kept his labours to himself. At the same time, of course, Henry withdrew not a step from his position as supreme head, and several papists died as traitors to mark the king's determination on that point. In those years the Church was, on the face of it, truly Henrician: as Catholic in doctrine as Rome itself, but schismatically divorced from Rome as a body of Christians. Yet from the first the existence of an anti-papal Protestantism on the continent jeopardised this idiosyncratic compromise. Sooner or later, the reformers would grow stronger; sooner or later, the 'Henricians' would realise that they could only maintain their Catholicism if they abandoned the royal supremacy. It was because he saw this that Henry never trusted Gardiner or the other orthodox bishops and left the country at his death in the hands of a Protestant boy with overwhelmingly Protestant advisers. In the last resort the king could not destroy what he and Cromwell had built. The essence of the Henrician Reformation lay in the sovereign national State's triumph over the Church in England; the changes in religion—in faith and dogma—usurped the place of first importance only when Henry was gone.

These changes did not, however, take long once the Crown had fallen into the powerless hands of Edward VI. The six years of his reign (1547–53) witnessed a revolution in religion as great as the jurisdictional revolution of the 1530's. Henry VIII was no sooner safely interred than the signs of Protestant triumph began to appear thick and fast. The late king's attempt to prevent any single councillor from gaining the ascendancy over the rest broke down at once: the earl of Hertford, with the assistance of Sir William Paget, had himself created lord protector and duke of Somerset and proceeded to rule in his nephew's name. Somerset certainly had some striking qualifications for the part. Not only was he the country's foremost military commander and the king's uncle, but he also suited the reforming party whose strength on the council gave him the upper hand. Unfortunately, his character and skill were not up to the task. Though generous, liberal in politics, and willing to remedy the griefs of the poor, he also proved arrogant, greedy and tactless in his dealings with his equals. Above all, he showed none of that penetrating political skill—that nose for the right moment and the right action—that had brought the Tudors so far. He began by removing the fierce laws of the last reign which had enabled the government to suppress religious dissent. The Act of Six Articles went, as did the treason acts; communion under both kinds was permitted; Cranmer published a book of *Homilies*, attack on which brought Gardiner to the Fleet. The government had shown which way they intended to go.

The Edwardian Reformation, which created a Protestant Church of England, proceeded in two clearly defined stages. In the first place it achieved a moderate Protestantism in the Prayer Book of 1549, supplemented by an act permitting the clergy to marry (1549) and an ordinal enacted in 1550. This last removed all vestiges of priesthood from the English clergy: they were to be simply ministers of the Word in the Protestant manner. The Prayer Book itself, containing a simplified set of services which centred on the Psalms, scripture readings, and appointed collects rather in the manner suggested by such Catholic reformers as Reginald Pole and the Franciscan Cardinal Quiñones, was plainly Protestant in its attitude to the sacraments of which only baptism and holy communion remained. The last proved the crux of the matter: the religious controversies of the reign concentrated on the sacrament of the altar—the quarrel between the mass and the communion service, and the problem of transubstantiation. Cranmer, whose mind devised and whose pen wrote nearly all the formularies and service books, had himself believed in the Real Presence as late as 1546, or at least he had never denied it in Henry's reign. But from 1547 he came under the influence of an invasion from the continent. The repeal of the repressive legislation attracted to England a number of the leading reformers, called in quite deliberately to assist the archbishop with his problem of discovering true religion and imposing it on the Church of England. Martin Bucer at Cambridge, Peter Martyr Vermigli at Oxford, John à Lasco and Francis Dryander—from Germany and Italy, Poland and Spain came some of the best known of the new theologians. The strongest influence on Cranmer was now Zwinglianism, embodied in that pope of Zürich, Henry Bullinger, to whom English Protestants were to look for aid and advice for some thirty years. But Cranmer refused to go all the way with Zwingli on the eucharist and arrived at a characteristic definition midway between the sacrifice of the mass and the mere commemorative service of the Swiss persuasion.

The first stage of the Reformation was thus Protestant enough, but somewhat reserved. True to his liberal temper, Somerset would not enforce the Prayer Book by more than a permissive act, nor did Cranmer feel sufficiently sure of his ground to abandon all contact with the Catholic past. But in the event the Prayer Book pleased few. The continentals accepted it with hesitation and decided against it as soon as Gardiner, since July 1548 in the Tower for publicly opposing Protestant preaching, discovered that it could be given a Catholic interpretation. The pressure on Cranmer to go further increased; in particular, 1550 brought to the fore the first of those puritan spirits whom English Protestantism was to produce in such quantity. Sincere, ardent, uncompromising, foulmouthed, and intractable, John Hooper proved a problem not only to political divines but also to such radicals as Nicholas Ridley, bishop of London. Neither Cranmer nor Ridley, least of all the council, felt inclined to respect Hooper's pernickety scruples over vestments and ornaments, but since good Protestant bishops were hard to come by they needed his services. In the end Hooper gave way to the extent of accepting the see of Gloucester (Worcester being added later), but his spirited defence of extremism helped to push the Church further into reform.

Nevertheless, the real pressure came from another quarter. After all, the English Reformation had never been the exclusive preserve of religion and theologians; politics and the lay power had always mattered more. In 1550 the lay power was in transformation. Somerset's enemies on the council outnumbered his friends; his policy of deliberately neglecting his colleagues had seen to that. In 1549, a year of crisis, the powerful gentry of whom the council was representative had had a bad fright when two simultaneous risings shook the State. Of these, the Cornish rebellion seems to have been in the main a reaction against the religious innovations: the Cornishmen complained of the alien Prayer Book and Bible, in a language as strange as Latin but less familiar. More serious was the great rising of the Norfolk peasantry, known from its leader as Ket's rebellion, which for a time established almost a separate political organisation in East Anglia. Here the main motives were agrarian grievances, especially the enclosure of common lands and arbitrary rents, while in religion Ket and his followers seem to have had Protestant sympathies. To Somerset's enemies these differences appeared immaterial; the disorders showed that he had failed in the first duty of Tudor governments. His religious innovations had provoked Cornwall; his social policy—investigations into illegal enclosures and attempts to enforce the law against the gentry themselves (1548)—had encouraged Ket and his men. These allegations were in part unfair, but that matters little. The council's indignation, fed also by the protector's personal ambitions and the failure of war in France, boiled over: under the leadership of John Dudley, now earl of Warwick and soon duke of Northumberland, they turned on Somerset, arrested him, and finally (1551) had him executed on a spurious charge of treason. The sorrow of the people at 'the good duke's' death both displayed the reason for his unpopularity with his equals and the essential impotence of this sort of popular feeling.

Northumberland's triumph was at first designed to look like a Catholic reaction, but it soon turned out to be the prelude to an even more energetic pursuit of the Reformation. The duke, an able administrator and energetic politician, might have made a good servant to a typical Tudor monarch, but left in undisputed charge he proved far too unscrupulous and self-seeking to do anything but harm to the realm. Representing, with others, those rising men who depended on Crown bounty and confiscated lands for their start in prosperity, he could not but favour the most extreme anti-clerical policy. The dissolution of the monasteries had left behind much unsatisfied appetite which Somerset had served in 1547 when he carried through an intention of Henry VIII's by dissolving and appropriating the chantries. These small foundations, mainly intended to support a priest to say masses for the founder's soul, were certainly obnoxious to the reformers who denied purgatory and disapproved of intercessory prayer; they were also landed property. The notion that their dissolution destroyed a flourishing system of grammar schools has recently been shown to be untenable; on the contrary, the sixteenth century did more than its predecessor for education, and some of the nationalised lands were in fact used to endow it.[1] But the bulk assisted the landed gentry. All that now remained for the plundering were the lands of the secular clergy, especially the bishops, which could best be confiscated by displacing the existing prelates and extorting concessions from their successors. Self-interest thus dictated a Protestant policy to

[1] Joan Simon, 'A. F. Leach and the Reformation', *British Journal of Educational Studies*, 1955, destroys the accepted view.

Northumberland; if, like Cranmer and Somerset, he had more genuine feelings in the matter they have never been observed.

Thus the reformers, English and foreign, who for a time had feared for their achievements, in fact found the new duke even more agreeable than the old. Cranmer soon produced a revised Prayer Book (1552) which discarded the remains of Catholic doctrine still found in its predecessor and came down entirely on the side of Protestantism, though he continued to believe in a spiritual presence in the eucharist which elevated that sacrament above the utter simplicity of the Zwinglian service. The book removed all those traces of 'popery' that à Lasco and the rest had objected to; as regards both doctrine and ceremonies the English Church had now followed the example of the continental Reformed Churches. A rigorous Act of Uniformity not only made all other forms of worship punishable by heavy penalties but also enforced attendance at the services of the state Church. In 1553 Cranmer added a coping stone to the edifice with the Forty-two Articles—a formulary of faith to which all the clergy were required to subscribe and which throughout is entirely Protestant, though not without those touches of backward-looking compromise which reveal the archbishop's essentially cautious approach to innovation.

England was now a Protestant country, at least so far as legislation and decree could make her one. In truth the changes at the top had as yet made little impression. Ardent Protestantism was found in some quarters. The king himself, since Somerset's fall something of a factor in affairs, held by it with the inhuman passion of an adolescent indoctrinated since childhood; the higher clergy had been carefully selected to include a growing number of men favourable to the new way of thinking (though the foremost preachers of the day, Hugh Latimer and Thomas Lever, being men given to criticising the powers that be, held no episcopal appointments); with some at least of the gentry and the products of the universities, a genuine belief in the reformed religion came even before the interests of the landowner. But no one was more fully aware than Cranmer that the truth as he now saw it would have to be inculcated in the nation, both clergy and laity, by a prolonged course of propaganda and enforcement, and his projected code of canon law—the *Reformatio Legum Ecclesiasticarum* completed in 1553 but never enacted—was designed to provide weapons in this fight. The country at large seemed at best indifferent; the old forms of worship continued to be used in many parts where the clergy and the local magistrates had no joy in the innovations. It has been said that the Edwardian Reformation went but skindeep. There is insufficient evidence for confident statements about its effective extent; but it is clear that, like the Elizabethan settlement later, its endurance depended on a period of use and enforcement, and that political accidents deprived its protagonists of the necessary time.

One other point is worth noting about the Edwardian Reformation:

it ended the Henrician type of royal supremacy in the Church, the personal and virtually despotic kind. Not only was the position of the supreme head weakened by the tenure of a child; the really important change occurred in the phrasing of statutes. Where Henry VIII used parliament to supply enforceability to decisions made and justified by the supreme head in person, the Edwardian parliaments participated in the exercise of the supremacy when the legally established form of worship became a schedule to an act of parliament. Elizabeth ultimately inherited her brother's rather than her father's position in the Church, adding weakness to it by being a woman and as such unfitted for the full headship; though she fought tenaciously to keep parliament from interfering in matters ecclesiastical, she could never deny their right to participate and had to retire to a second and lesser line of defence by quarrelling over the right to initiate legislation touching the Church.

As the year 1553 drew on it became plain that Edward VI had little time to live. Unless something were done he was bound to be succeeded by his sister Mary, Catherine of Aragon's daughter and an unshakeable adherent of the Church of Rome. To contemporaries such a succession signified a complete reversal of religious policy: in the sixteenth century governments everywhere dictated in such matters, and the cataclysmic changes in England are readily understood if one remembers that people held obedience to the lay power, whatever its religious views, to be enjoined by the divine law. Northumberland, however, had gone too far to hope to survive a turn of the wheel. From his fears grew the most outrageous and hopeless conspiracy of a century filled with many handsome specimens. Determined to maintain his power, the duke attempted to subvert the succession, exclude Mary, and crown instead Lady Jane Grey, heir to the Suffolk claim to the throne, whom he married to one of his sons. His daemonic energy and ruthless vigour carried the day in the council, but Edward's death in June proved his plot to be a mirage. The nation, resolved to have a true Tudor, acclaimed Queen Mary; as Northumberland moved against her into East Anglia, the council in London deserted him; in the end the princess succeeded to the Crown without any trouble at all. Northumberland, as was the way of things, suffered on the scaffold, but Mary's mercy for a time saved the lives of the other conspirators including that of the innocent sixteen-year-old pawn.

Thus there began the short period of the Catholic reaction, when for the last time England formed part of the Church which looked to Rome. Unfortunately for Mary, her policy, and her memory, it was also the first time that England formed part of the Habsburg territorial complex. Mary's overriding ambition was to restore the realm to the true faith, to obtain papal absolution for the sin of schism, and to eradicate heresy. Charles V, on the other hand, saw in the accession of his half-Spanish cousin a fine opportunity for bringing England within the circle of power which his family had built up by skilful and lucky marriages. From first to last the two policies never ran on sufficiently parallel lines. The emperor welcomed England's return to the papal fold, but he wished to prevent vigorous action against Protestantism and a sincere restoration of Mary's simple faith because he feared that such steps would lead to disruption and therefore lessen England's value to his own European policy. He felt this the more strongly because he intended to secure Mary's hand for his own son, Philip, archduke of Burgundy, a marriage which was in fact celebrated early in 1554 after the strong opposition of part of the English council had been overcome. The opposition and hostility of the nation never relaxed: Philip was at best but tolerated, while Englishmen and Spaniards discovered the ancient truth that contact between nations of very different temper and traditions is more likely to produce enmity than amity. The Spanish match pleased the queen, but it involved the country in somebody else's war, resulted in the loss of Calais, destroyed unity and purpose in the English government, and did not even prevent the persecution of Protestants which Charles V, however much he approved it in principle, saw to be a serious mistake in the circumstances.

The total sum of the reign's achievement has often been described as sterility, a verdict from which only the earnest partisan will find it easy to dissent. England was restored to Rome. The instrument chosen to bring about this consummation of Mary's devout wish was Reginald Pole, cardinal of England, who unfortunately turned out to be one of those honest and brilliant theorists who make such indifferent statesmen. Some thirty years earlier Thomas Cromwell had warned him not to suppose that the teaching of the philosophers could be applied to the things of this world, but this lesson Pole (some may think, to his credit) never learned. After he had broken with his kinsman Henry VIII in 1536, he was for a time employed in futile campaigns to raise opposition to the king among the monarchs of Europe; thereafter he retired to a congenial life of study and religion. Now, however, his hour had struck. Fetched from retirement, he journeyed towards his native land with papal bulls of absolution in his pocket and eager to restore the realm to its ancient obedience. He met two obstacles. One was the fear of the English ruling classes— everybody who mattered, that is—that a return to Rome would involve a surrender of the lands taken from the Church since 1536. The other was Charles V's desire that no disturbing factor should enter into England until his son was safely established there. Thus from late in 1553 until November 1554 the pope's legate waited in the Netherlands for licence to cross the narrow seas and carry out his mission of reconciliation.

In the meantime Mary tried to get some of her Counter-Reformation from parliament. To her mind, the anti-papal legislation was invalid in itself, but she had to yield to those, including Gardiner (now chancellor and chief minister), who declared that only parliament could undo what parliament had done. The first parliament of the reign (October 1553) repealed the Edwardian legislation but refused to re-equip the government with the secular weapons against heresy which Somerset had discarded. The second (March 1554) would do nothing at all, except attaint the participants in Sir Thomas Wyatt's recent rebellion which had, among other things, led to the execution of Lady Jane Grey and her relatives in the Tower. At last in November that year, Philip having now consolidated his position as king of England and full reassurances having been given that the secularised lands would not be mentioned, Pole was allowed to come to England, and a third parliament met to repeal the Henrician legislation and humbly beg the legate for the pope's forgiveness. The work of twenty years thus vanished overnight; the schism healed, all that remained was to punish its surviving authors and stamp out the remnants of heresy.

In fact, the rest of Mary's reign centred round the great persecution which is all that remains of her in the general memory. The third parliament re-enacted the old heresy laws, but even before that signs had appeared that action would be taken. Edmund Bonner, bishop of London (with Lincoln and Norwich the diocese most affected by Protestantism), had angered the politicians by trying to proceed against heresy before the laws were in force again. Gardiner, too, showed that his own desertion of the papal cause in Henry's reign had not weakened his determination to deal with the consequence of such weakness in others. Mary and Pole, convinced of the need to eradicate heresy, must take much of the burden of guilt; personally gentle and merciful as they were, they had the fanatic's fatal gift of being able to distinguish between the individual (to whom one is kind) and the cause (for which one kills).

The council found it easier to approve the persecution because by and large only the lower orders were involved. The leaders of Protestantism had fled abroad in some numbers; throughout the reign, English communities at Frankfurt, Geneva and Strassburg were carrying on, not without internecine quarrels, the traditions of English Protestantism and preparing for the day of their return. Four of the leaders, however, suffered: Hooper, Latimer, Ridley and Cranmer were burned as relapsed heretics. The rest of the 273 known victims who perished in the fires of Smithfield and elsewhere were mostly small men—artisans, shopkeepers, labourers—with an astounding proportion of women. Many of them were fanatics and some may have held opinions (Anabaptist and the like) for which a Protestant government would also have persecuted them. None the less, and not without justification, this concentrated attack and the deliberate spreading of the burnings *in terrorem populi*, reinforced admittedly by John Foxe's successful propaganda work (*Acts and Monuments*, first published in 1563), made the English for centuries hate Catholicism as a cruel and persecuting religion. Life was always cheap in the sixteenth century; the age was full of easy killings at law; yet a case-hardened generation reacted with horror to these burnings for religion's sake. Whatever else one may think of the persecution, it was a political error of the first magnitude.

The worst feature of the Marian restoration of Rome was that it contented itself with persecution and attempted nothing like a true spiritual revival. There were no signs of religious fervour or eagerness to lead men in the right way: Pole was old and worn out and even in the end suspect of heresy, while the other bishops had long ago lost their integrity. Everything remained political. Before the reign ended, Pole was to be excommunicated by a mad pope for purely political reasons, and Mary was to see her husband and her spiritual father at loggerheads. The truth is that in England only Protestantism, however thinly spread so far, represented a genuine spirit of religion. The country may have been attached to the mass and the old ways, but the old ways were eminently distinguished by the absence of real conviction or genuine faith. Admittedly conviction and faith were to produce conflict and persecution, but the history of Mary's reign itself shows that such results may be achieved not only by fanatics but also by the worldly. If England was to be rescued from the creeping corruption of self-seeking and greed which had spread ever wider since the restraining hand of government had failed in 1547, she would need not only a return to good government but also an infusion of an active faith. In the 1550's Rome could not offer this; perhaps unfortunately, and certainly much to Elizabeth's annoyance later, Geneva could.

When Mary and Pole died on the same November day in 1558 they knew that their policy had failed. They had ejected suspect clergy and seen heretics burned; on the face of it, England was as soundly Catholic as she had been before Henry VIII misdoubted his marriage. In fact, however, the reign had destroyed Rome's chances of ever again ruling the English Church. The war, the loss of Calais, the ascendancy of Spain had combined with the reaction against the persecution to turn the nation at last away from its past. Anti-clericalism, dislike of the Papacy, and eagerness for Church lands were no weaker than they had been thirty years earlier; now experience of Spanish and popish influence had further prepared the ground for an acceptance of Protestantism of which there had been few signs during the violent advance of Edward VI's day. Worst of all for the future of Catholicism in England, Mary never produced the child for whom she longed both as a woman and as a queen. She would be succeeded by her sister Elizabeth, Anne Boleyn's daughter and thought throughout the reign to be a danger both to the Catholic reaction and the Spanish dominance.

These were fears that the event proved right. Whatever her own private religion (a point never quite settled), Elizabeth found herself the virtual nominee of the Protestant faction. The exiles flooded back, refreshed by their sojourn in the new paradise. The parliament that met in January 1559 contained its enthusiastic core of good Protestants, and they pushed the queen farther and faster than she had intended to go. By the summer of 1559 the Acts of Supremacy and Uniformity had once again broken the link with Rome and restored the royal supremacy (weaker than Henry VIII's in theory and foundations but as formidable in his daughter's hands) and the Protestant Prayer Book to the Church of England.

CHAPTER VIII

ITALY AND THE PAPACY

IN the states of the Italian peninsula, as in the rest of central and western Europe, the news of the activities and doctrines of Luther, followed by those of Zwingli and later by those of the Anabaptists, the Anti-Trinitarians and Calvin, fell on ground ready to receive it. Among the numerous ecclesiastics, memories of Savonarola's preaching were not always propitious; thus the best-known Italian translator of holy scripture along Lutheran lines, the Florentine Antonio Brucioli, was violently hostile to Savonarola.[1] But there were the hopes raised by the Fifth Lateran Council (1512–17) especially in certain Florentine and allied circles in contact with the Venetian patrician and Camaldolese hermit, Blessed Paolo Giustiniani (1476–1528);[2] there was a desire for greater morality and austerity of life in the laity, the hierarchy and the curia; people were fully aware of the 'abuses' originally devised to meet the needs (in money and staff) of the financial administration and the centralised policy of the Church, not just the needs of the Holy See as an Italian state in matters of politics and war. There was also a strong desire for a more spiritual conception of Catholic religious life: for men like Giustiniani (and his friends included Gasparo Contarini, a Venetian nobleman, later to become famous as a cardinal) the consequences of such an infusion of the spirit occupied pride of place. These leanings were not in any way meant to affect the spheres of dogma, liturgy, discipline, traditions, the fundamental structure of the Church, or the papal authority, but would, it was hoped, be capable of supplying these with energy enough to purify the Church 'in capite et in membris'. Among the laity stirrings similar to those of the clergy were often to be found; but judgments more like the classic attack on clerical vices by the historian Francesco Guicciardini were also common.[3]

Expressions of this sort cannot be interpreted as favouring the actions of Luther, of the princes who protected him, or of his followers. They were manifestations of anti-clericalism among the laity, and of an 'anti-curialism' among many ecclesiastics which lacked any real conciliarist basis. Nor must the at first rapid spread of the doctrine of justification by faith, and the widespread and considerable interest taken in it by

[1] G. Spini, *Tra Rinascimento e Riforma, Antonio Brucioli* (Florence, 1940.)

[2] H. Jedin, 'Contarini und Camaldoli', *Archivio Italiano per la storia della pietà*, vol. III (1953). This aspect of Giustiniani and his friends has only recently been set in perspective, and research is in progress for the publication of his writings and letters. And see below, p. 278.

[3] On the whole period, cf. H. Jedin, *Girolamo Seripando* (Würzburg, 1937: 2 vols. with documents; Eng. translation, without documents, London, 1956).

humanists, theologians, preachers and the common people, be taken to mean that the reformers north of the Alps were gaining converts; the doctrine had been discussed by theologians and philosophers in the fifteenth century, and while the German and Swiss reformers used it as a dogmatic basis for the reorganisation of the hierarchical structure of the Church and its relationship with the laity and the civil authorities, for the majority of Italian ecclesiastics interested in it the expectations it aroused were of a kind to encourage merely conferences and discussions, and propaganda among individuals, often accompanied by semi-clandestine activities and a sort of political ambiguity which is characteristic of the Italian Protestant movement in its higher reaches. Thus when P. Carnesecchi[1] procured certain of those ecclesiastical benefices whose bestowal by the curia on persons unwilling to carry out the duties attaching to them was bitterly criticised as an abuse, he and his friends rejoiced at it; such benefices made it possible to assist poor and persecuted Protestants.

After the Italian expedition of Charles VIII of France, the Italian states had become theatres of war and their courts the object of diplomatic rivalry among the great powers. The ambitions of Cesare Borgia, idealised by Machiavelli because of the chances of unity and independence which they had offered to Italy, were but a memory a mere fifteen years after the death of Alexander VI and his son (1503). Julius II (1503-13), continuing the work of Cesare Borgia, thoroughly reorganised the civil and military administration of the States of the Church. His attempt to extend the papal dominions to their ancient boundaries brought him into conflict with Venice. But his military and political action in the international field, designed to promote 'the freedom of Italy' (*libertà d'Italia*) against France, Spain and the Empire who were disputing the Italian territories amongst themselves, succeeded only in fighting off the power of France and left the policy of the Holy See in the control of the other powers. Nevertheless the watchword 'freedom of Italy'—the independence of the Italian states from France, Spain and the Empire under the implied hegemony of the pope—remained the guiding principle of the papal policy until 1559. Having once again consolidated the Papal States, Julius II called the Lateran Council (1511) which should have initiated the work of Catholic reform. Though Leo X (1513-21) lived through the beginnings of the Lutheran Reformation and the resumption of the struggle between the powers in the rivalry of Charles V and Francis I, he continued the policy of Julius II. He assisted the imperial side in return for additions to the Papal States and benefits for the Medici family. Adrian VI (1522-3) during his short pontificate could do little in politics for the cause of reform. Clement VII (1523-34), on the other hand, was above all concerned with the enlargement and consolidation of the Medici interests and, profiting from the confused situation, attempted to gain lands and

[1] Cf. below, p. 266.

fiefs for his relatives. However, the eventual consolidation of Charles V's power, which put an end to these efforts, was not the sole reason for Clement's change of policy when he aligned the Holy See against Spain rather than France; as pope he regarded the imperial supremacy and ascendancy as dangerous to the Church, the more so because Charles V did not refrain from intervening in favour of Catholic reform and a general council. Thanks to the weakness of Clement VII, his French alliance and his Medicean policy, the programme of 'freedom of Italy', interpreted as equivalent to 'the liberty of the Church', had changed its meaning since the days of Julius II. After Charles V had permitted the sack of Rome, the forces of the Italian states ceased to offer firm support to the Papacy; Florence rebelled against Medici rule, Venice attempted to seize papal territories, and the French ally showed himself incapable, blind and unfaithful. In 1528, in return for a promise to restore Florence to the Medici, Clement VII deserted the 'Italian' cause (as Andrea Doria had done before him) and altogether abandoned the idea of Italian liberty. Yet it was only in 1530 that the Medici returned to Florence as its dukes; they were henceforth subject to Spain and closely tied to the Holy See.

With Paul III (1534–49) the policy of the Papacy, internally devoted to the strengthening of the Papal States, changed internationally to a neutrality which was not only a deliberate programme but also proved effective. Since Charles V's ascendancy in Italy was henceforth un-contested, it was also in the interests of the Papacy as an Italian power—and of the pope as a member of the Farnese family who enriched and aggrandised themselves even at the expense of papal territories—that the Holy See as an international power should remain neutral. At the same time, this was in the interests of the Catholic Church itself; peace was needed for the preparation of the council and the carrying through of Catholic reform. Pier Luigi Farnese, a son of the pope and favourably disposed towards France, was killed in a plot planned by the Spaniards (1547); on the other hand, the anti-Spanish conspiracy of the Fieschi in Genoa (1547) failed, as did that of Burlamacchi in Lucca, directed against the Medici and therefore against Spain (1546). Under Paul III the policy of the Holy See—leaving aside the pope's nepotism and the internal problems of the Papal States—began to be less concerned with Italian issues as such and more with the issues of religion and the Universal Church, that is, with the problem of the general council. While Clement VII had always put off calling one, Paul III began to issue summons from 1536 onwards. But the difficulties caused by the wars, by French sabotage, and by disputes with Charles V over its organisation, postponed its opening until December 1545.[1] The choice of venue fell upon Trent, near the borders of the Habsburg possessions but an Italian city independent under its prince-bishop. Owing to the plague and the fear of imperial

[1] Cf. also above, pp. 171 ff.

interference (from Innsbruck—much nearer than Rome), the council was in 1547-9 transferred to Bologna and then prorogued by the pope. The fact that at Paul III's death in November 1549 Reginald Pole's chances of succeeding were considerable shows how by this time purely ecclesiastical interests had got the better of Italian political interests. Julius III (1550-5) took no active part in Italian questions (the wars of Parma, 1551, and Siena, 1553-4) except in vain attempts at pacification. The neutrality which he observed did not reflect deliberate policy but was imposed by necessity, for the Holy See found itself in a disastrous financial position. In 1551 Julius III reopened the council at Trent, but he was once more forced to prorogue it when the religious wars in Germany endangered the town. He had no share in the Jesuit advance in Europe and beyond, or in the Catholic restoration in England. The pontificate of Marcellus II (1555) was too brief to be of any consequence. Under the Neapolitan Paul IV (1555-9) the papal policy of neutrality was temporarily suspended; the pope resumed anti-Spanish activities which in the end led to a war. Despite the intervention of Henry II of France, the Spanish troops of Philip II not only re-established Spain's supremacy in Italy (1556) but at St Quentin (1557) finally overcame those of France. On this occasion, though for a brief moment only, Venice allied herself with the Papacy, while Cosimo I of Tuscany confined himself to acquiring Siena as a Spanish fief. After 1556 the Carafa pope devoted himself only to his family and to the problems of Catholic reform and Counter-Reformation.

It will be seen that to begin with (1518-34) the Italian religious scene was dominated in the curia, and in the circles connected with it, by the conflict between the emperor and the popes over the question of the council. Throughout the whole period it is to be noted that Italian writers of anti-Lutheran treatises—there were at least sixty-three of them before 1536—did not deal with strictly Italian questions but concerned themselves rather with those which formed part of the general ecclesiastical debate, conducted in the main by Dominicans and Franciscans. At first the traditional theme *De Potestate Papae* predominated. Many even of the churchmen who were interested in the Pauline doctrines as propounded by Luther and in that great novelty, their application (favoured by peoples and princes) to the reform of the Christian Church, city by city and state by state, were not so much concerned with the Italian situation and the Church in Italy as with the fate of the Catholic Church and Christianity in general. The division of the peninsula into various states, the confusion arising from the loss of 'Italian liberty' or independence, and the presence of foreign civil and political authorities (French, Spanish and imperial) had resulted in the absence of a specifically 'Italian' Church. Giberti and his few companions stood alone. During this first period there occurred some individual conversions to the new German and Swiss doctrines.

It must be noted that, generally speaking, historical research into the whole Italian religious movement for the period 1519–63 has confined itself to studying the diffusion of Protestantism in Italy. No modern research has taken into account the differences between the various states, and those between the cities and the countryside; none has attempted to establish the characteristics and true meaning of a movement which up to a point made its presence felt everywhere in the monasteries and among the clergy, in schools, courts, offices and shops. It involved not only differences in dogma or doctrine and the general behaviour of intellectually or socially outstanding individuals, but also affected such things as popular religion, the lives of the lesser clergy, and the administrative and economic structure of Church and State.[1] However, from a general Italian point of view it can be said that sympathy with and interest in the ideas and practical schemes of reform established beyond the Alps penetrated all social levels from the peasant to the prince, from the artisan to the professor of law. Even after the work of ecclesiastical repression had begun the movement enjoyed the favour of many prelates and some princes and the benevolent tolerance of others.

We have least information about the early years (1519–30). Some names of individuals are recorded because they fled to Protestant countries or suffered some sensational condemnation; the authorities, whether favourable or not to reform of the Church in the Catholic sense, fought the new heresy only in its open and avowed forms, as when the Epistles of St Paul and the writings of the reformers were read and used openly for polemical purposes. But except to the ecclesiastical authorities, and not even to all of them, the dangers represented by the new preachers of repentance did not seem very great amid the misery of wars and occupation, and there was also some uncertainty as to dogma. The first to distribute the works of Luther and Melanchthon in Italy was a bookseller of Pavia, Francesco Calvi, a friend of Erasmus; this was as early as 1519 and done purely in the way of business, with no intention of promoting religious propaganda. Round about 1519 the works of Melanchthon, published pseudonymously, were read in Rome and in the curia, until they were denounced. The commercial centres of Pavia, Venice, Bologna and Milan, and the university of Padua acted as distributors. Luther was the man most talked about, and heretics in Italy were known for a long time generically as Lutherans: in one case at Ferrara the prosecutor spoke of 'sacramentarian Lutherans', a term that would have horrified both Lutherans and Zwinglians. In any case, except for the Waldenses who allied themselves with the Zwinglians (and later with the Calvinists) and

---

[1] M. Berengo and A. Ristori are investigating Lucca; E. Pommier is studying Anabaptism; and cf. S. Caponetto, 'Origini e caratteri della Riforma in Sicilia,' *Rinascimento*, vol. VII (1956), pp. 219-342; F. Chabod, *Per la storia religiosa dello Stato di Milano durante il dominio di Carlo V* (Bologna, 1940).

resumed proselytising after 1532, it was a story of individuals, not groups. Not even at the court of the famous duchess of Ferrara, Renée of France, was there any real proselytising: her court simply harboured converts. She had come to Ferrara in 1528, a deeply religious woman with strong humanist interests which subsequently widened to embrace the new religious and doctrinal movement.

However, individual cases or isolated groups occurred even earlier (1521, 1523, 1524, 1530). In 1531 Lutheran doctrine seems to have been fashionable among the students of the university of Padua. In the city of Venice the anxiety of the authorities not to interfere with German trade by imposing a rigorous censorship on religious discussion, together with the traditional caution of the senate, its concern for the interests of the printers, and the many foreigners at the university of Padua, assisted propaganda by the innovators and the dissemination of their writings which had begun in the monasteries as early as 1520. The year 1530 saw the beginning of trials, condemnations and executions, but the dominant note in the record is one of complaints from the ecclesiastical authorities about the indifference or excessive tolerance of the civil authorities, for example in the matter of control over books by transalpine heretics; and preaching on texts from St Paul, obviously very fashionable, was widespread. The political relations between the Venetian government and the Holy See, varying with the ups and downs of international politics, also influenced the situation.

In the kingdom of Naples, apart from Waldensian colonies in Calabria who behaved like their co-religionists in Piedmont, the movement was largely confined to the capital and became important only in the following decade. In other cities and states, too, the movement began to make its presence felt towards the end of this early period (Bologna, 1533) or in the next decade. It did not, however, remain confined to localities. Preachers (drawn nearly always from the Franciscan, Carmelite, Augustinian and Benedictine orders) moved from city to city, favoured by the fact that repressive action was still carried out at episcopal level—by each bishop in his own diocese—and in a manner which differed with place and individual. Zeal in supervision was variable, and the repression of heresy was often even accompanied by an uncompromising correction of the most notorious and scandalous abuses. Thus by moving from place to place preachers could avoid all danger and carry the new teaching elsewhere. In the form of one confession or another it also attracted people who were tied to no particular locality, principally members of religious orders, aristocratic ladies and various humanists of clerical origins whose mutual intercourse cut across political and administrative boundaries. Their presence was especially noticeable in those states which depended directly or indirectly on the emperor. During this early period, because of the desire to promote the convocation of the general council, because of the emperor's political struggle against the Francophil Clement VII, because of Erasmian influences in the imperial chancery (which suited the 'imperial' policy of Charles V seen as the representative of all western Christendom), and also as a means of political pressure on the popes, those who inclined to the new doctrines and to a criticism of ecclesiastical, and above all papal, abuses were given considerable freedom of movement in practice if not in theory.

The bishops' action should have been promoted and coordinated by the Papacy which soon began to issue bulls, briefs and missives reviving (on information received) the themes of the encyclicals against Luther, the Lutherans and their followers of other denominations. In fact, however, by the side of the Dominicans and Franciscans, who from the very beginning urged a pamphlet war against Luther, there were others in the curia, especially during the pontificate of Clement VII, who were so favourable to a reform of the Catholic Church that they often looked upon the champions of a Church renewed in religion, morals and institutions—champions who arose in the various dioceses of Italy, in the convents, or in aristocratic society—without any desire to persecute and even at times with sympathy.

These were the leaders of what came to be called 'Catholic reform' and what at this early stage may be called evangelism: a movement, that is, for the renewal of the traditional Catholic religious life through emphasis on ethics and religion, on the gospels and the epistles of the Apostles. This emphasis in no way implied a rejection of the dogmatic, liturgical and hierarchical tradition, and still less of the unity of the Church, but was simply a means of purifying all these and restoring them to their evangelical beginnings. It was linked with movements both European and Italian for the reform of standards and the conduct of the clergy including not only the administration of the Church but also morals, instruction and education at all levels, alms-giving, charitable works, the care of the poor, hospitals, and so forth. In the fifteenth century much had been achieved, as for instance the reform and reorganisation of the orders. These movements now resumed their work with a certain tendency to revive the religious activity and conscience of the secular clergy, a tendency often accompanied by attacks on the orders, especially on the Mendicants. Generally speaking, the protagonists were people born in the previous century who had entered the curia or Church life under Leo X and Clement VII with ecclesiastical titles but frequently with political duties. One of the most famous and typical of these, Matteo Giberti (1495–1543), thought by his contemporaries the model of a bishop and a diocesan reformer, was during this early period secretary and political adviser to Clement VII whose anti-imperial and anti-Spanish policy he inspired and guided in the conviction that this was the policy which would lead to the 'freedom of Italy' and the freedom of the Papal States as one of the principal powers of Italy. At the same time, however, Giberti was said to be one of the earliest members of that group of ecclesiastics of an austere life, given to prayer and charitable works, who were determined to renew the Church in order to renew Christendom, a group (*Oratorio del Divino Amore*) which included Gaetano di Thiene, Luigi Lippomano, Gian Pietro Carafa (the future Paul IV) and Giacomo Sadoleto, and was soon to be connected with men like Gasparo Contarini, Reginald Pole and others. It was only in 1528, after the failure of the anti-Spanish policy which he had pursued in the curia, that Giberti retired to his diocese and completely devoted himself to it, thus acquiring his fame among his contemporaries. He founded a printing press which published religious works, especially the Fathers, and, gathering round him men of great religious, literary and political repute, occupied himself with instructing his flock, both the lower clergy and the people, in faith and morals. Unfortunately, there is no modern study of this figure.

By the time that Clement VII's pontificate was nearing its end men like Giberti were taking part in the government of the Church in different ways. Frequently they acted as protectors of those bishops who in their sees were trying to promote a reform of the moral standards of the people, the return of the clergy to a stricter discipline, instruction, and a simple, comprehensible and edifying style of preaching. Naturally, they incurred accusations of heresy from their adversaries. With the pontificate of Paul III these men, on the explicit instructions of the pope himself, assumed the direction of the reform movement of the Church from within. The names of new cardinals, amongst whom many mentioned above are to be found, and such writings as the *Consilium de Emendanda Ecclesia* (1536) were the more striking manifestations. The movement, demonstrating the pope's willingness to act directly, also provided an alternative to the imperial propaganda on behalf of Catholic reform in the Erasmian sense and of the council. By this time the Papacy as a spiritual authority could no longer keep to general declarations of neutrality whilst pursuing its own policy as an Italian state; it had to be truly neutral. However, neither this, nor the increasingly urgent need of a positive reply to the questing faithful and to the accusations of Lutherans and Zwinglians, constituted the whole problem: interest in the new doctrines and their preaching was producing signs of restlessness in the more serious-minded clergy, and the controversy, emerging from the monasteries and studies, was spreading through the courts and the lower orders. Without any departure from tradition, this necessitated certain departures in philosophico-theological methods and interests. Because of this, as also because of the middle position in theology which many of these men sought to take up on many fundamental questions of dogma, and even because of the persecution which several of them subsequently suffered as favourers of heresy, a sort of historical legend has grown up round them; a legend which sees them as men who wanted to renew and really reorganise the Church, providing her with new organs adapted to the new society and to the newly emerging European political scene. Because of their conciliatory spirit they have been spoken of almost as if they had been 'liberals'; did they not recognise the need for reform and therefore admit a good deal of right and reason in the reforming activities north of the Alps, and did they not show (privately) tolerance towards those who studied and discussed the new doctrines?

In point of fact they tended to be backward-looking in anything that concerned the reform of the Church. They wished to restore the good old days, removing the abuses, decadence and corruption which to a certain extent justified the Protestants in public opinion. The famous *Consilium* proposed to eliminate and correct abuses in the curia which had become evils of the Church; to suppress dangerous philosophical teaching; to remove Erasmus's *Colloquia* from the schools; to institute a censorship of books. Even in the most serious problems they adhered to the traditional point of view, as in the matter of the relations between bishops and non-resident clergy, or those between bishops and the orders (especially the preaching and confessing orders) which the *Consilium* resolved in such a way as to reaffirm the bishops' authority. The middle position in theology in general started from an undogmatic spirituality which was patristic, or philosophically Neoplatonic, or of a Pauline type of evangelical piety in origin, all these positions dating from the preceding century or from the period before Luther. The new situation produced among theologians by Luther, Zwingli and later Calvin, who had epitomised the practical consequences of the new doctrines by the creation of new systems of Church organisation, was not taken into account; and formulae of compromise were sought to maintain or restore that which above all else seemed most important and necessary, that is to say, the unity of the Church. Moreover, many of the Lutheran evangelical formulae were not considered heretical in themselves; especially in the hands of Melanchthon and after the publication of the *Augustana* (1530), the reforms achieved by Luther and the Protestant princes and cities did not seem so dangerous and inflammatory as the extreme and scandalous Zwinglian reform. There thus appeared signs of the assumption that the 'revolutionary' period of the Lutheran Reformation was over; it was acquiring an institutional character and, in spite of polemical formulae and changes in organisation, was reverting to tradition. This, however, was only one aspect of the question, and a general one at that; even the most famous representative of that very group failed to bring about an agreement at the Colloquium of Regensburg (1541), though one was desired and attempted. Luther disowned Melanchthon, the pope disowned Contarini.[1]

The movement in favour of Protestantism or 'Lutheranism' quickened and became more intense in the years between 1535 and 1549. In Piedmont, the Waldenses enjoyed some freedom under the French government

[1] Above, p. 179.

because the occupying forces included members of the reformed Churches even in their higher ranks, and because the civil authorities adopted a tolerant attitude. In the duchy of Milan the movement spread and grew stronger with the support of the local civil authorities and in spite of the decrees of the Inquisition. In 1539 Austin friars were preaching heresy to a following of laymen and a few Franciscans; in the years thereafter those concerned were not only clergy but in one case even a merchant. In 1541 an investigation into the activities of Lutheran and Zwinglian students at Pavia developed into an attack on the preachers who had spread the new doctrines at Milan, Tortona and Pavia and who until the arrest of the students had not been denounced by anyone. Later there were cases at Pallanza (1543 or 1544), Cremona (1547) and especially at Casalmaggiore where a Franciscan preacher, who had adopted Calvinism and gathered round him a dozen disciples and propagandists, had captured almost the entire town and also made converts at Cremona. Between 1547 and 1548 some thirty people were arrested—presumably the ring-leaders, who would be the most convinced and active—and these included gentlemen landowners, members of the middle class, a doctor, an apothecary, artisans and a peasant; both rich and poor. Throughout the whole period episodes of this nature recurred; friars preponderated, but in Cremona a strong group of laymen was arrested and tried between 1550 and 1552. There, too, the men were of different social classes: a doctor, a cobbler, a bookseller, a goldsmith, a merchant, a servant and a lawyer. Most of those involved were gentlemen of leading families; and the authorities deplored the fact that the evil was spreading from the populace (artisans and peasants) to the gentry. This time the group was a properly organised community which was in contact with other similar communities, a congregation on the Calvinist model; even after this dispersion there are records of it down to 1576. The groups received some indirect and involuntary aid from the continual resistance of the local civil authorities to the interference of the inquisitors.

Religious disputes are recorded in Mantua about 1541, but there is no earlier information. In 1545 a denunciation accused laymen, ignorant of Holy Writ and grammar, artisans by profession, of arrogating to themselves the right to discuss religion. In 1539 one source suggests that heretics, protected by Cardinal Morone's vicar, were more dangerous and active at Modena than elsewhere. Here a Sicilian, Paolo Ricci (called Lisia Fileno as a humanist, and probably to be identified with Camillo Renato, later the master and mouthpiece of the Anabaptists and Anti-Trinitarians in their Grisons exile), gathered a small community together which apparently met regularly in private houses. The group was composed not only of scholars and men of substance, but also of uneducated and illiterate men; it comprised not only men but also women, and they argued about faith and the law of Christ not only in private houses but in the market place, in shops and churches. The fame of Modena spread north of the Alps, and Bucer sent a letter of congratulation and exhortation to the brethren in that city. Ricci, who was arrested and taken to Ferrara, abjured, but several Catholic preachers who were sent to Modena refused to go because of the general opinion that the town was completely Lutheran and dangerous. The official attitude to scholars was still one of persuasion and benevolence. In 1542 Cardinal Giacomo Sadoleto wrote to Ludovico Castelvetro—the philosopher, literary critic and philologist who in 1555 had to flee to the Grisons because in the course of a literary disputation the poet Annibal Caro had denounced him as a Lutheran— to warn him that doubts about his orthodoxy had been raised in consistory; but he contented himself with the assurances given by Castelvetro on behalf of himself and his whole group. From then on the public movement ceased and the clandestine movement is obscure, but four of the names of 1539 reappeared in 1555.

These years too saw the greatest Calvinist activity which centred on Renée of France. Calvin's journey to Ferrara in 1537, to preach at the duchess's court and with her favour and blessing make proselytes, created a sensation, but the French preacher's stay (his name was only discovered later) was short owing to the intervention of Duke Ercole II. Calvin's letters to Renée, full of encouragement and exhortations but also of reproaches for hesitations and weakness, reveal that same blend of political calculation over the action of converted princes and faith in the miraculous power of the Word of God preached in all its purity which we find in Zwingli ten years earlier. In Italy, too, the reformers' conviction that as the chosen instruments of Providence they were carrying out a work willed by God led to the same mixture of active conspiracy and ascetical spirituality. By converting a few important prelates and a few princes they hoped to repeat the successes of Luther.

Even after she had left Italy, the duchess continued her correspondence with Calvin, Bullinger and C. S. Curione; she had earlier intervened to defend persecuted Protestants like the then celebrated Fanino Fanini of Faenza. In this instance the duke supported her, seeking to delay the execution of the death penalty which Fanini had incurred by resuming his preaching after a previous recantation. It was important to Ercole II that he should keep the favour of the population of the Romagna which had common boundaries with the Papal States and Tuscany. Also to be found at Renée's court were the humanist Fulvio Pellegrini Morato and his daughter, the learned Olimpia Morata, famous in Protestant circles for her humanist teaching and her wanderings after she left Ferrara in 1551. By her own account, at any rate, Olimpia Morata typified the conversion from Pomponazzi's kind of humanism with its rationalist bias to Calvinist Christianity. All this did not, in fact, amount to very much, but it had great notoriety. The duke was obliged not only to keep an eye

261

on the duchess, which in any case had been done right from the beginning, but also to keep her outside the city, confined in a large villa where she lived till his death when the hostility of her son Alfonso, a devout Catholic, forced her to return to France (1559). The Papacy enjoyed feudal rights over the duchy of Ferrara and was always trying to annex it to the States of the Church, an ambition in which it succeeded towards the end of the century; the Este could not afford to allow Renée's policy to go forward.

On the Venetian mainland, Vicenza was a strong centre of Protestantism. In 1546 Paul III addressed himself directly to the *podestà* and captain of the people there, with a reference also to the forthcoming meeting of the council at Trent, in order to shake them from their 'tepidity'. Strong groups of Anabaptists continued to exist there even after 1546 when mention of Lutherans ceases. Apart from talk of Anti-Trinitarianism there is not much information about Padua during this period, after the first wave of Lutheranism round about 1531; the students were left in peace, and only in 1550 was the question of Lutheran students at Padua raised before the Council of Ten. In Venice itself efforts at repression were half-hearted on the part of the senate and the Council of Ten, but during the pontificate of Paul III the papal nuncio was very active in denouncing and arresting Lutheran preachers among whom Franciscans predominated. The work was continued by his successor who, however, asked for powers to absolve those who repented and to grant a certain latitude in the reading of new books. Those involved were unfrocked friars and educated laymen, but also artisans, and this was worrying. The priests were less numerous. The fame of the Venetian movement became so great that in 1539 someone thought he could write to the senate in Melanchthon's name to offer advice on the reform of clerical abuses, pointing out, however, that the more extreme movements were being suppressed in Germany and warning them about the spread of the Anti-Trinitarian doctrines of Michael Servetus. In 1540 came the first Venetian edition of the *Trattato utilissimo del Beneficio di Jesu Christo crocifisso*, the most widely read Protestant tract produced in Italy which was also translated into French, Spanish and German.[1]

From 1541 the repression grew more intense. Nevertheless, that the movement continued in Venice is shown by the popularity of another book, the *Tragedia del Libero Arbitrio* of Francesco Negri of Bassano, also widely read and translated. There were three editions in quick succession, in 1546, 1547 and 1550. However, the most interesting Venetian case was that of Baldassare Altieri, a native of the Abruzzi and secretary to

[1] The author was the Benedictine monk Benedetto Luchino (Benedetto da Mantova), not Aonio Paleario as was believed for three centuries. Cf. B. Croce, 'Il "Beneficio di Cristo",' *La Critica*, xxxviii (1940), pp. 115–25; and B. Luchino, *Beneficio di Cristo* (introduction and notes by Mariano Moreschini, Rome, 1942).

Sigismund Harvel, English ambassador to Venice; he availed himself of his diplomatic immunity to engage in propaganda and especially to establish contacts among Lutheran groups. In 1542 he was deputed by the congregations of Venice, Vicenza and Treviso to write an account of them for Luther. Altieri turned for help in that direction, above all because the new situation had ushered in a time of flight, imprisonment and fear; he begged the wonder-working German reformer to intercede with the Protestant princes of the League of Schmalkalden to put pressure on the senate and obtain toleration of worship and conversions until the conclusion of the council. That this would have been sufficient to rekindle the movement and extend it considerably is a point on which Altieri is in agreement with other sources. For the time being he obtained nothing and had to revert to the protection of the English ambassador in Venice; however, from 1546 he was also able to represent himself as the agent of the landgrave of Hesse and the elector of Saxony, though not of the powerful Schmalkaldic League. In 1548 the English ambassador died, and Altieri, having been dismissed, sought help from Switzerland. In 1549 he approached Bullinger for the appointment of resident representative in Venice of Berne and Zürich, but all he got were letters of recommendation. In any case, the collapse of the Schmalkaldic League marked a change in Venetian policy towards both pope and emperor. Altieri died in 1552, and with him failed another attempt to involve the fate of the Italian Protestant group with politics and diplomacy. The history of the movement is similar in the regions of Istria and Friuli: preachers and reforming bishops were welcomed enthusiastically by a considerable part of the populace, but remained isolated at the time of the repression and were subsequently arrested or forced to flee.

The same thing happened in Lucca where, at practically the same time, there were gathered several famous figures: Peter Martyr Vermigli, Curione, Count Martinengo and Girolamo Zanchi, all afterwards leaders of the Italian movement well-known abroad, and the humanist Aonio Paleario of Veroli, a native of the Papal States who was to acquire fame through his trial and condemnation (1567–70) as well as through his progress from pantheistic humanism to the teaching of Valdés which is apparent in his writings. This group at Lucca was the first to be attacked by the Holy Office by means of pressure on the political authorities who, because of Cosimo I's struggle for hegemony in Tuscany, found themselves on the defensive. The Burlamacchi conspiracy (discovered in 1544: Francesco Burlamacchi was beheaded in Milan in 1548 after long and painstaking controversies) was directed against the Medici and Spain and may have contained an element of 'Savonarolism'. At all events, in 1545 the senate of Lucca compelled the citizens to go to mass and fulfil all their other obligations, and the edict was repeated in 1549. During this period dissatisfaction began to impel a considerable number of families to migrate from Lucca to Geneva where, with Count Martinengo as their pastor, they formed the strong core of the Italian colony. The greater part of the emigration, however, took place between 1559 and 1560.

Little is known about Florence. There were some religious disputes in 1525, but contemporaries and historians were and still are preoccupied with the loss of Florentine liberty and with echoes of Savonarola. In 1544 Pietro Gelido, Cosimo I's agent in Venice, showed an interest in Lutheran literature and then fled Italy. In 1548 Ludovico Domenichi, a copyist and translator who also produced a version of Sir Thomas More's *Utopia*, was sentenced to ten years' imprisonment for translating and printing Calvin's *Nicodemiana*; he was, however, pardoned. In 1551 a veritable Spanish *auto-da-fè* was held at Florence, involving public recantations by twenty-two people and the burning of heretical books. Princess Caterina Cybo (d. 1557), who lived in retirement in Florence, was in touch with the circle of Valdés but not apparently with any local groups. There is no information available for Pisa, but in the other Tuscan university town, Siena (which passed to the Medici in 1552), disputations were held in the *Accademia degli Intronati*. In 1541 the city authorities had to pass a decree prohibiting the discussion of doctrines condemned by the Church, and it was necessary to repeat this in 1545. There was talk, too, of blasphemy. In 1548 it was the circulation of heretical books that was most worrying, and a list of the names of suspects included people in every walk of life. The presence of German Lutheran students gave some cause for concern.

In 1543 a very severe Roman edict was required against heretical books; it mentioned Rome, Ferrara, and Bologna as the centres of publication and distribution. Groups from Bologna and Modena were corresponding with Bucer at Strassburg to seek clarification in disputes over the eucharist. In 1549 many people from Bologna were sent to the Holy Office at Rome, but they were set free after Paul III's death; at their own request they were then tried and acquitted under Julius III. In 1550, however, it was thought necessary to institute a tribunal of the Inquisition at Bologna. The Protestant movement was here connected with the university and linked with groups at Modena and Ferrara.

The years 1535–50 witnessed the appearance, consolidation and spread of the Anabaptist movement and Anti-Trinitarian tendencies; at the same time, the group centred upon Valdés also began to develop.[1] These movements had this in common that they extended over various parts of Italy and were not localised. The people who took part in them were in contact with one another and moved from Sicily to Milan without any local attachment to dioceses, monasteries or courts, but simply as individual members of large communities with virtually no formal organisa-

[1] *Valdesiani*, the disciples and followers of Juan Valdés; not to be confused with *Valdesi* (Waldensians).

tion, though Venice can be called a centre of Anabaptism (of which it supplies most of the evidence), while Naples was the centre of the Valdesiani. The position of this last group was between the Catholics, Lutherans and Calvinists on the one hand and the Anabaptists and Anti-Trinitarians on the other. The movement was aristocratic, comprising nobles, leading ecclesiastics, humanists and great ladies. It spread through the halls of great houses and monasteries, through courts and chanceries, as well as through conversations and correspondence. It cannot be said to have had an organisation of even the most elementary kind, such as was that of the Anabaptists; as in the case of the Anti-Trinitarians, one is faced simply with an intellectual stream. Yet nearly all the Valdesiani were in direct or indirect contact with Juan Valdés until his death; they were and remained in touch with one another, and the preaching of one of their number, Bernardino Ochino, attracted and moved crowds. It must also be added that the movement was peculiarly Italian, not only in that it extended throughout the peninsula but also in that nearly all the followers of that Italianate Spaniard were themselves Italians. In addition, the greater number of religious and intellectual leaders who favoured religious and ecclesiastical reform in Italy, even beyond or against the desires of Rome, at first adhered to his circle, whether they were in contact with Valdés himself or with his friends.

Juan Valdés, a brother of that Alfonso who held office in Charles V's chancery and (like his brother) an Erasmian humanist, had come to Rome in 1529 in the emperor's train and remained at the court of Clement VII as imperial agent. When Clement died Valdés went to Naples where he settled permanently in 1534. There he gathered round him a group of friends who rested their discussions and meditations upon religious questions solely on the authority of scripture and the Fathers. Preferring to dwell on ascetic and mystical subjects, they took for granted, explicitly or implicitly, a general belief in the fundamental tenets of salvation by faith and Christ's sacrifice and of the soul's direct relationship with God. This enabled them to avoid clearly defined theological positions and to attribute no essential importance to the precepts, rites and sacraments of the Church; considering observance or non-observance of these indifferent (*adiaphora*), Valdés advised his followers not to neglect them if they proved necessary for other reasons, but to interpret them in a mystical sense. Thus, unlike Renée of France and her followers, Valdés's group had no need to celebrate the Lord's Supper according to the Calvinist rite, nor to avoid hearing mass, as was demanded of Lutherans and Calvinists. Valdés himself, in fact, died most devoutly in the bosom of the Catholic Church (1540).

Among his followers and visitors we find a future strict Calvinist like the Marquis Galeazzo Caracciolo of Vico, the Capuchin general Bernardino Ochino (later to die among the Italian Anabaptists who had migrated to Moravia), Isabella Briceño (a noblewoman who died in Basle among the Zwinglians), as well as the Princess Caterina Cybo and the celebrated Giulia Gonzaga who both withdrew to Catholic nunneries and, though suspected, were not touched by the Inquisition—though no doubt their rank had something to do with that. Both these last died in the bosom of the Church, as did Vittoria Colonna who, though not in direct contact with Valdés, was the protectress of Bernardino Ochino and many other Valdesiani. One document lists eleven bishops and archbishops among the friends and followers of Valdés, as for example Girolamo Seripando, a future cardinal and general of the Austin friars, who right to the very end remained a leading figure at the Council of Trent. In his youth Seripando was a friend of Valdés and adhered to the theory of 'Plato as an introduction to Paul' which Cardinal Pole propounded; later he became the protector of many accused of heresy and procured light punishments and their mitigation. However, later still (1549) this same man was to prohibit the discussion, by either side, of those doctrines which were the subject of controversy between Catholics and heretics, urging that only questions dealt with by the early doctors of the Church should be disputed and not modern ones. In 1550 he even abandoned this return to Christian antiquity and ordered an absolute embargo on controversial questions; if discussion was inevitable, the questions were to be treated with such lucidity as to remove every possible suspicion that heresy might be favoured.

Very different and much more typical of the more consistent Valdesiani were the fortunes of another of Valdés's visitors in Naples, Pietro Carnesecchi. Of noble birth and keen intelligence, possessed of a good humanist and legal training, Carnesecchi was one of the most brilliant men at the court of Clement VII who made him apostolic protonotary and his own secretary. He remained in Rome until Clement's death and was in contact with Giberti and the 'Oratory of Divine Love' at Rome. In 1540 he frequented Valdés's house in Naples and in 1543 the circle of the cardinal of England, Reginald Pole, at Viterbo. In the same year he went first to Venice and then to France to the court of Catherine de Médicis. In 1545 he faced his first trial, but—partly owing to the intervention of Catherine and Cosimo de' Medici—he was acquitted on all counts. After continuing his travels in France he went to Padua and Venice where he was in touch with high-ranking prelates and protectors of the new doctrines. Things changed with the pontificate of Paul IV. Carnesecchi was summoned before the tribunal of the Inquisition in 1559. Failing to appear, he was condemned as a heretic and his possessions were con-fiscated. So great was his danger that he fled to Geneva. In 1561, again through Cosimo de' Medici's intervention, he succeeded in having his condemnation rescinded and regained possession of his property. Hence-forth he lived in retirement at Florence. However, Cosimo was ultimately forced by political necessity to give in to Pius V who had resumed

Paul IV's activities against heretics. While Carnesecchi's letters to the inquisitors and his depositions in the long and exhausting process appear humble in character, tortuously and fearfully intent on avoiding precise statements, he died like a gentleman. He went to his death 'fashionably dressed in a white shirt, with a new pair of gloves and a white handkerchief in his hand as though to his wedding', as Cosimo's agent wrote from Rome in 1567.

The intransigents like Carafa (Pope Paul IV) had been right to look with suspicion upon the 'evangelism' of the Valdés, Pole and Giberti circles—whose members were often the same—and upon the friends of Vittoria Colonna and Giulia Gonzaga. For although it is true that these circles included high-ranking prelates, essentially faithful to the Roman Church and the pope's authority, it is also true that they produced heretics and enemies of Rome. On the other hand, there are signs to suggest that it was often the very intransigence and zeal of the Theatines (to take an example among the zealots) which drove men like Bernardino Ochino and Vergerio far from Rome.

It would seem that Calvin's words inviting his fellow-countrymen to an open profession of faith and to war were written for Carnesecchi, before his dignified death. In them Calvin poured scorn on the 'delicate protonotaries' who were pleased to possess a pure faith and would not fight and take risks. Calvin's writings on this subject (in part directed at Renée of France) seemed to fit the Italian situation so well that they were several times and by different people translated into Italian. An Italian edition was begun, but this did not see the light of day, or was even circulated, until 1553 when it was at last published in a small volume at Geneva. The volume contains an important admonition to the reader which discusses the question of flight in the face of persecution. The Italians are advised to choose exile unless they have a call to be ministers of the Word or are absolute rulers. The author of this preface was no optimist: 'It is well known that there are Churches in Italy and congregations...where everything is slight, cold and of little value...'; it is no great misfortune to abandon these 'since it is perfectly clear that there is scarcely any good in them'. Thus those who have left or are about to leave cannot be accused of leaving the Italian churches empty (since there are altogether or very nearly none), nor of having helped the enemy, nor of having given up the struggle, because they can fight better by preaching and writing from abroad. At all events this writer applies the peculiarly Calvinist term of 'Nicodemists' to those he addresses, though he points out that in other matters Calvin was referring to the French situation and not the Italian.[1]

[1] D. Cantimori, 'Nicodemismo e speranze conciliari nel Cinquecento italiano,' *Quaderni di 'Belfagor'*, 1 (contributions to the history of the Council of Trent and the Counter-Reformation; Florence, 1948), pp. 12–23. And cf. *Del fuggire le superstizioni che ripugnano a la vera e sincera confession di fede...composta già da M. Gio. Cal. in lingua latina e tradotta...ne la volgare italiana* [da Francesco Cattani (?)] (*sine loco*, but Geneva, 1553).

In essence 'Nicodemists' meant those who were disposed to live as Catholics, while treating dogmas and sacraments fundamental to Catholicism as matters indifferent to salvation—for if there was uncertainty over justification by faith, there was none over the mass and purgatory—and even condemning some Catholic practices and doctrines as un-Christian. According to Calvin, they appealed for justification to the example of him who came to Jesus by night, that is secretly (John xix. 39).

Certainly, 'Nicodemism' was very popular in Italy, largely through the influence of Valdés's teaching, but it was not confined to the immediate or distant followers of Valdés. Conscious and explicit formulations of this position are attested for Genoa in 1544 and for the Waldensian valleys—carried there by a Florentine—about 1555. There is, however, no detailed or accurate study of the subject. The position was closely involved with what people expected of the council: by a providential intervention it might make reconciliation possible, while by keeping alive the play of influence and intrigue in the courts and the curia it encouraged hopes which depended upon the interaction of politics and diplomacy. This explains why many Italian exiles, though not strictly members of Anabaptist or Anti-Trinitarian groups, appeared to Calvin as sophistical and ambiguous unbelievers, and why they were shocked when they failed to find in exile that freedom of thought and religious discussion for which, more than for any dogmatically defined truth, they had left Italy. This comes out most clearly in the protests of Camillo Renato and many other Italians after the burning of Michael Servetus, protests which—though not exclusively in Italian hands—were to develop into legal and theological theorising about religious toleration ('Socinianism').

Anabaptists and Anti-Trinitarians were not identical because not all the former, even in Italy, were opposed to the doctrine of the Trinity. Nevertheless, the first Italian Anti-Trinitarians were to be found among the Anabaptists. Lelio Sozzini died in the house of an Anabaptist, and his nephew was on good terms with the sect. These examples indicate that, distinct as these two radical religious movements were in Italy, they yet had close relations. Both spread clandestinely through the different classes of the population, among artisans, peasants and the lower ranks of the clergy, among lawyers, teachers and humanists. The Anti-Trinitarian peril was denounced to the Venetian senate in 1539. Servetus himself thought of going to Venice in 1554, and it was there that Postel published his *Apologia* for Servetus. In 1555 Anti-Trinitarianism was mentioned in papal bulls, while the first detailed information, derived from the confessions, revelations and accusations made by an Anabaptist during his trial, dates from 1550. In that year a genuine council of Anabaptists was held at Venice to discuss the tendencies towards Anti-Trinitarianism which had appeared in a group of their members, in the main apparently from Vicenza. Delegates came from various parts of

Italy and from the centres of emigration. Within the movement there were Italians from Pisa, Naples, Tuscany, the Papal States and Sicily, but the greatest contribution at this council or congregation of Venice came from the Anabaptist communities of the Grisons and those of Vicenza, Padua and Treviso, cities on the Venetian mainland. It was from this Venetian gathering that the legend arose that the Anti-Trinitarian movement had originated in Vicenza in meetings organised as early as 1546. But that there were Anabaptist propagandists in those parts during those years or even earlier is borne out by the lengthy depositions of the Anabaptist mentioned above: they show also that the Italian Anabaptists, too, had adopted the Mennonite system of itinerant preaching. After these revelations the Anabaptist groups were easily taken by surprise, arrested and dispersed. Some of them managed to flee to Moravia from where a little later (1559) they tried to send two emissaries, arrested by the Inquisition, to convert the Anti-Trinitarian brethren left behind in Italy to more moderate positions. It is to be noted that in Vicenza the Anabaptist movement spread rapidly after the Lutheran movement had been suppressed, probably because the Anabaptists explicitly professed 'Nicodemism' in order to meet the need for greater vigilance in the situation brought about by the Catholic Counter-Reformation.

According to the testimony of a man tried for heresy in 1550, there were heretics in Valdés's circle at Naples who maintained that Jesus was only a divinely inspired prophet and who denied the Virgin Birth; the informant accused Valdés of sharing these views. Perhaps he merely tolerated them. What is certain is that there were declared Anti-Trinitarians among his friends and disciples. The historian of Unitarianism, E. M. Wilbur, calls Valdés a 'liberal Catholic', but he also thinks that he was 'if not a pioneer, at least an herald of our movement'.[1]

Faced with this religious situation in Italy, the signs and suspicions of which were plentiful, the Papacy found itself constrained to take more and more systematic measures. It was not that the old laws, when applied, were not severe enough, but that the novelty and size of the heretical movement, the secrecy maintained by large groups of adherents, the solidarity of the humanists and the protection that various groups enjoyed at the courts, with bishops and cardinals, and in the curia, and lastly the dogmatic and doctrinal uncertainty arising from the hesitations and delays in the calling and activity of the general council, necessitated new weapons and measures of repression. From 15 January 1524—the day on which the papal nuncio in Venice was ordered to put into effect the decrees of the Fifth Lateran Council on preaching and the censorship of books—to 1543, there are on record some eighty papal briefs sent to Italian bishops and prelates for action to be taken against Lutheran

[1] *A History of Unitarianism, Socinianism and its Antecedents* (Harvard Univ. Press, 1947), p. 33.

heretics. In the last decade the spread and intensification of the movement was such that the traditional inquisitorial system entrusted to the bishops in their separate dioceses and territories proved quite inadequate. Pushed on by one of the 'Catholic reformers' of 1536 (Cardinal Carafa), Paul III therefore created by the bull *Licet ab initio* of 21 July 1542 a new central organisation, the famous 'Holy Office' of the general Roman Inquisition. The bishops' tribunals and the local inquisitions were to be subject to this supreme tribunal; they were to follow a uniform procedure determined by the Holy Office, to send copies of the proceedings to Rome and await guidance from Rome on the judgment to be pronounced in each case; often they even sent prisoners to the Roman tribunal, while in other cases the Holy Office sent down its commissioners instead. Thus before the Reformation in Italy had achieved the united character towards which it was tending, and before it had taken root among the people, the Holy Office arose as a unitary organ of repression and control which under Carafa's energetic guidance rapidly produced a change in the situation. The famous cases of Bernardino Ochino and Vergerio are typical. Ochino, who had achieved great fame as a preacher and been elected general of the new Capuchin order, had come into contact with Valdés whose inspiration was thereafter noticeable in his preaching. His fame may be said to have spread throughout Italy, and the enthusiasm of the crowds who came to listen had protected him from the episcopal and local inquisitions. However, when he was summoned before the new tribunal at Rome he preferred emigration (1542).[1]

Emigration had started several years before, but at first it was sporadic, involving sometimes wild extremists and often occurring on the borders of the northern states of Italy. Emigration properly so called developed gradually and tended to increase after Ochino's flight. However, while many of the best known suspects made their way to Switzerland, Strassburg and England, many remained in Italy and put their hopes in the council and in the protection of their friends, a protection which was often effective because it came from bishops, cardinals and princes.

At long last, after much discussion, the council opened its sessions in 1545. Believers in Catholic reform and the followers of Valdés hoped that it would first of all issue decrees concerning the reform of the Church and would then proceed to a definition of justification by faith which would permit of the humanistic and evangelical interpretations of St Paul's message. Great hopes were placed in the presence at the council in 1546 of members of the 'reform group'—people like the cardinal of England, Girolamo Seripando, and many others. Despite subsequent disillusionment among prelates and aristocracy, these hopes continued to survive even after the famous trial of Vergerio, as the trial of Carnesecchi shows.

[1] Cf. below, p. 284.

Vergerio had been Clement VII's nuncio in Germany and a reforming bishop in his diocese of Capodistria. In 1549 he emigrated and became the leader of the few truly Lutheran Italian exiles and a councillor to Duke Christopher of Württemberg, seeking in vain to contest the primacy of the 'sacramentarian' C. S. Curione who had fled in 1542. The hopes centred on the council were kept alive with patience and dissimulation until the propitious moment should come for appearing in the open. It was expected to arrive when the friends of reform had succeeded in passing resolutions on points of dogma which would allow some latitude of interpretation and action. Essentially it was the ambiguity of such a position which compromised Cardinal Morone who in May 1557–June 1560 was imprisoned, tried but not condemned by the Inquisition: things are not entirely to be explained by the zeal and rigid orthodoxy of Paul IV.

Besides these complicated hopes there was another simpler and more positive factor. Many people were reluctant to flee. The spirit which inspired them, and which was purely religious, made it a duty not to abandon the flock, large or small, which they had gathered, even at the price of martyrdom—even if in actual fact they did not in the end prove capable of making the supreme sacrifice. This question was explicitly considered after the flight of Vermigli, and as we have seen it continued to be discussed. Hence the importance ascribed in Italian circles to the case of Francesco Spiera. Spiera was a wealthy lawyer of Cittadella near Padua, with eleven children. Having been converted to the new faith apparently by moral scruples arising from his legal activities and by the reading of certain books, he set about converting his family and the people he met with evangelical literature. Finally he started preaching in public. It seems that he got his following principally among the poor— 'pauperes et tenues homines'. In view of the fact that all the sources emphasize how neglected the poorer sort were in town and country even in matters of religion, this is very likely. Spiera was denounced and stood his trial. Fearing that a conviction might disinherit his children, he recanted in 1546; but, immediately overcome by this betrayal of Christ whose reproachful voice he seemed to hear, he fell into despair and profound depression. The doctors diagnosed his case as one of deep melancholia and prescribed various cures. The news of this occurrence spread to Padua from where visitors—some of them illustrious, like Vergerio and Matteo Gribaldi—began to come in 1547 and 1548, to console and observe Spiera who declared that he now knew himself to be damned. He died in despair in 1548. The case caused a great stir and led to the publication of various accounts. Vergerio left his diocese and Italy in 1549, but others interpreted Spiera's example as an admonition to continue to preach and to confront the Roman Inquisition.

We have now come to the end of Paul III's pontificate and have reached, after the brief interlude of Marcellus II, the pontificates of Julius III and

Paul IV. The tendency to place the moral, administrative, disciplinary and organisational reform of the Church in the forefront now began to give way before an inclination to proceed to the repression of the heretical movement. This repression was based on the most rigorous dogmatic orthodoxy and the systematic suspicion of all who failed to show profound subservience to the clergy or cast doubts on the most extreme theories concerning the papal authority, theories which had still not been made the subject of dogmatic definition and were therefore still legitimately open to discussion. From the time of Paul IV onwards, the Spanish type of severe and grave ecclesiastic predominated at Rome; the humanist was replaced by the theologian, austere and upright, harsh and uncompromising towards laity and heretics alike. In fact there had existed a single movement in the Church whose two aspects—Catholic reform and Counter-Reformation—alternately came to the fore. The fact that ecclesiastical policy settled down in the shape of the Counter-Reformation did not mean that the other aspect disappeared: elements of each can be discerned in the principal texts of the other.

The pontificates of Julius III and Paul IV (1550–59), though politically very different, saw the slow retreat, full of contradictions, of the Catholic reformers. Some followed the pattern of Seripando, while others (for instance Morone) were held in high suspicion. It should be recorded that Carnesecchi, though he failed to present himself, was absolved from his sentence a few months after Morone. One more case may be cited, that of Giovanni Grimani, the patriarch of Aquileia, who in 1549 was accused of favouring the Lutheran heresy. Obliged to resign the patriarchate in 1550, he was tried and acquitted in 1552; he remained in obscurity until 1561 when he started an action for his rehabilitation which he subsequently obtained from the council. His name had been mentioned for elevation to the cardinalate, but despite the persistent diplomatic intercession of the Venetian senate he was never successful. The leading actors were still largely the same, but they were now thin on the ground among the representatives of more rigorous and uncompromising tendencies. The new generation was beginning to appear: Carlo Borromeo and Michele Ghislieri were entering upon their careers. Many of the figures who had been in the forefront during the first twenty years of this story found age overtaking them; others emigrated. From being the promoters of reform, Morone, Pole and Seripando grew suspect of heresy; content at first merely to act as protectors of men persecuted for heresy, they finally emerged as the upholders of the most rigorous orthodoxy, despite the contrast that this represented with their former tendencies and ideas. The political situation which emerged in Italy even well before the treaty of Cateau-Cambrésis could not be changed. Its elements were the predominance of Spain, the alliance of the Holy See with Spain, and the recognition that an agreement with the Protestants (Lutherans and others) was impossible. The predominance of Spain meant that the Counter-Reformation became increasingly repressive. On the death of Paul III Reginald Pole failed of the Papacy although a strong party among the cardinals desired him in preference to another member of the college. Towards the end of Julius III's pontificate Pole became one of the leaders of the Catholic restoration of Queen Mary in England, much to the disappointment and scandal of his Protestant friends; however, this was not enough to dispel the distrust felt by the new pope, Paul IV, for the friend of Morone and Giberti. In 1558 Pole, too, disappeared from the scene. His will contained a declaration of his absolute belief in the Papacy which was criticised by Giulia Gonzaga and Carnesecchi; the letter in which he expressed his disapproval served to condemn the latter to death.

By the time of Pius IV (1559–65) the Italian situation was stabilised. The work of economic reconstruction had begun, after wars during which all the Italian states (Venice less than the rest) had suffered heavily, especially in their revenues. The result was a social distress which differed in form and degree but was everywhere considerable. The situation required not construction but reconstruction. The political scene had changed, but in spite of the dramatic character of events the adjustments were unimportant. From 1545 the Farnese family held the duchy of Parma and Piacenza, and despite the conspiracy which led to the murder of Pier Luigi Farnese in 1547 they maintained their hold. The hostility of Siena and the surrounding countryside towards its Spanish government showed itself repeatedly in various risings which, culminating in that of 1552 in which French forces assisted, led to the war of Siena participated in also by the Florentine exiles. The war ended with the capitulation of the city of Siena in 1555. Subsequently, with the departure of the French in 1559, fell Montalcino, the last relic of republicanism—republican not only in its constitution but because here the people really played their part in the government. After a brief dispute with Philip II (to whom Charles V had granted it in 1555), Siena with its territory and possessions, except for the 'Stato dei Presidi', passed in 1557 into the hands of Cosimo de' Medici. In 1554 died Bartolommeo da Petroio, alias Brandano, who throughout the Sienese district was regarded as a prophet and had expressed the restless discontent of the people there in religious form.

In 1556 Lucca concluded a gradual process by hardening into an aristocratic oligarchy. This process had passed through a crisis in the 'beggars' revolt' of 1531–2, a revolt of the new citizens and middle classes who were for the most part wealthy, supported by the poor and the common people. In 1557 the Roman Jews were shut up in a ghetto. The history of absolutist reorganisation in the Italian states—as in the grand duchy of Tuscany or the duchy of Savoy—belongs, however, to another period, although the earliest laws in that direction date from this, accompanied as they were by the usual disputes with the ecclesiastical authorities.

Essentially it was a consolidation of Spanish ascendancy, with passive resistance from Venice and the emergence under the shadow of that ascendancy of the power of the Holy See as the principal Italian state; the renewal of papal authority in the Church gave it greater autonomy and mobility. The tragic scandal of the trial of the Carafa family and its destruction in 1560–61 in no way weakened the Holy See, even though the trial plainly turned into one of the greater part of the pontificate—or in truth of the whole ascendancy—of Paul IV; on the contrary, the energy displayed increased the prestige of the Papacy. In 1562–3 Morone and Seripando helped the council, which had been summoned in 1560, to a positive conclusion but the questions dealt with were no longer solely or predominantly Italian, though according to the historian Paolo Sarpi the ascendancy of Italian bishops was remarked upon, an ascendancy which was often obtained by pressure and negotiations on the part of the Holy See with the interested parties or the Italian princes. This comes out particularly well in the negotiations between Pius IV and Cosimo de' Medici. In exchange for putting pressure on the Tuscan bishops to participate in the council and vote in the papal sense, and in spite of his bitter jurisdictional and financial disputes with the Tuscan clergy, Cosimo obtained special political favours from the pope; and so did Alfonso d'Este.

Like all the Italian policy of the Holy See, that of this period has from that time to this been interpreted by Catholic historians as an 'Italian policy', one, that is, which favoured the 'liberty' of the Italian states, peace in the peninsula, the Italian 'nation' and 'people'—in fine, the 'national unity' of Italy. The latest writer to hold this view is the Italian historian, Professor Pontieri, in an important work which covers the same period and problems as are dealt with here.[1] He also asserts that its rigorous and energetic pursuit of Catholic reform and Counter-Reformation enables the Papacy to claim 'the indisputable merit of having saved the religious unity of the Italian nation in an age which proved the precursor of so much disaster for the Church and for Italy'. And he remarks: 'In this unity Italy, though subject to the foreigner, found herself and in the fullness of time was to achieve the foundations and the crowning glory of her political unity.' In reality, things happened rather differently and not without a struggle. Of this the men of the Risorgimento, from Mazzini to Cavour, were well aware, though one must make allowances for the distortions and simplifications of politicians writing history. The 'crowning glory', as Croce explicitly and sometimes rhetorically observes, harked back to those very movements which the activities of Catholic reform and Counter-Reformation, by dint of the Papacy's alliance with Spanish power, succeeded in suppressing.

[1] E. Pontieri, 'Gli ultimi aneliti della independenza italiana', in *Nei tempi grigi della storia d'Italia* (Naples, 1949).

CHAPTER IX

THE NEW ORDERS

THE religious life, in its many various forms, is deeply woven into the texture of Catholicism. The state of the orders is usually a reliable indication of the health of the Catholic Church as a whole, and from early times the great formative periods of Catholicism have been marked not only by reforms in the existing orders but also by the creation of new ones, responsive in the first instance to the needs or the mood of a new epoch, though generally concealing surprising powers of survival and adaptability. The Counter-Reformation Catholic revival of the sixteenth and seventeenth centuries was no exception to this rule. The period was one which witnessed far-reaching changes in European society, and these set crucial and perplexing problems before a Catholicism resurgent, indeed, but no longer in enjoyment of a religious monopoly, faced with curtailed and shrinking frontiers in Europe, and in many places fighting for very existence. The history of the religious orders in this age shows the working out of the customary formula of restoration and new creation, but in a setting far more complicated and unfavourable than monasticism had ever faced before.

A comprehensive judgment on the state of the religious orders at the outbreak of the Reformation is extremely difficult to arrive at. The currents of reform of the previous hundred and fifty years, which had divided all the orders of friars into Observant and Conventual groups and had produced the various observant Benedictine congregations in Italy, Spain, Germany, Austria and France, had long been dying down, though they were by no means everywhere quite dead. Unsupported by any effective movement of reform on a more general scale, their successes had remained un-coordinated, localised and often no more than transient, and every aspect of contemporary society seemed hostile to further progress. The break-up of the common life and the decline of fervour, with all their moral consequences, were aided by a large variety of material factors and by movements of opinion critical of the whole monastic ideal. Riches and poverty seemed equally unhappy in their effects. The growing interference of the lay power, interested mainly in questions of monastic property but not limiting its interference to them, was on balance probably more harmful than otherwise and was able to exploit internal quarrels and the frequent jurisdictional strife between conventual and observant superiors. Except in England the disastrous system of commendams lay heavy like a blight. Individual dispensations from monastic obligations could be obtained from the Roman curia with shameless facility and often without the knowledge of the applicant's own superior. There was widespread deficiency in the training and education of novices and younger religious, both men and women. The adverse criticism of humanists and the growth of a spiritual attitude which decried the value of penance and formal observances were at length followed by the radical denunciations— and then the destructive practical triumphs—of the Protestant reformers. This is not to deny that respectable, even fervent, religious communities of men and women still existed, often in strange juxtaposition with the worst abuses in others, but the general picture is one of a special way of life struggling—like the Church as a whole—in the toils of its complicated entanglement with the social and material web of the secular world. Even among the monks of the Charterhouse—*nunquam reformata quia nunquam deformata*—there was much intercourse with lay-people, and especially in the houses with great influence for good, such as those in London and Cologne. What was lacking was the force of an independent spiritual energy backed at the highest level by a regenerate and single-minded ecclesiastical leadership capable of diagnosing and facing the real troubles. Until such conditions showed signs of developing, no lasting change for the better could be expected.

So far as the friars were concerned the position was all the more critical in that they performed a very large part of the Church's pastoral work, and it is interesting that so many of the first Protestant leaders should— like Luther himself—have come from the ranks of reformed and observan friars. But their extensive privileges and exemptions from episcopal control, brought to a climax in the bulls issued in 1474 and 1479 by Sixtus IV generated a high degree of tension with the episcopate; and the central object of Church reform—the reconstruction of the Church's apostolic efficiency—was permanently obstructed by this problem of the regulars and their exemptions, which the Lateran Council of 1512–17 considered but could not solve. In the event, it was the revival in overwhelming strength of the pastoral and charitable motives as an essential part of the new spirituality characterising the groups of earnest men in Italy and elsewhere from whose efforts the Catholic revival sprang, that created a new form of religious association, that of the clerks regular, of which the Jesuits, who did not however derive from the Italian milieu, are the most important example. These bodies, by supplying the Counter-Reformation Church and Papacy with well-organised, well-educated, obediently-conditioned, but non-monastic groups of pastoral workers, equally detached from the allurements of a worldly life as from the local ties and the liturgical and community observances of monks and friars, played a vital part in enabling Catholicism to put its own house into some order, to stabilise its boundaries with the reformers and to achieve some measure of adaptation to the new age. Similarly it was the pastoral motive within the Capuchin Franciscan revival that from the start gave it its popularity with its lay protectors and ultimately secured for it the support of Rome.

There was, however, for some time considerable doubt at Rome about the whole question of the religious orders. In the debates inaugurated by the reform commissions of Paul III in the 1530's the talk was more of suppressing orders than of encouraging new ones. Proposals such as the suppression of all Conventuals and the amalgamation of all other religious into three or four institutes, the total abolition of exemption from episcopal control, and the complete prohibition of new foundations, showed the degree of exasperation and defeatism reached in some quarters. But these radical programmes, whatever their attractions on paper, would hardly have been practical ecclesiastical politics, and only an extremist party favoured them. And it has been pointed out that in the well-known *Consilium de Emendanda Ecclesia* and other similar contemporary documents one does not find very much in the way of positive suggestions for reform, such as the better spiritual and intellectual training of young religious, or other practical measures akin to those by which, ultimately, the level of monastic life in the older orders was gradually raised. Throughout the period covered by this chapter the early apostolic successes of the Capuchins, Theatines, Jesuits and other new communities, the fruits of a degree of self-denying zeal that seemed incredible to contemporaries, stood out against a background certainly of expanding general effort but also of underlying uncertainty in regard to the reformability and even the continued future existence of some of the older bodies. Not until a general code for monastic reform had been established at the Council of Trent in its last sessions of 1563 was the firm basis laid for an accepted general policy which, as the Counter-Reformation advanced in greater self-confidence and under central guidance towards the end of the century, gradually, if often only fitfully, raised the general level of the great bulk of the older monastic institutions.

The various bodies of clerks regular were the outstanding creation of sixteenth-century Catholicism in the sphere of the religious orders. But it will be convenient here to deal first with the more important monastic revivals along traditional lines that occurred in the period under review. The new foundations of Camaldolese monks in Italy, though appearing merely to continue the type of the localised monastic reforms of the fifteenth century, have a wider significance by virtue of the personalities of the founders and their close connection with the leaders of other important contemporary devout groups in Italy, well-springs of the Counter-Reformation. Paolo Giustiniani and Vincenzo Quirini were Venetians of noble family and sophisticated education. In 1510 and 1512 they and others of their devout humanistic circle abandoned the world to enter religion among the hermit-monks at Camaldoli, from where they made the greatest efforts to persuade their friend Gasparo Contarini to join them. But though they effectively assisted the future cardinal to rack his conscience, they were not ultimately able to persuade him that his salvation lay solely in the cloister.[1] The Camaldolese order, deriving from the eleventh-century foundation of St Romuald, contained both hermits and coenobites. By the beginning of the sixteenth century it had also branched into Conventual and Observant houses. But new impulses towards the full, exact restoration of primitive observance were being blocked by the order's general, Delfino. Quirini died early, but Giustiniani soon became the leader of the reformers. In 1519 he was elected superior of the hermits and in 1520 left Camaldoli with a number of followers with whom he founded new reformed Camaldolese settlements elsewhere, at Massaccio, Pascelupo and Monte Corona. Here his views of the original ideals of St Romuald were put into effect, and a quasi-autonomous congregation of Camaldolese monasteries named after the foundation of Monte Corona eventually came into existence.

Giustiniani died in 1528. He was an influential figure in Italy among the many groups of zealous men seeking God through penance, charity and retirement from the world. He was a personal friend of Carafa and of St Cajetan and also of Farnese, the future Paul III. That men of his stamp should become hermits in one of the most severe monastic régimes that existed made a striking impression among both the devout and the scoffers of the age. But it is also significant of the trend of the times that even for this most contemplative order Giustiniani regarded a certain apostolic action as essential and with this in mind had seriously considered the possibility of making his reformed foundations in America. He was, however, ultimately convinced that his charity must begin at home. His movement had traits in common with that of the Capuchins, which it preceded, and it was at Massaccio that two of the earliest Capuchins, Ludovico and Raffaele da Fossombrone, found a temporary refuge from their pursuers in the Lent of 1526 and made the request—rejected by the Camaldolesi—for a permanent home among them.

The Capuchin movement, coming as part of the general spiritual revival that lay at the heart of the Counter-Reformation, was by far the most successful and the most lasting of the many attempts to return to the letter of the Franciscan rule that had marked the history of the Friars Minor from earliest times. It created in time a new independent order of Friars Minor, and it is hardly to be wondered at if it came to be regarded in some quarters as the true fulfilment of the prophecies foretelling the eventual restoration of the original way of life taught by the founder. In 1517 Leo X had sought to simplify the complicated Franciscan situation by grouping all the existing Franciscan bodies into two, and two only, separate organisations. The Conventuals accepted all the official 'interpretations' and mitigations of the rule. The more numerous Observants

[1] H. Jedin, 'Ein "Turmerlebnis" des jungen Contarini', *Historisches Jahrbuch*, 1951.

sprang out of fourteenth- and fifteenth-century movements of return to original simplicity from which, however, many of them had now declined; and it was intended to set aside houses in each observant province for those who desired a stricter life. But little or nothing was done about this, and the Capuchin movement, testifying to the endemic and irresistible appeal of the Franciscan ideal in Italy, arose among Italian Observants borne on a great wave of new enthusiasm for the strict letter of the rule, an enthusiasm which in any circumstances could probably not have been satisfactorily catered for within the existing observant framework.

The movement arose not in the 'enchanted land' of Umbria but in the marches of Ancona, across the mountains from Umbria and Assisi, in a countryside which had been the citadel of the fourteenth-century Spirituals and the cradle of the Observants. Matteo da Bascio, a simple-minded young priest of peasant origin, of the observant house at Montefalcone, felt himself called to live according to the strict letter of the Rule of St Francis and to observe all the precepts of the saint's last testament, the obligatory nature of which had been denied by Rome. He made himself a habit of coarse material with a four-pointed hood sewn on to it (in place of the softer material and separate rounded hood then worn) which he believed represented St Francis's own actual dress, and this form of hood became for the Capuchins an outward symbol—for which they fought tenaciously—of their revival of primitive Franciscanism. The beard, which was the second vital Capuchin external, may have been an importation from the Camaldolese monks, whose customs had some influence in Capuchin legislation. But just as his meeting with the lepers was a turning point in the life of St Francis, so, for Matteo, a decisive part in his story was played by his devoted work for the sick and plague-stricken in Camerino in the plague of 1523 and later again in 1527 after he had been joined by three companions—the brothers Ludovico and Raffaele da Fossombrone and Paolo da Chioggia, all, like himself, Observants desiring a stricter observance. The Capuchin movement was not starry-eyed but was solidly grounded in devoted charitable work. This linked the Capuchins with all the other Italian Catholic reformers of their time and was the cause of the enthusiastic support given them by the duchess of Camerino, a niece of Clement VII, without whose protection from the hostile attentions of the observant superiors little more might have been heard of Matteo, Ludovico, and the pointed hood.

Yet Matteo had no thoughts of becoming the founder of an order. All he desired, and all he obtained orally from Clement VII—probably with the concealed aid of the pope's niece—when he journeyed to Rome in the pilgrimage year of 1525, was private permission to live a wandering evangelical life, reporting once a year to his superiors, wearing his hood and beard, and seeking to observe the Rule of St Francis faithfully. That the spiritual impetus which his example generated found outlet in a new organisation was due to the character and energy of his early follower Ludovico da Fossombrone. Ludovico was an old soldier who still had the spirit of fight in him. After surviving several attempts on the part of his superiors to apprehend him, he succeeded in July 1528, the year after the sack of Rome, in obtaining the bull *Religionis Zelus* which marks the legal beginning of the new group of Friars Minor formed by those who had now gathered round the first four. The bull gave them permission to lead an eremitical life according to the Rule of St Francis, to receive others into their community and to enjoy all the privileges of the Camaldolese. In 1529 the first general chapter, held at Albacina, laid down statutes and elected Matteo as superior. After a very short while he resigned his charge into the hands of Ludovico. This irregular transmission of authority was apparently acquiesced in by the rest.

In the earliest constitutions of 1529 the new communities called themselves 'Fratres Minores vitae eremiticae'. But the 'eremitical' life envisaged was not, it should be said, the solitary hermit life such as was lived then by the hermits among the Camaldolesi and, outside formal religious orders, by numerous individuals in Italy who from time to time would descend from their solitary dwellings in the hills preaching penance and announcing coming tribulations. It was, however, apparently from their being acclaimed as such with cries of 'Scapuccini!'—the popular appellation for hermits—that the Capuchins got the name 'Fratres Minores Capuccini' which ultimately stuck, and which makes its appearance in a papal document for the first time in 1535. But community life and the apostolic work of preaching and care for the poor and the sick were of the essence of the Capuchin ideal, as of that of St Francis. The eremitical life meant for them, as it had meant for St Francis, the location of their community centres in quiet hill or country places, away from the immediate pressure of noisy town life, and generally off normal routes of travel, yet near enough to centres of population for the brothers to be able to exercise their vocation as popular evangelists and also be in touch with the sources of charity on which they lived. The large, fine town churches and houses of so many Franciscan communities all over Europe were to be forsworn. The brethren would live in small communities—for large numbers brought dangers—in the simplest mud and wattle hermitages, with tiny cells and the smallest oratory. In such conditions alone could they practise the absolute poverty, the extreme physical asceticism and the complete abandonment to prayer which was to be their life at home. From 1528 onwards such hermitages began to be constructed, the four earliest, already existing in 1529, being at Colmenzone near Camerino, and at sites near Pollenza, Albacina and Fossombrone (the home of Ludovico and his brother).

In these hermitages and the others that followed them, the spirit of St Francis and his first companions lived again. The earliest Capuchin sources and stories recreate the atmosphere of the Fioretti. Like the first Theatines at about the same time they sought to exemplify in an extreme, almost superhuman form, the virtues opposite to the prevalent vices and abuses of the time—poverty, chastity, penance, prayer, and a popular apostolate. All the mitigations and interpretations of the rule, especially in regard to poverty and property-owning, that the Conventuals and even in part the Observants had accepted at the hands of the Papacy, they specifically renounced. In food, sleep, space, comfort, they sought the absolute minima. They took literally no thought for the morrow and abstained even from begging save in moments of the most dire need. In their tiny chapels they followed an extreme simplicity in ritual and in the manner of reciting the canonical Hours. Two hours a day were set apart for individual prayer. There was thus a strong element of the purely contemplative life, which at a later stage grew much stronger in certain parts of the order. But the primitive spirit of Franciscan apostolic activity was amply safeguarded, and prevailed both at the start and later over all tendencies towards contemplative deviationism. The very example of a life of penance and prayer was indeed an aspect of their apostolate, though it was not the whole of it. Renouncing all the privileges and exemptions that had been heaped on the mendicant orders, they sought at first to subject themselves in their preaching and administration of the sacraments to direct episcopal control. Later, however, there came a change of policy. As preachers they self-consciously eschewed the elaborate, the rhetorical, the technically theological, and cultivated a direct evangelical and moral appeal. For this reason, and also in the name of Franciscan simplicity, they did not encourage theological study, their earliest members being either priests already, or else, like Raffaele da Fossombrone, lay-brothers. There prevailed at first the primitive system of a complete equality between priests and lay-brothers, even to the extent of placing lay-brothers in positions of authority. Towards the middle of the century, however, this had to be abandoned. On the other hand, it seems that not all the priests were preachers, and that throughout the sixteenth century the non-preachers were in a majority. And while, as with all the other orthodox reformers of the hour, a more frequent recourse to the sacraments of penance and holy communion was a central theme in their exhortations, they did not themselves hear confessions, save very exceptionally. It is not quite clear whether this was part of their policy of not encroaching on the ground of the parish clergy or whether it followed from their distrust of studies. It was maintained, however, in spite of all criticisms, certainly up to the establishment of the complete juridical independence of the Capuchins in 1619.

In 1529, the year of the first general chapter, there was effected, after some initial difficulties, a union between the foundation of Matteo and Ludovico and a number of Calabrian Observants led by Bernardino da

Reggio who wished to break away from their superiors in the name of reform. This signified a geographical widening of the movement started in the Marches which henceforward began to spread to many other parts of Italy. It also brought to the new foundation men from a region where the memories of Joachim of Flora and of his influence upon the Spirituals were not perhaps quite dead. Yet the Capuchin movement, as a whole, was noticeably free from the extravagancies of outlook and the visionary apocalypticism which the writings of Joachim had helped to encourage among the Spirituals and the Fraticelli. Ludovico early took the important practical step of founding a settlement in Rome. His forward policy included also foundations at Naples (1530) and in other parts of Italy. By the time of the second general chapter in 1535 the new order counted some 700 members, mostly recruits from the Observants. These years of Ludovico's rule, however, while they had established the order and seen a notable expansion of it, had also been marked by great difficulties, both internally and as a result of external influences. They were, in fact, years of more than ordinarily severe growing pains.

Ludovico's own position was anomalous. He had never been elected superior but had simply taken over from Matteo when the latter had resigned his own authority to him. He ruled as a monarch without summoning the general chapter, contrary to all normal Franciscan law and custom. In spite of his outstanding services to the movement, his autocracy, which became severe and harsh, led to an opposition which forced him to summon the general chapter of 1535. At this, to his astonishment, he was replaced as superior by Bernardino d'Asti. Thrown completely off his balance, he spent a year in unworthy intrigues which led to another chapter in 1536 held in the presence of the order's cardinal-protector. Contrary, however, to his expectations, the chapter again rejected his claims and re-elected Bernardino, at the same time accepting a revised version of the constitutions which the latter had had prepared. Ludovico's proud spirit was unable to acquiesce with suitable humility in this final rebuff. He retired in dudgeon to a hermitage where he spent the rest of his days in solitude. At about the same time, Matteo adopted once more the life of a wandering preacher after which he had always hankered, relying apparently on the oral permission given him by Clement VII in 1525. It is probable that he returned to a nominal dependence on the observant authorities and may even have abandoned the Capuchin hood. Not much is known of his later life. He witnessed as a chaplain the battle of Mühlberg in 1546—where Bobadilla, one of the first Jesuits, was also present—and died at Venice in 1552. It was a curious fate that withdrew the two founders from the Capuchin order. Matteo's personal venture had kindled the spark and given the Capuchins the basic principle that the observance of the rule was more important than the interests of the order; but Ludovico's had been the energy and the administrative ability that had fanned the spark into an enduring flame. At the moment of their disappearance the flame was saved and nursed anew by the skill of Bernardino d'Asti, the third founder as it were, and then by his successors Francesco da Jesi, Bernardino Ochino and Eusebius d'Ancona. All these four men who stabilised and perpetuated the Capuchin reform had come over to it from the Observants. And this points to one of the reform's greatest difficulties—the hostility of the observant superiors.

This hostility was perfectly understandable. Among the observant superiors there were certainly some who sympathised with the Capuchin ideals. But the development of the separate Capuchin organisation, by draining away the most fervent elements from the Observants, gravely jeopardised the projected reform of the latter. Matteo's personal appeal to the pope in 1525 was in fact typical of the countless dispensations given irresponsibly by Rome to individual religious which were weakening the communal bonds of monastic life and undermining the authority of superiors. The separate organisation of the new reform out of observant deserters could well appear irresponsible and mischievous. The rapid growth of the Capuchins and especially the secession to them of the local observant minister-provincial, Giovanni da Fano, who had tried in the first instance to suppress Matteo and Ludovico, only made things worse. In 1530 the Spanish observant general, Quiñones, was succeeded by the Italian Pisotti. It was an unfortunate choice. Pisotti did nothing to help reform within the Observants and tried to suppress the Capuchin 'schism' by force. Moreover, he was a vain and showy man who conducted his visitations with unbecoming pomp. His conduct only encouraged what he intended to end—the flow of Observants to the Capuchins. But it is characteristic of the papal court at this time, and of the vacillation of Clement VII, that the enemies of the Capuchins now found it as simple to obtain official documents undermining their position as their first promoters had found it easy to obtain the necessary sanctions for their establishment. The ebb and flow of document and counter-document, sometimes obtained from quite different officials, is too complicated to be followed here. But Pisotti's deposition in 1533 was not decisive since his successor was also hostile, and the death of Clement VII came as a blow since his niece, the duchess of Camerino, the Capuchins' principal supporter, was immediately deprived not only of her influence but of her territories too by Clement's successor, Paul III, in 1534. But it had been Clement himself who had yielded, early in 1534, to the Capuchins' enemies and decreed their disbandment and their expulsion from their settlement in Rome. All these attacks had been somehow met and warded off by Ludovico. By the time of his disappearance in 1536 the air was calmer. The Capuchins had obtained a new and even more powerful protectress in Vittoria Colonna, and in 1536 and 1537 Paul III confirmed their legal existence. To assuage the Observants, however, he forbade the reform to accept any further observant recruits or to make foundations outside Italy. He also required the superior of the Capuchins to seek on election formal confirmation from the minister-general of the Conventuals. This last arrangement lasted until 1619, when its abrogation finally made the Capuchins a fully independent branch of the Franciscan family. The prohibition against the reception of further Observants was probably all to the Capuchin advantage, since it enabled them to train their own men right from the start. Recruits were not lacking throughout the sixteenth and early seventeenth centuries, and it is noticeable that, though the order worked mainly among the poor and uneducated, it always attracted a notable number of aristocratic and well-educated subjects.

But in 1536 the Capuchins still had in front of them what was to be in some respects their most formidable trial of all—the apostasy and flight to Geneva in August 1542 of their Superior and most eminent preacher, Bernardino Ochino. There can be little doubt but that this disastrous event, which very nearly broke them, also served to give them a more acute sense of the prevalence and power of Protestant ideas which henceforward influenced their whole apostolate. Bernardino's success and popularity as a preacher had been immense. In 1541 his term as superior had been prolonged for a second three years, though somewhat against his wishes, and he was regarded as a model religious and an outstanding leader. But his concentration on the problems of justification, his reading of Luther's works, perhaps also the friendship of Juan Valdés at Naples, eventually led him to a position which, at some point not exactly determinable, he must have realised could have only one outcome. There were of course those who were wise after the event, but it has also been said that Ochino's sermons and works up to 1539 might still be accepted as part of the ascetical Catholic literature of the time but for his subsequent apostasy. In 1542, however, the atmosphere in Italy was growing more tense. Lutheran ideas were sensed to be at work. The Roman Inquisition was being re-established. The consciousness of hidden dangers was hardening ecclesiastical minds. Carafa was powerful. Ochino had already been censured by the nuncio in Venice for publicly criticising the imprisonment of an Augustinian. In the last months of his Capuchin life he was suspect at Rome. It was an invitation from Paul III to visit him that determined his flight.

The pope's first instinct was to suppress the Capuchins altogether. For four years they had been governed by a hidden Protestant. Who could now trust any of them? Their greatest stay—immense popular support— broke beneath them. Only the intervention of Cardinal Sanseverino, coupled with the skill of Francesco da Jesi, who took over the reins dropped by Bernardino, and the influence of Vittoria Colonna, stayed the execution. An enquiry was held into the doctrinal views of all the preachers in the order, who were required to submit written statements. The result was satisfactory. The preachers were re-licensed and the Capuchins survived. Soon they began to regain their popularity, and the years following Ochino's disappearance saw a steady growth of the Capuchins and their work under Francesco da Jesi, Bernardino d'Asti, and Eusebius d'Ancona. The influential lay-brother, St Felice da Cantalice, joined the order just after Ochino's apostasy and in spite of the prohibition on observant recruits numbers steadily grew. As early as 1535 separate provinces, to the number of eight, or perhaps twelve, had been erected. By 1550 the number had risen to about fifteen, and there were about 2500 friars. The organisation followed normal Franciscan lines, but there was apparently some preference for conventual as distinct from observant terminology. The superior, or vicar-general, sometimes, but perhaps inaccurately before 1619, called minister-general, was elected for three years. The constitutions were re-edited in 1552. A certain moderation of the original extreme austerities was then seen to be necessary. As the order developed, larger and more permanent houses were recognised as desirable. Settlements within towns were acquiesced in. A place was given to studies. The primitive recognition of complete episcopal control was not restated. The later monastic legislation of the Council of Trent in 1563 entailed certain further modifications to Capuchin life—principally in respect of the organisation of studies. In 1572 the prohibition on foundations outside Italy was withdrawn. The order then spread rapidly throughout the world, more than doubling its numbers, both of houses and members, between that date and the end of the century, and becoming second only to the Society of Jesus in its contribution to the Counter-Reformation.

The Capuchins were not, and did not claim to be, innovators. It was the appeal of an already venerable ideal to which they responded—that mixture of the active and contemplative life which was the ideal of the friars—and the new institute was only a reformed branch of an already existing order. But the new bodies of clerks regular arose in specific response to the challenge of the special problems of the age. Among the groups of devout priests and laymen found in increasing numbers in many Italian cities in the early decades of the sixteenth century—and among which the Roman Oratory of Divine Love, founded on the model of a similar institution at Genoa, is the best known[1]—preoccupation with personal sanctification, with the restoration of the dignity and efficiency of the priestly office, and with charity towards the suffering and the destitute came together to produce the foundation of the different institutes of clerks regular, pastoral priests living according to a rule and under vows. The foundation of the Theatines in 1524 was the joint work of four members of the Roman Oratory of Divine Love, of whom the

[1] Above, p. 258.

two outstanding were Gaetano da Thiene (St Cajetan), a native of Vicenza, and the Neapolitan bishop Gian Pietro Carafa, later Pope Paul IV. The idea seems originally to have been Cajetan's, but the organising drive was more Carafa's. The gentle retiring saint and the restless, fiery, yet learned bishop were complementary to each other, much as were the first Capuchins Matteo and Ludovico. The congregation took its name of 'Theatine' from the Latin form of one of Carafa's bishoprics —Chieti—which he now resigned. The name was a sign of Carafa's predominance. Though he and Cajetan, and later others, alternated as superior in three-year periods, Carafa, partly because of his episcopal orders, seems always to have thought of himself as having a special place of eminence. The rule was elaborated between 1530 and 1533 at which later date the order was confirmed by Clement VII, an action repeated by Paul III in 1536.

The Theatines were neither monks, nor friars, nor canons. They were a body of pastoral priests living together who took the monastic vows of poverty, chastity and obedience in order to live the apostolic priestly life in as perfect a manner as possible. They recited the Divine Office together but did not sing it as was then general among all communities of clerics; and though Cajetan himself seems to have ascribed importance to the recitation in common, the order early sought and accepted for some of its members dispensations even from its private recital in order to save time for other occupations. All the first members gave away their property and resigned their benefices before entering, accepting an absolute poverty which, like that of the Capuchins, rejected both fixed revenues and regular mendicancy. They set themselves the highest ideals in clerical behaviour and dress, carrying to an heroic extent the correction by example of the failures and abuses of contemporary clerical life. New recruits sometimes took a new name on entering. While not accepting the official charge of either parishes or hospitals, they were busy in preaching, in hearing confessions and exhorting to the more frequent reception of the sacraments, in charitable works for the sick and distressed, in study, and especially in preparing for the reform of the liturgy. Their life was retired and unobtrusive, and they did not preach in the open air like the Capuchins and the early Jesuits. But Carafa retained his position with Clement VII, who continued to use his services in various ways. The Roman house of the Theatines quickly became a centre of intense spiritual life and influence.

Important as was the impact of the Theatines on the clerical world, and highly valuable as were the services they were destined to render to Catholicism by their example and as a seed-bed of future Italian bishops, their influence in the first decades of their existence was limited by two factors. First, their restricted numbers. It was not only that the number of those who presented themselves for a hard and hidden life bereft of all external attraction—even that of a monastic habit—was necessarily small, but also that from the first the founders were acutely conscious of the danger of professing persons incapable of persevering in so difficult an existence. Thus the Theatines remained comparatively few in numbers—and largely aristocratic in composition. This reduced the number of foundations, though it did not wholly save the order from defections. The second factor was the sack of Rome in 1527 which drove the Roman community to seek refuge in Venice after it had suffered—and St Cajetan himself principally—appallingly barbarous treatment at the hands of the Spanish soldiery. At Venice it remained, and the Theatines did not return to Rome until 1557 when Carafa was pope and Cajetan in his grave. It seems reasonable to believe that their interests as an order suffered in consequence. There was an unsuccessful venture at Verona in 1528–9, and even the Neapolitan foundation, made in 1533, encountered serious difficulties in the early years. Until 1557 Venice and Naples were their only two houses. But it is testimony to the impression they made that the word 'Chietino' became currently used to denote a Catholic 'puritan'—whether cleric or lay—and was applied for a time in some quarters to the first Jesuits. For St Ignatius, however, who knew the Theatines in Venice in 1536 and 1537, the whole Theatine concept was plainly far too limited, though what exactly passed between him and Carafa on the subject during that period must remain to some degree uncertain.[1]

Nor is it clear that there was any direct inspiration from the Theatines behind the foundation of two further orders of clerks regular which it is customary to consider alongside of them, those known as the Barnabites and the Somaschi. The motive of active charity—inflamed by the spectacle of the suffering caused in North Italy by war, poverty and disease and the vices brought in their train—lay strongly behind both. Of the three founders of the Clerks Regular of St Paul, later known as Barnabites from their possession of the Church of St Barnabas at Milan, the leader, St Antonio Maria Zaccaria, was a native of Cremona and had been a doctor before he became a priest, Bartolomeo Ferrari had been a lawyer, and Giacomo Antonio Morigia a professor of mathematics. The foundation took place at Milan in 1533 and the first members were allowed to take solemn vows. In spite of their devotion to pastoral work and especially to the care and education of youth, the society adopted a way of life so severely penitential that reports of its singularity compelled Paul III to undertake an enquiry in 1535. As a result of this, however, he confirmed the order, exempted it from episcopal control and bestowed certain privileges on it. In 1537 it made foundations in Venice, Vicenza, Padua, Verona and elsewhere. Zaccaria died in 1539. The rule was

---

[1] Compare P. Paschini, *S. Gaetano Thiene, Gian Pietro Carafa e le origine dei chierici regolari Teatini* (1926), pp. 137–9, with P. Tacchi Venturi, S.J., *Storia della Compagnia di Gesù in Italia*, vol. II, Parte Prima (2nd edition 1950), pp. 79–80.

established in 1542 but did not take its final form until 1579. In the seventeenth century the Barnabites spread into France, Spain and Austria. They retained as part of their life the recitation of the Divine Office in choir and had a special choir dress which they wore over their normal priestly cassocks.

St Girolamo Aemiliani, who in 1532 founded at Somasca, near Bergamo, the congregation of priests who consequently became known as the Somaschi, had been a soldier. His foundation, made with a group of friends who had worked with him during the plagues of 1527, 1528 and 1529 at Verona, Brescia and Bergamo, reflected his revulsion from war and all its social consequences. His chief charitable work was the foundation of orphanages. The first members of his society did not take vows, and on Aemiliani's death in 1537 would have dispersed had it not been for the exertions of his chief follower Angelo Marco Gambara through whom the society was continued and confirmed by the pope in 1540. In 1547 it unsuccessfully sought incorporation into the Society of Jesus. From 1547 to 1555 it was united with the Theatines, but their spirit was different, and when Carafa became pope the union was dissolved. The restored Somaschi were nevertheless encouraged in their independence by Paul IV. Confirmed again by Pius IV in 1563, the society was elevated by St Pius V in 1568 to the status of a true religious order by the introduction of solemn vows and was given exemption from episcopal control. Like the Barnabites, the Somaschi enjoyed the high favour of St Charles Borromeo. They always remained a small order, but in the second half of the seventeenth century enjoyed a considerable expansion by undertaking educational work on a larger scale in colleges and seminaries.

The story of the Camaldolesi, Capuchins, Theatines, Barnabites and Somaschi illustrates the complex of inter-connected spiritual influences and motives that were at work in northern Italy at the time. All the founders who have been mentioned were in touch with most of the others and with reforming bishops like Lippomano and the influential Giberti of Verona who had resigned the office of datarius at the Roman curia; while the hand of Carafa—practically the only southerner among them—was everywhere. Carafa doubtless did much to keep alive the real interest felt by Clement VII and Paul III in all these movements; he was in close and sympathetic touch with the early Capuchins and was the spiritual director of Aemiliani. To get the complete picture of this expanding leaven of renewed Italian Catholic spirituality we must not forget two factors not always sufficiently stressed: first the spiritual influences deriving from members of the older orders, both of men and women, and secondly the spectacle of the physical sufferings of the Italian people in the first decades of the sixteenth century. A strong influence on St Cajetan, for example, was the Augustinian nun, Laura Mignani of Brescia, who was only one of several religious women of the time who had much hidden influence but are less well-known than figures like Vittoria Colonna. Carafa was always in close contact with his Dominican sister at Naples who herself made a reformed foundation for women. The Dominican friar, Battista da Crema, was an influential spiritual director who was consulted by St Cajetan and who probably prompted the foundation of the Barnabites, though his detachment from his own order in his last years drew down Carafa's reproaches. All, however, united in deploring the appalling consequences of the wars, the plagues, the famines and the poverty which racked the Italy of the later Renaissance. Every 'Oratory', every devout group, every new body of friars or priests, was concerned with the relief of the sick, the hungry, the destitute, the orphaned, the care of reformed prostitutes, or the construction of special hospitals for the victims of syphilis—a new scourge brought, it was said, by the French invading armies. The purely spiritual motive was of course predominant and basic, but it overflowed naturally and organically into the charity of social relief which was an essential element in the Italian Catholic reform.

The foundation of the association of priests known as the Congregation of the Oratory belongs to a later period. But it should be noticed here that in 1533 St Philip Neri, the future apostle of Rome, came as a young man from Florence to the Eternal City where for the next eighteen years he lived the curious hermit-existence, with its strange spiritual experiences, that preceded his decision to become ordained. As a boy in Florence, Philip Neri had imbibed from the Dominicans of St Mark's and from St Catherine Ricci the cult of Savonarola, nor did he ever forget what he originally owed to the order of St Dominic. But in Rome he came into contact with many other powerful currents of religious thought and influence, especially the early Jesuits; and his mature and developed spirituality, though springing basically from his own originality of character and temperament, had been shaped over many years of close association with all the varied spiritual forces that were alive in the Rome of the middle decades of the sixteenth century and that had produced, among other things, the new orders that have been described.

In 1535 there took place in Brescia an event of considerable significance in the history of religious associations of women. A number of unmarried women, drawn from all social ranks and mostly young—though including a few widows—formed themselves into an organised company dedicated to St Ursula. The members were to remain in the lay state, to live with their families, to worship in their own parish churches except for a monthly general communion in common, and to wear no uniform. But they were to lead a retired and mortified life according to a rule and under obedience to superiors, and to perform works of charity, in particular the instruction of young girls in Christian piety in their own homes. In 1536 the bishop of Brescia approved the foundation, which was put under episcopal control and had priestly assistance and guidance. Its founder and inspirer was St Angela Merici, a woman already 61 years old at the time of the foundation, who for many years had been widely known as a person of great sanctity and mortifications and a pursuer of good works. The spiritual atmosphere she breathed was that of the Franciscan Tertiaries, and she had made the pilgrimage to Jerusalem. It was said that in 1525 Clement VII had sought to persuade her to work in Rome. Her foundation, which spread rapidly in the north of Italy, especially in Milan, and later into France, was significant not only as a female response to the social and moral needs of the time but also as a lay venture which deliberately rejected monasticism with its vows and its enclosure. Education in the secular sense, save perhaps the teaching of reading and writing, was not at first contemplated and was not undertaken until 1595 when it was started at Parma in a community which had been monasticised and had readmitted the old social distinctions. For this lay institute for social works and 'Sunday school' teaching, in which class distinctions vanished, was turned within a century into a religious order, with solemn vows and dowries and strict enclosure, conducting schools for girls—a valuable work, but not the original scheme.

St Angela, who died in 1540, seems to have expected her Company to develop and adapt itself, and the papal bull of confirmation of 1544 provided for future changes. But the actual development negatived many of her basic ideas. Neither social nor ecclesiastical opinion in the Italy or France of the Counter-Reformation was prepared for the idea of a free religious association of lay-women privately pledged to virginity and social retirement but organised under a rule of life for the performance of good works. First a uniform, or habit (1546), then conventualisation in a common dwelling (Milan 1566), at length simple and finally solemn religious vows with enclosure transformed the company into an order. In this process St Charles Borromeo and the decrees of the Council of Trent with their strict principles of enclosure for all religious women played the leading parts. The era of lay associations on St Angela's lines or even of active nuns without strict enclosure was not yet. Analogous experiences befell the foundations of St Jane Francis Chantal and Mary Ward in the seventeenth century, and it is only with the Sisters of Charity of St Vincent de Paul that the tide begins to turn. None the less, from St Angela Merici and her maidens have sprung the many families of Ursuline convents which have been so prominent in the education of girls. For completeness' sake it should be noted here that Fra Battista da Crema and St Antonio Maria Zaccaria supported a small religious association of women founded in 1535 by the former's patroness, the Contesa Louisa Torelli, to help the Barnabite apostolate among women. In 1557 they, too, had enclosure imposed on them. The Capuchinesses, founded at Naples in 1538 by Maria Longa, the Spanish widow of an Italian official, were strictly enclosed from the start.

All the new foundations, however, were quickly surpassed in importance by the Society of Jesus, whose canonical beginning dates from 1540. In this body the basic idea of the clerks regular was carried to its farthest lengths and enriched by new elements. Founded by a Basque with nine companions who comprised another Basque, three Castilians, one Portuguese, two Frenchmen and two Savoyards, but no Italians, the society was international in composition and wide-ranging in purpose from the first, and though established at the centre of the Church in Rome, since it was formed to be offered to the pope, owed little that can be detected to the Italian environment in which the ten 'foreign' or 'pilgrim' priests—as the first Jesuits were called in Italy—had lived and worked for four years before the actual foundation.

Don Iñigo Lopez de Loyola, who later adopted the name of Ignatius, was born in 1491 at Azpeitia of a Basque knightly family with property at Loyola and elsewhere. Until his thirtieth year he followed the callings of a soldier and a courtier, excelling in feats of bravery and rashness, and delighting—or so he recorded in later life—in duels, dice and affairs of the heart. A grave leg-wound incurred in the defence of Pamplona against the French in 1521 laid him on a long bed of pain and idleness during which his reading of Spanish translations of the legends of the saints and of the *Life of Christ* by Ludolph the Carthusian, in default of secular romances, was accompanied by a religious conversion in which his ideals of service and adventure were turned into completely new channels. Seeking to emulate the saints in the service of God and his Mother, Ignatius on recovery bade farewell to his family and journeyed to the famous shrine of Our Lady at the Catalan monastery of Montserrat. Here, having made a general confession to a French monk and having probably received helpful spiritual advice, he dedicated himself in an all-night vigil before the holy image to a new life of penitence and service. Exchanging his knightly garments with those of an astonished beggar, he then retired for eight months to the neighbouring town of Manresa where he submitted himself to the harshest penances and austerities and underwent a series of extraordinary religious experiences and illuminations which formed the basis of his whole future career and were the foundations of his *Spiritual Exercises*. Here, too, he discovered the *Imitation of Christ*, that great masterpiece of the northern *devotio moderna*, which with the books read in his first illness constitutes the only direct and undisputed literary influence upon his spirituality. Leaving Manresa purged and illuminated, he made the pilgrimage to Jerusalem (1523), crossing Italy alone and barefooted. At Jerusalem he sought to join the Franciscans and to end his days in the Holy Land as a friar. Failing to make his point he returned to Barcelona and contemplated entering the Carthusian Order. But gradually his ideal of service to God widened. Instead of desiring no more than to hide himself in a life of obscure monastic penance he felt the impulse to bring to others the knowledge of the way to God as God had taught him at Manresa. He realised that for this he required to educate himself, a vital decision for his future, and there followed his early periods of study at Barcelona (1525), Alcalá (1526–7) and Salamanca (1527). But everywhere he went, men and women gathered round him whom he instructed in religion and whom he sought to direct according to the plan of the *Spiritual Exercises* already, it seems, written down in an early form.

Such unauthorised activity on the part of a mere layman could hardly fail to be frowned upon by the ecclesiastical authorities, already highly sensitive to the existence in Spain of persons claiming direct divine illumination. At Alcalá and Salamanca Ignatius succeeded in justifying his orthodoxy though not in avoiding some period of imprisonment. But the restrictions which the inquisitors sought to place upon his activities as a spiritual teacher caused him to seek a freer field outside Spain for his studies and for his apostolic endeavours. Hence the years at the university of Paris (1528–1535), which were another turning point in his life when his whole horizon, in many senses, was enlarged. Here too he gathered round himself and formed the disciples who were destined to make the foundation with him, with six of whom—Le Fèvre, Laínez, Salmerón, Bobadilla, Rodriguez and Francis Xavier—he took the famous vow at Montmartre on 15 August 1534 by which they dedicated their lives in poverty and chastity to the service of God, either in the Holy Land or— should they be unable to do this—by offering their services to the pope. After they had completed their studies the companions met again in 1537 at Venice, the port of embarkation for Palestine, their number now enlarged by the addition of Le Jay, Broet and Codure. Ignatius was already there, completing his studies and familiarising himself with the Italian situation; it was at this time that he came into contact with Carafa and the Theatines. Those who were not yet priests, St Ignatius included, were there ordained, and the companions separated to work in different Italian towns until they could embark for the Holy Land.

But hostilities between Venetians and Turks made the journey impossible in 1537. After waiting a little longer, they decided to fulfil the alternative proposal of their Montmartre vow and offer themselves to the pope. In preparation, Ignatius, with Le Fèvre and Laínez, went to Rome to reconnoitre. In a chapel at La Storta outside Rome in November 1537 he was strengthened by an experience of a mystical kind in which he claimed that God had 'set him along with his Son', and in Rome his exertions soon commended himself and his companions to many in places of influence. He successfully defended himself against charges of heresy and irresponsibility raked up from his past in Spain and Paris, and at length, early in 1539, with backing from the highest ecclesiastical powers, he called his companions to him to decide on their future. The group now solemnly debated whether, in order to make themselves more effective as instruments in the hands of the pope, they should form themselves into a religious society or not. By 24 June they had unanimously reached the decision to remain united and to add a vow of obedience to a superior to their vows of poverty and chastity. They drew up a document in five chapters in which the essential principles of the Society of Jesus and its work appear on paper for the first time. It can hardly be doubted that Ignatius was the predominating force in all this and that the ideas now sketched were not new in his mind. The papal advisers to whom the document was submitted were, however, of divided opinions. Certain points in the proposals seemed new and strange; the atmosphere was against new foundations. It was almost certainly Cardinal Contarini who ensured a favourable outcome, and with some amendments the proposals were accepted. By a papal bull of 27 September 1540, *Regimini militantis ecclesiae*, the Society of Jesus—its name, which for long some found questionable, harking back to the experience at La Storta—came into existence. Ignatius was elected general in Lent 1541, and the six members then in Rome made their solemn vows in St Paul's Outside the Walls on 22 April 1541.

The long evolution of soldier into founder-saint was now complete and from this moment until his death on 31 July 1556 Ignatius of Loyola lived in Rome directing closely every side of his society's life and activities. The bull of foundation had cautiously placed a limit of sixty on the number of the professed members. In 1544 Paul III removed this, and Julius III shortly after his election in 1550 published the important confirmatory bull *Exposcit debitum* which had been prepared under his predecessor and in which the aims and structure of the society were more fully set out. Both these pontiffs warmly supported the Jesuits and heaped privileges on them in recognition of their value. Under Paul IV, however, the atmosphere became somewhat cooler. Papal help was withheld from certain Jesuit institutions, and after Ignatius's death an attack was made on the life-tenure of the generalship and the fathers in Rome were forced to recite their office in common like the Theatines. Pius IV, however, again allowed the society to observe its own constitutions. These, with the accompanying declarations, constitute a long and elaborate document in ten parts. They are the full working out of the five short chapters of 1539 and were the work of Ignatius himself, accomplished between 1547 and 1551 with the aid of his secretary Polanco, a graduate of Padua, who did most of the drafting. They were accepted by an assembly of the professed fathers in 1551 which also vetoed Ignatius's attempt to resign the generalship. The next few years were a period of rapid expansion. Whereas we have about 920 letters of Ignatius written between 1540 and 1549, for the years 1549 to 1556 the number is no less than 6740.

Useful activity marked all the declared aims of the society. Apart from the sanctification of its own members, these were the 'propagation'—the word 'defence' was added in the bull of 1550—of the faith and the promotion of the good of souls by preaching, teaching, retreat-giving, ministration of the sacraments and all spiritual and charitable works of mercy, including specifically the instruction of boys in the truths of Christianity. Everything was ordered with this pastoral aim in view, especially the revolutionary abolition of the common recitation of the office and the abstention from the singing of high masses. Fasts and severe corporal mortifications were to be no normal part of the life, and even the prayer of the Jesuit was to be so conditioned as to keep his will and his mind fixed on active tasks and away from the temptation of the contemplative ideal. The rejection of the ways and spirit of monasticism went farther than any clerks regular had yet gone and was a great stumbling-block to conservative critics who chose to see in this special policy for a special society a condemnation in principle smacking of Erasmian humanism or even of Protestantism. The practical successes of the society, however, were largely due to the revolutionary features which marked it at so many points, coupled with the long training of its members.

The intending novice was first submitted to a 'first probation' in the form of a thorough-going examination of character and motives carried out according to the set directions of the first chapter of the constitutions. The novitiate itself lasted two years instead of the hitherto customary one, and instead of being undergone in unbroken seclusion included wherever possible a period of service in a hospital and the making of a pilgrimage barefoot and begging. Then came an even more radical innovation—the intrusion of a period of indefinite length, called the scholasticate, between novitiate and profession. This was, in effect, a period of education, in humanities, philosophy and theology, as might be suitable; and it might also include employment in preaching and in charitable works. The scholastic took simple vows of poverty, chastity and obedience and pledged himself to enter the society proper if, whenever, and in whatever grade of membership, his superiors should decide. If in due course he were accepted for membership he was then ordained and submitted to a kind of second spiritual novitiate of one year, called the 'third probation', or 'tertianship'. After this he was incorporated into the society in one of three possible ways. Those who had not reached the highest intellectual or cultural level but could be useful in purely spiritual functions became 'formed spiritual co-adjutors'. The others became fully professed members taking solemnly the usual three vows and could not thereafter normally be dismissed. Of these, again, some were allowed to take a fourth vow which reflected the original intention of the founding fathers. This was a vow of direct personal obedience to the pope should the latter send them to work in foreign missions. The 'professed of the fourth vow' constituted the innermost core of the society and were its governing body. In 1556 out of about 1000 members only forty-three had been admitted to the fourth vow; eleven others were solemnly professed and there were five spiritual co-adjutors. The gradation of membership, which also included formed temporal co-adjutors (lay-brothers), was one of Ignatius's most ingenious inventions. The grades appear to reflect the successive stages of his own career. It has also been suggested that he may have been influenced by the Venetian constitution or by discussions on the constitutions of 'ideal societies' which took place in intellectual circles in Venice during his time there.[1]

Ultimate power in the society and the interpretation of the constitutions lay with the general congregation of the fathers professed of the fourth vow or their elected representatives. This body did not, however, meet at fixed intervals but only to elect a new general or at the summons of the existing general. In very exceptional circumstances it could be brought together to deal with an insane or gravely incompetent general. But while all monastic reforms in the preceding 150 years had sought safety in temporary superiors—even with Benedictine abbots—and in regular capitular assemblies in the manner of the friars for the control of business and the election of officials, the Jesuit general was chosen for life and the society knew no capitular organisation. The general nominated to all the important posts throughout the whole society and during his life-tenure was controllable only by his—elected—assistants. It was laid down that there should be four of these. In practice the general appeared supreme and may not unreasonably be regarded as reflecting in the sphere of ecclesiastical polity—like the Counter-Reformation Papacy itself—the new spirit of centralised autocracy characterising the early sixteenth century. Conversely, the virtue of obedience was held in special esteem and was particularly inculcated by Ignatius who wished its perfection to be the special mark of his followers. The society was conceived as an instrument in the hands of the pope to serve Christ and his Church. Similarly, the individual Jesuit lay in the hands of his superiors. The similes of the corpse—*quasi cadaver*—and of the stick-in-the-hand were not, however, original; they were drawn from the Franciscan and other medieval rules. But Jesuit obedience functioned without the limiting factors of an exact monastic rule and limited external activities, and the very variety and variability of Jesuit work widened, as it were, the potential area of its application. There was, too, an obedience demanded of mind and spirit in conformity with the special attitudes of the society in many spiritual and theological issues, something which could press more closely than the general duty to 'think with the Church'. Yet the conception of Jesuit obedience as essentially military is not the whole

[1] J. Crehan, S.J., 'Saint Ignatius and Cardinal Pole', *Arch. Hist. Soc. Jesu*, xxv (1956), pp. 11–12.

truth. The amount of care for individual temperaments which the constitutions specifically require to be shown by superiors, and which is exemplified in Ignatius's own skill in dealing with his subjects, is very remarkable, and many early Jesuits showed a truly Renaissance variety and independence of character within the society's prudent and elastic framework. Behind the Jesuit spirituality lay the *Spiritual Exercises*, that remarkable technique of systematic, purposeful prayer and meditation, regulating and focusing the will and the affections, a technique which, it is clear from the records, produced in numberless individuals a changed life, or a permanent re-kindling of fervour in new resolutions, thus reproducing in varying degrees of intensity Ignatius's own conversion, from the experiences of which the *Exercises* took their origin. The *Exercises* were one of the Jesuits' most powerful spiritual weapons in their general apostolate as well as the basis of their own spiritual training. The text, written with extreme care by Ignatius, is in effect his instructions for directors giving the exercises. A Latin translation of the Spanish original was approved by Paul III in 1548 and printed then for the first time.

The Jesuits pledged themselves to accept no bishopric or ecclesiastical dignity save by express papal command. They also prudently refused the spiritual direction of communities of women, and an ill-advised and embarrassing attempt on the part of Isabel Roser, one of Ignatius's earliest followers in Barcelona, to establish a female community in Rome under Jesuit obedience failed. They refused, too, the direct administration of parishes, but soon established a whole series of important religious and charitable organisations in Rome and elsewhere. In these ways they followed in the footsteps of the Theatines. But the special and wider activities which had come to distinguish them by 1556 showed the immense difference between the scope and the vision of the two institutes. These activities were, first, education and learning, secondly, missions to infidel and heathen lands, and thirdly, engagement in the fight against Protestantism outside Italy.

The Jesuits no more than the first Ursulines were founded as a 'teaching order' in the strict or exclusive sense of the words as later exemplified in the foundations of St Joseph Calasanctius and St Jean-Baptiste de la Salle. But St Ignatius well understood the scandal and havoc caused by an ignorant clergy and though he never became a great scholar himself he was determined that his own 'reformed priests' should be men of the highest cultural and educational standards consistent with their priesthood, men capable of giving an up-to-date and intelligent presentation of the faith they preached to Catholic and infidel alike. Not for nothing did he gird his own loins for study, draw his co-founders from fellow-students at Paris, institute the scholasticate, and restrict the fullest membership of the society to the best scholars. Some of the first Jesuits were, indeed, outstanding in ecclesiastical learning, and also in humanities, and commended themselves to Paul III as much by their doctrinal and scriptural expositions as by their pastoral efficiency. The future importance of the Jesuits as dogmatic and moral theologians and controversialists was latent in the society from the start and was foreshadowed in particular by the attendance of Laínez and Salmerón at the Council of Trent in 1546 where they met with such success that when they returned there in 1552, to play an important part in the discussions and also make the society more widely known, it was as accredited theologians of the Holy See. The colleges provided for in the constitutions—which, unlike the houses of the professed fathers, were allowed to enjoy fixed revenues—were intended for the education of members of the society, in humanities, philosophy and theology. The courses might be attended at established universities or be given by fathers of the society. The first college was established at Padua in 1542, and Ignatius drew up rules for it which became classical. A second was established at Coimbra a few months later. Others followed, the most important being the Roman college inaugurated in 1551. In 1556 Paul IV gave the society authority to confer degrees on its own students at this college.

So successful was the educational system elaborated by the society for the training of its own members that it soon came to be eagerly sought after by others. The task of running what we should now call secondary schools for boys—overlapping the sphere of university education as it then did—was not implied in the original Jesuit aim of teaching boys their religion. Ignatius was not at first eager to see it develop. Outside pressure, however, forced the pace. The first admission of lay boys to a Jesuit college for the humanities course took place at Goa in 1545 and was held justified by the special conditions of the Indian mission. Then in 1546 at the request of the duke of Gandía—later, as St Francis Borgia, to be general of the society and already secretly professed in it—a Jesuit was permitted to hold a course in arts for laymen at Gandía University. At length, at the earnest insistence of the viceroy of Sicily, Ignatius conceded the principle and a boys' college was opened at Messina, in 1548, the success of which led to other irresistible demands. At Ignatius's death the society had over thirty colleges for lay youths and had embarked irreversibly upon its career as the educator of the upper classes of Catholic Europe. No one could be less truly called a 'child of the Renaissance' than Ignatius who had early and decisively rejected the Erasmian outlook; but it was the Jesuits with their high academic standards in Latin and Greek who incorporated much of the scholarship and not a little of the humanistic spirit of the classical Renaissance into orthodox Catholic education. The purging of the classical texts in the interests of morality and Christian doctrine was no doubt objectionable to the whole-hearted humanist, but understandable from the Jesuit point of view on the object of Christian education. It was not until 1599 that, after numerous earlier experimental forms, the final version of the Jesuit educational plan, the *Ratio Studiorum*, was produced.

French influences were strong in early Jesuit studies. Ignatius insisted on adherence to the Paris system of teaching which was strange in Italy and often much disliked. The first rector of the Roman college—whose courses were soon thrown open to laymen—and a number of early Jesuit teachers in Rome and Gandía and Messina were Frenchmen. Paradoxically enough, in France itself the society made only small initial headway. In Paris both bishop and university, with their Gallican outlook, distrusted a body so heavily privileged by the Papacy and tending to overlap the university's sphere. In 1556 there were only two Jesuit communities in France, at Paris and Billom, and the first was in a somewhat equivocal legal position. In Portugal, on the other hand, there were already six communities, in Spain over twenty, and in Italy even more. In Italy the society was more quickly successful than elsewhere in overcoming the opposition of established local teachers and faculties who were unwilling to yield immediate place to the foreign priests with their Paris methods— and who made a principle of taking no fees.

It is a mistake to suppose that the Society of Jesus was founded specifically to combat Protestantism. As a Spaniard, Ignatius turned his eyes more readily to the Muslim world and the Orient than to the heretics in Germany. The extraordinary career of St Francis Xavier in India and the Far East, already ended four years before Ignatius died, represented the earliest Jesuit ideal which never waned. The quick and warm support of the Portuguese Crown promoted early missions in India, based on Goa, in Brazil, and in Ethiopia, this last being on the way out, with two Jesuits consecrated as bishops, at Ignatius's death. There was also a mission to the Congo. At the end of his life Ignatius toyed with plans for colleges in Jerusalem, Constantinople and Cyprus. In the Spanish-controlled New World, however, the Jesuits were late-comers, following in the footsteps of the earlier Augustinian, Franciscan and Dominican missions. But during his time in Paris, in Venice, and indeed in Rome itself, Ignatius doubtless came to appreciate the import of the Protestant movement. Nevertheless it was on the express command of Paul III, not on Ignatius's own initiative, that the first Jesuits went to investigate the German situation. During the 1540's Le Fèvre, Le Jay and Bobadilla went to Germany separately as assistants to Cardinal Morone and other papal representatives. Called to many places by both lay and ecclesiastical potentates who sought their advice, they made contacts and collected impressions and information so far as their ignorance of German permitted, and made some attempt at cultivating relations with Protestant leaders. But all came separately to the same conclusion, that only a new generation of priests and laity trained in a new and more positive, confident, Catholic mentality could save German Catholicism. Jesuit colleges were soon being asked for. The first permanent Jesuit settlement was made at the key-point of Cologne in 1545. The outstanding figures were Canisius and Kessel, both natives of the Low Countries. The settlement suffered at first, like that at Paris, from the attitude of the city authorities who supported the opposition of the university and other elements hostile to the new teachers. But Cologne was a vital place for Catholicism in Germany and was of great importance because of its close links with the Low Countries whence came so many of the early Jesuits. Later settlements such as those at Ingolstadt and Vienna had easier beginnings. At Ignatius's death the society had struck certain roots in Germany and had gained the favour of the Bavarian Wittelsbachs and of the Habsburgs—despite Bobadilla's outspoken condemnation of the Interim. It was also in charge of the German college founded in Rome in 1552 at the instigation of Cardinal Morone for the education of German boys suitable to be prepared for the priesthood, which was the first boarding college undertaken by the society. Later the Jesuits were to direct a number of seminaries and play a large part in training secular priests of many nationalities. Cardinal Pole was in sympathetic touch with St Ignatius and his young society. He was concerned with the abortive mission of Broet and Salmerón to Ireland in 1541, and though the suggestion of a Jesuit mission to England during the Marian restoration of Catholicism did not materialise—Ignatius had other commitments seemingly more important—Pole's plans for a more systematic education for priests which figure in the decrees of the Council of London of 1555-6 and on which were modelled the Tridentine decree of 1563 on seminaries, were clearly influenced by Jesuit practice and experience.[1]

In 1554 Ignatius's health was seen to be failing. He was given three assistants. Nadal was made vicar-general and made visitations of great importance in Germany and elsewhere. After Ignatius's death, however, it was Laínez, one of the original ten, who became vicar-general and was elected second general in 1558, the general congregation having been delayed owing to various difficulties raised by Paul IV. At Ignatius's death there were about a thousand Jesuits—the vast majority still novices or scholastics. They were distributed among about one hundred settlements of different kinds—professed houses, colleges, residences—and grouped into a dozen or so provinces covering Italy, Spain, Portugal, France, Germany and the Low Countries in Europe, and India, Japan, Brazil and the Congo. Perhaps a fifth to a quarter of the houses were outside Europe, but no fewer than 170 of the Society's members were living in Rome. Demands for colleges and foundations far beyond the society's resources in men and money were coming in. But the society was still in some ways in an experimental stage. The Italian element in it

[1] J. Crehan, S.J., op. cit.; V. P. Brassell, S.J. Praeformatio Reformationis Tridentinae de Seminariis Clericorum (Manresa, 1938).

was not yet strong. Not perhaps until the rule of the first Italian general, Claudio Acquaviva (1581–1615), did the elaborate provisions of the constitutions become fully and smoothly operative and the society stand forth with all its mature characteristics. Its unique character and immense potentialities were, however, already sufficiently apparent in 1556. It was the spearhead of the pastoral, active spirit of Counter-Reformation Catholicism, international, confident, determined, uncompromising, yet at the same time flexible, adaptable, ingratiating, modern. Taught by its founder, it sought to be on good terms with the highest authorities in both Church and State and to turn their power and patronage to good account. But, in the tradition of its founder, too, it was determined that nothing should be allowed to stand against its will to serve the Church according to the aims and spirit of its institute. Both central and singular in the Church, it was destined to have a far-reaching influence not only on the progress of the Counter-Reformation but upon every side of the life and spirit of modern Catholicism.

CHAPTER X

THE EMPIRE OF CHARLES V IN EUROPE

THE sixteenth century was an age of prophets. Luther, Zwingli and Calvin interpreted the Word of God, challenging the claim of the Roman Church to its own uniquely-valid interpretation. These prophets found their armed champions in Knox, Coligny and William of Orange. The Catholic Church countered them with her own arms, with Loyola, with Philip II and the Inquisition. But for more than a generation, before the religious conflicts erupted into open war, the political and religious life of Europe was dominated by a very different fighter for God: the Habsburg emperor Charles V, the last medieval emperor to whom the religious and political unity of Christendom was both the ideal purpose of his life and a practicable object of policy. 'Caesar is not a doctor of the gospels,' wrote Erasmus in his dedication to Charles of his paraphrase of St Matthew, 'he is their champion.' 'God's standard bearer', the emperor called himself when, in June 1535, he weighed anchor at Barcelona to wrest Tunis from the Turks.

Charles had good reasons for his belief. 'God has set you on the path towards a world monarchy', said the grand chancellor Gattinara, in 1519. Marriage alliances and inheritance had given Charles this unique opportunity. In the fifteenth century the houses of Austria and Burgundy had become united in northern Europe, those of Aragon and Castile in the south; but the marriage of Philip of Burgundy and Joanna of Castile, at the beginning of the sixteenth century, produced a similar union between the northern and southern houses only through a series of unexpected deaths. As a result, Charles inherited the Habsburg possessions of Austria, Tyrol and parts of southern Germany, the Netherlands and Franche-Comté and, south of the Alps, Spain with her new American colonies and the Spanish dominions in Italy, Sicily, Sardinia and Naples. To Charles V, this inheritance was a sacred trust, the evidence of a divine intention as well as the material means to carry out this intention. Others had jealously claimed some of his provinces without just title; but, with God's help and his own unceasing efforts, he had always managed to preserve his inheritance undiminished for an heir. Thus wrote Charles to his son in his secret instructions and testaments. At one time or another during his reign, Charles himself or a member of his family sat as ruler or consort on nearly every royal throne of Europe. Dynastic alliances had appeared as the effective instrument of God's will, and dynastic alliances remained the emperor's favourite policy throughout his life, the only type of policy he chose freely for the enhancing of his power in Europe.

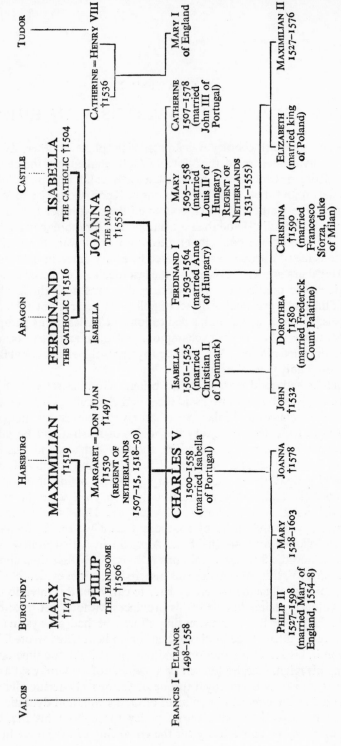

THE FAMILY OF CHARLES V

'For that which God most commends [to princes] is peace', he admonished his son in 1548. All wars which he had waged against Christian princes had been forced on him.

Only against the infidel was offensive warfare justified. Charles saw his task as the divinely appointed one of leading a united Christendom against the external enemy, the Muslim Turk and, later, against its internal enemies, the Lutheran heretics.[1] To this end the houses of Burgundy, Austria and Spain had been raised and united in his person. To this end Charles supported the legitimate rights of its members, even against the dictates of reason of state: he refused to accommodate Henry VIII in the divorce of Catherine of Aragon and pressed for decades the impracticable claims of his niece Dorothea to the Danish throne. To this end, too, he insisted that the members of his family sacrifice themselves to his imperial policy just as he sacrificed himself; for thus he wrote to his sister, Mary of Hungary, who had protested against the proposed marriage of their barely twelve-year-old niece, Christina of Denmark, to the duke of Milan in 1535.

For most of Charles's contemporaries his imperial position had no such transcendental significance; least of all for the men responsible for the young prince's smooth entry into the inheritance of his many lands. Charles had lost his father in 1506 at the age of six and had inherited from him the possessions of the house of Burgundy: Franche-Comté with the claim to the duchy of Burgundy (since 1477 in French hands) and the provinces which were then called *les pays de pardeça* and which came to be known as the Netherlands (*les pays d'embas*) only from the 1530's. These were the duchies of Luxemburg and Brabant, and the counties of Flanders, Holland, Zeeland, Hainault and Artois, together with a number of smaller counties and lordships. Charles's mother, Joanna of Castile, who survived until 1555, was insane and incapable of government. In consequence, the regency for the child was undertaken by his grandfather, the emperor Maximilian I, acting through his daughter, Margaret of Austria, dowager duchess of Savoy. Margaret's regency was brought to an end in January 1515 when the estates bribed Maximilian to have the young prince declared of age.

Within a year of this event, Ferdinand of Aragon was dead (23 January 1516). The whole inheritance of the Catholic kings, Ferdinand and Isabella, now fell to Charles of Burgundy. To Guillaume de Croy, lord of Chièvres, the effective head of Charles's government, the problem was

---

[1] This is substantially the view of P. Rassow, *Die Kaiser-Idee Karls V* (1932); *Die Politische Welt Karls V* (1947). Fifty years ago, E. Armstrong, *The Emperor Charles V* (2nd ed. 1910), argued that the emperor's policy was purely defensive, with all his actions forced on him by others. K. Brandi, *Kaiser Karl V*, vol. I (1937; English transl. by C. V. Wedgwood, 1939); vol. II, *Quellen und Erörterungen* (1941), in the fullest modern biography and an exhaustive critical bibliography, maintained that Charles's policy was more positive, with the increased greatness of the house of Habsburg as its ultimate aim.

neither new nor unexpected. Little more than ten years before, the Burgundian nobility had accompanied Charles's father, Philip, to Spain and had helped him to make good his claims to the crown of Castile. Since then, Spanish grandees had lived at the Burgundian court and had been admitted to the Order of the Golden Fleece. Spanish merchants were familiar figures in Bruges and Antwerp. For Chièvres and the great seigneurs in his council the question of whether or not to accept the Spanish succession never arose; it was only a question of how to achieve it. Chièvres was the leader of the old Walloon nobility. By culture, family ties and the possession of estates near or even across the French border they were traditionally francophile. Now, Chièvres had to reconcile the 'English' party with whose help Margaret had governed. He had to win over Maximilian and Henry VIII into full co-operation and induce Francis I to maintain a benevolent neutrality (Treaty of Noyon, 3 December 1516).

Having none of Gattinara's or Charles's sense of imperial mission, Chièvres could afford to leave France in control of northern Italy if this meant peace and amity with his powerful neighbour. When finally, in September 1517, he concluded a truce with the old enemy of the Habsburgs, Charles of Guelders, Burgundian diplomacy had won its major objectives—peace in Europe and freedom from all interference with the Spanish succession.

The situation in Spain itself was much more problematical. The union of the Spanish Crowns had not meant the union of the Spanish kingdoms, and there were still powerful forces in each which would gladly have seen a return to separate rulers. In Castile, despite the efforts of Isabella, the power of the Crown was still far from firmly established. At every royal death, the old antagonism between grandees and towns broke out into open strife. Since Isabella's death the regency of Castile had been in the hands of her old minister, Cardinal Ximenes de Cisneros, archbishop of Toledo. After Ferdinand's death, Ximenes was well aware that only the early arrival of Charles in Spain could assure him a smooth succession. The nobles, trying to profit by the interregnum, were attempting to regain their old control over the towns. Toledo and Valladolid were in revolt against their corregidors, the royal representatives in the city administration. The cardinal's attempt to raise a militia of 30,000 was sabotaged by both towns and grandees who feared for their own power. Ximenes had to give way for fear of more serious trouble. Most difficult of all, and most embittering, was the problem of royal appointments. The Spaniards accused the Netherlanders of greed and place-hunting. In fact, the court at Brussels was careful to hold its hand in all but a few cases; but, in Spain itself, Ximenes' secretary wrote that government was impossible without giving benefices and rewards (*mercedes*).

The eighteen months which it had taken Chièvres to prepare for Charles's departure had been too long an interregnum for Spain. When Charles landed there, in September 1517, his supporters were already disillusioned, while nobles and towns were sullenly apprehensive of the expected rule of the foreigner. The cardinal-regent lay dying, for joy at the king's arrival, as Charles's court jester maliciously said. Charles himself, young, ugly and inexperienced, speaking no Spanish and surrounded by Burgundian councillors and courtiers, did not initially make a good impression. The Spaniards contrasted the magnificence of the Burgundian court, its tournaments and balls, with the sober and inexpensive habits of the Catholic kings. Only three bishoprics were given to foreigners, but these included the see of Toledo, for Chièvres's nephew, and it was easy to regard this as plunder for the Burgundians. Moreover, it appeared that those Spaniards who had been in the Netherlands were preferred to those who had served the king's cause in Spain. In February 1518 the cortes of Valladolid presented Charles with far-reaching demands and much pointed counsel as a condition of the country's homage and of a grant of 600,000 ducats payable over three years. The court was accommodating and, if relations were not cordial, Charles was now the acknowledged king of Castile.

The estates of the realms of the Crown of Aragon had preserved even greater liberties than those of Castile. It took much longer than in Castile to come to terms with the cortes of Zaragoza and Barcelona and to obtain from them 200,000 and 100,000 ducats respectively. Chièvres preferred not to repeat this delay in Valencia. With the Crown of Aragon Charles had now inherited the old Aragonese empire, the Balearic islands, Sardinia, Sicily and Naples. It was a union of kingdoms each with its own history, its own traditions, obligations and enmities. The necessity of defending southern Italy from the Turks inevitably brought Charles V's empire into collision with the Ottoman empire, quite apart from Charles's view of himself as the champion of Christendom. The rival Aragonese and Angevin claims to Naples brought Charles into collision with France, a collision which the purely Burgundian policy of Chièvres had at least temporarily been able to avoid. Defence against the Turks inevitably turned into a struggle for the control of the central Mediterranean. Defence against the French inevitably turned into a struggle for the control of Italy and hence, as the emperor's advisers Gattinara and Granvelle were later to argue, into a struggle for the dominant position in Europe. Even without Charles's election as emperor, Castile's traditional friendship with France (maintained despite the francophobia of the Castilians) was now irretrievably broken, and similarly broken was the Walloon nobility's policy of Franco-Burgundian amity.

There remained the final step in Charles's succession, the succession to the Austrian and South German dominions of the Habsburgs and his election as king of Germany which carried with it the crown of the Holy

Roman Empire.[1] With the pope supporting Francis I and the electors still undecided, Margaret of Austria suggested that both pope and electors might be more easily induced to accept Charles's younger brother, Ferdinand, than the powerful ruler of the Netherlands, Spain and half of Italy. Charles's sharp reaction from Barcelona reads like a programme for his reign. Experience had shown, he wrote, that even such a virtuous and victorious prince as the Emperor Maximilian had been in constant trouble to safeguard his patrimony and imperial rights; but he, Charles, with the power of all his great kingdoms and dominions, would be feared and esteemed among other princes, would obtain true obedience from the subjects of the empire and defeat the enemies of the faith. This would be greater glory for both Ferdinand and himself than acquiring dominion over Christians. Charles promised, however, to work for Ferdinand's election as king of the Romans, that is as heir presumptive to the imperial title. In the end, Charles was elected unanimously by the German electors (28 June 1519).

The election was peculiarly the triumph of the new grand chancellor, the Piedmontese Mercurino Arborio di Gattinara who had been appointed to his office in 1518. A brilliant lawyer and superb administrator, an enthusiastic humanist and admirer of Erasmus, he had risen in the service of Margaret of Austria. For the next twelve years he did more than any other person to shape the development of his master's political ideas, then still in the youthful stage of the chivalrous quest for personal glory in the tradition of the Burgundian court. In his own memoirs, in speeches to the Spanish cortes and the Netherlands states general, in memoranda for the emperor and his council, Gattinara reiterated his belief that the imperial title gave Charles authority over the whole world, for it was 'ordained by God himself...and approved by the birth, life and death of our Redeemer Christ'. It was Dante's imperial idea revived. Like Dante, Gattinara, his learned and historically conscious compatriot, saw the centre of imperial power in Italy. Not the personal possession of Milan or of other territories, but the friendship and support of the Italian states and all Christian princes (guaranteed, no doubt, by Habsburg military power) were to assure the emperor his position as moral and political leader of the world. In time Charles made these views his own, with little of the Italian's humanist learning, but with an even greater emphasis on the religious and dynastic aspects of his position. When Gattinara died in 1530, Charles had grown up to intellectual and moral independence. From thenceforth he dispensed with a grand chancellor. Long years of power had heightened his sense of responsibility and had developed his slow and unoriginal mind to self-assurance and mastery of politics, making him tower over his contemporaries both in the constancy of his ideals and in the flexibility and shrewdness of his tactics. At thirty-four he wrote to his younger

[1] Cf. below, pp. 338f.

sister Mary, dowager queen of Hungary and recently appointed regent of the Netherlands, to console her over the troubles of her task: when she had had as much experience as he, she would no longer despair over difficulties. Years later, Mary was to complain to their brother, Ferdinand, 'that the emperor is difficult and does not always think well of a matter if it does not come from him'. Thus, self-assured and masterful, in his later years a little sceptical, the emperor appears in Titian's famous portraits.

Not all contemporaries, not even those in his own dominions, could accept Charles's and Gattinara's view of the empire as standing for peace among Christians and the defence of Christianity against Muslims and heretics. Gattinara's Italian policy was ascribed to his possession of estates in the duchy of Milan. His policy of moral leadership for the emperor became suspect when, after the battle of Pavia, he urged the annexation of Dauphiné and Languedoc. With an imperial niece married to the duke of Milan and imperial troops in control of its fortresses, the emperor's claim that he was preserving the independence of the duchy had a hollow ring to the Venetians and the French. Europe saw Charles V's empire primarily in terms of power, and in this view originated the permanent hostility of the only other European power of comparable strength, France, and the intermittent hostility or at best cool friendship of the lesser independent powers, England, Denmark and the Italian states. Moreover, Charles's very insistence on his religious aims and their fusion with his political ends helped to make insoluble two problems which were difficult enough in any case: his relations with the German princes and his relations with the pope. To the Protestant German princes the emperor's policy represented the double threat of imperial and religious coercion; and since the Catholic princes were equally alarmed about the emperor's political power, they never gave him the political support which alone would have enabled him to solve the religious question.

The pope seemed to be the natural ally of 'God's standard bearer', and Charles never ceased to hope that such he would prove to be. But Clement VII and Paul III, in their capacity of Italian princes, were as alarmed as their twelfth- and thirteenth-century predecessors at seeing Naples and Milan united in one hand. They therefore never stopped intriguing with France against the imperial power in Italy. Of this fact Charles was fully aware. What he never fully understood was that the popes, as spiritual heads of the Christian Church, could never entertain the emperor's claim to be the ultimate arbiter of the religious troubles which afflicted Christendom. It was unacceptable that at Augsburg and Regensburg the emperor's theologians should attempt to reach a compromise with the Protestants binding on all Christians;[1] it was intolerable that a secular prince should take the initiative in reforming the Church

[1] Above, p. 179.

and should threaten to summon a general council. The threat of the Turks and Protestants held pope and emperor together in uneasy alliance and only once, in 1527, did the underlying hostility break out into open and disastrous warfare; but the emperor's inability to induce the Papacy to co-operate whole-heartedly in his policies was one of the major weaknesses of his position.

The very existence of Charles V's empire—the uniting of a number of countries under the rule of one person—thus raised problems which the individual countries either would not have had to face at all, or, as the histories of France and England demonstrated, would have had to face in a much more tractable form. Added to these difficulties was the unprecedented problem of governing this diverse collection of states. In the last analysis, the empire of Charles V existed only in the person of the emperor. It was not even called an empire. That name was reserved for the old Holy Roman Empire, here distinguished by a capital letter from the empire of Charles V, a term which should be clearly understood as a purely modern designation; when Charles V's contemporaries used a collective name for his dominions at all, it was *monarchia*. There was much confusion in the minds of contemporaries as to the significance of even that venerable institution, now that it had suddenly acquired such a powerful head. To Gattinara, at least, it was clear that the personal union of the states of the empire must be matched by a functional union. By training and experience, Gattinara belonged to the school of Roman lawyers, mostly natives of Franche-Comté, who had helped the dukes of Burgundy to weld the Netherlands into a functional union by the establishment of the councils and courts through which they governed the provinces.[1] His authority as Burgundian grand chancellor was now extended to cover all of Charles's dominions. The Council of State, the only one of the councils to which great nobles were admitted and which advised the emperor on all imperial matters, was extended to include Spanish and Italian members, as well as the Burgundians. Characteristically, Gattinara saw his emperor as legislator for the whole world, 'following the path of the good emperor Justinian', reforming the laws and simplifying legal procedures, so that all the world would want to use them and that 'it would be possible to say that there was one emperor and one universal law'.

Nothing came of this vision. Nor did anything come of Gattinara's plan for a treasurer-general to whom the treasuries of all the emperor's dominions should render account. After Gattinara's death and the abolition of his own office of grand chancellor, the other all-imperial institutions regressed even from the very modest level they had attained. The central control of the empire became more and more a matter of personal control

[1] Below, pp. 441, 445.

by Charles and those advisers whom he chose to consult on any particular issue. The enormous amount of paper work (of which only a small part has been published) was handled by two distinct institutions: by a Spanish secretariat of state, continuing traditions inaugurated by the Catholic kings and responsible for the affairs of Spain, Italy and the Mediterranean; and a French secretariat, based on Burgundian traditions and responsible for all affairs north of the Alps. The old German imperial chancellery continued to function independently in purely technical matters, but politically it was dependent on the French-Burgundian secretariat. Inevitably, these developments led to a great increase in the power of the secretaries of state. Both the Spanish secretary, Francisco de los Cobos, and the French-Burgundian secretary, Nicolas Perrenot, seigneur de Granvelle, another Franche-Comtois, were men of great ability; but neither their functions nor their personalities made their position and influence comparable to that of Gattinara before 1530.

More than ever Charles, and Charles only, represented the empire. He governed it like the head of one of the great sixteenth-century merchant houses where the junior members of the family served as heads of the foreign branches of the firm. There were great advantages in having members of the Habsburg family as governors-general, regents or even kings in his dominions. They were locally more acceptable than even the greatest nobles of non-royal blood and much less likely to be involved in local feuds; their employment as his personal representatives accorded with Charles's own views of the central role of the dynasty in his whole position. The Netherlands, the Empire and Spain after 1529 were always, at least nominally, entrusted to a Habsburg or his consort. Only for the Italian dominions had non-royal viceroys to be appointed. In the event, the emperor's policy proved a success in all but one disastrous case[1] and his family served him loyally and, in the persons of his two governors-general of the Netherlands, his aunt Margaret of Austria (1518–30) and his sister Mary of Hungary (1531–55), with more than common skill and devotion.

If Charles V trusted his governors and viceroys and if he, unlike his morbidly suspicious son, Philip II, was prepared to keep them in office for decades and uphold them against local opposition, he yet reserved the ultimate control over policy and over the administration entirely to himself. He and his secretaries were in weekly correspondence with his governors. Despite the delays caused by the enormous distances the couriers had to travel; despite the emperor's notorious tardiness in taking decisions; despite the frantic appeals of governors and generals for fuller powers to cope with an emergency—despite all these difficulties, the emperor insisted on taking all important decisions himself, relying only on those councillors who were travelling with him on his constant

---

[1] Cf. below, p. 332.

journeys from dominion to dominion. The system achieved the control he desired, but at the cost of lost opportunities and great inefficiency. Once, at least, during the revolt of the Comuneros, it came near to ruining his power in Spain.[1]

Apart from the regular political correspondence, the viceroys and governors were bound by the instructions they received when they entered upon their office. They had to follow the advice of the privy councils which Charles appointed for them. He reserved all important appointments to himself, and the administration of any one of his dominions was therefore never the governor's administration but always the emperor's. In his political testament of 1548 he counselled his son not to let his viceroys usurp more authority than he had given them; while Philip should not believe all complaints which were levelled against them, he should never fail to listen to such complaints so that governors should not become absolute and his vassals despair of obtaining justice. It was sound advice, followed fairly and reasonably by Charles himself, but was later pushed to extremes of suspicion and duplicity by Philip II.

The emperor was determined to keep control not only over public appointments, but also over all other forms of patronage. He had the reputation of being slow to reward service; but a minister or a servant could always hope that, in the end, he would be given a *grazie* or *merced*: an ecclesiastical benefice, a title, a pension, a castellanship or one of the host of minor offices and sinecures with which the emperor could make a man rich without loss to himself. Great lords and ministers were willing to serve the emperor in the hope of such rewards, and lesser men, in turn, attached themselves to the lords and ministers. Viceroys and governors, sometimes even provinces and cities, had their agents at the emperor's court to represent their interests by a judicious distribution of gifts among councillors and secretaries. Some of these grew rich. Cobos, so Charles himself thought, did not take presents but had received many *mercedes* and desired more. The younger Granvelle, who succeeded his father as one of the emperor's principal advisers, was not above taking presents, though he liked to appear to refuse. The Granvelles, father and son, were reputed to have accumulated property to the value of a million ducats.

The position of Charles as the dispenser of all patronage explains much of the passionate longing of his subjects to have him reside within their particular country. As patronage had been Ximenes' most important problem before Charles's first visit to Spain, so it remained a key problem of all his viceroys and governors. Margaret and Mary, in the Netherlands, were given lists of persons to whom, and to whom only, benefices and offices were to be allotted in strict order as they fell vacant. In vain Margaret protested. She could not obtain the support she needed for the

---

[1] Below, p. 319.

emperor's service if she could never reward those who supported and worked for her. Her reputation, she said, had suffered badly when such appointments and grants as she had made had been revoked by the emperor. In the end, she pleaded at least to be allowed to dispose of a third of the benefices. But the emperor refused even this request.

Undoubtedly, the emperor's policy was effective in concentrating political control over his dominions in his own hands, but it remained a constant source of grievance to his subjects and made the work of his governors extraordinarily difficult. The subjects will more readily obey the prince himself than his governor, wrote his sister Mary at the end of twenty-four years of this experience, for, however much good sense the latter has, he is not as useful to them and hence there will always be a greater number opposing than assisting him.

The emperor's failure to develop a non-personal institutional organisation for his empire was not, however, the result only of the very personal view he took of his office, but also of the attitude of his different dominions. He was no Alexander or Napoleon who had conquered his empire, but the hereditary and legitimate ruler of each of his states whose laws and customs he had sworn to maintain. The Sicilians prided themselves on their voluntary allegiance to the house of Aragon and alarmed the Spaniards by dark hints of another Sicilian Vespers, should their privileges not be observed. The Spaniards maintained that the title of king of Spain was better than that of emperor of Germany and desired Charles not to use this latter title when he was in Spain. The Germans were particularly suspicious of foreign troops and their fear that the emperor was arranging the 'Spanish succession' of his son was one of the main reasons for his loss of authority in Germany at the end of his reign. The Netherlanders, the original architects of his empire, resisted even attempts to bring their own provinces into closer union. In 1534 the governor-general proposed to the states general a defensive union with regular financial contributions from each of the provinces for a standing army. The proposal was rejected; 'for if we accept the project,' the states general said, 'we shall undoubtedly be more united, but we shall be dealt with in the manner of France,' that is, lose our liberties. The particularism of the emperor's dominions was a fight not only against centralisation but also against autocracy. While Charles seized all opportunities which presented themselves to strengthen the Crown's authority in each of his dominions, he never attempted a full-scale attack on the liberties of his subjects in any of them. Any attempt to create an imperial administration would have been regarded as just such an attack.

In these circumstances, it is not surprising that Charles failed to develop an economic policy for his empire or even to conceive of an economic unity of his dominions in the way in which contemporary rulers of single states were beginning to think of the economic unity of their kingdoms.

In this field, as in others, only Gattinara understood the full implications of empire. He had proposed a common imperial currency. But nothing ever came of this proposal.

The emperor's policy in economic matters consistently followed the line of least resistance, a line determined by vested interests, local traditions and the overriding financial necessities of the imperial government. The monopoly of the oceanic trade was, indeed, firmly upheld; but, characteristically, it was reserved to the Castilians. Yet Castile was quite unable to provide the manufactures which the Spanish colonists overseas demanded. So far from taking advantage of the excellent colonial market which paid for its imports in solid gold and silver, the Castilians were alarmed at their own exports to which they ascribed the high prices in their kingdom. The Cortes of 1548 even petitioned for a prohibition of exports to the Indies, now that the colonists should have had sufficient time to build up their own industries. It was the very reverse of a mercantilist or imperialist attitude. The emperor did not accept this petition; nor did he accept an earlier one (1542) for the prohibition of the export of all raw materials from Spain, a prohibition which would have broken the most important economic link joining his two greatest dominions, the Spanish wool trade to the Netherlands. Admission of all the emperor's subjects to the Spanish colonial trade would have benefited all parts of his empire. The effect of the Castilian monopoly was that French, English, Venetian and Genoese merchants and manufacturers competed on equal terms with the Catalans and Netherlanders in supplying Castile with goods for re-export to the Indies. Nor was there any attempt to maintain what was left of the economic links of the old Aragonese-Catalan empire, once, in its heyday, the rival of the Venetian and Genoese commercial empires. Barcelona had declined from its former greatness. Her merchants still bought grain in Otranto and Palermo, salt in Trapani and silk in Naples and Messina. But the Genoese, Venetians and Ragusans, with more ships and greater capital resources, had broken Catalan pre-eminence, and the Neapolitans and Sicilians preferred to sell their raw materials to Venice and Florence whose industries could supply them with finished goods.[1]

The expulsion of the Jews by the Catholic kings in 1492 had deprived Spain of the only important group of her citizens who might have played the role in the economic life of the empire which Spanish soldiers and administrators were increasingly playing in its political life. Into the void left by the disappearance of the Jews stepped, first, the South German bankers. In 1524 the Fuggers, already the owners of most of the mineral wealth of Tyrol and Hungary, leased Spanish Crown revenues from the three orders of knighthood, Santiago, Calatrava and Alcántara. By the

[1] F. Braudel, *La Méditerranée à l'époque de Philippe II* (1949), pp. 88ff. This is the most comprehensive modern work on the political, social and economic history of the Mediterranean countries in the sixteenth century.

end of the reign the Fuggers also controlled the silver mines of Guadalcanal and the mercury mines of Almaden. The Welsers, the second greatest German banking firm, also had occasional interests in these leases and tried to build up their own colonial empire in Venezuela, in the classic style of the Spanish *conquistadores*.[1] More important still than the Germans were the Genoese. Andrea Doria's change from French to imperial service, in 1528, gave them their opportunity. In the next decades, the Centurione, the Pallavicino, the Spinola, the Grimaldi and many others established themselves not only as the emperor's bankers, but as the greatest traders in the Spanish Mediterranean area. Colonies of Genoese merchants settled in every important Spanish and South Italian port. Their economic services were as indispensible to the emperor as the naval services of Doria's galleys. It was the final and decisive victory over their old rivals, the Catalans.

In the north, the Netherlands undoubtedly profited economically from the Spanish connection. Imperial finance dominated the Antwerp money market. But imperial policy did not prove as effective a help to the Netherlanders' economic interests as they had hoped. Nowhere was the divergence of interests within the empire more apparent than in the complex and tortuous relations between Holland and the Baltic powers after the expulsion from Denmark of Charles's brother-in-law, Christian II, in 1523.[2] To Holland the free passage of her ships through the Sound meant prosperity; its closing spelt heavy losses, unemployment and hunger, for the Netherlands were dependent on Baltic grain. For the merchants of Amsterdam it was vital that Denmark should not fall into hostile hands, especially those of their deadly rivals, the Lübeckers. For the merchants of Brabant and Flanders, Holland's difficulties meant their own opportunities, since the Lübeckers were subtle enough to offer them far-reaching concessions when they themselves were at war with Holland. For the emperor, the Danish problem was above all a question of the rights of his family. He supported first Christian II's attempts to regain his throne and, later, those of Christian's daughter, Dorothea, and her husband, Frederick of the Palatinate. Through them he hoped to extend imperial influence in northern Europe, even if this involved Holland in costly and unwanted wars. Only Mary of Hungary's government in Brussels did its best to reconcile the parties, at times bluffing effectively with the threat of the engagement of all the emperor's forces. Such an engagement, however, Charles was unwilling to make. For him Denmark was a side issue, compared with the problems of France and the Turks; rather would he allow the Netherlands to treat on their own with Denmark

---

[1] R. B. Merriman, *The Rise of the Spanish Empire*, III (1925), p. 534. This book, though old-fashioned, is still the best general history of Spain for this period; it contains useful bibliographies.

[2] Cf. above, p. 135.

and Lübeck, reserving for himself the right to support the claims of his niece. Hence it was more than twenty years before the relations between the Netherlands and Denmark were finally settled in the Peace of Speyer (1544), and it was the Danes who insisted that the emperor sign for all his dominions. It was a victory of the political and economic over the dynastic concept of empire; but the emperor accepted it only with great reluctance.

Within the different parts of the empire there were powerful forces willing to support Charles and his imperial policy. The Burgundian high nobility who had done so much to secure their prince the effective succession to his kingdoms remained loyal to the end even if, for most of them, Gattinara's and Charles's Christian ideals meant little more than the fashionable common-places of their knightly upbringing at the Burgundian court. It was enough to serve the most powerful prince in Christendom and to have the opportunity of appointments to provincial governorships or even viceroyalties, or to win fame by leading his armies against Frenchmen, Turk or heretic. Thus, too, thought the Spanish nobility. Their early hostility to Charles soon changed to enthusiastic support. More than the Netherlanders, they were in sympathy with Charles's crusading and imperial ideals. Had not the Castilians fought the Moors on their own soil? Had not the Aragonese achieved power and renown by their Italian conquests and wealth by the easy acquisition of Sicilian and Neapolitan estates or ecclesiastical benefices? The double lure of knight-errantry and plunder made the Spaniards imperialists in Europe as it made them *conquistadores* in America. Nor did the chances of promotion and high office hold less attraction for the Italian nobility. As king of Sicily and Naples, the emperor was their own prince as much as he was ruler of Spain and Germany. The Gonzaga, the Pescara, the del Vasto preferred the role of an imperial viceroy or captain-general to that of a provincial condottiere.

Next to the high nobility, the lawyers were the emperor's most enthusiastic supporters. Trained in Roman law with its imperial and absolutist traditions, many of them humanists and Erasmians, they found it easy to combine their sympathy for Charles V's imperial claims with the prospect of dazzling careers in the imperial councils. For the rest of the populations of the emperor's dominions the advantages of belonging to a world-empire appeared more doubtful. There were those, especially among the merchant class, who were able to take advantage of the political connections between Italy, Spain and the Netherlands. But, as we have seen, the economic links between the parts of the empire depended little on its political structure or on the emperor's policies. The Spanish hidalgos, the lower nobility, who flocked in their hundreds to serve under the emperor's standards in the Spanish *tercios*, represented a Spanish, rather than a universal, imperialism. For the mass of the population, the empire seemed to be the last chance of peace within Christendom—that passionate longing which had attached itself for centuries to the name of the Roman Empire. Now, in Charles V, it seemed to find its fulfilment. Or so it appeared to the crowds who cheered the emperor's, or his son's, entry into their city on his journeys from country to country; and so it was presented on the triumphal arches which greeted him—arches on which local Latinists displayed their learning and enthusiasm for the 'restorer of the Roman Empire' and the 'future ruler of the whole globe'. But it was just this longed-for peace which the emperor failed to give his subjects. When the court had passed on its way, the taxes remained to pay for wars which often seemed no concern of the single provinces. If loyalty to the emperor seldom wavered, his governors, foreign or native, were often hated, and the ruler's absence on his imperial duties was deeply resented. Ultimately, local interests and loyalties remained predominant in every case; the feeling of imperial solidarity never developed sufficiently to become an effective political force.

Wars and ever-increasing taxes seemed to be the lot of the emperor's subjects. They pressed on millions when the benefits of empire seemed to be reaped by a few hundreds. Every letter that passed between the emperor and his viceroys, every memorandum presented to him by his ministers, was directly or indirectly concerned with problems of finance; for only ready money would keep in the field the emperor's armies, keep afloat his galleys, the instruments on which, in the last resort, all his policies and the very existence of his empire depended. The emperor's financial needs became more and more the fulcrum around which his relations with his separate dominions revolved.

Nowhere was this clearer than in the Netherlands. Their great towns, as they were never tired of insisting, lived by trade and industry; they wanted peace. Their nobility, though personally as avid for glory in the field and as bored by peacetime pursuits as the rest of the European nobility, were sufficiently involved in their country's economic life to support this desire. In 1536 the governor-general herself, Mary of Hungary, pleaded with her brother to keep the Netherlands neutral in an approaching war with France. Charles declined. Such apparent weakness would only encourage the French and the Gueldrians to attack the provinces, he wrote.

If the wars with France were the more expensive and potentially the more dangerous, the wars with Guelders were the more destructive and the seemingly more senseless. Charles of Egmont, duke of Guelders, was perhaps the most determined enemy Charles V ever faced. Against the centralising policy of the Brussels government he stood for the independence of the small princes. With French money and support he equipped his marauding bands. His marshal, Maarten van Rossem, 'Black Martin', the bogey-man of Dutch children, spread fire and destruction through Holland and northern Brabant. In 1528 he sacked The Hague and barely failed to capture Antwerp and Louvain in 1542. Time after time, Holland and Brabant petitioned a willing governor-general to negotiate peace with Guelders. But Egmont, urged on by France, broke every truce and treaty. In the end his policy defeated itself. Friesland, Groningen, Drenthe, Overijssel and Utrecht came to hate the would-be defender of their liberties more than the emperor. One after another they allowed themselves to be conquered by the governors of Holland and Brabant. In 1538 Egmont died, still undefeated in his own duchy. His successor, William of Cleves, tried to continue his policy when the political basis for it had disappeared. In 1543 the emperor was for the first time free to turn his full powers against Guelders and bring the long, anomalous warfare to an end by the annexation of the duchy. The north-eastern frontiers of the Netherlands were now secure; but the war had lasted too long and had shown the Netherlands how little advantage they derived from the great power of their prince.[1]

Charles V pursued the traditional policy of the dukes of Burgundy of bringing the provinces into closer unity and providing them with more efficient and powerful government. Against these centralising policies the provincial estates and the states general set their traditional privileges and autonomy. Ultimately, the relationship between Crown and estates was one of power which in the reign of Philip II had to be resolved by open warfare. Under Charles V neither side was as yet willing to push its claims to extremes, nor even to pursue a consistent policy of attacking the powers of the other. The estates did not seriously question the right of the 'natural prince' to govern, nor his right to demand money for the defence of the country. The government regarded it as a matter of pride, or, at least, an effective propaganda point, that the Netherlanders lived in greater freedom than the French and that their prince did not arbitrarily impose taxes on them. Nevertheless, every new financial demand was stubbornly resisted and whittled down by the estates. Every government proposal had to be reported back to the provinces and towns. In Brabant, and before 1540 in Flanders, the petty bourgeoisie of craftsmen and gilds were represented in the town councils and had to approve all proposals. Since, in general, unanimity was required, the artisans of Louvain, for instance, were perfectly capable of holding up the decisions of the whole states general. Failing to induce the town councils to give their delegates full powers, the emperor pursued a consistently anti-democratic policy towards the towns. Wherever the opportunity arose, he excluded the gilds from municipal government. He did this in Tournai in 1522, in

[1] A. Jacopsz, 'Prothocolle van alle de reysen', MS. in Amsterdam Stadsarchief, transcript by E. van Bienna. I owe the opportunity of studying this transcript to the courtesy of Dr P. A. Meilink, of The Hague.

defiance of his own promises; he did it again in Brussels in 1528, and in Ghent in 1540, following rebellions by these towns against his governor-general. The patriciates who were left in control of the towns were, on the whole, more accommodating to his financial demands. But he and his governors failed completely in their attempts to make the estates give up their insistence on the redress of grievances before the discussion of new taxes. He did not even try to prevent the provincial estates from building up their own administrative machinery to control the collection and expenditure of the taxes they voted.

The estates prevented the establishment of absolute royal power as it existed in France. But the interests of the urban patriciates, and therefore the states general, were local and sectional; the privileges they defended were equally local and often opposed to the interests of other provinces. Thus, Holland insisted on her privilege of freely exporting grain even when there was famine in the rest of the Netherlands. In consequence, Charles V's regents were never faced with a general revolt. The states general remained a conservative force, capable of blocking important government policies, such as the union proposed in 1534/5, but unable and unwilling to challenge the Crown's control of government. Nevertheless, the position of the imperial government in the Netherlands was unstable and tended to deteriorate, especially after about 1530. For this deterioration the increasing financial demands of imperial policy were largely responsible. No one has yet attempted to work out in detail the history of Netherlands finance during the emperor's reign, nor is this surprising: sixteenth-century methods of accounting were haphazard in the extreme, accuracy in arithmetic was rare, and the imperial finance officers frankly admitted the general confusion. But there is plenty of evidence of heavy and increasing taxation and of the intermittent, but steadily increasing, groundswell of the discontent it caused. Twice, in 1522 and 1525, the regent Margaret of Austria feared the imminent outbreak of rebellion. In 1525 there were riots in Bois-le-Duc; in 1532 in Brussels. Relations between the estates of Holland and the governor, the count of Hooghstraeten, grew steadily more strained. The abbots of the great monasteries of Brabant, normally the steadiest supporters of the government, formed a secret federation in 1534 to resist the imposition of further taxes. Most serious of all was Ghent's refusal to contribute her share of the taxes voted by the states general in 1537. By 1539 the town was in open rebellion against the government, though protesting its loyalty to the emperor. As so often before in the city's stormy history, the gilds set up a democratic dictatorship and inaugurated a reign of terror against patricians and government supporters. The emperor himself had to arrive with a large army to reduce the town to obedience (February 1540).

In the last years of the emperor's reign the wars with France demanded larger sums than ever. Charles left his son debts amounting to four and a half million livres. Even so, the Netherlanders claimed that in five years they had given him eight million ducats in extraordinary grants. They complained that they were being made to conquer Italy for the emperor; they believed, rightly or wrongly, that he kept Spanish troops in the Netherlands to hold down the people. Rising prices, the decay of older centres of the cloth industry, such as Ghent and Leyden, the growth of a new rural and small-town textile industry in Walloon Flanders—all these changes were upsetting the equilibrium of Netherlands society and creating a revolutionary situation, immensely aggravated by wars and high taxation. From about 1530 onwards, Lutheran and Anabaptist preachers found a ready following among the artisans and labourers of the old industrial towns. Shortly after the emperor's abdication, Calvinist preachers were even more successful in Antwerp and Walloon Flanders. The country nobility, at least in some parts of the Netherlands, saw their rental income dwindle with rising prices. Few of them could supplement it, like the high nobility, from government offices. Their traditional local influence suffered from the encroachments of the central government and its courts. As yet, they were still completely loyal; but the ground was already prepared for their opposition in the following reign. Charles V's Burgundian origins and personal popularity to some extent masked the seriousness of the situation. But when the emperor pronounced his abdication in the great hall of the palace of Brussels, before the deeply moved states general and the weeping knights of the Golden Fleece (25 October 1555), the Habsburg political system in the Netherlands was already near to dissolution. A few months later (1557) the government had to declare its financial bankruptcy and the states general became all but unmanageable. A few years later, the religious and social troubles came to a head, and the Netherlands embarked on the eighty years of civil, religious and national war which broke up not only the empire they had so light-heartedly helped to create, but also their own country.

The history of Spain in the empire of Charles V stands in sharp contrast to that of the Netherlands; at the same time, it was equally dominated by imperial finance.

Earlier than any other dominion, Castile was faced with these demands, and her immediate reaction could scarcely have been more hostile. To finance Charles's return journey to the Netherlands and his imperial election, Chièvres summoned the Castilian cortes to the remote Galician town of Santiago (March 1520) to demand a new *servicio* even while the grant of 1518 had not yet expired. From the beginning there were difficulties. The court insisted that the delegates should have full powers. The towns, rightly fearing that their deputies would be bribed with money from the taxes they were asked to vote, tried to bind the deputies with definite instructions. The Toledans did not appear at the cortes at all. The other towns demanded the discussion of grievances before supply. Gattinara then adjourned the cortes to the port of Coruña where the court was already embarking (April 1520). By a mixture of bribery and concessions, eight of the eighteen towns represented in the cortes were now induced to vote the *servicio*; five maintained their opposition; the others were divided and did not vote. As the ships weighed anchor, on 20 May 1520, the revolution had already begun.

No one in Spain, not even Charles's own council, thought that the new taxes were legal or that they could be collected. Mobs attacked the houses of deputies who had voted for the *servicio* and, in Segovia, murdered them. Royal authority broke down in most Castilian towns. The council's ineffective efforts at repression, especially the burning of Medina del Rio Seco by royal troops, only added to the bitterness of the opposition. Throughout the summer and early autumn of 1520 the nobility raised no finger to help their king. They had not yet forgiven him his Burgundian councillors and their alleged plunder, and they were particularly angered by the appointment of a foreigner, Adrian of Utrecht, as regent. The rebellious towns, led by Toledo, formed a league and set up a *junta* that was in effect a revolutionary government. Adrian was driven out of Valladolid and had to seek refuge on the estates of the admiral of Castile, Fadrique Enriquez. The rebel leader, Padilla, captured Tordesillas and the insane queen-mother. It looked as if Charles's authority in Spain would collapse completely. Only full powers to pardon and to negotiate with the Comuneros could save the situation, Adrian wrote in ever more despairing letters. His demands were echoed by the admiral, Enriquez, and the constable of Castile, Iñigo de Velasco, both of them appointed co-regents with Adrian in the autumn of 1520.

At no time were the problems of effective imperial control over distant dominions more evident. In the end, however, Charles's and Chièvres's policy of making only such concessions as did not touch the basis of royal authority proved successful: suspension of the collection of the *servicio*, the appointment of Enriquez and Velasco, with the promise of no further foreign appointments, and Charles's speedy return to Spain. But for many months the issue hung in the balance, and it was no direct effort of his own which saved the situation for Charles.

In the towns, radical and popular elements were more and more gaining the upper hand. When the revolt spread to the estates of the grandees, these latter began to take alarm. The old antagonism between towns and nobles flared up again. In Andalusia, the nobles with their vast estates and large numbers of Morisco tenants were aware of their danger earlier than the Castilian nobility. From the beginning they prevented the spread of the Comunero movement to the south. Within the Comunero camp, rival factions manœuvred for control of the movement. During the winter of 1520–1, one after another of their moderate leaders from among the urban nobility deserted to the royalists. On 23 April 1521, at Villalar, the Castilian nobles and their retainers routed the Comunero army. Valladolid and the other towns of northern Castile at once made their peace with the king; only Toledo, the prime mover in the revolt, held out until October 1521.

The power of the monarchy was thus restored in Castile, never to be seriously shaken again during the reigns of the Habsburg kings. The towns kept much of their autonomy; but royal control was safeguarded by the re-establishment of the powers of the corregidors. The deputies to the cortes had now to arrive with full powers and their salaries were paid from the taxes they voted. All attempts to revive the principle of redress of grievances before supply met with a firm refusal: after their defeat of 1521, the towns had lost their power to insist. Charles did not need to attack the cortes any further. They were willing to vote taxes, and their petitions, often repeated session after session, could be granted or refused as the emperor chose.

Although the nobles had won the civil war, they could not, for that very reason, break their alliance with the monarchy. The monarchy, now that it could manage the cortes and afford a standing army, was the stronger partner. Charles systematically excluded the grandees from the government of Spain, much to the duke of Alva's chagrin. But he still had many prizes and titles to give to the nobles as a compensation for their loss of political power. More immediately important still was the 'nobles' exemption from taxation. It was not a privilege which the emperor admitted willingly. At the cortes of Toledo, in October 1538, to which nobles and clergy were summoned together with the eighteen towns, the government proposed an excise tax on foodstuffs from which there should be no exemptions. The nobles voted against it almost unanimously, Velasco dropping dark hints of commotions which always happened in Castile when any 'novelty' was introduced. To avoid an open rupture, Charles gave way; but he never summoned the nobility again to meetings of the cortes. The monarchy had won its political victory in Castile only at the cost of letting the nobility contract out of the financial obligations of the state and the empire.

The consequences for Castile were tremendous. Together with the Netherlands, it was Castile which supplied most of the financial needs of Charles V's wars. Government revenue from taxation rose by about fifty per cent during the emperor's reign.[1] During the same period prices

[1] The recent pioneer work of Ramon Carande, *Carlos V y sus banqueros*, vol. II (1949), has given us a better picture of Charles V's finances in Castile than we have of any other of his dominions. Leaving aside the revenues which the government obtained from the import of precious metals from Mexico and Peru, the taxes from the clergy and the *cruzada* (sale of ecclesiastical absolutions), and some internal tolls whose yields were either very uncertain or

roughly doubled. Since the population was rising, it is clear that the total burden of taxation diminished, rather than increased; but its distribution between the different classes of society changed radically. By far the greater part of ordinary revenue had originally been derived from the *alcabalá*, a sales tax paid by all classes, nobles included. At the request of the towns, the *alcabalá* had been converted into the *encabezamiento*, a quota payment by each town or village. This quota remained constant and its real value tended to diminish as prices rose. On the other hand, the yield of the *servicio* rose much more rapidly than prices. The hidalgos, who dominated the town councils and represented the towns in the cortes, willingly voted taxes from which they themselves, as nobles, were exempt. The weight of parliamentary taxation fell entirely on the *pecheros*, the non-privileged classes. As shown by the index, the money yield of these taxes nearly quadrupled against a mere doubling of prices, and the proportion which they formed of the total burden of taxes in this table rose from 8 to 19 per cent. The Crown's alliance with the nobility was shifting the burden of empire on to the shoulders of those least able to bear it.

The emperor's governments in Spain were perfectly aware of this situation. 'The common people who have to pay the *servicios*,' wrote Prince Philip to the emperor in 1545, 'are reduced to such distress and misery that many of them walk naked.' The poverty was so universal, he continued, as to extend not only to the emperor's direct vassals but also to those of the nobles to whom they could no longer pay their rents. Yet, the nobles as a class do not seem to have suffered. They were, in most cases, able to raise their rents at least as fast as their prices.[1] Together with the foreign merchants and bankers, they were the chief buyers of *juros*, the life annuities funded on government revenues. When, in 1558–9, the government sold land and villages belonging to towns on the royal demesne, it was the nobles who bought them.

With the influx of precious metals from America, prices rose more did not increase substantially during the reign, we can construct the following table of Charles's revenues:

REVENUES OF THE CROWN OF CASTILE
(in million maravedis)

	Circa 1516		Circa 1553	
	Amount	Index	Amount	Index
Ordinary revenues (mainly *encabezamiento*)	380	100	500	132·8
Maestrazgos (leases of revenues of the estates of the orders of knighthood)	51	100	89	173·7
Servicio (grants by the cortes)	37	100	136	370·0
Totals	468	100	725	155

[1] Braudel, *La Mediteranée*, pp. 631. This view is also supported by Carande in a letter to the writer, 30 January 1956.

steeply in Spain in the sixteenth century than elsewhere in Europe. The stimulus afforded by this influx of money and by an expanding colonial market might have been expected to promote a rapid economic development. But Spanish agriculture was backward. The armed shepherds of the powerful sheep-owners gild, the Mesta, drove their flocks over hundreds of miles, from upland to lowland, and from lowland to upland pasture, through the whole length of Castile, trampling down cornfields, breaking down fences and spoiling much cultivated land in a country whose arid soil was, in any case, wretchedly poor compared with the soil of England or France. Despite the violent hostility of the landowners, the government upheld the Mesta's privileges, since the Mesta paid generously for them. Much more than in England, it was true in Spain that sheep were eating men, and the dark side of the flourishing Spanish wool exports to Flanders was an impoverished Spanish peasant unable to buy the manufactures of his urban industries. The towns were unable to flourish because of the shortage of agricultural products and the unwillingness of those gaining by the influx of precious metals to invest in trade. Thus the Castilian towns had remained small compared with those of Italy and the Netherlands. Their industries were underdeveloped and unable to compete with foreign industries for the dazzling opportunities of expanding trade. Imperial taxation, falling more and more heavily on the *pecheros*, thus had reached the point, wrote Philip to his father in 1546, where the natives of this kingdom were abstaining from all manner of commerce.

If heavy taxation tended to discourage investment and economic enterprise by the Spanish middle and lower classes, the nobles did not suffer from this handicap. But the inclinations and traditions of grandees and hidalgos, formed in the centuries of struggle against the Moors, made them even more averse to economic activities than the rest of the European nobility. Church and army and, for the hidalgos, the study of law at Salamanca and Alcalá de Henares, followed by a career in the king's service, these offered more attractive opportunities than the ignoble occupations of commerce. The cortes constantly complained of the activities of foreign merchants; but when, in 1552, Philip raised the question of the gradual redemption of the *juros*, then amounting to a capital sum of some 6,200,000 ducats, the holders of the *juros* objected violently; they would not know where else, except in land, to invest their money, and they feared that the price of real property would rise too much.

Thus, to the amazement of foreigners, all the silver from Peru could not make Spain a rich country. American treasure helped to pay for the emperor's wars and made the fortunes of Genoese bankers, but far too little of it was invested in production so as to overcome the country's economic backwardness. As Charles V's empire became more and more a Spanish empire, the economic weakness of Spain became an ever more serious handicap in her struggle with her west-European rivals.

It was the smaller and poorer of the emperor's Spanish dominions which resisted most successfully the inroads of centralised government and the pressure of imperial finance. If the Aragonese and Catalans had made greater difficulties than the Castilians in acknowledging Charles as their king, at least they did not rise in revolt against him. Only in Valencia, the one kingdom Charles did not visit during his first Spanish journey, did a revolution break out. At first it was directed, not against royal authority, but against the nobility. While the Valencian nobles were reluctant to do homage to an absent king, the artisans and labourers of the city of Valencia hastened to protest their loyalty. The Valencian populace, already armed and trained to resist the danger of Moorish invasions, now organised in a *Germanía*, a popular Christian brotherhood, directed against the nobles and Moors (1519). Charles could not remain the ally of such a movement; but, as in Castile, he did little more than appoint a Castilian grandee, Diego Hurtado de Mendoza, as governor. For more than eighteen months the *Germanía* controlled most of the kingdom; but they failed to co-operate with the Comuneros, nor were they able to arouse the sympathy of the lower classes in neighbouring Catalonia. Their slaughter and forcible conversions of Moorish tenants on noble estates cut across the class appeal of their revolt without gaining them sympathy from the country nobility or from the clergy. The forces of the *Germanía* leader, Vicente Peris, were defeated by the nobles' troops in October 1521, and Valencia immediately voted in its municipal elections for a return to the lawful authorities; but it was not until 1523 that all resistance outside the capital was finally overcome.

The defeat of the *Germanía* did not, however, affect the older rights and privileges of the kingdoms of the Crown of Aragon. The Aragonese nobles ruled over their vassals like kings, having power of high and low justice. In Catalonia they had the right to wage private war. In the cortes they successfully maintained the principle of redress of grievances before supply, 'so that it was in the power of a cobbler, smith or suchlike person to hold up everything until he was satisfied'. Thus wrote the shocked Venetian ambassador, Contarini.

If in Aragon a person was arrested by royal order, he could put himself under the jurisdiction of the *justicia*, the highest judge of the kingdom who held his appointment for life and therefore was independent of royal pleasure and displeasure. Contarini claimed that Charles had asked the pope to release him from his oath to maintain this particular privilege. But there is no evidence that this step proved effective or that Charles at any time attempted a full-scale attack on the Aragonese and Catalan privileges or freedoms. If the grants of the Aragonese, Catalan and Valencian cortes were comparatively small and often hedged about with onerous conditions, it was doubtful whether these small kingdoms could be made to pay so much more as to make it worth while running the risk of a head-on clash. Moreover, his Aragonese and Catalan subjects had long been accustomed to shoulder imperial responsibilities and, at least for his Mediterranean policies, he found their traditions more helpful than those of the Castilians.

These traditions were the rivalry with Genoa for the trade of the western Mediterranean and with France for the control of southern Italy. In the first half of the sixteenth century two new problems appeared: the problem of North Africa and the Barbary pirates, and the rise of the Ottoman empire as a naval power. These problems, originally quite separate, became so interwoven during Charles V's reign that they finally resolved themselves into a struggle between the Spanish and the Ottoman empires for the control of the Mediterranean.

The North African problem was largely the result of the Spanish conquest of Granada (1492) and the forcible conversion of the Moors of Castile (1502). Almost for the first time in history the two shores of the western straits of the Mediterranean were now under separate and hostile political control, their commercial and cultural links broken. But, although the Christian reconquest of the Iberian peninsula was now complete, Spain remained a multi-racial society, the only one in western and central Europe. Within her borders, the forcibly converted Moriscos were a constant threat; for the African Moors—many of them refugees from Andalusia thirsting for revenge—raided the Spanish coasts and often received help from the Spanish Moriscos. Christian Spain reacted in two ways: by internal assimilation and by external conquest. In 1525 the emperor extended the Castilian edict of forcible conversion to Valencia, and the Inquisition helped him to use it against the 'new Christians' of both Muslim and Jewish origin. Externally Spain reacted by the attempt to conquer North Africa. This was the policy of Queen Isabella and Cardinal Ximenes. It was broken off after initial successes because Spanish energies were side-tracked by Aragonese policy in southern Italy.

Until the early 1530's Spain's problems in the western Mediterranean were still largely separate. The oldest, the Genoese-Catalan rivalry, had been solved by the Spanish-Genoese naval alliance which made Andrea Doria captain-general of the emperor's galleys in the Mediterranean and which sealed Genoese commercial supremacy over Catalonia. In the meantime, however, Spain's failure to complete her North African conquests had brought a bitter revenge. In 1516 the Moorish rulers of Algiers called on the pirate brothers Barbarossa to capture from the Spaniards the Peñon, the fortified rock at the harbour entrance. It took Khair ad-Dīn Barbarossa thirteen years to achieve this aim; but, long before, he made himself master of Algiers and acknowledged himself the vassal of the sultan at Constantinople. For the first time in centuries, the

Christians were faced by a really powerful hostile naval force in the western Mediterranean, a force whose raids were a constant terror to the small coastal villages and towns of Spain and Italy. Worse was to follow. As a counterstroke to Doria's capture of Coron in the Morea (1532), the sultan appointed Khair ad-Din Barbarossa pasha and grand admiral of the whole Turkish fleet. With more than 100 ships he ravaged the coasts of southern Italy in 1534 and then threw his forces against Tunis and expelled its Moorish king, an ally of Spain.[1]

The emperor's Italian provinces were now seriously threatened, not only by pirates but by the full naval strength of the immensely powerful rival empire of the Turks. Effectively, it became a struggle for the control of the central Mediterranean; under Spanish domination, it would protect Sicily and cut off Barbarossa from Constantinople; under Turkish domination, it would keep the Muslim forces united and open the road to attacks on Italy and the western Mediterranean. Concentrating all his forces for the first time and leading his troops in person, Charles conquered La Goletta and Tunis in 1535. It was perhaps his greatest personal triumph, his vindication as a Christian knight and crusader. But Barbarossa was not crushed. Within weeks he retaliated by raiding Port Mahon in Minorca. More serious still was Doria's defeat at Prevesa, in September 1538, caused largely by distrust between the allied imperial and Venetian fleets. The Prevesa campaign had been the one serious attempt by the imperialists to carry the war into the eastern Mediterranean. There can be no doubt that this was the emperor's ultimate aim, with the conquest of Constantinople as the final prize. In August 1538 Mary wrote in great alarm from the Netherlands to dissuade her brother from his grandiose plans. The difficulties of operating over such distances were enormous, she argued; France, only recently reconciled, was quite unreliable; the pope and the Venetians would give little help; they risked little, while the emperor alone risked irremediable loss; his dominions needed peace above all, not further adventures. After Prevesa, Mary's views prevailed and the emperor's offensive actions had strictly limited objectives. Even these were often unattainable, as the disastrous failure of the emperor's own expedition against Algiers demonstrated in 1541.

The Turks, for their part, also made only one serious attempt, during the emperor's reign, to penetrate in force into the western Mediterranean. This was in 1543.[2] The Franco-Turkish alliance, discussed as early as 1525 and openly acknowledged in the 1530's, was potentially the most deadly danger the emperor had to face in the Mediterranean. Yet the Turks did not follow up their 1543–4 expedition. Even with French bases available to them, the distances were too enormous; the hazards of operating more than a thousand miles from the home base were as great for the sultan as they were for the emperor. The Spaniards completely failed to conquer a

[1] Cf. below, pp. 517 f.   [2] Cf. below, p. 531.

North African empire. Compared with the Indies, or even with Italy, North Africa offered few attractions to Spanish soldiers in search of plunder. Economically, the Spanish strong-points were a liability. The Venetians and other traders to the Barbary Coast preferred the Moorish ports. The Spaniards kept up their North African garrisons purely for strategic reasons. Yet they substantially maintained their naval supremacy in the western Mediterranean basin. The Turkish bases were too far from the heart of the Christian Mediterranean to challenge this.

In sharp contrast to the deterioration of Spain's position in North Africa was her successful defence of the Aragonese empire in Italy against France.[1] Sicily, the oldest Italian dominion of the crown of Aragon, was indeed never seriously threatened. As in Aragon itself, the emperor here succeeded to a small and relatively poor country whose estates enjoyed the most far-reaching privileges. In the Sicilian parliament clergy, nobles and towns had defended these privileges successfully against the encroachments of Spanish viceroys. At the very beginning of the reign, in 1516, they rose against a hated viceroy, Hugo de Moncada, and forced him to flee from Palermo. The nobles who led the rising protested their loyalty to Charles, and their envoys at Brussels obtained at least the replacement of Moncada by another viceroy, a Neapolitan, the duke of Monteleone. But, when neither Charles nor Monteleone showed any sign of revoking Moncada's unpopular edicts, a new rising broke out in 1517. This time it was led by members of the Palermo bourgeoisie, and it spread through most of the island. Amid murder and pillage, it soon became a social revolt against the nobility. The nobles reacted by assassinating the leader of the movement in Palermo and when, six months later, Spanish troops arrived, the situation was already under control.

Unlike the revolt of the Comuneros, the Sicilian revolts of 1516 and 1517 (and an abortive conspiracy of nobles in 1523) had little effect on the balance of political power. The Sicilian nobles and towns were fundamentally loyal to the Crown of Aragon. They cherished the memory of the Sicilian Vespers of 1282, their one supreme assertion of national will; but, as the spirit of national unity disappeared in bitter party feuds and in the rivalry of Palermo and Messina, the Sicilians lost almost completely their capacity for united action. Whereas in the Netherlands the defence of sectional liberties and privileges led eventually to a revolution against the centralising policy of the hispanicised monarchy, in Sicily the similar interests of nobles and towns only led to more internal wrangles and feuds. For, as in Aragon and Catalonia, the monarchy made no serious attempt to interfere with the country's privileges. Hampered in every action by these privileges and inadequately supported from Spain, successive viceroys fought a losing battle against the proverbial corruption

[1] Cf. below, pp. 342 ff.

of Sicilian officials, the venality of the Sicilian courts, the blood feuds of the barons and the ubiquitous bandits who were often, like the modern Mafia, protected by the local nobility. No longer, as in the fourteenth century, could the noble factions plunge the whole country into civil war; but they and their armed retainers still attacked each others' castles and cities, and their feuds had to be settled by regular peace treaties, guaranteed by the viceroy.

Finance was the key to the government's policy, as it was throughout the emperor's dominions. After centuries of external peace Sicily was now threatened with invasion by the Turks. Charles V's last two viceroys, Ferrante Gonzaga (1535–46) and Juan de Vega (1547–57), had to construct completely new coastal defences, maintain the Sicilian squadron of ten galleys and the *tercio* of Spanish infantry in the country, and train a native militia to beat off Moorish raids. These raids made the Sicilians appreciate the naval protection which Spanish rule provided against worse calamities. But parliament increased its 'donative' from an annual average of 100,000 scudi to only about 175,000 during the emperor's reign, a period when general prices rose in at least the same proportion. Apart from Aragon and Catalonia, Sicily remained the most lightly taxed of the emperor's kingdoms. When he abdicated, a new proverb became current in Italy: 'In Sicily the Spaniards nibble, in Naples they eat and in Milan they devour.'

The financial problems of Charles V's government in Naples were, indeed, relatively easier than in most of his other dominions. The kingdom's parliament was incomparably weaker than that of Sicily. The city of Naples itself had no vote in the granting of the donative; though it sent its deputies to the assemblies, it had its own representative institutions for this purpose. The clergy were not represented at all, and the nobles were too sharply divided into an Aragonese and an Angevin faction ever to have seriously thought of making parliament into an instrument of their political aspirations. There was no question of demanding redress of grievances before supply; the emperor and his viceroys dealt with petitions entirely as they thought fit. Thus Charles could draw large sums from the kingdom and send them abroad: 1,750,000 ducats between 1525 and 1529 for the imperial armies in northern Italy; 300,000 for his coronation, in 1530; 150,000 in 1543 and 175,000 in the following year, with another half million ducats in 1552—all sent to Milan and Germany. But there were limits to what even the strongest of the emperor's viceroys could screw out of the country. Repeatedly, the viceroy, Pedro de Toledo, refused imperial requests for money or declined to accept bills of exchange drawn on his government. With the increasing urgency of the Turkish menace, the cost of defence was rising steeply. From about 1530 the emperor had to help with Spanish money. But, if the coasts of Apulia and Calabria suffered at times from Khair ad-Din's raids, the Neapolitans were as conscious as the Sicilians of the protection afforded them by Doria's galleys.

There were, however, good political reasons for not exasperating the Neapolitans too far. The old feud between Aragonese and Angevins did indeed make co-operation of all nobles against the government impossible. The Aragonese faction had received much land confiscated from those who had supported Lautrec's invasion of 1528. Many more estates had been given to Spanish and Genoese supporters of the emperor who settled in the kingdom and intermarried with the Neapolitan nobility. All these were loyal; yet they and the Neapolitan towns were as proud as the Sicilians of their voluntary allegiance; they prized their privileges just as highly; their wealth and the authority they wielded over their estates were perhaps even greater. The barons imposed arbitrary taxes on their vassals and prevented them from appealing to the royal courts. The very judges of these courts were subject to their pressure if they came from baronial territory. A revolt by even one of these lords could be dangerous, as the prince of Salerno demonstrated in 1552 when he tried to bring the French and the Turks into the kingdom at the most critical moment of the emperor's reign.

It was therefore both politic and just that the Crown should take a stand against these excessive powers of the nobility. The protection of the poor and the weak against the rich and the powerful became the key-note of the instructions which Charles V gave to Pedro de Toledo in 1536. He had appointed this Castilian grandee in 1532 to rebuild a country ravaged by French and imperial troops, and to clear up the legacy of oppression and injustice left by a long period of weak government. A rapid succession of short-lived viceroys, some of whom, like the Netherlander Lannoy, did not even pretend to understand Neapolitan conditions, had been quite incapable of dealing with corrupt royal officials, tyrannous barons, and bandits protected by great lords. For twenty-one years Toledo battled against these evils by edicts and executions. His success was very limited. Eighteen thousand persons had been condemned to death during his viceroyalty, he told the Florentine ambassador in 1550, and he did not know what more he could do. The instructions to his successor, in 1559, paint a picture of conditions in the kingdom almost as dark as those of 1536.

But Toledo's policy succeeded in keeping nobles and people divided. Only once did they combine, and immediately imperial rule in Naples was in the gravest danger. In 1547 Charles V wanted to introduce the Spanish Inquisition into Naples. In Sicily it had already been introduced by Ferdinand the Catholic and had, at first, been very unpopular. In 1516 the Palermitans chased the inquisitors from their city together with the viceroy. Only towards the end of the emperor's reign did it become more popular through the immunities from royal jurisdiction which it offered to its thousands of lay familiars. The Neapolitans reacted even more violently than the Sicilians. Nobles and burghers of the city of Naples formed a union; the *seggi*, their representative assemblies, took over the city government; there were clashes with Spanish troops and the viceroy's warships fired on the city. Soon it was rumoured that the 'union' was negotiating with the French. Finally, Toledo offered the withdrawal of the Inquisition as a special favour granted to the burghers rather than to the city as a whole: enmity between burghers and nobles was a safer foundation for Spanish rule, he judged, than the Inquisition. In Naples, the very privileges of the nobility and their strength in local government redounded to the advantage of the viceroy; for much of the popular hatred of foreign rule was diverted on to the native nobility. As a result, and despite the Neapolitan mob's taste for rioting, Naples remained, on the whole, a contented part of Charles V's empire.

In Sicily and Naples, Charles V was hereditary king; in Milan he had no such rights. When the last Sforza duke, Francesco II, died in 1535, imperial troops under the marquis del Vasto were already in control of the duchy; but for years the emperor was uncertain how to settle the succession. During the negotiations with France, the cession of either Milan or the Netherlands to a younger son of Francis I was discussed in the imperialist camp. Charles himself and his Burgundian councillors, notably Granvelle, wanted to keep the Netherlands and give up Milan. Castilian nationalists, such as Archbishop Tavera of Toledo, supported this view, both from a dislike of Spanish entanglements in Italy and from the dislike of giving up an hereditary dominion in favour of a conquered one. But the majority of Spaniards, such as the duke of Alva, and the Hispano-Italians insisted on the retention of Milan as the key to Spanish power in Italy.[1] In the end, the Netherlands were not given up and Milan was successfully defended. But, in practice, the Spanish party had won. Prince Philip was invested with the duchy (1546); its affairs in the emperor's councils were entrusted to Cobos; the command of its fortresses was given to Spaniards or Neapolitans. Milan became a military outpost of Spain.

The Spaniards did not materially change the administration of the country by its traditional authorities, any more than they did in Sicily and Naples. The Milanese nobility were relatively poor, and politically weak through their division into the Guelph and Ghibelline factions. Hence, where in Sicily and Naples the viceroys' powers were limited and counterbalanced by the surviving powers of old feudal institutions, in Milan the powers of the governor-general were similarly limited and counterbalanced by a more modern, semi-autonomous civil service, consisting of the senate and the professional city administrations it supervised. Only at his peril could the governor-general quarrel with the senate, as Ferrante

[1] Chabod, *Lo stato di Milano*, pp. 39 ff.

Gonzaga found in 1554 when the senate induced the emperor to send an investigating commission to Milan and to recall his governor-general.

Senate and city magistrates might limit the governor-general's administrative authority; unlike the Sicilian parliament, they could not limit his powers to raise taxes. The large imperial army in Lombardy had to be paid, and it had the power to see that its pay was forthcoming. The protests of the towns, and even of the civilian governor-general, Cardinal Caraccioli, were ineffective against the halberds of del Vasto's *Landsknechte*. After Caraccioli's death in 1538, del Vasto combined the two offices of governor and captain-general (1538–46), as did Ferrante Gonzaga after him (1546–54). The Spaniards could now impose taxes at will, subject only to the fear of a rebellion in the duchy, with the immediate danger of renewed French intervention.

Yet, if the Spaniards 'devoured' in Milan, Milan also devoured Spain. In 1535 Granvelle had hoped that the duchy would pay not only for its own defence, but would contribute to imperial expenses. The disillusionment was rapid. Seven Perus would not suffice to meet all the emperor's needs in Lombardy, wrote the Spanish ambassador in Genoa in 1537. Four decades of war had left a terrible legacy of poverty and ruin. In the war years of 1536–8 Spain had to send more than a million ducats for the army in Lombardy, while Milan paid some 600,000. In the last five years of the emperor's reign, Spain equalled the Milanese defence contribution of about two million ducats. The cost of the Spanish garrison left the government of Milan with an almost permanent deficit. The duchy itself, however, recovered under the peace which Spanish rule finally provided. In the second half of the sixteenth century, its population increased and vigorous reconstruction of its cities and industries gave Lombardy another fifty years of prosperity before the disasters of the seventeenth century.

It was his election as king of Germany which had given Charles V his right to the imperial title and with it the moral justification to pursue his imperial policy. It was in Germany that, in the end, his imperial policy met with the most complete and irretrievable disaster. Charles kept his promise to his younger brother, Ferdinand. He made over to him all his rights to his hereditary dominions in Germany (1521–2) and also appointed him head of the *Reichsregiment*, the imperial government of Germany. In 1531, after his own coronation by the pope, Charles induced the electors to elect Ferdinand king of the Romans. Charles must have known that this step gravely prejudiced the prospects of his own son, Philip, to succeed him as emperor and that it even prejudiced the future existence of the combined power of the house of Habsburg. But Philip was only four years old. If Charles himself died prematurely—and his many wills and testaments show that he always bore this contingency in mind—it was essential to have a successor who would defend both the Habsburg claims in the Empire and the child Philip's rights in the Netherlands, Spain and Italy. Most important of all, Charles needed the strongest possible representative in Germany. In his instructions to Ferdinand in 1531 Charles allowed him much wider powers than any of his viceroys or governors. But he demanded to be consulted over the bestowal of high noble titles, and he insisted that his own appointments should be maintained and all his commands observed. In practice, therefore, Charles continued to control imperial policy in Germany.

The crux of the German problem was the alliance of Luther's reform movement with a number of the German princes. For more than twenty years Charles tried to minimise the importance of this alliance and to solve the religious question within the framework of a general reform of the Church. He changed his policy only when these attempts had definitely failed and when the Schmalkaldic League of Protestant estates began to intrigue with France.[1] Still striving to keep the religious and the political problems apart, he struck at the Protestant princes, ostensibly as rebels against imperial authority, in order to deprive the reform movement of its political backing. His victory at Mühlberg was to have provided the basis for a solution of both the political and the religious problems of Germany. In fact, it solved neither. The Council of Trent and Bologna was the pope's council and remained unacceptable to the Protestants. The German princes, Protestant and Catholic alike, were more unwilling than ever to increase the constitutional powers of the emperor by a thorough reform of the imperial constitution. Despite his victory and immense prestige, Charles was not strong enough to coerce all the princes. He tried to by-pass the problem by proposing a league of princes with the emperor at its head, in which each member was to pay a fixed contribution for a league army. The idea was not new. In 1519 the Swabian League, of which Charles was captain by virtue of his Austrian and South German possessions, had expelled the francophile duke of Württemberg from his duchy. The army of the league had been a most useful asset to Charles during the imperial election campaign and, in 1520, it had enabled him to acquire Württemberg. He did his utmost to keep the Swabian League in being: but since, in the eyes of the German estates, his power was dangerously great already, they were unwilling to continue it. On several occasions before the Schmalkaldic War, the emperor returned to the idea of forming a league, but never with more than partial success. His more comprehensive scheme in the autumn of 1547 fared no better. The Empire 'would be reduced to servitude,' said the elector of Brandenburg, and the princes rejected the scheme.

The failure of this plan precipitated the crisis over the imperial succession. Philip was now a man. The war against the Protestants had shown

[1] Cf. above, pp. 181 ff.

that only with the help of money and troops from Spain and the Nether-lands could the emperor uphold his authority in the Empire. More than ever, Charles was convinced of the correctness of his analysis of 1519.[1] There is no direct proof that in the winter of 1546-7 he contemplated asking his brother to resign his title of king of the Romans in favour of Philip; but Ferdinand's extremely sharp reaction to rumours of such an intention leaves little doubt that this was the ideal solution that Charles was contemplating. Ferdinand's attitude and that of his son, Maximilian, and the extreme hostility of the Germans to the idea of a 'Spanish succession', induced Charles to give up the idea. In acrimonious debates between the senior members of the Habsburg family a compromise was finally arrived at, in 1551. Ferdinand was to remain king of the Romans and succeed Charles to the imperial title, but was himself to be succeeded by Philip, with Maximilian succeeding Philip in his turn.

Neither side was satisfied and, for the first time, the unity of the Habsburg family was seriously impaired. In 1552 Maurice of Saxony and other German princes, in alliance with Henry II to whom they promised Metz, Toul and Verdun, attacked Charles and forced him to flee from Innsbruck for his life. Their success was at least partly due to the equivocal attitude of Ferdinand. The flight from Innsbruck and the Treaty of Passau with the rebellious princes undid the results of Mühlberg. The virtual collapse of his authority in Germany, together with his failure to retake Metz from the French (winter of 1552-3) convinced him that his imperial programme, as he had conceived it in 1519, had failed. The Church had not been reformed in such a way as to bring the Protestants back into the fold; neither had the Protestants been finally crushed by force of arms. Italy was secure, but France remained as threatening as ever and, so far from joining in a crusade, was the ally of the infidel. The Empire remained intractable and the next emperor, while still enjoying the alliance of the Spanish-Burgundian branch of the house of Habsburg, would no longer himself dispose of its full powers. His position would, inevitably, be much weaker than that of Charles; his interests would be purely central-European. Charles V's abdication, in 1555-6, was his own recognition of the failure of his imperial idea, the failure of the last attempt to re-establish the medieval concept of Christian unity under the leadership of emperor and pope.

Charles himself retired to a country palace built against the monastery of San Jeronimo de Yuste in Estremadura. There he held court and continued, amid his devotions, to take a lively and often active interest in the fortunes of his empire until his death in 1558. For the empire itself did not break up with his abdication. Its nature, however, was already beginning to change. From a universal, Christian empire, with a Burgun-dian core and inspiration, it was becoming a Spanish, Catholic empire

[1] Cf. above, p. 306.

with a Castilian core and inspiration. The inadequacy of the all-imperial administration was one of the weaknesses of Charles V's empire. But the old Aragonese empire possessed at least the rudiments of an imperial administration in the Council of Aragon, the supreme court for the realms of the Crown of Aragon in Spain and Italy. The Council of the Indies, for the Castilian overseas empire, functioned in a similar way, but with much wider competence in administrative and political matters. It was on these models that, in 1558, Philip II founded the Council of Italy. This provided Spain and her Italian dominions with a much closer administrative integration than any other group of states had possessed since Roman times.[1]

The Netherlands were economically the most advanced and wealthiest of the emperor's possessions. 'These are the treasures of the king of Spain, these his mines, these his Indies which have sustained all the emperor's enterprises', wrote the Venetian Soriano in 1559. But even as he wrote, it was no longer true. Against the greater wealth of the Netherlands, Spain provided its rulers more willingly with money. From about the middle of the century, the flow of American silver to Spain increased rapidly beyond all previous expectations. The wars in Italy and Germany showed more and more clearly the superiority of Spanish infantry over all other troops. Until Gattinara's death in 1530 the emperor's council was a genuinely international body, with the Burgundians predominant. Adrian of Utrecht was his regent in Spain; two Burgundians, Charles de Lannoy and Philibert de Chalon, were his viceroys in Naples. The Burgundian-trained Piedmontese, Gattinara, was his most influential adviser. But, in the last half of his reign, Spaniards and Hispano-Italians monopolised all high positions south of the Alps and, in their turn, they began to appear in Germany and the Netherlands. Some, as Ferrante Gonzaga, drew the logical conclusion from this trend and advocated the deliberate transformation of Charles V's empire into a Mediterranean monarchy. He suggested that Spain should withdraw from Germany and the Netherlands, neither of which could be held permanently. In Spain itself, Illuminism and Erasmianism, the great intellectual and spiritual forces behind the emperor's earlier vision of Church reform and reconciliation with the Protestants, were dying; their last exponents were imprisoned or in flight before the growing power of the Inquisition. With St Teresa and St Ignatius, with the Jesuits and the Inquisition, and above all, with its new king, Philip II, Spain now became the intellectual as well as the financial and military spearhead of the Counter-Reformation in the age of the wars of religion.

[1] For the councils of the empire see also below, pp. 445 f.

CHAPTER XI

THE HABSBURG-VALOIS STRUGGLE

IN western historiography the rivalry of Habsburg and Valois during the first half of the sixteenth century has become a classic tragedy. On many occasions the historians have played out the drama—the course of events, the salient features, the springs of action; one after the other, indeed, they have given themselves to sorting out the facts and to simplifying the generalisations. François-Auguste Mignet, well known as one of the experts, as the ring-master of this huge quarrel, has reduced the first phase to the period from the election of Charles to the Empire in 1519 until the Peace of Cambrai in 1529. In this decade, everything was tried. From the moment the die was cast the quarrel was an elaboration, a repetition of conflicts and tedious altercations.

From 1519 to 1529 the two dynasties struggled for the great arena of the European peninsula and the western Mediterranean. After 1529, even after February 1525 on the occasion of the great battle of Pavia, the failure of the Valois was a check to their future career, although this is not to say that their adversaries were any more successful. Does history still divide men and governments, once and for all, into conquerors and conquered?

Indeed, to turn one's attention once more to the long struggle is to be tempted by the progress of research, and even more by the transformation in the scope and explanation of history, to create an image rather different from the traditional one. Although the spotlight is reserved for the main characters, it is worth while to go beyond the executives and the background actors, right to those collective forces which, to be sure, have not formed the whole of history, but which have had a large part in shaping its destiny. A consideration of the evolution of institutions, of the 'imperial vocation' of the sixteenth century, of the waves of economic growth, will necessarily uncover perspectives other than those outlined, even though with great skill, by Mignet. This will, indeed, make something new and lessen the emphasis on the personal responsibilities and the faults and merits of the taciturn, wise and calculating emperor or the errors and follies of Francis I—that gambler to be fêted in the heady day of success at Marignano, early in his reign, but severely criticised in the gloomy moments of failure for too great a pursuit of pleasure—the pleasure of governing. The Venetian ambassadors show him obsessed with the acts, words and plans of 'Cesare'. For him also this struggle was the great affair of his life. Indeed these men, who were not so free in action as one would like to believe, acted and collided time and time again because of greater forces which so often—even if not always—imposed on them an unavoidable competition.

Then again, a fresh history of this long debate cannot be confined to the prologue 1519–29, although these years were, without doubt, decisive. The epilogue of the play too, after the *Paix des Dames* of 1529, needs the attention of spectators aware of history. Thirty years of conflict, of subterfuge, of movements, advances, retreats, thirty years which pass without falter from 1529 to the Treaty of Cateau-Cambrésis in 1559, make up, when all is said and done, a third of a century, not without important changes. Francis I disappeared first, in 1547; in 1555 Charles V retired from the world, to die in September 1558. The finale of the struggle was the almost sensational halt—the diapason note—of Cateau-Cambrésis.

Thus it is necessary to exercise caution in prolonging the play beyond the early days. Above all, it is not to be confined to the narrow scene of Europe. The whole world is, more or less, directly or indirectly, in question. If Spain had not held the Atlantic and, beyond, America with its bullion and treasure, could it have played such a great role, imposed its rule, and taken first place for such a long time? That it could not, the devoted studies of Fernand Braudel have clearly shown. It was Spain, more than his golden crown in Germany, that made Charles V—Spain and the mines of America. *Nervus belli est pecunia*: such was the wisdom of nations. All this must not be forgotten, neither gold, silver, nor the dimensions of a world which was far larger than Europe, with all her diverse and intriguing problems.

The 'imperial vocation' of the sixteenth century has often been spoken of, and nothing is more correct if by this we mean the search, the necessity, as well as the horror, of overall domination, soon to be called universal monarchy. Yet this vocation needs to be qualified in two ways. It is necessary, first of all, to replace it in its context; for the struggle for first place was between super-states—that is, states of depth and expanse—and in the sixteenth century the future lay indeed with states of depth, commanding territory, men and resources. The smaller states disappeared: those that were not swallowed up were the exceptions. This tendency diminishes the personal drama between Valois and Habsburg. In the second place, Charles V was not the first who, in the words of his adversary, wanted 'to be master everywhere'. The dream, even if not realised, of universal dominion accompanies the history of a Europe always mindful of having been one in the bounds of Christendom. The policy of Charles V was, moreover, a legacy, built from older dreams as well as from innovations. Charles was haunted as much by the shadows of the past as by 'Renaissance' ideas like the pursuit of glory, the point of honour, the eager constant search for ways out of his difficulties, the surrender to the fickle favour of his star of fortune.

Yet it is not only a question of legacies when one speaks of Charles V, who is beyond doubt the most worthy hero of the politics of his age. Admittedly he was heir—or victim—of at least two legacies. Immediate (and close at hand) was that which allowed him to enclose the France of the Valois with the heavy chain of his states and his pretensions. This will soon be shown. The other legacy is more complex, though no less important; it is deeper and more difficult to ascertain, to weigh and to judge. In the sixteenth century, Europe was and remained Christendom. It was, moreover, whether it liked it or not, Christendom face to face with Islam, regenerated by the successes of the Turk. Before the capture of Constantinople, even more after the taking of that city in 1453, the pressure of Islam increased dangerously. The threat stretched from Granada (only open to the Christians in 1492) to Greece; it surged along the southern shores of the Mediterranean, along the coasts of Asia Minor, to penetrate the expanse of the Balkans. Beyond this jousting-ground, Islam covered huge areas, reaching the negro races, the Red Sea, the Persian Gulf, the Indian Ocean, India, and even China, passing through the depths of central Asia. Europe could continue to exist only in so far as she was able to resist this hostile mass.[1]

As in the past, the temporal head of Christendom, as distinct from the spiritual primate at Rome, took over the leadership of the crusade and the inevitable conflict with Islam. Thus in the fifteenth century the long-sustained efforts of the dukes of Burgundy—simple dukes—in carrying on this honourable struggle raised them without royal or imperial crown to the first rank of Christendom. Thus again, in 1494, the seemingly empty projects of a crusade by Charles VIII before he entered Naples were more seriously intended than one might think, showing an 'imperial' attempt on the part of France. Later, France's agreement, her 'parallel action', with the Turk after Pavia (1525) marked the end of such a dream. This same dream lived again and became incarnate in the thought and person of Charles V. Everywhere, in the shadows cast by his sceptre, he set himself in the van of the crusade: at Naples (where in 1480–1, the Turk had laid siege to Otranto during two mortal years); at Vienna, which the Turk pressed in vain in 1529; even more in Spain, this Spain of the Catholic kings, drawn up facing the African coast—Spain, a living crusade. He established himself in the Mediterranean, the sea of the crusades: at Tunis in 1535, where he triumphed and at Algiers, where he failed in 1541 within sight of the ancient sea, he was indeed a crusader, nearly three centuries after St Louis. He would have been the last of a long line had not, on 7 October 1571, his natural son Don John of Austria triumphed over the Turkish armada at Lepanto and taken all the laurels of this romantic honour.

All this gives to the imperial experience of Charles V, in body and in

[1] Cf. also above, pp. 324 ff. and below, ch. XVII.

336

thought, a special shape which later ages question and scarcely approve. As always, Europe demanded and then refused the authority which could organise and unite her. In the face of strength, the weaker members clung together. The dominant power was exhausted in an endemic struggle, which was always breaking out afresh. Europe was at once for and against Europe. In the sixteenth century and even earlier, the nation states exploded a Christendom which in the Reformation was to experience other and even more serious trials.

This was a legacy wrapped in the past: it was also a legacy near at hand, which Charles, born in 1500, did not cease to inherit during his first twenty years. Gradually, by himself, he was to make his presence felt in a coalition of states. He was master of Naples, Sicily, Sardinia, with footholds in Africa, captured after a struggle by the Spaniards between 1506 and 1511. Thus the first 'Mediterranean' empire of Spain was established. He was also the master of a vast American and Atlantic empire whose weight made itself felt more and more. He was, therefore, one of the great princes of Christendom—the first, if there had not faced him Francis I, seated on the throne of France since the death of Louis XII at the beginning of the year 1515. In that very year, at Marignano, Francis had conquered Milan and with it the control, both direct and indirect, of northern Italy, the very heart of the material life and power of Italy, then the first country of Christendom. So it seemed that the odds were even between the two princes, the one in the south of Italy, the other holding the north and in truth the better portion of this garden of cities; the former ruling the Spains, the latter France. Yet Charles V held in addition the Low Countries, that other Italy and other dominant economy: Antwerp was a world centre. It is true that the prestige and riches of France weighed heavily in the balance. It is true also that Italy has never been taken over by barbarian invaders; the French in the north succeeded no better than the Spaniards in the south. Even Spain was not prepared to submit to a Fleming—Charles of Ghent as he was in 1516—as the future was to show. Finally, America was not yet the gushing reservoir of precious metals which was to astound and even sustain the whole century. It was on the Netherlands, not yet on America, that Charles put his early hopes of empire. But this is to jump ahead: the balance may seem to the historian, and even more to the contemporary, to waver between the two men who were to face each other in conflict. A last remark, however, before the curtain rises: chance must not be thought to have had too great a part in the formation of Charles V, for he was, after all, the result of scheming marriages, all negotiated under the pretext of *raison d'état*. In these marriages the Catholic kings, hand in hand with the Habsburgs, had long in advance encircled France, their over-riding ambition. Charles V's position was created in this absorbing, long-sighted game of chess.

It is now easier to organise this chapter through the sequence of the years. Three acts are clearly distinguished: the period from the imperial election of 1519 to the coronation of the emperor at Bologna in 1530; the indecisive years from 1530 to 1550, ending at Mühlberg (1547), that great ephemeral success, or at the Interim of Augsburg (1548), or even at the Peace of Augsburg (1555)—years during which Germany and not France was the centre of these complicated struggles; the last decade which in every respect also has a dramatic unity, right up to the bankruptcies and exhaustions which preceded Cateau-Cambrésis (1–3 April 1559), when France recovered her role.

Maximilian, Holy Roman Emperor (uncrowned in Germany)—another of Charles's grandfathers—died on 12 January 1519. Without more ado, the race was open for the new election. Everything seemed to be permitted in the contest. Without the slightest shame, the electors put themselves up for auction—more often twice than once. The pope, speaking of Charles, had said that 'money will make him king of the Romans' and we might as well add 'or nothing will'. The king of France also had riches at his disposal and the desire to seize the title and prestige, the possibilities which it offered. In addition there were the division and ill-feeling among the German princes, all concerned with themselves. Finding money, then, was a first care, coming before all else. Charles, in Spain, exacted from the cortes the promise of a subsidy. Then he turned to the financiers, those new overlords of the century. Jacob Fugger promised him 300,000 florins, and soon Charles had the support of other German bankers, the Welsers, and of financiers from Genoa and Florence. All these merchants as a result were detached from the French cause.

At the beginning, both Charles and Francis seemed to carry the college of seven electors by four votes. After March, however, the Very Christian King knew that for him the race was lost, even though he had the support of Leo X, 'ready to do anything [Francis] wished to prevent the election of the Catholic king', on good grounds: 'Do you know how many miles there are from here to the borders of his lands? Forty miles!' But this fear and this connivance were not sufficient. Outclassed, the French candidature nevertheless raised the expenses well above what was anticipated. In the end, the election cost the winner 850,000 florins, of which 543,000 had been put up by Jacob Fugger and 143,000 by the Welsers. The king of France had paid cash in gold coin, the Catholic king in bills of exchange on Augsburg. The bill was a promise; was it worth the same as payment in cash? However, the elector of Mainz received some 100,000 florins with the promise of an annual pension of 10,000. The Swabian League, with an army under Franz von Sickingen, had declared for Charles, and its aid was psychologically considerable; cost—171,360 florins.

Indeed, in all this largesse and prodigality France had had meagre resources; the capacities of the financial markets of Lyons and Genoa showed themselves to be insufficient. There is good evidence of this in the stealthy efforts on the part of Francis I to debase his gold coinage in June and July 1519. Against Francis had also weighed the consideration, important in itself, that he was looked upon as a foreigner by opinion in Germany. A neighbour of Germany, he would have been a more effective master than the distant Catholic king. Even more, did he not govern his people 'heavily'? Finally, to alienate the Habsburg was to overlook the troubles on the frontier, the threat of the Turk. All these considerations carried their weight.

In any case, at Frankfurt, on 28 June 1519, Charles was elected—unanimously: an ironic detail. The news was brought to him at Barcelona on 6 July, but among those who congratulated him the French ambassador was not numbered. The success, whatever its cost, was huge. Yet, to promise was one thing, to pay was another. The debts to the Fuggers remained for a long time unsettled. It was necessary to make them concessions (notably mining) in the Tyrol; then in Spain in 1525 to cede them the lease of the three Orders, the *Maestrazgos*—almost a state within a state. This is but the obscure side of their brilliant history.

Again, did the election settle everything? In order to judge it fairly we must estimate and comprehend the meaning of the Empire, or at least as much of it as can be comprehended. This is scarcely easy, for a thousand obstacles obstruct the way: the Lutheran revolt, setting the nets and snares of political complications; the rising of the Comuneros of Castile striking Spain to the heart (1521); in Germany, the war of the imperial knights (1522–3) and the dramatic Peasants' War (1525); abroad, itself all-absorbing, the first of the great wars with France; and the attacks of the Turkish forces which redoubled in violence. In all this, two dates are to be compared: 1521, the beginning of the conflict with France, and 1522, the capture of Rhodes, when the Mediterranean opened dangerously to the Turkish drive and advance. All Christendom, now in hazard, paid heavily for the fratricidal strife.

Yet let us return to the scene in Germany. The important Diet of Worms opened there on 28 January 1521. In the first place, the redoubtable problem of Luther's revolt was raised and Charles had come to find the great adversary of his life.[1] By the famous Edict of Worms the new doctrines were forbidden; but to forbid was not to conquer. Did the young emperor, indeed, have the time to dedicate himself to the problems of the Empire at a time when Europe was gradually being eaten by flames? Wisely, Charles ceded to his brother Ferdinand the lands of the Austrian heritage. The cession was confirmed on 7 February 1522 by the Convention of Brussels. Ferdinand thus took charge of the five Austrian

---

[1] Above, pp. 81 f.

duchies—that is, Austria, Carinthia, Carniola, Styria and Tyrol—and later (1530) became king of the Romans. Through him, and through his aunt, Margaret of Austria, governess of the Netherlands, Charles undertook, with the assistance of his family, the government of his too vast empire, fatefully so discontinuous. It encircled France. Nevertheless, France broke its unity and dislocated it from the very beginning.

Thus he was constrained to leave Germany to its quarrels; to disturb as little as possible that dangerous hornets' nest and leave the religious quarrel as a fire in a brazier. Had this not been so, he would have struck at the princes of Saxony and Hesse who were so ready to support and protect Luther; or at those rich cities which welcomed the new religion— Nuremberg, Augsburg, Ulm, Strassburg and later Magdeburg; or have brought to obedience the grand master of the Teutonic Order, who, after his marriage with the daughter of the king of Poland, confiscated the order and made himself the first duke of Prussia, adopting the doctrines of Lutheranism. Yet, what was the emperor to do in view of all his other distractions? To wait and temporise—this was the line for the young emperor. He did it without much success on the occasion of the Diet of Augsburg in December 1525, but more effectively at Speyer in June 1526, with the complicity of the German princes. In any case, even if he had wanted and had been able to strike down Protestant heresy, he was then without the essential support of the pope. Everything favoured a compromise, and one was reached in the Recess of 27 August 1526 which declared:

We, the Electors, Princes, Estates of the Empire...while waiting for a Council, [have agreed that] everyone [is] so to live, govern and conduct himself as he hopes and trusts to answer to God and his Imperial Majesty.

The appeal to a council, even more the principle recognising the authority of each prince's conscience, could not but favour and did favour the new doctrines. Yet this was necessarily a surface calm. The opposing parties were forming: the League of Torgau (1526), formed by the Protestant princes of Hesse, Saxony, Prussia, Lüneburg, together with the reformed cities, was the other half of the League of Cognac.[1] A spark could have set fire to Germany, but that was to come later.

It was Francis I—or rather the struggle between king and emperor— that saved Germany. After the election of Charles to the Empire, war could not be delayed any longer. It was only a question of getting the money together, to contract for men, to buy and solicit alliances. Francis I, indeed, was not without means. The victory of Marignano had planted his authority in the heart of northern Italy. By the *paix perpetuelle* of 1516 he had the virtual support of the Swiss cantons, and of the best infantry in Europe by the agreement of 1521 which allowed him to

[1] Below, p. 343.

raise an army of 16,000 in the cantons. However, there was a small drawback: Zürich, under the direction of Zwingli, kept out of the agreement.[1] But the big question was rather whether the king had or did not have the support of England against the emperor. Hence the manœuvres near Calais, the over-magnificent meeting between Henry and Francis on the Field of Cloth of Gold (7 June 1520). The festivities ended, however, if not without expense, at least without issue. Diminutive England conducted herself as best she could, now on one side, now on the other, weighting the balance now in favour of the Very Christian King, now in favour of the emperor. Yet the choice, except perhaps in 1528, was not so free. Wolsey favoured the Papacy, and England was prepared to bow before the great power of Charles V. It remains to see whether it was wise to go to the emperor. Indeed, did not England share the responsibility for Pavia? Henry VIII and his advisers had illusions about the strength of France. They gambled for the emperor and perhaps they played badly.

Charles V, however, did not waste time in isolating the king, who had been rash enough to encourage the insurgent Comuneros, crushed, fortunately for Charles, at Villalar on 23 April 1521.[2] Soon after, the emperor signed a secret pact with Leo X on 29 May 1521. Then, on 19 November, the combined armies of pope and emperor descended on Milan; the city, unable to resist, was taken and Francesco Sforza was at once restored there. The blow was direct and hard. Even more important were the negotiations, conducted personally, between Charles V and Henry VIII. By the Treaty of Bruges of 25 August 1521 the alliance was confirmed. Charles was to marry Henry's daughter Mary; both were to declare open war in March 1523. These agreements were confirmed on the occasion of Charles's visit to England by the Treaty of Windsor of 19 June 1522. The two allies decided to invade French territory together in May 1524.

All these arrangements strengthened the already strong position of Charles V. The armed expeditions into France had begun in the spring of 1521, directed especially against Burgundy. It did not help that an excursion by Francis I into Navarre fell short and ended in disaster. Yet it was not on the fringe of France or of Spain that the war was to find its outcome, but in Italy—the land of rich cities, of fertile plains, where princes and armies could be sustained by pillage and conquest. This mosaic of states hostile one to another, and of armies with their disputes and animosities, made Italy an ideal battle-ground. The gates were ever open. For France, two points were essential—Milan and Genoa; the latter, as has been pointed out, the mistress of a fleet of ships and galleys able to carry on the war at a distance.

Thus in 1521 the papal and imperial forces under Prospero Colonna and Lescaire chased Odet de Foix, Viscount de Lautrec, and the French

---

[1] Above, p. 100.   [2] Above, p. 320.

army from Parma and Piacenza and, almost without striking a blow, seized Milan. The next year, Lautrec joined with a Swiss army in the northern plains. Through impatience, however, he gave battle at Bicocca under unfavourable conditions (27 April 1522)—a severe defeat which cut short the effects of the French offensive and sent the discouraged Swiss mercenaries creeping back to Switzerland. As a defeat is not an isolated event, the imperial forces turned on Genoa, took it by main assault and consigned it to pillage (30 May 1522).

A few months earlier Leo X had died (1 December 1521). In his place was elected Adrian VI of Utrecht, formerly tutor to Charles V. He attempted in vain to follow a policy of neutrality between the two adversaries and to concentrate their efforts against the attack of the Turks in the east. Gradually he was drawn into the cogs of the Empire, openly, a bare month before his death in September 1523. Then the imperial candidate Giulio de Medici replaced him, to become after his election Clement VII. Here was a new triumph for the emperor. The Papacy seemed well in tow.

In France also Francis I had found things in disorder and in need of success. In 1523 there came the treason of the constable of France, Charles of Bourbon. It was the climax of a period of confusion and struggle. In the spring of 1521 Charles of Bourbon had lost his wife Suzanne, daughter of Pierre and Anne of Beaujeu. She had no living issue. By her will she had established her husband as full heir. The king and the duchess of Angoulême both claimed the inheritance. Then the constable, after negotiating with the enemies of the king, took flight in the autumn of 1523, finally reaching Burgundy and the service of Charles V. In July of the following year, in company with Spanish generals and the marquis of Pescara, he crossed the Alps, invaded France, penetrated Provence and laid siege to Marseilles. In the middle of these misfortunes, there occurred a small favourable event: in 1523 Andrea Gritti, sympathetic to France, was elected doge of Venice. However, Francis I, redoubling his efforts to find money, put his queen's and his own silver plate in pawn. On 13 August 1524 he was in Lyons demanding all the available plate 'since the affair in which I am engaged at present cannot be carried on without a large sum of money'. In the face of these preparations, the imperial troops abandoned the siege of Marseilles. On 12 December 1524, alarmed by the success of the emperor, Clement VII, Venice and Florence joined in secret alliance with France. This was the reason for Charles V's anger against the pope, who had been his protégé. The French troops meanwhile entered Italy once more, a detachment marching on Naples, the main body remaining in the north. Milan again changed hands.

In February this northern army was well-entrenched in the park of Mirabello near Pavia; it had everything to gain if it remained stationary.

But against all reasonable counsel it challenged the imperial forces. In the battle which followed on 24 February 1525, the French army received a crushing defeat. Francis I was taken prisoner. From Italy he was soon conducted to Madrid. Was Pavia lost by the instability, rashness and all the faults of the king, or won by the courage of the Spanish troops and the quality of the German *Landsknechte*, those rivals of the Swiss mercenaries? Whatever the cause, the battle was to have immense repercussions. Charles's victory overturned the balance in Europe. France, since Marignano the first military power, was knocked down. The vengeance of the Habsburgs threatened the recalcitrants, of whom Clement VII was not the least. All the problems were reframed in new terms: Europe had a master.

From his Spanish prison, Francis I with an ill-grace accepted the terms of the Treaty of Madrid (14 January 1526). He restored to his conqueror the Burgundian heritage seized by Louis XI, the suzerainty of Flanders, Artois and Tournai, and so the duchy of Burgundy. He renounced in addition his claims to Italy, to Milan, Naples, Genoa, Asti. The last humiliation was that Charles of Bourbon was to be pardoned and restored to his possessions and lands. Francis was to marry Eleanor, sister of Charles V. Although admitting that he was a prudent calculator, wishing to be reasonable to his victim, can we say that Charles was moderate? His policy attempted to be universal, directed against the Turk. Clause XXVI of the treaty stated:

La principale intention desdits Seigneurs Empereur et Roy Très Chrestien a esté et est de par cette dite Paix particulière pouvoir à l'universelle, et par conséquent aux emprises contre le Turc et autres Infidèles et autres Hérétiques....

A month later, Francis I, free once more, crossed the frontier of the Pyrenees, leaving his two sons as hostages. In reality, the French position was not as desperate as might be believed from contemporary accounts. The fear of Habsburg domination was, it may be said, a good counsellor. The defeat of France at Pavia, in destroying her position of eminence, immediately attracted allies. Everyone thought of defending himself against the emperor. Louise of Savoy, regent during her son's captivity, had a fairly easy task. Her appeals for help did not go unheeded. On the morrow of Pavia an appeal was made to the Turk, who gave a favourable reply: this will be discussed later. At the same time, the envoy Gian Giacomo Passano opened negotiations with Cardinal Wolsey in England. All these efforts ended in the Holy League of Cognac (24 May 1526) in which Rome and Venice rallied to the French cause, aiming at the destruction of Spain's influence in Italy. This league was accepted by Florence, then by Francesco Sforza, expelled from Milan by the Spaniards on 24 July 1526. Henry VIII was sympathetic to the alliance without being a declared member.

The league helped France to regain breath. Other powerful help came from the Turk's victory at Mohács in August 1526, giving almost all Hungary to the infidel. The blow struck Ferdinand and Charles V himself. The latter's feelings amid these new reverses can be imagined: especially his feelings against Clement VII. In order to give the greatest publicity to his cause, he sent on 17 September 1526 an open letter to the college of cardinals. A few months later, on 6 May 1527, the imperial army entered and sacked Rome; Clement VII had to take refuge in the castle of San Angelo. This was one of the most frightful and dramatic events of the century. In November the pontiff accepted in full the agreements proposed by the emperor, but avoided their immediate execution by escaping to Orvieto (16 December 1527). Doubtless, Charles denied responsibility for the sack of the city. This did not prevent the 'judgement of God' from dogging his cause. For many years the Papacy was to depend on the emperor, despite occasional gestures and acts of independence.

Events in themselves, however, continued to favour France. On 17 May 1527 Florence expelled the Medici and declared a republic under Niccolo Capponi. By the Treaty of Westminster (30 April 1527) Francis I attached Henry openly to his cause. In July Lautrec once more marched into Italy at the head of an army, ran through the duchy of Milan—without, it is true, taking Milan itself—and in conjunction with Andrea Doria and the Genoese fleet succeeded in expelling the imperialists from Genoa, where French dominion was proclaimed under Teodoro Trivulzio. Finally, the Assembly of Notables (16 December 1527) assured Francis that he could raise the necessary levies to pay the ransom of his sons.

The situation, however, remained fragile. The adversaries were exhausted by such a long struggle. One event could change everything, one way or another. It was at Genoa that the dramatic blow was struck. The campaign of 1528 had been notable for the penetration of a French army under Lautrec to the south of the peninsula, and Naples, besieged, was about to surrender. The blockade was made effective by the Genoese fleet of Andrea Doria, which cut off contact between Naples and Spanish Sicily. At this point, Genoa, or rather Andrea Doria, changed sides. The loyalty of Genoa to the French cause was already in doubt. In 1527 the Genoese had sent an envoy, Vincenzo Pallavicini, to Lautrec to demand the restitution of Savone which the French threatened to develop to the disadvantage of Genoa. Jacques Colin, the French delegate, on several occasions between October and January 1528 advised the king to retain the precious city. In June 1528 the discontent of Andrea Doria was well known, with the result that Charles V tried hard to detach him from the French cause. On 7 June 1528 Jean de Selve wrote to Montmorency, then at Paris, 'the emperor was working on Andrea Doria to win him over and by means of Doria to promise liberty to the city of Genoa'. Doria, indeed, put himself up for auction, asking Charles V for the recognition of Genoese independence and then for 120,000 scudi to be paid in Italy in two successive years. He refused the offers of Clement VII. On 4 July he sent orders to his nephew to retire with the fleet from before Naples. He soon besieged Genoa (9 September), finally restoring the republic under an aristocratic constitution. Francis I tried to reply to the blow. In August he schemed to raise a fleet in Brittany, and set sail for Italy to re-establish the situation. In October, Clement VII suggested that he should offer Savone to Genoa. All this was in vain. The consequences of the defection of Genoa grew. The French army before Naples, decimated by disease, bereft of its leader by the death of Lautrec, was forced to retire (28 August).

The rallying of Genoa to the side of the emperor, or rather of Spain (where its financiers were already so powerful)—this *rapprochement* was also one of the great events of the sixteenth century. It sealed an alliance which was not only political. It established Spain in Italy more strongly than before, for Italy lived both by land and by sea. Thus the maritime key-positions of western Italy were handed over by the *condottiere* admiral of Genoa to the emperor.

In this situation, was a general settlement far off? By the Treaty of Barcelona (29 June 1529) the emperor came to an agreement with Clement VII. The latter undertook to recognise Ferdinand as king of Bohemia and Hungary; the Medici were re-established in Florence. Peace was also concluded with France. By the Treaty of Cambrai (3 August 1529), called the *Paix des Dames* because it was negotiated by Louise, the queen mother, and Margaret, the aunt of Charles V, Francis I renounced his claims in Italy, as well as his right as suzerain in Flanders and Artois. In return, Charles V agreed not to press his claims to Burgundy. The possessions of Charles of Bourbon and the prince of Orange passed to France, whose allies—Robert de la Marck and the duke of Gueldres—were abandoned. The duchy of Milan was given to Francesco Sforza. Francis I was to marry Eleanor of Austria. The ransom of the two princes was fixed at two million écus, of which 1,200,000 were to be in a single payment in gold.

This settlement, clearly extensive, opened a new period in the relations of Francis I and Charles V. A new era began. 'I see two good things in this peace', declared Clement VII; 'the first is that the king of France will receive his sons and will not be tied to the emperor any more....The other good thing is that the emperor cannot but go to Germany, both for the affairs of the Turk, and also on account of the Lutherans.'

The two decades from the Ladies' Peace (1529) to Mühlberg (1547), formed a well-defined period in the political dialogue between the Valois and the Habsburgs. The last part of the reign of Francis I (he died before Mühlberg) was marked by less active and less violent conflicts. The war certainly continued intermittently, but a war of movement was faced with growing difficulties. In Italy, the installation of artillery, the construction of concealed ramparts and even more the reconstruction of stone walls which formerly had been breached so easily—all these advances of the engineer and military technician made fortifications more secure.[1] It was no longer possible to make a carefree entry into Milan, as in the days of Lautrec.

There was a second reason, in itself sufficient: Charles V and Francis I were not in conflict, except for two wars in 1536–7 and 1542–4. Economic conditions, doubtless, did not favour these long wars which swallowed up the finances of princes and kings. Did the reason lie in the wise judgment of Francis I? This would be saying a great deal. At the beginning, perhaps, he considered that it was a personal matter between him and *Cesare*. However, about them, between them, ready to oppose them as well as reconcile them, there were the other powers—Henry VIII and a restless Papacy. In the light of this situation we must appreciate the powerful offensive of Turkish Islam in the years before 1540–1 and a Germany which slowly but surely prepared for the explosion of Mühlberg. The policy of Francis I—whether it was wisdom aforethought or not—was revealed in the impact of events which he did not cause and of which he did not pay the cost.

In the struggle of Valois and Habsburg, there was a third great force—the Turkish empire. The Turk entered the struggle well before the years 1529–30, at the very moment in 1519 when Charles V was receiving congratulations from all over Europe on his election to the Empire. Even before this, the Turkish threat had become a political reality—in the Balkans, in central Europe, and above all in the Mediterranean on which the wealth of the western world was still dependent. Wherever the Turk advanced he stumbled on weak states, either corrupted from within or too small to give any substantial protection to Christendom. This was only too true in the Mediterranean in the case of Italy which, facing both west and east, displayed ominously dangerous divisions and weaknesses. It was true also in central Europe, where Bohemia and Hungary were fragile bulwarks. Belgrade and Buda-Pest were the important outposts in the south. Were they going to surrender? Already in 1520 Hungary appeared ill-prepared for her task and responsibility. The kingdom was disturbed from within by the ideas of the Reformation, and it suffered from the weaknesses of the monarchy. Lewis II and his court party (the great feudal lords) leaned in favour of German influence; they were opposed by the national party formed largely by the Magyar gentry under John Zápolyai, the *voivode* of Transylvania. In attempting to take advantage of these dissensions, the policy of the Habsburgs added to the chronic weakness of Hungary, weak both in body and head. Moreover,

[1] Cf. below, pp. 491 ff.

in the shadow of politics there stood big business. The Fuggers, who had extensive undertakings in Bohemia and Hungary, principally in the copper and silver mines (for instance) of Neusohl and Kremnitz, pushed forward their interests under cover of the German infiltration. Their exports and the recovery of profits excited the criticism of the nationalists, and above all of Zápolyai.

In the Mediterranean, there was the same alarming situation. Under the sultan Selīm the Terrible (1512–20) the pressure of Ottoman power became explosive. After the victory over Persia at Tchaldiran (1514), the Turkish armies seized Syria and Palestine (1516), then Egypt (1517), and received in turn the submission of the sherif of Mecca. All these successes were inevitably threats to the safety of the west. Against this peril, which can be imagined, there were drawn up the weak lines of defence of the Venetian and Genoese empires, and in particular the very real weakness of the Knights Hospitallers, encamped in Rhodes. Beyond this area of contention, there was the danger of the Barbary corsairs, whose striking rise under Khair ad-Dīn marked the early sixteenth century.[1] On all sides, it must be noted, directly or indirectly or even both at once, the power of the Habsburgs was threatened. In Hungary and the Mediterranean the conflict was on two fronts, and indeed on three if one considers the struggle with France. In thus defending himself on all sides Charles V exhausted his immense power.

On 22 September 1520 Sulaimān the Magnificent succeeded the sultan Selīm. Under him, blows of incredible power were struck at Christendom. It was now the hour of destiny. In 1521, in the first spring of his reign, Sulaimān left Constantinople (10 May). On 8 July, en route, he took Sabacz, and by the end of the month completed the investment of Belgrade. The threat was very serious. The pope had drawn attention to the crisis, and, indeed, Hieronymus Balbus had appeared before the Diet of Worms (3 April) as the envoy of the king of Hungary. Charles V, however, was too occupied with the problems of Germany and the revolt of Luther to pay much attention to his demands. Belgrade was left to its fate. At last it gave in (28 August) before the guns and explosive mines of the Turks. Venice, aware of her own weakness, hastened to make peace with the sultan, receiving confirmation of her commercial privileges, the right to have a consul at Constantinople and permission to keep Cyprus, all this in return for a tribute of 10,000 ducats.

How in 1522 Sulaimān turned his efforts against Rhodes is described below.[2] Victory came slowly to the Turks, but the siege passed without help and reinforcements. It was the year of Bicocca, and the appeals of the pope for a truce raised no answer. Adrian VI wrote to Charles V that if Rhodes or Hungary fell into the hands of the Turks he doubted whether the princes of Christendom combined could ever recover them. In 1524

---

[1] Cf. above, pp. 324 f., and below, pp. 518 ff..   [2] Pp. 510 f.

Lewis of Hungary once more called for aid. In February 1525 came the disaster of Pavia. France proceeded to establish contact with the Porte. The regent sent an agent, then in December an embassy, to which in February 1526 the sultan replied favourably. Thus Turkey entered the 'concert' of Europe. Hungary remained isolated; Poland had renewed a truce in 1525; Venice was tied by her treaty. The struggle between Francis I and Charles V was also a part of this general indifference to the eastern question which the historian must note and take into full account.

Lewis II, king of Bohemia and Hungary since 1516 (he was then ten years old), reigned over a divided country—divided, as already noted, politically, socially and religiously. The national party gained strength from all the economic difficulties, which were made clearly evident by the great devaluation of 1521. It was in opposition to the German influence and the court party that its leader John Zápolyai grew in stature. Lewis gave way to this xenophobia in 1524, and again in 1525. The allies of the Fuggers at court were replaced and their mines confiscated. Later, Anton Fugger (who took over control after the death of Jacob in 1525) estimated the loss at 206,741 florins. Then, in August 1526, came the devastating Hungarian defeat—'con grandissima estrage', as a Venetian ambassador reported—at Mohács.[1] Lewis was killed, Hungary was open to invasion, if not conquest. Ten days later, the victors entered Buda.

Mohács, like Pavia and perhaps more than Pavia, had immense consequences. From that moment, the Habsburgs found themselves in the breach. Ferdinand, brother of Charles V and imperial vicar, brother-in-law of the late Lewis, inherited on his own account not only the plans and prejudices of the German court party, but also the claims to the crowns of Hungary and Bohemia. He now found himself bound to defend Christendom against the infidel. It was partly ambition and partly prudence, for the lands of Ferdinand, as an observer remarked in Germany, were put in the greatest danger. Self-defence was also the defence of others. At Prague on 23 October Ferdinand was proclaimed king of Bohemia, and at Pozsony, on 17 December, the nobility of Hungary accepted him as their king. He at once found himself opposed by Zápolyai, who had also been elected king, this time by the national party at Stuhlweissenburg on 10 November. The prospect of an anti-Habsburg movement, taking the Empire in the rear, attracted the attention of the League of Cognac. Zápolyai, however, was distracted by offers of mediation and defeated at Tokay on 26 September 1527 by Ferdinand, who then had himself crowned on 5 November.

Mohács, then, entailed the loss of at least two-thirds of Hungary.[2] The Turk gradually entrenched himself. In the Habsburg part of Hungary, Ferdinand established his authority. With him, the Fuggers regained

[1] Cf. below, p. 512.   [2] Below, pp. 522 ff..

possession of their mines and industrial undertakings which they continued to exploit until about 1540. Zápolyai meanwhile took refuge in the mountainous regions of Transylvania and turned towards the sultan, who recognised him as king and vassal. In 1538, however, he came to terms with Ferdinand. Yet, after the great battle, the kings, princes and lords of Hungary scarcely counted for anything. The great dispute was between the German *Reich* and the Ottoman empire, and the latter, at least until 1540, did not lessen its pressure. The Turkish attack, indeed, continued along the Danube, and in September 1529 the Turkish flag was planted before the very walls of Vienna. On this occasion Germany paid heed to the mortal danger. The diet, assembled in March at Innsbruck, had voted 120,000 Rhenish guilders for defence against the Turk; in May, the Diet of Speyer promised an army of 16,000 men and 4,000 cavalry. The failure of the siege is described elsewhere.[1] At Vienna the tide of the Turkish invasions in Europe had reached its high-water mark. The event was of very great importance, showing as it did both the enormous strength of the sultan and the limits to his power. The setback before Vienna in 1529, the reverse before the small city of Güns in 1532, the small success in that same year of the fleet under Andrea Doria during a raid on Cherchell, a small port on the African coast near Algiers—these events both great and small showed that the Turk was not invincible, and that it was possible to check his impetus. However, until the years 1540–1 he was still able to strike some terrible blows. The gravity of the situation, terrifying to the contemporary, is confirmed in the light of history.

The moment has now come to complete the presentation of Germany which was more and more to pass to the forefront in the affairs and preoccupations of the emperor. Two essential movements developed which in the light of events assumed aspects of varying importance. On the one hand, beginning quietly and almost imperceptibly, there was a powerful and aggressive resurgence of active Catholicism—the great sweeping movement of the Counter-Reformation noted by German historians. On the other hand, the Protestant movement did not cease to make progress and to consolidate the uncertain grip which it had on Germany. Resurgence of Catholicism and expansion of Protestantism— the two movements were complementary and are to be explained one with the other. The victory of one meant anxiety for the other, and fear and success constantly changed sides. In spite of its conspicuous prosperity in the first half of the sixteenth century, the world of Germany could not continue indefinitely. The two movements clashed and from an early date prepared for the explosion of the middle of the century.

About the year 1530, the obvious success of the Lutherans is to be

---

[1] Below, pp. 514 f.

noted—or rather their steady progress towards consolidation. The groups which had signed the *Protestation* of Speyer began to take on a more definite form. At Schmalkalden, from 22 to 31 December 1530, the princes discussed the question, and at a second meeting on 27 February 1531 officially set up the famous league. Its members were the landgrave Philip of Hesse, the elector of Saxony, the dukes of Brunswick and Lüneburg (that is, Philip, Otto, Ernest, and Francis), Prince Wolfgang of Anhalt, the counts of Mansfeld (Gebhard VII and Albert VII), the cities of Strassburg, Ulm, Constance, Reutlingen, Memmingen, Lindau, Biberach, Isny, Lübeck, Magdeburg and Bremen. The league was defensive: 'On all occasions', the agreement stated, 'that any of us is attacked for the Word of God and the doctrine of the gospel or for any other thing connected therewith, all the others will come to his aid at once as far as possible and will assist in delivering him....' This league, however, did not clear away the obstacles to a stricter union of the Protestants. A chance circumstance changed this situation. Zwingli, the troublesome factor, disappeared on the battlefield of Cappel on 11 October 1531. His defeat encouraged the Protestants to settle their differences and close their ranks. The league soon made decisive progress and its military organisation was completed in November and December 1531. The elector of Saxony and the landgrave of Hesse were to share the leadership. There were new recruits: Göttingen, Goslar, Einbeck, Hamburg and Rostock, then in 1537, Augsburg, Frankfurt and Hanover. The Protestants thus established themselves strongly in northern Germany, but the character of their grouping and defence was a reply to the menacing foundation of a robust Catholic movement which even on the political level became a great force in history. In Germany these years flickered past like patterns in a kaleidoscope.

There were many reasons for this. All the bridges between Protestantism and Catholicism were not disrupted in a day. A whole party of moderation aimed to reknit the fabric of the Church. The German historians, for example Karl Brandi and even more Peter Rassow, have rightly attributed a first-class importance to attempts at reconciliation made at the time of the dramatic Diet of Augsburg in 1530. In spite of the emperor and of Melanchthon, these attempts finally failed.[1] Nevertheless, they reveal not only a state of mind but also a very complex situation. Outside the variations and profundities of the spiritual life, we must not forget the implications of politics within and beyond the Empire. In the west there was the hostility of the French, and in the east the war with the Turk. Thus steps in the direction of religious war needed retracing. At the Diet of Nuremberg in 1532 the problems and the necessary expense of the war in Hungary were uppermost in men's minds. The struggle abroad and the settlement of domestic issues resulted in the

[1] See above, pp. 93 f.

formal Peace of Nuremberg of 23 July 1532 which pronounced the end of all religious war in Germany and so suspended the prosecution of the elector of Saxony as well as the other law-suits against the Protestants: 'Nosque pro conservanda pace et concordia publica in Imperio et praecipue ut communi Christiani nominis hosti, Turciae videlicet, eo melius et acrius resisti, eiusque crudelissimi conatus adversus Christianum sanguinem...averti possint....'

All these elements—all or near enough—make it easier to understand, from a central stand in Germany, the course of events through the whole of the second act of the dynastic struggle. The difficulty, as always, is to arrange the scenes and to note the explanatory concordances, the chain of cause and effect. In this, we should not forget a basic rule: peace in Germany, with the alternations of Catholic and Lutheran ascendancy, with the false alarms of domestic war, those flashes which did not start the blaze—this peace depended on the wars abroad in the east and the west. Now the latter broke out in 1536-7 and 1542-4; the former came fairly frequently. There was a constant alert rather than open war. It existed continually on land and sea, expressing itself in pillage and raids which were cruel but brief and local. The Habsburgs, it must be noted, did everything, on all sides, to limit the destruction, expense and effort. They knew very well indeed how to negotiate at the court of the sultan—not perhaps the emperor himself, who did not want to lose face in the bargaining, but rather his brother who was placed in Vienna and whose possessions made him a neighbour of the Turk. So they discussed things as neighbours. In 1532, after the dispatch of ambassadors to Constantinople, the sultan and Ferdinand agreed on a perpetual truce (in reality, only short-lived). For the king of the Romans it was humiliating in form but profitable in substance. After all, the sultan had other worries (the wars in Persia in 1534, 1548, 1553)[1] and other ambitions. At the request of the king of France and of Barbarossa (who had been appointed captain-general of the sultan's fleet), he threw himself into a great war in the Mediterranean—so fierce a war that it did not spare Venice and saw the retreat and defeat in 1538, near Prevesa, of the imperial fleet. The Mediterranean was on the point of becoming a Turkish lake.[2] On the Hungarian frontier the war reopened in 1542, ending in 1547 with a truce of five years, only to break out afresh in 1551. All these instances indicate an unending war between Islam and the Habsburgs, and, it should be added, it was not an insignificant struggle. However, the Turk was not the only infidel. There were Moslems in Spain, even though they were often half-converted; and facing Spain and Italy there were the Barbary corsairs. In 1535 Charles V in person took Tunis, but he failed in a dramatic attempt against Algiers in 1541.[3]

[1] Below, pp. 516 f., 524 f., 528. [3] Below, pp. 518, 531.
[2] Below, pp. 519.

The wars with France were also intermittent. It required a startling event to bring Francis I and Charles V to war after the *laissez-vivre* of seven years of peace. In 1535 Francesco Sforza, duke of Milan, died heirless. His death provoked once more the endemic stimuli of the Italian wars. All Italy lived by a thousand appetites and animosities. It was not even a free Italy, for the Spanish domination had made huge advances since 1529. Charles could not afford to give way. As emperor he was suzerain of Milan. He arranged the succession and positioned his troops. At this, Francis I, consumed by his old enthusiasms, revived his old claims which in the heat of the moment seemed so lawful. Milan was close to his heart. He redoubled his plans for war, his appeals for help, above all to the Turk. Without the Turk, there would be no fleet. Without a naval diversion in the east, how could he prevail against such a powerful adversary? Henry VIII and the Lutherans decided to remain neutral spectators. Sulaimān turned on the pressure in Hungary and sent his fleets westwards. On this occasion, contrary to what has been said, there were neither 'capitulations' nor formal alliance, but rather, in the old and always apt description of the historian Jorga, 'parallel action' by the two powers.

War entailed extraordinary expenditures. Charles V naturally turned at once to his financiers. The Fuggers advanced him 100,000 ducats on 14 April 1536 at fourteen per cent, to be repaid in bullion from the New World. On 26 February 1537 another loan of 100,000 ducats was made. In addition, a very rich fleet arrived at Seville. In this same year of 1537, the famous *escudo* was minted, a lighter coin in gold. By itself, it showed that all was not well with the economy of the vast, sprawling Spanish empire.

The war, however, was not to be extensive. Francis I invaded Savoy and Piedmont, where Turin was seized in April. To counteract this, Charles V sent his army for the second time into Provence, and for the second time the expedition did not succeed. In the north, Charles of Egmont (d. 1538) put his lands under French protection, but after his defeat at Heiligerlee gave up Groningen. It was, in fact, a small war and a short war. It was ended by the intervention of Paul III in the Truce of Nice (18 June 1538). This was for ten years; it confirmed the Treaty of Cambrai, and both adversaries were to retain their conquests, Francis I keeping Savoy and two-thirds of Piedmont, the other third remaining in the hands of the emperor. Thus, according to the French historians, France captured lands which protected the kingdom. This truce was followed in July by personal negotiations at Aigues Mortes between Charles V and Francis I. They soon came to an agreement against a trinity of infidels: the Turk, the Lutherans and the English.

From all this—after a brief struggle between the two adversaries, followed by the emperor's voyage through France to the Netherlands where Ghent was in revolt—it must be remarked that France had gained a much-coveted gateway into Italy. Yet, even then, the diplomacy of the Very Christian King did not refrain from troubling the scene. On this occasion, Charles V felt himself sufficiently strong and secure to invest his own son Philip with the duchy of Milan. It was scarcely conceivable that Francis I should resign himself to the *fait accompli*. On the pretext of the assassination near Pavia (3 July 1541) of two French agents, Rinconi and Fregosi, returning from Constantinople, Francis I declared a fourth war against Charles V in 1542. He at once appealed to the Turk. The combined fleets of France and Barbarossa took Nice but failed to capture the city's fortress. After the French victory at Ceresole in April 1544—its importance must not be exaggerated—the emperor operated from the Netherlands and gained some territory in the north of France—St Dizier in Champagne on 17 August, in September Château Thierry and Soissons. Henry VIII established himself before Boulogne. The Swiss troops were deserting the French armies. Isolated, Francis I asked for peace. This was soon concluded at Crespy on 18 September 1544. Charles gave up his claims to Burgundy; Francis renounced his own on Naples as well as Flanders and Artois. His second son, the duke of Orleans, was to marry a princess of the imperial family (March 1545), but his death on 9 September 1545 returned Milan into the hands of Charles V.

These wars in the east and in the west, even in the south in Italy and the Mediterranean, saved Germany from the logical consequences of her domestic problems. These considerable benefits, however, were short-lived. They were even more so when the Protestants received some assistance from the Catholic side. Indeed, before turning to the events leading to Mühlberg, it is worth showing the very characteristic growth of Protestantism in the period more or less of the French wars.

There was a small war, but a war nevertheless, ending in the restoration during the summer of 1534 of the duke of Württemberg to his duchy. Fifteen years earlier he had been expelled by the Swabian League, and now he was re-established (and with him Protestantism was proclaimed) by the Schmalkaldic League. Philip of Hesse organised the affair. The Schmalkaldic carried out the invasion in April 1534, with the open support of Francis I who was only too happy to receive Montbéliard in return for his intervention. At the end of June, all was settled in the Peace of Kadan (29 June 1534)—or at least appeared settled.[1] The paramount problem, the very prospect of peace in Germany, remained without settlement. Other events favoured the Lutherans, especially in Brandenburg and Saxony. In 1535 the Catholic Joachim I of Brandenburg was succeeded by Joachim II, who at first was attached to the Catholic League of Halle, but later in 1538 refused to enter the Catholic League of Nuremberg. By 1540 he was already Lutheran. In 1539 there was a similar change in the duchy of Saxony. In this year Duke George, a loyal

[1] Cf. above, pp. 165 f.

Catholic, died. He was followed by Henry, a Protestant, and then in 1541 by Maurice, also a Protestant. These were small changes, but in themselves significant. German Protestantism was spreading over the map. Another small event, of which the details are of no great concern, came at this time. The years 1538–9 were the occasion of the complicated Jülich-Cleves-Berg succession problem.

The success of one meant fear for the other. The fears of the Catholics ended in the League of Nuremberg (10 June 1538) which the Habsburgs were to organise after the Schmalkaldic model. Its members were the emperor, Ferdinand, the dukes of Bavaria and of Saxony, the two dukes of Brunswick, the archbishops of Mainz and Salzburg. Advantages and setbacks came one after the other, and in 1540 a famous scandal was to strike at the very heart of the Schmalkaldic League when Philip of Hesse moved away from the league and entered into an alliance with Charles V (13 June 1541).[1] He abandoned his former ties with England, France and Cleves, promised to aid Charles, and agreed to recognise Ferdinand as Charles's successor. This affair opened a considerable breach in the ranks of the Schmalkaldic League. It gave Charles the opportunity of conquering the very important duchy of Gueldres. In 1543 Charles carried off the assault on Düren (24 August) and accepted the submission at Venloo (6 September) of Duke William, who returned to Catholicism in 1546.

By this time the situation had changed considerably. Indeed, the conflict in Germany assumed a more serious character. In July 1542 Henry, duke of Brunswick-Wolfenbüttel, an isolated Catholic prince, saw his state overrun by John Frederick of Saxony and the landgrave of Hesse. He took to flight, and his lands were at once converted to Lutheranism. Charles was at that moment scarcely in a position to intervene, since he might easily provoke a hostile alliance of France, Sweden, Denmark and Scotland. Even the pope was not to be trusted. For the moment Charles V had the friendship of Henry VIII, whose increasingly Catholic reforms in England had alienated him from the cause of Protestantism in Germany. On 11 February 1543 these two powers entered into a secret alliance against France, an alliance which the emperor published in March and Henry VIII in May. Nevertheless, the hour to strike Protestant Germany had not yet come. It still had a tendency to lean towards Francis I. In April 1541, as Contarini remarked, the latter warmly encouraged the Protestants to resist Habsburg domination, and even declared that he was not without sympathy for their doctrines. As mentioned above, in 1542 the Very Christian King declared war on the emperor. From this moment it would have been rash to act decisively in Germany. Charles V was careful and prudent; he knew how to wait. In September 1544, after Crespy, he was free from this constraint. One of the treaty clauses left him at liberty to bring about

[1] Cf. above, pp. 179 ff.

la réduction de notre sainte Foi et Religion et union chrétienne et obvier à l'extrême danger et hazard où elle se trouve, et afin de parvenir à la pacification générale d'icelle pour aussi pouvoir mieux entendre et s'emploier unanimement à la répulsion des turcs et autres infidèles.

For a quarter of a century after the Diet of Worms, however, everything had been prepared long in advance for the aggressive policy of Charles V in Germany.[1] He had already purchased support. Maurice of Saxony in 1542 had withdrawn from the Schmalkaldic League and, during the war with France, had followed the armies of Charles V. On 19 June 1546 he signed a pact of neutrality with Charles. It need scarcely be added that the diplomacy of the Habsburg was without equal in the buying of support, in the softening of consciences. In order to detach the young duke from the Protestant cause, the emperor played on his personal ambitions. After all, did he not wish to add the electorate of Saxony to his own duchy? On 27 October 1546 Maurice received a formal promise of this coveted honour. In addition, as was to be expected, the very Catholic duke of Bavaria took his place at the side of the emperor by a treaty of 7 June 1546. On 9 June Charles V completed an agreement with Paul III who, at the Council of Trent, had promised him an army and a large subsidy. In May 1546, intent on war, the emperor began to mobilise his troops. Yet, on this eve of battle, everything was not entirely as the emperor could wish. After the Peace of Crespy Philip of Hesse had re-entered the Schmalkaldic League. For their own part, the Protestants prepared for the inevitable conflict. During the winter of 1545–6 (December–February) the League carried on their discussions at Frankfurt. At the Diet of Regensburg (after June 1546) the Protestants opposed the Council of Trent and asked in vain for a national council. War was already on the way.

At the beginning the Protestants had a considerable military advantage —an army of 50,000 men, 7,000 cavalry, and 110 pieces of artillery. They had a brilliant commander in Sebastian Schärtlin von Burtenbach, whose strategy aimed at closing the Tyrol passes to the imperial armies, at cutting them off from Italy, and at breaking up the communications of the Empire. However, firm control and leadership were lacking; these plans were abandoned and gradually the Protestants lost the initiative. The years 1546–7 witnessed a curious turn of fate. Within a few months the great personalities disappeared from the scene—Luther (1546), Barbarossa (1546), Henry VIII (January 1547), Francis I (March 1547). Left alone, the emperor grew in stature, helped on occasion by good fortune, which, to be sure, reserved its favours for the young. It was sufficient for him to wait and be patient, to count the days. Gradually he carried off the cities—by the end of 1546 he had taken Memmingen, Biberach,

---

[1] Cf. above (pp. 181 f.) for a somewhat different view of the emperor's policy.

Heilbronn, Esslingen, Reutlingen, Frankfurt; in January, Augsburg and Strassburg; in February, only Constance still held out, while Catholicism was again restored in Cologne. He then turned against John Frederick, who had invaded the territory of Maurice. On 13 April he entered Saxony; on the 24th of that month, in the mists of the Elbe, he won the decisive battle of Mühlberg. John Frederick fell into his hands; Philip of Hesse surrendered on 20 June. The success of the emperor, as at Pavia, seemed complete. Maurice of Saxony received the promised electorate, and with it Wittenberg and the rich mines of Saxony.

The power of the Habsburgs had never been greater, more insolent, and yet, at the same time, more fragile. The collapse of this impressive position in the decade following Mühlberg formed the last phase in the dramatic dynastic struggle.

With the mid-century, Europe approached a great turning-point. Within only a few years the predominance of Spain was to make itself felt during the turbulent wars of Charles V, and the Empire and Germany were to pass into the shadow of history. The emperor lost his prestige, and his German Empire its economic power. Indeed, another Europe emerged, one can almost say a Spanish Europe, which was more open than that of Charles V to the Atlantic and the problems of the world. The Mediterranean lost some of its importance, and the Turk, that furious hornet, was bottled up. Yet rather than deal with this vast history we must turn to the closing destiny of Charles V. In these dramatic years the pace quickens, and in it he squanders his life-force.

The war of the Schmalkaldic League had been an expensive affair. Already in February 1547 the Fuggers had remarked that they 'were tired of imperial loans' in view of the delays in repayment. At the very moment when the imperial policy should have thrust forward and incurred new expenses it became calculating, a careful husband of its scanty funds. It was a costly frugality, for everyone, both friend and foe, was raised against Charles either secretly or openly. For his own part the pope, Paul III, did not wish the Council of Trent to become an imperial tool. In January 1546 he withdrew his troops from the army of Charles V. In March he sent the Council to Bologna, away from the direct influence of the emperor. With good reason he became alarmed at the nomination of Ferrante Gonzaga to the government of Milan. Paul III, however, died on 10 November 1549.

The sudden conquest of Protestant Germany was not sufficient in itself. It was necessary to organise this victory and reintegrate Protestantism in the unity of Christendom. The result could not but be authoritarian, and therefore difficult. The Diet of Augsburg, assembled on 1 September 1547, accepted on 30 June 1548 an Interim with a Catholic bias. The compromise gave satisfaction neither to the Lutherans nor to the Catholics.[1] It was

[1] Cf. above, p. 183.

easier for the emperor to declare (in July 1548) that the seventeen provinces of the Netherlands were free and no longer subject to the laws of the Empire: politics more than religion supported the decisions of authority. The revolt in Germany spread. At Königsberg in February 1550 a defensive league was set up against the Habsburgs, with Hans of Küstrin, John Albert of Mecklenburg, and Albert, duke of Prussia. After June French envoys entered into the important negotiations with Maurice of Saxony which led to the agreement of Lochau (5 October 1551) and then to the Treaty of Chambord (15 January 1552), completed by William of Hesse and John Albert of Mecklenburg (19 February). The king of France, the new and sombre Henry II, promised his allies an army and subsidies. In return, they ceded him the three bishoprics of Metz, Toul and Verdun. These agreements were supported by Sulaimān and favoured by the differences arising between Charles V and Ferdinand on the subject of settling in advance the succession to the imperial crown.[1]

Imperial diplomacy, strangely enough, trailed after the German and European conspiracy, thinking that it could emerge without recourse to war. It temporised and was finally deceived. Mary of Hungary, the regent of the Netherlands, in vain recommended that Maurice of Saxony should be seized by any means available. Thus, the inevitable occurred. On 13 March 1552 the French opened the campaign in Germany, their first attack no longer occurring in Italy. An army of 35,000 penetrated Lorraine and occupied the three bishoprics. At the same time, Maurice of Saxony and the margrave of Brandenburg-Culmbach invaded the south of Germany and surprised Charles V. He was obliged to flee to Innsbruck, then across the snowy Alps to take refuge at Villach. Yet his morale remained unbroken. On 4 April 1552 he wrote to Ferdinand: 'If I am to choose between a great disgrace and a great danger, I will take the part of danger....' He called Anton Fugger to his aid. The merchant of Augsburg, not wishing to see his enterprises thrown into danger, made out a loan of 400,000 florins to the emperor. Meanwhile, thanks to Ferdinand, and not least to the equivocations and calculations of that extraordinary commander, Maurice of Saxony, everything quickly changed. The kingdoms of Charles V, above all Spain, saved the old emperor. Charles returned to Augsburg, joined forces with the duke of Alva and, with the support of German Catholic strength, besieged Metz which had been captured from the Empire by the French. The city was well-defended by Francis of Guise, and Charles was obliged to retire on New Year's day, 1553. However, at Sievershausen (9 July 1553) Maurice of Saxony was killed at the very moment of victory over the margrave of Brandenburg-Culmbach. The latter, again defeated at Steterburg (12 September 1553) and Schwarzach (13 June 1554), fled to France.

After this reverse Charles V, now prematurely old and racked by bodily

[1] Above, p. 332.

ills, realised and accepted his defeat. It was no longer a question of settling German affairs by force. By the Peace of Augsburg, to which he did not wish to put his hand, religious peace was established between the Lutherans (but not all Protestants, for it excluded Calvinists) and the Catholics. Later, this settlement was to be summed up in the formula 'cuius regio, eius religio'. There followed Charles's abdication, retirement and death.[1] The imperial crown fell to his brother Ferdinand. His son, Philip II, received Spain, the lands of the New World, Naples, Milan, Franche-Comté and the Netherlands. A settlement was not far off. The acceptance of failure in Germany, the division of government, the preponderance of Spanish interests, above all, in 1557, the great national bankruptcies of Spain and France which shattered the nerves of war—all these were elements making for an end to the dispute. Thus peace was signed at Cateau-Cambrésis (1–3 April 1559). France gave up Savoy and Piedmont, and with them her claims on Italy. She retained, however, five fortresses, including Turin, Saluzzo and Pignerol; and in the north, the three famous bishoprics of Metz, Toul and Verdun. In Italy the Medici took Siena in fief; Lombardy was divided—the west to Savoy, the south and east to the Farnese and Gonzaga. With this great settlement came a pause in the diplomacy of Europe.

The Treaty of Cateau-Cambrésis has the reputation of being one of the great treaties of modern European history. Many of its decisions were to endure for over a century. It lasted, and this, for history, was a great advantage. Yet why did it last? There were at least two sets of reasons. The first concerns the economic situation of the period. After the peace all the activities of Europe, perhaps of the world, were stimulated. A more vigorous blood circulated. In the second place, the middle of the century was, as we have said, a watershed, a turning-point. It was not so much the closing of a period as an opening on the future. The second half of the sixteenth century was to reveal and uncover the long, substantial lines of Spanish domination. The centre of gravity of Europe, indeed of the world, broke away from the lands of central Europe. Charles V had instinctively appreciated the equivocal position of his reign; he realised that the heart of his empire was in Spain. His abdication settled the matter. It showed clearly the domination of Philip, leaving Germany to somnolence, abandoning France to domestic troubles. The Treaty of Cateau-Cambrésis was successful without knowing it, for it was the charter of a new Europe, gravitating towards the west, where the Atlantic Ocean brought precious and new life. The Turk could still show his active aggressiveness in Hungary, but Hungary was overcome and brutalised. For central Europe there was paralysis, and soon for Italy, the Italy of golden cities, decadence. The path of the future lay, even more than in Spain, across the Atlantic and the seven seas of the world.

[1] Cf. above, pp. 332 f.

CHAPTER XII

INTELLECTUAL TENDENCIES

I. LITERATURE: THE PRINTED BOOK

BY 1520 printing had become the normal method of circulating books. Already the invention had been pointed out as one of the most important in the history of mankind and a start had been made to collect the antiquities of typography.

Despite the interest of sixteenth-century antiquaries, and of an almost uninterrupted scholarly investigation from then until our own day, the early development of printing remains remarkably obscure. For this there are several reasons. To begin with, the new technique began as a jealously guarded trade secret, all the more so as the printed book for some time competed with if it did not positively simulate the manuscript. In the second place, the earliest books were invariably popular works, those most likely to be worn away by time and frequent use, leaving no remains or only fragmentary remains of their existence. It was of their very nature, moreover, that for long they did not appeal to the collector of fine books and so failed to appear systematically in contemporary libraries. And finally, the expertise of the student of early printed books has all too seldom been joined to a sufficiently profound knowledge of the manufacture and distribution of manuscript books; each department has tended to be studied in isolation; and the next great steps in exploring the fifteenth-century book trade will be taken only when the evidence of the manuscript and the evidence of the printed book are taken together.

On one matter there can fortunately be no dispute. The fifteenth century unquestionably saw a sharp rise in the demand for books, which need provoke little surprise. Literacy was rapidly increasing among both the gentry and the urban bourgeoisie. The management of an estate no less than the management of a business was dependent on written accounts, while the groups of experts who had needed letters in the past— clergy, lawyers and bureaucrats—were certainly not smaller in number. If the fifteenth century witnessed a decline in the quality of university education, it saw a singular increase in the quantity of it, while secondary education made rapid strides. The consequent need for books was by no means restricted to the professional requirements of the classes just mentioned—though these were considerable enough. It equally affected the literature of devotion and relaxation. Besides the Latin bibles and service books of the priest, vernacular scriptures and mystical works were much sought for by both religious and lay persons, while chroniclers, poets and writers of romances found audiences in both castle and town.

How many manuscript Latin bibles, breviaries and other service books survive is probably beyond calculation: all the great libraries possess many copies. But of the English bible some two hundred manuscripts survive; there are no less than sixty manuscripts of Mandeville's *Travels* in their French form; of Froissart's *Chronicle* we possess about a hundred manuscripts; and of the English *Brut* chronicle over a hundred and twenty manuscripts in English have been enumerated. These are all large books—expensive to produce and designed from the start as permanent possessions. Their established bulk serves to indicate the volume of more ephemeral and more personal literature produced by the book trade in the later Middle Ages—the school books like the *Donat*, works of devotion like the *De Imitatione Christi*.

By the end of the fourteenth century the book trade was secularised. The *scriptoria* of monasteries and the zeal of individual priests still occasionally produced copies of texts, but in normal circumstances the clergy and the laity turned to professional scribes for books and there is no doubt that public requirements were anticipated by the copyists. Popular works were constantly manufactured and, though their production did not keep up with demand, many books were no longer specially commissioned by each customer. Highly organised as the manuscript book trade was, especially in university centres where the need for books was matched by an equal need for textual accuracy in reproduction, it must have worked under considerable difficulties in view of the growing volume of custom. Under university patronage and with academic sanctions a bookseller and manufacturer might make a good living, as he might when protected by a monopolistic gild; but often the copyist was both overworked and unable to profit from the scarcity of the product, for any clerk could earn an honest penny by turning to copying. It was doubtless economic pressure as well as the promptings of piety which led to the formation of those associations of copyists at Deventer and elsewhere in Holland at the end of the fourteenth and beginning of the fifteenth centuries, which formed the kernel of the Brethren of the Common Life. Similarly there were technical advances which increased the output of books. Chief among these was the manufacture of paper. Originally imported from the Orient, paper began to be produced in Spain in the twelfth century and in Italy during the thirteenth. By the first decade of the fifteenth century paper mills are found in most West European countries and the original contempt for the new material was fast vanishing, though even in the sixteenth century printers occasionally used parchment for a few *de luxe* copies intended for presentation. Given ample supplies of a relatively cheap material for books, other innovations followed. Books were multiplied piecemeal—the exemplar being broken up into gatherings and handed out to the copyists. Smaller texts were copied, by a process akin to later 'imposition', on the unfolded sheets, as the survival of a few uncut manuscripts bears witness. Extremely popular and short works were sometimes cut on wood and reproduced in considerable quantities, the methods of printing designs on linen cloth here offering an example which was followed first by the makers of playing cards and the *Heiligen* sheets (the saint's picture and a brief inscription) before it was adopted by the makers of 'block' books. These developments are all found in the early fifteenth century and continued to be employed after the invention of printing.

By a long tradition, fortified by documentary evidence which is not entirely free of ambiguity, the invention of printing by moveable metal type is credited to John Gutenberg (Johann Gensfleisch), a native of Mainz. That moveable type had been evolved in China centuries before is no diminution of Gutenberg's originality, for the Chinese script put insuperable difficulties in the way of the free development of the new art, and in any case there is no positive evidence that knowledge of Chinese printing contributed to the western invention. If there are clear indications that in other centres in Europe (as Haarlem and Avignon) experimental printing was being investigated at about the same time as Gutenberg was at work, this simply confirms that there was a general anxiety to find ways of expediting book production. And if with Gutenberg we must associate the capitalist Fust and Fust's son-in-law, the copyist Schoeffer, this merely indicates that contemporary business men and scriveners were not slow to see the advantages offered by the new method of manufacturing books.

The 42-line bible produced by 1456, even if it was not made by Gutenberg himself, represents the first great achievement of the process he had developed and it comes at the end of at least a decade of printing by Gutenberg and his associates. The fragments which alone survive of earlier printing are revealing enough of the public aimed at by the new venture: an apocalyptic German poem, a Donatus, an astronomical calendar; while a printed papal indulgence of 1454 (with blank space for the recipient's name to be filled in by hand) indicates a further field in which printing was soon to be much used. Finally, in the splendid Psalter produced by Fust and Schoeffer in 1457, a colophon for the first time gives the printer's name and the date of publication. Many later books lack such precise dating, but from then on the chronology of printing is more certain and it is possible to follow with a fair degree of certainty the diffusion of the new process in Europe.

Though there are odd hesitations and delays in various parts of the continent, what chiefly impresses the historian is the rapidity with which printing spread. From Mainz it moved to Bamberg and Strassburg (by 1458). German printers had already produced a devotional work in Italian before the first books were produced in Italy itself, by Sweynheym and Pannartz at the monastery of Subiaco (1464–7) and then at Rome (1467 onwards). Venice, to be the most celebrated home of early Italian printing, had a press in 1469. In France three Germans began printing in the Sorbonne in 1470, the year in which dated printing begins at Utrecht. In Spain a Fleming began printing at Valencia in 1474, and at the same time William Caxton produced at Bruges the first book designed for the English market: he was printing at Westminster from 1476. By the start of the sixteenth century practically every country in Europe had its press and its native printers. In the larger towns a number of printers are found. In smaller centres a press was often at work intermittently by 1500: a total of forty-five places are associated with printing in France, sixty-four in Germany, nearly eighty in Italy. Areas where the demand for books was smaller had both fewer printers and fewer centres: in England a press existed for a short time at St Albans, and, besides London, continuous printing is found in the fifteenth century only at Oxford. The bigger centres, like Paris, catered for foreign demand. Thus it came about that in Scotland a press was established in 1508 only to last till 1510, and printing there does not have a continuous history for a further thirty years.

In about a generation, therefore, printing was established in practically the whole of Europe. In the main the speed of its progress was due to its being in every sense a continuation of the existing trade in books. While the production and distribution of printed books obviously raised new problems of finance and marketing, the books themselves were a staple commodity which had long featured as an item in commerce, albeit as a minor, luxury item in international trade. The import and export of books now became a considerable feature of long-distance exchange. Book fairs—of which the most important were at Frankfurt, Leipzig, and Lyons—facilitated wholesale dealings, and certain towns developed book production into a major industry: Venice and Basle were the most important in this regard, closely followed by Paris. As for the economics of production, we know all too little about the size of editions (which in the first century of printing seldom fell below 200 copies and seldom rose much above 1000 except in the case of a few school books) and the costs of production to hazard guesses at the profits of the printer-publishers in early days. It is certain that the printer ventured his own capital only on books for which there was a certain sale—school books, works of popular piety and of established reputation—and for more speculative works, and especially for new books from little-known authors, normally sought to share the risks (and the profits) with the author or some third party. The printer-publisher in a big way of business—an Aldus at Venice, a Froben at Basle, an Estienne in Paris—clearly needed very considerable capital to acquire and maintain the machinery, varied founts of type, the paper, ink and other raw materials, as well as to store the finished works, some of which were exceedingly bulky and might take years to sell. Such men clearly enjoyed a measure of prosperity and even greater esteem while never making large fortunes. At the other end of the scale were dozens of smaller establishments, frequently employed on jobbing work for the big houses, and a considerable number of fugitive presses, often itinerant, whose stock and materials could be put in the back of a cart. But by the middle of the sixteenth century a distinction between publishing and printing was emerging, and printing was effectively concentrated in the largest towns of Europe.

The new technique for long made small difference to the author. Copyright was at first non-existent and later was secured through the precarious monopoly obtained by municipal or royal privilege; and even this protected the publisher, not the author. Unless he was in partnership with the printer, the author was usually paid in kind, receiving an agreed number of copies of the book. This remuneration, slender as it was, came normally only from the publisher with whom the book was originally placed. Printers felt entirely free to reproduce texts initially produced by others, especially if they were not in the same area, and a popular work (many of Erasmus's fell into this category) was printed up and down Europe without the author's knowledge or approval, still less to his profit. After the establishment of printing the author was thus as dependent on his patron, on obtaining a reward in Church or State, as he had been before. Only a tiny handful of writers—again Erasmus is the best example—can be said to have earned a living from their pens, and in Erasmus's case this was principally due to his editorial work with Froben. On the other hand printing ensured a far wider celebrity than had been possible before and it made reputations more quickly, of patrons as well as of authors. Petrarch and Froissart would not have been better-off or less dependent on private subvention if their books had been printed, but their fame would have grown more rapidly and travelled farther afield.

If the importance of the patron remained unimpaired for centuries and the chances of plagiarism and piracy were vastly increased, the adoption of printing had a more immediate significance for literature in respect of censorship. The supervision of literary works from the viewpoint of their moral, theological or political orthodoxy had been difficult enough in the centuries of manuscript, but a resolute bishop or inquisitor could go far to destroy heretical views as expressed in books, when only a few copies were involved. Once printing began, such total repressions became almost impossible. Yet, coinciding as it did with the growth of religious divisions and political autocracy, sixteenth-century printing was regarded with suspicion and intolerance by a number of vested interests. Given the freedom of circulation enjoyed by the printed book, and often the inaccessibility of the author, the book itself became the subject of prohibition and possession of condemned works an offence. In this the Church took the lead. There was earlier evidence of papal disquiet but the two decisive steps correspond to the limits of this volume: in 1520

Leo X prohibited the dissemination and reading of books tainted with Lutheranism; and in 1559 Paul IV issued the first papal Index. The interval between these two dates was filled by isolated prohibitions and prosecutions which culminated in the issue of systematic lists by the theologians in Louvain and at the Sorbonne. To be effective, such condemnations, those of the pope no less than those of the faculties, needed the support of the civil authorities. Princes and magistrates were often tardy and fickle in responding to the demands of the orthodox, and as far as the author of a prohibited work was concerned he could console himself that censorship by the Catholic authorities was a positive advertisement in Protestant communities. Erasmus's high reputation in Protestant countries undoubtedly rests in part on the total condemnation of all his works by the Index of 1559. As for the Protestant censorship, it was naturally less ambitious and far less effective, for the reformed Church was divided into a score of obediences and had even less coherence than Catholicism. Yet where reformers controlled a small state, as in Geneva after 1542, a censorship no less anxious and irresponsible can be seen at work. It is proper to stress that the control of opinion by Churches was in the event to be frustrated by the printed book. It is none the less true that the fear and uncertainty of persecution bedevilled the life of many a conscientious and quiet writer and printer. Robert Estienne, driven out of Paris by the nagging persecution of the doctors of theology, migrated to Geneva in 1550 and there had to submit with grace to a system of licensing to which even Calvin paid at least lip service. Finally it should not be forgotten that there were a few movements and individuals whom Protestants and Catholics combined to despise and persecute. Concerted intolerance could still go far to stifle opinion: of the 1000 copies which were printed of Servetus's *Christianismi Restitutio* (Vienne, 1553) only three copies seem to have survived, of which one is defective.

It has been estimated that during the so-called incunable or cradle-period of printing, up to 1500, at least 30,000 different editions were produced in Europe.[1] In comparing this, both in quantity and in subject-matter, with the output of manuscripts in the first fifty years of the fifteenth century the historian is gravely handicapped. While incunables have been catalogued with a fair degree of completeness, we are without any similar analysis of later medieval manuscript books. While there seems to be no doubt that more new books made their appearance after printing was established (contemporary authors represent about a sixth of incunable titles), it seems probable that the types of work issued corresponded very closely to the types of literature already popular and well-established. Printing fed on a growing literacy and greatly contributed to the further spread of literacy. But the groups involved, though larger, were no different from those which had earlier patronised manu-

[1] Aside from single sheets of proclamations and the like.

script booksellers. In England the book trade reflects the conservative interest of the northern world. Religious works bulk large (very large if we include liturgical works imported from the continent), followed by law and school books. These categories, which respond in large measure to the needs of professional men, are those which provided the bulk of late medieval manuscripts. About half of Caxton's output was religious in the broadest sense. Wynkyn de Worde's output, that of a printer in a large way of business, is significant: about forty per cent of his publications were directed towards the grammar school curriculum, about twenty-seven per cent to religious works of one kind and another, not counting the forty different liturgical books he issued before his death in 1535.[1]

In Italy, while popular devotion, legal works, bibles, missals and other service books bulked large, early printing reflects also the scholarly, educational and moral preoccupations of humanism.[2] Indeed, Italy witnessed two crises of overproduction in 1472, at Rome and at Venice, due to the eagerness of the printers to anticipate the demand for this kind of literature. Such crises seem not to have occurred north of the Alps where output was more cautiously related to actual demand. All in all about half the total production in Europe prior to 1500 was probably of religious books, and Germany, France and England contributed largely to maintain this proportion. Of the 130 or so incunable editions of the Vulgate only twenty-seven come from Italy; there were eleven editions of Mallermi's Italian translation of the Bible compared with fifteen editions of the scriptures in German dialects. Of Thomas à Kempis's *De Imitatione Christi* no fewer than seventy editions were printed by 1500.

The books published in the first decades of printing reflect the taste of an earlier generation: the books themselves reflect the physical charac-teristics of manuscripts. Printed in types cut to copy as closely as possible the book-hands of the scriveners of the area of publication, the page of print was loaded with black ink, and rubrication by hand as well as the occasional use of vellum instead of paper were intended to add to the illusion that the new article was exactly the same as the old. A dis-criminating book collector like Federigo, duke of Urbino, would have scorned to have a printed book in his library; if such an attitude was not shared by humbler men, there is no doubt that much early printing was ugly. It is, therefore, a matter of some cultural and literary importance that by the end of the fifteenth century a different approach to book design manifests itself. In this the lead was taken by printers and publishers at Venice and notably by the Frenchman Jenson (d. 1480) and by Aldus Manutius (d. 1515). Italian printing copied local scripts, but these were

[1] H. S. Bennett, *English Books and Readers, 1475–1557* (Cambridge, 1952), pp. 188, 242–76.
[2] Victor Scholderer, 'Printers and Readers in Italy in the Fifteenth Century', *Pro-ceedings of the British Academy*, vol. XXXV (1949).

predominantly humanist, and the adoption of 'Roman' and 'italic', together with a clearer ink and a less densely-printed page produced by the early decades of the sixteenth century volumes which were, perhaps, no longer mistakeable for manuscripts but which were often beautiful in themselves. Nothing illustrates better the diffusion of at any rate certain elements in Italian humanism than the spread in northern Europe during the sixteenth century of the civilised typography of Italy. Outside Germany 'black-letter' gradually fell into disuse until it survived mainly to meet the requirements of a few conservative customers, notably the lawyers. From the 1520's the lead in fine typography and in the publication of scholarly books passed from Venice to Paris: this, too, corresponds to cultural trends of a larger kind.

This is not the place to discuss the significance of the printed book in the evolution of pictorial art, but it is appropriate to indicate briefly the implications of printing for scholarship. The importance of this is generally acknowledged so far as early publishers made available in quantity scientific and literary texts. The production of a series of modestly-priced and compact editions of the classics was begun by Aldus at Venice and continued by other publishers. Less easy to estimate is the effect of print on the technique of scholarship. The index to a manuscript volume was an idiosyncrasy of its possessor: the index to a printed volume had to meet the requirements of a larger public, its composition was an exercise in abstraction and led to a more critical appraisal of the text. The gloss surrounding a legal or religious passage in a manuscript was reproduced in printing by 1480, but clearly was less advantageous than the footnote. Even more clear was the ease of reference made possible by the existence of large numbers of more or less identical copies of a work. We accordingly move, with printing, into an era of intense cross-referencing from one book to another, lexicographical activity which would have been inconceivable without the facilities of the printing press. The seal was set on the printed book as an instrument of learning by the publication in 1545 of the first systematic general bibliography, Conrad Gesner's *Bibliotheca Universalis*.

The literature of the period 1520–59, to which we must now turn, was disseminated almost entirely by the printed page, and the general influences of the new process discussed above must be borne in mind. It is, however, far less easy to generalise about sixteenth-century printed books than about incunables, for the simple reason that, while books printed prior to 1500 have been more or less exhaustively listed by scientific bibliographers, our knowledge of subsequent publications is by no means as comprehensive. There is a systematic list of publications in England covering the sixteenth century in the *Short Title Catalogue of Books printed in England, Scotland and Ireland, 1475–1640;*[1] this takes in also books printed in English abroad, but (apart from Latin service books) not books printed abroad in other languages designed for the English market or by English authors, of which there were a considerable number. With this invaluable work as a basis, knowledge of both the quantity and the quality of English literary works in the sixteenth century is more securely established than is the case with the output of continental writers. With the exception of the partially complete author-catalogue of the *Bibliothèque Nationale* in Paris, none of the great continental libraries has a printed catalogue of books and the student who seeks an overall view of sixteenth-century literature must perforce consult the printed catalogues of the British Museum. The dangers of this are evident if one recalls that it has been reckoned that the Museum's holding of French books before 1600 'represents not much more than a fifth of the editions known to have been printed at Paris, and less than a sixth of the output of the French provinces'.[2] It is thus impossible to analyse by bulk or subject the publications of the sixteenth century in the manner possible with printed books in the second half of the fifteenth century. On the other hand a large number of authors have been made the subject of bibliographical study, and a number of important printers and publishers have been investigated.

That the total volume of publication had greatly increased by 1520 compared with 1500 there can be no doubt. This growth in the number of books manufactured each year continues in our period and in the case of England it has been estimated that for every book printed in 1500 four were printed in 1550. There is no reason to suppose that the rise in continental output was smaller; it was probably much higher, particularly in France where no inconsiderable portion of the book trade was devoted to the Spanish and Italian markets, and where before the disintegration of Christendom large numbers of service books were printed for sale in England and Germany. Even after the Lutheran Reformation in Germany and the Henrician Reformation in England, Paris, Basle and other great centres of publishing continued to produce learned works which had an international currency. If only three books by Cicero were published in England in Latin between 1520 and 1559 (*Philippics* 1521, *De senectute* 1535, *De officiis* 1558), this does not mean that English scholars lacked new editions of Cicero in the original, but only that the source for such texts was Venice, Paris, or Basle. The older British libraries are strewn with memorials of the classical educational texts of the continental publishers of the sixteenth century.

---

[1] A. W. Pollard and G. R. Redgrave, London, The Bibliographical Society, 1926; reprinted 1946, 1948; at present under revision.
[2] *Short Title Catalogue of Books printed in France...from 1470–1600 now in the British Museum* (London, 1924), p. iii. Similar catalogues cover Spanish (1921) and Portuguese books (1940).

If there had ever been any real possibility that revived Latin, the Latin of humanism, would develop into a language capable of containing the imagination and reflection of western Europe, the four decades we are considering saw this finally disappear. Italy still possessed the largest number of Latin speakers and writers; but a multitude of vernacular writers showed that almost any subject could be adequately treated in Italian, even if there was still debate (as we shall see) as to what constituted Italian. In France and in Spain the aptitude and ambition of vernacular writers is less evident than in Italy, but is none the less marked. A similar trend is evident in Britain and Germany, though in the latter area to some extent, and in northern and eastern Europe generally, Latin was still virtually a necessity, for the vernaculars were not yet capable of embodying even much ephemeral literature, let alone works of serious import. Yet dependence on Latin outside the Romance area was in the nature of things unlikely to persist. If Latin could not grow further in the lands where it had deep roots, it could scarcely flourish in the areas of Teutonic or Slavonic speech. The trend to vernacular writing is, then, a characteristic of European literature in this period. For all that, an enormous volume of literature was still composed in Latin.

The prestige as well as the utility of Latin was very great. Both ensured a living for the man of Latin letters. Princes and noblemen liked to see their names at the head of epistles dedicatory; so did professors and burgomasters, bishops, councillors, soldiers. Such men had patronage at their disposal in Church and in State. Italian republics and dukes, cities and kings in trans-Alpine Europe, needed Latin clerks to deal with their international correspondence. Busy men of affairs were less important as a public than the scattered intelligentsia of Europe, who also figure largely in the dedications of the Latin writings of the sixteenth century. This contributes an air of coterie to much of this literature: scholars writing for scholars. But though there is truth in this it is only a partial truth. Every country had its scholars—in schools, universities and administration. These men were a small enough proportion of their own communities, but taken together constituted an enormous public, international in character, incapable of hearing a Frenchman in French or a German in German, but eager and able to share in a literature which knew no national boundaries. Such a public accounts for the vast bulk of mid-sixteenth-century Latin writing, while the very quantity of it discourages investigation. Our libraries still contain the great folios of this forgotten Latin; the great *terra incognita* of the history of European civilisation lies today not in manuscripts but in printed books; the Latin literature of the Renaissance has had no historian.[1] Yet at the time the

[1] As is pointed out by Paul von Tieghem in his valuable long essay, 'La littérature Latine de la Renaissance', *Bibliothèque d'Humanisme et Renaissance*, vol. IV (1944), pp. 177–418. This is the only useful general discussion of the subject. In default of a full-scale work it is

patrons and public of Latin included practically all the intellectually eminent and many of the politically influential. This should warn us not to minimise its significance.

The old division between Latin and the vernacular had (with certain notable exceptions) allocated to Latin all serious literature, to the vernaculars all that was popular and ephemeral. This dichotomy, though apparently influential among fourteenth- and fifteenth-century humanists, was progressively challenged by the Latin men of letters. By the sixteenth century a great deal of writing in genres previously monopolised by vernacular was undertaken under the stimulus of the example of the literature of antiquity. Poetry (lyrical, narrative, philosophical and epic) was attempted; drama had its Latin-writing disciples; satires, *jeux d'esprit*, popular morality and works of fiction were all regularly composed in Latin; Greek and oriental texts were translated into Latin as often as into the vernacular; and there was much admiration for collections of letters aiming at the excellences of Cicero and Pliny. This, the lighter side of Renaissance Latin literature, has left few enduring monuments beyond the example it offered to the vernaculars of one and the same vehicle being used for delight as well as for sublimity and scholarship. Poetry of all kinds was prolifically composed, most of it of an amatory or mundane complexion, though everywhere, and especially in Reformation Germany, religious themes are found. Much of this poetry is extremely accomplished and some of it is moving. What makes it important, however, is that it greatly influenced later vernacular writers, and judged by this standard the *Basia* of the Dutch poet Johannes Secundus (d. 1535) demands notice here, and so does the Christian epic of the Italian Vida (d. 1566), his *Christiad* (1535), as well as his *Poetica* (1527). Elegies, eclogues, satires and epigrams distinguish a galaxy of other writers too numerous to mention. Theatrical pieces, composed often for pedagogical purposes, were soon adapted to the needs of propaganda and polemic. Between 1530 and 1560 religious drama in Latin enjoyed a remarkable popularity in Germany and the Low Countries, Naogeorgus (Thomas Kirchmeyer, d. 1563) being one of the most important authors of this kind of play. Elsewhere in northern Europe religious plays were only less in evidence, the much read and much translated *Jephthes* (1542) of George Buchanan (d. 1582) illustrating this. This tradition was to be exploited in favour of Catholicism by Jesuit dramatists later in the century.

In the field of satirical writing and popular morality the greatest figure is Erasmus (d. 1536), whose activity as a scholar will occupy us later. The *Adagia*, frequently reprinted and extended, were more than a collection of proverbs, frequently being developed into essays on currently debated

still profitable to consult H. Hallam, *Introduction to the Literature of Europe in the XV, XVI and XVII Centuries*, 1837–9 and later reprints.

topics. The *Colloquia* (1518), soon departing from their starting point as a manual of Latin conversation, became racy dialogues of biting satire and comic censure. In these types of literature Erasmus had imitators but no equals. In another field Erasmus represents the tastes of the period—his letters. First published in 1516, these were later expanded in collected editions. They represent only a fraction of his correspondence and were selected and revised before publication. The *labor limae* even more obtrusively colours the letters of other celebrated Latinists of the period; even in the case of a Sadoleto (d. 1547) or a Bembo (d. 1547) it could justly be said that their epistles were composed as exercises, *scriptae magis quam missae*, as a contemporary put it.

An air of unreality tends to hang over the types of neo-Latin literature we have just considered, but it does not equally blur the appreciation of the Latin scholarship of the period. To the writer of a serious work Latin still offered in most areas of Europe the only language of precision besides being the only means of crossing linguistic frontiers. It was, moreover, traditionally associated with erudition, and in practically every subject terminology and method indicated it as the vehicle of composition. Theologians, scientists, educationalists, philologists and historians therefore normally wrote in Latin. The content of a good deal of theological literature is discussed in detail elsewhere in this book.[1] Here we may merely observe some of the consequences of the Reformation in this department of scholarship. The first effect was the influence of theological values in all speculation.

It is no more easy to distinguish theology and philosophy during the Renaissance than it is during the Middle Ages, but in the anxious decades that followed Luther's challenge to Rome the speculative thinker found his works scrutinised for their theological implications with a rigour characteristic of the thirteenth century. The theologians on each side devoted their best energies to demolishing their opponents. In this polemic the very grace and culture of the Italian apologists of Rome seemed insufferable in Lutheran circles. Luther himself was content 'to bellow in bad Latin', and it was long before the influence of Melanchthon made good style a characteristic of Lutheran debate. On the other hand Béza and, to an even greater extent, Calvin, were Latinists of no mean order. Midway between the papalists in Italy, at Louvain and in the Sorbonne, and their opponents stood for a time Erasmus, lonely in a world where violent dogma was destroying good letters and 'Christian philosophy', as he called it. Neoplatonic or pantheistic doctrines which had seemed innocuous at the start of the century were now anathema in all religious camps. Lucretianism (like that of the Italian Palingenius, d. 1543?) and Anabaptism such as tinged the works of the Dutch play-

---

[1] Cf. chapters III–IX. Other scholarly works in Latin are discussed in section 2 of this chapter and in ch. XIII.

wright Gnapheus (d. 1568) were equally proscribed. The mixture of Averroism and Stoicism propounded by Pomponazzi at Padua (d. 1525) was regarded with hardly less disapproval. The contemporary rise in the prestige of Aristotle in all areas and of St Thomas among Catholics, important as these developments were to be for the future, is swamped by the urgent and acrid theology of controversy and condemnation.

Historians in Latin abound. Later critics have distinguished in this field a division between the followers of Flavius Blondus (Biondo, d. 1463), an exponent of antiquarian exactitude, and those of Aretinus (Leonardo Bruni, d. 1444), first of the great rhetorical writers. But by the sixteenth century these two schools were in practice much assimilated, and the new historiography—closely associated with the new diplomacy—shared the characteristics of both. Humanist writers tended to a fine display of language; orations abound, both in direct speech and in *oratio obliqua*; names of persons and institutions are latinised sometimes out of recognition. Yet, ornate and polished as many of these histories were, they are yet full of a new critical sense, avoid the mythical and doubt the legendary, base themselves on authentic source material, and usually accept (albeit unwillingly) the unstylish and compromising terminology of the Christian calendar and chronology. Italian principalities and republics took the lead in the new history and at first it was practised elsewhere mainly by emigré Italians: Paulus Aemilius (d. 1529) in France, Polydore Vergil (d. 1555) in England, Marinus Siculus (d. 1533) and Peter Martyr (of Anghiera, d. 1526) in Spain. Soon native writers acquired the new manner, as is exemplified by the Spaniards Antonio de Lebrija (Nebrisensis, d. 1522) and Sepulveda (d. 1573?) and the French continuator of Paulus Aemilius, Arnoul le Ferron (d. 1563). Germany (in historiography as in other fields) resisted the Italian manner, continued an interest in the universal chronicle which was elsewhere unfashionable, and was rent by disputes which sought arguments in a confessional treatment of the past. Some of these works had enormous success in Protestant lands, as did the *Chronicle* of Johannes Carion (d. 1537), later expanded by Melanchthon (1558–60). On the imperialist side the *Commentarii* of Sleidan (Johann Philipson, d. 1556) were equally noteworthy. One general work only was in the humanist tradition, the *Rerum Germanicarum libri iii* of Beatus Rhenanus (d. 1547); there are a number of regional historians of merit. The religious controversy in Germany had, however, one important result: it provoked the collaborators known as the 'Centuriators of Magdeburg' under the leadership of Flacius Illyricus (d. 1575) to produce an ecclesiastical history of a quite new kind, the first volume of which appeared in 1559; the *Annales ecclesiastici*, the Catholic reply of Baronius (d. 1607), as revised and continued by others, is still a work on which historians rely today. Italy had at this time a considerable number of highly reputed Latin historians, but the real originality of the Italians in this field (apart from the polished but superficial biographies and the contemporary history composed by Paulus Giovius, d. 1552) lay in vernacular writings. And it is for their ubiquitous influence on vernacular historiography that the Latin historical writers are important. With the historians we may perhaps link two men predominantly legal in their training and interests—Guillaume Budé (d. 1540) and Andrea Alciato (d. 1550). Budé's fame has survived less as a writer on legal antiquities and more as a Greek scholar; Alciato is best known not for his historical approach to civil law but for his *Emblemata* (1531), a collection of moral symbols which was frequently issued in illustrated editions and profoundly influenced the iconography of the later Renaissance.

The approach of Budé and Alciati in their technical writings was essentially philological, and philology, in a broad sense, accounts for much of the learned Latin of the sixteenth century, and much that was both valuable and influential. To go no further than the work of Erasmus after 1520: in secular literature we find editions of Cicero, Seneca, Suetonius, Curtius, Aristotle, Ptolemy, and translations of Galen and Xenophon: in patristic texts Jerome, Cyprian, Arnobius, Hilary, Irenaeus, Ambrose, Augustine, Lactantius, Origen, and translations of Chrysostom and Basil. This formidable list must be augmented by the productions of many other scholars, individually less productive, together adding up to the publication of practically all important (and many unimportant) texts of Greek, Latin and Christian antiquity. The *editiones principes* of these works have been listed on several occasions, even if we cannot make confident statements about the number of occasions on which the more popular texts were re-issued. It is clear, however, that the example of Aldus in publishing modestly priced, authoritative and compact editions of the classics was now widely followed in France and Germany; and that the Venetian leadership in Greek printing had now passed to Paris, where Robert Estienne (d. 1559) was a scholar-printer in the grand manner.

Though reactionary clergy were suspicious of humanism and sometimes openly hostile to the study of Greek and Hebrew, religious bitterness on the whole did not seriously impede classical scholarship; a respect for a republic of classical letters was a sentiment fragile perhaps, but none the less pervasive. In one field, however, sectarian animosity played havoc: Bible scholarship. The Lutheran movement coincided with the issue of Erasmus's New Testament (1516 Greek and Latin, 1519 the new Latin version), and the final publication of the edition of the Polyglot Bible inspired by Cardinal Ximenes (Alcalá, 1520). Erasmus's critical approach had already been indicated by his edition of Valla's *Adnotationes* (1505); the team of scholars assembled by Ximenes were more cautious in their approach. But the fury of the attack on the new application of learning to the scriptures, led by theologians whose suspicions had been aroused by the evangelistic proclivities of many of the scholars concerned and notably Erasmus himself, knew no bounds. The consequences were immense. Erasmus was compelled to revise his text in a direction he knew to be false (notably in the case of the famous interpolation in 1 John v. 7); Robert Estienne, whose great edition of the Vulgate (1538–40) remained for centuries the main scholarly edition, incurred the censure of the Sorbonne and had ultimately to leave Paris for Geneva (1550); and one of the effective resolutions of the Council of Trent made the Vulgate text sacrosanct for Catholics, while Protestants were extremely chary of a scientific approach to it. Much of the philological equipment of the scholars who laboured on the Greek, Hebrew and Latin scriptures was, on the other hand, defective. The science of paleography was unborn and Erasmus considered an eleventh-century MS. as ancient. Catalogues did not exist of many of the relevant libraries of manuscripts, and it was hazard and chance proximity that led to the collation of the texts used even by so indefatigable a worker as Estienne.

If the sixteenth century lacked the aid of paleography, it acquired systematic lexicography. The interest of the fifteenth-century humanists in this direction had been intense but erratic: individual authors had been studied, but as a general dictionary the student's best aid was the dictionary of Calepinus (Ambrogio Calepio, d. 1511) which did not match the quality of most of the texts to which it was perforce a guide. In 1531 Robert Estienne published the first edition of his *Thesaurus*. Reprinted in 1536 and 1543, this work grew larger and more reliable, offering an example to the compilers of lexicons not only of the classical language but also of modern languages. It was Henri Estienne (d. 1598) who performed the same work for Greek (1572).

Robert Estienne's *Thesaurus* improved on earlier works by excluding 'non-classical' authors. This brings us to the most vexed and interesting problem of neo-Latin literature in the early sixteenth century: Ciceronianism, its advocates and opponents. For a variety of non-stylistic reasons the study of Cicero had loomed large amongst humanist preoccupations in the late fourteenth and fifteenth centuries. Yet, while admiration for his style was widespread, the livelier Latinists were for long in practice free of consistent obedience to his vocabulary and syntax; *grammatica* was tempered by *genialità*; and Valla, the ablest linguist of the early fifteenth century, delivered a broadside at the Ciceronians of his day. Valla's very exactitude, however, signalised the dawn of a new epoch in criticism. Intermittent debates followed—between Politian and Paolo Cortesi, Gianfrancesco Pico della Mirandola and Bembo, in which both in numbers and influence the Ciceronians slowly gained. The final campaign was more bitter than these earlier skirmishes. Erasmus, who had thought much about the problem at any rate from 1516, published his *Ciceronianus* in 1528: the issue at once became entangled in questions of national prestige and religious orthodoxy. Italy, overrun by French and German troops, had taken refuge in her cultural ascendancy as a compensation for her political weakness. The 'imperialism' of Leo X and succeeding popes encouraged this sentiment. Rome had become the centre of a rigid Ciceronianism which was the symbol both of a defeated people and a Church still clinging to its ecumenical mission. Erasmus's attack was wounding not merely to a handful of scholars but to emotions of patriotism and pride in the religious primacy of Rome. Erasmus failed entirely to understand the nature of this identification of classical and Christian Rome: his opponents—lacking his originality, stung by his irony, confident of their linguistic purity—were totally oblivious of the suspicion of paganism and irreligion which their vocabulary aroused in northern Europe. Erasmus catalogued the verbal ingenuity of the Roman school (*Jupiter* for *Deus*, *Apollo* for *filius*, *factio* for *haeresis*, *christiana persuasio* for *fides*, *legati* for *apostoli*, *patres conscripti* for *cardinales* and so forth) and concluded, 'we profess Jesus in our mouths, but it is Jove and Romulus we carry in our hearts'. The Italian coteries assaulted Erasmus not only as a barbarian but as a Lutheran heretic, one who was patently undermining universal Christendom by advocating an eclecticism at once ugly and impious. The storm thus reflects more than merely literary questions and it is highly significant that the most active opponents of Erasmus lived in France—Julius Caesar Scaliger (d. 1558) and Étienne Dolet (d. 1546). Even in Latin literature the age of Italian leadership was passing away. So, too, was the period when Latin could claim attention as a vital vehicle of original literature. The pedantry and purism of the exponents of Latin (and Ciceronianism and *Virgilianità* were dominant for a further century even in Protestant lands where they had originally met resistance) went far to destroy its hold on the imagination of creative writers. Latin became merely part of the curriculum; the vernaculars laid claim to life.

In considering vernacular literature it is important to remember that at this time Latin and the vernacular were often used by the same writers, and that even writers who normally wrote in a vulgar tongue were steeped in Latin at school. The exceptions to this, though not negligible and though significant of later trends, are small in number. In style, in vocabulary, and in their literary ambitions writers of Italian and French were by the mid-sixteenth century profoundly affected by classical antiquity and by Renaissance Latin works. Since Italy was the main centre of humanist activity it is hardly surprising that Italian literature at this time displays a maturity much greater than is to be found north of the Alps. Renaissance Latin had aimed to be the medium of all experience; it offered an example of fixed orthography and grammar, and transmitted a rich but disciplined set of forms. Such an object lesson was presented to all

Europe in the course of the sixteenth century: and Italian itself could display to less advanced literatures the further stage of a vernacular moulded by its intimate association with revived Latin. For, besides their Latin models in antiquity and modern times, the sixteenth-century Italian also had before him the example of the vulgar writing of the fourteenth-century writers, Dante, Petrarch and Boccaccio. These men were regarded with almost as much veneration as Vergil and Cicero. The Italian, in short, had not only ancient but also in practice modern 'classics', though of course the canon of Italian literature was by no means firmly established by the sixteenth century.

The principal monuments of Italian literary excellence, which will be referred to in the ensuing pages, provide the main evidence for the superiority of Italian writing at this time. But three other peninsular developments are also suggestive of a sophistication to which northern Europe could not as yet pretend. The first of these is the debate as to the very value and nature of the Italian vernacular itself. The *questione della lingua* comprised two very different problems: was the use of a vernacular compatible with serious composition? and, if so, which of the various Italian vernaculars should be employed or should an Italian be developed which could transcend provincial dialects? Though the first question was still debated in the sixteenth century, it had already been answered in practice and Bembo's *Prose della volgar lingua* (1525) provided a theoretical defence of the vernacular all the more telling in that it was the work of one of the most accomplished Latinists of the day. The controversy went on; conservatives deplored the decline in Latin scholarship and pointed out that *trecento* masters themselves had used Latin for serious works; but the abundant harvest in the vernacular was a sufficient answer and Giambattista Gelli (d. 1563) even argued that it was a waste of time to learn ancient tongues. The other and ensuing dilemma was less obviously resolved. Bembo (although a Venetian) gave his support to Tuscan, but here provincial rivalries of a political kind came into play, for Italy had no capital city and Rome, Naples, Lombardy and Venice could challenge the cultural primacy of Florence. Indeed, it was from the background of the small court of Urbino that the Lombard Baldassare Castiglione urged the case for a courtly Italian, the language of gentlemen, eclectic and refined, the solution which had been offered two centuries earlier by Dante in his *De Vulgari Eloquentia*, where he had advanced the claims of a language 'illustrious, cardinal, and courtly'. This issue consequently remained a lively one. But in practice the existence of the fourteenth-century masterpieces of Dante, Petrarch and Boccaccio (the *Tre Fontane* of N. Liburnio's grammatical study, 1526) provided a standard or norm which the sixteenth-century writers for the most part accepted, while the 'imitation' of them was sedulously advocated by many theorists. Thus *Fiorentinità* and *volgare illustre* were far from being mutually exclusive in practice and what remains significant in the prolonged debate is the maturity of the vernacular which was being analysed.

A second facet of Italian precociousness is seen in the remarkable verse of Teofilo Folengo (d. 1544). Macaronic writing was no new thing when Folengo published his *Baldus* in 1517. It sprang naturally from a world in which Latin mingled with the vernaculars of common life and is found in medieval poetry; and it nearly always carried satirical overtones. But Folengo's hexameters raise the *genre* to a new level. Couched in the framework of the prevailing Italian epic, his poem has a compulsion and a racy realism which display an astonishing flexibility in both the Latin and Italian languages he was blending, and which were entirely consonant with his cynical purpose. Equally his verse is a tribute to the Italian public which called for four editions by 1552, as well as other works in the same manner, and which could relish the anti-rhetorical twist of Folengo's mind. Such ingenuity of manner and spirit are not uniquely Italian: Rabelais read Folengo and reveals a certain indebtedness to him both in vocabulary and in his approach to the mock-heroic. But *Baldus* could only have emerged in a society where literacy in both Latin and vernacular was widely diffused, where bourgeois values were explicitly accepted, and where high seriousness was not called for in a writer.

The third phenomenon peculiar to Italy was the prestige accorded to Pietro Aretino (d. 1556). Aretino's fame, which enabled him to curry favour with the great, to hobnob with pope and emperor and to live at Venice in considerable style, was entirely due to his ruthless pen. The profits of authorship were in his case vast, for he procured patronage by the threat of vitriolic attack and rejoiced in his power to make and break reputations. His work was journalism, whether he was writing astrological prognostications, obscene satires such as the *Ragionamenti* (1534) or works of lush conventionality such as his *Umanità di Christo* (1534). All was grist to his mill, and his trenchant, lithe style raised the vernacular to a point where the colloquial, the intimate and the informal were capable of perfect expression. This is more particularly seen in his letters, of which six volumes appeared between 1537 and 1557 and which provoked the emergence of a fashion for publishing vernacular correspondence. Aretino depended on a society where actuality was regarded as a merit, where literature was permeated by urban values, and where the public demanded to be amused and intrigued rather than elevated.

Elsewhere in Europe the audience to which vernacular writers could aspire was both smaller and more conservative. The Italian towns dominated the culture of the Peninsula. Elsewhere the bourgeoisie though important was not determinant: artistic modes and manners were coloured by older aristocratic and ecclesiastical values, or by popular elements as yet unassimilated in the current of polite literature. Paris and London were rising centres, but France and England were still lands where cohesion depended on the gravitation of magnates to a king; the same is true of the Iberian kingdoms; and in Germany the large and flourishing cities expressed their cultural aspirations in old-fashioned and largely religious terms, sharing in this way an attitude displayed by the aristocratic elements in the country. The patronage of letters by the Italian princes of the fifteenth and sixteenth centuries went far to transposing Italian melodies to a key in which they could be appreciated in northern Europe: but it was long before the resulting harmonies lost the courtly artificiality they thus acquired. What struck northern European writers about the Italian scene was the erudition, the scholarship of the Italians, not their ability to achieve popular realism. Bembo rather than Folengo or Aretino, the rhetorical rather than the anti-pedantic writers, were what non-Italians admired in Italian literature. It is significant that Joachim du Bellay (d. 1560) in his *Deffence et Illustration de la Langue françoyse* (1549) lifted nearly all his arguments for the vernacular from Italian sources, and especially from the *Dialogo delle lingue* of Sperone Speroni (d. 1588) while being both inspired by, and desiring positively to rival, the triumphs of Italian literature, viewed as a medium almost as refined and perfect as Latin and Greek. Some aspects of these processes may be revealed by a brief review of the main types of literature in the principal countries of the continent.

In poetry, during the decades we are considering, there are few outstanding writers. In Italy the period between Ariosto and Tasso is—despite the large number of poets—relatively arid. Petrarchism was dominant: even the opponents of the convention were constrained only to parody the Petrarchists. Exquisite and polished though they were, the verses of the Petrarchisti and Bembisti, which were composed by small coteries in all the Italian towns, rank as minor art; the verse of Francesco Maria Molza (d. 1544), Galeazzo di Tarsia (d. 1553) and Luigi Tansillo (d. 1568) live on only in anthologies; of the three women poets, Veronica Gambara (d. 1550), Vittoria Colonna (d. 1547) and Gaspara Stampa (d. 1554), only the last rises above the frigidity and perfectionism to which emulation of Petrarch normally led. The burlesque verses of Francesco Berni (d. 1535), though they too are Petrarchist in manner, fall into another category, for their parody mirrored a more popular and richer strain in the Italian scene, the satirical spirit already noted: his revision of Boiardo also responded to popular taste. Only one poet carries profound conviction, Michelangelo (d. 1564). Among the mellifluous versifiers of the day his harsh lines struck a discordant, anguished note; he alone broke out of the prevailing convention to speak with his own voice.

Yet if Petrarchism was inherently a limitation in Italy, its effect elsewhere in Europe was highly stimulating. Italian influences in French verse are already evident in the work of Clément Marot, though his attraction lies less in his espousal of a new manner than in his witty and honest application of traditional forms and themes; his translations of the Psalms were a more significant innovation and linked him with the reforming element in France, with the Calvinists in Switzerland, and with Italy again, where he died in 1544. The majority of contemporary versifiers were content to employ the old devices of the *rhétoriqueurs*, but Margaret of Navarre (d. 1549), an even greater patron of letters than her brother King Francis I, reveals, like Marot whom she protected, both Italian influence and the current of reforming sentiment; in her case these combined to give her verse an individual note, reflecting her own spiritual difficulties. The decade following the death of Margaret saw, however, the establishment of a consistently novel poetical tradition: in 1558 was published Joachim du Bellay's *Antiquitez de Rome* and *Regrets*; and in 1560 appeared the first collected edition of the poems of Pierre de Ronsard (d. 1585). The intellectual and sentimental origins of the Pléiade, of whom du Bellay and Ronsard were the greatest luminaries,[1] go back behind the formation of the 'brigade' round Ronsard in Paris and its first manifesto, du Bellay's *Deffence* of 1549: they owed more than they were at first prepared to admit to the *école marotique*, to Mellin de Saint-Gelais (d. 1558) and to Maurice Scève (d. 1564?), the most illustrious of a group of poets at Lyons who mediated between Italy, and the Italian discovery of antiquity, and France. Du Bellay's *Deffence*, with its sweeping condemnation of medieval poetical manners and its trenchant demand for a French literature akin to and equalling the literature of the classical world, was too incoherent to have itself created a new mode. This was established not by theory but by practice; by du Bellay's own exercises in the Petrarchan manner and his nostalgic response to Rome as well as to 'la douceur Angevine'; above all by Ronsard, not content only to triumph in a minor key but attempting the ode, the hymn, and the lofty epic.

In Spain, as in England, Italian influences were also at work. Juan Boscan (d. 1542) deliberately attempted the use of Italian forms and his friend Garcilaso de la Vega (d. 1536) was even more successful in conveying the subtleties of platonic love in the new manner. Already in the fifteenth century Spanish writers had been influenced by Italy. In England the literary contact with Italy was still tenuous in the mid-sixteenth century, and the Petrarchan attempts of Sir Thomas Wyatt (d. 1542) were laboured; the earl of Surrey (Henry Howard, d. 1547) was much happier with the sonnet, and probably drew out of Italy the notion of using blank verse for his partial translation of the *Aeneid*. But in Britain the 'late medieval' frequently displays more spirit and accomplishment than the 'Drab Age' which succeeded;[2] no better proof of this is needed than the

---

[1] The other names traditionally included in the Pléiade are: J. A. de Baïf, E. Jodelle, Pontus de Tyard, R. Belleau and J. Dorat.
[2] The terms are used as in C. S. Lewis, *English Literature in the Sixteenth Century* (Oxford 1954).

flourishing of verse in Scotland in the first half of the sixteenth century. Scotland, even remoter from foreign influence than her southern neighbour, produced a series of important poets, Douglas, Dunbar[1] and (in our period) Sir David Lindsay of the Mount (d. 1552/5). These men were handling traditional metres and forms with skill and sensitivity; so with all his eccentricity was the English poet John Skelton (d. 1529). Behind Spanish, Scottish and English verse, and even more prominently in Scandinavia, lay a ballad tradition, popular poetry in the fullest sense, but as yet largely uncommitted to print. Nowhere, however, is the influence of Italy more absent than in Germany, hostile, as already noted, to much that Italian humanism stood for. Nowhere did medieval traditions flourish longer. Hans Sachs (d. 1576) was the most prolific of the German verse-writers. The hymns of the reformed Church, and notably of Luther himself, original as they are, belong in many respects to an older lyrical tradition.

This short review of European poetry shows that the mainly urban, refined, Petrarchan styles dominant in Italy had by 1560 been to a great extent received in France, to a lesser extent in Spain and only slightly elsewhere. A not dissimilar picture emerges from a survey of developments in the field of drama. In most parts of northern Europe the medieval stage still flourished in the sixteenth century: at any rate before religious purists discouraged them, mystery plays, rooted in the popular apprehension of religion, continued to attract large audiences. Indeed, the early sixteenth century witnessed some of the most elaborate productions of which record remains, like that at Valenciennes in 1547. But the mid-years of the century saw the mystery play falling into official disrepute among both Catholics and Protestants. Another traditional genre, the morality or dramatised allegory, was only submerged by rival types of entertainment in the second half of the century, though its potentialities for political satire made it often the target of criticism by princes and magistrates. The morality developed farthest in France. There the capital city had recognised companies, such as the *Enfants sans Souci* of which Pierre Gringore (d. 1538) was a member, and specialised entertainments, off-shoots of the morality proper, the *soties* and *farces*; the *farce* especially was tenacious of life and survived the supercilious contempt of the new poets. Here again Scotland provides an instructive comment, for in Lindsay's *Ane Satyre of the Thre Estaitis* we have a morality which in its construction and in the wit of its language can fairly claim to be a classic of its kind, although composed as late as 1540, when it was produced in Linlithgow. In France and in England chronicle plays make their appearance in the mid-sixteenth century; the English chronicle play was to be extremely influential in later dramatic development. So in Spain was the *auto sacramental*, a popular drama, religious in origin, and destined to reach its farthest evolution in the seventeenth century.

[1] Cf. vol. I, p. 190.

Only in Italy had a new type of drama reached a vernacular language by the middle of the sixteenth century. *Sacre rappresentazioni* are still found, but they were relegated now to remoter areas and to the uncultivated. In Italy as elsewhere the mystery play bequeathed a more permanent legacy in the comic interlude (*intermezzo*). This, however, was neglected by the humanists for a more learned type of play, based on the revival of ancient drama. Translations of Plautus and Terence, as well as contemporary Latin plays similar in character, were among the aristocratic entertainments staged at Ferrara and Urbino, and soon popular at Rome and elsewhere. These esoteric exercises were by themselves of only short-term interest: but they unquestionably provoked the more significant comedies of Ariosto and Machiavelli (the latter's play *Mandragola* is especially notable).[1] The vernacular comedy in Italy, however, in fact did not progress much from the point which it had reached by 1520; nor did tragedy.[2] On the other hand the combination of the form of classical comedy with the older intermezzo tradition produced the *commedia dell' arte*. This remarkable development, where the company played *extempore* from a repertoire of stereotyped plots and characters, has naturally left few memorials of its early beginnings (the earliest documentary evidence is a Paduan contract of 1545); it naturally did not appeal to writers; and they, cut off from the actuality of the theatre, no longer produced plays of theatrical as opposed to literary merit. Thus the popular theatre in Italy was practically divorced from literature. In other parts of Europe, as we have seen,[3] many plays were written in Latin and a number of Erasmus's dialogues are racy and dramatic. These compositions, many of them pedagogic in intention, exercised on the whole a beneficent influence on the development of the theatre. The marriage between scholarship and popular drama accomplished in the end so brilliantly in England, France and Spain, presumably owed much to the existence in these countries of centralised governments and capital cities.

The strength and variety of imaginative prose writing in Italy, on the other hand, is striking testimony of the wide diffusion of bourgeois values in the peninsula. As in poetry, so here the fourteenth century provided an exemplar of genius. Boccaccio's spirit continued to inspire novelists in the mid-sixteenth century, though the stream of invention was giving signs of drying up: artistry was succumbing to the desire merely to distract; or was (through the practices of the endless writers of dialogues and treatises on platonic love) tending towards euphuism. The Arcadian or pastoral novel was to come of all this, but realism was submerged only with difficulty. If it is lost sight of in many of the essays and dialogues, like the work of

[1] Cf. vol. I, p. 175.
[2] The prestige accorded to Vitruvius and the influence of theatrical architects are supposed to have had discouraging effects.
[3] Above, p. 369.

Giovanni della Casa (d. 1556), the *Galateo* (on manners), or the *Ragiona-menti d'amore* of Agnolo Firenzuola (d. 1543), it would still be hard to deny it to Castiglione's *Courtier*, which rings true as a picture of the charm and stateliness of the Urbino court. But the novelist proper was closer to the people and even in attempting to astonish and horrify drew on deeper and more popular traditions than the humanists as such could appropriate. The better novelists thus had a universality which gave their works a European appeal, and there were soon translations and adaptations north of the Alps of the stories of G.-F. Straparola (d. *c.* 1557), A. F. Grazzini (Il Lasca, d. 1584) and M. Bandello (d. 1561).

In the north, however, the taste for fiction had its own roots in both *fabliaux* and *nouvelles* and in the declining but still popular prose epic of chivalry. This last, indeed, enjoyed a revival in the first half of the six-teenth century. Vast and rambling chivalrous stories are characteristic of Spain in particular: *Amadis of Gaul* is more representative of Spanish taste than the realism of the picaresque *Lazarillo de Tormes* (1554). *Amadis* was immensely successful in France, where Lancelot, Tristram and the rest had maintained their hold, and in England a similar pre-occupation is reflected in the translations of Lord Berners (Sir John Bourchier, d. 1533)—Froissart, *Arthur of Little Britain, Huon of Bordeaux.* Chivalrous love is one of the ingredients also in the *Heptameron* of Margaret of Navarre; though the framework of this collection of stories derives from Boccaccio, the moral impulse is essentially northern.

The greatest and most original imaginative writer of northern Europe at this time is François Rabelais in whose work practically every aspect of the literary trends we have discussed is reflected—heroic, humanist, realist. By background a provincial bourgeois, in religion successively a friar, a monk and a secular priest, Rabelais was essentially a university man, graduating ultimately as doctor of medicine. In this capacity he entered the entourage of Jean du Bellay and with him made the first of several visits to Italy. These Italian contacts doubtless confirmed his humanist inclinations, but it was at Lyons that they were first encouraged, at Lyons that he published both medical and archeological works, and at Lyons that he issued *Pantagruel* in 1533. *Gargantua* followed in 1534 but the *Tiers Livre* did not appear till 1546; the *Quart Livre* came out in 1548. After Rabelais's death in Paris in 1553 there was a partial publication of the *Cinquiesme Livre* in 1562, and a complete edition in 1564.[1] The genius of Rabelais as it is revealed in *Gargantua, Pantagruel* and their sequels is multifarious; he has been claimed as an atheist, a Protestant, a Catholic; as an Erasmian humanist, as the first of the *honnêtes gens*; as last of the medievals, first of the moderns. His place today is assured by his satirical observation of the world he loved, by his display of an extraordinary

---

[1] It is now generally agreed that as it stands the *Cinquiesme Livre* is not entirely Rabelais's work.

humanist omniscience and an optimistic view of nature, especially of human nature. At the time it was the fantasy that appealed, the allegory both medieval and Renaissance, the mock heroics and burlesque, the didactic intervals (which grew longer in the later books) and above all the relish for words. This verbal intoxication may pall on the twentieth-century ear. Then it was the apt vehicle for the heady mixture of a Gothic and a Latin world, the Gothic world of giants and the Latin world of the abbey of Thélème, a popular northern and an exotic southern tradition, meeting and mingling in a joyous, exuberant and well-stocked mind.

The use of the vernaculars for imaginative writing was nothing new: it had been accepted as their role in the Middle Ages. It is therefore by observing the stages by which the vernaculars penetrated into the field of serious writing that we have the best measure of their growing autonomy. This was virtually complete in Italy, but in other countries progress was slower and far beyond the sixteenth century Latin remained an important medium for scholarship. Nevertheless the mid-decades of the century saw a remarkable advance, partly through translations and partly through the composition of original works.

The volume of translations was formidable. Although a good many works were translated from one 'modern' language into another (as, for example, French chivalrous romances were at this time put into German), the bulk of translation was from Latin and neo-Latin and from Greek; and certainly it was from the second type of translation that the vernaculars stood to benefit most in vocabulary, syntax, and style. Italy undoubtedly took the lead in translations, and in particular was noteworthy for vernacular versions of Greek authors, but France was not far behind. Much of this activity has not survived the test of time. Texts, both Greek and Latin, were faulty; translations of Greek originals were often made from imperfect Latin versions; verse was translated into verse at the expense of literalness; and at all times and in all ways the translator forced his author into the mould of sixteenth-century convention. It is, therefore, only when the manner of the translator and his text coincide that art as such (aside from the diffusion of ideas, however inaccurate) resulted. This was rare enough in our period, but the tendency to a secular morality in the public for whom he was writing, as well as his own scholarship, made J. Amyot's *Plutarch's Lives* (1559) a notable work. Translations of humanist Latin did not suffer from the difficulty of accommodating ancient ideas in modern language. Thus the translations of Erasmus's *Encomium Moriae* made almost at the time it was written (1511) have a vigorous sympathy which later versions necessarily lack (French and German 1520, Italian 1539, English 1549); much the same is true of More's *Utopia* (1516) in the earliest vernacular renderings (German 1524, Italian 1548, French 1550, English 1551).

Translations of the Bible fall into a separate category. The nature of the text precluded the brash treatment accorded to secular writings; a long tradition of whole or partial translations, which had already acclimatised many passages in the vernacular, circumscribed translators; and the whole question was soon a major issue between reformers and counter-reformers. So far as this last point is concerned it must be left to the general history of the Reformation. As far as the significance of the Bible in literature is concerned, two points must be made. First, the attraction of certain parts of the Bible was very great, irrespective of piety, to sixteenth-century writers: Marot in France, Wyatt in England found the Psalms a challenge. It is hard to see how earlier writers had avoided such a stimulus of a purely literary kind, and it may be that the atmosphere of bible scholarship was needed to release what was to be a permanent pre-occupation in later literature, to 'paraphrase' Holy Writ. The second point is the consequence for literature at a national level of vernacular versions of the one book which was generally read. Luther's German translation (1522 onwards) which reached 377 editions by his death in 1546, is deservedly the most spectacular and most often-quoted example. In linguistically as well as politically divided Germany the unifying effects of a compelling version of scripture was naturally a noteworthy event: Catholic versions (Eck's of 1537) failed to capture support, and the most that the orthodox could do was to modify Luther's text which became the greatest single contribution to the formation of a single German language. Elsewhere the Bible had less dramatic consequences, though everywhere in the decades from 1520 to 1560 translators were at work: Lefèvre d'Étaples and Olivetan for France and French Switzerland, Tyndale and Coverdale for England, Pedersen for Denmark and many others.

However novel translations of the Bible seemed in the sixteenth century, the practice was old enough. Theology, on the other hand, was the senior university discipline of the Middle Ages, and Latin was its natural means of expression. This state of affairs was hardly changed in the sixteenth century, but the religious controversy of the period was conducted increasingly in the vulgar tongues. Many of Luther's and Calvin's polemical writings were in German and French respectively. Even more impressive was Calvin's translation into French of his own *Institutes* (1541), the first occasion on which a theologian developed a learned thesis in a modern language. On the other hand, though Catholics were compelled to answer Protestants in their own terms and thus in the vernaculars, the association of vernacular theology (and Bible translations) with reform in religion hardened the attitude to these subjects of orthodox authority, from the Sorbonne's querulous hostility in the 1520's to the measured distrust of the fathers at Trent. The other sciences, in the hands of corporations with no call to publicise or proselytise, gave way more slowly—law (canon and civil), natural science, philosophy and medicine, though in the case of medicine a growing number of practitioners of a kind humbler than the lofty doctors led to vulgarisation of texts and treatises.

Only in one field did serious vernacular prose make considerable advances—history. For this, too, there were precedents in plenty. Vernacular historiography is found everywhere from the thirteenth century onwards, and the case of Commynes had shown that, even without humanist influence, a critical or analytical view of the past was emerging in northern Europe. It would be entirely wrong to underestimate the value of the older historiographical tradition in the sixteenth century. It was through versions of the *Grandes Chroniques* and not Paulus Aemilius that the average sixteenth-century Frenchman derived his knowledge of the past; it may indeed be doubted whether there was much explicit humanist inspiration behind the historical and antiquarian erudition of John Leland (d. 1552) or of Estienne Pasquier (d. 1615), who published the first book of his *Recherches de la France* in 1560; and it was something of a chronological accident that made the chronicler Edward Hall, to a great extent the representative of an indigenous town-chronicle tradition, transmit to other representatives of that tradition the views of the Italian Polydore Vergil. In Spain, in Germany and elsewhere the chronicle was still viable in the sixteenth century. Yet when this has been admitted, the importance for historiography and for political speculation of humanism is considerable. The elevation of the prince made politics, the princely science, a matter of absorbing interest; it was from history that the structure of politics might be discerned; and from the models of Greek and Latin a history could be written in which politics was given pride of place. Thus the preoccupations which produced humanist writings on contemporary or near-contemporary history were to have profounder results than those which influenced (in ways already described) the rewriting of national stories in a modern manner: in this sense Bruni was more appropriate as well as more fashionable than Biondo,[1] and the writings of what has been called the 'second Florentine school of historians' have an interest beyond the narrow subjects with which they dealt.

The 'second Florentine school' was Italian: Italian in language, Italian in interests and Italian in sophistication of style and sentiment. But what makes Niccolò Machiavelli (d. 1527) and Francesco Guicciardini (d. 1540) significant is the extraordinary relevance of their speculation to Europe as a whole. The *Prince* of Machiavelli, influential even in manuscript before its first complete publication in 1532, the *Discourses* and the *History of Florence* (published in 1531 and 1532) are thus prime documents in the history of political thought;[2] and so are Guicciardini's two histories, of Italy (first published 1561–7) and of Florence (not published till 1859). Viewed solely as histories, these works are fundamentally important. Machiavelli's Florentine history is far more modern

---

[1] Cf. above, p. 371. [2] Cf. below, pp. 460 ff.

than any humanist Latin history in its bold disregard for the chronicle tradition, its confident summary and analysis, its insistence on forces and movements rather than personalities. Guicciardini's originality as a historian is seen in the *Storia d'Italia*, meant for publication, rather than in the *Storia fiorentina*: it was a view of political history in terms larger than the provincialism which had in practice dominated both Italian and European historiography. The history of Florence is thus seen to be intelligible only in the context of Italian affairs as a whole, and diplomacy and war emerge as the links which inexorably bind state to state. Ironically, these works by men who had tried their hands at practical affairs were the product of their failure as politicians and were written in periods of exile and isolation. Yet that in itself was an event of some significance. The *otium* so much admired by humanists was not unwelcome, even to the Machiavelli who was consumed by his message, to the Guicciardini whose ambitions for himself and his family were equally oppressive. For both men the pen was a release. They turned to it only in part to convert others, and much more to clarify their own points of view: it is worthy of remark that so much of the writing of both men was only published posthumously. In the case of Guicciardini in particular one has the sense of an intro-spection deliberately guided and controlled, and emerging in a profound pessimism. The *Ricordi civili e politici*,[1] written for his own family and not for publication, is in some ways the most extraordinary work produced in the period we are here reviewing. History for Machiavelli could yield lessons: for Guicciardini all was relative, save only the human situation itself. 'Quanto è diversa la practica dalla teorica!' Looking back on his career as a papal official, Guiccardini confessed to a loathing of ecclesiastical ambition, greed and luxury which he admitted would have made a Lutheran of him had he not thought first of his career (no. 28); and his three ambitions were republican government in Florence, an Italy free of all barbarians, and a world free of 'the tyranny of these criminal priests' (no. 236). But he despaired of seeing this. Man who sees what is good does what is bad; plans are as like as not made only to be frustrated; the future is always uncertain. 'But yet one must not put oneself at the mercy of fortune like an animal, but as a man use one's reason. The wise man must be content to have acted for the best even if it turns out for the worst, rather than by a base design to have compassed a good end' (no. 382). De Sanctis (thinking of Aretino) wrote that sixteenth-century Italy died of laughing: Guicciardini suggests an opposite conclusion.

By the mid-years of the sixteenth century the victory of the vernaculars over Latin was assured, though outside Italy it was not yet an accomplished fact. What other general conclusions may be drawn from the above survey? The ubiquitous influence of Latin and the hardly less pervasive influence of Italian stand out as notable. The writers of Europe were

[1] Partial and unauthorised edition, Paris 1576.

schooled in Latin, they translated and emulated Latin and Italian authors. The good effects of this are sufficiently evident. It may be noted that with the good effects went certain others that were harmful. The dominant Latin and Italian models in verse injured as often as they helped native traditions; 'ink-horn' terms, at once learned and obscure, were more than all but the best writers could withstand—even Rabelais was compelled to list 'aucunes dictions plus obscures' contained in the *Quart Livre*. This led on to preciosity and euphuism, and encouraged a coterie spirit in vernacular writers analogous to that which disfigured humanists in Latin letters. Yet this was a small price to pay for an enrichment of vocabulary which in the sixteenth century in Spain, France, and England proceeded at an unprecedented speed, and for the diffusion of sentiments and forms which proved congenial and long-lived. How else could Sanazzaro's arcadianism have become Spanish with Montemayor, English with Sidney? How else could the sonnet have revealed in all the main European literatures resources which could only be released by a disciplined and aristocratic form?

It is, however, in its prose that we may come to have a more certain judgment of the intellectual climate, and it seems fair to say that the prosaic was gaining at the expense of the poetical in the literary furniture of the period. This is seen not merely in the rarity of the great poet, nor in the gradual dominance of values which relegated poetry to the theatre or the study. The values to which sixteenth-century writers increasingly attached importance were pragmatic: personal and public morality determined by rules which, however much lip service was paid to the moral philosophy of antiquity, were in fact the product of observation and experience. It is this which makes it necessary to be reserved in regarding the achievements in philosophy of the Pomponazzis or the Cajetans; academic philosophy, materialist or Thomist, was more irrelevant than it had ever been; it had (one might say) epic associations which made it out of tune with a society which was growing ever more bourgeois in tone. Machiavelli and Guicciardini in Italy, Rabelais in France, lead straight on to Montaigne. The Bordeaux burgess turned laird was to digest in his *Essais* the books discussed in this chapter and we can by reading him get a measure of what the sixteenth century itself found valuable in its own literature.

2. SCIENCE

IN the history of science the sixteenth century is a period of changes in ideas and methods slowly coming into being, not until the following century accomplished and accepted. The science of this time is far richer in medieval elements than in modern ones. Despite Renaissance and Reformation, despite the wonders reported from the two Indies, despite indeed the technical innovations of Copernicus and Vesalius, learned and unlearned alike had a picture of the natural environment in which they lived little modified from that of the fourteenth century. The imagery drawn from this picture was no less appropriate to Shakespeare than to Chaucer.

For science consists of the description and analysis of natural phenomena on the one hand, and their explanation on the other. Explanation is attained by referring that which seems complex and puzzling to that which is taken as simple, evident and natural; and the pivotal points of medieval scientific explanation remained unchallenged in the sixteenth century. In physiology and medicine the Galenic doctrine of the four humours; in ideas of matter and its mutable forms the Aristotelian conception of the four elements; in astronomy the inevitability of perfectly circular motions; in physics the dichotomy of violent and natural movements; these and many other scientific principles seemed as beyond question as at earlier times, as indispensable as the laws of inertia and the conservation of energy to modern scientists in accounting for a great variety of natural phenomena. Copernican and Vesalian modifications of description did not transcend these primary canons of explanation, nor did fresh development of the physical or intellectual operations of science seriously place them in jeopardy. It was not until the following century that protests against Aristotelian logical methods and the mere citation of the authority of the ancients were accompanied by assertions of the supremacy of observation, experiment and mathematical demonstration as criteria of the validity of scientific theories.

At the opening of the sixteenth century—and largely throughout its course—the sources of scientific knowledge were in the first place the writings of classical antiquity, and in the second the products of the great creative period of medieval science in the thirteenth and fourteenth centuries. Introductory and general surveys of the sciences, such as the popular *Sphere* of Sacrobosco or the *Chirurgia* of Guy de Chauliac, were nearly all medieval compositions. For more advanced work in physics and cosmology, for example, the whole architecture and much of the substance was provided by Aristotle; in anatomy and physiology by Galen; in *materia medica* by Dioscorides; in astronomy by Ptolemy. Though the age of translation from Arabic into Latin had long passed, there was still a demand for the classics of Islamic science, especially the medical writings, before the Hellenists won their victory over the Arabists in the mid-century. Comparatively few of the scientific books printed before 1500 were of recent authorship, and of these few many were frankly designed as distillations of traditional learning. The first and probably the most successful textbook of the new century, the *Margarita Philosophica* of Gregor Reisch (1503), is of the same kind. It contains nothing that was not taught a century earlier; it reflects no new spirit of the age, no fresh attitude to the natural world. Avoiding most of the logical subtleties of medieval philosophers, ignoring the criticisms of Aristotelian mechanics voiced in the fourteenth century, it presented a somewhat dull résumé of the vivid intellectual experience of the Middle Ages.

It would be difficult to overestimate the debt owed by Renaissance science to the natural philosophers and medical writers of the Middle Ages. Contempt for the inelegance of medieval Latin and distrust of the Arabisms imported into the pure Hellenic tradition of science could not justify the repudiation of this debt. For the later Middle Ages had naturalised Greek science in western Europe, largely through the mediation of Islam. Where the Roman empire had signally failed, medieval Christendom had succeeded. And it had created in the university an institution for the perpetuation of classical learning, so that Paris, Padua and Oxford became the natural heirs of Athens and Alexandria. Four centuries of effort in translation, teaching and commentary, in analysing, criticising and comparing the ancient authors, had restored the fabric of civilisation broken by social disaster and the barbarian invasions.

Moreover, the Middle Ages had modified or added to the classical example of scientific enquiry in ways which, when further developed, were to become highly significant for the progress of science in the sixteenth century and to contribute to the 'scientific revolution' of the seventeenth. In method, the medieval philosopher had laid greater stress upon the necessity for supporting general propositions by direct observation of and experiment upon particular phenomena. Applications of this sound conception were limited but notable. Human dissection, virtually impossible in antiquity, was an ordinary practice of the great medical schools even if formalised into an ocular commentary upon Galen's texts. The elementary facts of magnetism had been elicited experimentally and the compass applied to navigation. In optics the phenomena of refraction had been carefully studied, and an explanation of the formation of the rainbow greatly superior to Aristotle's and partly resting on direct experiment, was put forward. The Middle Ages too had seen important advances in the technical arts which yielded such innovations as the mechanical clock and the glass lens, and these played a vital part in permitting the construction of the tools of observational and experimental science in early modern times.

Equally remarkable is the fact that the conventional beginning of modern history does not coincide with the genesis of some of the strategic conceptions of the scientific revolution, but rather cuts arbitrarily across their pre-history. The astronomical innovations of Copernicus cannot be divorced either from medieval explorations of the Ptolemaic celestial geometry or from medieval discussions of the possibility of the earth's movement. The chemical theory of matter and its changes lingering on through a series of vicissitudes to the time of Lavoisier in the late eighteenth century was of medieval origin, stemming from Islamic alchemists. Most interesting of all was the evolution of the idea of impetus,[1] in direct opposition to the dynamical theories of Aristotle, from ancient roots to the status of a comprehensive mechanical theory in the fourteenth century. With little further revision the same theory was taught by the commentators on Aristotle's *Physics* down to the beginning of the seventeenth century; it was from the intellectual springboard of impetus mechanics, not directly from the ideas of Aristotle, that Galileo proceeded to lay the foundations of the modern science. Traces of the medieval view are firmly imprinted on his exposition of his discoveries, which owe far more to Jean Buridan and Nicole Oresme in the fourteenth century than they do to Aristotle or the Renaissance.

In the fifteenth century, the early age of the Italian Renaissance, science and philosophy lost for a time the momentum which had carried them from translation to original achievement. One interpretation of this phase in the history of science would emphasise both the slackening in the early sixteenth century of the intense medieval concern with the logic of scientific explanation, and the very literal attachment of Renaissance scholars to classical authorities. Against this others would point to the boundless interest and fresh outlook of Leonardo da Vinci, to a more genuine sympathy with the authentic spirit of Greek thought, and to the creative work of Andreas Vesalius (1514–64) and Nicholas Copernicus (1473–1543) as indicative of the regenerative impact of the Renaissance upon science. Opinions on Renaissance science differ widely and are confused by uncertainties in the definition of the qualities which the Renaissance in the broadest sense is assumed to have manifested, or to have introduced into intellectual history.

Significant cross-connections between science and the general movements of the Renaissance are nevertheless quite clear. Of these the influence of the invention of printing is the most obvious.[2] The labour involved in copying manuscripts had bestowed an artificial eminence on a few chosen texts, and limited the diffusion of new work. By the mid-sixteenth century even obscure scholars could possess a relatively large collection of books on a single topic. A Cambridge physician who died in 1551 had a library of more than 200 volumes, including over forty on medicine—a Greek Galen and many other of the most famous works by classical, medieval and contemporary authors. Such an assembly of authorities could only rarely have been found outside monastic libraries before the introduction of printing, which permitted comparisons of observations and opinions scarcely possible in the Middle Ages. Similarly it is inconceivable that without the agency of the printed book the new

---

[1] Below, p. 401.   [2] Cf. above, pp. 361 ff.

navigational science of the Portuguese would have spread so rapidly, or that the works of Vesalius and Paracelsus (c. 1493–1541) would have aroused such wide controversy. Somewhat earlier the effect of the press on the diffusion of polemical scientific writing is well illustrated in the vast literature provoked by the appearance of an apparently new disease, syphilis, at the end of the fifteenth century.

The production of the first scientific and medical books was relatively large. According to Klebs's bibliography (1938) there were more than 3000 editions of 1044 titles by about 650 authors printed before 1500. A high proportion, inevitably, came from the Italian presses. Although most scientific and medical works were to be written in Latin for two centuries to come, a few of the most popular medieval texts (the *De proprietatibus rerum* of Bartholomew the Englishman, for example, Mandeville's *Travels*, and such books as Caxton's *Gouvernayle of helthe*) were already available in the vernacular languages. Many more works of wide interest were so published in the sixteenth century, including treatises on medicine and surgery, on navigation, and on other branches of applied mathematics. Galileo, however, was the first modern scientist of genius to write extensively in his native tongue.

In science the communication of visual images was hardly less important than communication by the printed word, and just as letterpress printing stimulated the desire to recover the best and purest form of the knowledge of antiquity, correcting generations of scribes' and translators' errors (in that it offered a means of reduplicating copies free from them) so printing from woodcut blocks, and later the copper-plate, offered a way of multiplying illustrations free from mistakes and encouraged the idea of illustrating texts by means of appropriate figures. A confrontation of pictures in medieval bestiaries and herbals, and the rarer medieval anatomical drawings, with analogous woodcuts of the sixteenth century makes the difference striking. A drawing is harder to copy accurately than a piece of Latin prose, and there had been far fewer skilled draughtsmen than scribes. Taking advantage of the new technique, the first printed and illustrated anatomies and herbals appeared in the last decade of the fifteenth century. The next fifty years saw an enormous improvement in their standard.

The woodcut contributed greatly to the advance of surgical teaching, of botanical knowledge, and of anatomy. But to make its use fully effective the man of science had to collaborate with the artist, and here the flowering of the arts of drawing and painting in the Renaissance was of profound service to science. Setting aside obvious qualifications, medieval art was symbolic and idealist; Renaissance art was representational and realist. It had mastered perspective—the technique of rendering three-dimensional structures on a plane surface. The artist could represent to the reader, almost as to the eye of the actual beholder, the spatial relations of the parts of a machine or the organs of the human body, whereas the Middle Ages had conspicuously failed to conquer the graphic approach to scientific and technical matters. Artists themselves, from the time of Botticelli onwards, delighted in the accurate delineation of flower and leaf, the strain of muscles, the reflection and refraction of light. In search of a deeper understanding of the animal and human organism, and to enhance the realism of their work, painters like Michelangelo and Leonardo turned to dissection, far excelling in their sketches the standard of professional anatomical illustration. It is not surprising therefore that the superb figures in Vesalius's *De humani corporis fabrica* (1543) have been attributed to a member of Titian's school. In this small area of biological illustration, probably, communication between science and the spirit of the Italian Renaissance was closest.

Yet the sheer scholarship of the Renaissance also had its powerful effect. This was to direct attention to three chief tasks: the recovery of lost or neglected texts and knowledge; the search for Greek manuscripts to replace Arabic-Latin medieval versions; and the careful study and collation of the best available manuscripts to restore the original work. Such scholarship was generously devoted to the scientific works of antiquity. Much that was unknown to the Middle Ages became familiar in the sixteenth century. Lucretius's *De natura rerum*, discovered in 1417 by Poggio Bracciolini, was printed many times. By far the most elaborate, if also the latest, statement of Greek atomistic speculation—which had been known to the Middle Ages almost entirely from Aristotle's hostile references—the influence of Lucretius's poem is reflected in the mechanistic corpuscularian ideas of matter of the seventeenth century. Celsus's *De re medica*, a Roman compilation of Greek medical science almost unknown till 1426, aroused deep interest and was printed even before the works of Hippocrates and Galen. On mathematics and mechanical science the revelation of the Greek Archimedes (1544)[1] had a revolutionary impact; in fact the modern history of mathematics might be dated from this event. New texts, however, did not altogether replace more familiar authorities, nor were medieval treatises based on the Islamic tradition immediately rejected by the generality, though dubiously regarded by Greek scholars. Algebra flourished as healthily as geometry in the sixteenth century without fresh inspiration from Greek sources, for this branch of mathematics was an Islamic creation. And if anatomy was purged of its Arabic terms in favour of Greek equivalents, chemistry has retained its *alcohol* and *alkali* and much other philological evidence of its Islamic descent. Since medieval European science was almost uniquely Hellenistic in its ultimate origins, and since the sixteenth century never made

---

[1] Certain works of Archimedes had been translated from Greek into Latin by William of Moerbeke in the second half of the thirteenth century. Versions of these translations were printed in 1543. A new Latin translation of the Greek text was published in 1558.

a total rejection of the Arabic intermediary, the latitude for displacement under the influence of Renaissance classicism was not so very great. Controversies over modifications to Ptolemaic numerical constants introduced by 'Arabic' astronomers, or the 'Arabic' technique of venesection as opposed to the Greek, concerned matters of detail rather than fundamental ideas and methods. Nor were Renaissance experts on such matters necessarily more ingenious or invariably better informed than their medieval precursors.

The scholar-scientists of the early sixteenth century were most markedly active in medicine and natural history. No other author was so carefully or frequently edited as Galen. English scholars participated in the preparation of the Aldine edition (1525), and Vesalius (who had previously republished Johann Günther's *Institutiones anatomices secundum Galeni sententiam*) had a hand in the Giunta edition of 1541–2. The herbal, as developed by such naturalists as Valerius Cordus (1515–44) and Pietro Mattiolo (1500–77), was based firmly on the Greek text of the *Materia medica* of Dioscorides, supplemented as was required to fit the rather different flora of western Europe. The medieval herbalist tradition, still strong in the first printed versions (as late as the English *Grete Herball* of 1526), was completely set aside. The encyclopaedic naturalists Conrad Gesner (1516–65) and Ulissi Aldrovandi (1522–1605) took the practice of quoting from classical authors to its limit, though they had other and greater merits.

The learned Hellenism of the Renaissance was by itself incapable of inspiring originality of mind, if by that is meant a willingness to criticise the accepted canons of scientific explanation, to pursue untried methods of enquiry, and really to examine the facts. To doubt the essential correctness of Aristotle, Galen and Ptolemy was still in the sixteenth and early seventeenth centuries to risk denunciation as a blockhead, or worse treatment. The men of the Renaissance did not criticise medieval philosophers for adopting and teaching the Greek view of nature, but for departing from it. The latter's fault was in failing to comprehend antiquity and setting about a blundering, pedantic attempt to improve upon its wisdom. Scholasticism itself, not the philosophy on which scholasticism was founded, was the target of such thinkers as Erasmus and Pomponazzi. If the Middle Ages, by their regard for both 'Arabs' and Greeks as authorities in science and medicine, by their development and criticism of inherited ideas, by their progress in technology and practical science, show evidence of some leaning towards a recognition of progress in civilisation, the Renaissance turned more emphatically towards the emulation of classical antiquity. It is not surprising, therefore, that some Renaissance divagations from the medieval tradition seem to move backwards rather than forwards; that those genuine iconoclasts who, like Paracelsus, were as avowedly anti-Greek as they were anti-medieval, were as violently distrusted in the sixteenth century as they would have been at any earlier period.

In what sense then is it justifiable to speak of a 'scientific Renaissance'? From what has been said, it is apparent that there was no sharp break in the continuity of scientific thought, no outright rejection of the past such as was to occur later. There was, however, a more judicious attempt to understand, rather than merely recite, its legacy. With anatomists and botanists this might involve the comparison of a text with the results of patient visual examination; or (as Copernicus said) it might take the form of assuming the same liberty to devise and test fresh hypotheses that the ancients had allowed themselves. Here the greater range of Renaissance classical knowledge exerted its effect. Antiquity had not spoken with a single voice, and it is noticeable that Plato, the Pythagoreans and Archimedes are mentioned more frequently and favourably in the sixteenth century than formerly. With the attempt to understand literally what ancient science had really meant, strengthened by the humanist impulse and a greater interest in nature as actually seen rather than imagined, there disappeared much of the medieval accretion of verbal gymnastics, religious symbolism and plain fable.

Practical activity and the movement from the philosopher's study to field and workshop are discernible in every aspect of sixteenth-century science. Natural historians, proclaiming the beauties of nature as well as its moral lessons, travelled widely and sought eagerly for exotic species. Paracelsus enlarged on the practical medical skills of barbers, bathkeepers, and wise women. Agricola (1490–1555) and Biringuccio (c. 1540) described their experience of the mines, metal-works, and infant chemical industry, assembling storehouses of new facts and observations. Geometry was applied to cartography and navigation, gunnery and survey; such applications aroused new mathematical difficulties which were in turn surmounted. Much attention was paid, with good results, to methods of measurement and observation. Even the greatest scientific feats of the time were essentially practical; Vesalius transformed anatomy by dissection and illustration; Copernicus put a strange hypothesis into an exact mathematical form. And if the fundamental terms of scientific explanation remained little modified, there was a decisive improvement in the statement of ascertainable facts. By 1600 the world was better mapped, the stars in the heavens were more precisely charted, the structure of the human body was more exactly delineated, the operations of chemistry were more plainly described, than they had ever been before. It was in this respect an achievement solid rather than brilliant; its full intellectual fruition was delayed; yet it prepared the way for conceptions totally different from any entertained in antiquity, the Middle Ages, or the Renaissance age itself.

There were three notable trends in mathematics: towards an extension of the more complex Greek methods in geometry, as studied in the works of Archimedes and Apollonius; towards a greater mastery of algebraic equations; and towards the development of popular teaching, with a strong practical bias. As the advances in the more abstruse branches of mathematics had but a negligible effect on natural science they need not be considered in detail. Both the development of algebraic symbolism and the application of algebraic methods to scientific problems were innovations of the seventeenth century rather than the sixteenth. Before the publication of Descartes's *Géometrie* (1637) and indeed for some time afterwards, scientists, astronomers and practical mathematicians, following the Greek example, made almost exclusive use of a purely geometrical treatment of their problems. They were set out in such a way that their solution required the calculation of a length, an area or a volume. Such calculations were immensely facilitated by the re-discovery of the Greek analysis of the conics, by a wider use of trigonometrical functions, and most of all by development of the Archimedean method of calculating areas into the 'method of infinitesimals'. Through greater flexibility in the techniques available the prospect was disclosed of handling questions in mechanical science by geometrical reasoning, the method which proved so powerful as developed by Galileo, Descartes, Cavalieri and many others early in the next century.

At a more elementary level the endeavour to deprive mathematical skill of its mystery, and even of lingering traces of association with the forbidden arts, was very conspicuous. Increasing complexity in the management of banking, finance, and exchanges on the one hand, and in the navigation of ships, the direction of engineering projects and the conduct of wars on the other, offered many opportunities for the exploitation of the humbler kinds of proficiency in calculation. Particularly was this the case in a relatively backward country such as England, where the first arithmetic—Cuthbert Tunstall's *De arte supputandi*—was not printed until 1522. It was followed by four vernacular books by Robert Recorde, including the significantly named *Ground of Artes* (1540–2),[1] *The Castle of Knowledge* (1551)—the first English work on astronomy to mention Copernicus—and *The Whetstone of Witte* (1557), which introduced algebra. For practical geometry, taught in the Digges' English treatises on mensuration and survey such as *Pantometria* (1571), the basis was provided by Euclid's theorems which were conveniently summarised in most of the handbooks. An English translation of Euclid's *Elements* (with a preface by John Dee) was published in 1570; it had appeared earlier in other languages. The use of instruments for measuring heights and distances was widely taught. Works of the same kind as those written in England were also printed in most of the continental languages.

[1] No copy of the first edition is known.

Two specialised applications of geometry, both closely linked with astronomy, received much attention and were greatly developed. The art of constructing sundials was subjected to many curious refinements after the use of portable instruments had been simplified in the fifteenth century by adding a small magnetic compass so that the dial could be easily aligned on a north-south line. In principle, the hour of the day can be determined either by measuring the sun's displacement in azimuth from the meridian, or by measuring its height above the horizon, or by a combination of these measurements. In the two latter cases the instrument must provide some means of allowing for the seasonal variations in the sun's declination. It might also be desired to make the dial adjustable for use in more than one latitude. The geometrical problems involved in putting these principles into practice, as also in constructing fixed dials for a great variety of different situations and purposes, were examined in a large number of treatises, of which perhaps the most complete was Christopher Clavius's *Gnomonices* (1581).

Navigation was a more serious business. Throughout antiquity and down to the fifteenth century ships had been guided from port to port by the sailors' familiarity with prevailing winds, the sea-bottom, and suitable landmarks. In addition the positions of the sun and stars indicated roughly the direction of the ship's course. With the adoption of the magnetic compass in the thirteenth century a better estimation of direction became possible, but it did not assist the navigator to fix his position. Similar methods were employed in the coastal navigation of the sixteenth century and many textbooks on pilotage were printed, teaching for example the way to determine the state of the tide at a given port, and the 'Regiment of the North Star'. But the skill and memory of master-mariners was inadequate for the task of sailing southwards and westwards in the Atlantic or crossing the Indian Ocean. In oceanic navigation the ship might be out of sight of land for months; the navigator had to have new means of fixing his position, and charts on which positions could be plotted. The problem was partially solved in the fifteenth century by recourse to astronomy and geometry. Latitude was found by taking the height of the noon sun (with due allowance for the changing declination) or of the Pole. Longitude had to be more crudely reckoned from the ship's course, with an estimate of the distance sailed on each bearing. The chart then revealed the approach of the vessel to its objective. Africa, for instance, could be circumnavigated by sailing first west, then due south until the latitude of the Cape of Good Hope was reached, then 'running down the latitude' to the Cape.

Oceanic navigation based on the combination of the log and the chart, the magnetic compass and celestial observations, the one major technique of the age wholly derived from natural science and mathematics, was a Portuguese innovation. It required, besides some understanding of elementary scientific principles, skill in the manipulation of instruments and in the use of tables. It spread gradually to Spain and then to the rest of Europe, for mastery of it was indispensable to those who would enter the East Indian or American trades. The most influential exposition of this new science of navigation was Martin Cortes's *Arte de Navegar* (1556), which was translated into English by Richard Eden in 1561. Though its essence remained unchanged, improvements to the instruments and tables required were steadily introduced. Theoretically sound methods of measuring changes in longitude were also brought forward, but none was practicable for more than two centuries. Precursors of William Gilbert's great treatise *De Magnete* (1600) investigated the behaviour of the earth as a magnetic body, which proved more complicated than was at first realised. The displacement of the magnetic from the geographic pole was recognised and allowed for, but the expectation that the variation of the compass-needle from true north would prove to follow a simple regular law over the whole surface of the globe was falsified. By the end of the century the possibility of improving navigation by further scientific research was widely acknowledged, while a host of advisers offered to teach the unlettered seaman how to mend his ways.

Geography and cartography, closely linked with navigation, advanced rapidly through the age of exploration initiated during the last decade of the fifteenth century. Another, not wholly harmonious, influence in this period was that of Ptolemy, whose *Cosmographia* was first printed in 1475. Renaissance attempts to redraw the map of the world according to his directions did not pay sufficient heed to medieval additions to knowledge. When it was realised that Columbus's discovery was not part of Asia, when the extent of the Pacific Ocean was revealed, and when explorers' reports were analysed, Ptolemaic geography was finally outmoded. Reasonably accurate maps of the explored regions of the globe appeared in the second half of the sixteenth century through the labours of Ortelius and Mercator. Careful mapping of restricted localities in Europe began in the late fifteenth century, and by 1600 the application of survey by triangulation to map-making was well understood. No attempt was yet made, however, to measure accurately the length of a geographical degree (and hence ascertain the size of the earth). Methods of projection, of special importance for marine charts, were investigated; here the great step forward was the introduction of Mercator's projection (1569) since this yields a map particularly suitable for navigational purposes. Its mathematical basis was first fully explained by Edward Wright (1599).

The most striking and extensive use of geometry was in calculating and predicting the motions of the heavenly bodies. This was not merely a question of abstract scientific interest, nor of practical concern only to navigators, for judicial astrology and similar superstitions still held a secure place in the minds of men. When the Copernican system of the heavens was debated, some of its earliest exponents hastened to point out that it would not at all disturb the traditional astrological calculations. Neither the Renaissance nor the Reformation restrained credence in astrology, or indeed any established superstition. Rather, through the suggestion that all kinds of knowledge were fit subjects for human enquiry, through quickening interest in the esoteric lore of the ancients, and through the decline of a purely Christian outlook upon the natural and supernatural worlds, there was a greater tendency to see man as subject to the play of mysterious powers. The dangerous mysteries were cultivated rather than shunned; philosophers as well as poets frankly attributed the accidents of life to the dispositions of the stars; physicians and alchemists regulated their operations by them. It was normal to view signs and portents—comets, monstrous births, new stars—as indications of misfortune and divine displeasure. The future conjunctions and oppositions of the planets and the occurrence of eclipses were thus not of interest to a few astronomers alone but to the multitudes who read the popular almanacs.

The problem faced by Ptolemy in the second century A.D. had been to construct a pattern of regular geometrical motions representing the observed movements of the heavenly bodies about the apparently fixed platform of the earth. If, as Ptolemy concluded, the earth formed the stable centre of the universe, then the sun, moon, planets and fixed stars revolved around it once in a day, making a westerly progress. But in addition, sun, moon and planets were seen to make a contrary easterly movement, at varying speeds, against the background of the stars. Further, although Ptolemy believed, as everyone believed before Kepler, that all these movements were perfectly circular, it was apparent from observations that only the sun and stars moved in circles with the earth, the pivot of the universe, at their centre. Ptolemy was able to account for the observed positions of the planets and the moon only by supposing that they moved in circles (epicycles) about a centre which itself moved in another perfect circle (deferent) about the earth. After ascribing suitable values to the periods of these various motions and to the radii of the numerous circles, computed from observations, he was enabled with the aid of various subsidiary hypotheses to construct a geometrical figure of the universe from which astronomical tables could be calculated and predictions of future events made. His geometry, however, did not follow a completely uniform pattern and he did not aim to create a rigid system capable of being reduced to a few simple principles.

Nor did Ptolemy explain celestial phenomena in physical terms—indeed an exact physical interpretation of his geometrical figures was impossible. This was found rather in the works of Aristotle, describing a group of homocentric spheres bearing the heavenly bodies in their revolutions, the

397

different natures of earthly and heavenly matter, the cause and purpose of the phenomena, and so forth. Aristotle therefore was studied by natural philosophers and Ptolemy by mathematicians who were often, but not invariably, also assiduous in continuing the tradition of practical observing.

Nicholas Copernicus was the last great exponent of the medieval tradition of mathematical astronomy, though he used its methods to demonstrate a totally different assumption—that the earth itself was in motion, a planet circling the sun. The idea that the seemingly westerly revolution of the whole heaven is an illusion resulting from a real rotation of the earth on its axis had been familiar enough in the Middle Ages without winning conviction. The idea that the five planets might have the sun rather than the earth as the centres of their orbits had been another natural alternative to the Ptolemaic scheme. But none since Aristarchos had taught that both sun and stars were fixed, and the earth a body rotating on its axis while at the same time revolving in an orbit round the central sun. The great virtue of this heliostatic system was that besides relieving the universe of the need to rotate once in each day it made possible the omission from the geometrical representation of each planet's motion that element which could now be attributed to the actual annual revolution of the earth. Thus Copernicus could claim with some justice that his system was mathematically more simple and harmonious than Ptolemy's.

It was on considerations of this kind, strictly transcending scientific evaluation, that he was forced to rely in asserting that the heliostatic hypothesis was not merely mathematically feasible, but true in fact. For Copernicus's celestial geometry is no more than Ptolemy's inverted and put to slightly different uses. He retained the perfect circles, epicycles and deferents, even the Aristotelian notion of celestial spheres is still present. In computing his periods of revolution and the radii of his circles he relied on Ptolemy's work and the observations Ptolemy had quoted, supplemented by a number taken from Islamic astronomers and a very few of his own. As a consequence, despite the fundamental difference in hypothesis, the Copernican and Ptolemaic geometries are interchangeable, that is, the relative positions of the heavenly bodies as seen from the earth are the same at any moment, no matter which system is used to calculate them. There could be no observational test of an astronomical kind to distinguish between them, nor could the heliostatic system yield more accurate predictions than the geostatic. Copernicus's first aim was to show that the heliostatic hypothesis was not just mathematically absurd, that it need not be less accurate than its rival. To do more was beyond his scientific competence. Yet inevitably he sought to do more, to justify his conviction that the established view was wrong. In so doing he turned to questions of probability rather than fact. Was it more likely that the whole heaven would rotate, or the earth only? Was it more likely that the little earth or the great fiery sun would occupy the central position in the spheres? Was it more natural to believe that the fixed stars were comparatively near—not much more distant than Saturn—or that they were so vastly remote that they gave no hint of the earth's annual revolution? Was the earth a unique body, or of the same kind as the planets and therefore capable of a similar motion?

In dealing with these questions Copernicus entered a realm of thought different from that of the mathematical astronomer. In proportion as he sought to show that the heliostatic system was a true representation of the phenomena and not a mere calculating device, he moved from the territory of Ptolemy into that of Aristotle. For if the earth circled about the sun the Aristotelian explanations of physical phenomena no longer made sense. It could no longer be true that heavy bodies fell down towards their natural place at the centre of the universe, if that did not coincide with the centre of the earth, or that light bodies rose from the centre towards the regions of air and fire. If the globe rotated and revolved, it could not longer be true that the heavy elements, earth and water, moved naturally only in a straight line downwards. Moreover (it had been urged long before), if the earth moved how could the stability of objects and buildings on its surface be maintained? Every explanation in physics and mechanics assumed that the earth was fixed in a central position, and each suggested that it was Copernicus, not Ptolemy, who was in error. But Copernicus was a mathematician, not a physicist nor a philosopher; he had neither the wish nor the talent to effect the profound change of view required to give a physical meaning to the heliostatic hypothesis. Certainly he proposed a few modifications to Aristotelian conceptions, suggesting for example that circular motion was natural and proper to all spherical bodies like the earth and moon, but he left the main difficulties unresolved. Thus he condemned himself in the eyes of most contemporaries as one who would sacrifice all sound scientific thinking for the sake of mathematical elegancies.

Their attitude was not merely obscurantist or prejudiced. For, if there were serious discrepancies in the Middle Ages between the mathematical-astronomical view of the cosmos and the natural-philosophical view, Copernicus had enlarged rather than reduced them. Aristotelian physics and the heliostatic hypothesis were mutually contradictory, though Copernicus gave allegiance to both; it is not surprising that few followed his lead, the majority preferring safer, traditional opinions. They saw, justly, that if Copernicus was right Aristotle was wrong; and that if the *Physics* was rejected, a vacuity of thought took its place. Not until Galileo in 1632 sketched the outlines of a new natural philosophy, consistent with the idea of a moving earth, was the dichotomy overcome and from this time the heliostatic system began to gain adherents rapidly.

There was indeed almost as much discussion of the 'Copernican reform' of astronomy before the publication of *De revolutionibus orbium coelestium* in 1543 as in the forty years after that event. Copernicus was a respected astronomer, having worked for some years in Italy, and rumours of his great work were abroad twenty years before its printing. His *Commentariolus*, a first sketch of the new astronomy, seems to have had some circulation in manuscript and there is a record of Copernicus's ideas being explained to Clement VII in 1533. Nothing indicates that the heliostatic theory was at this time stifled by clerical hostility or that the learned world (with a few exceptions) was other than indifferent to it. The position became less favourable to the Copernicans towards the end of the century. So long as the stars were imagined to be borne round by a sphere the universe could be thought indefinitely large in comparison with the earth, yet of a finite size. If the earth moved and the sun and stars were fixed, however, it was possible to conceive that there was no definite boundary to the universe, that starry space receded infinitely far from the sun on all sides, even the nearest star being necessarily almost unthinkably remote. This idea was embraced by the English mathematician Thomas Digges (d. 1595). But there was nothing very new in supposing that space was limitless: Nicole Oresme in the fourteenth century had discussed (and dismissed) the idea that there might be other universes beyond our own, of which we know nothing. Speculation of this kind, on the possible plurality of worlds and the existence of souls in them, had been considered philosophically absurd and theologically dangerous long before it was taken up by Giordano Bruno at the end of the sixteenth century. The condemnation of Bruno and his burning in 1600 created a notorious scandal in Protestant eyes; it also had the effect of directing Catholic opinion firmly against Copernicanism and led on to the still more famous trial of Galileo. Astronomical discussion was embittered by its confusion with theological issues; that this happened was not, however, a necessary consequence of Copernicus's innovations.

First steps towards greater accuracy in astronomy, based on improvements in observation, had been taken by Peurbach and Regiomontanus in the second half of the fifteenth century. Neither the heliostatic hypothesis, nor the refinement of instrument-making techniques which took place in the sixteenth century, had borne much practical fruit of this kind before the time of the Danish astronomer Tycho Brahe (1546–1601). Tycho was an anti-Copernican, specifically not for mathematical reasons but because the movement of the earth seemed to deprive physical phenomenon of all hope of explanation. The astronomical system he favoured gave to each celestial body the same relative motions as the Copernican, assuming the earth to be fixed and the sun and stars revolving about it. This was the logical response to the heliostatic geometry and robbed the Copernicans of any mathematical or observational argument in their favour. Scientifically, however, this system was the least significant part of Tycho's work. He was the supreme observer of his age whose records were not outdated for another two generations. The observatory (Uraniborg) where they were collected, built on the island of Hveen in the Sound under the patronage of Frederick II of Denmark, was unprecedented in Europe as an organised centre of research. Tycho designed his own instruments, many of which were adapted as precisely as possible for a single purpose, employing for their manufacture the finest German craftsmanship. He made a careful study of the various errors involved in making angular measurements with open-sighted instruments, and having invented means for reducing them as far as possible, realised the necessity for making appropriate corrections.

Like all his predecessors, Tycho was engrossed with the problem of planetary motion. Since, however, observations of a planet's position are most easily conducted by reference to the positions of adjacent fixed stars, his first task was to prepare a new catalogue of star-places. To this end he devised a new method of determining celestial longitudes. Both in this task and in his observations of the planets he improved on previous standards of accuracy by a factor of at least two. His range of error was about four minutes of arc, a limit which was to prove of critical importance for the future of theoretical astronomy, and indeed for the whole of physics, for it enabled Kepler to establish the 'laws' of planetary motion in an elliptical orbit. Thus Tycho, like Vesalius in anatomy, by painstaking application to the attainment of descriptive accuracy, laid the foundations for changes in ideas of which he himself had no foreknowledge. Yet his own direct influence was by no means wholly conservative. Neither Aristotle nor Ptolemy could claim his allegiance, save in his belief in the fixity of the earth; particularly he confounded the dogma of the unchanging nature of the heavens by his discussion of the nova of 1572, and proved that comets were not meteors (phenomena of the upper air) but truly celestial bodies.

In the sixteenth-century treatment of physics there was little change from the medieval pattern except that, under the influence of Archimedes, mechanics stood out more clearly as a distinct, mathematical branch of science. Aristotelian explanations—which essentially linked the physical properties of bodies with those of the four elements (earth, water, air and fire) of which they were thought to be composed, and with the four qualities (dryness, wetness, coldness, heat) associated with the elements— were still accepted. Discussion of the 'latitude of forms' (that is, the estimation of the degree of a quality possessed by a body) in the medieval manner continued. Medieval modifications to the Aristotelian theory of motion arising from the concept of impetus[1] were also taught without

---

[1] Essentially, that the action of being moved by some agency (such as muscular force, or the natural tendency of heavy bodies to descend) conferred upon a heavy body an 'impressed virtue' or 'impetus' to continue in motion. This impetus was the cause of the residual

important alteration. Fourteenth-century geometrical analysis of the effect of impetus, considered as the cause of the acceleration of falling bodies, was repeated and held by some to justify the important conclusion that falling bodies have a 'uniform difform' motion, one, that is, which could be taken as equivalent to a uniform motion, the motion of the body at the mid-point of its fall. But the clarification of the new concepts obscurely suggested by medieval and sixteenth-century authors, and the discovery of a mathematical analysis which made it possible to relate time, velocity and distance in a single formula describing the motion of a uniformly accelerated body, awaited the genius of Galileo. His confutation of the Aristotelian theory that heavier bodies fall faster than light ones by a demonstration at the Leaning Tower of Pisa is now generally regarded as a myth, but the same experiment was certainly performed by others about 1590.

More solid progress at a humbler level was made in statics and hydrostatics. Medieval study of the Greek theory of the lever and equilibrium in general had not been inconsiderable; the medieval treatment was still represented at the beginning of the sixteenth century. By 1586, however, Simon Stevin (1548–1620), who is otherwise notable as an exponent of the decimal system and as a practical engineer, had solved many further problems with the aid of the principle of virtual velocities, which he applied to the action of non-parallel forces. Here he came very close to the conception of vector-quantities. He was also the first to discuss 'Pascal's paradox'—that the pressure of a liquid on a surface varies with the area of the surface and the height of the column of liquid above it, irrespective of its cross-section. Galileo, another eager student of Archimedes, carried out similar investigations which were extended in his work on the strength of materials in later years. It was during his Pisan years too that Galileo first became aware of the isochronism of a swinging pendulum.

This was an important period in hydraulic engineering in which both Stevin and Galileo played a practical part and to which some of their theoretical studies were consciously related. The application of science to mechanical engineering occurred less readily, though the sixteenth century yielded a fertility of minor inventions. In optics what little was done was wholly practical. Following Alberti (1404–72), Dürer and others wrote on the geometry of perspective, otherwise there was little new in the theory of light and colour. A number of circumstantial reports indicate empirical experimentation with lenses and mirrors and the invention of telescope-like devices a generation or more before the authentic discovery of the 'Galilean' type of telescope about 1609. Here

motion of such bodies after the action of the moving agent ceased, and of the acceleration of freely falling bodies. Aristotle's explanation of these movements is very obscure and unsatisfactory.

again, perhaps, it is in practical developments that the change from the medieval world is most clearly seen.

Chemical knowledge and skill were transmitted to the sixteenth century by two distinct channels, the industrial and the alchemical. In antiquity and the Middle Ages there had been a close connection between them, and it may well be that some industrial techniques—for example those of distillation and of dissolving and recovering metals with the aid of mineral acids—were borrowed from the alchemists' laboratories. Alchemy was distinguished by its mystical philosophy and by the unintelligible jargon in which the preparation of the Great Work was described. Industrial procedures—the extraction and purification of metals, the manufacture of soap, glass and alum, the extraction of dyes and drugs—were usually described in as plain a language as the writer could command, with little attempt to explain the processes in terms of any theory. Taken together these two aspects of the chemical tradition amounted to a large body of experience in the preparation by chemical art not merely of a growing number of saleable commodities but of a larger number of substances which were as yet no more than curiosities.

New ideas and new practices render the developments of the sixteenth century more complex still. Alchemy of course persisted; there was an intensified interest in industrial experience; and there occurred the double development of the iatrochemical school stemming from Paracelsus, part esoteric and mystical with strong alchemical leanings, part rational and empirical with potentialities for future organisation into a true science.

By the beginning of the century alchemy had already ceased to contribute to the growth of chemical arts and ideas, though the legacy of its theories continued to inhibit the formation of less imaginative modes of explanation until the seventeenth century. The pursuit of alchemical chimaeras continued vigorously, however, stimulated by the Paracelsian influence; even Robert Boyle (1627–91) and Isaac Newton (1642–1727) were incapable of simply dismissing it. Many treatises falsely ascribed to the giants of the Middle Ages—Albertus Magnus, Arnald of Villanova, Raymund Lull—enjoyed an extensive circulation, and one of the great collections of writings in the art, the *Artis auriferae quam chemiam vocant*, was published in Basle in 1572. Many new alchemical tracts were composed also. While the 'puffers' prolonged their futile and often sordid operations at the furnace (as depicted, for example, by Brueghel in 1558), the 'adepts' rose to high flights of linguistic and pictorial symbolism. To this period belongs the fullest flowering of alchemical imagery seen, for example, in the *Rosarium philosophorum* and Thurneysser's *Quinta essentia* (1570). But the first half of the following century is even more packed with alchemical activity.

Alchemical writings turned to the past, their authors claiming to

26-2

expound an ancient wisdom. Another class of books presaged the industrial expansion of chemistry in the future, though also representing old traditions. A work on assaying, doubtless continuing a manuscript tradition, had been printed in German as early as 1510. Particularly in Vanoccio Biringuccio's *Pirotechnia* (1540) and Agricola's *De re metallica* (1556) there was given a very complete account of everything involved in metal-working, from the assay of ores and mining through roasting, smelting, the separation of metals and refining to the manufacture of alloys and the technique of casting. For the economic production of the precious metals in Europe (here the account is enriched by Lazarus Ercker's treatise of 1576) reliable knowledge of the content of the ore, careful control of the processes by which the gold and silver were isolated, and precise assays of the purity of the metals during their refining were essential. Hence the assayer, who was also charged with preserving the exactitude of currency alloys, effected the first introduction into any branch of chemical science of the accurate measurement of mass, which has ever since been of critical importance.

The range of chemical topics discussed by Biringuccio and Agricola was by no means restricted to metallurgy. Between them they describe the manufacture of glass and gunpowder, the preparation of alum, vitriol, sulphur and other minerals, and the composition of several re-agents. Agricola's more traditional writings on geology and mineralogy are also important, and his account of mining technology is unique. Other authors followed more narrowly the same line. Ercker's treatise on assaying has already been mentioned; it was translated into English as late as 1683. A long series of treatises on the most important operation in the chemistry of the time, distillation, stretches from Brunschwig's *Liber de arte distillandi* (1500) through the centuries. With the growing taste for spirits (which physicians rather encouraged than reproved) the distiller was becoming a manufacturer; distillation also figured in the preparation of many non-alcoholic spirits used medicinally and indus-trially. There was no full account to succeed the manuscript treatise of Cipriano Piccolpasso (1524–79) on the great Italian ceramic industry, with its superb empirical control of the chemistry of glazes and pigments, but its lack is somewhat recompensed by the books of the great French potter, Bernard Palissy (1524–89). The Venetian glass industry was well served by Antonio Neri's description of 1612. Many other authors, including Cornelius Agrippa at the beginning of the century and Baptista Porta at its end, reveal interest in and knowledge of various aspects of chemical technology, such as the treatment of metals, dyeing and colouring, or the jeweller's art.

Thus as alchemy sank more deeply into mysticism, its assertions of practical success increasingly doubted by experienced metallurgists, the industrial chemical arts offered ever greater incentives to fruitful enquiry.

Their processes and methods (in outline at least) no longer confined within the secrecy of the workshop or gild, they drew attention to the contrast between the detailed phenomena of chemical change exploited by craftsmen and the vacuous generality of philosophical or alchemical explanations. But the technological writers were masters of fact; their knowledge was fragmentary and unorganised, their observations haphazard and sometimes misleading. Chemistry as a systematic, explanatory science could not spring from this source alone.

Upon this double tradition of chemistry impinged the violent and irrational personality of Paracelsus (c. 1493–1541). Like Luther he was a totally unmodern man who nevertheless assisted the genesis of the modern world. He neither possessed nor desired the classical scholarship of the learned philosophers and physicians of his day, directing his appeal by passionate denunciation of the ancients, by extravagant claims for his own wonderful insight, and by proclaiming his own miraculous cures, to the lower levels of literacy and the humbler exponents of the medical art. His position was a simple one. Orthodox medical men were totally ignorant of the mysteries of life, disease and death which only he, Paracelsus, understood. Most of his ideas on these topics were of the cruder medieval kind, and even his contemporaries thought Paracelsus superstitious. He regarded everything—animal, vegetable and mineral—as having its virtue for human use, to be known by its signature.[1] The art of the physician was to recognise the disease and to know how to procure the 'virtue' required for its cure. The art of the pharmicist was to extract the virtue in medicines and multiply its efficacy. Here Paracelsus entered on new ground which for reasons that he could not have anticipated have given him a place in the history of chemistry. For he believed that virtues were to be extracted by pyrotechnical operations, by the boilings, solutions, precipitations and distillations practised by the alchemists. By his rule every factitious product of chemical art should find its proper place in the pharmacopoeia, alongside the few natural minerals long established in it. Even the numerous poisons yielded by chemistry had their hidden virtues.

This doctrine was not entirely unheralded. Alcohol, antimonial and mercuric compounds, and the mineral acids had already been recognised as meritorious drugs by some physicians, though rejected by others. Paracelsus, however, advocated the complete substitution of chemical remedies for the involved herbal preparations later called 'Galenicals'. He himself added practically nothing to chemical knowledge, but his followers of the iatrochemical school experimented boldly in the laboratory and in their (often unlawful) practice. By the early seventeenth

---

[1] The doctrine of signatures exploited a more or less arbitrary resemblance between the symptoms of a disease or a part of the human body and a substance or species. Thus the walnut in its shell, reminiscent of the brain in its skull, was indicated as a cure for ailments of the head.

century the term 'chemistry' was customarily applied to a distinct occupation, the preparation of medicaments by chemical processes. Chemists were further distinguished by their explanation of what happened in terms of the 'tria prima' (salt, sulphur, mercury). The practical successors of Paracelsus, who did not hesitate to rebuke him for his wilder assertions which were taken up by charlatans, and who were also often alchemists too, discovered and described for the first time many new reactions and substances, and took the first small steps towards a genuine chemical theory. In Andreas Libavius's *Alchimia* (1597), despite its title the first chemical textbook, the sixteenth century provided the model for the empirical treatment of chemistry which was to be so fruitfully developed during the next century and a half.

At the opening of the sixteenth century there were no botanists, zoologists or physiologists, and very few anatomists. On the other hand there were many medical men (and a few others) who were interested in these subjects, for they can all be said to have had some existence as appendages to medicine. As with medicine itself, the study of living nature was strongly influenced by Greek writings and ideas, especially in the first half of the century; continuity with the classical world, under the dominant authority of Aristotle and Galen, is even more obvious than in the physical-mathematical sciences. And in contrast to the latter, observation and description were the chief occupations; theoretical developments are of little significance. Whereas the tradition of science had been confined to the Mediterranean basin, the men of the sixteenth century were confronted by a world extending from the northern tundra to the South African cape, from the East to the West Indies. They responded to its challenge with a not unworthy attempt to catalogue and comprehend its richness of living species, though reluctant to confess that this had been unsurmised in antiquity.

Although Aristotle had written three major zoological treatises (*Historia animalium*; *De generatione animalium*; *De partibus animalium*)—works which reveal an astonishing range of enquiry and knowledge, and which were unexcelled before the later seventeenth century—the direct medieval inheritance was in this respect particularly feeble. The bestiary, with its legends and its heavy symbolic overlay, was the chief organ of medieval zoology, despite such exceptional evidence of first-hand observation as occurs in the *De arte venandi cum avibus* (*c.* 1248) of the Emperor Frederick II. The Renaissance tended to shift the stress from the universal to the particular, from the symbol to the reality, while at the same time enhancing the importance of the hitherto neglected material on animals and their behaviour available in Aristotle, Pliny and many other classical authors, but its effect was not markedly apparent before the middle of the century. Even painters seem to have found plants more inspiring subjects than animals: Leonardo's study of the flight of birds is characteristically unusual, but his inspiration seems to have been mechanical rather than biological.

The revival of biology belongs to a period when the Renaissance, an exclusively Italian phenomenon no longer, was transforming the art and scholarship of France, Germany and other still more remote parts of Europe. In zoology Conrad Gesner (1516–65) of Zürich was its greatest figure with Ulissi Aldrovandi (1522–1605) of Bologna as his close rival; it was assisted by such Frenchmen as Guillaume Rondelet (1507–66) and Pierre Belon (1517–64) and the Englishmen John Caius (1510–73) and William Penny (c. 1530–88). The explanation of their activity must be sought partly in religious devotion, partly in aesthetic appraisal, partly in sheer curiosity; it was generally accompanied by massive learning. For these men were scholars even more than they were observers and collectors —and the undisciplined urge to collect marvels produced strange results at this time, as in Aldrovandi's own museum. Compiling from almost every respectable author, their grasp was not satisfied by biological considerations of morphology and habitat but extended to philology, legend, proverb and dietetics. They rejected some, though not all, of the medieval fabrications of the crocodiles' tears and barnacle-goose kind; they assembled the beginnings of a corpus of sound information on animal species. This was the greatest achievement of these so-called 'encyclopaedic' naturalists—combined with their efforts towards procuring realistic representations of the creatures they described. Graphically, however, the zoological writers were less successful than the botanical. The tally of the immense variety of living and moving things was begun, but to the sterner scientific disciplines of classification and embryology, comparative anatomy and physiology, the sixteenth century naturalists contributed little new. They were certainly far from replacing Aristotle.

The situation in botany was more promising and ripened more swiftly. Herbal lore was an essential element in medical art, and in knowledge of authorities and field experience a few medieval herbalists had maintained a scientific tradition. The early printed herbals initiate no new trend; again a new phase begins late, and in the north rather than in Italy. Its commencement is generally assigned to the publication of Otto Brunfels's book (1530) because Brunfels, though unremarkable as a writer, had the good sense to employ an artist to make illustrations from actual specimens. Leonhart Fuchs's herbal (1542) is even more imposing—it is outstanding as a work of art—in that Fuchs was a man of deep learning and wide experience. Yet his work, like that of many of his successors, shows a utilitarian rather than a scientific mentality in its author. Of intrinsic biological problems he—and they—seem largely unaware; his horizon was limited to recognition and medicinal usefulness. Many other herbals, Latin and vernacular, illustrated and unillustrated, were published in the following half century, the pioneer English contribution in this new vein being John Gerard's (1597). All were modelled, directly or indirectly, on Dioscorides; plagiarism was common, and printers bought or stole each others' woodcut blocks.

In the latter part of the century collectors were extending their range widely and intensively over western Europe, and even to the New World and the East. Fuchs described maize, Gerard the common and the sweet potato, Matthias de l'Obel tobacco, and naturalists were eager to establish in their gardens the non-indigenous species described by such botanically-minded travellers as Garcia del Huerto and Nicholas Monardes. Under this pressure the old habit of identifying at least every group of plants with species described by the ancients broke down. It was realised that the flora of the north-west, and still more that of the lands beyond the sea, was distinct from that of the Mediterranean region. The ancients who had been ignorant of such drugs as guaiacum, such delicacies as chocolate, were clearly not omniscient; as clearly, the riches of the natural creation varied from continent to continent. Such discoveries suggested the need for a 'method' which would bring out the relationships between the thousands of plant species, and also permit their classification on principles less arbitrary than those of alphabetic or other groupings. A method could only be based on the selection of certain morphological characteristics to be used as criteria of relationship and classification; from the nature and use of this selection arose the problems of systematic taxonomy figuring so largely in the history of botany during the next two hundred years. In this direction, especially through the ideas of Andreas Cesalpino (1519–1603) and de l'Obel (1538–1619), the sixteenth century made important advances; generally, there were great developments in collection, arrangement and description. Moreover, the progress of botany as a study in its own right was assisted by the separation of the pharmaceutical interest, marked by the publication of the first official pharmacopoeias (Florence 1498, Nuremburg 1551, Augsburg 1564). But the sixteenth-century naturalist was more concerned with the plant as a specimen than with its functioning as an organism. Just as study of the animal as such remained much where Aristotle had left it, so knowledge of the plant level of existence had advanced little if at all beyond that of his pupil Theophrastus. Biology had begun one of its great tasks—that of enumeration—but a fresh onslaught on the other, the investigation of the conditions and processes of the living state, was to come very much later.

In this respect only the study of man himself is unusual. Knowledge of the gross structure of his body was revised and clarified; old ideas of its working in health and subjection to disease were criticised; even man's psychology was less dogmatically considered than before. Without displacement of the main pillars of Greek and medieval thought on these topics, there were shifts of emphasis and modifications of detail productive of fruitful controversy. These in turn reflected on medical practice, giving new indications for treatment, softening a little the unyielding tradition of book-learned medicine inherited from the Middle Ages. It became more creditable in the physician to be willing to observe and experiment.

Anatomy was the primary medical study, recognised as indispensable to medical qualification. The achievement of the sixteenth-century anatomists was shaped by their duties as university teachers, to lecture by Galen's book and also demonstrate its truths upon the body. This was the established procedure of which the Renaissance brought out the full potentialities, refining the technique of dissection, correcting but not abandoning Galen, welding together verbal description and visual experience. For Galen's anatomical treatises were not suddenly replaced, even by Vesalius's *Fabrica*—William Harvey in 1628 built his arguments on Galen's views even while effecting a new synthesis of recent anatomical discoveries—and none of the great practical anatomists of the preceding century had set out to prove flatly that Galen was wrong. Rather they were surprised afresh as each of his errors was revealed. As elsewhere in science criticism was not so much directed against the genuine classical learning which newer standards of scholarship brought to light as against its medieval interpretation. The very motives leading men to dissect and occasionally to experiment seem to have been the desire for a full understanding of Galen's words (in this way dissection was complementary to the efforts of the textual scholars), and the search for material which would enable them to comment faithfully upon these words and illustrate them. Since Galen's anatomical treatises were the most useful extant, they must be mastered before they could be superseded.

When men like Berengario da Carpi (1470–1550), Vesalius, and Bartolomeo Eustachio (1520–74) turned to dissection as a means at once of research and instruction they were therefore still within the Galenic framework. But anatomists had no wish to confine their knowledge to the audience of the lecture-room, and in using the printing-press some adopted graphic representation to supplement their texts. Indeed, after a time text became in some instances subservient to illustration, as in Vesalius's *Epitome*. The principle was not wholly new; besides a rare medieval anatomical drawing, some coarse woodcuts had been published before the beginning of the century, but the serious history of anatomical illustration begins in the time of Berengario and Charles Estienne (1520–30). From their fairly crude figures there is a rapid ascent to the magnificent woodcuts of Vesalius (1543) and the perhaps technically superior copper-plates of Eustachio (c. 1552), both of which were frequently copied.[1] The preparation of illustrated anatomies still further

___

[1] Vesalius's cuts were tremendously popular; they are revived (with slight modifications) in Diderot's *Encyclopédie*. Eustachio's plates were also much re-used in the eighteenth century, when they were discovered and first printed.

promoted application to dissection, for the excellence and usefulness of the artist's work was in direct proportion to the skill and experience of the operator. Here, moreover, the learned, scientific study of anatomy was quickened by artistic insight. Leonardo's anatomical sketches, unexcelled in their own or any time, are well known, and he was not unique in this passion. Graphic realism provided an unprecedented vehicle for instruction in anatomy; and it is to its draughtsman— whoever he was—that Vesalius's *Fabrica* owes much of its fame and significance.

The *De humani corporis fabrica* (1543) was the highest achievement of Renaissance anatomy and the greatest feat in the attainment of scientific accuracy before Tycho's work in astronomy. Vesalius was no theorist—he exposed the chief factual impediment to Galen's explanation of the heart's action without endeavouring to frame an alternative—and he castigated his authority far more often on grounds of fact and procedure (for example, referring to the human body structures found only in animals) than for his interpretations. Despite such criticisms Vesalius's treatment of human anatomy was closely modelled on Galen's; but Galen thus elucidated, revised and illustrated was far more useful and accessible to contemporaries than were Galen's own writings. The way was cleared—though not fully traversed—for a return in anatomy to actual observation of the body, and Vesalius founded at Padua a school which was capable of proceeding farther in this way than he himself. In comparative anatomy, in the dissection of particular organs, in the study of embryology, the Italian successors of Vesalius initiated modern branches of science. Laboratory dissection was placed in a firm position as the chief tool of zoological investigation, with man as its principal subject, and the techniques of the anatomist were made to serve enquiries remote from their original demonstrative purpose.

The consequences of the advanced anatomical knowledge of the sixteenth century were, however, only to be worked out in the next. So also with human physiology: the first great step, related directly to the work of the Paduan anatomists, was Harvey's theory of the circulation of the blood (1628). Changes in ideas of how the body works were more closely linked with broad changes in outlook and medical experience than with specific anatomical discoveries. The French physician Jean Fernel (1497–1558) was in his mature years equally hostile to belief in the influence of the heavens on the body and to faith in magical remedies. His scepticism sprang from experience of the futility of these superstitions, from reason, and from confidence in the Galenic doctrine. It was not grounded on any new scientific facts or ideas. For Fernel the body and the diseases afflicting it were within the sphere of rational causality and not at the mercy of mysterious forces, but his causes are Galen's causes and his physiology is Galen's physiology, logically and coherently presented.

Fernel had no conception that physiology could be investigated by experiment, being certain that it could not be enlightened by cutting up dead bodies from which the governing spirit and its 'faculties' had passed away; the functioning of the body could be 'known only by meditation' upon the physician's experience. The sole challenge to such orthodoxy came from the Paracelsians, who rejected the theory that digestion was effected by heat. Instead they supposed that an 'archeus' or internal chemist inhabiting the stomach separated the harmful 'tartar' in food from the beneficent parts which were converted into 'mercury' and absorbed. This fantastic conception, though winning little favour at the time, had some indirect effect in encouraging the development of more plausible 'chemical' theories in the seventeenth century.

It follows that changes in medical practice also owed little to the more conspicuous advances in the medical sciences. Vesalius took part in a controversy on blood-letting: but it can scarcely be found that his anatomical experience influenced his arguments. Servetus, the earliest exponent of the 'lesser circulation' of the blood from the heart through the lungs and back, is tediously traditional when he orates on syrups. Medical practice was inevitably more responsive to variations in the incidence of disease, to changes in the pharmacopoeia attributable to the influence of Paracelsus and the admission of outlandish drugs, and among the best physicians to accumulated observation, than it was to work at the dissecting table. The progress of surgery was, however, directly related to the satisfactory teaching of anatomy. This was generally recognised, and there was a corresponding tendency for the social standing of the surgeon to improve as he strove for higher learning and skill. The operative parts and practical parts of medicine seem indeed to have been more genuinely progressive than the theoretical.

Without doubt the world of science was wider at the beginning of the seventeenth century than it had been in the early years of Copernicus and Leonardo da Vinci, and men were traversing it more freely. Scientific curiosity was flourishing outside the universities and was proving more creative among the laity than among the clergy, for so long almost the sole guardians of learning. In Italy and elsewhere scientific clubs were springing up, lectureships were being founded, vernacular works of importance were being written. Practical science—mathematical, physical and chemical—was developing apace; soon Bacon would emphasise the utility of natural knowledge and set the artisan's experience almost at the same level as the philosopher's insight. Though major challenges to the hitherto unquestioned authority (and veracity) of classical authors were few, and though these challenges were resisted by the vast majority, they had been made and they were to prove fruitful. Even within the limitations of ancient sources there was a wider and deeper familiarity; the legacy of Greek science was less narrowly cramping, less dogmatic, less tightly homogeneous, than it had seemed in the Middle Ages.

All this represents a growth, an intensification of the trend of medieval science rather than a deflection from it. Almost everything that happens in the history of science in the sixteenth century has a medieval precedent and would have been comprehensible, if repugnant, to earlier generations in a way that the science of the age of Newton was not. Significantly, attempts to re-state fundamentally the aims and methods of science were made (by Francis Bacon, Galileo, Descartes and indeed by almost every major figure) in the seventeenth century, not in the sixteenth. In the latter period reason and logic were esteemed in their due spheres; mathematics was rising in prominence as an analytical technique; the importance of experiment and observation was admitted; but though men used all these elements in building their picture of the natural world, they by no means supposed them to constitute its totality. Propositions that the seventeenth century was to qualify as religious, metaphysical, or superstitious passed without question in the currency of sixteenth-century science. The old impediments to the full development of a scientific attitude—credulous faith in authorities, superstition, appeals to Providence and Divine Will, failure to observe and verify—were not yet overcome, indeed they were in some respects more troublesome than ever. Nature was capable of working in very odd ways and producing strange creatures, and no one dared yet to impose limitations on her oddity. The concept of the 'law of nature', the foundation of a mechanistic science, was itself unformulated. A salve applied to a weapon *might* heal a wounded man; there *might* be mermaids, animals with human heads, cockatrices, salamanders living in the fire; metals *might* grow like moss in the veins from which they were dug. It was hard to distinguish the unverified from the impossible, and only rarely were men inclined to doubt a supposed effect on account of the lack of a sufficient cause. The very decline of the influence of the classics allowed a more marvellous and disorderly view of nature to be taken, until the classics were replaced by a new, more rigorous, scientific method.

The sixteenth century witnessed technological progress and gave to Europeans first-hand knowledge of three-quarters of the globe. It gave them many new facts, and new fables. But it had furnished no new principles for distinguishing fact from fiction, or for facilitating the cumulative acquisition of organised facts that Bacon was to see as the chief immediate task of science, save its few examples of systematic observation. Nor did it offer new theories to correlate and account for facts that were already familiar, in relation to the falling of heavy bodies, the attraction of magnets, the mutations of light and colour and the 'transmutations' of chemistry, for example, even though some workers on all these subjects were aware of the frailty of the only theories they could give. It was a century of contrasts, between mysticism and incipient mechanism, between idolatry and criticism of the classics, between tedious conservatism and bold originality of hypothesis. The resolution of these antitheses, the framing of a new philosophy of nature and new theories appropriate to it, the forging of new tools of scientific enquiry, were to be the great achievements of the seventeenth century to which the sixteenth transmitted much that was valuable in the way of suggestion and exploration.

CHAPTER XIII

SCHOOLS AND UNIVERSITIES

THE rapid developments in educational theory and practice witnessed in this period have deservedly attracted much notice. There was a significant increase in the amount of speculation on the aims and methods of teaching and a number of institutions were established which actively practised new principles. Consideration of the question is, however, far from simple. On the one hand it is necessary to define the nature of the programme of educational reform in order to estimate, if possible, the degree to which schools and universities genuinely displayed a fresh approach. On the other hand one must disentangle the movement for reform in teaching from the movement for reform in religion, for the latter had marked repercussions in this field, not only confusing the issue for contemporaries but bedevilling later interpretations of the subject with confessional prejudice. Was there an advance in education or a regression? Did, or did not, the Reformation compromise and frustrate the Renaissance? Even the value of a classical education, which was adopted so firmly at this time as an ideal of pedagogy that it lasted invincible for over three centuries, has lately been called in question. On one point fortunately there can be little doubt. The novel attitudes which obtruded in the sixteenth century were not victorious suddenly. They modified existing machinery only gradually, and for much of the time over most of Europe the educational facilities of the mid-sixteenth century were what they had been for some centuries before. It is therefore necessary to begin by surveying the traditional structure of schools and universities.

Even more important, one must bear in mind that for a large majority the formal instruction of the school, which had developed from purely clerical needs, had little relevance. That this was the case with the peasantry, who formed the vast bulk of the population of Europe, needs little demonstration: the seasons, the sky and the agricultural wisdom of their forefathers were schoolmasters for most men. True, priesthood offered a sure way for the humblest boy to improve his social status and that of his family; the desperate efforts of Thomas Platter to find teachers indicate the prestige of letters in an unlettered Alpine valley; but few boys had his persistence and there was in any case room in the Church for only a handful of recruits. In towns, though there it was easier to find teachers, systematic instruction in Latin was less important than the practical study involved in apprenticeship, as lengthy and as carefully controlled as the arts course at a university. Even for the gentry and nobility, especially outside Italy, the subjects which really mattered were provided in the age-old way: riding and the use of weapons, hunting; an eye for a rich heiress, a good estate, and a sound animal. It is true that the gentlemen of the late Middle Ages found reading and writing more than mere graces. To comprehend complicated estate accounts one needed not only literacy, but if possible a smattering of the law and a head for figures. But such practical attainments were not offered by school or college training. A tutor of sorts was therefore a not uncommon member of the great man's household, and the children of the gentry usually had a domestic chaplain from whom they might learn their letters, or the services of the local priest; accounting procedure was acquired by the hard way of profit and loss, and the law by both exuberant litigation and an increasing habit of turning at least one member of the family into a lawyer.

The modern distinction between primary, secondary and university education was not made in the Middle Ages, but in fact teaching then fell into the same categories. Primary education, the instruction of young children in reading and writing, was widely available, though it was seldom endowed adequately and therefore tended to be intermittent. As with all other teachers, the elementary schoolmaster or mistress required the licence of the bishop, though one may doubt whether this was always obtained by the man or woman who earned a little extra by sharing an ability to read, write and reckon with a handful of children on a purely *ad hoc* basis. There were, however, more regular schools. The need for choristers made the song school a regular feature of the late medieval chantry and church; here reading and elementary instruction were part and parcel of the musical training. The writing school is another type of school which is found in all western countries, though it, and its humbler relation, the ABC school or reading school, were often in the hands of men whose qualifications were slight: at Launceston in the 1540's the ABC school was kept by 'an aged man chosen by the mayor', and at Glasney, also in Cornwall, it was kept by the bellringer. Most frequently the local priest was the local schoolmaster: the 'pedant who keeps a school i' the church' of Shakespeare; an episcopal synod at Chartres in 1526 prescribed a school in each parish where 'a priest or clerk may be found able to teach the alphabet and the creed'; and the convocation of Canterbury in 1529 required 'all having cures...to teach boys the alphabet and reading'. The curriculum of these elementary schools was based on a conjunction of the alphabet with Latin and vernacular versions of the Lord's Prayer, the Creed, and other prayers and graces. These, which were to develop in England into the 'ABC and Primer', were an introduction to the basic tenets of the faith as well as to the elements of reading, and were relevant to the further education of the clerk which lay behind elementary instruction itself. But many who had no desire to become clergy attended elementary schools; and it is significant that in the larger towns there is much evidence for the existence of schools where practical arithmetic was taught, the 'reckoning' needed by merchant or steward. There are good grounds for supposing that elementary education of the kind described was increasingly available in the later fifteenth and early sixteenth centuries: in England the movement is associated in particular with the multiplication of chantries; on the continent the Rhineland, for example, seems to have had many schools—at Xanten we find the master of such a school complaining in 1491 that he and his assistant are overworked, and a few years later five elementary teachers are employed at Wesel, while schools are found in even small Rhenish villages. Moreover, whatever entrance requirements they tried to preserve, many grammar schools in practice had elementary classes, the 'petties' or *petits*, taught either by a junior master or a senior boy.

The secondary or grammar school was even more closely associated with the Church and, like the elementary school, frequently developed alongside chantry and college. The grammar school master was more rigorously supervised by the ordinary (or, in certain university towns, by the authorities of the university) than his counterpart in the elementary school; and he was more jealous of the monopolistic privilege conferred on him by his licence. His function was the preparation of boys for higher clerical education at the university, and though his school might be saddled with very young pupils, in general his charges began their grammar at the age of seven. The grammar was Latin grammar, though instruction in the lower classes involved the vernacular, and the basic texts were the Latin service books and portions of the Vulgate, together with such textbooks as Donatus and Alexander de Ville-Dieu (Dolensis). The pupil then progressed to the *Dicta Catonis* and selections from Cicero, Ovid and Virgil. In university centres the grammar school was properly so termed; elsewhere, especially in large towns, the curriculum of the school occasionally covered most of the subjects of the university arts faculty. 'Latine loqui, pie vivere': if religious instruction was absent from the curriculum, it informed all the subjects that were taught and the aim was a preparation for that ecclesiastical institution, the university, where the boy was sent at adolescence. As with elementary schools, so with Latin or grammar schools, the evidence suggests a steady multiplication in the century prior to the Reformation, and there is no doubt that many boys attended school who had no intention of proceeding later to a university. The larger German towns had well-found establishments, often attached to the main church; in England it is clear that relatively modest towns had such schools attached to churches, chantries and guilds, as well as one or two 'private' grammar schools of which Winchester and Eton are the most famous. On the other hand the miseries of John Butzbach and Thomas Platter warn us not to paint too rosy a picture of the educational facilities available in the early years of the sixteenth century. The number of schools was perhaps increasing, but the quality of teaching was often very low.

The most impressive evidence of expanding facilities for education, however, is provided by the universities. A total of forty-five *studia generalia* had been created by the end of the fourteenth century, enough (one might have supposed) to cater for the needs of Christendom. But in the fifteenth century thirty-three more were erected[1] and up to 1550 there were added half as many more. The most noticeable feature of fifteenth- and early sixteenth-century foundations is that for the most part they are found in the countries where there were no great *studia* in the thirteenth and fourteenth centuries: Spain and Portugal, Scotland, above all the Empire, where in 1520 there were eighteen universities to compare with the five which existed by 1400. Theoretically the university still offered a training in arts leading on to professional training in the higher faculties of law, medicine, and theology, but in the early sixteenth century, as for long past, the faculty of arts in all universities contained a large proportion of youths who had no intention of graduating even as bachelors of arts, but who regarded a year or two as an undergraduate a desirable experience. For them attendance at the formal lectures on the prescribed texts in grammar, rhetoric, and logic had little relevance. It may be inferred that this element in the university was increasing from the grim introduction of corporal punishment in the colleges of Oxford and Paris: the rod of the schoolmaster was put into the hands of the don because the don was doing increasingly what was regarded as schoolmaster's work.

The structure of education sketched above was continuously if slowly changing. Already in the field of secondary education the schools associated with the Brethren of the Common Life, like the great school at Deventer, were breaking new ground: here in the eight large classes a boy was led up to the study of texts which at the time seemed unusual—a good deal of Virgil, Cicero, Horace, and Baptista Mantuanus—by teachers like Hegius (d. 1498) who were scholars as well as grammarians. Many pupils of the Brethren started a similar tradition in new areas; Dringenberg took it to Schlettstadt where Wimpheling was educated, and where John Sturm was later to be a pupil. Already in 1509 Colet had founded St Paul's school, no different in spirit maybe to earlier schools controlled by city companies, but much larger, better endowed, and devoted expressly to 'good litterature, with latin and greke, and good auctors suych as haue the veray Romayne eliquence joyned with wisdome, specially Cristyn auctours'; and prescribing not only the old familiar texts but also Erasmus's *Institutum Christiani hominis* and *De copia*. As for universities, many changes were in progress. At Paris and Oxford the colleges were rising fast at the expense of the university; commoners were everywhere

---

[1] For these figures see Rashdall (ed. Powicke and Emden), vol. I, p. xxiv; Dôle and Besançon are counted as one, see *ibid*. vol. II, p. 192.

more accepted than they had been; and specialisation was turning the *magister* or *doctor* into the *professor*. As for the teaching in the university, the very nature of the arts course and the tradition of licensing visiting teachers allowed for innovations, like the chairs of poetry in several continental universities, or the lectures given by visiting experts, like those of Aleander at Paris. In both school and university the printing press gradually affected teaching. Disputation, and dictation of text and commentary, remained basic, but the existence of cheaper books enabled commentaries to be more elaborate and dictation slowly declined. By 1520, for example, well over 250 editions of the *Doctrinale* of Alexander of Ville-Dieu had been published.

These changes were nevertheless not to be compared with the rapid advance in educational theory and practice witnessed in Italy during the fifteenth century, on which a great deal of sixteenth-century pedagogy elsewhere in Europe was to be based. The numerous towns of Italy, its flourishing universities, the existence of a prosperous and leisured bourgeoisie, are themselves among the reasons for the revival of letters. This in turn was above all an educational programme. The humanist *par excellence* was the humanist educator. It would, of course, be false to suggest that the professional institutions which provided for the educational needs of trans-Alpine Europe were there absent or essentially different: Bologna laid its impress more or less deeply on all northern universities and the example of Paris was equally influential in the *studia* of the peninsula. But when interest in Latin antiquity and in ancient moral attitudes began to be cultivated the Italian universities, virtually independent of Church control and lacking important theological faculties, were well placed to respond. The older universities like Bologna and Padua were by no means hostile and gave considerable, if intermittent, encouragement to the new scholarship, while Florence (and later Pisa), Pavia and Ferrara were even more the homes of humanist teaching. Equally significant was the way in which Italians speculated on the principles of education, and the conclusions to which they came. This is revealed briefly by the stress laid on the Ciceronian dictum, 'virtutis laus omnis in actione consistat', in a letter from Vittorino da Feltre to Ambrogio Traversari. That this was the sentiment of the leading schoolmaster of the fifteenth century is hardly more remarkable than that he addressed such an observation to the pious monk and future saint, for piety and sanctity in earlier days had been at odds with the life of action, just as the clerical education in the Middle Ages had neglected the citizen or layman as such. For Vittorino, as for other Italian educationalists of the time, the aim of instruction was not scholarship alone, nor technique alone, nor the inculcation of dogma. Existing 'schools'—whether the officially encouraged professional education of cloister and university, or the less systematic but equally professional teaching undergone by merchants' sons in towns or the children of the gentry in the courtyard and bower—were thus of small use. Italian theorists in this field were consequently at one with the general spirit of humanism and shared a conviction that ancient moral teaching, 'honestas gravitasque morum', was complementary to Christian values, and that knowledge in the arts and sciences could only be securely founded upon a study of the literature of antiquity. Letters were therefore a preparation for social life in its fullest sense: they inculcated ethical principles, they polished manners, and they deepened understanding. While such a preparation endowed a man with all the qualities necessary for public affairs, it was no small justification that they also refined and enriched the social intercourse of leisure.

The plans of education elaborated by Vergerio, Bruni, Aeneas Sylvius, Vegio and others are strikingly consistent. The early years of the child in the care of the mother, the tutor or preceptor who then undertook more formal instruction, and the larger school to which a pupil should go in his tenth year, are commonplaces of this literature. So are the subjects to be studied. While an encyclopaedic knowledge was regarded as an ideal, the concentration on the acquisition of a mastery of Latin, in which grammar was subordinated to an understanding of the best texts, was a more limited aim, and one which was reinforced by those feelings of proud patriotism which inspired much humanist activity. In the curriculum Terence was approved for his value in illustrating conversational Latin, Cicero as a master of prose both familiar and forensic, and Ovid and Virgil as poets. The historians were almost as highly regarded as these writers, for they provided a plentiful stock of moral instances, and the ethical content of the selected author was as important as his literary worth. To Latin, taught as far as possible as a living language, Greek was added, though it was studied generally for a shorter time and few, even of the teachers, aimed at speaking it. A chief justification of Greek was that it alone enabled a full elucidation of Latin and a similar end lay behind the study of ancient geography and natural history. While the humanist who was specially interested in physics or mathematics was clearly bound to deepen his knowledge of these subjects by studying the appropriate Greek and Latin writers, this formed no part of the ideal curriculum: geometry had a certain value as a school subject, but arithmetic was too akin to the reckoning of the shopkeeper to be of much service.

That these principles could be transmitted as readily as they were to the north of Europe in the sixteenth century is in part due to their having been elaborated mainly in the atmosphere not of the republics of Italy but of the princely courts. Though schools of a new or humanist type were established at Florence and Venice, the two great exponents of the new *ratio docendi* were Vittorino at the Gonzaga court at Mantua and Guarino Veronese at the Este court of Ferrara. Even in their day the habit of keeping a scholar of repute as tutor in a noble household was not a new one in Italy; thereafter it became a regular feature and is reflected in the general assumption of the educationalists that a *praeceptor* or *paedagogus* was the prime instrument for furthering the programme of studies. The group of children in the great man's entourage, composed of his own offspring and those of his retainers, clients and friends, is sufficiently medieval and sufficiently general in Europe; the Italian courts had adapted the existing practice by providing a trained schoolmaster, and as their court was situated in a town the schoolmaster could form the centre of the intellectual aristocracy of the community, as Guarino did at Ferrara. Accustomed as they were to the notion of a domestic tutor or chaplain, the princes and nobility of the north could follow suit by replacing him with a man chosen for his scholarship. There was, however, a certain difficulty of adjustment. The humanist schools of Italy were on the whole large; the northern practice among the leisured class was for a tutor and only a few children. Vittorino and others in Italy found no reason to discourage athletic and martial activity. This side of Italian experience found a ready acceptance among some educationalists in the north and clearly linked up closely with the traditional discipline of the gentry; but it found less acceptance with Erasmus or Vives, who regarded physical exercise solely as a means of keeping fit and not as a desirable end in itself. But these differences are small and what impresses one is the dependence of publicists and practitioners in northern Europe on the methods and aims of an earlier generation of Italians.

Among the northern theorists two are pre-eminent for their influence and originality, Erasmus and Luis Vives. Erasmus,[1] although not in any real sense a teacher, performed many services to education of a practical kind, some of which will call for notice later. His principles as such are mainly contained in the *De pueris instituendis* of 1529; other directly relevant works are the *De ratione studii* (1511), and the *De civilitate morum puerilium* (1530); but many other writings bear on questions of education.[2] For Erasmus education on the humanist plan justified itself by providing a direct approach to the scriptures and the roots of living Christianity, by its civilising powers and because it made available the sound scholarship of antiquity. The *seminaria pietatis*, the liberal disciplines, the duties of society and purity of manners were inculcated at the same time and in the same way, and were necessary to all men, unlike the technical or professional attainments provided in conventional teaching. The child, after learning from his mother both piety and the ability to write, and, when possible, the elements of Latin, should pass at the age of seven into the hands of his father, a schoolmaster or a tutor: few fathers

---

[1] Cf. above, pp. 369 f., 372 ff., for his literary activities.

[2] Cf. Erasmus's own lists of works 'qui spectant ad institutionem literarum', in *Opus Epistolarum* (ed. Allen), vol. I, pp. 38–9; vol. VIII, pp. 373–4.

were able to undertake the work, few schoolmasters could be trusted; a tutor was therefore the best solution, teaching a small group of boys. The tutor's task was to teach Latin by direct methods—conversation, the use of dialogue, and easy texts, with much oral and written composition—the constant aim being to extract the moral teaching of the works studied and to acquire fluency in self-expression. Rhetorical facility as taught by Quintilian was to be studied in Cicero. Greek was to be taught in a different way and in a somewhat different spirit: there was no attempt to acquire a colloquial mastery of the language, and it was to be regarded as valuable for the light it threw on the Bible, for its illustration of Roman literature and for its value in scientific subjects.

Juan Luis Vives (1492–1540) was as cosmopolitan a figure as Erasmus. A Spaniard by birth, his adult life was passed in France, England and the Low Countries. Like Erasmus, he too was the author of school books as well as of treatises on education itself. Of these last the most important was the *De tradendis disciplinis* of 1531. For Vives the home and the mother have more importance than they have for Erasmus, but he is in agreement that, though a school is best, a good tutor is more readily found than a good school. Ability to read and write a vernacular well was regarded as desirable by Vives, as it was by Italian educationalists by the end of the fifteenth century; and he is prepared to add vernacular historians to ancient historians as sources of moral instances. But by the study of language he meant the study of Latin, and its grammar should be a means to an end, not an aspect of dialectic. Here again we meet the direct method and a programme of reading culminating in Cicero, and in the study of Greek as an adjunct to Latin. Hostile as he is to logic and dialectic of the old-fashioned kind, he is prepared to admit mathematics and physics, though good textbooks are lacking. For Vives as for Erasmus, a profound religious impulse colours all education. Scholarship as such, though admirable, must be subordinated to the practice of a Christian life. The schoolmaster may thus be encyclopaedic, but for his pupils he must be more modest and contrive to instil an *eruditio* which will be compatible with *pietas*.

The third great exponent of educational doctrine in this period is Cardinal Giacomo Sadoleto (1477–1547) in his *De liberis recte instituendis* (1533). Again we find the absence of good schools deplored and recourse to a tutor advised. But in Sadoleto we find a greater stress on Greek, because of the current Platonic preoccupation of Italians, and an interest in *philosophia* which stems from the same root. Moreover, Sadoleto envisages an education which aims at covering in general fashion the whole field of knowledge, though he argues that each pupil should also cultivate a special interest and competence.

The programmes advanced by Erasmus, Vives and Sadoleto were essentially scholastic; although they extolled the civilising value of literature, they gave this a subordinate position. It would, however, be wrong to exclude those writers whose aims were educational in only a limited sense, and who made manners their chief interest. For Castiglione's *Courtier* (1528) and the *Galateo* (1558) of Giovanni della Casa very significantly affected the general view of the gentleman's qualities in northern Europe. Both books were widely translated and naturally appealed to French, English, and Germans for whom the gentry constituted the most influential single element in society, and for whom the new ideals of deportment, conversation and moral behaviour could be grafted on an ancient doctrine of chivalry: 'manners makyth man' was a medieval notion, and it was the manners which were changing, not the respect they were given. The fusing of the literary aims of Erasmus and Vives with the courtesy of Castiglione is clearly seen in *The Boke named the Gouernour* (1531) of Sir Thomas Elyot (d. 1546). Both Erasmus and Vives were products of the educational system they criticised and tried to correct. Elyot was not a graduate, yet the long tale of his works shows what intellectual accomplishments an active and intelligent youth could acquire in London and away from the university. His detachment from professional education enabled him to reflect more than most northerners the genial aim of the Italian educationalists. His purpose in the *Gouernour* was to liberalise the central figures of secular society; his 'governors' were all men with administrative responsibilities from the king's immediate officials down to the modest gentlemen who served as J.P.'s. For the children of such men he prescribes the Erasmian programme of Latin as a living language, and accepts the need of a tutor; but he is prepared (as Erasmus is not) to diversify the hard business of learning a language with music and drawing and physical exercise. The whole end is the acquisition of a wisdom, based on the teaching of antiquity, which will flower in social virtue and social usefulness.

What effect did the speculations of the theorists have on practical education? They unquestionably diffused the basic doctrines of the Italian theorists of the *quattrocento*; and they also lent new authority to the habit of sending the children of great men to school or of giving them a tutor, while the kind of tutor they prescribed, and who was more frequently appointed, was now a grammarian, not, as of old, a clerk. As a result, the landed classes accepted in the end the necessity of formal education. Their effect on the institutional side of teaching is harder to assess, for the theorists were above all thinking in terms of the family. In any case schools and universities were developing and changing, thus offering an opportunity for new methods, while not necessarily depending on them. In the field of textbooks the humanist contribution was great, as will be pointed out.

Three celebrated types of secondary education may be instanced as examples of humanist principles in action outside Italy: the Collège de

Guyenne at Bordeaux, Sturm's school at Strassburg, and the curriculum of the first Jesuit seminaries. It will be evident that these establishments—the first French and tainted with reform, the second German and avowedly protestant, and the third a celebrated 'instrument' of the Counter-Reformation—were broadly similar in their approach; and that they were employing methods which were by no means entirely novel. The Collège de Guyenne was provided with a group of 'notables lecteurs' whom André Gouvéa took with him when he left Paris in response to the invitation of the magistrates of Bordeaux in 1534. Under Gouvéa the school flourished and its curriculum in the mid-century became celebrated. The tenth, or bottom form, contained the *alphabetarii* or *abecedarii*, learning through the vernacular the elements of Latin on the basis of liturgical material and the *Libellus puerulorum*, a summary of inflections. The boy who could master this material, who could conjugate and decline his Latin, as well as write legibly, was promoted to the ninth form, the biggest in the school. Here a fluent command of French and above all of Latin was the aim; Cato's moral *Disticha* was read along with a more advanced grammar. In the eighth class a selection from Cicero's letters and scenes from Terence were the means of acquiring *locutiones*, and a weekly prose supplemented daily construing. The boy of fair ability attained the seventh class at the age of eleven or twelve, and embarked on a more elaborate treatment of the same texts; in the sixth and fifth classes larger texts were tackled, including a play of Terence entire, and a beginning was made of the study of prosody. In the fourth class there were more significant changes: an oration of Cicero was studied with a manual of rhetoric, compositions became longer and included verse, and a start was made on Greek. This set the pattern for the top three forms, though a little mathematics was taught in the third and later years: Cicero; Virgil, Ovid, Lucan among the poets; Quintilian; the historians, were the main texts studied, and composition now included the preparation of declamations. Disputations were a frequent device of the form-master, and, though French was freely used in the translation and commentary on authors, the aim was fluency in Latin speech as well as in writing. John Sturm (d. 1589) was appointed rector of the *Gymnasium* at Strassburg in 1538 and his curriculum—though he introduced Greek earlier and used Bible texts more—is virtually the same as that of Gouvéa and Vinet at Bordeaux. Jesuit schools, which began to multiply from 1546 onwards, were also very similar; the final *ratio studiorum* was not drawn up until later in the century but the main lines of the Jesuit programme are already evident in the constitutions of 1551. Grammar (Latin at first and then Greek) was taught in seven forms by the same methods as in Protestant schools, though there was much less brutality, a greater insistence on prizes and competition as a stimulus to zeal, and more ruthlessness in expurging from classical texts those portions considered inflammatory for the young. In their attention to the psychology of teaching the Jesuits were in advance of most practical teachers outside their order; but their aims were the same as those of other humanist educators: the inculcation of morality and manners by a rhetorical and linguistic training. When both Protestants and Catholics proclaimed the virtues of grammar it is hardly surprising that the classical curriculum dominated secondary schools so completely and so permanently.

The spread of the classical school is less remarkable if it is remembered that its organisation was itself not essentially new. The curriculum of medieval grammar schools is somewhat obscure, but larger schools were probably always organised in upwards of six forms. Hegius at Deventer had eight forms; the Breslau school in the early sixteenth century had nine. Wolsey's abortive foundation at Ipswich was to have eight classes; Eton in 1528 had seven but by the mid-century had dropped to the six which were to become engrained in English tradition. As promotions from one class to the next could be made quarterly or half-yearly, the variations between one school and another in the number of forms is made smaller. Even if the shape of the larger school had already existed, the speed is remarkable with which the new grammar ousted the old. One can trace the leaven at work in a man like Mathurin Cordier who taught at Nevers, then at Bordeaux, at Geneva, and at Lausanne, leaving wherever he went the imprint of a new approach to teaching; or in John Sturm, pupil of the famous school at Schlettstadt, whose reputation he was to dim by the academy he directed at Strassburg. The high repute of Sturm's school led to it being copied by many other teachers; it was visited by Calvin when he was considering plans for school development at Geneva; when Thomas Platter was appointed to the municipal school at Basle in 1541 he also consulted Sturm. In Protestant Germany the espousal by Melanchthon of the new curriculum lent at a crucial period the force of orthodoxy to educational reform: his advice was sought on educational matters by fifty-six towns; his influence was more directly seen in the Latin school at Eisleben (1525) and the *Oberschule* at Nuremberg (1526); and for ten years he himself kept a private school at Wittenberg. Melanchthon's influence is also seen in John Bugenhagen, whose ordinance for the school at Brunswick (1528) was also the basis of the regulations in seven other North German towns. The *praeceptor Germaniae* taught much to the Jesuits, his opponents, and not least that conscious system was essential to an efficient school. Backed by a powerful order, served by exceptionally well-trained teachers, it is no surprise that Jesuit schools multiplied: when the founder of the order died in 1556 there were over thirty schools run by the Jesuits for others besides their own novices, and the numbers contined to rise. Their success in Catholic Germany was very considerable.

The signs and symbols of the new curriculum were its textbooks even more than its texts. Donatus, the *Doctrinale* of Alexander of Ville-Dieu, the *Graecismus* of Eberhard of Bethune and other medieval grammatical works were still much used in the humanist grammar school: Melanchthon and the Jesuits both prescribed Donatus; and the grammatical works of Jean Despautère (van Pauteren, d. 1520), which improved only a little on the *Doctrinale*, was equally patronised. But they were used only for the lower forms, they were treated as grammars pure and simple, not as the subject of dialectic, and they gradually gave way before more up-to-date manuals. The dissatisfaction of the teacher with the old textbooks is shown by the number of schoolmasters who composed new ones. The presses of all large towns were constantly issuing works by local grammarians and pedagogues. England was far from being in the van of the movement, yet we find John Anwykyll, master of Magdalen College School, issuing his *Compendium totius grammatice* in 1483. His successor John Stanbridge moved to Banbury in 1501: his *Accidentia* was printed seventeen times between 1505 and 1550; and, aside from other frequently issued books, his *Vulgaria*, an English and Latin vocabulary, came out seven times between 1508 and 1529. Robert Whittinton's *Declinationes nominum* was printed sixteen times by 1533, and 128 editions of other grammatical works by him have been listed for about the same period. More important still, because better in quality and graced with the approval of Erasmus, were the efforts of Colet and the high-master of his school at St Paul's, William Lily. Lily's *Absolutissimus de octo orationis partium constructione libellus* and the *Brevissima institutio* of Lily and Colet were the basis of the grammar officially commanded by Henry VIII in 1540. On the continent the same process is at work: Melanchthon's *Grammatica Latina* had the same repute amongst Protestant school teachers as had later the *De institutione grammatica* of the Portuguese Jesuit Emmanuel Alvarez among Catholics. Many others could be mentioned some of whose works had more than local significance—as, for example, those of Rivius at Meissen and of Camerarius, who was a schoolmaster at Nuremberg before he taught in universities.

Even more characteristic of the new pedagogy were the books of conversational Latin which humanist teachers composed for their pupils. As with so much in humanist technique, the dialogue was a medieval inheritance and was closely related to a catechetical method associated above all with religious instruction. But the old form was filled with new meaning and the colloquy emerged. Though perhaps not the first in the field, Erasmus was undoubtedly the greatest of the colloquial writers, and the prolonged success of his *Familiarium colloquiorum opus* was perhaps due to the origin of some of the earlier pieces it contained in what little practical instruction Erasmus had himself given. Scribbled down in 1497, they were published by Beatus Rhenanus without Erasmus's knowledge in 1518. The first edition by Erasmus came in 1522; thereafter they were revised, extended and reprinted steadily; by the death of Erasmus in 1536 the work had appeared a hundred times. The earliest of the *Colloquies* were mere lists of phrases—'formulae salutandi'. Then came the 'percontandi forma in primo congressu' with two interlocutors, and then a 'domestica confabulatio'. These, however, are soon followed by the famous conversations in which Erasmus scourges contemporary follies, which belong not only to the history of education but to the history of religion and literature. Though bitterly attacked by the Sorbonne and condemned for their frivolity and worse by both Luther and Loyola, the *Colloquies* are found in school use all over both Catholic and Protestant Europe. They were, however, far from being alone in the field and a number of other books of similar type were composed which had no pretensions to the satirical approach of Erasmus. The *Paedologia* of P. Mosellanus, *Dialogi pueriles* of C. Hegendorff, and the *Dialogi* of A. Barland are all contemporaneous with Erasmus. Of many similar works, two had more than ordinary success, the *Linguae Latinae exercitatio* (1538) of Vives, and the *Colloquiorum scholasticorum libri quattuor* (1564) of Cordier. The importance of these books lies in the vivid reminder of the aim of the new grammar school curriculum—the acquisition of a command of Latin speech at once fluent, graceful and correct. This aim was also responsible for the importance attached (as already noted) to Terence and to Latin versions of the dialogues of Lucian which were prescribed at many schools. Equally it lies behind the Latin drama being actually produced—a feature above all of Sturm's method at Strassburg— which led in turn to the composition of neo-Latin dramatic pieces, more particularly in Germany and among the Jesuits.[1]

The new concentration on the humanities affected school teaching profoundly, as indicated. The impact on the universities was distinctly less marked. The sixteenth-century educationalist was less concerned about the quality of advanced work than about school teaching. The university as it existed in the sixteenth century was still primarily a professional institution, and while the arts faculties were naturally affected by a new attitude to literature and grammar, the senior disciplines of medicine, law and theology were markedly less responsive. In general it seems true to say that the new education was not regarded with general hostility by the older universities, though the Sorbonne was suspicious and at Oxford 'Greeks' and 'Trojans' for a time made an issue of the reception of the new learning. Many scholars of the new stamp are found in European universities; the school movement had had the effect of closing the gap between secondary and university education; editions of classical authors were addressed to both the senior forms of schools and students at universities. Yet the great monuments of advanced erudition are often curiously detached from academic roots. Erasmus was in no sense a university man. Robert Estienne's *Thesaurus linguae Latinae* (full

---

[1] Cf. above, p. 369.

edition 1543) was not a product of a university; nor was the Greek *Thesaurus* of his son Henri (1572). It is noteworthy that at Venice and Lyons, where so much learned literature was printed, there were no universities; and no one would associate the scholarly presses of Basle with its small and insignificant university. A new insistence on literature at the expense of logic may justly be attributed to the universities of Germany. Everywhere Galen and Hippocrates were studied in better editions and with greater attention to text rather than gloss, yet the medical faculty at Basle received Paracelsus at first with much the same respect that it paid to Vesalius, and it cannot be said that the mainly literary approach to medicine in universities was conducive to much progress: the accepted text reigned supreme, even if it was much improved.[1] Civil law was also taught from better texts, but canon law went into a decline which was, naturally, complete in Protestant universities and particularly in Germany. There, on the other hand, theological faculties assumed an importance which was as noticeable as that of the Sorbonne in Paris, though theological teaching at Wittenberg and elsewhere was fairly narrowly restricted to Bible exegesis and dogmatics.

If Greek and Hebrew are taken as tests of the new learning at the academic level (as contemporaries often assumed they should be) the relative failure of universities to accord a full place to liberal studies will be noted. Professors of Greek are found in most universities by the mid-century, and many of them were exceedingly learned and productive men. But their field of action was the edition of texts and above all of translations, and the slender apparatus of Greek which was all that even advanced educationalists allowed for in schools was quite incapable of giving the average student at the university enough groundwork for serious study. Even in the schools Greek was not invariably found till towards the end of the sixteenth century. In 1561 the statutes of Merchant Taylors' School (London) repeat the phrase used in Colet's statute for St Paul's half a century earlier: the headmaster should have Latin and Greek, 'if such may be gotten'. If Greek became an arts subject at universities it was not a compulsory one, except for the handful who entered a higher faculty. Hebrew was in an even less favoured position and was, of course, entirely restricted to theological teaching, as at Wittenberg, under the statute of 1546, where the professor of Hebrew was in practice teaching Old Testament exegesis.

The conviction that the languages, Latin, Greek and Hebrew, were of fundamental importance and yet not adequately treated in universities accounts for the development of tri-lingual colleges. Here the foundation of chairs in ancient languages at universities prior to the second decade of the sixteenth century hardly constitutes a precedent. Leo X's educational innovations at Rome and Cardinal Ximenes's at Alcalá are more sugges-

---

[1] Cf. above, pp. 391, 409.

tive of a new departure, but there is no disputing the original character of the foundation of the Collegium Trilingue at Louvain. Its founder, Jerome Busleyden, who died in 1517, left money for the establishment of a college in the university of Louvain where, in addition to student bursaries, provision was made for three lecturers who were to provide gratuitous instruction. They were 'to read and expound publicly to all comers, both Christian and other moral and approved authors, in the three languages, that is, in Latin, Greek and Hebrew'. Despite difficulties from theologians chary of the new studies because they were associated with heresy, and from other teachers who saw their audiences dwindle, the new college flourished. Reflecting Erasmian ideals, it directly enjoyed Erasmus's protection and counsel. Since it was detached from the normal university curriculum it proved attractive not only to students at Louvain university, but also to many gentlemen and visiting scholars, who could benefit from a modern approach to language and literature without being compromised by study for a degree. That the Trilingue at Louvain responded to a widely felt need may be inferred from parallel developments elsewhere. Richard Fox's foundation of Corpus Christi College at Oxford (1517), and Wolsey's college (1525) both reflect the same climate of thought, though less successfully than Louvain. In France a similar development culminated in 1530 in the appointment of 'lecteurs royaux'. In 1531 there were five: two for Greek, two for Hebrew, and one for mathematics; a regius professor of Latin was added in 1534; and thus a new Trilingue was established, which was in time to grow into the Collège de France. More was involved in this than programmes of purely literary reform: a new attitude to advanced study is shown at Louvain and at the embryo Collège de France. This is vividly illustrated by the career of Ramus (Pierre de la Ramée, d. 1572), a university man if ever there was one, but one whose unavailing attempts to rejuvenate traditional teaching encountered fierce resistance in Paris. For him the new royal foundation, where he taught from 1551 to 1562, was not an opportunity for radical innovation, but an environment for teaching the curriculum in a spirit of freedom which had died in the university itself.

All the educational changes noted above were carried out in a period when doctrinal disputes were growing harsher. Religious differences, between reformer and orthodox, and between one kind of reformed Church and another, influenced schools and universities in several important respects. Since the old school was essentially clerical and the newer school aimed at combining learning and devotion in a *pietas litterata*, a dispute about the nature of religion was to some extent a dispute about the character of education itself. Moreover, reformers attached importance to a direct approach to the scriptures which also had pedagogical implications. The destruction of old educational endowments was involved in the establishment of new ones, while the disorders attendant on reform physically disrupted some schools and universities and bequeathed traditions of *odium theologicum* which poisoned the atmosphere of lecture and classroom. Above all, the progress of the Reformation and Counter-Reformation increased the already considerable control over education exercised by the civil magistrate: the prince emerged as arbiter of the destinies of schools and universities.

The removal of the incentive of a career in the Church was a particular difficulty in Protestant countries. As already noted, the hope of securing preferment had been a powerful attraction among all classes in the pre-Reformation period. When that disappeared, so also (it seemed to many at the time) disappeared the serious scholar. The children of the gentry still went to school and university, but they had small ambition for the few posts available even in a relatively well-endowed Church like that in England, still less to be preachers in the continental reformed Churches. In one of his sermons Latimer complains that 'there are none but great men's sons in colleges and their fathers look not to have them preachers'. Similar complaints are heard from Germany. Luther himself in 1524 and again in 1530 connected the absence of the old priesthood with the paucity of candidates for learning and even advocated compulsory education under state sanctions. Even aside from the absence of numerous livings, the polemics of the reformers on the value of labour and the iniquities of the priesthood had a discouraging effect. The margrave George of Ansbach in 1531 blamed the situation on 'those preachers who inveigh so strongly against study and teach that children should be trained up as manual workers'. Yet if the vernacular Bible was the sole sure road to salvation, why should the child bother with Latin and Greek?

Merely on the level of provision of funds for education the process of reformation had a disturbing effect. Certainly it was the intention of those who confiscated Church lands that these should be in part reallocated to educational purposes. In 1543, for example, Duke Maurice of Saxony in agreement with the estates, allocated the endowments of three convents at Pforta, Meissen and Grimma to the provision of a school in each of these three places; yet the properties were the subject of much uncertainty and proved inadequate to the demands put upon them. Much the same is true of the schools established by town councils, such as the academy created from Carmelite property at Augsburg in 1531 where the town authorities had to add to the endowment. Prior to the Reformation there were large numbers of teaching posts attached to Church livings: these disappeared, and in general the teacher was dependent not only on fees but also on the fluctuating charity and irregular resources of a prince or a municipality. As a result, the most auspicious schools found it hard to retain the services of a good master, and time which should have been spent in teaching was consumed in the composition of memorials to the authorities, or in the exercise of a petty trade or in efforts to obtain another post. To send his class round the town begging was a frequent device of the German teacher. At Münster there were six different masters between 1537 and 1541. Moreover, the impetus to the provision of educational facilities had been directed mainly to the creation of Latin schools and the old 'writing' or 'German' schools were left to men who were failures in any more lucrative walk of life. At Frankfurt-am-Main in 1531 a shoemaker petitioned the council for permission to set up a German school on the grounds that times were bad; at Augsburg in 1551 a bookbinder made a similar request. There seems no doubt that in England the Reformation as a whole seriously disturbed the course of secondary and elementary education, but the severity of this may well have been exaggerated, and in particular the effects of the chantry commission established in 1547 probably had far less evil consequences than has been supposed.[1] At any rate the developments in England, like those on the continent, did not long interrupt the increase in educational facilities and they further encouraged the already noticeable trend towards the secular control of schools.

Though the agitated and complaisant dons of Oxford and Cambridge feared that Henry and his son might proceed to a more general dissolution, only the monastic colleges at Oxford and Cambridge disappeared as a result of the Reformation and the income of the majority of the colleges was not affected. In Germany the Reformation had more serious consequences for the finances of higher education. Endowments of colleges and of chairs were confiscated by prince or town magistrates, and prebends in collegiate churches attached to teaching posts were swept away. Three new universities, Marburg (1527), Königsberg (1544) and Jena (1558) in particular competed for funds with all the other political commitments of their princely founders. The local Maecenas often proved an unsteady support and university emoluments were as low as they were paid irregularly. As with schools, so with universities we find repeated protestations of poverty and endless claims for help: the distinguished professor of Greek at Heidelberg, Micyllus (Molshem), memorialised the university in 1537 on the impossibility of keeping up appearances on sixty florins a year even if he had been a single man, as he was not; the response of the university was to add a further twenty florins to his stipend; the elector palatine, who was then approached, suggested that Micyllus should be dismissed. Just as schoolmasters begged and peddled to make ends meet, so professors in universities were compelled to augment their pay by other means than teaching, and at Heidelberg the 1558 statutes allowed professors to retail a stipulated quantity of wine each year. In Catholic Germany, pay and conditions of employment were only less chaotic and there too an unwilling prince or town council had often to make good the devastation of mismanagement and inflation.

[1] Cf. above, p. 244.

To the disorders produced in finance and administration the changes in religion added the disruption of polemical theology and the vicissitudes occasioned by shifts in political control. In this respect also the experience of England was mild compared with the experience of Germany. The variations in Henry VIII's policies were reflected in the universities only to a slight degree: doctrine as such was for some time scarcely an issue, and the extirpation of heresy at Cambridge and Oxford hardly affected the universities. But under Edward VI and Mary, representing as these reigns did the two poles of contemporary religious opposition, the universities underwent something of the upheavals of continental institutions. At Oxford, for instance, under Edward Protestant theology was foisted on the university in the person of Peter Martyr and the university was rent by disputes over the nature of the sacrament; a good many dons left, only to return under Mary, when their enemies fled and two Spanish friars were introduced to undo the Protestant damage. In Germany theology was a more potent solvent, princely action more drastic. At Tübingen in 1535, for example, those teachers who adhered to the old faith were forcibly expelled; at Leipzig, by the advice of the theologians at Wittenberg, the duke of Saxony deprived all professors who did not accept Lutheranism in 1539. Equally demoralising were the perpetual disputes between theologians and the expressly tendentious nature of teaching in all subjects. Protestants disputed with Protestants: the differences between Luther and Zwingli provoked violent academic quarrels; especially after Luther's death the Lutheran camp was distracted by the disciples of Melanchthon and those of Flacius Illyricus.[1] Wittenberg adhered to Melanchthon, Jena was the headquarters of the Flacian party, and every Protestant university was disturbed by these disputes. Later Calvinism added to Protestant dissension. In those parts where Catholicism was maintained there were naturally fewer troubles of this kind, though the arrival of the Jesuits frequently provoked resentment which sometimes led to open hostility on the part of the old university, as at Ingolstadt in 1556 and at Vienna in 1559. In France there was doubt and division until a hardening orthodoxy compelled the moderate reformers, who had been numerous in university circles, to choose for one side or the other. The Sorbonne was the dogged champion of the old way and it was as truculent with the Jesuits as it had been with the 'lecteurs royaux'. Only in Italy, where university teaching was in general declining at this period, and in Spain where most universities pursued a medieval curriculum untouched by change, were there few doctrinal difficulties: in both countries an effective Inquisition exercised surveillance over university heterodoxy; in both countries the Jesuits were to dominate the educational scene.

The effects of the factors touched on above accounts for a general

[1] Cf. above, p. 184.

decline in university attendance, noted at the time and probably more severe in Germany than elsewhere:

Estimated yearly attendance at German universities 1501–1560 (average of 5-year periods)[1]

Years	Heidelberg	Cologne	Erfurt	Leipzig	Rostock	Greifswald	Freiburg	Ingolstadt	Tübingen	Wittenberg	Frankfurt an der Oder	Marburg	Königsberg	Dillingen	Jena	Total
1501–05	201	586	461	740	322	81	207	172	155	527	—	—	—	—	—	3346
1506–10	266	556	473	789	333	63	208	291	219	308	—	—	—	—	—	3687
1511–15	299	581	502	819	359	77	203	371	212	364	257	—	—	—	—	4041
1516–20	247	469	541	705	284	72	170	422	161	600	273	—	—	—	—	3850
1521–25	156	322	95	331	140	44	147	184	123	379	93	—	—	—	—	1994
1526–30	84	152	44	175	37	—	77	149	95	250	49	47	—	—	—	1135
1531–35	140	121	108	256	44	—	131	154	105	371	75	140	—	—	—	1645
1536–40	170	173	124	301	100	—	177	229	156	586	112	182	—	—	—	2307
1541–45	178	129	136	468	122	?	203	406	194	879	201	205	—	—	—	3121
1546–50	181	228	302	489	182	?	282	360	224	640	288	154	125	—	—	3455
1551–55	153	243	158	378	224	?	257	392	312	866	286	206	63	132	—	3670
1556–60	187	261	156	490	177	?	341	402	341	960	349	203	80	118	269	4334

The figures of attendance at the universities listed above are rising at the start of the century, continuing a trend which is almost unbroken during the fifteenth century. This expansion comes to a stop in the 1520's: for comparable figures it is necessary to go back to the early fifteenth century; and the high point reached in the quinquennium ending in 1515 is not attained again until 1556–60. There is no escaping the conclusion that in Germany the Reformation had very serious though temporary repercussions on university attendances. It has been claimed that a decline, similar if less severe, occurred at Oxford. The figures available do not lend themselves to any exact calculations, as matriculation records are not available at this period. There are, however, certain indications that there was a recession. The Register,[2] which is a defective document, records degrees being conferred for the first time on an average of over 150 persons *per annum* between 1505 and 1509; thereafter quinquennial averages seem to drop: 1520–24, 116; 1540–44, 70; 1555–9, 67. Yet in 1552 about 1000 members of the university were listed, and for a university now entirely collegiate in structure the total seems respectable enough. Numbers

---

[1] Franz Eulenburg, 'Die Frequenz der deutschen Universitäten von ihrer Gründung bis zur Gegenwart', *Abhandlungen der phil.-hist. Klasse der königl. sächsischen Gesellschaft der Wissenschaften*, Bd. XXIV (Leipzig, 1904), pp. 55, 102–3. The table omits Trier and Mainz and the dubious figures for Greifswald after the university there resumed in 1539. For Eulenburg's method of calculating the above figures see *ibid.* pp. 7–45. The Vienna figures show that the lowest point occurred in the 1530's; F. Eulenburg, 'Ueber die Frequenz der deutschen Universitäten in früherer Zeit', *Jahrbücher für Nationalökonomie und Statistik*, III. Folge, Bd. 13 (Jena, 1897), p. 543.

[2] Oxford Hist. Soc., ed. C. W. Boase, 1885.

rose again in Elizabeth's reign, and here too the religious and political disturbances of the mid-century seem to have had repercussions on attendance which, however marked, were not long-lasting.

All in all, the most significant single aspect of education in this period is the way in which it fell increasingly under the control of the secular authority, town council or prince. Admittedly this is not exactly a new phenomenon. At any rate from the fourteenth century, when the 'laicisation' of society in its broadest aspect began to be apparent, the university and to a less extent the secondary school were obvious targets for the ambitious civil ruler. As directly dependent on papal bulls, supranational therefore and peopled by students and doctors who looked to the curia for privilege and preferment, the university presented an aspect of the Church most calculated to interest sovereigns bent on controlling the Church in their domains. Moreover, the feeling was in the air that a country of any standing should have its own *studium generale*, just as in urban communities the town council frequently evinced similar sentiments. Hence in the fourteenth and fifteenth centuries we find much evidence of concern among princes and magistrates for the control of old universities and the establishment of new ones. In Italy, where the Church had played a small part in the university from the start, this was naturally most evident. But in the north universities were established by dukes and kings as symbols of their regalian rights; and such establishments were frequently bolstered up by a prohibition of study in any other *studium* which the ruler laid on his people. The great centres of the north, Paris and Oxford, were greatly humbled. Paris, though still cosmopolitan, was damaged by the lavish creation of universities in Germany, Scotland, and elsewhere in France; and by espousing Gallicanism found itself in a constricting alliance with the monarchy. Oxford was made obedient to the royal will by the events of the schism and by the episode of Wycliffe. At Oxford and Cambridge the chancellor was virtually a royal nominee, while royal munificence was a sorry substitute for genuine independence.

Developments such as these point the way to the supremacy of the prince finally brought about in the sixteenth century. In England the first major occasion for a display of the king's latent authority was the divorce of Catherine of Aragon; subsequent changes were accepted with a minimum of trouble, hasty messengers being despatched to ingratiate the university with whoever was regarded as powerful at court. The universities, like the monasteries, suffered visitation, and under Edward and Mary two royal commissions undertook a complete review of the universities. The sweeping powers of the commissioners were a forcible reminder that the king had become pope in England. Though in day-to-day administration the Crown had little incentive to intervene, its powers were enormous: at Oxford the royal inclination could settle the Greeks' and Trojans' hostilities; it could determine precisely who should vote in

433

the election of proctors. Behind the bland concern of Henry or his successors for the well-being of universities, the flustered dons discerned the terrible omnicompetence of king and parliament. The monasteries had been dissolved; so had the chantries; might it not be soon the turn of Oxford and Cambridge? Yet the influence of the Crown in England had important compensations. It protected Greek against conservatives; it founded lectureships in the liberal disciplines; the mild improvements in curriculum introduced by the Oxford commissioners of 1549 would have taken years to introduce without royal sanction and were on the whole in line with the university's needs.

In France the position of the king was very similar. It is a measure of the greater standing of the Paris theologians that they were able to persist in a resistance to Francis I's tolerant attitude to the new learning and Erasmian reform; but their resistance was in the end fruitless, and what helped them was a change in Francis I's attitude after the *Placards* of 1534; even then the incipient Collège de France survived as a result of royal protection. In Germany, the prince was even more obtrusively master of his seats of learning. As already mentioned three Protestant universities were created by princely action: Marburg, Königsberg and Jena. These institutions were at once faced with the problem of their status, for the true university required the granting by the pope of the right to confer degrees of universal validity, the *ius ubique docendi*. Marburg may have secured such a privilege from Charles V, as Jena did from his successor, but neither pope nor emperor would recognise the university of Königsberg. New institutions such as these were naturally intended to serve the interests of their creators. Marburg professors could be dismissed by the prince, who also was the judge of their orthodoxy. At Königsberg staff and students took an oath of loyalty not so much to the university as to the faith and the duke of Prussia: 'adversus... Principem...nulla me ratione ac via nec publice nec privatim, improbe, impie, seditiose, hostiliter consulturum, facturum moliturumve.' In older universities which accepted the new faith the process was not dissimilar, and at Wittenberg, home of Lutheranism, the university, endowed like the rest by an act of State out of the lands of the Church, had become by 1550 a function of the State Church. When Greifswald was re-opened in 1539 it was equally dependent on the liberality of the duke of Pomerania. Where the university lacked a prince, or, as at Erfurt, the prince was not at hand, the town council tended to assume control. Erfurt council imposed Protestantism despite the technical independence of the university; at Basle, the council and the university reflected rapid changes in the pendulum of religious obedience. But the municipal university which most clearly displays the control of the magistrates was Geneva. There in 1559 Calvin re-erected an *Academia Genevensis* which was completely under the authority of the local theocracy. The king's acquisition of control over the university in his lands was by no means confined to Protestant Europe. At Vienna Archduke Ferdinand from 1533 onwards brought the university under his direction, and a series of decrees, aimed at reform, put the institution in a state of utter subservience: overseers were appointed to enforce regular lecturing and the details of instruction were given close government supervision. At Ingolstadt the duke of Bavaria also issued 'reform ordinances' which had the same result. The only new university in Catholic Germany in the period was Dillingen, established by the bishop of Augsburg and recognised by the pope in 1551. The secondary school was obviously of less direct interest to the prince, although in Germany the local ruler occasionally interfered to secure religious uniformity among teachers, and in England the elementary Primer and the Latin grammar book were both regulated by government by the end of Henry VIII's reign.

The process of 'territorialization' of the world of learning was, as already indicated, at work before the Reformation, but in the decades covered by this volume it entered upon a decisive stage. No more in a sense than one phase of an attack by princes on the existence in their dominions of institutions which were aspects of a universal Church—monastic orders, canon law, universities—the subjection of the scholar was perhaps severer in its effects. It contradicted that hope of a republic of letters which had seemed attainable to humanists like Erasmus. It made inevitable in the long run the association of science and national prestige and gave governments the right to regard academic institutions as existing primarily for public purposes defined by the statesman. And for a time it produced a notable stagnation in higher studies as pursued in universities. This was most marked in Germany, and it has been plausibly argued that the decline in the vitality of German letters and German erudition began, before the Thirty Years War, in the 'stunted, lifeless, academic institutions' which resulted from the movements described above. Germany, however, is only a special case of a general phenomenon. The post-Reformation university in Europe as a whole entered on a period when, though its social importance was steadily mounting with the convention that youths of gentle family should attend for a while, its academic importance in the narrow sense tended to diminish. The enormous intellectual advances of the seventeenth century are only to a slight degree associated with the doctors and the dons of the moribund faculties. Ironically enough, when universities did revive in a much later period, it was in Germany that the renaissance took place.

It is proper to ask what practical consequences were involved in the educational changes we have considered. What was the response to the new grammar school and the university as changed by reformers, both academic and princely? This question is more readily put than answered, though some information is available.

As far as the bulk of the population is concerned, the peasantry had small interest in the professions of the humanist educator. Some indications there are of a positive craving for the literary facilities offered by schools among persons whom their station in society destined for the humbler tasks. Thus Robert Williams, 'keppynge shepe uppon Seynbury hill', in 1546 scribbled in a book he had just bought a devout condemnation of a prohibition (34 & 35 Henry VIII, c. 1) of Bible reading by all laity save the gentry and prosperous merchants. Yet Robert Williams was inspired by religion rather than by education, and the universal complaint of the schoolmaster was that in agricultural communities children attended classes only when it suited them: in Germany it was stated that the peasants sent their children to school only in the winter, and in the summer used them in farm work.

The grammar school was, however, directed at gentry and burgesses. Although clearly the tradition was growing that a period at school was a necessary part of the upbringing of a boy, there is a good deal of evidence that such attendance was perfunctory and not regarded highly by either boy or parent. What direct relevance had Latin grammar to the squire's son? For Elyot it was necessary to learn Latin to become a 'governor' in the full sense. Yet, in a period when secular administration was livelier than it had ever been, how many of the main 'governors' were scholar-gentlemen in Elyot's sense? Cromwell, who was emphatically not a university man, replaced Wolsey, who was: parents could scarcely be blamed for taking the hint, and Elyot was demanding too much when he urged that boys should not be taken from school when they were fourteen. The attendance of the gentry at school and university in the fourteenth and fifteenth centuries is well-attested and was clearly growing.[1] While this must have fertilised the mind of the occasional poet and statesman, for the majority it was a mere convention: what could the average squire find helpful in Latin grammar? As for the merchants, practical training in accounts and the acquisition of modern languages were not to be had at the grammar school. 'The wealthy citizen, therefore, after the first year or two, continued to send his boy to Switzerland, or England, to Venice or Bruges, to learn the great commercial languages.' Cordier in one of his colloquies explains that parents 'were restless under long-continued and apparently unprofitable instruction in Latin'. His plea that Latin was the proper language for international relations cannot have carried much conviction in mercantile communities. In fact, with few exceptions, the success of the sixteenth-century school seems to have been in inverse proportion to its humanist content. English grammar schools, which maintained an old tradition, gradually adopted a new curriculum, but they did so gently and without marked educational optimism. On the con-

[1] J. H. Hexter, 'The education of the aristocracy in the Renaissance', *Journal of Modern History*, XXII (1950), 1–20.

tinent, and especially in Germany, the tally of bankrupt academies is a long one. The success of Sturm at Strassburg, of Neander at Ilfeld, of Platter at Basle, was largely personal; such men, in Montaigne's phrase, had 'plutost la teste bien faicte que bien plaine'; and their achievements must be balanced against the failures of scores of humanist scholars of much greater intellectual attainments. The Collège de Guyenne at Bordeaux, where Montaigne went to school, was exceptional, just as his earlier home upbringing had been exceptional. For Montaigne enjoyed the kind of education prescribed by the theorists. He learnt Latin from the cradle in a household which had been geared by his father to the production of a model child. His mother and the servants picked up enough Latin to talk to him and he thus mastered the language 'sans art, sans livre, sans grammaire ou precepte, sans fouet et sans larmes'. Later at the school under Gouvéa, 'sans comparaison le plus grand principal en France', the boy had as teacher an eminent Grecian like Nicolas Grouchy and an outstanding Latinist like George Buchanan. Yet he felt his school days to have been without much fruitfulness; his facility in Latin declined; and the product of a humanist education of the most perfect kind used his Latin only to point a moral or adorn an opinion.

A further commentary on the school and university of the Renaissance is provided by the emergence of learned academies of various kinds. This is admittedly hardly a subject which falls within the history of education. Yet it is surely of some significance that in the Middle Ages such groups of adults, coteries drawn together not only by personal intimacy but by common intellectual pursuits, are hardly to be found. In Italy in the fifteenth century such associations develop, the pattern being set by the Platonic Academy at Florence. In Italy they are exceedingly numerous in the sixteenth century, some beginning to display a formal constitutionalism which was later to be one of the characteristics of the academic tradition, and some the specialisation which marks bodies such as the Accademia della Crusca at Florence (1552), devoted to the Italian language. In the north informal groups are found in humanist circles: the *sodalitas* which has been called the 'Adwert Academy' is an early instance; in a looser sense still 'Doctors' Commons' in London was, it seems, largely a club for scholars and above all for civil lawyers, while the Inns of Court performed a similar service for the common lawyers. In France in particular, much influenced by Italian example, the academic movement was noticeably strong. In the event, corporations of savants and amateurs of learning, stemming from these slender beginnings, did much in the centuries ahead to provide the inspiration for, and to control the evolution of, the scholarship and science which had formerly been the monopoly of the universities and schools.

CHAPTER XIV

CONSTITUTIONAL DEVELOPMENT AND POLITICAL THOUGHT IN WESTERN EUROPE

ALONG the western seaboard of Europe, the first half of the sixteenth century witnessed the consolidation of national states. The smaller countries were not affected. Scotland had to await the arrival of the Reformation in the 1560's and may be ignored in this survey; Burgundy was undergoing a process of centralisation which did not prevent her break-up and redistribution in the next hundred years; Portugal had already achieved all the organisation she was to have until the Spanish occupation in 1580. Thus the story must concentrate on three main units —England, France, and the Spanish kingdoms. In all these countries, medieval kingship began to fail early in the fifteenth century. The Hundred Years War with attendant and subsequent civil wars wrecked both the French and English monarchies, while the kings of Castile and Aragon developed sudden weaknesses in the face of local and class independence. The second half of the century therefore saw simultaneous attempts to restore strong monarchy as the only safeguard of law and order. The Catholic kings in Spain, Charles VII and Louis XI in France, the Yorkists and Henry VII in England—all pursued much the same ends by much the same methods. But if these restorers of peace and good government naturally used the means to hand and were therefore 'medieval', it is not surprising that the next generation, proceeding from there, should have more consistently invented and innovated. In England the break with Rome involved a constitutional revolution in which the independent national state was deliberately set up, administration reformed, the principle of legislative sovereignty worked out in practice. In Spain, the reign of Charles V gave much greater political unity to realms hitherto held together by marriage only; this and the introduction of Burgundian methods of government led to marked progress in centralisation. In France, the reign of Francis I witnessed rapid moves towards royal absolutism and consolidation disguised behind a façade of traditionalism. Everywhere, much the same problems elicited answers that, despite significant differences, had much in common.

Any discussion of constitutional problems must start with the monarchy. Kingship symbolised national unity and received a degree of homage which at times approached idolatry. The previous decline of medieval kingship laid the foundation for an exaggerated devotion to monarchy in the next age. For it was through monarchy that a species of secular salvation came, and one need not wonder at the submission to the new messiah. His position was strong: traditionally God's representative on earth, ruler and administrator, fountain of justice and head of the feudal hierarchy, he now stood out also as the saviour of his country and embodiment of its self-conscious nationhood. More practically, he was also the fountain of all honour and advancement. Men looked for favour and promotion at the hands of superiors whose service they would do in their turn: and kings commanded far and away the greatest amount of patronage. A growing ceremonial, most gorgeous in France but most formal in England, set monarchs apart from lesser men; the decline of the old nobility and the growth of a new one created by royal favour tended to make the highest in the land their creatures; the age looked ripe for a full blossoming of royal absolutism.

However, the many expressions of devoted sentiment and the evident signs of frequent despotic action must not disguise the absence of genuine absolutism and perfect monarchical rule. Charles V, handicapped by being not one king but several, succeeded in weakening the liberties of Castile but remained half-chained by those of Aragon and Burgundy. In England (as we shall see) it is possible to discern behind the bluster and wilfulness of Henry VIII a remarkable degree of constitutionalism and limitation upon the royal will. Even France, where under Francis I and Henry II long strides were taken away from the uncertainties of medieval kingship, was to demonstrate during the Wars of Religion how insecurely based these achievements were. All the same, the French monarchy came nearest to the ideal. The history of that endeavour went back to the closing years of the Hundred Years War when Charles VII began to create a monarchy capable of standing above the rival jealousies and free to tax and legislate at will. The work of Louis XI, Louis XII and Francis I resulted in a monarchy superficially still medieval, but in truth much more like the open absolutism of the seventeenth century. By 1546 a Venetian envoy thought that the French had handed over all their liberties to their king. Even though, in the customary manner, its power might be defined by the lawyers in laboriously contrived prerogatives—the rights to make law, appoint officers, decide on peace and war, exercise ultimate juris-diction and coin money—the French monarchy acted, where physical power permitted, without regard to limitations or defined rights. Its power to legislate was limited by the notion of unchangeable fundamental laws, but these proved meaningless in fact; the *parlements* of the provinces, and especially of Paris, could refuse to register an edict and thereby render it void, but they never did. In its theory, its powers, and its unconfined freedom of action, the French monarchy was a model to monarchists everywhere and, as early as the 1530's, a byword for tyranny to others. Charles V occupied a very different position, if only because he never ruled a unitary state. Even France remained in a way a conglomerate of fiefs and territories. Though policy and lucky accidents made possible the absorption of many of the great fiefs (Brittany between 1492 and 1532, Bourbon in 1523, Alençon in 1525, and ultimately—with Henry IV—the Bourbon lands of Navarre), and though one financial organisation covered the whole realm (the *généralités*), the kingdom remained a gathering of diverse provincial and social organisations, customs, and rights to which the monarchy gave unity by something like a series of individual contracts.[1] But this diversity and confusion was simplicity itself by the side of Charles V's empire. Stretching from the Netherlands to Sicily, from Castile to (for a time) Bohemia, it never had any unity except in the person of the ruler who retained his separate character in every part of his dominions. As has been seen, there was no such thing as an imperial monarchical organisation: only a series of rulers—from the Holy Roman emperor through the kings of Castile, Aragon, and the two Sicilies, down to the dukes of Milan and Burgundy, the counts of Artois, Flanders and Holland, and so forth, all of whom happened to be the same man.[2] In every one of his realms Charles's position was different. Even in the centre of his power, in Spain, he was reasonably absolute in Castile but subjected to remnants of oligarchic control in Aragon. Ferdinand and Isabella had of necessity been content to revive the monarchical powers of the Middle Ages, to suppress excessive noble influence, and to adapt such popular institutions as the *Hermandad* (a police organisation mainly supported by the towns) for their own monarchical purposes. Such unity as there was beyond the marriage of the rulers depended in part on the submission of the lesser country, Aragon, to the greater Castile and in part on the political uses of the Inquisition, established in 1481 and from the first so organised as to control both realms.

In these circumstances it is not surprising to find that Charles V made no major attempt to assert novel monarchical doctrines, but that on the other hand the very necessity of his person to the coherence of his dominions gave him an unusually strong hand in asserting personal monarchy. He was least able, perhaps, to do so in the Low Countries. Though he completed the Seventeen Provinces by acquiring Tournai (1521), Friesland (1523), Overijssel and Utrecht (1528), Groningen (1536) and Guelders (1543), and withdrew Artois and Flanders from French suzerainty (1529), and though he used the advanced organisation of that agglomerate duchy as a model for his heterogeneous lands in general, he rarely visited the Netherlands after his early years and left them to the efficient administra-

---

[1] Cf. R. Doucet, *Les Institutions de la France au XVI siècle* (1948), vol. I, p. 36: 'Le caractère contractuel de cette royauté au xvi⁰ siècle, qui constitue une transition entre la royauté féodale de passé et la royauté absolue qui acheva de s'organiser au temps de Louis XIV.'
[2] Cf. above, pp. 308f.

tion of female relatives. In the fifteenth century the provinces had been given a precarious unity through a central bureaucracy (largely staffed by legists from Franche-Comté) and a general assembly of estates; but to the end of Charles V's reign the provincial estates mattered more than the states general, provincial customs and privileges remained untouched, and the individual provinces obeyed him neither as emperor nor as king of Spain, nor even as archduke of Burgundy, but only as their own territorial duke or count. The failure to establish a true monarchy in this small but diverse territory explains much about Philip II's difficulties in the next generation; it also throws light on Charles V's attempts to govern other vaster and equally diverse territories with some degree of uniformity.

Yet over and above the individual organisations stood the ruler, assisted by men whose interests transcended borders and were attached to him alone. If there is no particular doctrine of monarchy to be discerned in Charles V's practice—if it is true that he had to play the chameleon as he passed from one realm to another—it is also true that the impressive and wise ruler that Charles became offered a practical example of monarchical rule to which most of his dominions submitted. With all the growing bureaucracy demanded by the complications of financing and governing so vast a realm, unity and survival—and thanks to Charles's foibles all action, too[1]—continued to depend on the monarch. In this inchoate, untheoretical way, Charles V moved away from the medieval constitutionalism of his Netherlandish and Aragonian heritage towards a bureaucratic absolutism in which Burgundian technique and Castilian power were to play the biggest part.

By comparison with these giants, the task of the English monarchy looked relatively easy. Admittedly, it was the last to recover from the medieval decline: the French revival was well under way by the reign of Louis XI (1461–83), Ferdinand and Isabella could abandon their own version of the *Hermandad* by 1498, but dynastic war in England went on till 1485 and its repercussions can be seen in attacks on potential claimants down to the end of Henry VIII's reign. However, unlike his continental counterparts, the English king only needed to revive the powers and methods of medieval monarchy by re-applying the personal action of the king in his household. Medieval England had enjoyed the unusual benefits of a compact territory and, by medieval standards, an exceptionally powerful and effective monarchy. It is true that the early Tudors still had some consolidating to do: in 1536 Wales was incorporated with England, while a general act against franchises finally subjected all partially exempt regions to the national state and the king's writ. The problem of Ireland remained unsolved. Henry VII abandoned a promising but expensive attempt at Anglicisation in favour of the old uneasy reliance on local nobles; and Henry VIII (in 1540) abandoned Cromwell's policy

[1] Cf. above, pp. 309 f.

of conquest and infiltration—though a year later he embodied an empty claim in the new title of king of Ireland. Despite all this, the Tudors ruled a country which, as medieval conditions went, had long been uncommonly united. Above all, it obeyed one law—the common law of England, developed since the twelfth century and so ancient by this time that it stood in danger of ossification. As against this, France harboured a variety of provincial customs and laws. During Francis I's reign many attempts were made to produce a general code based on the Roman law, less because this offered support for despotism than because the only competent experts were civilians; but in the end only a partial codification of individual customs was achieved. Charles V's empire had as many codes as countries and the notion of one common set of laws was too absurd even to be considered.[1] The English common law might be thought inadequate and in need of reform (which it was), and by some even barbarous and worthy of abolition (which it was not); but it provided unity in the realm on a foundation of sectional and personal rights, while elsewhere unification with the help of the monarchical Roman law led to absolutism.

If subjects had their rights, so had the kings of England with their prerogative, a set of known privileges and a residue of undefined powers intended to enable a ruler to govern. In both England and France royal lands, customs, duties and rights attached to feudal lordship provided the basis of royal finance; and nearly all of this belonged to the Crown by prerogative right. But government was becoming ever more expensive, as internal and external administration demanded larger staffs, as war got much more complicated, and as the general rise in prices squeezed the fixed incomes of crowned heads. Here both Francis and the emperor were better off than Henry VIII: strictly speaking, extraordinary taxation always required parliamentary consent in England. There were ways of getting round this, such as allegedly free gifts (benevolences—declared illegal in 1483) or forced loans which were never paid back, but none of these expedients could be used too often or too blatantly, as Wolsey discovered in 1524 when a series of attempts to supplement inadequate parliamentary grants resulted in near-rebellion over a wide area and had to be given up. Nor could English kings make law, one of the prerogatives attached to the French monarchy. A notorious act of 1539 declared that royal proclamations had the same effectiveness as acts of parliament; but proclamations could not be used for major issues because they could not create treasons or felonies. They promulgated minor and temporary government orders, and the act was mainly intended to provide machinery for the enforcement of these. The English monarchy, unable to tax and legislate by its mere will, lacked the pillars upon which a true despotism could be erected—which is not to imply that it was ever intended to build one.

[1] Except by Gattinara; above, p. 308.

Against this must be set the fact of extensive king-worship in the England of Henry VIII—a profusion of adulatory and obsequious language which has often been allowed to obscure the reality of the situation —and the accident of politics which led to much thinking about monarchy in England. This was Henry's quarrel with the pope. It was always likely that the peculiar problems of national sovereignty would crystallise in such a conflict, for the Papacy claimed not only the spiritual allegiance of Latin Christendom but a species of direct rule over all clergy everywhere. The Spanish realms solved the problem by combining a solid adherence to the spiritual supremacy of Rome with a firm insistence on control over the national Church: the Crown made all appointments of bishops and the like and enforced obedience upon the clergy, but it put no obstacles in the way of the Spanish Church's jurisdictional and fiscal relations with the Papacy. After Charles V's victory in Italy, when the pope became the emperor's chaplain, the problem really ceased to exist. France had for a long time seemed most likely to sever her connections with Rome: in 1511 Louis XII, at war with Julius II, had even called a Church council on his own responsibility. But the compromise arrived at in the Concordat of 1516 established a situation very similar to that prevailing in Spain and gave the French Crown all it wanted.[1] It also left England as the pope's most valuable source of money and patronage, a fact which played its part in Clement VII's stubborn opposition to all concessions to Henry VIII.

Even so, however, that quarrel might in the end have been solved on similar lines (as Henry first hoped to solve it) but for the international situation which kept Clement unrelenting and the decision, taken under Thomas Cromwell's influence, to use the opportunity for a complete break. The most papalist of monarchies thus went right over to the other extreme. The step rested on a clearly conceived political doctrine. England was an empire—a state sovereign within its borders and free from all outside control—and it was governed by a king who also exercised the powers of supreme head in the national Church. The monarchy thus received the biggest single accession to its powers since its inception, and it matters little that precedents for such claims may be traced in the centuries before the rise of the papal monarchy in the Church (that is, before c. 1000). In theory, at least, Henry VIII's double role, even in the feeble hands of his son and the reluctant hands of his elder daughter, represented an elevation of kingship unparalleled elsewhere in western Europe. Whether in fact his monarchical position was equal to that of Francis I remains to be seen: his power over the Church was complete enough, and his personality sufficed to leave a quite illusory air of easy despotism.

In all the countries of the west monarchy thus became the necessary embodiment of statehood and acquired in the process both a more

[1] Cf. above, p. 211.

wonderful aura and extensive practical powers. That this development—however well foreshadowed, however incomplete—amounted to something new can be traced in the way in which these monarchies proceeded to build up a more sophisticated and more competent machinery of government. The similarities are marked, but attempts to trace ancestry and influence seem unlikely to lead anywhere. There occurred a general rejection of the medieval idea of administration—by the king, his friends and his entourage, or, to use the English term, his Household—and the gradual creation of what, making allowances for the age, one may call a professional and bureaucratic organisation. Under the influence of civil lawyers, fifteenth-century Burgundy had shown the way, and much of the system used by Charles V in Spain bore the imprint of his Netherlandish advisers. During the years of reconstruction both France and England had been content with traditional methods, but the sixteenth century saw notable innovations. The revolution was plainest in England where Thomas Cromwell produced a sudden and coherent set of reforms in the 1530's. Wolsey, content to govern as the single all-powerful head, still used the system of Henry VII, though he gave it a little more organisation than that king, personally in charge and only concerned with results, had thought necessary. The subject of administrative reform is much too wide to permit here more than a most cursory examination. Three main characteristic lines all contributed to the replacement of 'Household' by 'national' bureaucratic methods: the use of royal councils, the rise of new or newly important officials, and widespread reforms in financial organisation.

The characteristic instrument of sixteenth-century monarchy was the royal council. Councils had a long and complicated medieval history in which elements of royal ascendancy (choice of councillors, control of actions) mingled with ambitions to use councils as controls on monarchical despotism. The decline of the old nobility and the consolidation of royal power which marked the later fifteenth century generally produced councils chosen and controlled by the Crown and absolutely faithful to it. There then followed a growing bureaucratisation, marked both by the introduction of organisation (clerks, records, procedure) and by a tendency to specialise the various functions of the council in separate institutions. In 1497 and 1498 specific orders transferred the judicial work of the French council to an offshoot known as the *grand conseil*, political and administrative duties remaining in the hands of a body variously described as *conseil du roi*, *conseil privé*, or *conseil d'état*. Between 1534 and 1540, though without any specific order, the English privy council was created out of an inner ring of leading councillors vaguely discernible before within the large whole council; its final establishment in 1540 marked an organic division between it and the council as a court of law, the Court of Star Chamber. At the same time, the same men could and

444

did sit on either part of the council in both countries, a fact which, while it reminds one that sixteenth-century bureaucracy was never utterly clear-cut, must not be used to deny the perfectly obvious institutional distinctions. Francis I further relied on an inner ring within his council of state (even as only a few of the English privy councillors did most of the work), and Henry III later started subdivisions in that body (as did Mary Tudor in hers); but these further changes assumed institutional form only in the next century, when again they can be paralleled in England. In our period both France and England used restricted privy councils composed of a few reliable nobles and sometimes bishops, the great officers of state, and some professional politicians or administrators (England leaning to the former and France to the latter); the control was the king's, though in neither country was it common for the king to attend council meetings.

However, the monarchy which really exploited the council was that of Charles V. Things had moved in the familiar way in such constituent parts of the empire as Castile or Aragon or the Netherlands. In the former two, the Catholic kings reorganised the old royal councils by restricting their membership, imposing bureaucracy and paperwork, and using them as purely royal instruments. There had been little specialisation before the Habsburgs. In Burgundy, on the other hand, Philip the Good (1419–67) had established control through a privy council for affairs and a great council for justice. Charles V greatly developed these beginnings. He assisted specialisation at Brussels where the regent now had three councils —that of state for political affairs (and to accommodate the nobility), a privy council of professionals to administer, and a council of finance. In the Spanish peninsula three sets of councils existed. There were the honourable and somewhat formal assemblies concerned with general and elevated matters: a council of state, established in 1526, which, though ostensibly it advised on matters of state, was but a meaningless sop to the grandees, a council of war, convened when necessary, and the council of the Inquisition, sometimes one and sometimes two for the two kingdoms but always under one president. Secondly, each unit of the realm had its proper governing council: that of Aragon was given the complete organisation of that of Castile in 1522, and another was established for Italy in 1555 to assist Prince Philip on taking over there from his father. The needs of the New World led to the erection of the council of the Indies (1524). All these councils combined administrative and judicial functions, the latter predominating. This multiplicity was given coherence in part, of course, by the person of the sovereign, but in part also by the ascendancy tacitly vested in the council of Castile whose president acted as regent for the whole peninsula during Charles's absences. Lastly it must suffice to mention that within each kingdom there were further subordinate councils of the military orders, of the *Hermandad*, of finance, and so on, not forgetting the semi-official council of that strange and powerful sheepherders' association, the Mesta, all of them obeying the Crown and helping to diffuse royal authority throughout the realm.

The staffing of these councils and of the administration in general posed problems which in their intensity were really new. France and Charles's empire could rely on the services of large numbers of men trained in the Roman law and desirous of an official career either in diplomacy or internal administration, but England had to look elsewhere for its civil service (though some legists were employed there, too), especially after the Reformation had ended the old reliance on the Church.[1] The system which evolved grew straight out of a social organisation which placed each man in relation to a master or lord whom he served. The new civil service tended to be recruited from the servants of royal servants and ministers whose private households and offices provided the training. However, far too little is yet known about the lower ranks of the bureaucracy; there is more to be said about their betters. The old great officers did not relinquish their technical ascendancy. The lord chancellor of England and the chancellor of France remained the men of formal dignity, presiding for instance in privy council, but they lost their hold over administration and, except inasmuch as they were also leading councillors, also their contact with affairs. Wolsey was a medieval chancellor and as such chief—almost sole—minister; after him, chancellors were in the first place the highest judicial officers of the realm. The same happened in France, though there the ancient offices of the constable and marshals of France entered upon a new career as the nucleus of a general system of police. The fact that Gattinara as chancellor was really Charles V's chief minister from 1518 to 1530 makes that administration as 'medieval' as Wolsey's. While retaining all the old forms and offices, the century tended to look to new ones for the real work to be done.

The reason was simple enough: the sixteenth century faced novel tasks, or at least tasks of a quite novel degree of magnitude. Internally, centralisation and consolidation meant that the central authority now took on much that had hitherto been left to subordinate units; there was also a new sense of social responsibility, most marked in English paternalism, which put burdens on government. Externally, the new diplomacy (a whole new hierarchy of ambassadors and envoys, permanent and occasional, with their staffs) and the new needs of war demanded a developed organisation. In all countries the answer was mainly found in the king's secretary. Officers peculiarly close to the person of the monarch, used to writing his correspondence, in England also entrusted with the custody of the king's most private seal, commonly trained in a knowledge of

[1] The practice of taking orders as a start to a civil service career disappeared only gradually but was dead by the reign of Elizabeth. In all countries, but more particularly in England, it remained common to employ men of no special professional training—soldiers, often enough, in Spain and France, and gentlemen of breeding and ambition in England.

languages, and not overburdened with traditional tasks, they were eminently suited to the purposes of centralising monarchy. Even under the Catholic kings the real mainspring of government had been in two secretaries, Miguel Perez d'Almaza and his nephew Pedro Quintana. Charles V was familiar with a similar practice in Burgundy—Jean de Marnix, Margaret of Savoy's right-hand man, though he needed a titular office to sit in council, owed his importance to the inferior office of secretary—and naturally maintained it in all his dominions. After Gattinara's death in 1530 he left the office of chancellor vacant and ruled through Cobos and Granvelle, secretaries whom one must describe as secretaries of state.[1] Under each there were further ranks of secretaries in charge of departments and linking the various councils whose work it was their duty to prepare. It is not too much to say that the empire of Charles V was run by professional administrators of various eminence who generally bore the title of secretary.

England followed this trend at a relatively early date, largely because Cromwell used the secretaryship to make himself the all-powerful minister (1534). Before his day the office had been quite important because of its intrinsically close association with the Crown, but its holders had rarely sat in council and never been men of the first rank. Although Cromwell later took more distinguished offices, he started the English principal secretary on a career which never really lapsed and hardly even regressed —not even when for administrative reasons the office was divided between two men (1540). France was a little slower in turning king's secretaries into leading ministers of state: it was not until 1547 that their real power was acknowledged by the formal establishment of the office, while the title *secrétaire d'état* dates only from 1559. In a monarchy more given to defining and organising by decree than that of England, these dates do represent a belated arrival at the position which Cromwell, without the full title, had occupied in the 1530's. In part this was due to the fact that the French monarchy had found in the masters of requests another office to take the strain of centralised and bureaucratic monarchy. Originally appointed to exercise a general equitable jurisdiction on the king's behalf and numbering eight when the office was first defined in 1493, these officers proved so useful that by the middle of the century there were more than sixty of them, employed now as general watchdogs for the Crown. Equipped with vague but immense powers, they supervised all central and local administration, finance, the army, problems of heresy—'une délégation illimitée de l'auctorité royale' (Doucet). There was nothing remotely like them in either England or Spain, though the former borrowed the title for four harmless jurists charged with the settlement of poor men's lawsuits.

All these reforms and developments took money; altogether, government, as already explained, was becoming unprecedently expensive. This

---

[1] Cf. above, p. 309.

is not the place to investigate the actual finances of the three realms: they were never very secure—Henry VII stood out for centuries as a wonder for wise men because he actually accumulated a reserve—and the strain of war was always bringing bankruptcy near. France and Spain helped themselves by increasing the burden of taxation which tended to fall on those less well able to pay; the former also used sale of offices and a tenth from the clergy, while the latter had the notorious wealth of the Indies. Charles V in fact greatly increased the revenue from his Spanish dominions; but prices rose faster.[1] The English Crown, unable to do much about taxation both direct and indirect, staved off disaster by appropriating Church revenues: in 1534 it acquired the right to clerical first fruits and an annual tenth, and in 1536–40 the dissolution of the monasteries temporarily made the government very wealthy. But the problem of greater interest, because it was in a way the real financial problem of the century, was one of collection, that is of financial organisation. Governments could never be really sure of getting their due. None of the three ever quite solved this, simply because they lacked sufficient physical means of control. England for a time looked likely to produce a genuinely reformed system. Henry VII, using his usual household methods, had developed the royal Chamber into a great collecting agency overshadowing the ancient and cumbersome Exchequer. After Wolsey had given the system a little more definition but less efficiency, Cromwell undertook fundamental reforms by divorcing financial machinery from household control. His plan involved the creation of parallel collecting agencies (revenue courts), each of which was to deal with a particular section of the revenue and to pay its surplus into a central treasury. The minister fell before the scheme was complete, and his successors, beset by the difficulties of the 1540's (war, depression, inflation), had to abandon its more ambitious aspects. By 1554 the financial machinery of England was settled for a century or more: control reverted to a partially reformed Exchequer which handled nearly all the royal revenues but unlike Cromwell's planned courts had neither the staff nor the time to exploit government rights to the full. The centralisation which Cromwell had desired was up to a point achieved, while many of the modern methods of Henry VII's and Cromwell's introducing were retained. But the ponderous and tradition-ridden Exchequer with its wooden tallies, with its entrenched officers and their petty jealousies, could not secure the ease of administration to which Cromwell had aspired. This was not restored until further reforms were undertaken late in the seventeenth century.

In many ways the machinery in France and Spain—countries where the Crown disposed of wide taxing powers—was much simpler. Until 1523 French revenue had been administered by two sets of officials: the royal lands by the four treasurers of France under the *chargeur de trésor*, and

[1] Above, p. 321.

the much larger 'extraordinary' revenue (*gabelles, aides, tailles, traites et impositions foraines*) by the four receivers general of finance. In that year the branches were combined and a central treasury was established under a *trésorier de l'epargne*, with a *trésorier des parties casuelles* to administer the more recent and casual revenue. Further reforms attempted a progressive centralisation of all revenue in one organisation, though this was never quite accomplished. The problem of audit was solved by the appointment in 1547 of two controllers, replaced by one controller-general in 1554, a reform for which England waited till the nineteenth century. In Spain, Charles V had inherited from the prudent Ferdinand a careful organisation centring upon the two *contadores mayores*, or chief treasurers, and the daily meetings of a financial board (*contraduria*) assisted by three secretaries (*porteros*). The detailed organisation of receivers, treasurers and controllers, which in England and France was tackled at different times with varying success, proved sufficient in Spain; all the emperor felt compelled to add was a supervising council. This was set up in 1523 under a Burgundian expert, the count of Nassau; under Philip II it was to develop into that highly bureaucratic clog on efficiency, the *consejo de la hacienda*. The troubles of Spanish finance were less exclusively administrative than those of England whose resources could never be properly mobilised; they arose rather from the magnitude of the emperor's political tasks and a mistaken reliance on American bullion.

One aspect of the central government remains to be dealt with—the administration of justice and enforcement of law which all sixteenth-century governments would have admitted to be their first concern. In fact this is to make an anachronistically strict distinction between ordinary and judicial administration. Following the custom of centuries, the sixteenth century conceived of government as primarily engaged in enforcing the law and deciding disputes between parties; all, or nearly all, the institutions already mentioned had a mixed character, council and court combined. Thus the Court of Augmentations, set up (1536) to handle the confiscated monastic lands, was run by a council of chief officers who dealt with such questions as the disposal of evicted monks, the sale and lease of lands, and the collection and expenditure of revenue, but who also acted as judges in straightforward lawsuits arising out of the lands in their charge. The *parlement* of Paris, far and away the most distinguished of the superior courts of France, never altogether forgot that it had really originated in the king's general entourage and never ceased to try to exercise 'conciliar'—political and administrative— functions despite royal attempts to restrict it to its primary, judicial work. Yet the story is by no means all confusion. There were ancient courts everywhere which were true courts and no more, and, as the history of the French and English privy councils has shown, a genuine division of functions was certainly not outside the century's comprehension. Though space forbids a discussion of any but the more important central courts, it must be remembered that there were also—quite apart from the general system of Church courts—ancient popular courts, feudal (seigniorial) courts nearly as ancient, and local offshoots of the central royal jurisdiction. One of the chief characteristics of the century was the gradual supersession of all inferior jurisdiction by the Crown's authority.

In this particular task England was once again placed unusually well. She had not only a common law but also a system of common law courts, centralised at Westminster but equipped with means to do justice throughout the country. King's Bench, the most honourable of them, dealt with criminal cases and those touching the Crown; Common Pleas (the busiest) with civil cases between party and party; the Exchequer with revenue cases. Unfortunately these courts had proved themselves both too formalised in their procedure and too inflexible in their law to cope with changing conditions: too often in the fifteenth century they failed to do justice or enforce law and order. The former failure had already led to the growth of the Court of Chancery, administering a yet developing body of rules designed to vary the law so as to fit the needs of justice and therefore called equity; under such active chancellors as Wolsey, Thomas More, and their successors this court acquired permanence, institutional character, and a great deal of business. To make up for the other deficiency of the common law courts, and to supply sufficient justice in an increasingly litigious age, the early Tudors (here again Wolsey was a moving spirit) developed the residuary jurisdiction of the royal council, first by attracting business to formal sessions of the council and later by establishing conciliar courts. The Court of Requests, dealing with the civil pleas of poor men and anyone else who could get a hearing, existed by 1530 and received its never very extensive organisation in the next twenty years; the Court of Star Chamber, primarily designed to deal with riots and other crimes short of felonies, always remained in one sense the judicial session of the council out of which it had grown but was nevertheless from 1540 at the latest a true separate court dealing only with legal matters. Star Chamber's original task—the suppression of disorder and the punishment of men too powerful and influential to be dealt with by the ordinary courts—was soon accompanied and even outstripped by the settlement of private disputes, thinly disguised as Star Chamber matters by the introduction of imaginary riots into the bill of complaint. Other conciliar courts enforced the law in the unsettled borders (Councils of the North and the Welsh Marches) or dealt with special problems, like the revenue courts of which Augmentations was the prototype and Wards and Liveries (1540–1643) the longest lived. Though these courts owed something in their procedure to the Roman law, the law they enforced was the law of England—common law, statutes, and in the case of Star Chamber proclamations.

It is probably true to say that, size for size, neither France nor Spain could boast so extensive and intensive a system of law courts. But a simpler structure of royal central jurisdiction did not imply either less law or less litigation; it reflected the fact that these countries had come later to unification under one judicial ægis and did not need to duplicate earlier courts. France had a number of superior courts at the centre, most of them fiscal, but only two need to be noticed here. One was the *grand conseil*, already mentioned, which, though organised in 1497, did not come to full flower until the reign of Francis I. This king used this off-shoot of his council to co-ordinate justice and override the varieties of law and jurisdiction which distinguished France. Its competence was virtually unlimited in both civil and criminal matters, but the only really consistent factor in its work was the interest of the Crown. Much more than Star Chamber, it was a weapon of royal centralisation, entirely subject to the king's control, and its heterogeneous yet single-minded purpose was recognised in the consolidating ordinance of Henry II (1552). It was well for this court that no estates met between 1484 and 1560: on both those occasions protesting voices were raised against it. But it was too useful to the Crown—and too necessary, one may add, to France in the prevailing state of law and legal administration—to be cut down in power. The same cannot be said of the other great court, the *parlement* of Paris. Although technically only one of several provincial *parlements* or high courts, it exercised a superior influence by virtue of its antiquity, the reputation of its lawyers, and its detailed organisation to which the first half of the century added a good deal. It had grown out of the king's general council, of which fact the so-called *lit de justice*, a meeting in the king's presence, was a reminder; yet it had largely escaped from royal control until the sixteenth-century monarchy began to apply some pressure. Henry II's *chambre ardente* was a temporarily successful move to deprive the *parlement* of criminal jurisdiction;[1] the court's theoretical power to hold up legislation by refusing to register it remained theory. But as an ordinary court of first instance and appeal—provided it submitted to royal authority—its competence, too, was unlimited, and it also exercised a general surveillance over the realm at large. To kings like Francis I and Henry II who could make it toe the line it offered yet another weapon in the armoury of a centralising and absolutist monarchy.

Needless to say, Charles V disposed of no judicial organisation for all his realm, except inasmuch as he himself could be petitioned for redress in hopes of evading or improving upon the ordinary courts. In the Nether-lands the privy council tried to get some consistency into the multiplicity of provincial codes and courts, but the slow work was not far advanced when Charles laid down his crowns. In the peninsula, on the other hand, much had been done to give good and fair justice to the separate kingdoms.

[1] A court which for a few years (1547–50) monopolised cases of heresy; above, p. 224.

These inherited from the Middle Ages central courts called indifferently *chancellarías* or *audiencias* which administered as a rule set codes of law resting upon Germanic custom but owing much to the Roman law. The Catholic kings extended this system to Granada, Valencia, and other outlying parts; they also secured better and swifter justice by adding more judges and sessions to the individual *chancellarías*. The reign of Charles V saw no important reforms: on the whole the efficiency of the courts seems to have declined without a resident monarch to supervise them, and Spain began to suffer from that besetting trouble of early modern Europe—vast arrears of unsettled litigation. In Aragon Charles did a little to break down the ancient safeguards against despotism. The office of *justicia* (regent, justiciar and protector of liberties rolled into one) had been curbed by Ferdinand who imposed on it a controlling council of five royalist legists; this was first (1518) enlarged to seven and then abolished (1528) because the emperor, wishing to respect the forms of Aragonese liberties, preferred to make sure that supporters of the monarchy were elected *justicia*.

This sketch of monarchical government in the western kingdoms, very incomplete as it must necessarily be, has illustrated the degree to which, the methods by which, these rulers established, extended and deepened their centralised power. The work was rarely pursued consistently for any length of time, being constantly interrupted by such prior interests as wars, religion and diplomacy. Charles V could never devote to his territories the sort of organising attention that Spain had had from Ferdinand of Aragon or Burgundy from Philip the Good. In England the administrations of Henry VII and Cromwell, both intent upon improving the machinery of government, were islands in a sea of general and often ill-considered political ambitions. France perhaps went at the task with the greatest persistence, but she owed this less to her kings than to the large body of trained and devoted legists and civil servants. Not only was the work done patchily, not only was there neither hope nor often the slightest intention of destroying all the liberties and diversities of the past in the general process of cleaning up: one must never forget the common failure to translate the firm resolves of government into effective action and ready obedience in the localities.

Until fairly recent times, centralised governments have always found it very much more difficult to carry out their policies and orders than to devise them. The effectiveness of sixteenth-century governments varied a good deal. They were usually capable of suppressing actual revolt, and they commonly had means at their disposal to coerce occasional resistance to their authority. But to a degree which it is now hard to understand they depended less on physical force than on mystique, and if opposition was widespread but not violent it could usually be successful. Anyone who thinks, for instance, that the break-away from Rome was forced upon a reluctant England by Henry VIII's tyrannical government had better study what happened when the people who mattered—the gentry especially, but also merchants and craftsmen, yeomen and even husbandmen—really disliked a government measure. They disliked paying taxes, and Henry VIII's only retreats before his own nation were always in face of this dislike; they would not obey regulations forbidding certain exports and imports, and the government's economic policy remained at best a barely breathing letter. In neither case was failure due to want of trying. Though the kings of France and Spain possessed better means of control, they could not have claimed markedly greater success in the day-to-day running of their countries: indeed, in the sixteenth century England was still the best and the most governed country of western Europe. While messages and orders and reports took days or weeks to travel to and fro, while countries remained half-empty with great stretches of wilderness to hide the evildoer, while local preoccupations and prejudices continued to sway juries and justices, centralised government could never become total or totalitarian government.

These points must be kept in mind if the picture presented by local administration is to be properly judged. In all the countries in question little was added in this period that could be called new. Everywhere there existed quite well-designed machinery, inherited from the past, for the execution of the central government's orders. Some of it was by this time only a survival from the past, like the English sheriffs and the French *gouverneurs* (suppressed in 1542 but revived three years later to please the great nobles)—officers who had once been the king's loyal servants, had then succumbed to disruptive feudalism, and were now little more than personal honours. The financial organisation of the *généralités*, reformed in 1542 so as to provide a uniform system of eighteen tax districts, gave French government a control over the most difficult problem of all to which neither England nor Spain could offer a parallel. But the main form taken by local government organs was judicial. In Castile and Aragon the problem had been one of towns: control the towns and you controlled the country. The Catholic kings therefore established their hold by means of the *corregidores*, royal officials attached to the municipal administrations and soon in control of them. England had her justices of the peace, local gentlemen appointed to administer the law; throughout the century their duties and sphere were constantly being enlarged until they were not only magistrates of summary jurisdiction but also social administrators. The French system relied on an ancient office, that of the *bailli* or *senechal* who was not unlike the English justice in the sense that he tended to be a great man of his locality but very different in another way because his territorial sway, personal standing and powers of rule were much greater. The *bailli* represented the king in all matters (financial, judicial, military), and so he still did in the sixteenth century though it has been remarked that he often acted more like the representative of his *bailliage* at the king's court. Partly in order to lessen the local ascendancy of these great men, the office was rendered less personal by the addition of many inferior officials: from 1523 each *bailliage* had its *lieutenant criminel* and *lieutenant civile*, while further *lieutenants, procureurs du roi, avocats du roi,* and so on, swelled the establishment till there appeared bureaucratically organised courts, a development never experienced by the English local justices. An edict of 1554 consolidated the system and erected a general police organisation for the realm. This was the basis on which the full bureaucratic absolutism of the *ancien régime* could arise in the next century, though it is important to remember that before that happened the semi-feudal *bailli* had to make way for the *intendant*.

For the time being, in any case, even the French Crown could not boast of real control in all parts of its dominions. It was not weakness of machinery but difficulties of communications and coercive power that stood in the way, as well as the apathy of the remote country which always does so much to explain the ascendancy of capital cities in national politics. As things stood, local men had to run local affairs. Nothing exceptional was implied by the English reliance on unpaid local worthies: the French administration, appointed and to some extent paid by the Crown, also of course utilised local material, and so did the Spanish. The French practice of selling offices worked in favour of local men and local independence; it made for the creation of an hereditary bourgeois bureaucracy to replace the old hereditary nobility in the running of the provinces. The English system may have been potentially less under Crown control, but in practice the Tudor council kept a careful and reasonably effective eye on the justices to whom the loss of the commission would have been quite as serious a matter in the social structure of the shire as dismissal would have been to any salaried official. Over their own agents, at least, governments exercised sufficient control; only a major rebellion producing an unusual situation could endanger this, as when the gentry of northern England joined in the Pilgrimage of Grace. The warnings already given against overestimating government power in this period must be balanced by the realisation that all these monarchies had a tighter hold and operated more formidable weapons of power than had been seen in that part of Europe since the fall of Rome.

So far we have been concerned with the details of royal government. We have looked at the machinery through which the rulers of the western kingdoms expanded their power, consolidated their territories and their hold on them, and to all appearances developed absolutist tendencies always inherent in monarchy. But all these countries had institutions of the other part: representative assemblies existed, not only in the English parliament, the French and Burgundian estates general, the Castilian and Aragonese cortes, but even in such lesser units as the French and Netherlandish provinces, in Catalonia and Valencia. In fact, from the thirteenth century onwards all Latin Christendom had seen a rapid spreading of such assemblies; they were as typical of Germany, Scandinavia, Hungary and the rest as of western Europe, and they were as typical of late medieval politics as was monarchy itself. Of course—and this is undoubtedly important—they were much more intermittent. But they existed, and a German scholar has seen in all these states a structural dualism—a *Doppelpoligkeit*—between ruler and representative assembly which seemed to him, and has seemed to others, the critical constitutional question from the fourteenth century onwards.[1]

Yet it is by no means certain that this dualism was the outstanding feature of late-medieval assemblies. They were, after all, royal creations, dependent on the royal summons for their very existence. Naturally enough, they were usually called because they could serve some royal purpose. The most obvious royal purpose was money, and all these assemblies claimed and exercised powers of granting taxes. In France they lost control in 1440 when the Crown equipped itself with direct powers to tax; in Castile they in effect abandoned their power after 1538. In both countries their consequent lack of usefulness just about killed them. Moreover, except in England where everyone, nobles and clergy as well as the commons, paid taxes, this role had always been of least interest to the politically most powerful estates, with a necessary weakening of their enthusiasm for those expensive and protracted meetings. As regards legislation, the French estates never had much chance of extorting statutory remedies for grievances in the manner of the English parliament. In the Spanish cortes these powers varied from the tight hold of the Aragonese assembly to the rudimentary attempts made in Castile; but in the sixteenth century, the monarchy everywhere in the peninsula established an exclusive right to make and promulgate laws. Nevertheless, for their useful functions assemblies were convened frequently, except in France where none met between the obstreperous body of 1484 and the crisis estates of 1560: until repeated failures to extract financial co-operation discouraged him, Charles V called the cortes of Castile some fifteen times, though he contented himself with but six meetings of the still more difficult cortes of Aragon.

The other reason for which kings used assemblies was political: these meetings helped on territorial unification and symbolised it. The English parliament had achieved much in that direction in the fourteenth century, though as late as 1536–40 Henry VIII employed his parliament for the same purpose when he called elected representatives from Wales, Cheshire and Calais. It was Burgundy that demonstrated this aspect most fully: here the calling of the states general was designed to override provincial particularism and give a firm foundation to the monarchy. It worked only

[1] O. Hintze in *Hist. Zeitschr.* vol. 141 (1929).

within limits; until the reign of Philip II the states general tended to remain an ornamental body, while the real work, even of taxing, went on in the individual provincial assemblies. Louis XI of France copied principle and practice, so that for a short time (1468–84) there were important plenary meetings of the French estates. But, equipped as it was with independent sources of revenue and a growing bureaucratic organisation of the realm, the French monarchy thereafter preferred to do without estates rather than face criticism. In the Spanish kingdoms, too, the cortes had received early encouragement as royal weapons against local or noble independence, and they were still playing this part under the renovated monarchy. But because of the very different levels of constitutional development reached in Castile and Aragon, and the ancient separation of the two kingdoms, no meeting for all Spain was called until 1709. The cortes of Portugal, incidentally, underwent a rapid decline in this century and ceased to participate in the making of law.

While then these assemblies really had no life apart from the will of the Crown, the latter's needs and the claims which estates had established over them gave some a chance to oppose the monarchy and limit its liberty of action. This was so in Aragon and above all in England. The English parliament had a history of privileges won and powers developed at the expense of royal absolutism, and even though in the fifteenth century it had fallen into the hands of factions, constitutionally it had only gained in the process. However, events under the Yorkists and Tudors at first suggested that it, too, was only an adjunct to the power of the Crown. Henry VII called it to endorse his policy and grant him money; he ceased to call it when he needed neither. The first few years of Henry VIII saw four parliaments, called to help finance a war; then Wolsey took over and only one more parliament met before his fall fourteen years later, and that one a failure from the king's point of view. The parliament of 1523, stubbornly contesting the government's demands for supply, displayed the kind of behaviour which in 1538 convinced Charles V that he could no longer use the Castilian cortes. Thus there was something like a crisis also in the history of the English parliament: during Wolsey's rule it was by no means certain that it alone of all that welter of assemblies would survive the sixteenth century not only alive but vastly more important. On the other hand, it did enjoy certain advantages over similar institutions elsewhere. It controlled extraordinary taxes which the Crown had no other legal means of levying. Though legislation might be devised by the government (the common modern practice anywhere), it also could not become effective until agreed to by the two houses of parliament; the Crown had no independent powers of law-making except by proclamations whose limitations have already been described. Parliamentary statute was recognised as the supreme and very nearly the only way of adding to or amending the common law of the realm: it certainly was the only way if new treasons or felonies were to be created. As to composition, it has been shown that the traditional view of the superiority of the House of Commons with its mixture of knights and burgesses over the merely bourgeois French 'third estate' arose from a misunderstanding of the latter, but the House of Commons was a much more self-conscious institution than any lower estate in Europe. Its numbers (growing from 300 upwards, as against the 38 procurators of the towns in the Castilian cortes or the 150 or so members of the *tiers état*) and its social homogeneity (the towns never played so great a part as on the continent and since 1400 at least had increasingly looked to the gentry for representatives) were enough to distinguish it from similar bodies elsewhere. The English parliament, as it emerged from the Middle Ages, was better fitted for survival than any estates or cortes; but its sudden rise to importance was a matter of political circumstance and statesmanlike perception.

The crisis came in 1529 when Henry VIII realised that he would not get his divorce without a fight. As western monarchs usually did in such a situation, he called his parliament; too much has been made of an action which in itself proclaims customary procedure rather than political genius. And for some three years parliament proved of little enough use; the problems to be solved were too great and too unprecedented for the minds then in charge. Until 1532 Henry could think of nothing better to do with parliament than to have it threaten the clergy and remedy abuses; it was helpful to have a vague sort of support given to his intentions, but he was told that parliament could not free him for re-marriage, as he had hoped. But for the twist given to things by the arrival in power of Thomas Cromwell, parliament would have remained barren and might well have been discarded like its fellows on the continent. But Cromwell's plan for the cutting of the knot involved two main lines of thought. For one, he encouraged the king to make a reality of his claim to undisputed supremacy in his dominions; theology, the king's own ingrained conviction, and past history back to Constantine, were pressed into service to declare the papal supremacy a usurpation. But these were words: the stroke of genius lay in the second prong of the attack. In order that the royal supremacy should be enforced it was necessary to create new treasons—new offences which the courts would punish—and parliament was the proper maker of such laws. Yet parliament, it could be said, and was so said before 1533, could not touch the sphere governed by God's law of which the canon law was a proper reflection. To this conception Cromwell opposed, in practice and in theory, the view that within a body politic only the positive enacted law made by the sovereign legislator has binding force, and that in effect that legislator is not limited in any way. Here, of course, lay the essence of monarchical despotism, if one cared to make it so; in the England of the 1530's, however, it was made quite plain that sovereign legislative power rested with the king-in-parliament and not with a single royal despot. The history of law-making in England had tended in that direction; Cromwell was a parliamentarian by training and predilection; yet the clarity with which the question of sovereignty was put and answered remains remarkable, as does the assurance with which in that king-worshipping age the ultimate power in the State became vested in a constitutional and limited monarchy. The vigour and assertive arrogance of Henry VIII and Elizabeth have up to a point disguised the truth: though autocrats by temperament they were never despots because they could not in their persons make law. The manner in which Cromwell carried through the break from Rome established parliament as a permanent and indispensable part of the constitution.

All the countries with which we have dealt unmistakably grew in one direction: greater cohesion and consolidation, stronger and more intrusive government, centralised monarchy. This was as true of England as of the rest, though thanks to her history England had less far to go in this agreed direction and therefore the less need to break with her past. In none of the kingdoms was monarchical despotism achieved in this period; practical difficulties, historical obstacles, and remnants of feudal thought stood in the way. However, in the realms of the Valois and Habsburg Crowns the trend towards absolutism was clear and maintained; setbacks notwithstanding, absolutism came in the end. Those weapons of royal government that alone were capable of turning against the Crown—the assemblies of estates—were discontinued or reduced to cyphers. Only in England, parliament, so far from weakening, entered upon a new life in this period when it (and it included the king) became the sovereign organ of a sovereign national State. The old dualism was resolved by the creation—in fact, though few saw it—of a mixed sovereign body. The consequences for parliament were striking: within two generations, structure, procedure, attitude, and methods of governmental management had become recognisably 'modern'. It is not for nothing that the parliaments of the 1530's first provide evidence of large-scale plans of government legislation, of committees in Lords and Commons, of free speech in a real sense, of government management in the house and government influence on elections. The parliamentary system which had to be reformed in the nineteenth century took its shape in the sixteenth, when all other representative institutions declined.[1] On the face of it, the power of the Crown was more evident in England, too; but the discerning eye can surely see beyond to the essential 'constitutionalism' of the Tudor monarchy.

How far were these trends and events reflected in contemporary thinking upon the State? Generally speaking, significant political thinking

---

[1] The states general of the Netherlands had a great future, but their history is one of republican rebellion and quite different from the development of the 'royal' type of estates in England.

occurs only when there are significant political upheavals. Spain, as is not surprising in view of its pretty placid internal state, could show no writings of note. Early in the century both France and England produced backward-looking traditionalist interpretations of the State. Claude de Seyssel, who published his *La Grant Monarchie de France* in 1519, accorded the king supremacy and absolute rights within his proper sphere but held that he was limited by the divine, the natural and the customary laws. Like so many others he used the metaphor of the body politic to express his conviction that the State was an organic and corporate unit in which the head might indeed rule but in which the other parts had their indefeasible rights.[1] He admitted that bad or dead customs were for the king to amend and had to agree that in France the king could invade property rights by means of his taxing power; but, full of admiration for the balance he saw in the French constitution, he insisted on such traditional restraints as extra-human law, counsel and consent. Christopher St German, a common lawyer who produced several treatises culminating in *Doctor and Student* (1528), similarly stressed the existence of a law independent of man; though he admitted both the extent of the royal prerogative in England and the law-making power of parliament, he retained the medieval safeguard of the law of nature, or, as (in the manner of English lawyers) he called it, law of reason. These men were traditional lawyers and of an older generation; St German was to be overtaken in his eighties by the Reformation of which he approved without grasping its significance to his view of the State.

One freak of pre-Reformation writing in England must not go unnoticed. In 1516 the young Thomas More produced his *Utopia*, a description of an imaginary island kingdom ideal in every respect except that it was not Christian. *Utopia* was partly a dream and partly a passionate and often shrewd criticism of contemporary conditions in England. Its constitutional theme is, however, thin; it was neither derived from observation of the England he knew nor influential upon it. Moreover, like all the constructions of moralists, Utopia is on reflection a frightening community. Highminded, honest, not without humour (none of More's thinking could be that), the book is also oppressive, narrow, puritanical and intolerant. More disapproved of private property as the cause of all evil—a Christian tenet rather than the proto-communism that has been read into it—but he also, following the father of all these imaginings, Plato, applied commonplace and deadening standards of utility to all men's doings. Many social customs of the Utopians are reasonable, generous and wise; yet the total effect of their polity should make a thoughtful man turn and run. The work owes its reputation in part to its

---

[1] Edmund Dudley, in his *Tree of Commonwealth* (1509), was alone at this time in varying the metaphor: his purpose—to bring home a conception of organic unity in the State—was much the same.

radical social ideas which (though they were based on an insufficient under-standing of England's economic problems) have pleased later radicals; in part to its noble attack on amoral statesmanship; but in the main to its attractive style and the author's charming personality. The More of *Utopia* was a humanist, a moralist, rather than a commentator on events; but he did not ignore the world around him. The outstanding mind among early sixteenth-century thinkers went much farther in studying fact. This was Niccolò Machiavelli.[1] He was dead by 1527; his experience was confined to Italy, already a political backwater in the period here dealt with; and it cannot be shown that he influenced anyone—writer or statesman—before 1560.[2] On the other hand, his attitude to politics—universal and narrow at the same time—is particularly typical of the generation after his death, so that he must be considered here.

Born in Florence in 1469 Machiavelli made an official career as a diplomatist, was secretary to the Council of Ten from 1498 to 1512, and after the restoration of the Medici lived in reluctant retirement. He owned a sharp eye, though it must be remembered that his experience was really confined to diplomacy, and the peculiar diplomacy of Borgia and Medici Italy at that; he read widely among the ancients and looked upon republican Rome as everything he passionately wanted modern Italy to be; and he undoubtedly had a malicious liking for appearing more cynical and shocking than he really felt. His relevant works are *The Prince* and *The Discourses upon Livy*. The latter are generally recognised to have more of the essential Machiavelli in them, but the former—more cynical, less thoughtful—is the better book and it is therefore small wonder that he has tended to be judged by it. What matters in Machiavelli's thinking are his aims and methods, rather than his conclusions. He wished to teach statecraft as it really was and ought to be, as his experience and study had shown it to him and free from the moral precepts which he could not find outside the books. He failed to see that the devices he described are not improved by publicity. Machiavelli's real originality lay in his analytical method. It was not as new as is sometimes suggested for a writer to look at reality in his interpretation of politics, but Machiavelli carried the notion through with severe and dedicated logic. He tried conscientiously to base all his theories only on ascertainable fact: these things, he said, have happened, such is the manner of their happening, and these are the lessons they teach. It was a revolutionary approach to politics because for one thing it eliminated the claptrap about invisible laws and similar conventions of no reality in life, and because for another it subordinated everything to the test of expediency. Machiavelli's question always was

[1] Cf. also vol. I, pp. 177 f.

[2] The old view of Thomas Cromwell as a deliberate Machiavellian will not stand up to investigation (G. R. Elton, 'Thomas Cromwell's Political Creed', *Trans. R. Hist. Soc.* 1956).

'is it conducive to the end in view?' and never 'is it right?' This, of course, has earned him his bad name, but he was after all correct in thinking that his question, and not the question of the moralists, moves most men, and politicians especially, in the conduct of their affairs, and that therefore the true political philosopher must give it full weight.

Machiavelli knew very well how revolutionary his method was and he regarded it with much pride. All the same, it was much less truly inductive than he and his admirers have held; there were weaknesses in it which cannot be ascribed to the difficulties of the pioneer. In the *Discourses* in particular he was more concerned with the facts of history than those of experience, and he used them selectively, without much critical sense, to support a preconceived theory. He tended to be dogmatic about the efficacy of causation and the use of parallels in history; his whole method demanded some such dogmas, but Guicciardini, for instance, was more sanely sceptical about historical precedents and the force of selected examples. Nor was Machiavelli's own experience diversified enough to save him from a narrow application of his revolutionary doctrine; he never seems to have got beyond the questions of military and diplomatic action to the problems of economics or the structure of the State. He had, in fact, no considered view of the State but confined himself to studying its preservation by the use of power. It must be understood that Machiavelli's concentration on the problem of power marked a great step forward in the understanding of politics and was, philosophically speaking, an act of liberation. Further, Machiavelli, who liked to present the picture of a relentlessly cold analyst and observer, was in reality a man of over-powering passions, especially political passions, as his whole deluded attitude to ancient Rome shows. Lastly he committed the common error of 'realists': he over-rationalised human nature, with the result that he held it in an excessively low esteem and ascribed to men a power of divining their interest and acting upon it which in such pure form they do not possess.

These reservations make it unnecessary to dilate at length upon his conclusions which consist, by and large, of quite reasonable if often short-sighted maxims for the conduct of irresponsible government.[1] He preferred republics to princes, even for the purposes which he hoped to see realised in Italy—another example of his failure to understand his own world and of his attachment to Livy. If his immediate influence was small, his ultimate place must be high. For however imperfectly he may at times have practised his own teaching, he was great because he grasped the importance of looking at things as they are. His astonishing insight into some men's actions, his clear realisation of the problem of power and how to preserve it, his very refusal to erect a system or impose a moral, raise him above those comfortable writers who repeat with unction the

[1] Cf. also vol. I, pp. 273 f.

conventional nonsense of the past and profess to know and teach that which is right.

We return to lesser but immediately more significant writings. The French monarchy's march towards absolutism did not go unnoticed by the publicists, and defenders of royal power arose particularly among the students of the Roman law. Legists like Grassaille and humanists like Budé linked hands to free monarchy from the theoretical limitations inherited from the feudal and religious theories of the past. They did this by greatly expanding the position of the prerogative until they saw *merum imperium*—unrestricted authority—in monarchical rule. Though such old stage properties as fundamental laws and the need for counsel were retained, they were rendered nugatory by the denial of practical limitations on the royal freedom of action. Above all, these theorists began to distinguish a double power in the king: an ordinary power by which he governed under and according to the law, and an absolute power which enabled him to ignore even the positive law if the interests of the State demanded it. It is interesting to see how the traditional paraphernalia are preserved, while the deductions drawn from them arrive at a very different monarchy from Seyssel's. Perhaps it ought to be pointed out that these theories reflected the progress of the French monarchy; they did not inspire it. Less absolutist notions also survived: as late as 1555 Guillaume de la Perrière published a *Miroir Politique* whose insistence on the supremacy of the law Seyssel would have heartily applauded. The real political crisis in France came after 1560, with the outbreak of the religious wars; and so, naturally, did major political writing.

England, on the other hand, had her crisis in the 1530's, and the Reformation produced some interesting writing though no great thinkers. The important thinkers of the political Reformation in England were Aristotle and Marsiglio of Padua; the actual writers owed much to these. This is less noticeable in the theological defence of the royal supremacy— dull statements of caesaro-papism like Edward Foxe's *De vera differentia regiae potestatis et ecclesiae* (1534) or Stephen Gardiner's *De vera obedientia* (1535). The work of Cromwell's group of propagandists, writing in the vernacular, excites more interest. Humanistically trained and employed by the government, they wrote from conviction and with an enthusiasm for the new state of affairs which reminds one that to many the Henrician Reformation came as a great breath of liberty. The leading names are Thomas Starkey who published his *Exhortation to Christian Unity* in 1535 but left the larger and more original *Dialogue between Lupset and Pole* in manuscript; and Richard Morison, a diplomatist as well as a publicist, who wrote among other things *A Remedy for Sedition* (1536) and *An Exhortation to Stir All Englishmen to the Defence of their Country* (1539). Their works, and those of others, not only defended the royal supremacy but, significantly, also adhered to constitutionalism and the supremacy of the law; rejecting extremes they admired the middle way and saw the importance of social and economic reforms if the political changes were to endure. Despite Henry VIII's personality, no English writer can be found who preached absolutism on the French model; but in the country which had in practice arrived at the concept of legislative sovereignty there were not even tentative steps towards a theory of it. On the other hand, the practising theory (if the term be permitted) of the Reformation statutes—whose preambles contain many significant political ideas ultimately coming from Cromwell himself— shows quite a coherent notion of what was happening: the statutes not only define precisely the whole concept of national sovereignty (Act of Appeals, 1533), but also adumbrate a statement of the legislative supremacy of the king-in-parliament (Act of Dispensations, 1534). It is, however, probably true that the very lack of an incisive and powerful mind among the writers saved England from losing the comfortable and useful instinct for often impalpable 'limitations' which alone makes the rigour of legislative sovereignty supportable.

CHAPTER XV

CONSTITUTIONAL DEVELOPMENT
AND POLITICAL THOUGHT IN
EASTERN EUROPE

THE three kingdoms of Poland, Bohemia and Hungary were among the largest in sixteenth-century Europe. Together they filled the area bounded by Germany, the Baltic, Russia and the Balkans, or, in the terms of physical geography, the basins of the Oder, Vistula and middle Danube. They occupied a central position also in respect of political development, for while they lagged behind the western European states they were in advance of Russia and Turkey. It is this central position which constitutes their historical interest: the balance of power between the landowners and the monarchy was so even throughout the century as to give to their relations, whether of conflict or co-operation, a significance that illuminates the more decisive conflicts which were at the same time being waged in the extremer parts of Europe.

The accession of Sigismund I 'the Old', of the Jagiellon dynasty, to the Polish throne in 1506, and of Ferdinand I of Habsburg, brother of the Emperor Charles V and already ruler of the complex of the hereditary Austrian lands, to the thrones of Bohemia and Hungary in 1526, may be said to mark the beginning of the conflict, for they both succeeded to *fainéant* kings against whom the landowners had virtually had things all their own way. The kingdoms to which they acceded were still medieval in the looseness of their political structure. Sigismund's inheritance was not even in name a kingdom but a *rzecz pospolita* or *respublica*; the half-dozen duchies into which the kingdom of Poland had fallen apart in the twelfth century had not yet all been brought under the direct rule of the king, for the duchy of Mazovia was not incorporated until the failure of heirs to its last duke, who died in 1526. East Prussia was not fully subject to the king of Poland until 1525, and even then its Hohenzollern duke, Albrecht, enjoyed almost as much sovereignty as a vassal of Poland as he had done as grand master of the Teutonic Order. Moreover, more than half the territory which Sigismund ruled, the grand duchy of Lithuania, had no organic union with the kingdom of Poland other than that of a common sovereign until the Union of Lublin in 1569.

The territories to which Ferdinand succeeded when he was elected king of Bohemia in 1526 constituted an even looser dominion. They were technically 'the Lands of the Crown of St Wenceslas', which comprised the Czech lands of the kingdom of Bohemia and the margravate of

Moravia, the dozen or so duchies of Polish-German Silesia, the two separate Wendish-German duchies of Upper and Lower Lusatia, and various islands of unassimilated duchies and lordships such as Cheb (Eger), Kladsko (Glatz), Loket (Elbogen) and Opava (Troppau). Ferdinand's Hungarian realm was the least unitary of the three, for 'the Lands of the Crown of St Stephen' comprised two distinct kingdoms: the kingdom of Hungary and the kingdom of Croatia. Within Hungary was the inassimilable principality of Transylvania, itself compounded of the three partly autonomous Magyar, German and Szekler 'nations'. Croatia comprised three disjunct parts: Dalmatia, central Croatia and Slavonia.

What gives to this part of sixteenth-century Europe its homogeneity is the great economic supremacy that was enjoyed and exploited there by the landowners, who, however large or small their estates, were nobles, *una et eadem nobilitas*, as the phrase ran in Hungary. This class, the *szlachta* of Poland, the *šlechta* of Bohemia, the *köznemesség* of Hungary, unrestricted by any rule or custom of primogeniture, conscious of its power and jealous of its profitable privileges, by means of its virtual monopoly of economic power had a dominant position in central Europe. The landlords together with the Crown, the Church and the towns owned every acre of land, and as the century progressed the share of the lay landlords was steadily increased by acquisition of Crown lands in pawn, of Church lands by confiscation, and of town lands by coercion and forfeiture. Feudal jurisprudents like Verböczi could assume that the 'nation' was co-terminous with the Crown and the landlords without feeling argument or justification to be necessary.[1] The political power of the nobility was based on the local or county assemblies. In Poland they were called 'little diets' (*sejmiki*), and there was usually one in each palatinate, altogether thirty-seven in Poland and a dozen in Lithuania. They were composed exclusively of the landlords. The *sejmiki* were not perpetual organs of local administration and justice, which in Poland was still exercised by local officers of the Crown. Their function was primarily parliamentary. To them were directed royal writs for elections to provincial or national parliaments; the 'pre-parliamentary' (*przedsejmowe*) *sejmiki* then proceeded to elect their paid representatives to the lower house and mandated them on the general lines of the agenda which had been sent with the writs of summons. The representatives of the *sejmiki* then assembled in provincial assemblies, of which there were six, where they concerted the policy to be pursued by the province in parliament. After the parliament was dissolved the representatives reported to the local 'reportorial' (*relayine*) *sejmiki*, which took steps to execute the laws which had been enacted, gave their assent to any taxes granted at a

---

[1] For the economic policy of the lords, cf. above, pp. 35 f. It rested upon the freehold —almost sovereign—rights of the owners of 'estates' which were consistently extended at the expense of both Crown and peasantry.

higher rate than had been agreed to beforehand by the *przedsejmowy sejmik*, and appointed the officers to collect the tax in the palatinate.

Local assemblies (*sjezdy krajské*) in the Bohemian lands were similar to but less powerful than those in Poland. The powerful local councils (*landfridy*) which had assumed wide legislative, administrative, judicial and financial powers during the anarchical interregnum of 1439–58 had since then been emasculated by the centralising policy of King George of Poděbrady and the oligarchs of the Jagiellonian period, and at the date of Ferdinand's accession they met only to elect members of parliament and some local officials and to provide for the execution of statutes. Ferdinand still further weakened them by forbidding the *sjezdy* to assemble without royal summons under penalty of death. Very different was the position and power of the counties (*megyek*) in Hungary, for Ferdinand so urgently needed to win the support of the nobles in his civil war with his rival John Zápolyai and his successors, and their Turkish allies and suzerains, that he dared not assault their privileges in local self-government. Indeed, the survival of the Hungarian county was perhaps the best guarantee of the continuance of the relatively autonomous position of Habsburg Hungary down to the *Ausgleich* of 1867. The Hungarian county court was not an occasional assembly, but a permanent committee elected by the assembly (*megyegyülés*) of the nobles of each county, exercising judicial, administrative, economic and financial functions; the county assembly not only had the elective functions of the Polish *sejmik* but was also an effective local legislature.

The highest organ of the nations of central Europe in the sixteenth century was the parliament or diet, where from time to time the estates (*Stany, Stavy, Rendek*) of each kingdom, principality, province or *land* assembled to join, normally with the ruler, in the exercise of sovereign functions. The large number of these parliaments in the three central European kingdoms is at once a sign of their importance and a symptom of their vulnerability. In Poland there were the general parliament (*sejm walny*) of the kingdom, the provincial parliaments of Great Poland, Little Poland, Kujawia, Royal (Western) Prussia, Ducal (Eastern) Prussia after its incorporation in 1525, and Mazowia, which was an autonomous appanage until the extinction of its cadet line in 1526. Lithuania had its own parliament until it was amalgamated with the Polish *sejm* by the Union of Lublin of 1569. In 'the Lands of the Crown of St Wenceslas' the parliament (*sněm*) of the kingdom of Bohemia had certain sovereign rights over the whole, but much power was left to the parliaments or diets of Moravia, Upper and Lower Silesia, and Upper and Lower Lusatia. There were also the autonomous estates of Cheb, Loket, Opava and Kladsko. Occasionally, for the purposes of a coronation, to deal with a crisis in public order (1511, 1518) or, most often, to provide subsidies for the Turkish war (eleven times between 1530 and 1595), there would be convened a general parliament of delegates from all the parliaments of the Bohemian Crown. But such general assemblies were regarded with suspicion by the estates as instruments of royal exaction, and no attempt was made to develop them into a permanent instrument of sovereignty for the whole Bohemian complex of states. In 'the Lands of the Crown of St Stephen' there was also a multiplicity of parliaments. The estates of the kingdom of Hungary were duplicated during the civil war, Ferdinand's supporters meeting usually in Pozsony (Pressburg, Bratislava) and Zápolyai's in Budapest; the principality of Transylvania had its own parliament, for most of the century a sovereign body independent of the Hungarian king and parliament; the kingdom of Croatia, in so far as it was not occupied by the Turks, enjoyed three parliaments, in Zagreb, Dalmatia and Slavonia. It is an interesting commentary on the conventional conception of Ferdinand as the enemy of parliamentary government that it was he who endeavoured to create a supreme parliament for all his dominions. He summoned all the estates to such a common or federal parliament at Brno in 1528 to try to make Austrian currency universal throughout his dominions; similar congresses of estates were summoned to Linz in 1530 and 1541 to provide money for the Turkish war. As the Bohemians refused to attend any assembly outside their own borders Ferdinand tried to assemble the parliaments in a general congress at Kutná Hora (Kuttenberg) or Prague in 1534 and 1541, but there the Hungarians either did not appear or refused any subsidy. The opportunity to establish an estates general for the Habsburg lands was made abortive by the jealous particularism of the national estates themselves.

The composition of the parliaments of central Europe in the sixteenth century illustrates the dominance of the landlords. They were essentially meetings of the estates, but the only estate whose presence was necessary everywhere and always to constitute a parliament was that of the nobility. The king if he were present in person or by his lieutenant was an estate of parliament; but after a demise of the Crown, if there was either no immediate male heir or only an infant, the parliaments convened without royal summons to proceed to the sovereign act of election. In each parliament the nobles were the largest and most powerful element, but they were usually not a united force, for the divergent interests of the wealthy magnates and the gentry were reflected in the existence of two chambers (*curiae*). The Polish parliament (*sejm*) comprised an upper house, the senate, and a chamber of representatives (*izba poselska*). The senate was composed of the Catholic archbishops and bishops, the provincial governors (*wojowodowie*), the castellans, the crown marshal and the court marshal, the chancellor, vice-chancellor and treasurer. Until 1529 it had 87 members; from 1529 to 1569, as a result of the extinction of the Mazovian appanage, it had 94, and after the union with Lithuania 140. The Polish senate was formally a body of central and local officers of the

Crown and royally nominated prelates, but because these officers and prelates were all, except for a few *novi homines* and royal favourites, drawn from the great noble families, it was a chamber which represented and exercised the oligarchic policy of the great landholders. Voting in the senate was *viritim* and probably by majority. The lower house of the Polish parliament was, with the exception of the representatives of the city of Cracow and, after 1569, of Wilno, a homogeneous assembly of the *szlachta*. Every adult male of noble birth had the right to sit and vote in the chamber, but the cost in time and money kept most of them away. In the early part of the century the senate nominated half the members of the chamber, but from 1520 the middle nobility fought this practice and after 1540 it apparently ceased. A statute of 1520 introduced the practice of the election of members of the chamber by the *sejmiki*, and the king undertook to pay the expenses of not more than six representatives from each constituency. Despite the efforts of Sigismund II to keep the number of members small, the size of the chamber increased from 45 in 1504 to 93 in 1553, to 110 in 1569 and 158 in 1570. Elected members were bound to attend. There is evidence that important constitutional laws, such as those of 1548, 1553, 1563 and 1565, were decided by a majority vote. But in less important matters there was a fatal tendency to seek to secure a unanimous vote or at least a vote *nemine contradicente*. There was as yet no *liberum veto*, though an individual *sejmik* could and sometimes did refuse to accept a statute as applicable to its own area.

The Bohemian parliament (*sněm*) was tricameral. The upper house was undisguisedly a House of Lords (*curia dominorum* or *magnatum*); every *pán* (lord) who was accepted as such by the house itself and whose nobility was at least four generations old was a member; it was therefore not a house of royal ministers and local governors like the Polish senate, but a co-optative assembly of the wealthiest landlords. It had no clerical members, for the episcopate of Bohemia had disappeared in the storms of the Hussite wars and was not restored to a place in the legislature until after 1620. The second *curia* in the *sněm* was that of the gentry (*vladykové*), or, as they were coming to be called, the knights (*rytíři*). Every gentleman who had a coat of arms and who was inscribed in the 'land books' as having an estate had the right to a seat and vote. There were some 1500 such noble families. But the member had to maintain himself; therefore, as in Poland, only the richer and more important attended. The poorer nobles elected from two to six representatives in their district assemblies who were maintained during the parliament at the king's expense, but every noble had the right to attend. After 1526 Ferdinand tried with considerable success to prevent the election of nobles to parliament, so that the second chamber came to be the virtual monopoly of the richer nobles of the middle aristocracy. It numbered usually between 100 and 200 members, never more than 300. The third estate in the Bohemian parliament was that of the burgesses. This exceptional phenomenon is witness to the greater power and wealth of the towns in the lands of the Bohemian Crown. They had secured and consolidated their participation in the *sněm* during the Hussite period and, though the lords had been successful in excluding them between 1485 and 1508, they had in the latter year secured their readmission. They were strong enough even to survive the punitive measures of Ferdinand I who sought to punish their part in the rebellion of 1547 by reducing their representatives to the status of a merely consultative council of the royal *camera*; however, by the time of his death in 1564 the urban estate had regained its former position as an integral part of the parliament. Thirty royal towns and six 'dower' towns sent representatives to the Bohemian parliament and six royal towns to that of Moravia.[1] The urban members of parliament were nominated and paid by the town councils; smaller towns would sometimes consent to be represented by their larger neighbours. The three houses of the Bohemian parliament had since 1440 deliberated separately and each decided by a majority of votes. In the *plenum* of the three houses which gave final assent to its acts, each house had one vote and to be effective this vote had to be unanimous.

The Hungarian parliament (*Országgyülés*) was the most purely aristo-cratic in sixteenth-century central Europe. It was composed of two Houses (*tabulae*) of which the upper House was a small assembly of the heads of those great families whom it was customary to summon in-dividually to Parliament and of the two archbishops, the bishops and a few of the heads of the greater religious houses. As most of the great offices of state were held by prelates or magnates, the Hungarian house had much the same oligarchical character and predilections as the Polish senate. The lower house (*tabula inferior*) was an assembly of undefined composition. Early in the sixteenth century the nobles were summoned to it *viritim*, but gradually the practice of electing representatives from each county prevailed. In 1552 the king declared that he did not wish to burden the gentry with the trouble and expense of attendance in parlia-ment and invited them to send delegates. But some were invited in-dividually as late as 1572, though for the last time. The Hungarian towns had but an insignificant place in the parliament: eight 'free' towns and two of the 'mining-towns' (*bányavárosok*) of Upper Hungary were re-presented, but their delegates, if they came at all, did not compose a separate House but were swamped amid the gentry of the *tabula inferior*.

Though the estates of the kingdoms of Poland, Bohemia and Hungary were the organs of the landowning nobility, there was in many respects a coincidence of interest between king and parliament. In Hungary the

---

[1] The towns were also represented in the parliaments of Silesia and Lusatia. It is also worthy of remark that there were houses of Catholic prelates in Moravia, in both the Silesias and in Upper, but not Lower, Lusatia.

perpetual Turkish danger affected Ferdinand I as much as it did the Hungarian people; he needed the taxes he could extract from the lords' serfs and the towns as much as the lords needed the Habsburg armies for the defence of their estates from the assaults of Sulaimān and his pashas. Ferdinand also dared not offend the liberties of the Hungarian nobility for fear of driving them into the camp of his rivals in Transylvania. For that reason the constitutional history of sixteenth-century Hungary has much in common with that of Tudor England; in both countries it was a period of mutually useful but increasingly uneasy collaboration between Crown and parliament, but with two important differences. In Hungary local government was in the hands of the aristocratic county assemblies and not in those of nominees of the Crown responsible to the privy council, and the Crown was still elective. Ferdinand realised that these were the two weak points in his position. Much as he would doubtless have liked to weaken the parliamentary and comitial power of the lords, he needed their support too much to do more than subject the national central administration to the authority of his monarchical instruments in Vienna. In this limited field he was very successful. The Hungarian *concilium regis* was given nothing to do and the title of king's councillor became merely honorific. The *camera regis* he refashioned in 1528 on the Austrian and Bohemian models; it was suspended during the Turkish crisis of 1528 to 1531, then revived as the *camerae administratio*, merely to administer the budget assigned to it by the *Hofkammer* in Vienna, to which it was made completely subject in all except certain matters of customs and trade administration by edicts of 1548 and 1561. An even more effective measure in bringing the government of Hungary under the direction of Vienna was the suspension of the office of palatine (*nádor*) of Hungary from 1532 to 1554. In 1554 Ferdinand did permit the parliament to elect the able and loyal Tamás Nádasdy as palatine, but after his death in 1562 Ferdinand would have no successor. The palatine as '*locum tenens regis et generalis capitaneus*', chief justice, president of the council and 'official intermediary between the nobles of the realm and the emperor' was indeed too independent of outside control for Ferdinand's purposes. For most of his reign he therefore appointed, not a palatine, but a lieutenant (*helytartó*) who as such had no authority over Ferdinand's military forces in Hungary. His two lieutenants, Elek Thurzó and Archbishop Pál Várdai, had a lieutenancy council which was the chief instrument in maintaining Hungarian statehood and the independence of its judicature during the reign.

As soon as he became king of Hungary and Bohemia Ferdinand reformed the central Viennese offices of state to become policy-making and probouleutic bodies for all his dominions. These central departments were exclusively manned by Ferdinand's German ministers and officials, though some of them had secretaries or committees for Hungarian and

Bohemian affairs. They were the court chancery (*Hofkanzlei*), the court chamber (*Hofkammer*) which gave instructions in financial matters to the local chambers, the court council (*Hofrat*) and the all-important privy council (*Geheimrat*), whose four or five German members advised the king on foreign policy and his personal and family affairs and produced the agenda for the Bohemian, Hungarian and other parliaments.

Ferdinand's other great concern was the elective character of his monarchy. In 1526 the estates of Moravia had recognised his wife, Anna, sister of King Lewis, as lawful heir, and she had transferred her rights to Ferdinand; and the Silesian estates had accepted him 'as hereditary and elected king'. But the Bohemian parliament merely elected him from a number of candidates and had insisted that he publish a *revers*, in which he declared that the estates had freely elected him, that his successor would not be king until he had been crowned, and that any foreign successor must take the oath at the frontier before he entered the realm. In his coronation oath Ferdinand had to swear that he would preserve the Bohemian estates in their 'orders, rights and privileges' and alienate nothing from the lands of the Crown. In Hungary in 1526 Ferdinand's initial position had been even more delicate. Zápolyai had already been elected by a majority of the lords, and therefore to establish himself at all Ferdinand had had to agree in the election diet at Pressburg to maintain the laws and customs of the realm, not to introduce foreigners into his Hungarian council, nor to give estates to foreigners. After his election Ferdinand made a declaration, as he had already done for Bohemia, that he owed his throne to a true and voluntary election. It was Ferdinand's contribution to the establishing of the Habsburgs on the Hungarian and Bohemian thrones that he was able to go far towards blotting out this uncongenial page from the acts of his reign. In 1539 he took the first tentative step by requesting the Hungarian parliament to recognise that he had succeeded by hereditary right; the request was not granted, but in a statute of 1547 the Hungarian estates went so far as to declare that they thereby 'transferred themselves to the government and power not only of His Majesty, but also of his successors for ever.' Near the end of his life Ferdinand asked that Maximilian should be crowned without election; the estates demurred but did not persist, and in 1563 the parliament allowed Maximilian to be so crowned in his father's life-time. Even the one condition the parliament had made, that a palatine should be elected, was not complied with by the king.

Ferdinand's efforts to make his Bohemian crown hereditary illustrate even more clearly his patient opportunism. In the year after his election the corrupt and stupid Bohemian magnates induced the *sněm* to declare that the king's adult heir might be crowned in his father's lifetime provided that he swore to preserve the 'freedom of the land'. In 1541, by an accident which Ferdinand was quick to exploit, the Bohemian land books, in which were recorded all the solemn acts of state, were destroyed by fire; Ferdinand saw to it that, when new ones were compiled to replace them, the *revers* of 1526, in which he had confessed himself but an elected king, was omitted. In 1545 Ferdinand attempted a positive step by drawing up a *revers* which averred that 'the estates of Bohemia had recognised and accepted Queen Anna as heir to her brother Lewis, and had then elected and accepted Ferdinand of their free and good will'. The estates were acute enough not to allow so dangerous a declaration to be entered in the land books. A better opportunity came as a consequence of the abortive rebellion of 1547, the most fateful crisis in Bohemian constitutional history before 1618. In 1546 the long-maturing conflict in Germany had erupted in the Schmalkaldic war. Ferdinand tried to get the Bohemian parliament to provide him with men and money to fight the Protestant German princes; but the Bohemian lords with unusual and inopportune rashness decided to back John Frederick of Saxony. Hardly had they begun to assemble in arms for this treasonable end when his defeat and capture at Mühlberg put the whole body of Bohemian liberties at Ferdinand's mercy. Never did he show his political astuteness better than in the way he used this opportunity. Since the king knew that he would have the lords' support in the oppression of groups whom they regarded with sectarian and economic jealousy, he made the Bohemian Brethren and the towns the scapegoats for the lords' offence. Against the Brethren a decree of exile was pronounced; the towns were deprived of self-government, their elected magistrates were replaced by royally appointed *hejtmans* and commissioners (*rychtáři*), and their real property was made forfeit. To the guilty lords Ferdinand not only gave a pardon, but he won their support by a declaration that 'his majesty has no desire to act in respect of what affects the liberty and privileges of the estates.' Characteristically, he used his triumph of 1547 to persuade the cowed Bohemian lords to insert the *revers* of 1545 in the 'Land Ordinance' of 1549 and to declare that 'the privilege of the Bohemian lands embodies this principle that the eldest son of each king shall become king of Bohemia after the death of his father'. In the same year the Bohemian parliament tamely accepted Maximilian II as hereditary and unelected king in his father's lifetime, just as it later accepted and proclaimed Maximilian's son Rudolf II two years before his father's death.

Constitutional development in Poland in the sixteenth century did not result in any strengthening of monarchical power such as the Habsburg rulers achieved in Bohemia and, to a less degree, in Hungary. Indeed, the extinction of the Jagiellon line in 1572 and the subsequent failure of Henry of Anjou and Stephen Bathory to establish either a Valois or Transylvanian dynasty on the Polish throne, set Poland on that course of aristocratic anarchy which was to make it a byword for political ineptitude. It is not that either Sigismund I (1506–48) or Sigismund II (1548–72) was incompetent or unaware of the task that the sixteenth century set to European rulers. Sigismund I had indeed the makings of an autocrat and under the instigation of his second wife, Bona Sforza, who brought to Cracow the statecraft of the Milanese despots, he struggled to assert his authority. So too did his son, Sigismund Augustus, at least until 1562, when he seems to have resigned himself to sharing his authority with the *szlachta*.

The constitutional position of the Polish monarchy was already weak when the century began. Casimir IV (1446–92) had deliberately preferred the possibility of territorial acquisition to the assertion of his domestic authority and had made many concessions to the *szlachta* to purchase their support for his designs on Silesia and Prussia. His two sons, John Albert (1492–1501) and Alexander (1501–6), succeeded not by right of primogeniture (they had an older brother, Vladislav, king of Bohemia and Hungary) but by elections for which they had to pay by concessions, and their reigns were too full of military disaster and too short for them to be able to check the growing power of the oligarchical senate. Alexander's famous constitution of 1505, known as *Nil novi*, conceded the principle that 'from henceforward nothing new may be established by us or our successors, without the full consent of the council and delegates of the lords, which might be harmful to the Republic or to the harm or injury of any private person or directed towards a change of the general law and public liberty'.

Sigismund the Old, the youngest of Casimir's five sons and the third of them to occupy the Polish throne, was blessed with a stronger character, greater political perception and a longer reign than his two predecessors; he also had a son and heir, a most valuable asset which had been denied them. In 1530, when the young Sigismund was only 10 years old, Queen Bona and her husband jockeyed the *sejm* into electing him king of Poland, so that he could at any moment step into his father's shoes without further ado. But the nobles soon realized the folly of this act. They continually harassed Sigismund I, clamouring for what they called 'Execution of the Laws'. This famous programme, first promulgated at the Diet of Bydgość (Bromberg) in 1520, demanded the summoning of a national *conventus justiciae* which should collect all laws, reform, unify and codify them, and put them into effect; it was a programme to perpetuate and effectuate the whole complex of aristocratic privilege that had been extracted from the monarchy during the last two centuries. Annexed to this proposal was a demand for the *egzekucja dóbr*, that is, the re-purchase by the Crown of its alienated lands. The parliaments also pressed continually, and eventually with success, for the exemption of the *szlachta* from the jurisdiction of the ecclesiastical courts. The first considerable success was achieved in the parliaments of 1538 and 1539 at Piotrków and Cracow, where Sigismund I was compelled to promise that he would never infringe the laws or issue constitutions *sua sponte*; he also was made to declare that the election of his son in 1530 was not lawful and that after the death of the younger Sigismund the new king would be elected with the participation of the whole nobility. All that Sigismund had therefore secured was the succession of his son in 1548 without further election.

The reign of Sigismund II Augustus was preoccupied with the growth and pretensions of the now largely Protestant nobility and with the long and costly struggle for Livonia and White Russia with Ivan the Terrible,[1] so much so that he had neither the leisure nor the opportunity to pursue the constitutional conflict with success. In 1562 he conceded the 'execution' of Crown lands illegally alienated since 1504. In 1569, when the Crowns and parliaments of the kingdom of Poland and the Grand Principality of Lithuania were united by the Union of Lublin, he was unable to prevent the extension of the legal and economic privileges of the Polish *szlachta* to the whole of the vast Lithuanian principality. Sigismund Augustus died in 1572 with no son to succeed him, leaving the Crown to be put up to auction by the now supreme and sovereign nobles. They used the opportunity with disastrous success, binding their chosen candidate, Henry of Anjou, to the most rigid promises to respect all their liberties, political, social, economic and religious, as set out with brutal clarity and devastating detail in three documents: the *Pacta Conventa*, the religious charter known as the *Warsaw Confederation*, and the *Henrician Articles*. This last summed up the victory of the *szlachta* in the clause *de non praestanda obedientia*: 'if the king act against these laws, liberties, articles and conditions, or do not fulfil them, he thereby makes the nobles free of the obedience and fealty they owe him'. The dynastic disasters which followed confirmed the victory of the Polish lords. Henry of Anjou had been in Poland but a few months when he seized the opportunity of succeeding his brother Charles IX as king of France to desert his uncomfortable Polish throne in 1574. His elected successor, Stephen Bathory, prince of Transylvania, had no leisure from his wars with Russia to do more than begin an attack on the Protestant Polish communities; dying in 1586, he too left no son. The *szlachta* elected to succeed him Sigismund III, the first of three kings of the Vasa dynasty. But it was already too late. Poland lay firmly in the dead hand of the landowning minority, robbed of the opportunity of political greatness which its size, wealth and national genius might have made possible had this sixteenth-century conflict between class and nation been differently decided.

Of the three nations with which this chapter is concerned it was only the Poles who made any scholarly attempt to rationalise the practice of aristocracy. The Polish magnates and officers of state were more closely in contact with French, Italian and German scholars than were the

[1] Cf. below, pp. 558 ff.

Czechs, so long cut off by their heresy, or the Magyars, culturally less advanced and preoccupied with the Turkish peril. Magyar and Czech political theory has to be gleaned almost solely from the 'Law Books' written by such sixteenth-century Bractons as Viktorin Kornel of Všehrd and István Verböczy. Kornel's book, *Concerning the laws of the Bohemian land*, was put into its final form by 1508. It largely consists of a description of the manner in which the land court (*zemský soud*) exercised its jurisdiction and of legal procedure connected with the land registers (*zemské desky*); in both these central organs of the landlords he finds faults and suggests reforms, for Kornel, deputy secretary of the land registers, approached problems with a lawyer's and a bureaucrat's desire for efficiency and wished to abolish the more grievous and arbitrary privileges of the lords in the interest not only of the State but also of the peasants. By far the most famous and important legal treatise of this type was István Verböczy's *Tripartitum opus iuris consuetudinarii inclyti regni Hungariae*, compiled at the request of King Uláozló (Vladislav) of Hungary and approved by him in 1513. It was never given statutory validity by the Hungarian parliament, but it came to have decisive authority for the courts of law and remained the foundation of Hungarian constitutional and private law for more than three centuries. The *Tripartitum* is primarily concerned with the law of real property, and the whole of its long first part —devoted to the law of inheritance, forfeiture, contract, dower and wardship—is frankly customary law. Verböczy accepts without argument that the origin and justification of the ownership of real property and the noble status that goes with it is the reward of *praeclara facinora* by the prince, whereby a mutual relationship is established: 'For the prince is elected solely by the nobles, and the noble receives his nobiliary dignity from the prince.' The second part of the *Tripartitum* is concerned with judicial process in criminal cases and is introduced by a discussion on legislative authority in which Verböczy says that fundamental laws (*constitutiones*) can only be made by the co-operation of prince and people and that such laws 'bind in the first place the prince himself who gave them to the people at its request, in accordance with the principle: 'Obey the law which thou thyself hast made.' The third part of the *Tripartitum* deals with subordinate legislative bodies: the Croatian and Transylvanian diets, the counties, the royal and chamber towns, and the gilds. The whole work concludes with a statement of the legal and judicial position of the serfs (*jobbagiones*) which says that though the peasants had formerly the right to change their place of residence, this liberty had been forfeited by their recent rebellion, an act of treason which has caused them to be made subject to their landlords *mera et perpetua rusticitate*.

It was a constant grievance of the Polish lords that they had no such authoritative statement of their liberties and privileges as Verböczy had provided for the Hungarians. In their parliamentary agitation for such an 'execution of the laws' the Polish publicists and civil servants produced a spate of treatises and speeches which taken together provide a fairly homogeneous theory of estates sovereignty. Perhaps the ablest single work of this kind is the 'Instruction for the making of a good ruler' which Stanislas Orzechowski addressed to the newly crowned Sigismund Augustus in 1549, under the title of the *Subditus Fidelis*. Having stated his thesis that 'the equestrian order is the foundation of the realm', he goes on to say that

the king is chosen for the sake of the kingdom; the kingdom does not exist for the sake of the king. For the Law, since it is the soul and mind of the kingdom, is without doubt more powerful than the kingdom, and consequently than the king.... If therefore any flattering Tribonian or Ulpian in the Roman service tells you that you are supreme in your realm, deny it and tell him that the law reigns in your country.

Orzechowski is quite sure that Poland is the only home of liberty. In his *Oratio ad equites Polonos* of 1553 he asked:

Can you show me any country which you have seen or of which you have heard which is free, except Poland?...The Bohemians, who are of your blood and race, how much have they preserved of their laws?...I say nothing of England which has seen its two great lights, its own senators, John bishop of Rochester and Thomas More, slain by the axe of the public executioner.

The greatest achievement of the political thinking that was stimulated by the Polish constitutional experiment of the sixteenth century was the *De Republica Emendanda* of Andrzej Frycz Modrzewski, written in 1551 and printed in 1558. It begins with a Ciceronian definition of the State and of the ideal of a mixed constitution. The king should be elected, chosen not for his birth, but for his knowledge of the art of governing;

since therefore kings of Poland are not born, but elected by the will of all the orders, it is not right that they should use their power to make laws or impose tribute of their own will. They do all things with the agreement of the orders and according to the prescription of the laws.

No law can be made unless it have the approval of the *ordo equestris* and of the senate. As the estates are in duty bound to save the State from the danger of royal tyranny, so it is the duty of the king to prevent oligarchic privilege from acting unjustly. Modrzewski does not limit himself to abstract theory; much of his book is devoted to the exposition of the positive functions of a well-ordered state: provision for education, the control of trade, care for the poor. There is one chapter (XVIII) on the duty of the State to build workhouses which might have been written by Edmund Chadwick himself. His conscience was troubled by the fact that, in contrast to Germany, Poland permitted the existence of serfdom. Again and again he insists that the law is not merely aristocratic privilege but must be equal for all: 'if we remove from the serfs the right of calling their lords to account we have robbed them of all liberty. If we give the lords the power of judging their serfs in their own cause, we destroy the principle of just judgement.' The *De republica emendanda* ends with a passionate attack on a fiscal system whereby the whole cost of national defence is imposed by lords, themselves free of tax, on the shoulders of the wretched peasants. Modrzewski's faith that if the harmonious constitution of the Polish republic can be purged of its injustices it can become the most perfect of states may be the funeral oration of medieval Europe, but it also contains within itself the idea of a state where justice is sovereign and the public good the supreme end of government and law.

A NOTE ON CONSTITUTIONAL DEVELOPMENT IN GERMANY[1]

THE Holy Roman Empire of the German nation had ceased to be anything like a political unit long before 1519, when Charles V was elected into the Habsburg preserve of the imperial Crown, after a great expenditure of cash and promises.[2] But the idea was not dead, and the fervours of sixteenth-century nationalism in Germany encouraged hopes of a revival. Luther and his followers never tired of appealing to a supposedly united Germany. Even the princes showed quite a genuine attachment to the empire and the imperial conception, though it has to be admitted that in the last resort territorial independence and religious dissent always overcame their feelings on this score. It might have been different if Charles had been 'German' instead of universal in his aspirations. He could not regard Germany either as his own country or as the centre of his dominions; though he himself cherished a profound belief in the idea of empire it was not to him a specifically German empire. This is understandable enough: there was no reason why a French-speaking Burgundian, ruler of so many diverse territories and dependent for the essence of his power on Spain rather than central Europe, should think of himself as a German. But while one must ignore those who even today will not forgive Charles for not being German enough, it has to be realised that he was particularly ill-qualified to exploit the imperial dignity for the purpose of creating a united German state.

Of course, the fault was very far from being his alone. His grandfather's time had witnessed the culmination of various attempts to give reality to the empire by constitutional reform.[3] But neither the creation of a few common institutions, nor the attempt to turn the diet into an instrument of unity, nor the expedient of creating intermediate units between princely territories and the empire (the 'circles'), had had any success at all. The idea of a *Reichsregiment* was revived in 1521 when

---

[1] This Note requires an explanation. A chapter on constitutional developments and thought in Germany was to have been contributed by Professor E. Hassinger of the university of Freiburg i.Br. who, to his great distress, was unfortunately prevented from completing the task by the onset of an illness which to the last seemed likely to leave him alone sufficiently long for the chapter to be written. When the decision to abandon it had finally to be taken, it was too late to look elsewhere for someone to fill a gap which could hardly be left entirely blank. The editor therefore found himself compelled reluctantly to swim in very unfamiliar waters. This Note is not expected to replace the missing chapter, but it may at least show that the problem was not simply forgotten.

[2] Charles was compelled to agree to the first of those *Wahlkapitulationen* (election charters), common practice after him, in which the emperors promised to observe the old laws and the liberties of the princes.

[3] Vol. I, ch. VII.

Charles left Germany for Spain, and for nearly a decade his brother Ferdinand struggled to make a reality out of the feeble instruments of civil and military control which this regency commanded. The opposition of the estates and the contemptuous neglect of its orders by the Swabian League wrecked the scheme, which was allowed to die away round about 1530. In 1559, when Ferdinand had inherited the imperial dignity, he at last succeeded in organising a few mildly effective imperial institutions: an imperial chancery under a head (the vice-chancellor) who was to have a history of some importance, and two courts—*Reichshofrat* and *Reichskammergericht*—whose adoption of the Roman law was to have lasting effects on German jurisprudence. But by then such feeble expedients, though they served the interests of the house of Austria, could no longer pretend to assist in restoring political unity to the Empire.

The diet's failure was less excusable. Not only had it been the chosen instrument of the reform party round about 1500, but, assembling as it did all the more powerful interests in Germany, it also offered a ready stage to any serious efforts at co-operation and integration. In practice, the diet (*Reichstag*) was mainly used as a weapon of princely independence against the emperor. From 1497 onwards its resolutions had nearly always taken the form of a rescript (*Abschied*), a treaty between the emperor and the estates; Charles V's attempts to use it as a tool of imperial authority, underwriting the emperor's decisions, were doomed from the first. Its constitution also worked in favour of particularism. In effect the estate of electors decided everything; even the estate of princes had little chance of altering their superiors' resolves. As for the lesser nobility, the *Reichsritter*—ruined in any case as an independent force after the failure of Franz von Sickingen's Knights' War (1522)—or the imperial cities, their voices never gained an effective hearing in this assembly of territorial rulers. Though it was only after the 1555 Diet of Augsburg that meetings of the *Reichstag* became congresses of diplomatic representatives from the various principalities rather than assemblies of estates, the tendency had been there for a long time. The diet was therefore dominated by those who favoured particularism rather than by the friends of union. Elsewhere in western Europe representative institutions often proved useful to the centralising policy of a strong Crown; in Germany, royal weakness and the unrepresentative character of the estates combined to destroy the best instruments for consolidation that the age knew.

What hope of better things there was rested rather in local and subordinate leagues. The circle organisation of 1500, though it endured and was to have a little administrative significance, never proved sufficiently organic to rob the independent territories of their sovereignty. More promising seemed such less ambitious schemes as the great Swabian League, formed with imperial encouragement in the later years of the fifteenth century. Intended to preserve the imperial peace (*Landfrieden*) in the important south-western area of Germany, it disposed of a formidable armed force (over which both Maximilian and Charles exercised at times considerable powers of control) and attracted not only cities and lesser feudatories but also some princes. In the end even Bavaria joined it, though such thorns in the duke's side as the cities of Ulm and Augsburg were among the leaders of the League. Its greatest days came early in the period. In 1518–19 it triumphed easily over Duke Ulrich of Württemberg; in 1519, its forces, encamped outside Frankfurt, are thought to have exercised a marked influence on the election of Charles V; from 1523 it ignored and overrode the orders of the *Reichsregiment* in its proceedings round the upper Danube and upper Rhine. But the defection of Sickingen deprived it of an important commander and the support of the imperial knights, and after 1530 it passed into dissolution.

Nevertheless, it had set an example. Leagues multiplied after the formation of that of Schmalkalden in 1530 (p. 350), so much so that when Philip of Hesse was later approached with a request to join a reconstituted Swabian League he replied that he already belonged to far too many such alliances. However, the League of Schmalkalden also demonstrated that the principle of partial confederation could easily work against imperial unity instead of towards it. Charles V alone in later years remembered the advantages for authority which the Swabian League had possessed in 1519; his plans for effective unification continued to depend on the formation of associations, and the negotiations which followed his victory over the Protestants in 1547 turned upon his proposal for a general German League. They came to nothing: as the Swabian League had already demonstrated, the hopes of such a body lay in the continuing strength of elements other than the territorial princes, and by 1547 these elements, whether imperial cities or lesser nobility, had passed into eclipse. The disruptive ambitions of individual rulers triumphed over all attempts at unification. To the princes, and especially the electors, Charles's aims were dictated by innovatory and foreign ideas. When they claimed to be protecting ancient liberties against the emperor's centralising activities, they were not entirely hypocritical, but they certainly sounded the death knell of the old Empire. The alliance which after 1550 Maurice of Saxony led against Charles, the emperor's defeat and humiliation, the Treaty of Passau (1552) and finally the negotiations of 1555—as between independent sovereigns—terminated a phase in the history of Germany which had been effectively dead for a long time and was only given spurious life by the energies of Charles V.

These energies had received surprising assistance from the event which in the end was to make quite sure of German disunity. At first blush the Reformation must strike one as the ruin of all remaining hopes of unity. Through conflicts over religion and uniformity it added a new element of discord; among some princes it produced an even fiercer determination to preserve their freedom on which alone the continued existence of the new faith depended; though Luther's success owed much to German nationalism, the Reformation in the end submerged that passion. When the Protestants of 1529 refused to accept a majority decision of the diet (p. 93), they had a good enough case in law but were denying the age-old traditions of the Empire and disposing for good and all of any hopes that still attached to the estates. Thus, because the Reformation managed to establish itself and in the process confirmed German particularism, its part in this historical development is plain. But for a time its effects might have been very different. It was the outbreak of religious dissension which drove Charles V into action and kept him in the field to battle for something like unity in his German dominions; without it he would very probably have been content to allow Ferdinand to run affairs in that half-hearted agreement with the princes and other estates which had characterised Maximilian's later years. And it should be recognised that Charles's personal character—his shrewdness, determination and persistence—was of signal importance in the history of Germany in those years; it goes a long way towards explaining the unrelenting struggle. When the decision of Speyer (1526) that each prince should use what religion he pleased (as he would answer to God and his imperial majesty—but only Charles's toughness made the second reservation at all significant) was at last embodied in treaty form at Augsburg in 1555, the emperor had kept the pot boiling for thirty years by his resolve to create a monarchical system in Germany in order to restore religious unity.

Moreover, the Reformation gave Charles half a chance of success by splitting the ranks of his opponents and providing him with a party among the princes: it compelled the Catholics into an unwillingly close alliance. The very extent of his triumph in 1547, however, altered things. The princes recovered their traditional attitude, secular interests overcame religious concerns, and Charles's inability to exploit his victory was entirely due to the restoration of the princely phalanx. Yet it had been a closer thing than is often realised. If Maurice of Saxony had died in 1548 instead of 1553, if the depredations of the Margrave Albert Alcibiades of Culmbach in 1552-3 had not alienated some support from Charles, if the emperor had not been a tired and lethargic man at that critical juncture—these ifs may be as futile as such hypotheses usually are, but they should remind us that Charles came near to defeating the Reformation in Germany and to creating there better conditions for monarchical government, just because the religious split gave him allies in the work.

However, in the end particularism stood victorious over the corpse of imperial hopes. The future of Germany lay with the territories, the individual lands ruled over by electors, princes, counts, and the rest. Within these virtually sovereign states, constitutional developments were very much on the lines common in the west. That is to say, most of them displayed that increase and consolidation of monarchical power which is typical also of France and Spain, though like those countries they remained as yet too encumbered with the limitations and customary rights of the past to justify talk of absolutism. The princes reorganised their finances, developed new fiscal organs (chambers) out of their curial offices, and enjoyed a good deal of income independent of any tax-granting assemblies. They relied increasingly on councils of trained civil servants, usually civil lawyers; so for that matter did the towns, and few things strike one as more extraordinary in sixteenth-century Germany than the commonly high academic qualifications of those burghers who held office in cities both great and small. As was usual in the period, paternalism accompanied centralisation; some princes replaced the ordinances of both gilds and empire by laws of their own on trade, labour, poor relief, and so forth. At the same time the territorial diets (*Landtage*) seem to have passed through a period of increasing importance. This is a subject on which little is at present known, though work in progress should reveal more in time. The diets played a considerable part in financial matters: in some regions they took over and guaranteed the debts of the ruler, with the result that they supplanted him in the control of finances generally. Their composition tended to change as towns declined and the landed gentry and nobility gained economic strength; this was particularly the case in the north and east. Nowhere does there seem to have been any serious rivalry between prince and estates. The prince remained the effective ruler, though his liberty of action was somewhat limited by the existence of a body whose chief characteristic, nevertheless, was readiness to co-operate and share in the tasks of government. Here as elsewhere in the west, changes in the direction of true autocracy came later. However, one must not leave this subject without a word of warning. It is almost certainly a mistake to speak of the German states as though they were all cut after one pattern. What has been said may reflect present agreement on the major outlines, but though much yet remains to be done it is already becoming apparent that ultimately the differences between the various principalities may look quite as big as the similarities.[1]

[1] I owe this information to Dr F. L. Carsten of the university of London, at present engaged in studies in the constitutional history of Germany in the sixteenth and seventeenth centuries.

CHAPTER XVI

ARMIES, NAVIES, AND THE
ART OF WAR

THE forty years between the accession of Charles V in 1519 and the treaty of Cateau-Cambrésis in 1559 were more decisive for the evolution of the art of war than any subsequent period before the late eighteenth century. The previous generation had been a period of real transition; different arms, different methods of fighting, old and new, had been used side by side, their respective merits still uncertain. The successful defence of Padua had seemed to show that inner defences could effectively supplement old-fashioned walls; at Novara, the traditional tactics of the Swiss were resoundingly vindicated; the handgun still found less general favour than the cross-bow. But in this later period certain definite breaks with the past were made, and the modes of warfare for two centuries were anticipated. Fortification was systematised on the basis of the bastioned trace, and the temporary emphasis on internal instead of external defences was reversed; the cross-bow was rejected; the massed self-sufficient column of pike disappeared; no army henceforward dared to take the field without some balance between the three arms, cavalry, infantry, artillery; every army sought and found a unit of organisation some way between the hundred-odd strong band and the huge and unwieldy 'battle'; the arquebus and the pike came to be used habitually together, and the former began to give way to the musket; the pistol appeared on the battlefield and was responsible for the emergence of a new medium cavalryman, the pistoleer. New weapons demand fresh tactics. The fact that armament was more or less stabilised by 1559 meant that tactics by that date had reached a stage of comparable definition. Strategy is largely determined by recruitment, finance, transport, the relationship between fortification and siegecraft, and the composition of armies. Each of these particulars took on a lasting form in this period. Armies relied on foreign mercenaries who went home if their pay was not regular; even the wealthiest state found it difficult to produce enough money at regular intervals in a long war; transport, including all but the heaviest siege guns, became as fast as the roads could allow; sieges took so long that armies were immobilised for periods that placed a great strain on finance and supply, and, on the other hand, garrisons had to be so large that an army on the march had to strip itself of a great proportion of its effectives in order to police newly conquered land and protect its bases. Armies of similar composition avoided conflict and fenced warily until a very definite opening for attack appeared. The tempo of warfare slowed.

After Pavia (1525) pitched battles became rare. The paymaster and quartermaster challenged the importance of the general. Propaganda and the handling of morale became ever more crucial as what had always been a battle of wits became increasingly a war of nerves.

All this is not to say that in a period of definition there were none of the characteristics of a period of transition. Generals could still act with the recklessness that brought disaster to de Thermes at Gravelines; the exploits of a civic militia could still shine among those of the professional soldier, as at Siena in 1552-3. The Turks who had stormed the scientific defences of Rhodes in 1522 were seven years later repulsed from the old-fashioned walls of Vienna. But, on the whole, these years saw such a rapid withering of the old branches of the traditional Tree of Battles, and such a luxuriant extension of the new, that it showed a very different appearance.

The spread of new military ideas and their consolidation was helped, of course, by the fact that there were hostilities somewhere in Europe throughout most of the period. Lessons were quickly learnt, conclusions could speedily be put to the test. Progress was aided, too, by the cosmopolitan nature of armies; generals learnt not only from the enemy but from their own mercenaries. And men were not only waging war, they were writing about it, and thus knowledge came to be pooled even more quickly.

Two motives, it is true, caused some delays in publication. There was the traditional fear that dangerous knowledge might be put at the disposal of the infidel. The publication of works on fortification was safe enough, for Christians were not the aggressors, but it was considered hazardous to print advice on how towns and men might be blown up or defeated in the field. Such, at least, was the argument. But if no one went so far as Valturius had gone in the presentation of a manuscript of his *De re militari* to the sultan in 1463, large numbers of technical works did appear, and any reticences can be better explained in terms of monopoly rather than high thinking: as long as Italian secrets about gunnery and fortifications were kept, for instance, other nations would be forced to employ Italian founders and engineers. Of the three countries which produced most of the military literature, France was most notable for analysts and annalists—our knowledge of contemporary warfare would be poor without the work of Fourquevaux, Montluc and la Noue; Italy for theoretical and technical works—the works of Biringuccio and Tartaglia underlay nearly everything written on artillery for two hundred years; and Germany for encyclopaedic descriptions of armies and their organisation—the *Kriegsbücher* of Fronsperger and Solms constitute complete illustrated guides to the art of war, from the composition of an army, its tactics and its arms, to the smallest detail of administration.

It is not to be expected that writers on military subjects were exempt

482

from the passion to cite classical precedents; the very greatness of Rome was due in the first place to her armies and only second to the arts which flourished under their protection. As in the previous generation, the works particularly of Vegetius and Frontinus continued to be ransacked, and Aelian, Polybius and Caesar, Modestus and Vitruvius still spoke to willing ears. Their ideas were not swallowed whole, but the most practical writer on a technical subject was glad to add to his opinions an echo of ancient authority. Even Machiavelli—and no one allowed his eye to be deflected more easily from modern war to ancient gossip about war—said of classical precedent (in his *Arte della Guerra*, 1521) that 'I would not follow it exactly in every particular, but in such ways only as may best suit the circumstances of the present times'. After comparing the respective merits of ancient and modern infantry for instance, he decided that the ideal unit should be made up half of men armed in the Roman manner, with short sword and shield, half in the modern Swiss fashion with pikes and arquebus. Giovanni Battista Zanchi, writing on fortification in 1554, said that in spite of gunpowder the best way of treating his highly specialised subject was to deduce rules from ancient as well as modern practice.

Ancient practice, indeed, was not always irrelevant. When Vegetius says: 'It is much better to overcome the enemy by famine, surprise or terror, than by general action, for in the latter instance fortune has often a greater share than valour', he is speaking for any commander of the mid-sixteenth century. Again, the Romans, being without stirrups, used cavalry for missile rather than shock tactics; their emphasis was on heavy, steady infantry and a nimble, worrying body of horse. As first pike and then arquebus did much to render the medieval charge of heavy cavalry ineffective, this Roman combination came into favour once more. Nor was the new fortification without precedent. Across the Adriatic the late-classical defences of Diocletian's palace at Spalato, with their hexagonal gate towers and square towers set diagonally at the corners, showed how missiles could be deflected and a curtain covered by projecting works which did not suffer from the disadvantage of the older round towers, namely that a space at their heads could not be reached by fire from other parts of the defences.

If the ancients had anticipated much of the strategic and some of the tactical and technical needs of the sixteenth century, there was one new element which they had not foreseen: gunpowder. Frontinus spoke for the old world alone when he referred to weapons 'the invention of which has long since reached its limit, and for the improvement of which I see no further hope in the applied arts'. The modern world saw the conduct of battles turned upside down by the new arm and could not afford to pay much attention to advice given in ignorance of it. Yet the fascination of the ancient writers remained. In contrast with the present, their wars seemed so masterfully planned, their armies so rationally trained, their battles so orderly. This impression was largely due to historians like Livy who described combats as they should have been rather than as they were, and to Vegetius who was describing the art of war again as it should have been, making ardent propaganda for an idealized past and an organisation more complete and efficient than any could be in practice. This completeness enslaved even men as practical as Albrecht Dürer. In his work on fortification he devoted a whole section to the detailed town-planning of a fortified place. It was based on Vegetius's analysis of a fortified camp—a practice already given up by the Romans themselves. No general tried to arrange a camp on these lines in the sixteenth century. There were a few occasions on which practical points of organisation were taken over from Roman usage, the 'legion' of Francis I, for instance, with its 6000 men divided into units of 100 each under a 'centennier' (centurion). But while most of what had been written about Roman armament and tactics was rejected as inapplicable to an age of gunpowder, everything that was said about the morale and discipline of Roman armies was listened to raptly: arms had changed but men remained the same.

Every author who dealt seriously with military problems as a whole was concerned with the material of armies, with men and their morale. Time after time battles that should have been won were lost by indiscipline or failure of nerve. Idle and unskilled officers infected their men. Waste and peculation added to the cost of war. Campaigns were hampered by desertion, by the alienation of a countryside through brutal plundering, by the difficulty of following up a victory because of the disintegration of troops indifferent to everything but loot. The best equipment, the shrewdest tactics, the most inspired leadership—without steady and dependable troops they were all useless. The problem most concerned native troops, hastily and unselectively recruited, dismissed as soon as possible, but it was raised too by the behaviour of mercenaries, all too often feckless and truculent, unwilling to fight a day beyond the payment of their wages, however desperate the position of their employers. Every army had its disciplinary machine, the provosts with their officers and their gibbet. But a busy marshal's court and a row of crooked necks did not necessarily lead to men behaving more steadily under fire; even the death penalty exacted by the Turks and the Swiss for cowardice could not make a good soldier out of a slack and frightened one.

Both morale and training go to the making of a good soldier. And morale itself is affected by training and discipline. 'Good order makes men bold, and confusion cowards.' 'In war discipline is superior to strength.' 'Length of service or age alone will never form a military man, for after serving many years, an undisciplined soldier is still a novice in his profession.' The first sentence is Machiavelli's, the others come from Vegetius. There is perfect agreement. On questions of discipline and morale the advice of the ancients could be taken without qualification. Even writers on technical subjects reflected the general preoccupation with the human element in war. To defend a fortress, wrote Dürer, there was needed 'above all a religious and virile population, really capable of defending themselves'. In the matter of military discipline, wrote Fourquevaux bitterly in 1548,

all things were better done by the ancients than they are by us. Their soldiers were more orderly, more painstaking, more virtuous and better men of war than we are.

The Roman soldier was laboriously drilled according to set rules, he was subject to a stern discipline, took great pride in his profession and came of a stock by nature hardy and abstemious.

French, Italian and English writers did not hesitate to compare their own troops unfavourably with those of nations which seemed to display some of the ancient virtues. The Spaniards were widely admired. Unexcitable and steady by temperament, they were used to a hard life and suffered one gladly. For the Spanish gentleman the military was the highest of all professions. The men were well trained in garrisons at home before being drafted to the field. The Swiss, too, were hardy and used to privations. They were painstakingly drilled—the life of a pikeman depended on the steadiness of his comrades. Till their confidence was shaken at Bicocca (1522), the Swiss were convinced that they were the best troops in the world. Their preference for killing rather than taking prisoners, their refusal to sacrifice order for plunder, their ruthless punishment of waverers—these harsh characteristics singled out a race who had established their freedom by arms, and by arms were still extending their boundaries. The German professional soldiers, the *Landsknechte*, shared some of the steadiness and *esprit de corps* of the Swiss but none of their patriotism. For them morale, entirely divorced from the cause they were fighting for, was solely the product of professional self-reliance. But most quoted, most praised, and most envied, were the Turks. And the reproach to the western soldier was all the graver when he was disparaged by comparison with an infidel. 'Their military discipline has such justice and severity as easily to surpass the ancient Greeks and Romans', wrote Giovio.

The Turks surpass our own soldiers for three reasons: they obey their commanders promptly; they never show the least concern for their lives in battle; they can live for a long time without bread and wine, being content with barley and water.[1]

Visitors were impressed by the perfect order preserved on parades and in camp. The Turks saved their aggressiveness for war and did not, as did western soldiers, swagger and royster and brawl in peace time. Moralists,

[1] *Turcicarum Rerum Commentarius* (Paris, 1539), p. 83.

in fact, idealised the Turkish character in order to reprimand Christian backsliders as a whole, but one characteristic of the Turks they and the military reformer found equally significant: they esteemed 'those happy and blessed, that died not at home, amidst the sorrow and lamentations of their wives and children, but abroad amongst the outcries of their enemies, clangour of armour and shattering of spears'.[1]

Much of this praise was due. The permanent troops had been rigidly trained from boyhood. They owed the sultan an unquestioning loyalty. Their religion urged them uncompromisingly to war against non-believers. There was no snobbish disinclination to serve on foot. Promotion was regular and not by birth but merit, in marked contrast to France and England where—Thomas Audley grumbled in Edward VI's reign—many a man 'was made a Capitaine before he was a souldier'.[2] The old soldier was guaranteed a livelihood on retirement. The planning of campaigns was not hampered by any conflict between the military and their political employers, because the Turks did not know the western distinction between military and civil administration. Some of these virtues could not be reproduced in the west for religious and sociological reasons, nor was any western country organised basically for war. But reformers in the west were not only, for this reason, crying for the moon: they were celebrating the perfection of a luminary already on the wane. Their glamourised version of the Turkish armies neglected its faults. The janissaries were dangerous in peace as well as in war. Educated for battle, they were good for nothing else, and as the century progressed they increasingly came to show the disadvantages of a Praetorian guard, more the master than the servant of the State. Their fighting quality declined, too, when they were allowed to marry, and when, towards the end of Sulaimān's reign, the sons of janissaries were admitted to the corps: their exclusive loyalty to the sultan was in this way twice mitigated. Moreover, Turkish victories were due no less to sheer numbers, as in Cyprus in 1522, or to the political disunity of their enemies, as time and again in Hungary, than to their military efficiency. And while their tactics and armament tended to stand still during the sixteenth century, and their discipline slightly to fall off, European armies showed themselves more open to innovation and increasingly capable of the trained steadiness essential for the proper handling of modern weapons. Yet it was clear even to those who knew the Turks best and therefore feared them least, that, in contrast to the European powers, their possession of a large standing army gave them a great advantage.

The Italian wars had shown the disadvantages of mercenaries clearly enough. When unpaid they either marched home again, or, as at Bicocca,

---

[1] Johannes Boemus, *De Omnium Gentium Ritibus* (Augsburg, 1528), lib. 3, c. 2.
[2] 'A Treatise on the Art of War', in *Journal of the Society for Army Historical Research* (1927), p. 133.

insisted on action before action was ripe. Even if paid, their reliability was doubtful. On the eve of Pavia 6000 Swiss, fully paid, marched off to protect their own borders when they heard that Chiavenna had fallen. Even after behaving magnificently they were liable to spring unwelcome surprises on their employers, as when the *Landsknechte*, after helping to save Vienna, demanded triple pay and threatened to sack the town if they did not get it. Loyalty to particular captains, like Frundsberg or Giovanni dei Medici, could sometimes override personal ends, but commonly money was the only motive that could keep mercenaries in the field, and of all the essentials of war, ready money was hardest to come by.

Mercenaries, wrote Fourquevaux in his widely-read *Instructions sur le Faict de la Guerre* (1548), have no stake in the country and are not fighting to defend their homes or possessions. They get preferential pay and retire loaded with gifts, yet—as Pavia showed—they are by no means always victorious, and they do not even bear the brunt of the battle but leave the position of real danger to the native troops who thus take most of the risks of battle but get none of the credit for victory. These arguments, which incorporate the main points of Machiavelli's criticism of mercenary troops, are, of course, one-sided. The employment of mercenaries did bring definite advantages. They were always available, Swiss, German or Italian. They were highly trained and bore better and more up-to-date arms than national troops, grudgingly equipped by the State. They could remain in the field for as long as they were paid without worrying about crops spoiling or businesses going to the bad from neglect. Apart from the Swiss, who had enough national feeling to refuse to fight each other or to imperil the fortunes of their own country, mercenaries would attack whoever they were told, irrespective of race or creed. German *Landsknechte* fought in thousands against the Empire. Italian troops helped the French in their peninsular wars. Catholic Italians helped crush the rebel Catholics of Devon and Protestant Germans the rebel Protestants of Norfolk in 1549; the Swiss helped Catholics attack their co-religionists in the French civil wars. Mercenaries, moreover, would as willingly help their employer defend his territory as attack someone else's, while national troops were prepared to defend their immediate neighbourhood in case of dire need (when they might fight very gallantly, as did the Florentines in 1529) but were not eager for foreign service, though soldiers were always forthcoming from poor countries like Spain and poor classes like the lesser nobility of France.

There were, on the other hand, positive objections to a standing army. First and foremost, of course, was the cost of keeping it up in peace. The upkeep of garrisons, parks of artillery and household troops was already enough for the estates who had to foot the bills for their betters' military schemes. The unruly behaviour of troops was another good reason for seeing as little of them as possible. When the Knight in the *Discourse of the*

Common Weal (*c.* 1549) describes the French legions, the English husbandman replies:

God forbid that we have anie such tirantes come amongst us; for as they saie, such will in the countrie of fraunce take pore mens hens, chickens, pigges, and other provision, and paie nothinge for it; except it be an evell turne, as to ravishe his wife or daughter for it.

And the same objections were being raised across the Channel, as numerous royal ordinances show. At a time when firearms gave the professional soldier an advantage over the peasant with his bill and bow, a standing army could be a political threat, as well as promise of insolence and aggression. And if the soldier was a menace to peaceable folk when he was in service, they had still more to fear when he was on leave or discharged. To employ mercenaries was to shift the burden of this social dislocation on to the country of supply. Yet again, not all governments thought it safe to arm their own subjects. Machiavelli had had to plead hard for his militia. 'Rome continued free four hundred years, and Sparta eight hundred, though their citizens were armed all that while; and many other states have lost their liberties in less than forty years.' Even in the perilous years 1512 and 1524, however, the Florentines would not allow the subject towns of the *contado* to raise troops to defend themselves and thereby help Florence herself.

Though many of the objections to a standing native army concerned their existence in peacetime, when at worst they could cause disturbance, all the objections to mercenaries concerned actual campaigns which they could turn into defeats. In spite of the disadvantages of native troops, therefore, efforts were made to raise and train them, and to use them to supplant at least a proportion of mercenaries. One drawback was that modern armies needed a combination of various specialised arms: artillery, heavy and light horse, pikemen and arquebusiers, and excellence in some of these categories depended, in the last resort, on racial characteristics as well as training. In spite of reverses, the Swiss and German pikemen remained the best in Europe: France made numerous attempts to produce her own, but never with success. Italian arquebusiers remained in demand long after other countries had trained their own. No one country in fact could provide high quality in all arms: some supplementation through mercenaries was necessary. A second drawback lay in the character of certain arms: the pike, the arquebus and, after the middle of the century, the musket, required long and consistent training. But all that states could afford, and civilian prejudice would tolerate, was a system of native reserves, called up for muster and drill at somewhat long intervals, with a nucleus permanently engaged on garrison duties.

The problem did not confront England in an acute form. Her continental campaigns were infrequent and short, the Channel—reinforced by Henry VIII's coastal fortifications—was an effective bar to invasion. Northern levies twice proved enough to defeat the Scots, at Flodden (1513) and Solway Moss (1542). Londoners were sufficiently reassured by their trained bands. The only permanent troops were the king's yeomen and the garrisons of Calais and Berwick. Unspurred by pressing danger at home England remained, except in the realm of naval armament, a stronghold of military conservatism. Henry VIII carried on a flirtation full of second thoughts with the arquebus, but the bow remained by far the more important missile weapon. Pikes were introduced but so gradually that foreign pike had still to be hired for his last campaign in 1543–5. Similarly, Burgundian cavalry—England, like Spain, bred very few horses heavy enough to sustain full armour and barding—and Spanish and Italian arquebusiers were used up to the end of the period.

The problem facing the empire was graver, for although Spain, Germany and the Low Countries could provide the full variety of arms, the demands of frontiers on the east, south and west were very great, and while Germany was a reservoir of heavy infantry and medium cavalry (*Reiter*) it was not an easy one to tap. A fairly high general level of prosperity made the profession of arms unattractive to the majority, and Maximilian's attempt to infuse the *Landsknechte* with a feeling of loyalty and reverence to the house of Habsburg had failed. Even when they fought for their own country their loyalties were first and foremost to their captains; as imperial servants they were intransigent and difficult to combine. Peace transformed them from soldiers into brigands. There were attempts in the middle of the century to awaken the long dormant feudal service; the imperial commisary, Lazarus von Schwendi, for instance, hoped that the Turkish menace would overcome the long tradition of service by (indifferent) substitute or cash. He wanted a standing army on full pay, unvitiated by the trade unionism of the *Landsknechte*. The venture failed, but at least the diet, by its ordinances of 1548, 1551 and 1555, bound the *Landsknecht* close to the State and deprived him of some of the privileges he so consistently abused.

It was France, however, the most aggressive of European states, who felt the need to establish a standing army most urgently. The *ban* and *arrière-ban*—the horsed levy of tenants owing military service for their fiefs—continued to be used, though its usefulness was constantly declining as infantry, and especially highly trained arquebusiers, became more and more important. Many of the keenest recruits preferred service in the regular heavy cavalry—the *gendarmerie*—or, after 1534, in the regular infantry, the legions. There were attempts to reform these levies. From time to time the categories exempt from liability to serve were reduced; a move was made to revise the faulty records of military obligation; in an effort to make the service less burdensome, the obligation to serve abroad was temporarily cut down from forty days to the time necessary to pursue an enemy away from French frontiers. Plans were made for the *ban* and *arrière-ban* to produce infantry and medium cavalry instead of the old heavy man-at-arms and his horsed assistants. In spite of these attempts the levies never made a good showing, and in spite of nationalist prejudice in their favour they were despised by military experts who advocated the creation of an entirely new body to take their place.

The *franc-archers* still survived, but raised as they were for short periods, armed with a medley of weapons and lacking in discipline, they were of little use and disbanded in 1535. Another fifteenth-century corps still survived, the *compagnons d'ordonnance* or *gendarmerie* of gentlemen volunteers, and they still provided the solid cavalry basis of French armies. Their service was regular, in that they had to muster three times a year to receive their pay and be inspected, and about one-half of their number was away on leave in peace-time while the other half remained on garrison duty. Their usefulness declined as the Italian wars went on and the heavy cavalryman played a decreasing part in deciding the fortunes of a battle, and though the corps remained in being, much of its prestige had disappeared by the middle of the century. They tended to be reactionary, haughtily intolerant of discipline, and to look upon military service as a perquisite of rank that could be waived if it was inconvenient. More professional in feeling, of course, were the French household troops, the Scots and Swiss Guards and the archers, but their numbers were small, and, again, the Scots and the archers fought as cavalry.

Native infantry was recruited for the occasion in bands by captains who held the king's commission. These men were volunteers and behaved well on the battlefield, but as they were dismissed wherever peace was made, their aim was to make as much out of periods of hostility as they could by plunder; having, in many cases, no peacetime niche to return to, they remained in arms, living off the countryside until war should break out once more. These *aventuriers* were a lively argument for the establishment of a regularly paid infantry corps. Such a corps was organised in 1531, when legions, each of 6000 men, were recruited in Champagne, Picardy, Normandy and Languedoc. Pains were to be taken to select good men; their uniform and arms—pike and arquebus in proportions that varied from legion to legion—were to be provided by the king. Nobles were attracted by exemption from service in the *ban* and *arrière-ban*, commoners by tax exemptions and the chance of promotion into the nobility. In peacetime there were to be two musters a year for the majority, while the *cadre* of each legion remained permanently in arms. The creation of the legions was attended by much enthusiasm and publicity. Fourquevaux wrote his book largely for their guidance. But the hope that they would replace *aventuriers* and mercenaries turned out to be illusory within a decade. The cumbrous administrative machinery was faulty; the men were often poor soldiers and they behaved badly in action in 1543. And when an attempt to reorganise them had failed in 1558, attention was switched to the progress of a second, more lasting experiment, the creation of *regiments* of a less unwieldy nature. In the middle of the century France still depended on *bandes* of infantry, especially on some, like the *bandes de Picardie* and the *bandes de Piemont*, which were so regularly re-employed that they can be looked upon as equivalent to permanent troops; and in 1543 and 1549—sad concession to the failure of the legions—the old dependence on Swiss mercenaries was confirmed by new treaties. Sixteenth-century wars were not to be won by clapping civilians into uniform and giving them a Roman name.

The character of these wars was largely determined by technical developments. New weapons demanded new tactics, new tactics dictated changes in the composition of an army. Again, new weapons, by forcing a changed attitude to battle, affected strategy and the length of campaigns; and in this way they had repercussions on government as a whole, internally from the point of view of finance and supply, externally from the point of view of foreign policy and diplomatic activity. It is essential, therefore, to say something about weapons and their evolution. Particularly is it essential to look at the development of fortification, for the change in the tempo of warfare brought about by this science was the most important single influence on sixteenth-century strategy. When armies could render themselves almost invulnerable by carefully designed temporary fortifications in the field, and when city walls became stronger than the guns of a besieger, then a war of battles eagerly sought and readily accepted and of cities quickly falling to the victor—the sort of war that Charles VIII's invasion had brought to Italy—was no longer possible.

The problem was to protect walls from guns and, to a secondary extent, from mining. The outlines of the answer had been anticipated in the previous period. It had been seen that walls must be lowered, to provide a smaller target, and thickened to increase their resistance to shot and sustain retaliatory armament. As walls sank, so did the defenders' range of vision, and wide ditches, and outworks beyond them, became increasingly necessary to keep the attack a safe distance from the main defences. As walls thickened, it became more difficult to see what was happening immediately underneath them; flanking observation, as well as flanking fire, was needed, and the use of the bastion was consolidated, the type which presented an acute salient angle to the field supplanting the rounded variety. The systematically planned bastioned trace—a curtain with bastions at regular intervals—still lay in the future; even at Antwerp (1540) and Hesdin (1554) the fortifications had an *ad hoc* air, with the bastions irregularly spaced. Gun ports and embrasures continued to enlarge their external, at the expense of their internal, splay, and the use of large low ports *à la française* was discontinued as they were too vulnerable to storming parties. Various attempts were made to compensate for the slow rate of fire of the defenders' guns during an assault, either by increasing the tiers of fire—as Francesco di Giorgio had suggested, in the lobes of his bastions—or, as this led to structural weakness, by the building of outworks, casemates, or cavaliers, which supplemented the fire from curtain and bastion. Neither method was systematically exploited in this period, reliance being placed on intensive fire from light arms and on subsidiary defences inside the walls, ditches covered by ramparts. Generally speaking, cities were attacked before they had undertaken large-scale refortification on modern lines. The defenders were forced, therefore, to supplement their existing fortifications from within, and reconcile themselves to the frequent defence of breaches, as happened at Vienna (1529), Boulogne (1544) and Metz (1552), where, as the surgeon Ambroise Paré recorded in his *Voyages*,

everyone was employed in carrying earth to make up ramparts by night and by day. Princes, lords and captains, lieutenants and ensigns—all carried the basket, to encourage the soldiers and citizens to do the like—as they did. Yes, even ladies and gentlewomen, and those who had no baskets, helped with kettles, panniers, sacks, sheets and with whatever else they could carry earth in, and all in such a way that no sooner had the enemy broken down the wall, than he found an even stronger rampart behind it.

By the end of the period the theory of fortification had got a long way ahead of the practice. The ideal fortified city of the textbooks, for instance, was round, and actual towns were not. Differences in terrain meant that the ideas of the experts were not universally applicable. But the most important checks on progress were existing fortifications. Every town had its defences, and reconversion was very expensive; Dürer, the only theorist to appreciate this fact, suggested defence work as a form of poor relief. Citizens and rulers felt proud of the lofty walls and were loath to cut them down; only the extreme urgency of their position in 1526 led the Florentines to reduce some of their towers. The usual aim was to modify the walls a little to exploit the defensive utility of cannon, and a little more to protect points of special danger, and to leave it at that. There were few new large-scale works of fortification, like Antwerp's (1540), and there were not even many new fortresses: Michele Sanmicheli's S. Andrea on the Venetian Lido and Henry VIII's works on the English south coast were exceptions to the general rule of adaptation. Theoretical writers of the 1520's, like Dürer (1527) and Valle (1528), devoted much of their space to new ways of defending existing walls. The fortifications of Verona were gradually re-modelled from 1520, but Verona was in a crucial strategic position on the main road from the Brenner, and the inadequacy of its defences had been shown by the fighting of 1509 and 1516. As late as 1552 Metz was still adapting its old works, filling towers with earth to turn them into make-shift bastions.

The changes in the art of fortification that gained wide theoretical assent in this period can be seen by comparing Machiavelli's *Arte della Guerra*, published at the beginning of it, with Niccolò Tartaglia's *Quesiti, e Inventione diverse*, published in 1546. Machiavelli, drawing on his own experience of the siege of Pisa and on what he had heard about the siege of Padua, concentrates on adapting existing walls and preparing internal defences. Tartaglia, while admitting that there must be some way of dealing with an enemy who has breached the walls, concentrates on keeping him at a distance with fire from walls planned afresh with mathematical precision. In storming Machiavelli's defences, an enemy, after climbing or breaching the town wall, would find himself on the brink of a deep wide ditch, commanded from the top by guns firing from a rampart made from the spoil thrown up on the town side, and flanked in the bottom by casemates firing along it. Tartaglia's ideas are developed in the course of a dialogue with the prior of Barletta in which the prior asks him if he does not think that the new fortifications of Turin —an angle bastion at each of the city walls, and a gun platform half-way along each wall—are the finest possible. Tartaglia says no. They are good as regards *materia* (brute strength) but poor as regards *forma* (design). Walls should not be straight, but curved. The enemy should never be able to get nearer to the curtain than he is to a bastion. At any moment he should be open to the fire of at least four banks of artillery. The prior's reaction to these opinions, which were rapidly becoming commonplace, was: 'If this were true, artillery would have lost much of its reputation in taking cities.'

Tartaglia's theories had already been put into practice in England. The reconciliation of Francis I and Charles V in 1538 meant that Henry VIII was faced by the possibility of a joint invasion on their part levelled against any point on the entire east and south coasts. Accordingly he pushed forward an elaborate system of coastal defences, building forts and block-houses at intervals from Hull to Milford Haven, concentrating on the Thames, the Downs, Southampton, the Isle of Wight and Falmouth. A number of them survive in fair condition: Deal and Walmer in the Downs, Hurst Castle in the Solent, Pendennis and St Mawes on Falmouth Haven. They have nothing in common with earlier English fortifications. They were fortresses, and nothing else: the efficacy of the design was in no way compromised by the needs of a dwelling house. They were built directly by the State and not, as had been the custom, by an individual or corporation under licence from the Crown. There were no examples of recently-constructed fortresses in England to act as a brake on independence of design. There was no native school of engineers. The fortresses, therefore, were built by imported experts, like Stephen von Haschenperg, in the most modern manner. While not uniform in plan, all lie low, are sunk in moats, have curved walls and rounded parapets and are provided with several banks of gun embrasures, some of them (as at Sandown and Walmer) showing a nearly full external flare. The political danger faded, and these fortresses were never put to the test. If they had been, it is very unlikely that they would have been taken by storm. The defence of Rhodes had shown how effective even old walls could be when assisted by modern devices: its bastions had helped assault after assault to be beaten back, even when the *fausse-braie*, or outer wall, had been pierced.[1] Within the last thirty years, wrote Fourquevaux, there has been a revolution in the fortification of cities. As everyone is busied with re-making their defences, 'the conquest of a country from now on will be hard indeed'.

The development of artillery continued under the active care of monarchs who valued guns for the prestige involved in their ownership as well as for their effectiveness. The fabrication of guns and gunpowder became more widespread as each nation endeavoured to produce its own. There was still a wasteful multiplication of types, involving formidable problems of supply and, in some particulars, downright inefficiency, for stone balls continued to be used, though far inferior to iron, because they could be made to size on the spot, to supplement gaps in supplies of ammunition. At the siege of Boulogne (1544) the English were still using artillery of eleven different calibres, each requiring its own carriage and shot. It is perhaps worth giving particulars of four of the more lasting types, medium guns whose characteristics remained more or less constant for the next hundred years.

	Weight (lb.)	Calibre (in.)	Range (yd.) Point blank	Range (yd.) At 10° elevation	Rate of fire in rounds *per diem*
Culverin	4000	5½	460	2650	60
Demi-culverin	3000	4½	400	2400	70
Saker	1500	3½	360	2170	80
Falcon	800	2½	320	1920	120

Though the monster guns of an earlier age had been supplanted by others more nimble and accurate, Henry VIII indulged his nostalgia for these impressive but unwieldy tubes by confronting the garrison at Boulogne with vast dummy guns of wood which had small real ones strapped on their backs.

As there was no uniformity of bore, so there was none of material. Iron and brass guns were produced side by side. Brass flowed better in the mould and was more suitable, therefore, for large guns. On the other hand, the heat of firing made it soft and liable to explode. Iron built-up guns had the advantage that they could be made by local smiths, but they were heavier and less accurate than cast guns and fell out of favour in this period. Gun-making became the specialised, centralised business it was to remain. There was a considerable increase in accuracy. Guns were

---

[1] Cf. below, p. 511.

better bored, carriages better adapted, the gunners' quadrant did something to obviate the need for wasteful and elaborate sighting shots, some attention was paid to the study of ballistics. As cast iron replaced forged iron in the making of mortars they became increasingly useful in siege work and by the middle of the century were throwing an effective explosive shell. If the very large gun was used decreasingly in siege work, the very light one began to disappear from the field. German gunsmiths had developed a light gun that could be drawn on a four wheel carriage at a gallop, and it was used at Renty in 1554, but it was already an anachronism. The musket was coming into use, and with a similar calibre it was almost as effective and far easier to transport.

Apart from the stubborn retention of the long-bow in England, the period saw the final triumph of fire-arms as missile weapons. The crossbow disappeared from battle in the 1520's, not without some conservative regret. The arquebus was open to the criticisms that it was unreliable in wet weather and that its rate of fire was slower than the bow's. But the maximum killing range of an arquebus of the best Italian make was about 400 yards, which compared favourably with the range of a long-bow and equalled that of the cross-bow; the arquebus was also decisively superior in shock and impact and therefore in killing power. Interestingly enough, it was in the years that saw the speediest development of firearms from the handgun to the musket that, in the east, the range of the bow was enlarged to a degree that has proved impossible to recapture. The weapon used was the short composite bow, and even to qualify for admission to the archers' guild founded by Mehemmed II and fostered by Sulaimān the Magnificent, it was necessary to have shot an arrow at least 630 yards, while the highest class was reserved for those who had exceeded 770 yards. These ranges were achieved, however, with light flight arrows, exploiting the wind, and there is no indication of how useful from the points of view of accuracy and impact they would have been in battle. The short-bow was known in Europe, but several factors counted against its adoption: the heavier armour used in the west: extreme difficulty of manufacture and of obtaining trade secrets from an infidel country: most of all, the rapid extension of firearms—which had been used, of course, almost from the first, by the Turks themselves.

The arquebus had been shown to be so effective by the troops— Spanish and Italian—who had first used it on a large scale, that German and Swiss infantry (the latter particularly after Bicocca) employed a proportion of shot with their pike. In Spain the respective value of the two arms, man for man, was reflected in the higher pay offered to the first-class arquebusier than to the best pikeman. Fourquevaux, who was one of those who regretted the sudden dropping of the cross-bow, said of the arquebus that 'it is very good, as long as it is used by skilful men, but at the present everyone wants to be an arquebusier: I know not whether it is to take higher wages, or to be lighter laden, or to fight further off'. And he adds a useful reminder of the waste entailed by giving the arquebus to unskilled men: 'For this negligence is cause that in a skirmish wherein 10,000 shots are fired, not so much as one man dies, for the arquebusiers content themselves with making a noise and shoot at all adventure.' The musket, soon to overtake the arquebus, was still in this period in its embryonic form: a heavy match-lock of one inch bore, used in siege work. Its long barrel was supported by a mounting, so that it resembled a small piece of artillery. A version of it, with a portable rest, had been seen in the field in the 1520's but it was a difficult weapon to handle, its improvement was slow, and its widespread use lay in the future.

The arquebus was used by mounted troops, but it was not a satisfactory cavalry weapon. It required two hands to fire, and before the invention of the wheel-lock (in which a piece of pyrites is held against a rapidly revolving steel wheel, set off by a spring when the trigger is pressed) the conserving of a lighted fuse was an additional snag. It was probably necessary to drop the reins, or even to dismount, before getting in a telling shot. But as the wheel-lock spread during the 1520's, the cavalry carbine and the horse pistol appeared, both prepared for instant use and carried in saddle holsters. These weapons, especially the heavy pistol, which came into use in the 1540's, had, as we shall see, an important effect on cavalry tactics. With firearms as a whole, as with guns, no uniformity must be looked for. Much experimentation was going on; specimens of superb craftsmanship, hardly less effective than the best arms of the following century, were produced in small numbers for the wealthy, but the arms used by the rank and file—particularly non-mercenaries—were conservative, simple and cheap.

In spite of the great development of firearms, armourers had never been busier. Gunpowder had led to armour being strengthened: from now on it was heavier, solider, and, except for the gratification of individual whims, more rounded in contour. Daunted by the threat of gunshot wounds and the blood poisoning which so consistently followed them, the soldier who could afford it insisted on armour proofed against shot—resistant, that is, to small-arms fire at ranges greater than point-blank. These suits were specially strengthened on the front of the head piece and the breastplate: the tasses and lames of the pauldrons were also thickened, though here great protection was given by the normal overlapping of the plates. This heavier armour was inconvenient, but firearms made it essential even in hot countries like Spain and Italy where the wearing of full armour had previously lagged behind the north of Europe. The additional weight was particularly galling to infantry, who frequently preferred to remain nimble and under-protected to being prisoners of their own defences. There were complaints that men treated their armour as army baggage rather than personal equipment and in case of surprise were therefore slow to put it on. And they were criticised for wearing it so seldom that in action they were scarcely able to sustain its weight.

One of the justifications of the tourney was the practice it gave in wearing armour. And the tourney itself dictated important changes in the nature of armour, changes that came to a head in this period. The gap between battle practice and tourney practice was at its widest; the same armour would hardly do for both. Nor was a suit of armour designed specially for the tourney of use by itself; each version of the combat was characterised by the administering of a different sort of blow, with lance, sword or mace, on horseback or on foot, and for each the armour had to be adapted to give the best protection where it was most needed. This was done partly by the substitution of one piece for another, partly by the addition of reinforcing pieces. The suits of field-harness and foot-fighting armour made in 1547 for the Archduke Ferdinand of Austria had 34 alternative and reinforcing pieces. This was not unusual; up to 100 were known. And the level of craftsmanship was maintained by the intelligent patronage of monarchs like Charles V and Henry VIII whose fashions were followed by their courts. The weight of armour had some influence on tactics. The heavier it was, the less able was a horse to travel fast with its wearer. The charge in line (*en haye*), developed in the previous century to replace the dense ambling advance in column, lost its power of impact when delivered at a walk, or even at a trot, and the sixteenth century saw a return to the column, with weight of impact a substitute for dash. But the most important single factor that affected tactics was, of course, gunpowder.

In spite of the increased mobility of gun-carriages, artillery played a less important part in battle than firearms. Writers like Machiavelli and Fourquevaux, when describing imaginary battles, allow the artillery to fire only a shot or two before being masked by an advance or silenced by enemy cavalry. This was an exaggeration, but there were, in fact, few examples as yet of a prolonged initial cannonade before an open battle. The main utility of artillery was to strengthen an entrenched position, as at Bicocca, to bombard the enemy out of one, as at Ravenna, or to break up a formation as naval artillery fire broke up the Scots left wing at Pinkie and the French right wing at Gravelines. The Turkish device of keeping an artillery reserve behind between the lines of cavalry to open fire on an enemy who broke through was as successful at Mohács in 1526 as it had been at Tchaldiran in 1514, but it was not copied in the west, partly, no doubt, because Christian troops were less happy about artillery firing from the rear.

Bicocca (1522) and Pavia (1525) demonstrated once and for all that tactics would have to be revised in face of the arquebus. The first demonstrated its power in a fortified defensive position, the second in the open field. The main victim at Bicocca was the Swiss infantry, at Pavia the

French cavalry, each the best representative of its type. The Swiss, who had chosen to attack in spite of the advice of Lautrec, the commander-in-chief, steadily advanced against arquebusiers firing from a rampart behind a sunken road. Their losses were enormous, and though they reached and began to storm the imperialist position, they were so weakened that pikemen coming up through the arquebusiers were easily able to push them back. At Pavia, the marquis of Pescara met a charge of heavy cavalry by dispatching his arquebusiers forward to harass the advance, using every cover they could—and there were plenty of hedges and small brakes of trees in the parkland over which the battle was fought—and retreating where necessary into the protective ranks of pikes. Brantôme quotes a Spanish source which emphasises the novelty of these tactics (*modo de pelear por si nuevo y no usitado, y sobre todo maravilloso, cruel y miserable*) and himself calls them 'a confused and novel form of fighting which is easier to imagine than to describe';[1] a useful reminder that, as tactics became more open with the use of skirmishing arquebusiers and smaller blocks of troops, descriptions of battles tended to become increasingly artificial. The French complained bitterly of the novelty of these tactics but took the lesson to heart: from 1529 horsed arquebusiers were attached to the *gendarmerie*, and horse pistoleers were employed as soon as the German *Reiter* had shown how effective they could be. After Pavia, moreover, cavalry was no longer used against arquebusiers. It was used against other infantry, or to attack pike supported by shot if they were already frontally engaged with other troops. As both foot and horse began to avoid direct movement against arquebusiers, shot ceased to be a decisive arm. The great victories of gunpowder were Ravenna, Bicocca and Pavia, before any reasonable counter had been worked out. From the mid 1520's shot, though it remained essential, became a secondary arm.

Though the proportion of horse to foot fell to something like one to seven or eight during this period, cavalry still retained a decisive influence in war. Light horse was still needed for scouting and raiding and to harass troops already engaged. Heavy cavalry still performed the invaluable function of halting a body of infantry by repeated charges, so providing artillery and missile troops with a stationary target, as at Pinkie. As pike infantry became more regularly stiffened with shot, the charge home declined in favour and—though the virtues of the manœuvre were hotly contested—tended to be replaced by the caracole, in which a column of medium-heavy horse armed with pistols advanced in steady order to close range, each rank filing away after firing, the next coming up to take its place. The advantage of this tactic was that a continuous stream of fire poured into the enemy. The disadvantage was that it required a very steady nerve to come close to infantry that contained arquebusiers

[1] Ed. Lalanne, vol. I, p. 337.

and take careful aim, and as most riders were right-shouldered it meant that they could only file off to the left, a characteristic that halved their usefulness. But some sort of medium-heavy or heavy cavalry remained essential; armies very deficient in horse were inevitably the victims of those better equipped with this arm.

Much of the social stigma attached to infantry service had disappeared by the middle of the period. This was due to a number of reasons. In some countries, like Spain, where the mule was the main riding animal, and England, where horses were of slight build, there were fewer horsemen because there were less mounts. Monarchs had publicised the growing tactical importance of infantry by an occasional dramatic gesture: Charles V marched a short distance with his pike-men, just as Maximilian had done before him. The increasing popularity of the foot-tourney among noblemen accustomed them to the sight of a gentleman in armour on his own legs. And firearms helped to make foot service more popular, though it made the recruitment of pike so difficult that the Swiss and Germans had no need to be anxious for their market. Both arms were needed. Pike alone was vulnerable to shot, arquebusiers alone were vulnerable to any body of cavalry that charged in without presenting too leisurely, or too broad, a target. If there were pikes to break the impact and give the arquebusiers time to re-load, or arquebusiers to thin a charge before it hit the pikes, then the odds were heavily against the cavalry. In this period of experiment the problem was to find the best way of combining the two. At Ceresole (1544) two experiments cancelled each other out. Both French and imperialists had placed shot behind the first rank of pike with orders not to fire until the armies had actually met: the French pistols and the Imperialist arquebuses blazed out at the same moment, levelling the foremost pikes, but not effecting a changed balance of power.

The same idea had occurred to Thomas Audley whose treatise on the art of war was written in Edward VI's reign. His ideal battle order was based on a huge square of infantry, either exactly square (a reminder of the very deep Swiss formations) or twice as broad as it was deep. This was to be composed of five units. The first five or six ranks were to be pike, with an optional rank of shot after the first rank of pikes; the second unit consisted of halberds or bills, the ends guarded by small squads of pike, in case the inferior weapon were attacked in flank by horse; in the middle was another unit of pike; behind that a combination of halberd and bill guarded by pike like the former one, finally, pike alone again. This mass was to be guarded by a 'sleeve' of shot (archers as well as arquebusiers, this being an English order) on either flank; beyond that, in each case, the guns, and beyond them, the horse. In front of the whole array was a long, thin line of missile troops, archers and arquebusiers mingled. In combat, this skirmishing line made as much trouble as it could before retiring, then the main bodies closed line to line, the aim being to have enough cavalry to hold the enemy as well as enough to send round to gall his flank.

There is nothing very progressive here. And, on the whole, battle orders remained reactionary until the third quarter of the century. This was partly due to the fact that once the lessons of gunpowder were learned there were very few large-scale pitched battles, and partly to the difficulty of combining new levies and professional mercenaries in cosmopolitan armies whose loyalties were often divided between commander-in-chief and unit leaders. The tradition of large mass opposed to large mass (the medieval battle) lingered and was reinforced by the memories of the deep Roman battle order, with its units of mutual support, *principes*, *hastati* and *triarii*. Difficulties of brigading certainly fostered the mass at the expense of smaller, freer units presenting a more elastic front. The legion of 6000 men and the *tercio* of 3000 were attempts to secure units of manageable size. Several small 'bands' had been grouped under a common command. But there was still no corps that combined a considerable overall size with disciplined self-contained units, like the regiment of the future with its companies. Armies remained less effective than the sum of their parts would suggest.

Shortage of money affected strategy in that it affected the size of an army and its transport, and sometimes tactics as a lack of ready cash—*point d'argent, point de Suisse*—might lead to the defection of a unit; but it did not seriously affect the decision whether to go to war or not. The problem was rather easier for the country attacked: owing to exemptions, out-of-date assessment and ineffective collection, sixteenth-century taxes seldom dipped as deeply into men's pockets as it was intended they should, and under the threat of war the apparently over-taxed could usually spare a little more. France, a constant aggressor, who could plead but not prove compulsive need, succeeded time after time in finding money for fresh adventures, using now general levies on the kingdom as a whole, now loans from individuals and corporations, now special levies on a particular section of the community, like the clergy. And there was always the prospect, for armies serving abroad, of compensating poor and irregular pay by loot and ransom.

With every technical advance, the amount of capital sunk in an army increased. Guns, gun-carriages, and their ammunition trains represented a growing expenditure, and though much of this was borne in peace as well, getting the contents of an artillery park on the move involved the hiring of some thousands of animals. A medium weight gun required ten horses, a large one up to twenty yoke of oxen. As the state's investment grew, so did its reluctance to allow the spoils of war to be dissipated among individuals. Ideally, war should pay for itself, as it had (it was held) among the ancients where a great proportion of plunder was handed over to the State and the remainder distributed equally among the troops, less an allotment to the legion benefit fund. The legal right of soldiers to plunder—at least in a technically 'just' war—was not challenged: *jus belli infinitum*. But attempts were made to prevent the State being entirely uncompensated, as well as to regulate looting in the interests of discipline. The 1527 Articles of War of Ferdinand I were among the most lasting and representative codes of the time. They forbade plundering without permission; precise order was to be observed until this permission was given by signal. Any artillery, ammunition, powder and stores of provisions were to be reserved to the emperor. Cities taken by surrender were not to be looted. The fact that these Articles were issued in the year of the sack of Rome indicates how necessary such rulings were, and how difficult to enforce. Men were intent on making a fortune out of the wars, and many—like Sebastian Schertlin von Burtenbach, who took part in the sack—returned with enough booty to buy an estate and a noble name. So much was stripped from the towns and villages through which an army passed—clothes, utensils, animals, besides more valuable goods—that attempts had to be made to restrict the allowances of baggage that encumbered an army's progress. But where all parties were interested, such restrictions were bound to be ineffective. It is doubtful, moreover, if the State would have gained by effectual checks on plunder, or by appropriating more to itself, for loot remained a lively attraction in recruiting.

Wars, besides, were not embarked on after a sober inspection of expenditure and prospective return. Glory, prestige, adventure—these were all-powerful incentives still and affected those who decided upon war just as booty and ransom did those who fought in them. Four times between 1525 and 1558 France set off on the impossible task of seizing Naples with neither naval supremacy nor effectual control of Lombardy and central Italy. The chivalric romances that had helped to inflame the adventurous nobles (as opposed to the careful politicians) in the circle of Charles VIII were still read, and, indeed, the period saw a resurgence of admiration for the life of arms, for the military virtues. The grandiloquent romances that inflamed Don Quixote were not alone responsible for this; so was the sober tribute of the Romans. 'How much superior is the art of war to all others', Vegetius had written in his third book, 'by which our liberties are preserved, our dignities perpetuated, and the provinces and the whole empire itself exist.' And the sentiment is exactly paraphrased in Guillaume Duchoul's 'Epistre au Roi' in his *Discours sur la castramentation et discipline militaire des Romains* (1556). The same theme recurs in the speeches made in 1528 to the Florentine militia in order to stir their enthusiasm for their new and unfamiliar trade. Pier Filippo Pandolfini praised the discipline of arms 'la quale supera tutte le altre scienzie et virtù'. Luigi Alamanni exhorted them to look upon their military service with as much 'riverenza et candidezza' as they brought to divine service.

Bartolommeo Cavalcanti described the Good Soldier in terms that a moralist might have taken over verbatim for a sketch of the Good Man. In these cases the Christian virtue of fighting was emphasised quite naturally because there was still a strong Savonarolist conviction that Florence was Christ's chosen city, and that her rivals were his rivals. But praise of the military virtues were quite conventionally pitched so high that there was ample justification for Rabelais' own ironical version in the Prologue to Book III of *Gargantua and Pantagruel*.

I believe indeed that war is called *Bellum* (a fine thing) in Latin, not out of anti-thesis, as certain botchers of old Latin tags have believed, because they saw but little beauty in war, but positively and literally, because in war every kind of beauty and virtue shines out, every kind of evil and ugliness is abolished. That wise and pacific king, Solomon, knew no better way of expressing the ineffable perfection of divine wisdom than by comparing it to an army with banners.

Christian pacifist scruples, though still voiced by a few in the Erasmian tradition, found little support with regard to European wars, though they proved a useful stick with which to beat the cruelty of Spanish aggression in the New World. Fourquevaux's impatient dismissal of them represents the majority view. As long as wars are not fought simply from ambition or revenge, they are lawful.

In my opinion it is to no purpose to allege the contrary out of Holy Scripture, saying that a good Christian ought patiently to suffer injuries and wrongs, without resisting those who would strike him or take away his goods. For I believe that that was only spoken to the Apostles and their like, who had to have humility and patience if the doctrine they preached was to bring forth good fruit.

The military writer was conscious of two audiences: the Europe of rival states, and Christendom. 'I do not aim only to help members of the great family of Christians one against the other,' Dürer wrote in his work on fortification, 'but above all to assist those who are neighbours of the Turk against the power and arms of these infidels.' The idea of a crusade still lived, but a crusade involved not a denunciation of war as such, only a canalisation of it. Between the extreme opinions—on the one hand that Christian principles must be more firmly instilled to counteract man's natural pugnacity, on the other that Christianity is to be deplored for having sapped man's martial vigour (Machiavelli's view)—lay the acceptance by the great majority of war as an inevitable feature of social life, good or bad only as it affected the lives of individuals or the reputations of states. It was reflected in the peacetime recreation of the noble, and his tourney was echoed in the often savage *Fechten* of the commoner. It filled the chivalric romance and was the burden of much of the ever more widely read literature of Rome. Nor did such reading present war only in its noblest aspect—selfless sacrifice, refusal to accept political servitude; it stressed as well the importance of finding quarrels in a straw, and (from such books as the *De strategematis* of Frontinus) the importance of winning battles however cruel or oblique the means employed.

Machiavelli had complained that war had become so humane, and there was so little to be feared from defeat, that men were no longer prepared to undergo the rigorous training necessary for success in arms. This impatient generalisation was hardly supported by the facts. The Turks seldom took prisoners, unless terms had been granted in good time to a garrison. Even then the terms were not always observed: after the surrender by agreement of Buda in 1529, the garrison were massacred as they marched out. Nor did the Turks make the distinction between nobles, usually preserved for ransom, and common soldiers. And they were not alone in their summary attitude to the defeated. The Swiss were almost as consistent and were greatly feared for their boast that they took no prisoners but killed all who fell into their hands. And other nations were on occasion equally merciless, as were the French when, on the fall of the Château le Compte near Hesdin in 1552, they ordered all prisoners to be killed out of hand and not held for ransom. More common practice, however, was for a commander to order his men to grant quarter when it was clear that the enemy was beaten beyond all hope of recovery. Those who were capable of paying a ransom would then be held, while those who could not were, if they were lucky, stripped and allowed to go free, the problem of the unremunerative prisoner being too complicated for sixteenth-century military administration to face. But mercy was accorded by grace rather than from any sense of obligation, moral or legal. When Metz was relieved, the French went out to dress the wounds of the Spaniards who had been left behind by their retreating comrades, 'which we willingly did,' said the surgeon Paré, dourly adding 'and think they would not have done the like towards others'.

When it is remembered how scanty was the concern shown for an army's own wounded, it appears less remarkable that concern for the enemy's should be uncertain. Medical care was most perfunctory. Great lords took their own surgeons with them, and sometimes these men were able to care for the common soldier, but their first concern was naturally for their employer and his friends. The *tercio* allowed one medical man for every thousand troops; the English force of some 32,500 men who took part in the war of 1544 had no surgeons directly employed by the army, nor was regular provision made by French armies. Mary Tudor left an endowment for a hospital for poor, aged or disabled soldiers, and Coligny's ordinances of 1551 suggested a levy of the troops themselves to provide a fund for the provision of hospitals. In France the maimed soldier was not, it is true, entirely uncared for. Some were placed in monasteries where the king possessed the right of collation (these were usually bought off by the aggrieved monks for a pension); others were placed in fortress towns where they were given a pittance in exchange for nominal duties. But this accounted for a very small number. The regular provision of a medical corps, the setting up of proper military hospitals, and a system for compensating the disabled soldier, had to wait for the establishment of large regular armies. But if there was little medical service available, its quality began to improve in this period, particularly with regard to the treatment of gunshot wounds. Until the publication of Ambroise Paré's *La Methode de Traicter les Playes faictes par Harcquebutes*, in 1545, these wounds had been treated largely by cautery. His introduction of saner and less drastic treatment led to an immense saving of lives; and within a decade four more authors published books on the treatment of wounds, three of them concentrating on gunshot injuries.

Although there were few pitched battles at sea between 1519 and 1559, and no decisive one, it was a period of great activity in shipbuilding and sharply mounting expenditure on navies and every item of their equipment. As the size of armies grew, so did the number of transports and escorts needed in combined operations: Charles V attacked Tunis in 1535 with some 25,000 men; the French sailed against the south coast of England ten years later with nearly 60,000. Political rivalries led to an armaments race between the powers whose frontiers were most vulnerable to attack from the sea. Venice set herself the ideal of a reserve of one hundred war galleys to reinforce her patrol vessels in time of emergency. This meant an establishment of warships greater than that of any Atlantic power, but, even so, it was only in alliance with other navies that Venice could hope to match in numbers the war galleys of the Turks and their north African supporters. In the north the main challenge came from France, and Henry VIII's enthusiasm for the navy meant that England, apart from matching numbers, tried to outstrip her rival in matters of design and administration. And if political rivalry dictated numbers, prestige insisted on size; every ruler wished to have at least one vessel of awe-inspiring appearance, and to the Scottish *Great Michael* of 1511 and the English *Henry Grâce à Dieu* of 1514 the French added the *Grand François* in 1527, the Swedes their *Elefant* in 1532 and Portugal the cumbrous *São João* in 1534. Even the Knights of Malta, attracted by these vast hulls with their brilliant ornament and impressive armament, bid for the limelight by launching a prodigy of their own, the *Santa Anna*, in 1525. Merchant vessels of one thousand tons burden and more were not uncommon, and their cargo capacity justified their size, but these huge warships were like the unwieldy 'prestige' bombards of the early days of gunpowder; glory apart, the money would have been better spent on several products of a smaller size.

Shipbuilding activity was also stimulated by experiments in design, the modification of existing types and the introduction of new ones. The main concern of Mediterranean naval architects was to improve the speed and manœuvrability of the heavy galley. This type had been used up to the 1530's as strongly defended cargo vessels, especially by the Venetians. With a heavy armament and large crew they were able to defy raiders, and as long as they carried precious cargoes the freight charges covered the otherwise excessive proportion of crew to cargo space. The recession in the spice trade made them uneconomical, and, as naval armament was improving at the same time and a type of vessel which gave more protection to the oarsmen than the light galley afforded was needed, the heavy merchant galley became a warship. They were constructed mainly for cargo-carrying under sail and their rowing and fighting qualities had been sacrificed: the problem was to make them as fast and, if possible, as handy as the light galley. Three solutions were offered. The first, and least practical, was to have more than one deck of oars. Picheroni della Mirandola submitted plans to the senate for galleys with two and four decks respectively, but as the upper deck oars on the bireme would have been some sixty feet long, and on the quadrireme over one hundred and eighty, it is not surprising that the plans were rejected. Venice in fact built no multiple-decked galleys. A second suggestion was that more oars than the usual three should be rowed from one bench, one man to each oar. Galleys with four oars to the bench, one man to each oar, were known, but when Vettore Fausto, public lecturer in Greek eloquence at Venice, offered the senate his version of the all-conquering quinquireme of the ancients—five oars to the bench—there was much debate and hesitation before the Arsenal was directed to build a prototype. In a public speed-trial in 1530 the quinquireme, despite its complexity, beat a standard three-oar-to-the-bench galley amid great excitement, but no successor to Fausto's vessel was built; the future was to lie with a third principle of design, that of having one oar to the bench worked by several, commonly five, men.

While in the south the emphasis lay on the improvement of the galley and the round-ship as independent types, in the north there was an effort to combine them in a ship that would join the handiness of the galley to the seaworthiness and solidity of the round ship. After much experiment with sail plan, gun positions and oar arrangement, a compromise emerged towards the middle of the century in the galleon, more nearly flush in silhouette than the carrack, higher and bulkier than the great galley, almost exclusively dependent on sail, but capable of being worked by oars in an emergency, and adding the galley's heavy armament fore and aft to the traditional round ship's weight of broadside fire. All these experiments with design (in the south there appear to have been even experiments with armoured hulls) meant that the cost of each ship was enhanced by the degree to which it differed from a constructional norm. In the development of the fighting vessel this period was a crucial one, but the evidence is to be found more clearly in account books than in combat.

As far as merchant shipping was concerned, the previous generation had settled the fundamental distinction between oar and sail, long-ship or round-ship, in favour of the round sailing ship. There were features that suggested that the same decision might now be made for ships of war. Modifications of the sails and tackle of round-ships had put them firmly ahead of galleys for general seaworthiness, and, encircled by guns, they were floating fortresses that could beat off the attacks even of a large number of galleys, as was shown from time to time in the Mediterranean itself, as at Prevesa (1538) when a becalmed Venetian sailing galleon beat off a series of galley assaults. On the other hand galleys suffered from several serious weaknesses. Unlike the round-ship they were frail to any broadside shock, and their motive power could be crippled even by a glancing blow which damaged the oars or the overhanging rowing deck. Because of their length they were difficult to turn smartly, and as it was only safe to fire powerful guns so that the recoil was absorbed by the length of the ship these could only be traversed (and in most cases elevated) by movement of the vessel itself. Moreover, the winds that shattered Charles V's fleet on the Algerian beaches in 1541 (and prevented the Turkish galleys from intercepting him) showed that galleys were only dubiously reliable in winter. Yet, for all this, the galley remained the main warship of the Mediterranean; not only did the great galley influence the design of northern sailing ships, but true galleys were built for use in the Channel and the North Sea.

Warship design could not be decided only by shipwrights' arguments. Tradition counted for much, though one should beware of seeing the northern races' hatred of forced labour as a reason for the failure of the galley to establish itself in their waters. The oarsmen in Christian galleys were almost all free men, voluntarily recruited, permitted some cargo space of their own, and idle for the greater part of any voyage when use could be made of sail. It was the difficulty of getting free men to behave well in port and return to their vessels on time that was one of the main reasons for suggesting, as a Venetian *provveditore* did in 1556, that more convict crews should be employed. A far more important factor that prevented the shipwright's ideal from being put uniformly into practice was the composition of the dominant fleet in any particular waters. As long as the Turkish war fleet was composed of galleys, it would have to be met by galleys. A fleet of round-ships was helpless in a calm when sufficiently outnumbered, or when matched by the heavy long-range guns which great galleys were bearing by mid-century. Nor could round-ships alone force galleys into an engagement they were not prepared to accept. Nor would one type of galley suffice—the comparatively cheap light galley, for instance, even if used together with heavy round-ships. A fleet of galleys could only be tackled effectively by a comparable force, light galleys sustained by, and supporting, heavy galleys. Joint operations between sail and oar were always unreliable because of the vagaries of the wind. At Prevesa Andrea Doria was on the point of coming to grips with the Turk when the wind failed. Not wanting to be separated too much from his round-ships he called off the attack. The Turks also stopped, hoping to draw the galley force, which was inferior to theirs, forward on its own. Doria refused to be drawn, and as a result there was no general engagement. Antonio Doria, in his unpublished 'Discorso delle cose turchesche', emphasised that, as sail and oar behaved so differently as wind and sea varied, the round-ship should never be admitted to the line of battle, but should be used only for transport, supply and reserve. And in the same way, because the French used galleys, the English were forced to meet them with rowing vessels of their own, as when the English row-barges protected their round-ships from D'Annibault's Italian galleys in 1545.

There was an additional factor that prevented the consideration of ideal fighting qualities alone. There was still a close connection between merchant shipping and ships of war. No navy was large enough to be independent of merchant auxiliaries; no country was rich enough to use its fighting ships exclusively for war. In England, for instance, merchant shipping of a certain size was subsidised by the Crown with an eye to supplementing the navy, and naval vessels were hired to merchants during times of peace. The character of warships was inevitably influenced by the type of vessel most useful for trade. The oceanic interests of the Atlantic powers forced them to think largely in terms of the round-ship, while the shrinking oceanic carrying trade of the Venetians enabled them to counter the Turkish galleys with galleys of their own without sacrificing commercial convenience too much to military necessity—though by the middle of the century the contrast between merchant and naval shipping was sharper in the Mediterranean than in the north; the constant Turkish threat to Venice, and the decreasing usefulness of the galley as a profitable cargo-carrier, meant that she was forced to lock up capital in a specialised war-fleet a century before the Atlantic powers were forced to do the same. Similarly, the exceptional use of men-of-war as patrol vessels in the north had long been a commonplace to the Venetians, reconciled since the growth of Turkish sea power to thinking of a navy in terms not only of occasional impressive fleet concentrations or profitable merchant ventures but also of unremunerative vigil.

When fleets came in contact with one another their behaviour was still tactically analogous to the behaviour of two armies. Neither in theory nor in practice was there yet any clear suggestion that naval tactics were *sui generis*. The voice of antiquity was conservative and inexplicit. The Romans had relied on the superior weight of their ships to bear down any rival and concentrated on coming to grips as soon as possible, the real work of destruction being accomplished by boarding parties of legionaries. Naval matters did not therefore occupy much space in the writers *de re militari*. When Vegetius was writing Rome was little concerned with naval affairs, and he was more concerned with sea lore than with sea war, spending most of his space telling the commander when it was safe to embark and how to find his way to an enemy; accepting the sea-land analogy, there was no need to go into details of what happened when he found him. As a result, very little was written about war at sea by theorists, and the commanders of fleets, many of them military men relying on subordinates in matters of navigation, determined tactics in the light of their own experience on land. In the case of galley warfare this was perfectly natural; intricate and closely controlled manœuvres could be planned independent of the wind. But it is remarkable that the same principles dominated plans for the fighting formations of sailing ships. Thus Alfonso de Chaves, writing of Spanish round-ships about the year 1530, emphasised that

a regular order is no less necessary in a fleet of ships for giving battle to another fleet than it is in an army of soldiers for giving battle to another army. Thus, as in an army, the heavy cavalry form by themselves to make and meet charges, and the light horse in another quarter to support, pursue and harass; so in a fleet, the captain-general ought to order the strongest and largest ships to form in one quarter to attack, weaker ships in another quarter apart, with their artillery to harass, pursue and give chase to the enemy if he flies, and to come to the rescue wherever there is most need.[1]

The aim was an attack, on a widely extended front (using, as a result, only guns that could fire forward) so that the larger ships could grapple and board the enemy as quickly as possible, aided when necessary by the lighter craft standing by for any emergency. The only difference from purely galley tactics is that whereas a flank attack was effective against galleys, it was perilous against the broadside of the round-ship, which was not easily sunk, moreover, by ramming. Another version of these Spanish tactics is given in the two sets of sailing orders made out for the English fleet in 1545. It was to attack the French in a main body divided into three ranks supported by oared wings and by a reserve. When the first rank met the first line of the enemy it was to sail between his ships and then turn to attack them in the rear at the same time as the English second rank, commanded by the admiral, came up to engage them frontally. This was not, of course, a manœuvre that could be transferred to the land, but the battle order is basically a military one, as was every order that depended on frontal attack in extended ranks like lines of soldiers anxious to get to grips. Naval tactics proper had to wait until the pitched battle had become influenced by the running fight—the full use of broadside fire

[1] *Fighting Instructions 1513–1816* (ed. J. S. Corbett, Navy Record Society, 1905), p. 7.

and the dependence on artillery rather than boarding; when, in fact, off-fighting was realised to be the most effective form of engagement between sailing ships. This development (irrelevant for galley navies) was only to come in the last third of the century. It was not the fruit of experience gained in pitched battles, but came about when the opinion of mariner veterans of small running fights made itself felt in councils of war previously dominated by soldiers. But these new tactics had to wait also for the development of improved gunpowder that would allow the short guns most easily handled in broadside fire to improve in range and striking power. By the 1550's, while galley warfare continued with little change in the Mediterranean, the nature of war at sea had undergone a revolution in the north, as technical improvements in the design and arming of ships, coupled with the decline of the military analogy, led to the supremacy of off-fighting. Henceforward skill rather than numbers would decide the issue. Once a frontal engagement of the old type was joined, orders could no longer be passed and a disorderly mêlée followed in which weight was the main advantage. In off-fighting a fleet could be controlled to some extent (for signals were still rudimentary) throughout an action, and, though boarding still took place on occasion and the large ship with a large crew retained some advantages, the odds were in favour of the handier vessel. After the middle of the century the arts of war by land and sea began to diverge in manner as well as in matter.

CHAPTER XVII

THE OTTOMAN EMPIRE, 1520–66[1]

TOWARDS the end of his reign Selīm I had been preparing for a new offensive, but no one could be sure where the blow might fall. Now, in September 1520, the great sultan was dead. As the news became known in Christendom, men felt that a dark shadow had been banished, an imminent peril suddenly dispelled. Sulaimān, the only son of Selīm, was said to be ill-versed in affairs and of a quiet nature, a prince, therefore, who would be little inclined to war. Seldom has prediction been more rash or doomed to swifter disillusionment. In 1521 Sulaimān marched against Hungary.

The campaign had been organised with meticulous care: the *beglerbeg* of Rumeli moved towards Sabacz, the sultan following with most of his household regiments; the grand vizier Pīrī Pasha, with a strong contingent of janissaries and ample provision of siege guns, made for the main objective, Belgrade, which Mehemmed II had tried but failed to capture in 1456. At the same time the Akinjis[2] rode out in two columns, the one to effect a diversion against Transylvania, the other to devastate the lands between the Sava and the Drava. The fall of Sabacz and Semlin severed the routes leading to the north and west of Belgrade, so that Sulaimān was now free to assail the great fortress. Guns bombarded the walls from an island in the Danube, a fierce assault drove the garrison into the citadel, an Ottoman flotilla, sailing upstream, cut off all relief by water. The end came when dissension broke out between the Hungarians and their Serbian mercenaries, the former wishing to prolong, the latter to abandon the defence. Belgrade surrendered on 29 August 1521.

Sulaimān turned now to the conquest of Rhodes. The Knights of St John had long harassed Muslim commerce, plundered vessels bearing pilgrims towards Mecca, slain and enslaved the subjects of the Ottoman sultan, their depredations being so severe that in 1480 Mehemmed II had tried to seize the island, though without success. The fate of Rhodes had in fact been decided in 1517 when Selīm I conquered the Mamluk sultanate: thereafter the Ottomans could not suffer the continued existence of this 'pirate-stronghold' athwart the sea-routes from Istanbul to their new provinces of Syria and Egypt. Yet the fortress was almost impregnable, and Sulaimān was well aware that the knights were making elaborate preparations to defend it. The bitter fighting of 1522 was to

---

[1] For an analysis of the structure of the Ottoman state, cf. vol. III, ch. XI.
[2] I.e., raiders, volunteer light-armed horsemen serving for the reward of plunder and captives.

underline how much the sultan owed in this campaign to his father, Selīm, who in the last years of his reign had strengthened and improved the naval resources at his command, with the intention, as it would seem, of subjugating the island.

The invasion fleet arrived at Rhodes on 24 June 1522. More than a month passed in the landing of troops and munitions, in work on trenches and on sites for the siege artillery. Sulaimān, marching through Asia Minor with strong reinforcements, crossed over to Rhodes late in July. Attempts to storm the fortress made it clear that mining and bombardment of the walls alone offered a prospect of success. There now ensued a stubborn and protracted conflict, the Ottomans, in their intermittent assaults, losing heavily in men and material. With the onset of winter, rain and cold so hindered the conduct of the siege that the sultan was induced to hold out generous terms of capitulation, but it was not until 21 December that the knights, worn down to the limit of their endurance, yielded on promise of freedom to withdraw unmolested to Europe.

There were grave events, too, in Syria and Egypt during the first years of the new reign. Memories of their former splendour still survived amongst the Mamluks whom Selīm I had incorporated into the Ottoman régime, and now, with the accession of Sulaimān, the more dissatisfied elements believed that the time had come to regain their independence. The pasha of Damascus, Jānberdi al-Ghazālī, once a Mamluk amir, had risen in revolt in 1520–1, had besieged Aleppo in vain and then suffered defeat and death while resisting a punitive force sent against him from Istanbul. Unrest and intrigue were rife in Egypt, leading to disturbances on the death of the pasha, Khā'ir Beg, in 1522 and thereafter to a more serious rebellion in the winter of 1523–4 when the new Ottoman pasha Ahmed, in alliance with some of the Mamluk begs and Arab chieftains, tried to crush the janissaries stationed at Cairo and so make himself the real master of the land. His ambition was doomed to failure, for in view of the rivalries amongst the Mamluks and also between the various tribal confederations there could be no question of a united resistance to Ottoman rule. The revolt, although suppressed without undue trouble, convinced Sulaimān of the need to modify the settlement improvised at the time of the conquest. He entrusted the task to his grand vizier Ibrāhīm who in 1524–5 carried out in Egypt an extensive reform of justice, finance and administration, reshaping the government on lines that it was to retain, in essentials, until the rise of Muhammad 'Alī almost three centuries later. Ibrāhīm created a balance of power and privilege between the pasha, the janissaries, the Mamluk begs and the Arab tribes. Henceforth, the alignments and tensions among them were to exert a dominant influence on the course of events inside Egypt. In time, the delicate equilibrium now established would break down in favour of the Mamluks and to the disadvantage of the pasha; but this change was as yet far in the future, and in the meanwhile the reforms ensured to Egypt a long interval of firm and beneficial rule.

It was three years since Sulaimān had gone to war. Amongst the janissaries inaction bred resentment which, in March 1525, flared out in a sudden tumult, warning the sultan not to defer too long the preparation of a new campaign. The grand vizier, recalled from Cairo, arrived at Istanbul in September and the decision was made to launch a great offensive on the Danube. Sulaimān marched against the Hungarians in April 1526. Progress was slow and difficult because of bad weather, and it was late August before he crossed the Drava near Eszék. The advance continued through a region of marshes and swollen streams, under persistent rain and occasional mist, until the Ottomans reached the plain of Mohács.

The Hungarians faced a desperate crisis. Bitter rivalries ruined all prospect of a prudent and united resistance.[1] No effort was made to hold the line of the Drava, nor would the Hungarian nobles agree to withstand a siege in Buda in the hope of prolonging the defence until the approach of winter should compel the sultan to retreat. The critical weeks of mid-August were wasted in acrimonious debate, and the final choice fraught with extreme danger: to risk a field battle against a foe much superior in numbers and armament, and this before the men of Zápolyai, before all the Croatian levies and the troops summoned from Bohemia had arrived.

To the east of Mohács flowed the Danube, to the south and west of the plain were low wooded hills, which masked the advance of the Ottoman columns: in the van, the frontier warriors of Semendria; next the *sipāhīs* of Rumeli and then, of Anatolia; behind them, Sulaimān with the janissaries and the regiments of household cavalry; and in the rear, the warriors of Bosnia. It was 29 August 1526. The Hungarians had no intention of fighting on the defensive behind their waggons and carts. Their heavy cavalry, in a first violent charge, hurled back the troops of Rumeli against those of Anatolia, but was itself halted when the begs of Bosnia and Semendria, who had moved to the left through the hills, came down from the west into the right flank of the Christian advance. King Lewis now led the rest of his horsemen in a second assault, cut through the *sipāhīs* of Anatolia and rode headlong into the janissaries and the guns ranged around the sultan. A terrible artillery fire shattered the Hungarians, massive flank attacks drove them in rout towards the Danube. Soon the king and most of his nobles were either dead on the field or else drowned in the river marshes, only a few remnants of the broken army escaping under cover of rain and darkness. Sulaimān reached Buda on 10 September. One week later the Ottomans began to cross the Danube to Pest. The Akinjis, who had ravaged far and wide in the direction of Raab (Györ) and Komorn, were recalled, the rich booty and all the guns

[1] Cf. above, p. 348.

found at Buda shipped downstream. Swiftly the sultan retreated, first to Szegedin and thence to Peterwardein and Belgrade, after a campaign resplendent with the most famous of all his victories.

During the return march news had arrived of revolt amongst the Turcomans in Cilicia who were angered at the conduct of Ottoman officials sent out to make a register of their lands and wealth for purposes of finance and administration. There was trouble, too, in Karaman, where a certain Kalender-oghlu and his dervish adherents roused the Turcoman tribes against the Ottoman régime. For almost two years the troops of Anadolu, Karaman, Amasia and Diyarbekir, with the aid of reinforcements from Damascus and Aleppo, were engaged in a fluctuating war, so serious as to demand at last the personal attention of the grand vizier, Ibrāhīm Pasha. By tactful diplomacy and the bestowal of fiefs he induced the Turcoman begs to abandon their alliance with Kalender-oghlu. Thereafter, the defeat and death of the rebel were soon achieved, but, even so, a further outbreak occurred in the Taurus region, and it was not until the summer of 1528 that the last embers of revolt were extinguished.

Meanwhile, a fateful conflict had arisen beyond the northern frontier. Lewis, king of Hungary and Bohemia, had married a Habsburg princess, Maria, sister of the Archduke Ferdinand and the Emperor Charles V, while Ferdinand himself had taken as wife Anna, the sister of Lewis, and had then received from the emperor the government of Austria and its dependencies. When Lewis died at Mohács, leaving no child to succeed him, Ferdinand laid claim to the rich inheritance. If he could realise his ambition, Hungary and Bohemia might be welded, with Austria, into a formidable barrier against Ottoman aggression. The sultan would then be confronted, not with a mere Hungarian king, independent yet weak, as Lewis had been, but with a prince who belonged to the greatest dynasty in Europe, to a house tenacious in the extreme of its rights and privileges and, despite vast commitments elsewhere, able to muster on the Danube, in time of dire need, resources far above those which Sulaimān had overcome at Mohács. Although Ferdinand soon acquired the Bohemian Crown, no facile success awaited him at Buda. He had first to defeat a rival candidate, the *voivode* of Transylvania, John Zápolyai, whom the native faction amongst the nobles had raised to the throne in November 1526. One year later Ferdinand was acclaimed king at Stuhlweissenburg, his troops having driven the Transylvanian to take refuge on the border with Poland. Zápolyai now turned to Istanbul for aid.[1]

The sultan, though regarding the Hungarian realm as his own by right of conquest, knew that indirect control, comparable with that which he wielded in Wallachia and Moldavia, would be far less arduous to win and maintain than a permanent and direct occupation. If he were to establish a dependent prince at Buda, a cordon of vassal states would then cover

[1] For the way in which the issue appeared to Ferdinand, cf. above, pp. 348, 470.

the northern frontier of his empire from the Black Sea almost to the Adriatic. He therefore welcomed the appeal of Zápolyai, bestowed on him the kingdom of the dead Lewis, and swore to guard him against the enmity of Austria. Soon ambassadors arrived from Vienna demanding that the Ottomans relinquish all the fortresses which had fallen to them along the Sava and on the Croatian border during and since the campaigns of Belgrade and Mohács. In bitter scorn Ibrāhīm, the grand vizier, wondered that Ferdinand did not ask for Istanbul, while the sultan, in a final audience, gave to the envoys the ominous message that he himself would come to Vienna and restore what the archduke demanded: 'Bid him therefore have all in readiness to receive me well.'

A major offensive on the Danube was a stern test of Ottoman military skill and resource. The campaign season extended, in the Hungarian wars of Sulaimān, from mid-April to the end of October, but the distance to Belgrade alone was so great that the sultan could seldom cross the Sava in force before the first days of July. The march was often slow and laborious, for the weather seems to have been bad even in summer, the official war diaries of Sulaimān referring constantly to storms, cold winds and relentless rain.[1] Problems of supply and transport were especially hard to solve. Rivers had to be spanned by means of pontoon bridges, a feat that required high technical ability; roads had to be made over difficult ground—and Hungary was a land of many streams and marshes. The Danube flotilla could only share to a limited degree in the movement of guns and munitions, most of which were needed for immediate use in the field and had therefore to be loaded on waggons and carts, on camels and other beasts of burden; yet, owing to the harshness of weather and terrain, the loss of animals was not infrequently severe. Ample reserves of food were essential, since the retreat might lie through territories swept bare of sustenance by the Akinjis during the forward march or else waste and barren from the devastation wrought, by Christian and Muslim alike, in the raids of former years; and always, in the last phase of a long campaign, a new danger might arise—the premature and sudden onset of winter.

Never were these difficulties more evident and more formidable than in 1529. Sulaimān left Istanbul on 10 May, did not reach Belgrade until mid-July and only on 27 September stood at last before Vienna. Because of incessant rains and flooded rivers, he had lost a vital month in which Ferdinand was able to garrison the city with a powerful force of veteran soldiers. Time was short, food already becoming scarce, and the Ottomans were far from their nearest base. If they were to take Vienna, it would have to be quickly or not at all, but the Christian defence held out against every assault. On 14 October the sultan gave the order to retreat. 'Snow from evening until noon next day', 'much loss of horses and men

---

[1] Cf. the diaries in J. von Hammer, *Geschichte des Osmanischen Reiches*, vol. III (Pest, 1828), pp. 621–25, 639–44, 647–52, 665–71.

in swamps', 'many die of hunger'—so ran the story of the grim march to Belgrade. And yet the campaign was not a complete failure, for it achieved one important result: Zápolyai ruled again at Buda.

The Archduke Ferdinand had not the means to launch a vigorous counter-offensive. His troops were ill-paid and discontented, his need of money acute. The German princes, though prepared to aid him in the hour of danger, would never fight a long and costly war on the Danube for the benefit of the Habsburgs. Nor could he depend on receiving prompt assistance from the Emperor Charles V, now deeply preoccupied with the conflict between Catholic and Protestant. Ferdinand tried, therefore, to make peace with the sultan, offering tribute in return for the possession of all Hungary, but the attempt met with no success. He himself would not abate in the least his claim to the whole kingdom, while Sulaimān was adamant in his refusal to abandon Zápolyai.

The sultan left Istanbul in April 1532, his declared aim being to seek out and crush the combined forces of Ferdinand and Charles V. He crossed the Sava in the last days of June, followed the Danube route as far as Eszék, and then turned to the north-west through Babocsa and over the river Raab, until he came to the little town of Güns. Here, in a desperate and brilliant defence sustained for almost three weeks, a small garrison resisted the full weight of the Ottoman assault, yielding at last on 28 August. Most of the summer was now gone, the rains were frequent and prolonged, and meanwhile, as the sultan must have known, German, Italian and Spanish veterans had been able to join the troops of Ferdinand at Vienna. Sulaimān, having no mind to renew the bitter experience which he had suffered three years before, abandoned his original purpose and, from this moment, the campaign assumed the character of an immense razzia. The Akinjis rode far into Austria, while the main army moved through the mountain valleys of Styria towards Graz where the Tatars of the Krim Khan were let loose along the river Mur. It was a march 'wearisome as the Last Judgment'. The sultan now retreated across the Drava and then swept with fire and sword down the whole length of Slavonia to the Bossut, an affluent of the Sava. Here the raids came to an end, for beyond this stream lay Sirmium, a region under Ottoman control. On 12 October Sulaimān arrived once more at Belgrade.

After two exhausting but indecisive campaigns against Austria the sultan realized that time and distance were enemies at least as formidable as the power of the Habsburgs and that, unless he committed himself to the conquest of a permanent base far to the north of the Sava, he would have little chance of inflicting on Ferdinand a sudden and catastrophic defeat. He therefore granted peace to the archduke in June 1533. The 'king of Vienna' was to retain what he then held of the Hungarian realm. He could also make a separate agreement with Zápolyai subject to the approval of the Porte. Sulaimān had in fact conceded little more than a truce without time limit. A prince dependent on his favour would continue to be master of Buda; his own word would still shape the future course of events on the Danube. Meanwhile, he had obtained an immediate advantage: freedom to deal with urgent affairs in the east.

The Ottoman frontier with Persia was ill-defined. The direct rule of the sultan extended, in the north of Asia Minor, only to Erzinjan and Baiburd, the lands beyond these fortresses remaining under the control of Turcoman begs who gave allegiance, as their need dictated, now to Istanbul and now to Tabriz; in the south, it embraced western and most of central Kurdistan, but not the region around Lake Van, where the forces of the shah were still active. The war of 1514–16 had died down into a smouldering tension along the frontier. No formal peace had been made between the sultan and the shah. Feuds and incursions continued to disturb the border zones, and the odium which divided the orthodox or Sunnī Ottomans and the Shī'ī Persians was no less fierce than before.[1]

While Sulaimān was marching towards Güns, the troops of Karaman, Amasia and Diyarbekir, with detachments from Syria, were fighting in Kurdistan against the khan of Bitlis, who had gone over to the shah. The defection of this border chieftain brought home to the sultan the need to consolidate and strengthen the unstable frontier in Asia Minor. There was a further ground for war, in that the Persian governor of Baghdad had offered submission to the Porte, only to be murdered before Ottoman aid could be sent to him. Sulaimān did not intend to forego so opportune a pretext for the conquest of Iraq.

As soon as peace had been concluded with Austria, the Grand Vizier Ibrāhīm hastened towards Kurdistan, but on receiving news that Bitlis was once more in Ottoman hands, he retired into winter quarters at Aleppo. In the spring of the next year he moved against Persia and by mid-July had taken Tabriz. Shah Tahmasp, mindful of the crushing defeat which his father, Ismā'īl, had endured at Tchaldiran in battle with Sultan Selīm (August 1514), preferred to abandon the city rather than face the janissaries and the Ottoman field artillery. Sulaimān left Istanbul only in June 1534. During his advance he traversed almost the whole of the frontier zone, passing through Erzinjan to Erzerum, then south to Lake Van and eastward to Tabriz, where he joined Ibrāhīm Pasha on 28 September. There now ensued a most formidable march across the mountains of western Persia. 'Snow as in deepest winter' beset the land, food was scarce, the loss of transport animals severe, but at last, on 30 November, the sultan entered Baghdad. He remained there until April 1535 and then, having provided for the defence and administration of Iraq, withdrew northward through Kurdistan to Tabriz. The shah was still determined to avoid all risk of a great battle. To these tactics of evasion the sultan

[1] On the rise of the Shī'ī Safawids and the danger of this movement to Ottoman rule in Asia Minor, cf. vol. I, ch. XIV.

could find no effective answer. Tabriz was in the heart of Azerbaijan, a mountainous area far removed from the nearest Ottoman base. An attempt to hold this region would be a most doubtful venture, as long as the army of the shah remained intact—yet the prospect of destroying that army, rapidly and at one blow, was almost negligible. In late August Sulaimān gave the order to retreat. The campaign had achieved two notable results: the formation of a new province at Erzerum on the eastern frontier, and the conquest of Iraq.

In 1536, soon after his return from the Persian war, the sultan bestowed on France commercial privileges similar to those which Venice had long held in the Ottoman empire. This agreement was the visible symbol of the growing friendship that united the king of France and the sultan. In the years following his defeat and capture at the battle of Pavia (1525) Francis I had striven to bring about a sustained Ottoman assault against Austria, hoping thus to relieve the Habsburg pressure on his own realm.[1] Sulaimān, aware of the benefit to be won from an understanding with a Christian state hostile to the Emperor Charles V and the Archduke Ferdinand, welcomed an appeal so close to his desire for effective control of the Hungarian kingdom. And yet, as the campaigns of Vienna and Güns had shown, the war on the Danube ensured to Francis I no decisive gain and even worked to his disadvantage, in so far as it rendered the German Protestants less willing to join him in overt resistance to the emperor and forced them, for their own interest, to make common cause with Austria against the sultan.

There was, however, a second front which offered a prospect of more favourable co-operation. The maritime resources of Charles V had been much increased in the Mediterranean. Genoa, dissatisfied with the conduct of her French allies, deserted to the emperor in 1528—an event of the first order, for the republic possessed the sole fleet which might have secured to France an effective command of the sea. Moreover, in the same year and with the approval of Charles V, the Knights of St John established a garrison at Tripoli on the African shore and in 1530 accepted from the emperor the task of defending Malta. Spain, which had long aspired to the conquest of the Muslim principalities in North Africa, seemed now to be on the verge of achieving her desire. The vital issue was one which Sulaimān, as the greatest of all Muslim rulers and also as the overlord of Algiers, could in no wise disregard: was North Africa to be preserved or lost to Muslim rule? Only a bold offensive at sea could avert the danger of Christian domination. At the same time, if the Ottoman fleet were sent against the emperor, it would serve, in respect to France, as an admirable substitute for the galleys of Genoa. To Sulaimān, no less than to Francis I, war in the Mediterranean appeared to be of more immediate advantage in their conflict with Charles V than further campaigns on the Danube.[2]

[1] Cf. above, pp. 343, 352 f.   [2] Cf. also above, p. 351.

The sultan had great arsenals at Istanbul and Gallipoli, good harbours along the Aegean and Levantine coasts, abundant timber in Asia Minor and ample supplies of labour for his shipyards. The main defect of his naval organisation was a lack of competent sea-captains and of an efficient high command able to match the skill and experience of the Venetian and Genoese admirals. One event, above all, warned Sulaimān of the urgent need to eliminate this weakness. The ministers of Charles V had advised their master to strengthen the defences on the Italian coast, especially in Apulia, and at the same time, as the best means of deflecting the sultan from the Danube, to begin a vigorous sea offensive in the eastern Mediterranean. In September 1532 the Genoese commander, Andrea Doria, led his fleet, reinforced by papal, Maltese and Sicilian squadrons, to the conquest of Coron in the Morea. Ottoman troops recovered the fortress in April 1534, but only after a wearisome siege prolonged by the aid that Doria was able to bring to the Spanish garrison which he had left there. Sulaimān was preparing to march against Persia, yet he could not leave the sea unguarded in his absence. The danger of a new raid by Doria to the east of Malta, no less than the growing threat to North Africa and the problem of co-operation with France, demanded immediate measures to ensure that the naval forces of the sultan would be reorganised and then employed with the greatest energy and effect. A splendid instrument was available for this purpose in the community, or tā'ife, of corsairs at Algiers, veteran sailors trained and hardened in ceaseless forays against the Christians. Their famous leader, Khair ad-Dīn, came to Istanbul at the sultan's bidding[1] and brought with him his own captains and naval technicians. He built new ships, sailed forth at the head of the Ottoman fleet and in August 1534, eight months after his arrival at the Porte, captured Tunis, thus neutralising the hold which Charles V had won over the narrow waters of the central Mediterranean. It was only a transient victory, for in July of the next year the emperor conquered the town and restored its Muslim ruler as a vassal prince supported and controlled by Spanish troops stationed in the fortress of La Goletta. Khair ad-Dīn however, escaped to Algiers and in the autumn raided the Balearics and the coast of Valencia.

Francis I, in the hope of regaining Milan and Genoa, made war once more on the emperor in 1536. The sultan was willing to co-operate against the common foe, but did not move until his naval preparations were complete. In the summer of 1537 he marched to Valona on the Adriatic, while Khair ad-Dīn sailed with a much enlarged Ottoman fleet to Otranto and laid waste the adjacent lands. The king of France had found the war expensive and unprofitable and, far from invading Milan, was even now negotiating with the emperor for a truce on the Italian front. Sulaimān

---

[1] Khair ad-Dīn had made submission to Selīm I (1512–20) in return for aid against the Christians.

declined, therefore, to run the risk of crossing the Adriatic in force. Doria was cruising in the Ionian sea, and, having no reason to fear a French attack on Genoa, might yet concentrate his warships and attempt to wrest from Khair ad-Dīn command over the strait of Otranto. In August the sultan abandoned the raid on Apulia and struck at the Venetian island of Corfu.

Sulaimān had no need to look far for grounds of accusation against Venice. The Christian corsairs who preyed on Muslim shipping in the eastern Mediterranean had long been accustomed to sell their plunder and obtain supplies in the Venetian harbours of the Adriatic and the Aegean. In Dalmatia and the Morea the Cretan, Greek and Albanian mercenaries of the Signoria were often involved in local conflict with the Ottoman begs. The tension had grown in the years since Khair ad-Dīn began to reorganize and improve the naval forces of the sultan. Now more than ever before, Venice felt the need to strengthen her squadrons in the waters near Corfu, each time that the Ottoman fleet sailed out from Istanbul. The republic acted thus from mere precaution, but there was a real danger that her captains, although warned to behave with the utmost forbearance, might fail in self-control under the strain of constant watchfulness and restraint. A serious 'incident' could well bring disaster to Venice, for she had lost much of her former influence at the Porte. Ibrāhīm Pasha, throughout his career a staunch friend of the Signoria, had been executed in 1536, and now, amongst the officials and ministers who were high in the favour of Sulaimān, no one enjoyed more prestige than Khair ad-Dīn—and he was the advocate of a ruthless offensive at sea. If trouble came, Venice would find it difficult to appease the anger of the sultan. Venetian patrols did in fact seize a number of Ottoman ships at the time of the raid on Apulia and then committed the fatal mistake of attacking a small squadron which had on board an ambassador bearing letters of complaint from Sulaimān to the Signoria.

In reprisal Ottoman troops laid waste Corfu, but withdrew in September 1537 on discovering that the main fortress could not be taken save at the cost of a prolonged siege. Venice, realizing that all hope of peace was now dead, welcomed the prospect of an alliance with the pope and the emperor. Articles of agreement were signed in the spring of 1538, yet it was not until the autumn that the naval forces of the league at last assembled for a joint campaign against the Ottomans. The decisive moment of the war came on 28 September when Khair ad-Dīn defeated the Christians off Prevesa in the Gulf of Arta, a success due in no small measure to the conduct of Doria, who was resolved to maintain his fleet intact and therefore left the brunt of the fighting to the Venetian and papal commanders.[1] The battle was in itself only a minor affair, the allies losing but few of their ships. None the less, it marked a more ominous phase of the conflict for

[1] For a different interpretation of Doria's action, cf. above, p. 507.

naval supremacy: the Ottomans had met and repulsed the combined strength of the two fleets alone capable of thwarting their ambition to win control of the Mediterranean. From this time forward until Lepanto in 1571 the initiative at sea was to rest largely with the sultan.

Venice obtained no real advantage from her league with the emperor. Indeed, the sole achievement of the allied fleet was to take Castelnuovo on the Dalmatian coast in October 1538, but even this modest gain was soon erased, for Khair ad-Dīn recovered the fortress in August of the following year. The republic viewed the alliance as a means of protecting her dominions in the Adriatic and the Levant, whereas Charles V, concerned above all with the defence of the western Mediterranean against the raids of the Algerian corsairs, regarded it as no more than a limited commitment and would not risk the destruction of his naval forces for the benefit of the Signoria. Venice, despairing of effective aid from the emperor, now sought to end the ruinous conflict. Her need of peace was the more urgent in that she drew from the Ottoman lands indispensable supplies of grain, a traffic which the war had so restricted that in 1539 she was suffering from a grave dearth of corn and found it difficult to feed her citizens. A truce arranged in this same year led, after long discussion, to the settlement of October 1540. Venice paid a high price for the renewed favour of the sultan, ceding her last strongholds in the Morea (Napoli di Romania and Monemvasia) together with the islands which she had hitherto controlled in the Aegean Sea.

Meanwhile, Sulaimān had begun a naval offensive against yet another foe, the Portuguese, who, in the distant waters of the Indian Ocean, were attempting to sever the trade routes along which the spices of the East flowed to Syria and Egypt, there to pass into the hands of merchants from the great commercial centres on the northern shore of the Mediterranean. The Portuguese conquered Goa in 1509, thus securing in western India an admirable base from which their fleet could dominate the sea-lanes leading towards Arabia. Sokotra, guarding the approach to the Bab al-Mandab, had been taken in 1507. Thereafter, although never successful in their efforts to capture Aden, the Portuguese were able to penetrate deep into the Red Sea—indeed, in 1541, Estevão da Gama carried out a daring raid even as far as Suez. An alliance was also sought with Christian Abyssinia which had long been in conflict with the Muslim amirs of the Sudan. In the Persian Gulf, too, the Portuguese were no less active, Ormuz (occupied in 1515), Maskat and Bahrain being the chief harbours under their control.

The Mamluk sultan, Kānsūh al-Ghaurī, anxious to retain the large revenue that he derived from the transit trade, sent to western India a small fleet which overcame a Portuguese squadron off Chaul in 1508, but was itself defeated at Diu in the next year. Despite this reverse, al-Ghaurī, with the aid of timber, guns and naval stores obtained from the

Porte, built new ships at Suez and in 1515–16 tried to gain effective command of the coastal towns in the Yemen, a campaign brought to a premature end when Selīm I conquered Syria and Egypt (1516–17), although local warfare continued on land between the Mamluk troops disembarked from the fleet and the Arab chieftains of the region.

The Ottomans now had a direct interest in the defence of the Red Sea, yet were for a long time so preoccupied with Balkan affairs as to give little heed to the danger from the Portuguese. The grand vizier, Ibrāhīm Pasha, during his visit to Cairo, reorganized the naval administration at Suez, with the result that the old Mamluk fleet sailed out in 1525 to exact from the Yemen a more than nominal obedience to the Ottoman sultan. The venture led to no great success. Not until after the conquest of Iraq, an event which indicated that to the conflict in the Red Sea there would soon be added war between the Ottomans and the Portuguese in the Persian Gulf, did the sultan at last decide to begin a vigorous counter-offensive.

The governor of Egypt, Sulaimān Pasha, was ordered to build a new fleet at Suez, a task which he began in 1537 and, impressing into his service Venetian sailors whom he found at Alexandria, completed in the spring of the next year. In August 1538 he captured Aden and in September, having crossed the sea to India, joined the forces of Gujarat in their attempt to seize the fortress that Nuño da Cunha had erected at Diu in 1535–6. The pasha, now far from his base, had not the means to undertake a prolonged siege, and the Christians at Diu held out in a stubborn defence. On 6 November Sulaimān Pasha abandoned the enterprise and withdrew to the Yemen, organised there a new Ottoman régime, of which the main centres were Aden and Zabid, and then returned to Egypt.

At the end of 1538 the Portuguese were still in control of the trade routes to Arabia and the neighbouring lands. The initial effect of their blockade had been severe, for Venetian merchants often found that almost no spices were for sale in the markets of the Levant. Indeed, the Signoria was compelled at times to obtain cargoes of pepper and other eastern commodities from Lisbon. And yet the old traffic, although disrupted and much reduced in volume, had continued despite all adversities. The Portuguese were able to restrict but not obliterate the Muslim commercial interests so long established on the coasts of Malabar and Gujarat. Their squadrons could enter yet had failed to win command of the Red Sea and might soon be confronted with a strong challenge to their domination in the Persian Gulf. If the sultan chose to persevere in a more active resistance to the Portuguese, the trade to Basra and Suez would no doubt regain much of its past splendour.[1]

The peace with Austria did not end local hostilities on the Danube frontier. The border warriors of Bosnia, Semendria and the adjacent

[1] For these Portuguese activities, cf. also below, pp. 596 f., 599 f., 604.

regions were *ghāzīs*, soldiers devoted to the *jihād*. To them the *ghazā* or razzia into the non-Muslim lands—the Dār al-Harb, that is the Abode of War—was an obligation of their faith as well as a means of material benefit in the form of plunder and of captives who could be sold as slaves. The Hungarian and Croat marcher lords in the service of Austria had, too, a code of behaviour not unlike that of the *ghāzīs* and fought no less in conscious defence of Christendom than in the desire to safeguard the territories under their immediate control. No decree from Istanbul, no edict from Vienna, could have halted the unceasing strife in the border zones where the razzia constituted, as it were, an entire mode of life with its own peculiar patterns of conduct and belief.

Along the Drava Ottoman raids became so troublesome that in 1537 a force of about 24,000 men—German and Bohemian troops, levies from Carniola, Styria and Carinthia—advanced southward against the fortress of Eszék. The frontier begs hemmed the imperialists into their laager near Valpó, cut them off from all supplies of food and fodder, and slew or stole most of the animals which had drawn their carts and guns. It was now late November. The Christians began to retreat, moving between lines of waggons and light field-pieces chained together. Snow-storms hindered the march and at last the long columns broke under the pressure of a fierce pursuit, the men of Carinthia, with the German and Bohemian regiments, being almost annihilated in a desperate battle fought on 2 December.

There was conflict, too, on the lower Danube. Moldavia retained, even at this time, a certain degree of independence in relation to the Porte, for the sultan, in 1529, had confirmed to the nobles the right of naming their own prince, subject to Ottoman approval of the candidate thus elected. The *voivode* of the moment, Peter Rareş, was suspected of intrigue with Vienna. His eviction, therefore, was considered at Istanbul to be desirable and indeed urgent. In September 1538 Sulaimān occupied Suceava, then the capital of Moldavia, raised a new *voivode* to the throne and annexed southern Bessarabia, henceforth to be a *sanjak* the revenues of which would maintain the Ottoman fortresses of Akkerman and Kilia. The sultan had reason to be well satisfied with this achievement. Moldavia would in future come under more effective restraint, and the land-route from the Crimea to the Danube, which the Tatar horsemen of the Krim Khan followed when summoned to the Hungarian wars, would be much safer than before.

It was now five years since peace had been made between the sultan and the Archduke Ferdinand. In the meantime, despite frequent missions from Vienna to Istanbul, no method had been found of reconciling the rival claims of Zápolyai and the archduke to the Hungarian Crown. Sulaimān defined his own attitude in the clearest terms when he told the Austrian ambassador, Schepper, in 1534:

...this realm belongs to me and I have set therein my servant....I have given him this kingdom, I can take it back from him, if I wish, for mine is the right to dispose of it and of all its inhabitants, who are my subjects. Let Ferdinand, therefore, attempt nothing against it...What Janos Kral[1] does there, he does in my name....

In 1538 Zápolyai made a compact with the archduke: each was to have the title of king and each to retain what he then held of the Hungarian realm, but on the death of Zápolyai (at this time unmarried and childless) his lands would pass to Ferdinand, with the proviso that due recompense be assigned to his queen and her issue if he should ever take a wife. To be effective, the compromise required the approval of Sulaimān—and his consent had not been asked. Moreover, a strong faction amongst the Hungarian nobles, with Martinuzzi, the bishop of Grosswardein, at their head, viewed with disfavour the prospect of Austrian rule. In 1539 Zápolyai married Isabella of Poland. His death in July next year, just after his queen had given birth to a son, led at once to a crisis of the first magnitude.

Martinuzzi, knowing that Ferdinand would seek to enforce the compact of 1538 and himself confronted with dangerous rivals at home, appealed to the sultan for immediate aid. Sulaimān realised that, in regard to the Hungarian problem, no return was possible to the solution of indirect control. The kingdom, torn by bitter feuds, could not be left to the nominal rule of Isabella and her infant child, John Sigismund, nor could a substitute be found for the young prince, the sole claimant around whom the 'native' faction might be expected to gather in defiance of Ferdinand. A new approach was needed, strong enough to curb the designs of the archduke. The sultan must have weighed in his mind the harsh lesson, learned before Vienna and Güns, of the difficulties involved in protracted warfare on the remote Danube. None the less, his final choice was one of permanent conquest. War, indeed, had become unavoidable, for in the meantime imperial troops were marching towards Buda. Sulaimān ordered the beglerbeg of Rumeli to reinforce its garrison and, in his furious anger, stormed at the ambassador who had arrived from Vienna: 'Have you...told your lord...that the kingdom of Hungary is mine? Why does he send an army into my kingdom? What is your purpose here and where is your honour? Your king wants only to deceive me...it is winter now, but summer will come again.'

In August 1541 the sultan encamped at Buda, the begs of Bosnia and the Danube, together with the partisans of Isabella, having earlier cut to pieces the Christian troops opposed to them. Of the ambassadors now sent to him from Ferdinand, Sulaimān demanded that their master return all the fortresses taken since the death of Zápolyai. The archduke was also to give tribute to the Porte for the Hungarian lands under his control before that event. John Sigismund and his mother were escorted to

[1] 'King John', i.e. John Zápolyai.

Lippa, there to rule over Transylvania as vassals of the sultan. Buda itself would be the centre of a new Ottoman beglerbeglik on the Danube. The next campaign was organised with minute care. In the summer of 1543 Sulaimān marched northward from Belgrade with an army of un-exampled power and splendour. Long camel trains carried food and munitions, the river flotilla bore the siege guns and also large supplies of grain and other stores, the janissaries and the mounted regiments of the household, the corps of engineers and the artillery had been mobilised in full strength. The fall of Valpó, Sziklos and Pécs to the beglerbeg of Rumeli cleared the road to Buda. Gran, the sultan's main objective, yielded on 10 August; Stuhlweissenburg was stormed on 4 September. Now that he had won a firm basis for Ottoman rule on the Danube, Sulaimān returned to Istanbul. The campaign of 1544 was entrusted to the frontier begs. Mehemmed Pasha, the commander at Buda, took Nógrád, Hatvan and also Visegrád, a strong fortress which hindered the movement of the river fleet to and from Gran. Meanwhile, the Bosnians captured Velika in Slavonia, raided into the region of Varaždin and, at Lonska, routed the levies of Styria, Carinthia and Croatia. The Archduke Ferdinand, seeing no hope of effective aid either from the German princes or from his brother, sought and obtained a truce in 1545. Sulaimān was not unwilling to end the war, his attention being now drawn towards the Persian frontier. After long debate, articles of peace, valid for five years, were signed in June 1547. Ferdinand, for the lands still under his direct control—the far northern and western areas of the kingdom—agreed to send annually to the Porte the sum of 30,000 Hungarian ducats.

There had been no serious conflict with Persia since 1536. None the less, local hostilities flared out from time to time in the border regions; the sultan and the shah still vied with each other for the uncertain allegiance of the chieftains, Muslim as well as Christian, of Armenia and the Caucasus. The flight to Istanbul of Elkāss Mīrzā, a brother of Shah Tahmasp, gave Sulaimān a favourable prospect of strengthening the eastern frontier. In the summer of 1548 he marched to Tabriz but found that the shah had chosen once more to abandon it, rather than fight a decisive battle. The sultan now withdrew westward to besiege the great fortress of Van which he had taken in 1534 and then lost to the Persians in the following year. After a brief resistance Van surrendered on 25 August and, with the adjacent lands, became the nucleus of an Otto-man frontier *vilayet*. Having wintered at Aleppo, Sulaimān moved to Erzerum and in September 1549 sent the Vizier Ahmed Pasha against the Georgians of Akhaltzikhé who, with the Safawid begs, had been raiding in the border zones between Kars, Oltu and Artvin. The vizier, in the course of a razzia which lasted for six weeks, brought the district around Tortum under more effective Ottoman control. In the meantime, Elkāss Mīrzā, engaged in a vain attempt to foment revolt inside Persia, had fallen into the hands of the shah. Being thus denied all hope that Tahmasp might be overthrown, the sultan returned to Istanbul, arriving there on 21 December.

The shah was now free to recover, if he could, the territories which had just been taken from him. In 1551 Safawid horsemen laid waste the region of Akhlat and 'Adiljevaz on the northern shore of Lake Van and also defeated the troops of Iskender Pasha, the beglerbeg of Erzerum. Sulaimān ordered the grand vizier, Rustem Pasha, and Mehemmed Sokollu, the beglerbeg of Rumeli, to recover the ground lost in Armenia. The campaign, planned to begin in 1552, was deferred until 1554, the sultan being confronted meanwhile with a grave crisis in the relations between himself and his son Mustafā. When at last the Ottomans did move against Persia, Sulaimān, and not the grand vizier, was in command. He set out from Aleppo in April 1554 and marched through Diyarbekir and Erzerum to Kars. The Persian border defences, especially at Erivan and Nakhjivan, were now subjected to a ruthless destruction and the rich lands of the Karabagh behind them devastated with fire and sword. If he could not destroy the army of the shah—withdrawn, as in former years, far ahead and to the flank of the Ottoman advance—Sulaimān meant at least to wreck the forward zones which had long been the main point of departure for Persian raids into Asia Minor. With his aim largely achieved, the sultan retired to Erzerum and there, in September, agreed to a truce with the shah. A formal peace, the first to be made between the Ottomans and the Safawids, was signed at Amasia in May 1555. Sulaimān abandoned all claim to Tabriz, Erivan and Nakhjivan, but retained Iraq, together with most of Kurdistan and western Armenia.

The conflict with Persia had been fought in a region so remote from Istanbul that, as a rule, it was June before the sultan could enter the territories of the shah. Problems of transport were hard to overcome, for, with Safawid horsemen harassing the Ottoman columns in the mountainous terrain of Armenia and Azerbaijan, the loss of camels and other beasts of burden tended to be severe. Each campaign, in terms of actual warfare, had to be carried out and finished within three to four months, a sudden onset of the long, harsh winter and the rigour of a snow-bound retreat being of all dangers the most to be feared. The shah, remembering the lesson of Tchaldiran, avoided all risk of a great battle, swept the mountain valleys bare of food and fodder, then withdrew, leaving his frontier begs to watch and hinder the Ottoman advance. To these tactics of evasion and the irremediable difficulties of remoteness, terrain and climate there was indeed no simple and effective answer. The victories of Sulaimān had brought the Ottomans to the extreme limit of valid and enduring conquest in the east. A war to annex Georgia, Persian Armenia and Azerbaijan would be certain to involve the state in a vast and onerous expenditure of men and material. Success might be even more harmful than defeat—for numerous forts and garrisons would be needed to hold back the Safawids and, at the same time, control the Turcoman tribes and the Christian peoples of the Caucasus. The campaigns of Sulaimān had made the issue clear: to rest content or to go forward? The hour could not be far off when a fateful decision would be taken at Istanbul.

Two years after his return from Persia in 1549 the sultan found himself once more at war with Austria. Martinuzzi, the bishop of Grosswardein, had long been the real master of Transylvania, despite the continued efforts of Queen Isabella and her partisans to end his domination. Aware that he himself was held in no great esteem at the Ottoman court—in 1548 Sulaimān had warned him not to disregard the interests of Isabella and her son—he began to intrigue with Ferdinand of Vienna. In 1551 he forced the queen to surrender Transylvania to the archduke and accept in exchange certain territories in Silesia. Ferdinand now sent Spanish and Italian soldiers, under the command of Giam-Battista Castaldo, to assume control of the main fortresses. The raid which Mehemmed Sokollu carried out against Lippa and Temesvár in the autumn of this same year convinced Martinuzzi that Sulaimān would unleash a massive campaign against the imperialists, as soon as the winter had gone. He sought therefore to act as mediator between the sultan and the archduke, hoping thus to maintain his own power in Transylvania, whatever the ultimate course of events might be. His conduct led the imperialists to believe that he was a traitor to their cause. Castaldo, armed with permission from Vienna to follow his own judgment, made a fatal error when, on 18 December 1551, he brought about the murder of Martinuzzi. By this deed Ferdinand lost all prospect of winning the Transylvanians to his side.

The war went badly for the archduke in 1552. At Szegedin 'Alī Pasha, the beglerbeg of Buda, routed a force composed of Spanish and Hungarian troops, took Veszprém in April and at Fülek, in August, won a second battle against the imperialists. Mehemmed Sokollu and the vizier Ahmed Pasha conquered Temesvár in south-west Transylvania (henceforth to remain under direct Ottoman rule) and then swept northward along the river Theiss to attack the fortress of Erlau. The Christian garrison fought, however, with such desperate courage that in October the Ottomans abandoned the siege. Although the war lasted until 1562, it led to no further change of real importance in the Hungarian scene, for neither the archduke nor the sultan could afford to launch a sustained offensive; the one because he lacked the means to do so, and the other because he was soon involved in a new campaign against Persia and in a prolonged and dangerous conflict over the succession to the Ottoman throne. The archduke, knowing that he would not be able to evict John Sigismund, the son of Zápolyai, through force of arms, made use of diplomatic manœuvre at the Porte in order to achieve his aim. Ambassadors sent from Vienna to Istanbul strove to draw the maximum advantage from the difficulties of the sultan and insisted that Transylvania should be ceded to their master. Sulaimān had no great desire to continue the war; yet, despite his deep concern in regard to the internal crisis, he was adamant in his refusal of this claim. When, in 1561, the sultan at last recovered his freedom of action, Ferdinand was left with no valid resource. The peace of 1562 renewed, in substance, the terms of 1547. Austria paid tribute to the Porte, and to the same amount as before—30,000 ducats. Transylvania was still a vassal state under Ottoman control.

The campaigns of 1541–62 had brought about the emergence of three distinct Hungaries: Austrian, in the extreme north and west, Transylvanian, east of the Theiss, and, between them, the territories which the sultan had conquered along the middle Danube. The Ottomans did not attempt to 'colonize' their new province *en masse* but created 'islands' of effective occupation in the neighbourhood of great fortified towns like Belgrade and Temesvár, Buda, Gran and Stuhlweissenburg, the begs and their *sipāhis* moving in armed columns from fortress to fortress and living in fact as a garrison in an alien land. The imperialists, too, evolved a military régime centred around their own strongholds, for instance, Kanizsa, Raab, Komorn and Erlau. Moreover, on the one side as on the other, minor forts, of the type known as 'palanka' (constructed from timber and earth and enclosed in wooden palisades), were raised to guard the main routes and river crossings. In the course of time, therefore, the fluid frontier zone where Christian marcher lord and Muslim beg waged unceasing guerrilla warfare tended to harden on more or less stable lines. The Archduke Ferdinand, although he lacked the means to fight a major campaign of reconquest, could and did find the resources to erect a formidable barrier against the Ottomans. Throughout his reign he devoted much care to the rebuilding and improvement of the Hungarian fortresses in his possession and often entrusted them to Italian, Walloon, Spanish and German troops, that is, to professional soldiers expert in the most advanced military techniques of the age. This effort to organise an elaborate defence in depth was far from complete when Ferdinand died in 1564, yet its effect was becoming apparent long before this date. The Ottomans, committed to the assault against a strong defensive armature and a foe resolved not to run the risk of a great field battle, had to conduct a war of sieges, laborious and wasteful in men and material—a war, in short, which could not fail to heighten the basic difficulties confronting them, of time, remoteness and terrain, of transport and logistics. The years of rapid conquest would soon be gone; victories now cost more and brought less reward than in the past. As in Armenia, so too on the Danube, the Ottomans had almost attained the farthest limit of valid and justifiable expansion.

It was the Ottoman custom that a sultan, on ascending the throne, should kill his brothers and their male children in order to dispel the danger of civil war. Princes of the blood lived, therefore, under a dire constraint, the more compulsive and intense as their father grew old, to prepare for the critical hour which would mark the commencement of a new reign. Of the sons still left to Sulaimān in 1552[1] the eldest was Mustafā, born of Gulbahār, a prince well aware that in Khurrem, the consort whom the sultan cherished with an abiding love, he had an implacable foe determined to achieve his ruin and thus win the throne for one of her own children. Khurrem had drawn to her side the astute Rustem Pasha who received the hand of her daughter, the princess Mihr-u-māh, and in 1544 became grand vizier, an office which he was to hold, save for one brief interval, until his death in 1561. The pasha strove to form and maintain a faction hostile to Mustafā, raising to power men who were dependent on himself.[2]

In their youth the sons of a sultan went out from Istanbul to administer provinces in Asia Minor, each of them having a small court, with officials and tutors to instruct him in a practical knowledge of how the empire was ruled. At this time Mustafā held the *sanjak* of Amasia. To counter the intrigues of Khurrem and the grand vizier, he had long sought to gain the trust of his personal entourage and to acquire favour with the Turcoman tribes, with the *sipāhīs* or 'feudal' horsemen under his control and also with the janissaries and the great dignitaries of the Porte. His endeavours were crowned with notable success, for in 1552, when Rustem Pasha came to Anatolia as *serdār* (general-in-chief) of the new offensive against Persia, there arose among the soldiers an ominous murmur that Sulaimān had grown too old for service in the field and that it would be better to set a young and vigorous sultan on the throne. Sulaimān had no choice but to assume command of the troops destined for the Persian campaign. He left Istanbul at the end of August 1553, having summoned his eldest son, with the *sipāhīs* of Amasia, to join him during the outward march. In October, near Eregli in Karaman, Mustafā appeared before his father and was at once executed.

It would seem that the sultan had good reason to act in this drastic manner. There existed a definite and increasing tension between the *sipāhīs* or 'feudal' class within the empire, and the *kullar*, the 'men of the sultan', that is, the janissaries, the mounted regiments of the imperial household and the numerous personnel educated in the palace schools. The *sipāhīs*, Muslim born and in general of Turkish descent, formed the main weight of the armed forces, yet had no access to power and privilege through the higher ranks of the provincial administration. The *kullar*, recruited from captives of war and from the *devshirme* or child-

---

[1] The sultan was now past the prime of life, for he had been born in November 1494 or, according to other sources, in April 1495.

[2] Sinān Pasha, the brother of Rustem held the office of *kapudan*, i.e., high admiral, in the years 1550–54. The grand vizier knew that, if the fleet were in safe hands, it would be difficult for Mustafā to cross the straits to Istanbul.

tribute levied in the Balkans, were converts to Islām, a *corps d'élite* trained to wield an almost exclusive control over affairs of state and to fill the great commands and appointments in the provincial as well as in the central régime. Now, in the reign of Sulaimān, social and economic stresses began to affect the status and attitude of the feudal class, rendering more burdensome the strain of frequent and remote campaigns and making the *sipāhīs* more aware and envious of the superior role accorded to the *kullar*. Distress in the rural areas also gave rise to the so-called *levends*, men uprooted from the soil, who had recourse at times to brigandage, often with the connivance of the feudal warriors, and welcomed a prospect of service in a cause as desperate as their own. Mustafā became, as it were, the focus and symbol of this unrest. To spare him meant in effect to run the risk, not of a mere revolt in Anatolia, but of a formidable rebellion founded on grave discontent and, still worse, fought with the aid of the *sipāhīs*, that is of soldiers expert in the art of war. How real the danger had been was made clear in the camp at Eregli, for among the troops assembled there the death of Mustafā evoked a reaction so tense that Sulaimān deemed it wise to dismiss the grand vizier Rustem Pasha, reputed to be the prime author of the tragic deed.

A bitter conflict was now to be waged between Selīm and Bāyazīd, the sons of Khurrem. The portents of a further crisis became visible in 1555, when Ahmed, the grand vizier, lost his life as a result of court intrigue designed to discredit him and so bring about the recall of Rustem Pasha. A brief revolt, also in this year, in the name of a 'false' Mustafā, was symptomatic of continuing disaffection within the empire. No irreparable breach occurred between Selīm and Bāyazīd as long as their mother remained alive. Khurrem, with the aid of Rustem, controlled among the dignitaries of the Porte a faction able to exert a strong and perhaps decisive influence on the course of affairs. Her ultimate purpose is still a subject for conjecture rather than categorical statement. Western observers at Istanbul inclined, however, to the belief that she favoured Bāyazīd.

The death of Khurrem in April 1558 hastened the onset of civil war. Selīm and Bāyazīd, profiting from the unrest in Anatolia, recruited armies of their own among the Turcomans, the *levends* and the *sipāhīs*. Aid was indeed forthcoming, yet only at a price fraught with grave consequence to the Ottoman régime and, in itself, indicative of the resentment which the 'feudal' class and its allies felt for the 'men of the sultan': the princes had to confer on large numbers of their troops the status of janissaries, thus promising them entry into the privileged ranks of the *kullar*. The storm broke in the autumn of 1558. Bāyazīd, no less than Selīm, had long striven to obtain from the sultan a *sanjak* close to Istanbul. A geographical advantage might well decide the conflict, for, if Sulaimān should die, the throne would no doubt go to the son who first arrived at the Porte and there seized the *khazīne* or state treasury. The sultan now transferred Bāyazīd from Kutahya to the more remote Amasia, Selīm being moved at the same time from Manissa to the more distant Konya in Karaman. Bāyazīd, fearing that compliance would mean the ruin of his cause, rose in overt rebellion and thus left Sulaimān no choice but to intervene in favour of Selīm. Defeated in battle near Konya in the summer of 1559, Bāyazīd withdrew to Amasia and then, despairing of success, fled into Persia.

The sultan assembled troops along the eastern frontier and sought to induce the Uzbeg khan of Transoxania and the chieftains of the Caucasus to prepare for war against the Safawids. He was, however, loath to begin yet another Persian campaign. The shah, too, although determined to profit from his good fortune, had little desire to become involved in a new and dangerous conflict with the Ottomans. He agreed, therefore, after two years of diplomatic manœuvre, to surrender the ill-fated prince in return for a large financial reward. Bāyazīd was executed in September 1561. The long crisis had come to an end. There is no means of knowing how much of private anguish it had inflicted on the old sultan, but a glimpse of the truth can perhaps be discerned in the tragic words which the Venetian Donini ascribed to him: that he was glad to see the Muslims freed from the miseries of civil war between his children and to feel that he himself could live out the rest of his life in peace and not die in despair.[1]

Meanwhile, since the campaign of Diu in 1538, there had been spasmodic warfare against the Portuguese along the shores of Arabia and in the Persian Gulf. The Ottomans, having brought Basra under their direct control for the first time in 1546, established there a small fleet and an arsenal. Pīrī Re'īs, sailing from Suez with a large squadron in 1551, raided Maskat and Ormuz, made for Basra and then returned to Egypt, leaving most of his command to be blockaded in the Shatt al-'Arab. A new admiral, Murād Beg, tried in vain to break out of the Gulf in 1552. Sīdī 'Alī Re'īs, a seaman who had fought at Prevesa under the great Khair ad-Dīn, left Basra in 1554, lost some of his vessels in action with the Portuguese and, after suffering severe damage in a storm off the coast of Makran, found refuge at Surat in western India where the remnant of his fleet was disbanded. On the African shore of the Red Sea the Ottomans had long held Sawakin and now, as a further safeguard against the danger of an effective alliance between the Christians of Abyssinia and the Portuguese, occupied Masawwa' in 1557. The war at sea continued, although on a minor scale, far into the reign of Murād III (1574–95) when

---

[1] Cf. the Relazione of Marcantonio Donini (1562) in Alberi, *Relazioni degli Ambasciatori Veneti*, 3rd Series (Florence, 1840), vol. III, pp. 178–9: '...dicesi comunemente che...al cielo disse queste o altre simili parole, cioè: Sia laudato Iddio, che sì come ho sommamente desiderato di vivere tanto tempo che io avessi potuto vedere li musulmani liberi dalla tirannide che loro soprastava senza che venissero all'armi tra di loro, così mi sia felicemente ora succeduto, che da qui innanzi mi parrà di vivere vita veramente beata; che s'altrimenti mi fosse occorso, sarei vissuto e morto disperatissimo....,

a certain 'Alī Beg, with a squadron based on the Yemen, carried out raids to Maskat in the 'Uman and to Malindi and Mombasa on the coast of Africa.

The effort to maintain, in the Red Sea and in the Persian Gulf, a fleet able to resist the Portuguese demanded of the Ottomans a vast expenditure in men and material. Stores and equipment, guns and timber had to be brought overland to Suez or else down the rivers of Iraq to Basra. Construction methods valid in the Mediterranean would not serve in Arabian waters. Technicians and crews must therefore be found with the skill needed to build and man ships of an appropriate type. And yet, despite these and such other difficulties as the lack of good harbours in Arabia, the Ottomans achieved no small measure of success. It was clear, even before Sulaimān's death, that the Portuguese had not the strength to win absolute command of the Indian Ocean. As the Muslim counter-offensive gathered weight and momentum, the ancient traffic through the Red Sea and the Persian Gulf began to revive. A rich commerce flowed once more to Egypt, Alexandria receiving in the years around 1564 cargoes of pepper equal and perhaps superior in volume to those which were then arriving at Lisbon. Aleppo, the terminus for caravans from Iraq and Persia, was now to flourish as one of the great spice and silk markets of the Levant. A precarious equilibrium had been established between the old traffic and the new. The balance would incline at last irremediably in favour of the sea route around Africa, but only when maritime nations far stronger than the Portuguese—the Dutch and the English—broke into the waters of the Indian Ocean and won for themselves a dominant share of the eastern trade.

In the Mediterranean, too, there had been prolonged warfare since the battle of Prevesa in 1538. Charles V, knowing that he would soon be in conflict once more with France, struck hard at Algiers in October 1541, hoping thus to forestall the danger of renewed co-operation between the corsairs and the French naval forces. A splendid armada sailed from the Balearics to the African coast and there, in a sudden storm, suffered damage so severe that the campaign was abandoned. Khair ad-Dīn took his revenge in 1543 when he burnt Reggio in Calabria and, uniting with a squadron under the Duc d'Enghien, captured the town, though not the citadel, of Nice. The Ottoman fleet, to the great disgust of Christendom, wintered at Toulon, the port, with most of its people removed to make room for the Muslims, becoming, as it were, a second Istanbul. There now ensued a period of relative calm, for the emperor signed a peace with France in 1544 and was moreover included in the armistice that Sulaimān granted to Austria in 1547. Meanwhile, Khair ad-Dīn had died in the summer of 1546, leaving behind him a number of captains well qualified to continue his work, among them the famous Dragut (Torghūd Re'īs) who conquered Tripoli in North Africa from the Knights of St John in

1551 and thereafter so harried the western Mediterranean that Philip II of Spain resolved at last to crush him. A powerful force sent against Tripoli, where Torghūd now ruled in the name of the sultan, met, however, with disaster, the Ottoman fleet, commanded by Piyāle Pasha, surprising and routing the Christians at the island of Djerba in May 1560. This brilliant success encouraged Sulaimān to attempt the conquest of Malta. The *kapudan* Piyāle left Istanbul with a splendid fleet on 1 April 1565, the corsair squadrons of Algiers and Tripoli being also summoned to the campaign. Most bitter fighting marked the course of the siege, but the Knights of St John held out with desperate valour until at last, in September, strong reinforcements came to their aid and so compelled the Ottomans to withdraw.

The Christian cause triumphed at Malta and again at the battle of Lepanto in 1571, five years after the death of Sulaimān, yet these celebrated victories led to no enduring advantage. A far more decisive campaign was waged in 1574, when the Ottomans conquered Tunis and so resolved in their own favour a vital issue of the sea war—whether North Africa would be saved or lost to Muslim rule. Algiers, Tripoli and Tunis now owed allegiance to the Porte and stood, moreover, on the threshold of a golden era as the three great corsair states of the Mediterranean. The threat of Christian domination had in fact been averted in North Africa for some two and a half centuries.

The agreement of 1562 with Austria became null and void on the death of the Emperor Ferdinand in 1564. Sulaimān, although willing to renew the peace, was angered at the outbreak of hostilities between the Emperor Maximilian II and John Sigismund of Transylvania. The refusal of his demand that the imperialists restore certain towns belonging to the *voivode* made war inevitable. The sultan marched once more to Belgrade in the summer of 1566. It was to be his thirteenth and last campaign. A powerful column under the Vizier Pertev Pasha had been sent off in advance to capture Gyula on the river Körös in western Transylvania. A much stronger force, with Sulaimān himself in command, moved towards Szigetvár. Of these fortresses the first yielded, and the second was stormed, at the beginning of September—but just before the fall of Szigetvár death had come to the old sultan.

The reign of Sulaimān owed its splendour to far more than the great campaigns of conquest. Administrators and statesmen of exceptional skill, like the grand viziers Ibrāhīm, Rustem and Mehemmed Sokollu, flourished at this time. Among the *'ulemā*—the theologians and jurisconsults trained in the *Sharīʻa* or Sacred Law of Islām—none were more illustrious than Kemālpasha-zāde and Abu Suʻūd. Bāki, the prince of poets, and Sinān, a famous architect, gave lustre to an age resplendent with the rich unfolding of all that is most typical in Ottoman culture and civilisation. The sultan devoted large revenues to frontier defence, as in the repair of fortresses at Rhodes, Belgrade, Buda and Temesvár, and to the building of mosques, bridges, aqueducts and other public utilities, for instance at Mecca, Baghdad, Damascus, Konya and Kaffa. Above all, he strove to embellish his capital on the Golden Horn and, in pursuit of this aim, did much to complete the enormous task, begun by Mehemmed II, of transforming Constantinople, impoverished and depopulated during the last years of Byzantine rule, into Ottoman Istanbul, the proud centre of a vast empire.

To his people Sulaimān became known as Kānūnī, the law-maker. He could not alter or violate the *Sharīʻa*, a code embracing wide areas of human thought and conduct which in the Christian world belong to the realm of secular and not of religious affairs. The edicts bearing his name, although to the western mind somewhat narrow in range and in character more interpretative than original, represent none the less a long effort to improve and adapt to the needs of a new age the complex structure of the Ottoman state. Men of his own time emphasized his zeal for justice and the Venetian Navagero paid high tribute indeed when he wrote that Sulaimān, provided he were well informed, did wrong to no one.

Among those who saw the sultan in all his power and splendour not a few have left on record their abiding impression of his personal qualities and character. Navagero discerned in his face a 'marvellous grandeur'. To Andrea Dandolo he was a monarch wise and just, yet ruthless beyond measure when danger threatened his empire or himself. Busbecq, describing how the sultan went to the mosque soon after the return of the Ottoman fleet from its brilliant success at Djerba, read in his countenance no more than a stern and impenetrable reserve, 'so self-contained was the heart of that grand old man, so schooled to meet each change of fortune however great'. The historian confirms, refurbishes and sometimes corrodes the fame of the dead. A final verdict on the true role of Sulaimān in the triumphs and achievements of his reign must rest with future research, but there is little reason to think that he will not continue to be for us, as he was for the Christian world of his time, the Magnificent Sultan.

CHAPTER XVIII

RUSSIA, 1462–1583

W HEN Ivan III succeeded his father, Vasily II, in 1462 a new era in the history of the grand principality of Moscow began. By the end of Vasily's troubled reign the hegemony of Moscow over the other Great Russian principalities and republics had been confirmed. But Tver, Ryazan, Rostov and Yaroslavl were still independent; the republics of Novgorod and Pskov and the town of Vyatka owed no allegiance to the grand prince of Moscow; and the Russian lands in the south west along the Dnieper and the upper reaches of the Oka were under Lithuanian control. Furthermore, the majority of the Great Russian people were still, in name at least, tributaries of the khan of the Golden Horde.

The early years of Ivan's reign were years of preparation for the major tasks that lay ahead. Before Ivan could set about the conquest of the Ukrainian lands from Lithuania, the eastern and southern frontiers had to be secured; before the remaining independent Great Russian states could be securely annexed to Moscow and the lands of Muscovy extended to the Baltic and the White Sea, Novgorod and her northern empire had to be subdued; and before Russia could emerge as an international power with her pride and dignity restored, the degrading Tatar yoke had to be thrown off.

There is little information of hostile activity on the western or southern boundaries during the sixties of the fifteenth century, and Ivan was able to concentrate his attention on the powerful and aggressive Tatars of Kazan. As a result of a series of campaigns against Kazan (1467–9), which apart from the great summer expedition of 1469 were little more than full-scale reconnaissances, not only was valuable experience in invading Kazan territory gained, but also a period of calm ensued and Moscow's eastern frontiers were not violated during the nine years following the armistice concluded in the autumn of 1469. With his eastern frontier thus temporally secured, Ivan was able during the following decade to devote his energies to the problem of Novgorod. The great autonomous republic had long been split into mutually hostile factions—the pro-Lithuanian oligarchy supported by the 'greater folk' (*bol'shie lyudi*) and the pro-Muscovite mass of the 'lesser folk' (*men'shie lyudi*). After the Peace of Yazhelbitsy (1456) it became clear that Novgorod could not maintain her traditional independence for long. Ivan had only to wait for the pro-Lithuanian faction to compromise itself sufficiently with Casimir, king of Poland and grand prince of Lithuania, for him to step in and save his 'patrimony' (*otchina*) from the hereditary enemies of Orthodoxy, thus rallying to his side the majority of the population and justifying his actions on religious grounds. The opportunity arose at the end of the 1460's when Novgorod appealed to Casimir, asking him to annex the city, to submit the archbishop to the jurisdiction of the metropolitan of Kiev and to send them a prince. Whether or not the Lithuanian prince who appeared in Novgorod at the end of 1470 came in fact as a result of Novgorod's invitation, his presence in the city probably decided Ivan to take action, and his departure (March 1471), hastened no doubt by the growing threat from Moscow, caused the pro-Lithuanian party to make a last effort to interest Casimir in their plight by proposing a treaty. But before it could be ratified, and before Casimir could offer any aid to his ally, Ivan had decisively defeated the Novgorodians (1471). Novgorod was forced to renounce all further dealings with Lithuania and to cede considerable areas of her northern empire to Moscow.

Yet the town still remained, in name at least, a 'free city' and retained her right to choose her archbishop. Only in the beginning of 1478 did she formally lose her independence. After an outburst of anti-Muscovite feeling within the city and an indignant refusal of the *veche* (popular assembly) to recognise the grand prince's sovereignty over Novgorod, Ivan surrounded the city (November 1477) and forced the republic to accept his terms. He demanded the removal of the assembly's great bell—in other words the dissolution of the *veche*—the abolition of the post of *posadnik* (locally elected mayor), and the complete sovereignty of the grand prince over the city. As for territorial demands, Ivan expropriated ten cantons (*volosti*) of the archbishop's possessions, half the land belonging to six of the wealthiest monasteries and all the cantons of Torzhok. But it needed still more drastic measures to subdue the enemies of Moscow in Novgorod. Reports of treasonable communications with Casimir and the Teutonic Order were the cause of Ivan's third campaign (October 1479), which was followed by mass executions and deportations. Towards the end of the 1480's further plots were discovered, as a result of which over 8000 of the wealthiest and most influential citizens were removed to the neighbourhood of Moscow and replaced by more reliable elements from the interior. In this same year (1489) the last of Novgorod's former colonies, Vyatka, was subdued by force. All the northern lands from Karelia to the Urals were now Muscovite territory. With her empire lost, her best citizens deported and her trade depleted (in 1494 Ivan closed the Hanseatic office in the city), Novgorod could no longer offer resistance to Moscow. Her subjection was complete. It was as though the last vestiges of political freedom had disappeared from the Russian land.

As for the remaining Great Russian territories still independent of Moscow at the beginning of Ivan's reign, none were in a position to offer serious resistance to the grand prince. In 1463 and 1474 the principalities of Yaroslavl and Rostov respectively were annexed by treaty. The fate of Tver was decided by the fall of Novgorod, for from 1478 the lands of Tver were surrounded by Muscovite territory; in the autumn of 1485, after the flight of her last grand prince, Tver willingly accepted the sovereignty of Moscow. The independent republic of Pskov only nominally retained her autonomy throughout Ivan's reign. Her annexation was merely a question of time. The same was the case with Ryazan, whose foreign policy was managed entirely by Moscow and whose princes were little more than vassals of the grand prince.

By the end of the 1470's the process of 'gathering together' the grand prince's patrimonies was more or less complete; in an emergency Ivan could rely on military support from all the Great Russian territories. Before applying himself, however, to his major task, the wresting of the Ukraine from Lithuania, Ivan had still to reckon with Casimir's ally in the south, the Tatars of the Golden Horde. In 1472 their khan, Ahmed, as a result of an agreement with the king, had invaded Muscovite territory, and Ivan, realising the danger of this partnership, sought an ally in the Crimean Tatars. At first Mengli-Girey, khan of the Crimea, was unwilling to commit himself. But after being temporarily driven out of the Crimea (since 1475 under Turkish suzerainty) by Casimir's ally, Ahmed, he agreed to a pact with Moscow (early 1480). Moscow and the Crimea were to act in unison in offensive or defensive war against Casimir and each agreed to help the other in case of attack by Ahmed. Yet in spite of this alliance Ivan can scarcely have felt himself secure at the beginning of 1480. For not only was the Livonian Order (as a result, no doubt, of an agreement with Ahmed) showing unusually intense activity on the borders of Pskovite territory, but Ivan's brothers, Andrey and Boris, chose this very moment to desert. Fortunately for Ivan, Casimir refused aid to the brothers, and in the autumn they were successfully persuaded to rejoin their elder brother in face of a Tatar invasion; for on 8 October 1480 Ahmed's armies had appeared on the river Ugra, the south-west frontier of Muscovite territory. After a preliminary skirmish both sides exercised extreme caution, Ivan through fear of, and Ahmed in anticipation of, Lithuanian intervention. But Casimir showed no signs of joining his ally. For not only did a timely attack by Mengli-Girey occupy him on his southern border, but also, according to the chronicles, 'he had his own internal disorders (*usobitsy*)'. Realising perhaps that a major campaign against Moscow was impossible without the co-operation of Casimir,[1] Ahmed withdrew his entire army. His capital was sacked by Tatars from the district east of the Volga, and he himself was murdered early in 1481.

The retreat from the Ugra marked the end, after two and a half centuries, of the Tatar yoke, raised Moscow's prestige in the eyes of the

[1] An equally convincing reason for Ahmed's retreat was given by the chronicler of Kazan who mentions a raiding party sent by Ivan to the lower reaches of the Volga.

Crimean and Nogai Tatars and enabled the grand prince to enter the field of European diplomacy, no longer as a vassal of the khan, but as a sovereign in his own right. Only Ahmed's children remained a nuisance and a potential danger to Moscow, a danger which Ivan sought to remove by diplomacy rather than by force of arms. Again he was obliged to seek the friendship of the Crimean Tatars, who after Ahmed's demise had entered into diplomatic relations with Casimir. In 1482 Mengli was persuaded to break with the king and invade his lands. The resulting sack of Kiev (September 1482) was a major diplomatic victory for Moscow. From now on Mengli was the firm ally of the grand prince. It was less easy to bring the Tatars of Kazan into the Muscovite coalition, but by taking advantage of dynastic strife within the khanate and by backing now the one now the other pretender to the throne, Ivan was able to secure his ends. In 1487 his armies placed Mengli's step-son, the pro-Muscovite Muhammed Emin, upon the throne. His accession won for Moscow the friendship too of the Nogai Tatars with whom Muhammed was linked by marriage ties. The coalition was too strong for the remnants of the Golden Horde. After several abortive attempts to invade the Crimea, the children of Ahmed were soundly beaten in November 1491, and although their final defeat at the hands of Mengli was inflicted only in 1502, from the beginning of the 1490's they no longer constituted a serious threat to the southern boundaries of Moscow.

Ivan's attempts to form a coalition with the western powers against Casimir met with less success. In 1483, by marrying his eldest son Ivan to Elena, daughter of Stephen IV of Moldavia, Ivan secured a valuable ally on the south-western borders of Lithuania. Diplomatic relations with Hungary, which began in 1482, were conditioned by King Matthias Corvinus's attempts to inveigle Ivan into a war with Casimir which would divert Poland from Hungary. But when in 1490 Matthias died and was succeeded by Casimir's son, Ladislas (Vladislav), king of Bohemia, and the kingdoms of Bohemia and Hungary were united under the Jagiello dynasty, all diplomatic relations with Moscow ceased. Relations with the empire were equally fruitless. The king of the Romans was intent on acquiring Ivan's aid in his struggle with Ladislas of Hungary. And when in 1493 Maximilian tactlessly suggested the formation of an anti-Turkish league which would include both Poland and Moscow, Ivan realised that no help could be expected from the Habsburgs. Diplomatic relations with the Empire died a natural death.

In spite of Ivan's diplomatic failures in the west, he was now in a stronger position than ever before to begin the war with Lithuania. Thanks to his neutralisation of Kazan and his friendship with the Nogai and Crimean Tatars his eastern and southern flanks were secure. Thanks to a timely and successful invasion of Livonia in 1481, resulting in a ten years' truce, he had nothing to fear from the Teutonic Knights. And by the end of the 1480's Novgorod had ceased to cause Moscow anxiety. The first Lithuanian war was a half-hearted affair, a series of frontier skirmishes and parleys, and by the end of 1491 it had virtually fizzled out. But in the following year Casimir died unexpectedly. The Lithuanians hastened to appoint his son Alexander grand prince of Lithuania, the throne of Poland falling to his elder son, John Albert. War along the whole frontier flared up. The weak Alexander was unable to cope with the situation. In vain he sought help from Poland. Willing to secure peace on any terms, the Lithuanian nobles at length proposed a marriage alliance between Alexander and Ivan. Peace was concluded in 1494. By the terms of the treaty Ivan, who insisted on the title of 'Sovereign (*Gosudar*') of all Russia', won considerable territorial gains, the whole of the Vyazma area and the minor principalities on either side of the upper Oka being ceded to Moscow. In the following year Ivan's daughter Elena, with the strictest injunctions to maintain her Orthodox faith, was despatched to Wilno, where she was married to the Catholic Alexander.

By the end of the century the time was even more favourable for Ivan to launch his major campaign against Lithuania. His scrupulously tactful relations with the Porte throughout the eighties and the nineties assured him of the continued support of the sultan's vassal, Mengli-Girey. His friendship with John of Denmark and his war with Sweden (1495–6), which had facilitated John's conquest of Sweden (1496–7), assured him of Scandinavian neutrality. And on the very eve of the war the intensification of anti-Orthodox propaganda and the attempt to enforce the principles of the Union of Florence upon the unwilling Orthodox population of Lithuania caused several Russian princes from the border districts to offer their services to Moscow.

The war began in the summer of 1500. One Muscovite army moved south and occupied virtually all the territory between the Desna and the Dnieper, reaching Putivl and Chernigov in the south and Gomel in the west. The remainder of Ivan's forces threatened the area of Smolensk. After the great defeat of the Lithuanians on the river Vedrosha near Dorogobuzh (July 1500), the position of Lithuania was desperate. Alexander tried in vain to turn Mengli-Girey and Stephen of Moldavia against their ally. The kings of Hungary and Poland offered Ivan their mediation and threatened him, should he not accept it, with their intervention. But the only active help Alexander received came from the Livonian Order. The Germans invaded the territory of Pskov, but their successes were cut short by an attack of dysentery. In retaliation Ivan despatched an army to Livonia. In the autumn of 1501 the Germans were overwhelmingly beaten at Helmed near Dorpat.

In 1502 Ivan resumed the attack against Lithuania. His aim was Smolensk. While his troops besieged the city, a vast army of Crimean Tatars ravaged Galicia and Volynia, reaching as far west as Cracow. But this gigantic raid was too southerly to assist the Muscovites, and in the autumn the siege of Smolensk was raised. Again the king of Hungary offered his mediation; this time his ambassadors brought with them to Moscow a plea from Pope Alexander VI to cease hostilities and join in a crusade against the Turks. Ladislas's offer was rejected, but in the following year a six-year armistice was concluded. The terms were wholly favourable to Moscow. Alexander (king of Poland since his brother's death in 1501) yielded the occupied territories of eastern Lithuania (roughly bounded by the rivers Desna and Sejm in the south and Dnieper in the west) and in the north the territory bordering the upper reaches of the western Dvina and Dnieper. Muscovy's new frontier thus constituted a direct threat to Smolensk and Kiev. Although Ivan had not succeeded in wresting from Lithuania all those lands that had formerly been Russian, at least the foundation for future conquests in the west had been laid.

Much of the success of Ivan's foreign policy and of his 'gathering of the Russian lands' was due to the fact that his reign was comparatively free from internal disorders. The grand prince showed himself capable of handling with skill not only foreign ambassadors, but also his own family and his boyars.[1] And by the end of his reign he had established himself as undisputed master in the land, feared and grudgingly respected by even the most conservative elements at his court. In all his dealings with his family he showed the same inflexibility of will and ruthless singlemindedness. For Ivan was not satisfied to be *primus inter pares* within his family: the 'Sovereign of All Russia', the 'Tsar and Autocrat' (the style used by the metropolitan at the coronation of his grandson) could tolerate no limitation of his power, no claim on the part of his brothers to what they considered to be their ancient rights. While Ivan, encouraged at every step by the official voice of the Church, progressed towards absolute autocracy, his brothers lagged behind, unable and unwilling to rid themselves of the traditional sense of equality within the princely family, the legacy of the early Ryurikovichi. The rule of primogeniture had indeed once and for all been vindicated by Vasily II, and we hear of no attempt by Ivan's brothers to claim the throne. It was rather their desire to defend their ancient rights as appanage princes, and their anger at Ivan's unwillingness to share his patrimony with them, that led them into disaffection and revolt. The trouble began in 1472 when Ivan's eldest brother, Yury, died childless. In his will he made no mention of his appanage which Ivan, much to the disgust of his remaining three brothers, proceeded to appropriate. In the following year treaties were drawn up between Ivan and his two eldest brothers, Andrey and Boris, according to which the latter promised to hold Ivan and his son as 'elder brothers', not to

---

[1] Boyars—here used to designate the hereditary aristocracy of Muscovite society. A special meaning (a specific senior rank in the governmental and military hierarchy) was common in the sixteenth century.

seek the throne of Ivan or his successor, and not to interfere in the escheat of Yury.

The brothers' grievances were still further increased when one Dmitry Obolensky-Lyko, who had fallen foul of the grand prince, exercised the ancient right of all 'free servants' (*vol'nye slugi*) and transferred his allegiance from the grand prince to Ivan's brother, Boris, only to be arrested on the latter's territory by Ivan and removed to Moscow. Although this was not the first instance of the limitation of the right to 'depart', it was the first time that this right had been denied in the territory of a member of the grand prince's family. Boris vented his grievances to his elder brother, Andrey:

> Our brother Yury died—all his patrimony fell to the lot of the grand prince and he gave us no share in it; together with us he took Great Novgorod—but to us he gave no share of the spoil. And now he seizes without judgment whosoever departs from him to us. He considers his own brothers lower than the boyars.

In 1480 the two brothers openly revolted against the grand prince. With their families and their courts they proceeded west to Novgorod territory in the hope of gaining the support of Casimir. Faced with the danger of internecine war, Ivan sent the archbishop of Rostov to plead with his rebellious brothers. But Andrey and Boris received no aid from any quarter. In the early winter they returned with their troops to defend the Ugra line against the Tatars. The rebellion was over. But in the critical years of preparation for the Lithuanian war Ivan could ill afford to risk another armed revolt within the country. By revising his treaties with Andrey and Boris (1481 and 1486) he forced his brothers formally to acknowledge his own territorial acquisitions (the patrimonies of Yury and Andrey the Younger, who died in 1481, and the lands of Novgorod and Tver) and to repeat their vows to abstain from all foreign relations. In spite of these declarations of loyalty, however, Ivan continued to suspect Andrey of treachery and waited only for a pretext to rid himself of his brother. In 1491 Andrey provided the pretext by failing to send his troops to the aid of the Crimean Tatars. He was perfidiously arrested and imprisoned with his sons. Three years later he died in prison. When the metropolitan interceded for him, Ivan is reported to have said: 'When I die he will seek the throne; if he himself does not get it, then he will stir up my children and they will war one with the other.'

Ivan's family troubles did not end with the removal of Andrey. In the late 1490's a dynastic crisis occurred in which were involved not only the leading representatives of the Muscovite aristocracy and the Church, but also the closest members of the grand prince's family. In 1490 the heir presumptive, Ivan Ivanovich, Ivan's son by his first wife, died. Ivan was faced with the problem of nominating as his successor either his grandson, Dmitry, the son of Ivan Ivanovich and Elena Stepanovna, or Vasily, his eldest son by his second wife, Sofia Palaeologa. Dmitry, as son of the late heir-apparent who himself had borne the title of grand prince, undoubtedly had the stronger claim. Furthermore, he and his mother appear to have been supported by the leading boyars at the court, who had little love for Sofia Palaeologa and who presumably saw in Dmitry the ideal prince—malleable, young and weak. Vasily, on the other hand, could claim imperial descent through his mother, niece of the last emperor of the east. To judge from the scanty references in the chronicles, his supporters were the *d'yaki* and the petty nobility at court, the 'boyar children',[1] the new class of *dvoryanstvo* or professionals who owed their rank and station not to their birth but to their service—in other words, men whose existence depended on the sovereign they served, the natural enemies of the privileged aristocracy and the fervent supporters of complete autocracy. Behind Vasily and Sofia there also stood the most influential churchman of the day, Joseph, abbot of Volokolamsk, who opposed Elena, if for no other reason, on the grounds that she was tainted with the heresy of the Judaisers.[2]

In 1497 the grand prince's hand was forced. A plot to seize the treasury and remove Dmitry from the scene was revealed. The ring-leaders, mainly boyar children and *d'yaki*, were summarily executed. Vasily was placed under palace arrest, and Sofia, accused of harbouring 'women with philtres' (with the aim, presumably, of poisoning Dmitry), fell into disgrace. On 4 February 1498 Dmitry was crowned grand prince of Vladimir, Moscow and Novgorod. Of the causes of this temporary set-back for Vasily and Sofia the chroniclers only mention the court intrigue. But it is interesting to note that in 1497 hostilities broke out again between Elena's father, Stephen of Moldavia, and Alexander of Lithuania, and that many of the executed boyar children had links with the courts of former appanage princes and with Muscovite emigrés in Lithuania. The triumph of the Elena-Dmitry faction, however, was short-lived. In January 1499 two leading boyars of the Muscovite court, Ivan Yurevich Patrikeev and his son Vasily, were forcibly tonsured, and Patrikeev's son-in-law, Semen Ryapolovsky-Starodubsky, was executed. Their removal was followed by the triumph of Vasily, who was crowned grand prince of Novgorod and Pskov. Three years later Elena and Dmitry were placed under arrest. Dmitry was bereft of his title of grand prince and Vasily was crowned grand prince of Vladimir and Moscow, autocrat of all Russia (14 April 1502). The chroniclers throw no light on the causes of Ivan's *volteface*. The persuasive powers of Joseph of Volokolamsk may have influenced Ivan in his decision to reinstate his wife and son. But the

---

[1] Boyar children—members of the service gentry descended from impoverished boyar families; *d'yaki*—originally clerks or minor secretaries who in the sixteenth century were employed in more leading positions, some of them even reaching the grand prince's privy council.

[2] See below, p. 545.

removal of the boyars may well have been more connected with Russo-Lithuanian affairs than with the dynastic problem; for the Patrikeevs and Ryapolovsky had been intimately concerned with the peace negotiations of 1494 and the betrothal of Elena and Alexander, and it is possible that they opposed Ivan's aggressive foreign policy at the time when Ivan was actively preparing for war with Lithuania.

Whatever the causes of the dynastic crisis of 1497–9, one fact clearly emerges: by the end of Ivan's reign the Muscovite aristocracy was shorn of much of its power and was no longer able effectively to oppose the grand prince. Indeed, in the second half of the fifteenth century a striking change took place in the relationship of grand prince and boyar, of sovereign and subject. The old appanage principalities had virtually ceased to exist as such. Only a few descendants of previous appanage princes retained their patrimonies on anything like the scale their fore-fathers had known. Many, ruined financially, their lands parcelled out among the members of their families or mortgaged to the monasteries, had no alternative but to enter the service of the grand prince of Moscow as 'service princes' (*sluzhebnye knyazya*). And with the emergence of 'service princes' at the court of Moscow, the old idea of 'free service' and 'free servants' naturally disappeared. For the essence of 'free service' lay in the right of departure (*ot'ezd*), the right of all freemen to choose which prince to serve. Formerly these rights had been freely exercised between one independent principality and another and had been guaranteed by every inter-princely treaty. But with the gathering of the Russian lands and the annexation by Moscow of virtually all the Great Russian principalities, freedom of service became an anachronism. A prince or boyar might transfer his allegiance to the grand prince. But to 'depart' from the grand prince to an appanage prince, or, worse still, to the grand prince of Lithuania, was little short of treason.

But merely to remove the traditional formula ('our boyars and free servants shall have freedom [to depart]') from inter-princely agreements was not sufficient to prevent defection. In the case of the distinguished boyar, Prince Daniel Dmitrievich Kholmsky, suspected no doubt of planning treachery or desertion, Ivan took more stringent measures. In 1474 Kholmsky was arrested. He was released only after signing a pledge of allegiance (*klyatvennaya zapis'*) in which he stated: 'I will serve my sovereign and his children unto death and will depart...to no one else.' Eight guarantors (including the metropolitan) stood security for him. In the event of his defection they stood to forfeit 8000 roubles. Although this method of binding a service prince to his suzerain by pledge and security had been practised in Tver and Lithuania as early as the second half of the fourteenth century, it was the first time it had been applied by a grand prince of Moscow.

It must not be imagined, however, that a prince or a boyar, on entering the service of the grand prince, was deprived of his territorial rights. In most cases he retained and continued to administer his freehold estates. Furthermore, he was free to dispose of his patrimony at will, to mortgage, sell, exchange or bequeath. But the Muscovite court and the Muscovite army was not staffed exclusively by the landed aristocracy. In many cases the princes and boyars entering the grand prince's service were accompanied by their retinues, their servants and their men-at-arms, who in turn became the 'service people' of the grand prince. With the gradual centralisation of the government during Ivan's reign which brought an ever-increasing number of men into the service of the grand prince, it became necessary to reward this 'service class' not with hereditary freehold estates, but with lands granted on a basis of life tenure, the ownership of which was exclusively conditioned by the terms of service of the tenant. This system of granting *pomestya* was not new; the first record of a grant of conditionally owned land can be found in the will of Ivan I. But it was only in the reign of Ivan III that the *pomestye* system became generalised, all but superseding the granting of patrimonies (*votchiny*) in reward for service.

The rapid growth of the *pomestye* system inevitably led to a land crisis. The private domains of the grand prince were insufficient to meet the needs of the government; so too were the state 'black' lands. The demand for land could only be met by distributing confiscated estates in annexed territories. Of these the lands of Novgorod provided by far the richest supply. Already in 1479 and 1484 we hear of small-scale evictions of tenants from Novgorod to the interior. But in 1488 and 1489 the first mass deportations took place. Over 8000 boyars, 'well-to-do folk' (*zhit'i lyudi*) and merchants were removed together with their families and settled in the eastern areas of the Muscovite territory. Their estates were distributed in *pomestya* among 'service men' from the 'lower lands', the districts of Moscow and her neighbouring territories. The exact dimensions of this mass resettlement (*ispomeshcheniye*) are not known, but from the details available it would appear that some 1600–1800 service men were thus rewarded. Of these the sources mention 73 members of various princely families, 175 representatives of old Muscovite boyar families and 280 '*posluzhil'tsy*', former bondmen of Muscovite and Novgorod boyars whose lands had been confiscated, professional soldiers who had received their freedom on entering the service of the grand prince. From an examination of the topographical details of the resettlement it is possible to assess the importance attached by Ivan to this latter category of *posluzhil'tsy*. The largest percentage of *pomestya* in the vulnerable frontier zones were entrusted to them; and later the garrison of Ivangorod (built in 1492 on the east bank of the Narova river opposite the town of Narva) was manned almost exclusively by former servants of Novgorod boyars. By thus remunerating his service men with land which it was in their own interest to defend, Ivan created in areas of potential danger efficient military cadres of men who owed their freedom and their land to their sovereign on condition that they rendered him faithful service.

Although the confiscated territories of Novgorod converted into *pomestya* amounted to something like a million hectares and although similar methods were employed in other districts annexed by Moscow, still further land was required by the State to satisfy the needs of the ever-growing service class. It was not surprising that Ivan should turn his eyes on the vast estates of the Church. During the fourteenth and fifteenth centuries the monasteries had increased out of all proportion to their former size and number. Thanks to their true colonising instinct, their acute sense of business, and their ability to exploit the pious generosity of the princes and boyars, the abbots filled their coffers and increased their domains, mainly at the expense of the impoverished landowners. Huge areas were bequeathed, mortgaged and sold to the monasteries. Their agents had no rivals on the land market. But the Church had no desire to sacrifice even a part of its wealth to the State. And the leading ecclesiastical polemicists were careful to surround the Church's possessions with an aura of inviolability. It is true that after the fall of Novgorod Ivan had expropriated considerable property belonging to the archbishop and the monasteries of Novgorod and in 1500 had converted an unspecified amount of Novgorod Church property into *pomestya*. But these were isolated cases. Secularisation of Church lands other than on Novgorod territory was clearly unthinkable without the blessing and co-operation of the hierarchy. The tradition of inviolability was too strong within the Church. Furthermore, the time had not yet come when the grand prince of Moscow could treat his clergy as he pleased; while preaching the crusade against the infidel Latins of Lithuania, he could ill afford to offend the representatives of Orthodoxy at home; a rift between Church and State would hardly present an attractive picture to those Orthodox elements in Lithuanian Russia whose support and desertion he was so anxious to obtain. The best he could do was to attempt to check the flow of privately owned lands into the hands of the bishops and abbots by forbidding landowners in certain newly annexed territories to bequeath or sell their estates without first informing the grand prince.

If Ivan was not willing openly to broach the question of the secularisation of Church lands, discontented elements within the Church were. At the conclusion of the Church council of 1503, convoked in Moscow to deal with certain flagrant abuses within the Church, the Elder (*starets*) Nil Sorsky proposed 'that monasteries should not own lands, and monks...should feed themselves by the work of their hands'. Nil himself undoubtedly acted from disinterested motives; for him monastic estates were 'the deadly poison of monasticism', corrupting the monk and distracting him from the true spirit of piety. But a later source states that many of Nil's supporters from the districts beyond the Volga had been expressly summoned to the council by the grand prince. Nil's proposal was countered by Joseph of Volokolamsk whose objections were frankly practical. Landless monasteries were unlikely to attract 'pious and noble men,' he said, 'and if there are no pious monks where shall we find metropolitans, archbishops and bishops?' The majority of the members of the council, who needed no persuading, supported Joseph. But they reckoned without the stubbornness of the grand prince. He demanded that an answer to Nil's proposal be brought to him personally. Three times the council's decision, bolstered up with canonical and historical justifications, was reported to him before he agreed to accept their findings. The 'possessors' or 'Josephians', as the supporters of Joseph were called, had won the day. And although Nil's followers, the 'non-possessors' or 'Trans-Volga Elders', held their ground in the ensuing polemical battles and were later to attract to their camp men of the calibre of Maxim the Greek and the Abbot Artemy, the question of the secularisation of Church property had been decided once and for all. Neither Ivan nor his successors were able to reverse the decision of the council of 1503; and throughout the sixteenth century the estates of the Church remained for the most part outside the grasp of the State.

In spite of the victory won by the Church in 1503 and the tenacity and astuteness displayed by her leaders, the relations between Church and State were already becoming one-sided during Ivan's reign. In questions concerning the faith the Church required the grand prince to sanction her decisions and to punish her wrong-doers; in political controversies she had no alternative but to side with the autocrat; and in the delicate task of formulating the relationship between the temporal power of the State and the spiritual authority of the Church, she found herself obliged by circumstances to recognise the superiority of the former. No one realised more clearly than Joseph of Volokolamsk the theoretical and practical limits of the Church's authority. In his campaign against the heresy of the Judaisers he saw just how obstructive the 'defender of the faith' could be if it suited his purposes. And the heresy was indeed a dangerous one, both to the faith and to the State. It was introduced into Novgorod from Kiev in 1470. Its members denied the fundamental tenets of Christianity and practised certain Jewish rites. It quickly spread to Moscow, infecting not only members of Ivan's court (including his daughter-in-law, Elena), but also, if we are to believe Joseph, the metropolitan himself. With unremitting tenacity Archbishop Gennady, and later Joseph, campaigned against the heretics. But there was little they could do without the co-operation of the grand prince who himself had been responsible in 1479 for the appointment of two leading heretics to important ecclesiastical posts in Moscow, and whose own daughter-in-law was tainted with the heresy. Ivan, it is true, had convened a Church council in 1490 against the heretics, but the punishments awarded to those found guilty were mild, and the heresy continued to flourish and spread. Joseph wrote to those in power; he talked in private with Ivan; he urged the grand prince's confessor to use his influence. At last in 1504, two years after the disgrace of Elena and her son, Ivan consented to convene a second council. Many of the leading heretics were excommunicated and burned; some recanted and were imprisoned; and although Ivan ordered their release a year later, Joseph's task was virtually completed.

It was no coincidence that Joseph's formulation of the theory of the supreme power of the sovereign was closely linked with the struggle against the Judaisers. Indeed, it was to the grand prince as protector of the faith that Joseph addressed his monumental work against the heretics, the *Illuminator* (*Prosvetitel'*): the tsar's main duty, he argued, was the safeguarding of Orthodoxy; the punishment of the wicked the responsibility and duty of the State. And so long as the grand prince was niggardly in these duties, the obedience due to the sovereign remained, in Joseph's definition, significantly qualified: 'obey not a tsar who leads you into impiety and evil'. It was only after the Council of 1504 that the sovereign received his apotheosis. 'The tsar by nature is like unto all men,' we read in the final chapter of the *Illuminator*, 'but in authority he is like unto God Almighty.' At the same time the ecclesiastical panegyrists of Muscovy were elaborating those theories of Moscow's Byzantine heritage which were later, during the rule of Vasily III, crystallised in the writings of the monk Filofey. Ivan was styled 'the second Constantine'; Moscow 'the third Rome', 'the new Israel'. But these theories were expressed almost exclusively by the Church. Little or no mention is made of Moscow's Byzantine heritage in the official writings of the day—in diplomatic correspondence, epistles, wills, speeches, decrees. The explanation of the grand prince's reluctance to make use of the extravagant formulae prepared by the Church and to lay claim to the heritage of his wife can be found in his foreign policy. The goal of his military and diplomatic ventures was not the conquest of Constantinople from the sultan, the suzerain of his Crimean ally, but the reconquest from Lithuania and Poland of the lands formerly possessed by his Kievan predecessors. The title for which he demanded recognition was not emperor of all the Orthodox east, but sovereign of all Russia.

Ivan died on 27 October 1505. His death was not marked by extravagant eulogies from the pen of the chroniclers. There were no signs of national mourning. Yet he had done more than continue the work of his predecessors. He was not just another descendant of the house of Daniel of Moscow, stubborn and uninspiring, reaping the harvest sown by his forefathers. He was distinguished from his predecessors and his immediate successors by a remarkable shrewdness and foresight, by an uncanny grasp of international affairs. His military campaigns may not have been spectacular, but they were highly successful. His diplomatic methods may appear clumsy, but they were effective. He had few of the attributes of the brilliant or popular ruler. His indecisive behaviour in the face of the enemy in 1480 evoked the censure of the populace and the reproof of the clergy. Disliked by his boyars, he nevertheless commanded their fear and respect. Of his private life we know little. His only pleasures to have been recorded were those of the table. In appearance he was tall, thin and slightly stooping. So awe-inspiring were his features that women were said to have fainted at the mere sight of him.

By his will Ivan assured his eldest son of complete political supremacy. Vasily received two-thirds of all his father's estates; the remaining third, consisting of towns and districts of lesser importance, was divided among his four brothers. Furthermore, escheats of any of the younger brothers were to revert without partition to the grand prince. In Moscow itself all the principal revenues derived from the law courts and the customs, which had hitherto been divided among the grand prince and his brothers, were allocated almost exclusively to Vasily. Even in their own territories Vasily's brothers found themselves deprived of many of their former rights. They were forbidden to mint their own coin or to conduct relations with foreign powers. In their estates adjoining Moscow and in the capital itself they lost not only their right to trade, but also the right to judge major criminal offences.

Vasily was thus firmly established on the throne. Ivan had good reasons for taking his precautions; both the Livonian master and the king of Poland expected Vasily's accession to be accompanied by internal disorders. But there were no manifestations of unrest. Dmitry and his mother remained safely in prison; their supporters maintained a healthy silence. And Vasily, though young, was not weak. If anything he was endowed with more stubbornness than his father. He was certainly more intolerant of those who opposed him, more autocratic in his bearing and more overweening towards his inferiors. He lacked only his father's greatness. He rounded off and consolidated Ivan's work with admirable efficiency—but no more.

The annexation of the two remaining Great Russian territories, Pskov and Ryazan, cost him little difficulty and no military effort. The first to be formally annexed was Pskov. Throughout the fifteenth century the republic had been almost entirely dependent on the grand prince of Moscow both for military aid against her western neighbours and for internal administration. Her affairs were managed by the grand prince's governor (*namestnik*) whose powers were steadily increased, while the authority of the popular assembly (*veche*) was correspondingly diminished. During the last thirty years of her 'independence' her military campaigns were exclusively directed by Moscow. Yet as an independent state, her domains were outside the reach of the grand prince. Only by formal annexation could he gain access to the estates of the landowners. In the autumn of 1509 a suitable pretext for ending the independence of Pskov arose. Vasily was quick to exploit a quarrel between his *namestnik* and the Pskovites. When arbitration failed he took matters into his own hands. In January 1510 the bell of the *veche* was removed; two *namestniki*, whose functions were mainly military, were appointed in lieu of the previous governor; the entire administration of the city was placed in the hands of a civil servant (*d'yak*); and 300 families of the leading citizens were deprived of their estates, deported to the interior and replaced by an equal number of families from the Moscow district. Pskov had become a province of Moscow. Eleven years later Ryazan was formally annexed when its last grand prince, who, in an effort to regain the independence of his forefathers, had entered into secret negotiations with the Tatars, was arrested by Vasily.

In the west Vasily's foreign policy was similar to that of his father. He consolidated and increased Ivan's gains in Lithuanian Russia, but was unable to continue his south-westerly thrust into the Ukraine. Sigismund I, who had succeeded his brother to the throne of Poland and the grand principality of Lithuania in 1506, began to prepare for war with Moscow early in 1507, in the hope of a grand coalition of Poland-Lithuania, Livonia and the Tatars of Kazan and the Crimea. But Vasily forestalled him by temporarily pacifying Kazan and attacking first. He also entered into secret negotiations with Mikhail Glinsky, the most powerful landowner in Lithuania, who despite his acceptance of the Roman faith became the rallying point of all the pro-Muscovite Russian elements of the population. In the first phase of the war (1507–8) fighting was desultory and inconclusive. Glinsky, after conducting harrassing operations in Polesie, deserted with his army of followers and his relatives to Moscow, and the Lithuanians were obliged to conclude a treaty (autumn 1508) whereby all the territorial acquisitions of Ivan III, with the exception of Lyubech on the Dnieper, were recognised as Muscovite possessions.

For four years an uneasy peace was kept. But in 1512, goaded on by Glinsky who sought richer rewards in conquered territory, and encouraged by the preparations of the grand master of the Teutonic Order to wage war on Poland with the support of the emperor, Vasily invaded Lithuania. His objective was the city and district of Smolensk on the upper reaches of the Dnieper. After two attempts (December 1512, June 1513) the Russians succeeded in capturing the city in July 1514. In spite of an overwhelming (but insufficiently exploited) Polish-Lithuanian victory two months later, Smolensk remained in Russian hands. The war, however, dragged on intermittently for the next five years. Notwithstanding his treaty of aggression with Maximilian (1514) and his offensive and defensive alliance (1517) with Albrecht, grand master of the order, Vasily could hope for no concerted action against his enemy. The Treaty of Vienna

(1515), concluded between the emperor and the king of Poland, nullified the former's pact of aggression with Moscow and demonstrated his duplicity; the war between Albrecht and Sigismund (1519–21) showed only the weakness and the decline of the order. After a series of bitter but fruitless campaigns, culminating in the massive invasion of Muscovites and Crimean Tatars in 1519, negotiations for peace were put in motion. In 1522 a five-year armistice (later extended to 1534) was concluded on the basis of *uti possidetis*. The immediate aim of Vasily's western policy had been achieved. Smolensk, the focal point of Russia's western defensive system, the cultural and economic gateway to the west and south, was securely in Russian hands, and was to remain so for a century to come.

The problems that confronted Vasily on his eastern and southern borders were graver and more complex than those which had faced his father. For whereas Ivan had managed to live in peace with the Crimean Tatars and had suffered little interference from the east, Vasily was, in the second half of his reign, faced with the menace of a pan-Tatar coalition, supported by the Ottoman Turks and organised by the Girey dynasty of the Crimea. The Crimean Tatars were no longer the firm allies of Moscow. Since the final defeat of the remnants of the Golden Horde in 1502 they had had no need of Muscovite military aid; furthermore, the eastern— and the most convenient—half of their traditional raiding territory was now under Muscovite control. But whereas the ageing Mengli had been content with razzias (twice in the first ten years of Vasily's reign Moscow's Ukrainian possessions were ravaged by Crimeans), his son Muhammed-Girey had more ambitious plans. In 1521 Muhammed-Girey's brother Sahib ousted the pro-Muscovite successor of Muhammed Emin, Shah Ali, from Kazan, and in the same year Muscovy was invaded on two fronts. A vast army of Crimean Tatars, reinforced by Nogais and Lithuanians, crossed the Oka at Kolomna, while an army of Kazan Tatars under Sahib closed in on Moscow from the east. The besieged capital was saved only by a timely attack on the Crimea by the Tatars of Astrakhan. The invasion of 1521, however, marked the beginning of the decline of the power of the Girey dynasty. Muhammed himself was killed in 1523 after a vain attempt to subjugate Astrakhan, and his successors were too occupied ousting one another from the khanate for the next ten years to prove dangerous to Moscow. Nor were the Turks, whom Muhammed-Girey had sought to entice into an anti-Muscovite coalition, willing or able actively to support their Crimean vassals in any major foreign adventures. Undaunted by Sahib's formal acknowledgement of Sulaimān II's suzerainty in 1524, Vasily was determined to remove the Gireys from Kazan by force. But only in 1532 did the Muscovites succeed in replacing Sahib's nephew and successor, Safa-Girey, by Djan Ali, the brother of the ex-Khan Shah Ali. Once more events had shown that Kazan was not strong enough, militarily or economically, to exist independently of Moscow. Her temporary allies, the Nogai and Crimean Tatars, were too remote and too engrossed in their own affairs to afford effective aid; her suzerain, the sultan, showed no inclination to intervene in her struggle for independence; and her merchants saw in Russia an ever-growing market for their wares rather than a raiding ground for her soldiers.

In his dealings with his family and boyars Vasily showed himself still more intransigent than his father. His brothers he frankly despised. 'Who', he is alleged to have asked his advisers in 1525, 'is to rule after me in the Russian land and in all my towns and provinces? Shall I give [the power] to my brothers? Yet my brothers cannot even manage their own appanages!' Treated with humiliating contempt, spied on by the agents of the grand prince, they were unable to assert their authority or actively to resist their brother. Their entourages were subject to the scrutiny of the grand prince who had no scruples in removing or replacing their courtiers. They were not even permitted to marry until the Grand Princess Elena had borne her husband two sons. The boyars too had little reason to be satisfied with the autocratic demeanour of their sovereign. No longer was their counsel sought in all matters of State; instead the grand prince was wont to consult his private secretaries (d'yaki), men far removed by birth and rank from the traditional advisers of the princes of Moscow. 'Nowadays', complained the disgraced boyar Bersen Beklemishev, 'our sovereign conducts all matters by confining himself with two others in his bed-chamber.' The long-established right of the subject to 'meet' (i.e. voice a grievance to) his sovereign was no longer encouraged, as Bersen himself had found to his cost. And the right of the subject to 'depart' from the grand prince was still further limited by the vigorous application of klyatvenniye zapisi. Nor was the aggressive foreign policy of the government viewed with favour by the majority of the boyars, for the frequent wars—particularly in the west—brought in their train fresh streams of border princelings to fill the already swollen court of Moscow and disrupt the minutely elaborated order of precedence.

In the Church—or rather in the predominantly 'Josephian' hierarchy headed by the metropolitan Daniel—Vasily found a willing partner and a subservient supporter. Not only was Daniel instrumental in the perfidious arrest of V. I. Shemyachich which led to the annexation of the latter's appanage, Novgorod Seversky (1523); in 1525, he also gave his sanction to the canonically unjustifiable divorce of Vasily and his barren first wife, Solomonia, and married the grand prince to Elena, the niece of Mikhail Glinsky, much to the disgust of his opponents within the Church, the Trans-Volga Elders, and of the majority of the boyars who had little desire to see the royal stock propagated. It was not until 1530, however, that Elena produced an heir, the future grand prince and Tsar Ivan IV. Three years later her husband died unexpectedly, having entrusted his infant son to the care of the metropolitan and his wife's uncle, Mikhail Glinsky.

The death of Vasily unleashed the forces of discontent in the court of Moscow. The unhappy minority of the grand prince was marked by an unprecedented struggle for power. Freed from the despotic control of Vasily, his brothers, his widow, his boyars all sought to establish their authority and all failed. Conspiracies, *coups d'état*, treason, banishment and murder followed each other in swift succession. Vasily's widow, Elena, aided by her unscrupulous lover, Prince Obolensky-Telepnev, survived as regent for five stormy years which witnessed the removal not only of Vasily's ineffectual brothers, but also of her uncle, evidently involved in a boyar plot to overthrow the government. But it was only after her death in 1538 that the boyars were given a chance to show their hand. As a result of a *coup d'état* engineered by the powerful Shuiskys, descendants of the princes of Suzdal, Obolensky was arrested and murdered and those boyars that had been imprisoned during Elena's rule were released. During five years of chaos and confusion the power swung from the Shuiskys to their rivals, the Bel'skys, descendants of Gedymin of Lithuania, and back again to the Shuiskys. The metropolitan see, the occupation of which depended on the favours of the party in power, twice changed hands. Crown lands were expropriated and arbitrarily distributed. The treasury was plundered. Towns and villages were ransacked. District governors vied with one another in greed, ferocity and corruption. Matters were not improved in 1543 when the thirteen-year old grand prince, incensed at the ignominious disgrace of his favourite, Vorontsov, had Andrey Shuisky murdered by the palace servants, for the Glinskys were quick to exploit the Shuiskys' downfall. For three and a half more years the anarchy continued. Even Ivan's solemn assumption of the title of tsar (January 1547) and his marriage to Anastasia, a member of the old Muscovite family of Zakharin, did not seemingly diminish the power of the Glinskys. It was only in the summer of 1547, when the rabble of Moscow, incited by a group of discontented boyars, seized and murdered Yury Glinsky, the tsar's uncle, that the rule of the Glinskys came to an end, and with it the Time of the Troubles.

If the young tsar's mind had been warped by the scenes of violence and depravity he had witnessed in childhood, it had also been poisoned against the boyars whose arrogance, egoism and sheer inability to govern he was never to forget. Yet the programme of the systematic and deliberate destruction of the boyar opposition was not yet begun; there followed instead a respite between the excesses of the boyars and the reprisals of the autocrat, a period of reform initiated by the so-called 'Chosen Council',[1] that private coterie of governmental advisers headed by the

---

[1] The *Izbrannaya Rada*, or Chosen Council, was the name given by Kurbsky in his *History of Ivan the Terrible* to the associates of Silvester and Adashev.

young and able favourite Adashev and the influential priest Silvester, and including in its numbers certain of the more public-spirited boyars. Information on Adashev and Silvester and their clique is scarce and indirect; little is known of the 'Council's' composition, functions or terms of reference; the extent of Ivan's participation in or approval of their reforming activity is uncertain. But there can be little doubt that the reforms carried through at the end of the 1540's and throughout the 1550's were far-sighted and shrewdly conceived. They aimed, first and foremost, at centralising and increasing the efficiency of the administration, a step necessitated by the vast growth of territory during the past hundred years and the failure of the central government to keep pace with this growth. They resulted, to a certain extent, in the strengthening of the service gentry at the expense of the boyars.

The most far-reaching of these reforms were in the field of local government. That relic of the appanage days, the archaic system of *kormleniye*, whereby provincial governors were 'fed' (*kormilis'*) by the districts they were granted in reward for service, levying large irregular dues, tribute in kind and various taxes (justice, customs, marriage, etc.), was hopelessly out of date. Not only did the local population suffer from—and repeatedly complain of—the abuse with which the *kormlenshchiki* exercised their authority—extortionism, violence, miscarriage of justice, lawlessness; but the State also suffered from the variegated practices adopted by individual governors, the complete lack of uniformity in this decentralised system of local administration and the difficulties of mobilising at short notice widely scattered commanders and their troops. Already during the minority of the tsar steps had been taken to remove the machinery of criminal justice from the hands of the provincial governors by creating the office of 'district elder' (*gubnoy starosta*), elected by district representatives from the local service gentry and 'boyar children', and aided by similarly appointed subordinate officials responsible for the apprehension, trial and punishment of criminals. Although the main purpose of these measures was the suppression of brigandage rather than the limitation of the juridical powers of the local governors (who indeed continued to receive dues from criminal proceedings), it was nevertheless the first step in the process of replacing the arbitrary power of the governor by the authority of locally elected officials. In the early years of the great reforms further limitations were placed upon the rights of the local governors. In 1549 the service gentry were freed from the jurisdiction of the governors, became subject only to the central organs of justice and received the right to judge the peasants on their domains. The great legal code of 1550 made obligatory the presence of elected representatives of the local population at the assizes of the provincial governors. At the same time an effort was made to regularise the taxes and legal dues a governor might levy. The final blow was struck in 1555 when all cantons were permitted by law (but not compelled) to replace their governors by elective authorities responsible for local administration, justice and the levying of dues, now paid directly into the Treasury instead of the pockets of the governors—a step which at once benefited the State (for the local authorities could be centrally and efficiently controlled by the government) and the population of the provinces who were now given the opportunity of freeing themselves from the arbitrary control of the *kormlenshchiki*.

Even more beneficial to the State were the measures taken to improve the efficiency and the conditions of service of the *dvoryanstvo*. In 1550 there occurred the first large-scale 'resettlement' (*ispomeshcheniye*) of Muscovite service men on Crown lands adjacent to the capital. The purpose of this resettlement was to provide approximately half the members of the central government and the Muscovite court (amongst whom were included the senior commanders of the army) with domains near the seat of administration and thus increase their efficiency and 'readiness for service', speed up mobilisation in case of war, and form reliable cadres of responsible administrators. By the decree of 1555 or 1556 the serviceman found his duties defined according to the size of his *pomestye*, was for the first time able to bequeath his fief to his son, provided the latter continued his father's service, and began to receive regular cash remuneration, as well as land, for his service. Steps were also taken to increase the efficiency of the army by limiting, but not abolishing, that clumsy and complex system of establishing social and official precedence by seniority of birth and service (*mestnichestvo*), and by raising the first cadres of a permanent standing army. At the same time the general centralisation of military command and public administration throughout the land was reflected in the creation and rapid expansion of various ministries (*izby*—later *prikazy*) manned mainly by *d'yaki* and centrally administering such affairs as military appointments (*razryadny prikaz*), distribution of fiefs (*pomestny prikaz*) and foreign affairs (*posol'sky prikaz*).

However much Ivan may have been in sympathy with the reforms, he was clearly unable to tolerate the reformers. In 1560 the 'Chosen Council' fell from power. Adashev was despatched to Dorpat where he died; Silvester was banished to the Solovetsky monastery. One has only to read Ivan's first letter to Kurbsky, who deserted to Lithuania in 1564, to realise the causes of the fall of Adashev's clique: opposition to Ivan on the question of the Livonian war, advocacy of an aggressive policy towards the Crimea, hostility towards Anastasia—or rather towards her family, the Zakharins—reluctance to admit the tsar to their council or to recognise his supreme sovereign power, unwillingness either fully to satisfy the service gentry or sufficiently to curb the power of the boyars. And, above all, treachery. For when in 1553 Ivan, seriously ill, commanded his cousin, Vladimir Andreevich of Staritsa, and the boyars to swear allegiance to his infant son, Silvester and other members of the 'Chosen Council' had refused to obey the seemingly moribund tsar and had sided with those boyars that supported the candidature of Vladimir as heir to the throne. While the behaviour of Silvester and his followers in the events of 1553 probably reflected a split within the leading governmental circles, a reaction against the Zakharins ('your son is still in swaddling clothes; the Zakharins will rule us', Adashev's father is reported to have said to the tsar) rather than support for a general uprising, an armed attempt to place Vladimir on the throne, yet their actions were interpreted by Ivan as part of a vast boyar conspiracy against his person.

The dismissal of Silvester and Adashev, followed by the removal, by murder and exile, of their partisans, was merely a prelude to the day of reckoning. Unbalanced by the events of 1564—defeat in Lithuania, desertion of his general, counsellor and friend, Prince Kurbsky, threat of invasion on two fronts—Ivan staged his theatrical *coup d'état* at the end of the year. With his suite he left Moscow for Alexandrovskaya Sloboda, halfway between Moscow and Rostov. One month later two documents from him arrived in Moscow; the one accusing the clergy and the ruling classes of treachery and of responsibility for all the disorders within the State since the death of his father and announcing his decision to abandon the throne; the other informing the merchants and the populace of Moscow that he bore them no ill will. If this was a ruse to sound the affections of the people, it was entirely successful. The merchants and the populace petitioned the metropolitan to send a delegation to the tsar, begging him to return. Few could have desired a return to the chaos of the 1530's; yet few could have dreamed of the chaos—and the terror—to come.

Ivan returned, and on his own terms. He demanded the right to deal with all 'traitors' in his own way, and he announced the formation of a 'special court' or *oprichnina* consisting at first of a thousand chosen men to be settled in certain districts from which all owners of patrimonies or of *pomestya*, if not members of the special court, were to be evicted and resettled elsewhere. The remainder of the State, known as the *zemshchina*, was to function as before, with its own council of boyars (*duma*), army, legal system and administrative organs. Only in matters of supreme importance, such as the declaration of war, were the boyars of the *zemshchina* to consult the tsar. The governmental organs within the *oprichnina* formed a complete parallel with those of the *zemshchina*, yet, it seems, they acted at first independently. The country was split into two. Later this duality of government was even further stressed by the temporary granting of the title of 'grand prince of all Russia' to the ex-ruler of Kasimov, the Tatar Simeon Bekbulatovich, as head of the *zemshchina*, while Ivan assumed the humble title of 'prince of Moscow' (1575-6). The number of *oprichniki* soon grew and with it their territory. Eventually the special court controlled approximately half the country, a vast wedge stretching from north to south, the *zemshchina* being gradually squeezed to the outer and less productive fringes. Certain streets and districts of the capital itself were reserved exclusively for the *oprichnina*. The members of the special court were picked from all strata of society, from the commonalty to the titled aristocracy. Even foreign adventurers found their way into its ranks. They wore distinctive uniform. They were united by an oath of unquestioning loyalty to the tsar and mortal hostility to the *zemshchina*. At best they were the chosen commanders and administrators of the new State; at worst, the executioners and secret police of the tsar.

Executions and banishments followed Ivan's return to the capital in 1565. When it became realised that open protest at the ravages of the *oprichniki* merely provoked further reprisals, the opposition went underground. Conspiracy appears to have followed conspiracy. The unmasking in 1567 of a—perhaps trumped up—plot to betray Ivan to the king of Poland was followed by three years of investigations and mass executions. Among the victims was the tsar's cousin, Prince Vladimir of Staritsa, poisoned together with his mother, wife and daughter. Reports of intended treason by the citizens of Novgorod—together with the city's failure to raise sufficient funds for the wars in the west—led to unparalleled massacres; the city was thrown open to the *oprichniki* who murdered and pillaged for six weeks. The toll of dead is said to have reached 60,000. The disastrous military events of 1571—the sack of Moscow by the Crimean Tatars and the failure of the Russians to take Reval (Tallin) after a seven-months' siege—were ascribed by Ivan to treachery and inefficiency within the armed forces of both the *zemshchina* and the *oprichnina*. Again there were mass executions. But the *oprichniki* were not always provided with convenient pretexts for their excesses. Whole cities suffered without the preliminary accusation of 'treachery' being even proffered. A metropolitan was strangled for daring to raise his voice in protest. It seemed as though the country was undergoing a bloody civil war, yet a one-sided civil war, for the forces of Ivan met with little or no resistance.

Yet was the *oprichnina* nothing more than a weapon for liquidating 'boyar treachery', a monstrous police force built up and trained to satisfy the bloodthirsty appetites and lusts of a paranoiac? Or was the *oprichnina* the far-sighted scheme of a statesman of genius, the logical continuation of the agrarian reforms of Ivan III and of the *izbrannaya rada*, a social revolution intended to achieve what the tsar realised was unachievable under normal circumstances, namely the creation of a new government, a new class of service gentry, reliable and free from the ties of tradition? Unfortunately the scarcity of unbiased sources—the very existence of the organisation was indeed painstakingly concealed from foreign powers— makes it difficult to assess the purpose or even the functioning of the *oprichnina.* Conclusions can only be drawn from the results. As a social experiment the *oprichnina* was, in the long run, successful. In stripping the hereditary aristocracy of its power and raising the status of the service gentry, it brought to a logical conclusion the process initiated, as we have seen, by Ivan III. But whereas Ivan III had contented himself with rendering harmless or removing a mere handful of potentially dangerous opponents, his grandson, by the wholesale methods of murder and eviction, attempted to reduce the entire aristocracy to the level of the service gentry and to replace them in all offices of state by his own chosen nobility. Yet though the boyar class as a whole, decimated by the purges of the 1560's and 1570's and financially ruined, gave way eventually to the new nobility and finally abandoned all claims to be the joint rulers and advisers of the grand prince of Moscow, Ivan none the less, in the middle of his efforts to destroy them, realised that he could not rule without them. The disasters of 1571 had demonstrated that the 'wretched little *voevodas*', as Kurbsky later styled the generals of the *oprichnina*, could not replace the experience and tradition of the boyar commanders. How clearly Ivan realised this is shown by the emergency measures taken after the sack of Moscow by the Tatars. The *oprichnina* itself was subjected to a purge and many of its most distinguished members were liquidated; it was forbidden, under pain of corporal punishment, to use the word *oprichnina*—from now on it was the 'court' (*dvor*); and a further 'resettlement'—this time in reverse—took place: certain confiscated patrimonies were in part returned to their original owners and the *oprichniki* settled upon these lands as *pomeshchiki* were themselves displaced and granted new lands. The significance of this measure becomes clearer still if we examine the effects of the *oprichnina* on the rural economy. The parcelling out of the large estates into *pomestya*, the excesses of the *oprichniki*, the instability of land-ownership and the subsequent impoverishment of the *pomeshchiki* caused the peasants from the central districts and the estates north of the Volga to seek safer and more profitable lands in the east, in the newly conquered territory of the Volga, and in the south, on the Don steppes, in the no-man's-land between the Russian and Crimean frontiers. Not even the steps taken by the government to bind the peasants to the land, nor the half-hearted attempts to secularise Church property, could avert the crisis in agricultural labour. The *pomeshchiki* were in many cases forced to resort to abducting agricultural workers from neighbouring lands in order even to subsist on their estates, let alone run them efficiently or make the requisite contribution to the war effort. Gradually the central and western rural areas became depopulated; in some of the districts of Novgorod adjoining the theatre of the Livonian war up to ninety per cent of the land lay fallow towards the end of Ivan's reign. The service gentry were unable to fulfil their military duties; the armies lacked manpower; the treasury became depleted. The *oprichnina* degenerated into little more than an instrument for squeezing resources for the long war in the west from an exhausted population.

It is significant that the great and lasting military achievements of Ivan's reign all occurred before the institution of the *oprichnina* and that the greatest—the conquest of the lower Volga—took place during the rule of the 'Chosen Council'. Throughout Ivan's minority the khanate of Kazan had again proved a thorn in Russia's side. In 1535 the pro-Muscovite Djan Ali was murdered and the Crimean Girey dynasty was reinstated in the person of Safa-Girey. Raid followed raid. A considerable portion of the Muscovite army was needed to deal with the frequent incursions in the east as well as the constant threat of invasion from the south. In 1545 the Russians went over to the offensive. Unrest and internal dissension rapidly decreased the military efficiency of the Tatars. Between 1546 and 1552 the throne of Kazan changed hands six times, now the pro-Muscovite party gaining ascendancy, now the pro-Crimean. Yet it was only after two further unsuccessful campaigns (1547–8, 1549–50) that Kazan fell (October 1552). Five more years of punitive campaigns against the rebellious Tatars and the peoples of the central Volga area were needed before the submission of the khanate was complete. The position in Astrakhan was complicated by the interests of the Crimean Tatars and the Little Nogai Horde, who supported the Crimean puppet khan, Yamgurchey, on the one hand, and those of the pro-Muscovite Great Nogai Horde on the other hand. But resistance to pressure from Moscow was negligible and in 1556 the Russians occupied the city without a struggle. The annexation of Astrakhan was followed by the recognition of Moscow's suzerainty by the Great Nogai Horde in the Caspian depression east of the Volga. The whole of the Volga was now in Russian hands. The eastern frontiers of the state were secure; the way was open for colonial expansion into Siberia and the Far East; and the great trade routes to central Asia, Persia and the Caucasus no longer lay through territory hostile to Moscow.

After the successful conclusion of operations in the east it was clear that the young and virile state of Muscovy could scarcely content itself with the *status quo* on the southern and western frontiers. Three possible courses of aggrandisement and expansion lay open to the government—the subjugation of the Crimean Tatars in the south; the annexation of the White Russian and Ukrainian lands under Polish-Lithuanian domination in the west; or the conquest of Livonia and the Baltic seaboard in the north west. The first of these courses was persistently urged upon Ivan by the government of the 1550's. From the earliest days of Ivan's reign the Crimean Tatars had shown themselves unwilling to negotiate with Moscow and had proved a constant menace. While not strong enough to mount and maintain a full-scale invasion, they were able to cause grave inconvenience and severe damage by their frequent raids, especially when these raids were launched in collaboration with Moscow's enemies, as in 1535 when a timely attack on the Oka assisted the Lithuanians' invasion of the Seversky district, or in 1552 when Devlet-Girey, urged on by the sultan and the king of Poland, attempted to divert the Russians from Kazan. The *Izbrannaya Rada*, however, met with little success in their advocacy of an aggressive policy against the Crimea. True, from 1556 to 1559 a series of raids along the Don and Dnieper were carried out against Tatar territory, but these were more in the nature of a reconnaissance for a major invasion which never took place. After the fall of the government in 1560 Ivan turned to the defensive in the south. A series of fortified lines (*cherty*) consisting of towns or strong points linked by a system of defensive works—trenches, palisades and ramparts—was created on the northern fringes of the steppes in the hope of blunting the spearhead of any Tatar invasion; and later a permanent frontier guard force was established to neutralise the diversionary and surprise effect of the raiders. The tsar was clearly unwilling to commit himself to a major campaign involving extended lines of supply and communication or to risk the danger of a war with the Ottoman Turks without the assurance or even the hope of military support from the west.

The constant menace to his southern flank together with the ever-growing unity of the Polish-Lithuanian state and the possibility of an East European-Baltic-Turkish coalition directed against Moscow dissuaded Ivan from attempting the annexation of the Russian lands in the west; the problem was shelved in favour of what appeared to be a far easier and altogether more rewarding task—the conquest of Livonia. There were indeed many reasons for embarking on such a course. Not least among these was the vulnerability of the country. The military power of the Order of the Knights of the Sword was in a state of complete disintegration; there was little unity between the order and the independent bishops; the archbishop of Riga was openly polonophile—the master, Fürstenberg, favoured agreement with Moscow. Strategically the seizure of Livonia would endanger the state of Lithuania not only in the east, but also along the whole of her northern frontier. But the economic advantages to be derived from such a course of action far outweighed all other considerations. Mastery of Livonia meant an outlet to the Baltic, and the possession of the town of Narva and of the great harbours of Reval and Riga meant direct trade with the west, the facilitation of the import of metal goods and arms and the export of Russia's natural resources; furthermore, a secure footing on the southern Baltic seaboard would remove the possibility of economic blockade by the western and northern powers.

For a quarter of a century Livonia was the corner-stone of Ivan's diplomatic and military endeavours. All Moscow's military energy was expended in the fruitless effort to conquer the Baltic lands—fruitless, because without a fleet the seaboard could not be seized or held, and because Moscow was not alone in her designs on Livonia. Her interests soon clashed with those of Denmark, Sweden and Poland-Lithuania in a four-sided struggle for the old possessions of the order and of the bishops. Yet the other interested nations were slow to move. A full-scale invasion in 1558 brought the whole of eastern Estonia (including Dorpat and Narva, but excluding Reval, which refused to surrender) into Russian hands; in the beginning of the following year the northern half of Latvia was added to their conquests. Only then did Russia's future opponents in the struggle for Livonia begin to show signs of alarm. The mediation of the king of Denmark resulted in the conclusion of a nine-months' armistice during which Lithuania signed a treaty with the new master Kettler (who had replaced the pro-Muscovite Fürstenberg), agreeing to defend the order in exchange for the temporary Lithuanian occupation of the south-eastern fringe of Livonia.[1] But it was only after further successful Russian operations in central Livonia in 1560, which led to the virtual collapse of the order, that the other powers actively intervened. By the treaty of 28 November 1561 all the possessions of the order were formally ceded to Poland-Lithuania, Kettler becoming a vassal of the Polish king with the newly-created duchy of Courland and Semigallia in the south-west as his fief. In the same year King Eric XIV of Sweden, at the request of Reval, occupied northern Estonia, while the possessions of the bishop of Oesel in the north-west had already been occupied by Magnus, brother of the king of Denmark.

Faced with the alternative of war with Sweden and Denmark for the northern districts, or with Poland-Lithuania for the southern half of Livonia, Ivan chose the latter. The steady worsening of Danish-Swedish relations culminating in the Seven Years War (1563–70), and the anti-Polish tendencies of Eric XIV, led to the establishment of friendly relations between Moscow and Sweden. Until the end of the 1560's Ivan undertook no campaigns against western Estonia. His only military venture of importance during this confused and complex period of diplomatic negotiation was the seizure of Polotsk (1563), the key to the main waterway (the western Dvina) to the Baltic and commanding the eastern approaches to the capital of Lithuania. Apart from the great Lithuanian victories at Ulla and Orsha between Polotsk and Smolensk in the following year—victories which, happily for the Russians, the Lithuanians failed to follow up—there were few clashes with Poland-Lithuania until the end of the following decade. Ivan, indeed, during the years of the radical reorganisation and the internal upheaval of the

---

[1] It is interesting to note that Ivan in his first letter to Kurbsky (1564) laid the blame on the *Izbrannaya Rada* for this granting of a vital breathing space to the order. '[I recall] how, owing to the cunning suggestion of the Danish king, you gave the Livonians a whole year to prepare themselves.'

Muscovite state, could do little more than maintain the *status quo* in Livonia and White Russia by diplomatic bargaining with Lithuania and attempt to form a coalition with England and Sweden. However, towards the end of the 1560's the international situation had from the standpoint of Muscovy considerably deteriorated. England expressed no desire to enter into an offensive or defensive alliance with Russia; hopes of a lasting Russo-Swedish pact were shattered on the accession to the Swedish throne of Sigismund's polonophile brother-in-law, John III, who ousted the mad Eric XIV in 1568; the fusion of Poland and Lithuania into a single state was finally achieved at the Diet of Lublin (1569); and at the same time the Turks were pressing Poland for a military alliance against Moscow. The only ally gained by Moscow in the general reshuffle was Denmark, annoyed by Sigismund's interference in her freebooting activities in the Baltic. Yet even Frederick II failed to assist his brother Magnus, the tsar's newly appointed vassal 'king' of Livonia and commander-in-chief of the Russian armies in the north-west, in the fruitless siege of Swedish-held Reval (1570–1).

Neither Moscow nor Poland-Lithuania were able or willing to embark on a major war at the beginning of the seventies. The king needed peace to put into operation the principles of the Union of Lublin and to consider the problem of the succession to the Polish throne; the tsar was wholly absorbed with the Tatar invasions (1571, 1572) and the need to set his house in order. Yet Ivan was far from uninterested in the affairs of Poland. During the interregna following Sigismund's death (1572–3, 1574–5) he twice proposed his candidacy, once for the Crown of Poland and once for the grand duchy of Lithuania. Whether or not he entertained serious hopes of being elected as king or grand prince, his chances were highly remote. After the flight of Sigismund's successor, Henry of Anjou (18 June 1574), Ivan's diplomatic manœuvres had clearly one aim only— to baulk the election of the sultan's vassal, Stephen Bathory, prince of Transylvania, by supporting the candidacy of the Habsburg Archduke Ernest. A peaceful partition of eastern Europe between the emperor and the tsar seemed an altogether better proposition than a strong king of a united Poland-Lithuania backed by the Porte.

With the election of Stephen Bathory to the throne of Poland (end of 1575) the Livonian war entered into its final phase. Taking advantage of the Polish king's preoccupation with the Danzig rebellion, Ivan threw all his resources into a last effort to conquer Livonia. Meeting virtually no resistance, the Russians overran the whole country (with the exception of Reval and Riga), pushing the scanty Polish and Lithuanian forces behind the Dvina. It was Ivan's last successful military venture. In the following year the tide of fortune changed. Deserted by Magnus, with no hope of an English or Austrian alliance, Ivan was powerless to resist the combined onslaughts of Poland and Sweden, together with the increasing threat of invasion from the Crimea. One by one Ivan's western strongholds fell—Wenden (1578), Polotsk (1579); in 1580 Stephen captured the strategic centre of Velikie Luki in an attempt to drive a wedge into Russian territory, thereby cutting off Ivan's forces in Livonia. It was only lack of money and the half-hearted attitude of the Polish diet that forced Stephen to abandon more grandiose plans for a full-scale invasion of Moscow, and to limit himself to extending the Polish corridor in Russian territory east of Livonia by attempting the capture of Pskov (1581). In the north nearly all the southern seaboard of the Finnish Gulf was in Swedish hands by the end of 1581. Further resistance by Ivan was unthinkable. Only the stubborn refusal of Pskov to capitulate spared the Tsar more humiliating terms at the peace treaty of Yam Zapolsky (January 1582) which was brought about by papal mediation. As it was, he renounced all claims to Livonia and the districts of Polotsk and Velizh; the only concession made by Stephen was the return of Velikie Luki. In the following year the whole of Estonia, as well as the towns and districts (*uyezdy*) of Ivangorod, Yam, Koporye and Korela were formally ceded to Sweden. Only the extreme eastern tip of the Gulf of Finland—the small coastal strip on either side of the mouth of the river Neva in the district of Oreshek—was left to Muscovy.

Ivan survived the Swedish treaty by one year. Worn out by a life of dissipation and torn by remorse for the death of his son Ivan, whom in a fit of ungovernable rage he had struck dead two years previously, he died suddenly on 18 March 1584 while playing chess. Although by the end of his reign the foundation had been laid for Russian sovereignty in Asia by the conquest and colonisation of the khanate of Siberia, and although the loss of Narva (1581) was to a certain extent compensated by the establishment of regular annual commerce with England and the Low Countries via the White Sea–northern Dvina route (discovered quite fortuitously by the English in 1553), Ivan left a sorry legacy to his son Fedor. The great venture in the north-west had failed. Russia was left with even less of the Baltic seaboard than before the war. In the west the frontiers remained much as they had been at the death of Vasily III. And in the south the threat of invasion was ever-present. But it was the internal condition of the country that presented the gloomiest picture. The long war in the west, the depredations of the *oprichnina* and the upheaval of agrarian economy had exhausted the country economically. The treasury was empty. The central and western districts were barren. Discontent was rife. Ivan had truly sown the seeds of civil war. Writing four years after Ivan's death, the English ambassador, Giles Fletcher, summed up the results of the reign in the following words:

this wicked pollicy and tyrranous practise (though now it be ceased) hath so troubled that countrey, and filled it so full of grudge and mortall hatred ever since, that it wil not be quenched (as it seemeth now) till it burne againe into a civill flame.

CHAPTER XIX

THE NEW WORLD, 1521–1580

I N a life of bold decisions, none was bolder or more significant for the future than Cortés's decision to rebuild the city of Tenochtitlán-Mexico and to make it the capital of the kingdom of New Spain. The site had many serious disadvantages. It was an island, marshy and reputedly unhealthy; it produced no food of its own, except the fish caught in the lake; its drinking water had to be brought by expensive artificial means from the hills of Chapúltepec, several miles away; it communicated with the mainland by causeways, and many among Cortés's following thought that these causeways, with their easily invested bridges, would be dominated by the Indians of the mainland rather than by the island Europeans. Moreover, a large Indian population still lived on the island, lurking among the ruins of buildings which Cortés had had pulled down in order to dump the rubble in the drainage canals, to facilitate the manœuvres of his cavalry. In short, the site might well be a trap, incapable of resisting siege, and peculiarly vulnerable in its provisioning and water supply.

Cortés, though certainly aware of the economic defects of the place, overrode the objections. He believed it to be as strong a site for Europeans as for Indians. Further, he probably wished to avoid a too rapid dispersal of his followers through the land they had only partly conquered, where they might still become the victims of their new vassals, or of their own disagreements. Finally Cortés was wise enough to appreciate the prestige of Tenochtitlán, its 'renown and importance', as he expressed it. Christianity has often sought to identify itself with the ruins of preceding civilisations in the relationship of new spirit occupying old forms. By re-occupying Tenochtitlán, by building churches and dwellings upon its temple sites, rather than leaving its ruins as a monument to Aztec grandeur, the Spaniards not only destroyed the pre-conquest appearance of the city; they also identified themselves with its traditions as a religious and political centre.

Throughout 1522 and 1523 the work of rebuilding went on. Immense numbers of Indian craftsmen and labourers were drafted to the city; according to the Texcocan chief Ixtlilxochitl, who directed the drafting, nearly the whole labouring population of the valley of Mexico was brought to work. Accidents and over-work caused the death of many Indians, and many thousands died in the epidemic of smallpox, introduced by Europeans, which raged throughout these years. With reason the missionary friar Motolinía listed the rebuilding of Tenochtitlán as the seventh of the ten 'plagues' which afflicted the Indians of New Spain. The whole work was carried out with breath-taking speed, directed by the Spanish commanders with the same ferocious energy that had made the conquest possible. The scale of the undertaking astonished contemporaries. The new city, in size, in grandeur and regularity of lay-out, vied with the greatest capitals of Europe. The island population in the 1520's was certainly not less than a hundred thousand people, bigger by far than Toledo or Seville or any other Spanish city in Europe. For its support it drew upon the products of a rich agricultural region of vast extent and commanded the services of a great system of tributary labour, inherited from Aztec times, whose capabilities in the early days seemed almost limitless. More significant still, it was a mixed city in which Spaniards and Indians lived side by side in their respective *barrios*. The rebuilding of Tenochtitlán began that fruitful intermingling of Spanish and Indian ways which has remained characteristic of Spanish North America ever since; and the founding of Mexico City provided the model which many later conquerors were to seek to imitate.

Spanish society was strongly urban in character. In Castile, fortified corporate towns occupied a position of privilege and power, as was natural in a country whose history had been filled with intermittent war, with constantly shifting frontiers. Noblemen, though they drew their income from land or, preferably, from the possession of flocks and herds, built their palaces in the towns. Rural life was for peasants, many of them *moriscos*. In the reconquest of Christian Spain from the Moors, the occupation or the establishment of fortified towns had been an essential precaution; and similarly, it was natural for the Castilian conquerors of Mexico to establish themselves in corporate towns, while looking to the surrounding countryside for their support. The principal functions of these towns in the early days were not economic, but military and administrative. Even the military aspect of their life soon lost its importance, for with a few exceptions—the Chichimecas of New Galicia, the Araucanians of Chile—the Indians were much less dangerous, much more acquiescent, than the Moors in Spain. It was as social and administrative centres, as the strongholds of a new ruling class, that the towns of Spanish America early attained their dominant position. Every leader of a conquering army made it his first care to establish towns, to get them legally incorporated and to instal his own immediate followers as the officers of municipal government. Of course the majority of such towns were not Mexicos; many of them were at first mere temporary camps of thatched huts; but they shared with Mexico the essential characteristics of legal incorporation, with jurisdiction over the surrounding country, control of Indian labour, and dependence upon Indian supplies for their subsistence.

In Mexico, as subsequently in most other towns of the Indies, the soldiers of the conquering army—or at least the more substantial among them, those who had financed themselves for the campaign—became the *vecinos*, the legally enrolled householders. From their number Cortés nominated the first city government, the *cabildo* of twelve *regidores* or councillors (in smaller towns the number of councillors was smaller). The *regidores* were to elect the two *alcaldes* or municipal magistrates, with them were to hold office for a year, and upon retirement were to elect their own successors, subject to Cortés's approval. Office was thus to circulate among the restricted group of *vecinos*. The *vecinos* were to get their living not by the exercise of any urban trade; for though among their numbers there were men of almost every calling, they thought of themselves as soldiers and in any case had not come to the Indies to ply their old crafts. They were to be supported by grants of *encomienda*. The system of *encomiendas* was not new; it had long existed in Spain in territory taken from the Moors, in the Canaries, and in the West Indian islands; but in Mexico it received more precise definition and a far more extended use. An *encomienda* was a native village, or part of one, or a group of villages, 'commended' to the care of an individual Spaniard—an *encomendero*—whose duty was to protect the inhabitants, to appoint and maintain missionary clergy in the villages, and to undertake a share in the military defence of the province. The conquering army was thus to be settled as a quasi-feudal militia, residing in towns of Spanish foundation, but living upon the country. *Encomenderos* were entitled by their grants to support their households by levying tribute from the villages in their care; tribute which in the early days took the forms both of food and cotton clothing, and of unpaid forced labour. A grant of *encomienda*, however, involved no cession of land or jurisdiction. *Encomiendas* were not feudal manors; nor were they slave-worked estates. In law, at least, the Indians remained free men, and their rights over the land they occupied were unimpaired. In the valley of Mexico, and in many other places, Indian land custom already made provision for the payment of tribute to overlord peoples, and for the support of chieftains and priests, of temples and community houses. The Spanish *encomenderos* stepped into the places of the Aztec rulers and drew the tributes and services formerly paid to them. As a means of initial settlement the *encomienda* was logical, indeed obvious. As a permanent arrangement it had grave disadvantages. The *encomenderos'* right to forced labour opened the door to ill-treatment and over-work, especially in view of the Spanish mania for building. The Indians' control of their land, whatever the law said, was also endangered; for if a community could not meet its tribute obligations, or if its headmen could be bribed, its lands might be offered for sale. Moreover, the number of Spaniards who could be supported by *encomiendas* was relatively small, for—in the early days at least—the grants were large. Cortés arrogated to himself a vast *encomienda* in the valley of Oaxaca, comprising officially 23,000 tributary heads of households, in fact many more. This was exceptional, of course, but *encomiendas* of 2000 and more tributaries were common. The humbler soldier who received no *encomienda* had two choices open to him. The conditions of colonial society at first being wholly unsuitable for small-scale farming or the practice of European trades, he could either remain the follower, the *paniaguado*, of a great *encomendero*, and live upon his bounty; or he could move on to fresh conquests and hope eventually to secure Indians of his own. Society in these circumstances was necessarily restless, factious and disorderly. The permanence of any governmental system, moreover, depended, among other things, upon royal confirmation. Cortés succeeded in securing confirmation of his initial arrangements—and prudently reserved a large proportion of the Anáhuac villages to the Crown—but Charles V and his advisers were naturally suspicious of the *encomienda* system, with its feudal implications, and royal second thoughts could be expected to modify it. Finally, the Church, as represented by missionaries of the mendicant orders, was unlikely to be satisfied for long with the perfunctory provision of religious instruction which the law enjoined upon the *encomenderos*; nor were the *encomenderos*—loyal sons of Church though most of them were—likely to welcome ecclesiastical intervention between them and their tributaries.

The conquest of New Spain was a spiritual as well as a military campaign, and the principal local opposition to the rule of swordsmen came from the soldiers of the Church—the friars of the missionary orders. The Franciscans were the first in the field in Mexico, as the result of a request made to the emperor by Cortés himself. The first Franciscans sent out in 1524—the famous Twelve under the leadership of Fray Martín de Valencia—and many of their successors, were strict Observants, carefully trained for their task. The same is true of the first Dominicans who, under Fray Domingo de Betanzos, went to Mexico in 1525. They were picked products of Church reform in Spain, representing both the radical churchmanship of Cisneros and the humanism and learning of Erasmus. Fray Juan de Zumárraga, nominated by Charles V as first bishop of Mexico in 1527, was a conspicuous admirer of Erasmus. The doctrinal books printed in Mexico under his direction—the *Doctrina Breve*, and the *Doctrina Cristiana* prepared as a catechism for Indian use—both show the profound influence of Erasmian thought; both insist on the primacy of faith over works and advocate the unlimited diffusion of the scriptures. The men who began the spiritual conquest of Mexico were thus daring religious radicals; but they were also members of a spiritual army whose leaders stood close to the throne. In the first decades of Mexican settlement they had almost a free hand, usurping, by royal direction, the pastoral and sacramental duties normally entrusted to secular clergy. Their leadership in the spiritual conquest ensured its efficiency and speed, and their impact upon colonial society in New Spain, despite the smallness of their numbers, was of explosive force.

The conversion which the missionaries sought to achieve was more than a mere outward conformity. Baptism was to be preceded by careful instruction in the faith, by preaching, by catechism, and by the establishment of schools in which the sons of leading Indians might be educated in Christian doctrine and European ways. The teaching, catechising and baptism of many hundreds of thousands could be achieved, by the small numbers of friars available, only by the concentration of Indians in urban communities close to the nucleus of church and convent from which the missionaries directed their enterprise. Naturally the friars settled in places where urban communities already existed; but such concentrations of population were rare in Indian New Spain. Outside capitals such as Tenochtitlán, Tepeaca, or Cholula, the great majority of Indians lived in scattered hamlets among their *milpas* of maize and beans. Much of the energy of the missionaries was therefore devoted to persuading or compelling the Indians to move into new towns built around church and convent and reserved for Indian habitation. By these means, they argued, new converts could have not only the moral advantages of urban life and missionary teaching, but also the economic and social advantage of segregation from lay Spaniards. A policy of racial segregation was followed, not for the comfort of Europeans but in order to protect Indians from the exploitation and demoralisation which might result from too close contact with Europeans, and to keep them under continuous ecclesiastical supervision. The success of the friars in establishing their ascendancy over the Indians was extraordinary and can be explained only in terms of Indian psychology. The Indians were accustomed to living in accordance with an intricate and continuous ritual which governed all their communal activities, including the all-important processes of agriculture. Ceremonial and work were intertwined and inseparable. The Spanish conquest, with its destruction of temples, its prohibitions of pagan dances, its forceful proselytising, weakened and in some places destroyed the old ritual organisation. Work—whether forced labour for an *encomendero*, or wage labour, or even subsistence agriculture —ceased to be part of a socio-religious ceremonial system and became a mere profane necessity. A void was created in the spiritual and social life of the Indians, which could be filled, though partially and often superficially, by the ritual of the Church and the activities of church-building. The friars understood this necessity; and the very numerous and very large churches which were built, with Indian labour, all over New Spain, though they owed their massive strength to considerations of defence, also owed their magnificence to a desire to replace the lost splendour of the pagan temples. Similarly, the splendour of ecclesiastical ritual—far more elaborate than was common in Europe—was an attempt to meet the Indians' longing for the old ceremonial life which they had largely lost. On the other hand, the policy of the orders necessarily interfered with the control of Indian labour upon which Spanish economic activity depended. It involved the preservation, and indeed the extension, of Indian communal agriculture, for the support of the mission towns. Moreover, the demands of the missions for Indian labour—and their success in securing it—for the purpose of building churches, cloisters and new dwellings, competed directly with the demands of the *encomenderos* and other lay Spaniards; and their exemption from episcopal jurisdiction was a source of indiscipline within dioceses. Inevitably the friars on one hand, the *encomenderos* and the secular clergy on the other, became embroiled in a complex struggle for colonial power. The struggle did not immediately become acute, however, because the conquest did not stand still. As the friars began their spiritual conquest, the lieutenants, rivals and imitators of Cortés were already moving out from Mexico in search of new empires to conquer.

Cortés himself never forgot that the discovery and conquest of New Spain had originated in attempts to find a route to the Pacific and so to the Far East. Mexico occupied and its valley secure, Cortés quickly resumed the search, whether for a strait between the oceans, or for harbours which could became bases for Pacific exploration. Of his subsequent expeditions, only those to Pánuco—the first commanded by himself, the second by Sandoval—had a purely Atlantic object; and they were undertaken chiefly to counter the slave-raiding activities of Garay, governor of Jamaica, in the Pánuco area. The other expeditions organised by Cortés were all intended to open exploration to the west and south. Between 1522 and 1524 Michoacán and most of the Pacific coast area as far north as the Santiago river were conquered and granted in *encomienda*. In 1523 Pedro de Alvarado led a well-equipped force through Tehuántepec into the region of the Maya cities of Guatemala, and Cristóbal de Olid was sent by sea to the bay of Honduras, to occupy the settled country there and to search for a strait. Both these expeditions encountered not only physical obstacles and stout Indian resistance, but also opposition from an unexpected quarter, from Pedro Arias de Avila's men exploring north from Darien. The two great streams of mainland conquest met along the southern borders of what are now the republics of Guatemala and Honduras, and a dangerous armed clash seemed imminent. To complicate the situation further, Olid repudiated Cortés's authority and set up an independent command. Cortés thought it necessary to deal with mutiny and possible civil war in person. It was the one serious blunder of his career. His army marched to Honduras across the base of the Yucatán peninsula, through appallingly difficult country in which abrupt mountain ranges alternated with dense rain-forest. One river and its riparian swamps had to be crossed by means of a floating bridge whose construction required the felling of over a thousand trees. Few horses survived the march, and the men who survived emerged from the forest broken in health and even, for a time, in spirit. Nevertheless, Cortés's presence sufficed to restore order among the Spaniards in Honduras—Olid had been murdered before his arrival—and to make diplomatic arrangements with the men from Darien which attached Honduras, for the time, to Mexico. Meanwhile Alvarado, as loyal as he was fearless and as capable as he was ruthless, had carried out a successful, rapacious and brutal campaign in Guatemala. The Mayas, vigorous, intelligent, with a developed city-building culture, lacked political unity, and Alvarado profited by the enmity between two principal peoples, Cakchiquel and Quiché, to support the one against the other and ultimately to subdue both. The Spanish city of Guatemala, on the first of its three successive sites, was founded in 1524, and *encomiendas* were distributed among its *vecinos* in the usual way. Upon hearing of Olid's defection Alvarado hastened north in an attempt to join Cortés, but his support proved unnecessary and the interruption of the settlement of Guatemala was brief. Alvarado succeeded in holding his men together and in standing off rival incursions from Darien. He visited Spain in 1527 and returned to America a knight of Santiago, with his government of Guatemala confirmed.

Cortés returned from Honduras to Mexico by sea in 1526. During his two years of absence local feuds and jealousies had distracted city and province, and a procession of hostile tale-bearers had left Mexico to damage his reputation in Spain. He was soon to be superseded; but meanwhile he resumed, with his old vigour, the business of organising New Spain, exploring its coastal provinces, and pursuing the search for a sea route to the East. The whole aspect of Pacific exploration had changed since the capture of Mexico. Ferdinand Magellan, the Portuguese navigator who entered the service of Spain, had left Seville on his west-ward voyage to the Spice Islands in the same year—1519—that Cortés had left Cuba to conquer Mexico. Magellan knew, though probably Charles V did not, that the Portuguese were already trading in the Moluccas and took a calculated risk in going there. The events of his voyage are well known: the shipwreck and the mutiny off the coast of Patagonia; the discovery and the terrifying thirty-eight day passage of the strait that bears his name; the seemingly endless crossing of the Pacific, which reduced the ships' companies to a diet of rats and leather; the inhospitable landings in the Ladrones and the Philippines, and the death of Magellan and forty of his people in a local war. Sebastián del Cano, the Spanish navigator upon whom the command devolved, sailed south from the Philippines with only two ships remaining, skirted the coast of Borneo, and in November 1521 reached the Moluccas. The Spaniards were well received by the sultan of Tidore upon whose territory they landed. They traded their merchandise for cargoes of cloves and established a warehouse at Tidore, leaving a small garrison to prepare for future expeditions. Then, since none of his company felt inclined to face the dangers of Magellan's strait again, del Cano divided his forces. The *Trinidad* set off across the Pacific for the coast of Mexico, and was captured by the Portuguese before she was many days out. Del Cano himself eluded the Portuguese and took his battered *Victoria* through the Macassar strait, across the Indian Ocean, round the Cape of Good Hope and back to Spain, with her precious cargo. She had been away for three years. It was a prodigious feat of seamanship, and del Cano shares with Magellan the honour of this astounding voyage. He was the first captain to sail round the world.

Del Cano's triumphant return to Spain produced two parallel sets of consequences. The first was a state of more or less open war between Spaniards and Portuguese in the Moluccas. The second was a series of outwardly amicable negotiations between Spain and Portugal in Europe. During these negotiations, Charles V sent out from Spain a second fleet for the Moluccas, under the *Comendador* Loaisa; and subsequently despatched orders to Cortés in Mexico to send ships across the Pacific to Loaisa's support. Loaisa's expedition was a disastrous failure. Only one ship of a powerful fleet reached its destination, to find the Tidore factory destroyed by the Portuguese. Cortés, very willing to establish a trade in silk and spices from the Moluccas to Spain through Mexico, fitted out three ships on the Pacific coast and sent them off after Loaisa in 1527, under the command of his kinsman Alvaro de Saavedra; but Saavedra fared no better than Loaisa. Only one of his ships reached the Moluccas and none returned. It became clear that whatever happened in Europe, the Portuguese were in command of the situation in the East and the value of the Spanish claim was depreciating. The emperor, at war with France and on the verge of insolvency, in 1527 conceived the ingenious idea of selling or pawning his claim to the Moluccas before it should depreciate still further. In 1529, despite the opposition of the Spanish cortes, the Treaty of Zaragoza was duly signed. By this treaty Charles V pledged all his rights in the Moluccas to Portugal for 350,000 ducats in cash, and an arbitrary line of demarcation was fixed fifteen degrees east of the islands. For forty years Spaniards in the New World concentrated their attention on the Americas and left the East alone. It was not until the 1560's that they resumed Pacific exploration in earnest and actually settled in the Philippines. Cortés's later Pacific expeditions were coastal reconnaissances, whose chief result was the discovery of Lower California.

In the year of the treaty of Zaragoza Cortés visited Spain to present himself at court, to defend and explain his proceedings in Mexico, and to urge his claims upon the royal gratitude. He would have done well, for his own sake, to have gone earlier, as Alvarado had done. It was characteristic of him that he did not leave his immediate tasks of exploration, conquest and settlement until interferences with his authority and attacks on his reputation made his position intolerable. In 1527 a court of appeal for New Spain had been established by the Crown. The president of this *audiencia*, Nuño de Guzmán, was a lawyer by profession but a *conquistador* of a particularly brutal type by choice. He had been governor of Pánuco during Cortés's absence in Honduras and had amassed a considerable fortune by shipping Indian slaves to the Islands, though presumably this was then unknown to the Crown. He was a personal enemy of Cortés and a trusted adherent of Velásquez, the governor of Cuba, who had done all in his power to thwart the conqueror since 1519. With his fellow judges he was empowered to initiate an inquiry into the truth of the charges repeatedly brought against Cortés at the Spanish court; an inquiry which dragged on for years, with many petty recriminations, and was a principal motive in Cortés's journey to Spain. In 1529 therefore Nuño was left in control of affairs in New Spain; but he was disliked by the 'old conquerors' and in addition became seriously embroiled with the mendicant orders, particularly with the powerful and uncompromising bishop, Zumárraga. Zumárraga opposed *audiencia* rule not as a partisan of Cortés, but as a zealous champion of the Indians of Mexico many of whom fell victims to the slave-hunting activities of Nuño and his colleagues in the vast *encomiendas* which they acquired, by confiscation, from the adherents of Cortés. Zumárraga reported to the Crown, with reason, that Nuño's treatment of the Indians might provoke an armed rising; he conducted in Mexico an impassioned campaign against Nuño culminating in a general interdict on the city. Nuño intercepted most of Zumárraga's letters, but some of his complaints reached Spain, and late in 1529 the decision was taken to remove from office all the *audiencia* judges and the treasury officials of the province. Nuño anticipated the news of his disgrace by leaving Mexico in 1529 with a large armed following to make a new *entrada* to the north-west of New Spain, where he achieved a successful and very destructive conquest in the area later known as New Galicia. However, he did not enjoy his new command for long; arrested in 1536 and sent to Spain, he died in confinement four years later.

Cortés was in Spain at the time of the decision to replace Nuño. He had arrived at court with appropriate gifts and a train of Indian acrobats and had been warmly received by the emperor. He had been granted the title of marquis of the Valley of Oaxaca, and his great *encomienda* there had been confirmed. Beyond these rewards, the emperor's advisers had to decide how far he was to be trusted, and what use should be made of his great abilities, in the dangerous situation which had arisen in New Spain. Their decision was characteristic. Cortés was to return to Mexico as captain-general, to command such forces as were available in case of trouble; but he was not made governor. Civil government was once again to be entrusted to an *audiencia*, and this time great care was taken to select judges whose ability and integrity were beyond question and whose personality and policy would be acceptable to the missionary interest. The president was Sebastián Ramírez de Fuenleal, bishop of Santo Domingo, and the saintly humanist Vasco de Quiroga was one of his colleagues. This committee of very able lawyers and ecclesiastics administered New Spain for five years, endeavouring, without much success, to enforce royal orders modifying the rough government which the *conquistadores* had set up, and dealing as best they could with the factions which formed and quarrelled around the person of Cortés. Finally the Crown reached the obvious conclusion that friars, Indians and *conquistadores* could be governed only by a single strong hand and appointed a viceroy with far-reaching powers; but once again Cortés was passed over. The first viceroy was a soldier and a diplomat, cadet of a great noble house—Antonio de Mendoza, who took over the government of New Spain in 1535.

Of Cortés there is little more to say. He offered to lead troops against Nuño de Guzmán in New Galicia, but the offer was refused. With the approval of the Crown, the government of New Spain took every possible measure to whittle down his privileges and possessions, to interpret in the narrowest possible way the rewards he had been given by the emperor. Even the Indians of his *encomienda* were to be counted, so that their number could be restricted to the agreed 23,000. His Pacific expeditions were opposed and frustrated, especially after the arrival of Mendoza who himself wished to organise the exploration of the semi-legendary 'Cíbola' to the north of the Mexican deserts. The energies of a great commander were thus more and more confined to business activities, to the management of his sugar and cattle properties in Oaxaca and his house property in Mexico City. Finally in 1539 Cortés wearied of the New World and returned to Spain, where he lived in comfort but also in boredom, supported by the revenues of the *marquesado*. His reputation as a commander of expeditions against semi-barbarous tribes was little valued in Europe. Neither his services nor his advice were sought by the Crown, even in fields such as North Africa where they might have been of value. He died at his house of Castilleja de la Cuesta, near Seville, in 1547.

The policy of the Crown in New Spain in the 1530's was aimed not solely at Cortés but at the whole *conquistador* society which he represented. It was intended to be both anti-feudal and pro-Indian; and for long the emperor's advisers assumed, uncritically, that the two were synonymous, or at least complementary. The *encomienda* was the key to the situation; or so the friars and the bureaucrats at that time believed. A frontal attack on the institution would be difficult and dangerous, though its ultimate abolition was the aim of the more radical of the Crown's advisers. Meanwhile, the Crown resolutely resisted attempts of *encomenderos* to make their *encomiendas* hereditary, or to assume feudal jurisdiction within their boundaries, and sought to whittle down their privileges and to reduce their number. Already in 1530 the second *audiencia* had secret instructions to begin the reduction, or the resumption by the Crown, of the larger *encomiendas*. This policy, it was hoped, would prevent the growth of a potentially dangerous class of colonial feudatories, release the Indians from an onerous servitude and strengthen the direct authority of the Crown.

By 1530, not only had the main lines of Crown policy been indicated; the main instruments for its enforcement had been chosen. Success depended upon replacing the self-appointed captains and governors of the initial conquest by salaried officials appointed by the Crown. Some of these officials were soldiers and some ecclesiastics, but the great majority were school-trained lawyers. The standing committee of the Council of Castile, which had been set up in 1511 to deal with the business of the Indies, was constituted formally in 1524 as the separate Council of the Indies, a predominantly legal body. It combined, in the manner characteristic of Spanish institutions at that time, the functions of a supreme court of appeal in important cases with those of an advisory council and a directive ministry for the supervision of colonial affairs. The power of legislation, also, though legally reserved to the king, must often have been exercised by the council with little more than a purely formal royal assent. Failing the personal intervention of the monarch, the empire had a legal bureaucracy at its head.

In the Indies, as in Spain, the professional lawyer was the natural and chosen agent of a centralising policy. *Audiencias* had already been established in Santo Domingo and in Mexico; by the end of the sixteenth century their number in the New World was to be increased to ten.[1] Primarily courts of appeal, they acted also as cabinet councils to advise the civil or military governors of their respective provinces. They might hear appeals against governors' decisions and actions and might report independently to the council. They were expressly charged with the protection of Indian rights, forming a connecting link between a paternal royal authority and a subject people of alien culture, counteracting the centrifugal tendencies of an avaricious and disorderly colonial society. The *audiencia* judges—the *oidores*—were necessarily, in the absence of colonial law schools, peninsular Spaniards, differing widely in training, temperament and interests from the *conquistadores*. Those among them who carried out their instructions literally often clashed with the *conquistadores* directly; those, on the other hand, who accepted the interests and way of life of colonial Europeans competed with them for the available pickings.

Not only the higher courts, but the provincial treasuries also, were staffed from an early date by officers appointed by the Crown, replacing

[1] Santo Domingo, 1526; Mexico, 1527; Panama, 1535; Lima, 1542; Guatemala, 1543; New Galicia, 1548; New Granada, 1549; Charcas, 1559; Quito, 1563; Manila, 1583.

the original appointments made by the conquerors. The royal *hacienda* was carefully separated from the general administrative and judicial system of the colonies. Each provincial capital had its treasury office, its strong-box, its staff of officials—treasurer, comptroller, factor. The officials were responsible for the collection of direct taxes such as the *quinto* on precious metals; for the collection and sale of tribute in kind brought in by the Indian communities held by the Crown; for disbursements, such as official salaries, authorised in advance by the Crown; and for the regular remittance of the surplus to Spain. Treasury officials were directly responsible to the *contaduría* section of the Council of the Indies. No payments might lawfully be made from the colonial treasuries without the prior authorisation of the Crown, so that no viceroy or governor could hope to establish a private kingdom with public money.

Not only did the Crown appoint higher officials in courts and counting-houses; it early began to weaken the power of the 'old conquerors' in their own strongholds, the corporate towns of the Indies. The revolt of the Comuneros in Spain in 1520–1 had made a deep impression on the young king, leaving him more than ordinarily suspicious of the privileges and pretentions of municipal corporations, and of the local magnates who often controlled them. The towns of New Spain, therefore, were able to secure titles and armorial bearings, but little else, by grant from the Crown. Their power of raising local taxes was severely limited, their *procuradores* were forbidden to meet together without express royal permission, and any tendency towards concerted action was sharply discouraged. Nothing in the nature of a colonial cortes was allowed to develop. At at early date also, the Crown secured control of the internal composition of the major *cabildos*. In Mexico, where at first the annual *regidores* had elected their successors, year by year, subject to the governor's approval, the Crown began to appoint *regidores* for life in 1525. By 1528 the whole body consisted of these *regidores perpetuos*, and elections, except those of the two *alcaldes*, ceased. Admittedly many of the men who received *regimientos* from the Crown were 'old conquerors', *encomenderos* or local notables of some sort; but others came straight from Spain with their letters of appointment in their baggage, and all owed their dignities to the favour of the king or of some high officer of state. In 1529 the Crown for the first time appointed the town clerk of Mexico, and one by one most of the principal offices of the city came into the royal gift. It was an extremely useful form of patronage, from the king's point of view, costing the treasury nothing. It effectively discouraged the growth of a spirit of municipal independence, without, however, abating the feeling of municipal dignity.

The coping was set upon this elaborate structure of royal patronage by the appointment of the first viceroy, with a stipend generous enough to place him above petty venality, but himself serving during royal pleasure.

The viceroy's powers were very great; but even he, lacking extensive local patronage, having little armed force at his disposal and no power to spend money from the royal chest, was in no position to make himself dangerously independent. Moreover, he was watched and to some extent checked by the *audiencia* judges and like all other officials had to submit to a *residencia*—a judicial investigation of his tenure of office—at the end of his term. Charles V was singularly fortunate in his first choice of a viceroy for New Spain. With Mendoza firmly in command, with everyone, in the manner characteristic of Spanish administration of the time, set to watch everyone else, the independent spirit of the *conquistadores* seemed safely under control, and the way seemed clear for the introduction of those reforms of native policy which the missionary friars continued to urge upon the government.

During these far-reaching royal interventions in New Spain, however, other *conquistadores* had been busy far away in South America; by the time of Mendoza's arrival in Mexico, another equally formidable empire had been subdued by Spanish arms; the work of missionaries and officials was to do again, in much less favourable surroundings. Ever since the occupation of Darien rumours had been current among the Spaniards there of civilised and prosperous kingdoms to the south, but the reality long eluded discovery. The chief political and religious centres of ancient Peru lay high up on the Andine plateau, guarded by the gigantic ramparts of the eastern and western Cordillera. Here, at heights varying from 9,000 to 13,000 feet, over a period of some four hundred years the Inca clan and dynasty of the Quechua people had established a military dominion which, at the time of the Spaniards' arrival, extended for nearly two thousand miles from north to south and had its capital at Cuzco. The Inca empire was held together by stern discipline based on communal land-holding and a far-reaching system of forced labour. Discipline was enjoined by an elaborate and magnificent cult of ruler-worship and enforced by a military organisation which maintained fortresses and stores at strategic points, and a network of mountain roads and liana-cable bridges all over the empire. The Inca polity was far more closely organised than that of the Aztecs in Mexico, and its communications were better, considering the extreme difficulty of the terrain; but the general temper of the Peruvians was less warlike, and human sacrifice had ceased among them before the Spaniards arrived. Their material culture was largely of the Stone Age, but they were skilled workers in soft metals, made more use of copper tools than did the Mexicans, and employed gold and silver freely, for ornament and even for utensils. They were accomplished and artistic weavers, using not cotton but llama and vicuña wool. They had no writing, but employed a system of knotted cords for keeping accounts, such as tribute returns. Their agriculture was based not on grain crops such as maize, but on roots, chiefly varieties of potato. Their cities were solidly and skilfully built of dressed stone, not of adobe. Like the Mexicans, they had no knowledge of the wheel; but unlike them possessed a beast of burden, though a small and relatively inefficient one, the llama.

In the century or so before the Spanish invasion the Incas had extended their domination north into modern Ecuador, south into Chile as far as the Maule river, and over the region of the well-developed and highly individual Chimu culture of the coastal plain of Peru. These relatively recent acquisitions were a source of weakness to the empire. It was from the northern coastal regions that rumours of Inca wealth reached the Spaniards in Darien, and their inhabitants, still resentful of Inca rule, received the European invaders with acquiescence, if not with enthusiasm.

Peruvian enterprise was initiated in Darien by a syndicate comprising two soldiers of fortune from Estremadura, Francisco Pizarro and Diego de Almagro, and a priest named Luque. All three had settled in Darien as *encomenderos*, dabbling also in farming and mining. Luque, though he took no active part in the conquest of Peru, seems to have provided most of the initial capital. The partners spent four years in voyages of coastal exploration, in which they collected enough evidence to encourage them to approach the emperor for a formal capitulation. Pizarro's journey to Spain coincided with the triumphal appearance of Cortés at the court—a favourable omen; and Pizarro secured an appointment as *adelantado* and governor of the kingdom which he undertook to conquer. He returned to Panama with his four half-brothers and other volunteers. Leaving Almagro in Panama to follow later with reinforcements, Pizarro finally set out in 1530 with about 180 men and twenty-seven horses for the conquest of Peru.

The arrival of Pizarro at Túmbez on the northern coast of Peru coincided with the final stage of a succession war in which the reigning Inca, Huáscar, was defeated and dethroned by his usurping half-brother Atahualpa who chose as his capital not Cuzco but Cajamarca in northern Peru. Reports of this conflict encouraged Pizarro, after establishing himself in the Túmbez region and founding the 'city' of San Miguel, to march inland to Cajamarca. Here, by means of a surprise attack under cover of a formal conference, the Spaniards succeeded in killing most of Atahualpa's immediate retinue and capturing the ruler himself. Aided by surprise, by a favourable political situation, and by a breath-taking boldness that frightened the conquerors themselves, Pizarro and his men decided the fate of the Inca empire in a single afternoon. Almagro, with 200 men, arrived shortly afterwards. The Inca forces, deprived of the authority of their ruler, were unable effectively to resist the conquerors' march, with about 600 men, on Cuzco, which was taken and sacked in November 1533. The gold looted from Cuzco, together with the room-full of gold vessels which Atahualpa collected in the vain hope of buying his freedom, was melted down, the royal fifth subtracted, and the rest distributed; enough to make every man in the army rich for life, though comparatively few lived long to enjoy it.

Despite the hardships, the almost incredible mountain marches, and the fighting that lay behind, Cuzco was the beginning rather than the end of Pizarro's worst difficulties. Hitherto the campaign had followed approximately the same lines as that of Cortés in Mexico, but after the capture of Cuzco the pattern of events diverged. Pizarro, unlike Cortés, did not establish the centre of his power in the ancient capital of the kingdom, but founded in 1535 an entirely new Spanish capital—Lima, the City of the Kings, close to the sea in the Rimac valley. The choice was natural on military grounds, for Cuzco was remote from the harbours on which Spanish Peru depended for reinforcements and supplies from the outside world, and its mountainous surroundings made the use of cavalry, the chief Spanish arm, difficult if not impossible; but by this decision Pizarro emphasised the division between Spanish coast and Indian mountain and lost one means of attaching the Peruvians to a new allegiance. Peru never experienced the rapid interaction of European and Indian ways which was characteristic of the early history of Mexico. Pizarro was in any case a man of a very different stamp from Cortés. He had the disadvantage of not being, in the conventional social sense, a gentleman. In Spain he was the illegitimate son of obscure peasants, in the Indies a warrior among warriors, owing his leadership to vaulting ambition, boundless courage, and skill in fighting. He was illiterate, and therefore dependent upon secretaries. Shrewd though he was, he lacked Cortés's charm and diplomacy, his sensitive understanding of human situations, his genius for attaching even defeated enemies to himself. The judicial murder of Atahualpa was a blunder, condemned by many Spaniards. Pizarro had, moreover, jealous rivals in his own camp, and serious disputes soon arose among the conquerors. The first news of trouble came from San Miguel, whose governor, Belalcázar, had marched north into the region of Quito at the invitation of some of its inhabitants to rid them of their Inca governors and to establish a conquest of his own. The situation was complicated by the unexpected arrival from Guatemala of the restless and warlike Alvarado who also had designs on Quito. First Almagro and then Pizarro hastened north to avert civil war. Almagro and Belalcázar (who were *compadres*) made common cause against Alvarado, who after an interview with Pizarro agreed to return to his own government. Belalcázar retained his conquest of Quito.

Meanwhile Hernando Pizarro, the conqueror's half-brother, who had been sent to Spain with news and presents, had returned with despatches granting to Francisco Pizarro the title of marquis, and to Almagro that of *adelantado* in a necessarily undefined area to the south of that governed by Pizarro. Almagro promptly claimed Cuzco as part of his grant; Pizarro refused to give up the city; and after a face-saving reconciliation

Almagro departed on an expedition to explore and conquer his southern kingdom. He was away for two years, during which his army traversed the bleak *Altiplano* of what is now Bolivia and penetrated far into Chile, returning by way of the coastal desert of Atacama. Almagro's people suffered great hardships from cold and hunger, from heat and thirst; they lost most of their horses and many of their own number; found no more cities and no plunder worth the name; and returned to Cuzco in April 1537 still more bitterly jealous of Pizarro's good fortune.

During Almagro's absence Pizarro had to face a dangerous and widespread Indian rising led by Manco Inca, a successor of Huáscar whom Pizarro tried, unsuccessfully, to use as a puppet ruler. Manco failed to make any impression on Lima, but invested Cuzco closely and cut the city off from reinforcements sent from the coast. Indian armies were too large to keep the field for long periods, with the primitive means of transport available, and after some six months Manco's army began to dwindle; but before Pizarro could take advantage of this weakening, Almagro arrived with his army from Chile, took Manco in the rear and defeated him, marched into Cuzco and seized the government of city and province. This was the origin of the first of the civil wars of Spanish Peru, the war of Las Salinas. Like many subsequent disturbances in Peru, the war was a quarrel not only between two factions of Spaniards, but between the coast and the mountains, between the cities of Lima and Cuzco. Lima won; Almagro, after many vicissitudes, was defeated in 1538, and strangled by order of Hernando Pizarro, who took him prisoner. He had been an open-handed and popular leader, and his death made many enemies for the Pizarros. Francisco Pizarro's own turn came three years later. In 1541 he was murdered in Lima by a group of the 'men of Chile'; and a second civil war, the war of Chupas, flared up between the partisans of the two dead chieftains.

Manco Inca, who after his defeat lived for ten years as a fugitive ruler, may well have reflected on the ironical fate which befell the conquerors of his people—little bands of armed spoilers seeking one another out and fighting to the death among great mountains, with an empire at their feet awaiting an organising hand. The area under Spanish influence had expanded greatly during the war of Las Salinas and afterwards. Belalcázar had extended his dominion from Quito through forest country inhabited by primitive tribes, north to Popayán, and beyond into the isolated but settled land of the city-building Chibchas. Here his advance met that of Gonzalo Jiménez de Quesada, who marched south from the Caribbean up the Magdalena river to the populous and prosperous savannahs of Bogotá. On this occasion the leaders, approximately equal in strength, agreed on a division of territory. Santa Fe de Bogotá became in due course the capital of the Spanish kingdom of New Granada. Belalcázar— who had added a new technique to the methods of conquest by driving a great herd of pigs along with his army, a source of food supply on the march and a great acquisition to the country—became governor of Popayán. Far to the south, Almagro's reconnaissances of Chile had been followed up by Pedro de Valdivia who founded the city of Santiago in 1541. Valdivia's conquest was unusual in two respects. As a result of Pizarro's death he found himself without a master and became one of the few elected governors in the Indies by the choice of the *vecinos* of Santiago, much as Cortés had been 'elected' at Vera Cruz. Finding no gold and no settled Indian culture, he succeeded in establishing a modest but soundly based Spanish farming community, in one of the loveliest and most fertile valleys in the world.

All these captains had been, in form at least, the lieutenants of Francisco Pizarro. Pizarro's death left a vacuum in Peru which only the Crown could fill. The war of Chupas, accordingly, differed from the earlier quarrels in that a royal governor despatched from Spain was actively engaged. The licentiate Vaca de Castro, president of the new *audiencia* of Panama, sent to Peru to investigate the disorders there, held a commission to succeed Pizarro in the event of the marquis's death; and accordingly on arrival assumed command of the Pizarro faction, turning it thereby into a royal army operating against an armed rebellion. The Almagro party was defeated, and many of its leaders executed; and, more difficult, Castro with a lawyer's skill and patience dissuaded Gonzalo Pizarro from claiming, sword in hand, the succession to his brother's authority.

Castro's part in the war of Chupas was a brief prelude to a far more drastic royal intervention which was to affect profoundly the course of events in both New Spain and Peru. For more than a decade the Crown had been urging its officials in New Spain to restrict the power and privileges of *encomenderos*. No effective action had been taken. Not only were the *encomenderos* well entrenched and locally powerful; the officials also quickly came to recognise the *encomienda* as the most powerful single instrument of the Spaniards in the colonisation of the Indies. The anti-feudatory and humanitarian legislation promoted at court by missionaries like Las Casas met opposition in the colony, at least until mid-century, from the officials entrusted with its enforcement, because every realistic administrator engaged in colonial government knew that without *encomiendas* there would be no colonisation. Even the missionaries were not of one mind. Many friars in the colonies—the Dominican Fray Domingo de Betanzos, for example—opposed the expropriation of *encomiendas*; and towards the middle of the century the mendicant orders were being forced, by episcopal attacks on their immunities, into an uneasy alliance with the *encomenderos*. Nevertheless, Las Casas and others of his mind maintained an unremitting pressure at court, and events in Peru gave support to their arguments. *Encomiendas* had been granted in Peru as in New Spain, but there had been little leisure for peaceful organisation. The constant

578

fighting had taken a far heavier toll of Indian lives and property than in New Spain, and the mitigating influence of the missionary orders had been far less effective. By the time that Peru was conquered, Erasmian radicalism within the Spanish Church had lost much of its vigour. Peru received no picked band of zealots comparable with the Twelve. The evangelisation of the Indians and their training in European crafts were far less successful than in New Spain; on the other hand, the indiscipline of colonial feudatories took far more dangerous forms, and the Crown had still more cogent reasons for attacking their privileges.

In 1542 the Crown, partly at the insistence of Las Casas, made a sweeping frontal attack on the whole *encomienda* system. The 'New Laws of the Indies' were a comprehensive code for the whole field of colonial government, but the most significant and revolutionary clauses concerned *encomiendas*. All *encomiendas* were to revert to the Crown on the death of their present holders; no official, lay or ecclesiastical, might be an *encomendero*; and the *encomiendas* of all who had taken part in the civil disturbances in Peru were to be confiscated immediately. This last clause, if interpreted literally, would have deprived every *encomendero* in Peru of his Indians forthwith. In New Spain Mendoza persuaded or bullied the *visitador* entrusted with the enforcement of the New Laws to suspend their promulgation indefinitely. Peru, however, had no effective royal government, and the first viceroy was appointed and sent out, along with the staff of a new *audiencia*, specifically to put the new code into operation. He was Blasco Núñez de la Vela, a professional soldier, an inflexible and unintelligent martinet. His insistence, against the advice of the *audiencia* judges, on the immediate enforcement of his instructions, provoked an armed rising, led by Gonzalo Pizarro, and a fresh civil war, in which Núñez was killed in battle, early in 1546. Gonzalo Pizarro became, for a time, the effective ruler of Peru. Had he repudiated his allegiance altogether, as his grim camp-master Carbajal advised, he might have established an independent kingdom. Habits of loyalty, however, though loose, were strong. Gonzalo Pizarro so little understood the growing bureaucratic absolutism of Charles V that he attempted, like a *conquistador* bargaining from strength, to secure royal recognition of his authority; but the time for such loose feudal agreements had passed. The attempt to negotiate merely enabled Núñez's successor in the government, the priest Pedro de la Gasca—having already, from Panama, secured command of the sea—to land in Peru, to detach many jealous individuals from Gonzalo, and eventually to raise an army which defeated him. Gonzalo and his principal lieutenants were beheaded in March 1548. Of the five violent and ungovernable brothers who had conquered Peru, only Hernando survived, to end his days in a Spanish prison. The establishment of order throughout the viceroyalty was a slow and difficult process; but by 1560 the viceroy—the brutal Cañete—was able to report that the southern realms were entirely at peace. Colonial feudalism of an armed and overt kind had been put down; in Peru, as in New Spain, the official replaced the *conquistador*.

Though inflexible in suppressing armed rebellion, the Council of the Indies had already received and digested Mendoza's cogent advice, and had recognised its mistake in pushing the *encomenderos* too hard. Both central and local governments were working towards a compromise solution. The *cédula* issued by the emperor at Malines in 1545 re-established the old rules concerning the succession of *encomiendas*; they were to run, as before, for two lives, a limit often exceeded in practice. On the other hand, a series of subsequent decrees in 1549 and 1550 prohibited the exaction of services by *encomenderos*, and in particular the employment of Indians as porters. The institution survived, therefore, but changed in character. No doubt *encomenderos* did extort illegal services, but in law they were entitled only to the tribute of their Indians—tribute paid partly in money and partly in produce, at rates fixed from time to time by the *audiencias*. The *encomienda*, so defined, was to become a mere pension to pay for the support—and to buy off the opposition—of the 'old conquerors' and their descendants. Villages which had not been granted in *encomienda*, or which escheated to the Crown in course of time, were entrusted to the care of district officers, *corregidores*; and these *corregimientos*, which were temporary salaried offices, not feudal grants for a term of lives, gradually replaced *encomiendas* as the normal reward for local services. The problem of inducing the Indians to work for wages, and to contribute to the economic life of a community wider than a single *pueblo*, was taken out of private hands and became a public concern. Though personal servitude had become illegal, governors were empowered to compel 'idle' Indians to seek employment, and all Indian villages were required to furnish a weekly quota of labourers for hire, for recognised public purposes; a system generally known as *repartimiento* in New Spain and *mita* in Peru.

In New Spain the legislation of 1545–50 was enforced with considerable success by the second viceroy, Luis de Velasco, who governed the province from 1550 to 1563, and by the *visitadores* whom he sent out for the purpose. In Peru, effective enforcement was not achieved until the time of Francisco de Toledo, the organising genius who in twelve years of government (1569–81), gave the viceroyalty of Peru its settled, permanent, bureaucratic stamp, and who, incidentally, ordered the execution of Túpac Amarú, the last recognised Inca prince. Enforcement would have been difficult, perhaps impossible, in both viceroyalties, but for powerful social and economic forces working in the same direction. Clearly the best way to prevent the use of Indians as porters was to encourage the breeding and use of pack animals; and the best remedy for a limited, semi-feudal society based on *encomiendas* was the provision of other occupations by which Europeans could earn a living, without outraging their prejudices on the subject of work unsuitable for gentlemen. In fact, in the second half of the sixteenth century *encomiendas* declined steadily in value, because of government interference, mounting inflation (since tributes were assessed largely in money terms), and decreases in the Indian population due to pestilence. At the same time more and more Indians—in New Spain at least—acquired European skills or developed their own crafts, either for wages or on their own account. The use of coined money spread, a money economy began to replace direct subsistence, and Spaniards discovered new sources of livelihood which far outstripped the old *encomiendas* in importance. Of these sources the most characteristic and lucrative were mines and stock ranches.

In the arid uplands of Castile from which most of the *conquistadores* came, pastoral pursuits, the grazing of semi-nomadic flocks and herds, had long been preferred to arable farming. The preference was social and military as well as economic; it was the legacy of centuries of intermittent fighting, of constantly shifting frontiers. The man on horseback, the master of flocks and herds, was the man best adapted to such conditions, in the New World as in the Old. There were, it is true, a few favoured localities such as Puebla in New Spain or Antioquia in New Granada, where Spanish landowners grew wheat for sale in nearby cities, or at the ports for victualling ships; but in most parts of the Indies, cattle and sheep raising became in Mendoza's time the principal occupation of the wealthier Spaniards. Every chronicler of New Spain mentioned, usually with astonishment and delight, the prodigious numbers of beasts which the country supported. Mendoza himself introduced the merino sheep, the basis of an incipient woollen industry which, incidentally, earned a sinister reputation for coercion and ill-treatment of Indian labourers in its *obrajes*. Of the spread of cattle, the price of beef in the Mexico market is eloquent evidence: in 1538, 17 maravedis the *arrelde* of 4 lb.; in 1540, 10 mrs; in 1542, 4 mrs. The price was fixed at the last figure by municipal ordinance, and penalties exacted for selling cheaper; for the city *regidores* were almost all ranch owners. With beef so cheap, no Spaniard need starve or work for wages, and great men who owned cattle ranges could keep open house and feed large bands of retainers. Except in the neighbourhood of big cities, the beef was comparatively unprofitable; the chief value of the beasts lay in their hides, for saddlery and for protective clothing, and in tallow, for making candles and for coating the hulls of ships as protection against marine borers. When hides and tallow had been removed, the carcasses of slaughtered cattle were often left to rot where they lay. In such conditions production, to be profitable, must be on a very large scale, and grazing grants went chiefly to wealthy settlers who could afford to stock them. The grants were loosely defined, initially in terms of radius from a fixed spot, and little attempt was made to survey boundaries. Naturally the beasts invaded the unfenced *milpas* of the Indian villages, despite repeated legislation, and despite the efforts of colonial courts to protect Indian property. In the valley of Toluca, forty-five miles north-east of Mexico, for instance, cattle were introduced in 1535. Twenty years later the valley carried 150,000 head. The Franciscans of Toluca reported that the local Indians, except for a few employed as shepherds or cow-hands, had fled to the hills, and the price of maize had gone up from ½ *real* the *fanega* to 4 *reales*. Some single owners, they said, had over 15,000 head, and government could do nothing because of the influence of ranchers and cattle-owning officials and of the secular clergy in Mexico City who lived on the tithes. Toluca was one example among hundreds. The spread of stock ranching was undoubtedly a major cause of depopulation in central New Spain, and over-grazing the principal cause of the soil erosion which has plagued Mexico ever since. In Peru, horned cattle were of less importance, but sheep, and pigs rooting in the potato patches, created similar conditions in many parts of the highlands. In both areas stock ranching, often combined with abuses of the *encomienda* system, tended to the destruction of Indian communal farming and to the establishment of European-owned *latifundia*.

First *encomiendas* and then stock ranches produced the accumulations of capital which made possible the large-scale mining of precious metals. Gold and silver mining in the early days of the conquest was a simple affair of prospecting and washing in likely streams; but about the middle of the sixteenth century, immensely productive silver veins were discovered at Zacatecas and Guanajuato in New Spain, and at Potosí— richest of all—in what is now Bolivia. Various forms of crude mass-production quickly took the place of the primitive washing process, and extensive plant—extensive for those days—was set up for extracting the silver from the ore, usually by a mercury amalgamation process. These developments produced lawless and exciting silver rushes, and special courts were hastily set up in the mining camps to register claims and settle disputes. The Crown claimed a share, usually one fifth, of all metal produced. A considerable body of officials was employed to weigh, test and stamp the silver ingots as they issued from the mines and to take out the royal share which, after authorised disbursements, was shipped to Spain, along with the larger quantities of bullion sent home by individuals, either as an investment, or in payment for European goods imported.

Although some Spaniards, and more Indians, worked small claims by hand, the typical silver miner was a capitalist on a fairly large scale. Mining and ranching were complementary, since the miners needed steady supplies of beef, leather and tallow candles, and often the same people were concerned in both. Mining, like ranching, bore hardly on the Indian population but in a different way. It created a great demand for pick-and-shovel labour; some of this demand was met by the import of negro slaves, but most of the work was done by Indians who, though paid, had to be recruited largely by coercion under the *repartimiento* system. Over-work and under-feeding, but even more the epidemics which spread in crowded conditions, took a heavy toll of Indians in the mines; and epidemic disease was carried by the mine-workers back to their villages. Those Indians who accepted European ways, more or less, who acquired European crafts or plied Indian crafts near European centres, were effectively protected against ill-treatment (though not, of course against disease) and could become modestly wealthy; so could the headmen who organised the labour supply; but Indians who stayed in their villages and tried to carry on in the old way had the worst of both worlds. In general, as the provinces grew rich and prosperous, so they grew less populous. In New Spain especially, the Indian population declined steadily, with sharp drops in the 1540's and again in the 1570's due to major epidemics; and the decline continued until the middle of the next century.[1]

Both New Spain and Peru produced silver; it was their chief value in Spanish estimation. But Peru produced much more silver than New Spain, and beyond bare subsistence needs produced little else. The conquerors of Peru remained a small Spanish community, with a good deal of specie at their disposal and with an avid desire for consumer goods. New Spain, on the other hand, where Spanish and Indian communities had begun to mingle and fuse, was industrious and productive and short of specie owing to the efficiency of silver-tax collection and the large private remittances made to Spain, especially by the Cortés estate. It became profitable to ship goods of Spanish origin down the coast to Peru to supplement the costly trickle of imports across the Isthmus. With these trans-shipments went Mexican products (mules, sugar, preserved fruit), European-type wares made in New Spain by Spanish or Indian craftsmen, and an interesting assortment of Indian wares—polished obsidian mirrors, lacquered gourds, feather-work tapestry and the like. The Cortés estate invested considerable sums in this trade, shipping chiefly its own products. In the 1560's the conquest of the Philippines by Miguel López de Legazpi[2] —who was a land-owner and had been an official in Mexico—led to the establishment of a regular trade across the Pacific between Manila and Acapulco; and as a result great quantities of silk and other Chinese goods were similarly trans-shipped to Peru. It was this development of the trade, and the resulting leak of Peruvian silver into the specie-hungry Orient, which led the Crown to intervene and eventually in the seventeenth century to prohibit trade between the viceroyalties altogether.

[1] A recent and well-documented study gives the following approximate figures for central Mexico: 1519—11,000,000; 1540—6,427,466; 1565—4,409,180; 1597—2,500,000. S. F. Cook and L. B. Simpson *The Population of Central Mexico in the Sixteenth Century, Ibero-Americana* 31 (Berkeley, Calif., 1948). Other writers differ considerably in their estimates of numbers, but there is general agreement on the downward trend.

[2] Cf. below, p. 612.

A close regulation of trade had always been characteristic of Spanish imperial policy, and the subordination of Pacific to Atlantic considerations was entirely consistent. The trans-Atlantic shipping of Spain was concentrated in the port of Seville, and from 1543 was a monopoly in the hands of the *consulado*—the merchant gild—of that city. The *consulado* was a powerful body, well able to defend its privileged position and to abuse it. By an elaborate series of fictions, merchant houses all over Spain became members by proxy of the Seville gild, consigning their cargoes in the names of resident Seville merchants. Even foreign commercial firms, German, English and Flemish, adopted this device, so that the genuine members of the gild performed a vast commission business which later came to overshadow their own legitimate trade. Seville was the bottle-neck of the Indies trade, a bottle-neck still further narrowed by the minute regulation which the Crown enforced through its agency, the *Casa de Contratación*. The *Casa* collected the duties on the Indies trade and received and transmitted the revenue shipped from America. It contained within itself a court for the settlement of commercial disputes, a hydro-graphical department, and a school of navigation. It inspected and licensed emigrants, to prevent emigration of Jews and heretics; ships, to ensure their sea-worthiness; and navigators, to ensure their competence. Some commodities might only be exported with special licence—firearms and negro slaves, for example. In general, the licensing regulations were an irritating hindrance to legitimate commerce, and a challenge to the ingenuity of law-breakers.

Sixteenth-century Spain was primarily a producer of raw materials, exporting wine, olive oil and wool in return for foreign wares; but it possessed industries also, and in some types of manufacture—silk, fine woollens, gloves, leather, arms and cutlery—Spanish craftsmen not only supplied a large part of the domestic market, but furnished a surplus for export to the Indies. The increase, between 1530 and 1594, in the population of such towns as Burgos, Segovia and Toledo, suggests that industrial activity was growing also; but it certainly did not grow fast enough to keep pace with the growth of demand in the Indies. There was a rigidity in the economic structure of Spain which made a rapid expansion of the export trade extremely difficult. Among the causes of this rigidity were the contempt widely felt for humdrum employment, and the resulting shortage of labour; the exclusive conservatism of municipal corporations and craft gilds; the privileges accorded to transhumant sheep-raising, which damaged arable interests and led to shortages of food; the large and growing proportion of people in unproductive occupations, especially the Church and the profession of arms; heavy taxation, which impeded the accumulation of capital; and constant European war. These factors particularly affected Castile, the kingdom most directly concerned; for the flourishing commercial centres of Catalonia and Aragon were committed to their Mediterranean connections and had no great interest in the Indies trade. *Mutatis mutandis*, many of these factors operated also in the Indies, making Spaniards there more dependent than they need have been upon native labour and imported European goods. The whole of the Indies was an eager market for cloth, weapons, tools and hardware of all sorts, books, paper, wine, oil and slaves. Except for oil and wine, —largely produced by *morisco* labour—Spanish merchants could not export these goods in sufficient quantities or at competitive prices. The Indies trade, therefore, was a standing temptation to slavers, smugglers and illicit traders, mostly Portuguese in the first half of the century, but later from northern Europe also. John Hawkins, who organised three large-scale voyages to the Caribbean with slaves and textiles in the 1560's, was the forerunner of many others, Flemish, English and Dutch.

The large proportion of silver in their cargoes made homeward-bound Indies ships a temptation also to marauders—privateers, chiefly French during the incessant wars between France and Spain, but later Dutch and English too; and pirates at all times. About the middle of the century it became necessary to send the bullion shipments under convoy. From 1564 two armed fleets were despatched from Spain every year, one to Mexico and the Gulf ports, the other to the isthmus of Panama. Both fleets wintered in America and reassembled at Havana the following spring for the return voyage. Each fleet consisted of from twenty to sixty sail, usually escorted by from two to six warships. It was forbidden for any ship to cross the Atlantic except in one of these convoys, unless special licence had been granted. The system, including the supporting cruiser squadrons based at Santo Domingo and Cartagena, and the for-midable defences at Havana, was planned by one of the greatest sea commanders of the time, Pedro Menéndez de Avilés, and on the whole it proved effective. Odd stragglers were lost in most years, but on no occasion in the sixteenth century was a whole sailing intercepted and defeated, and regular sailings were maintained for a century and a half. The successes of Drake in 1585–6 were achieved against coastal towns, and their results were purely temporary. On the other hand, the cost of the convoys was borne by a heavy and complicated series of duties on all goods carried to and from America; so the safety of the fleets was dearly bought, and the whole arrangement added greatly both to the delays of obtaining goods in the colonies and to the price of the goods when they eventually arrived.

Throughout most of the sixteenth century the Portuguese were among the chief illicit traders to the Spanish Caribbean settlements. They possessed, in the Azores, a useful port of call, and in West Africa a series of slave barracoons, maintained by agreement with coastal rulers. African slaves had been employed from the early years of the century in the sugar production of Hispaniola, and later on the Main and in coastal

Mexico. Traders licensed by the Spanish government to supply slaves to the colonies had to buy their slaves from Portuguese middlemen; and Portuguese slavers often ran cargoes across on their own account, either as sub-contractors or as smugglers. A transatlantic slave trade in Portuguese hands, therefore, was already established when, in the latter part of the century, a demand for slaves grew up in Portugal's own American possessions in Brazil. For the first thirty or forty years after Cabral's landfall the Portuguese, fully occupied in the east, made no use of Brazil except as a source of wild brazil-wood for the dyeing industry, and as a dumping ground for transported criminals—*degredados*. The coast was visited as much by French wood-cutters as by Portuguese; and it was partly the desire to assert the rights of prior occupation against the French which impelled the Portuguese government in the 1530's to take active steps to promote settlement there. In 1530 an armed fleet under Martim Affonso de Souza was sent to prospect the 3000 miles of coast from Maranhão to Río Grande do Sul, to eject French settlers and seize French ships. De Souza spent two years on the coast and founded the first two permanent settlements in Brazil: São Vicente, near modern Santos, and Pernambuco, the centre of the dyewood region, where the French had attempted to establish a fort. In 1533 John III divided the Brazilian coast—and, in theory, the hinterland to the 'line of demarcation'—into twelve captaincies which were granted to proprietary landlords known as *donatários*. The *donatários* were required to settle and defend their territories at their own expense, receiving in return extensive administrative, judicial and fiscal powers over such colonists as they could induce to emigrate; powers such as many Spanish *conquistadores* had sought and been denied. The Portuguese, however, could furnish neither the men nor the capital for the rapid settlement of Brazil by a system of purely private enterprise. Neither gold nor diamonds were found until late in the seventeenth century, and pioneering in the tropics held little attraction for men who could, if they chose, engage in the commerce of the East. Four of the original grants were never taken up; four succumbed to Indian attacks; two only—Pernambuco and São Vicente—had begun by mid-century to yield a profit to their holders; and French interlopers continued to visit the coast. In 1549 John III, recognising the weakness of the captaincy system for the purposes of settlement and defence, took the first steps towards the establishment of royal government: the proclamation of Bahía as the capital of Brazil and the appointment of Tomé de Souza as captain-general. De Souza already had considerable experience of administration and war in Africa and the East. The formidable expedition which accompanied him to his post included, besides soldiers, settlers and officials, six Jesuits under Manoel de Nóbrega; members of this newly founded order were to play a prominent part in the growth of the Portuguese empire in the Old World and the New, and their missions among the primitive Tupi-Guaraní peoples were to set a characteristic stamp upon the whole history of interior Brazil. Nóbrega remained in Brazil until his death in 1570; his ministry overlapped and influenced the government of that great soldier and administrator, Mem de Sá, captain-general from 1557 to 1572. Mem de Sá was perhaps the most effective and forceful of the founders of colonial Brazil. One of his major tasks was the eviction of the French from central Brazil, and the foundation (in 1567) of the settlement of Rio de Janeiro near the site of the principal French encampment. He was the first captain-general to devise and enforce a consistent native policy, intended to discipline the warlike, to convert the heathen, to protect those who submitted against enslavement and ill-treatment; in particular, to abolish cannibalism and to induce the Indians to settle in agricultural communities. These were among the aims of Spanish policy also; but the primitive forest Indians of Brazil were less promising neophytes than the settled peoples of central Mexico or highland Peru, and Portuguese policy was correspondingly less ambitious and less effective.

Portuguese society in Brazil was markedly rural in character. There were no Mexicos or Limas, and most of the 'towns' were mere hamlets. Apart from subsistence crops—native cassava and introduced maize—and the dyewood which grew wild, the principal product was sugar, introduced from Madeira. Sugar was best grown, in Brazil as elsewhere, on relatively large estates, with slave labour. The Brazilian Indians proved unsuitable as estate labour, but the Portuguese were better placed than other Europeans for obtaining slaves from West Africa, and by the end of Mem de Sá's government the pattern of 'great house', slave quarters and cane fields was established. By 1580 there were some sixty sugar mills in operation. The population amounted to roughly 20,000 Portuguese, 18,000 settled Indians, and 14,000 negro slaves. This thin scattering of people was confined to a narrow coastal fringe, the hinterland as yet untouched; but eight of the old captaincies possessed established settlements, and Bahía, the capital, had some pretentions to the title of city. Brazil was in this state, still almost empty of people but with a few scattered Portuguese settlements achieving a modest prosperity, when in 1580 the king-cardinal Henry, last of the rulers of the house of Aviz, died leaving a vacant throne. Philip II, by a mixture of bargaining, bribery, persuasion and force, asserted his own claim to succeed; and Portugal and the Portuguese possessions came under the rule of a Spanish king.

Already before 1580 the Spaniards had succeeded the French as the principal competitors for the control of Brazil. In 1536 Pedro de Mendoza had built his short-lived fort at Buenos Aires, the first move in a long rivalry in the Río de la Plata area, and his people founded Asunción in 1537. Orellana in 1541–2 had crossed the Andes from Peru, made his astonishing canoe passage down the Amazon, and established the Spanish claim to the Amazon valley west of the line of demarcation. Both at the northern and the southern extremities of the line, where it was thought to cross Brazil, Spanish activities continued to alarm the government in Lisbon. In practice, however, the Portuguese settlements on the northeast coast were remote from these activities; and even the events of 1580 had little immediate effect upon Brazil. In a *carta patente*, issued at Lisbon on 12 November 1582, Philip II undertook to leave both the commerce and the administration of the Portuguese colonies in Portuguese hands, and in general he kept his promise. Portugal and its possessions were simply one more addition to a heterogeneous collection of separate kingdoms, united only by allegiance to the Habsburg king. It was only by slow degrees, and incompletely, that the influence of Spanish bureaucracy permeated the easy-going society of Portuguese Brazil.

By 1580, then, Philip II was ruler of all the European settlements so far established in the New World. The achievement of Iberian conquest and government was an impressive one. The Crown had been well served, not only by soldiers and settlers, but by administrators, lawyers and ecclesiastics. Enduring kingdoms had been created; and a great body of statute law had been enacted, governing the relations between conquerors and conquered, and the authority of the Crown and the royal courts over them all. Much of this legislation—the New Laws, for example, and the *Ordenanzas sobre Descubrimientos* of 1573—was a model of enlightenment for its time. That it was imperfectly enforced is true, and not surprising. Most sixteenth-century legislation was imperfectly enforced; but, at least, the generous provisions of courts, staffed by salaried professional judges who might be expected to be reasonably impartial, ensured that the royal decrees were more than mere pious exhortations. Not only in conquest, settlement, legislation, government, but also in the abstract field of political theory, the Spanish achievement in the New World left enduring and memorable traces. Francisco de Vitoria's *Relectiones de Indis* contain the first systematic discussion of the right and wrongs of conquest, the beginning of modern international law. Juan Ginés de Sepúlveda wrote the first reasoned treatise justifying the subjugation and tutelage of primitive by more civilised peoples. Las Casas, in his refutations of Sepúlveda, wrote not only indignant catalogues of crimes, not only distinguished contributions to humanitarian literature, but serious and cogent defences of human liberty and constitutional government. It is a measure of the self-confidence of sixteenth-century Spain, and of Spanish respect for liberty and law, that in the days of Charles V—a great king and a great autocrat—treatises denouncing the excesses of the *conquistadores* (who, after all, were in a sense the agents of the Crown), treatises criticising the whole enterprise of the Indies, treatises even in some circumstances advocating tyrannicide, could be circulated and read without scandal. Conversely, the treatises describing and justifying the government of the Indies—many of them, like Juan de Matienzo's *Gobierno del Perú*, written by colonial officials—are for the most part temperate and well-informed. In theory and in practice, in policy and in law, the rapacity and the crusading zeal of the *conquistadores* quickly gave way to a sane, conscientious and prudent imperialism, an imperialism which could face its critics boldly and with confidence. Partly for that reason, the conquest proved remarkably enduring.

Imperialism, however, lays burdens, both economic and political, upon the homeland of the conquerors, and its rewards are often illusory. Many Spaniards—*conquistadores*, settlers and officials—made fortunes in the Indies which they could hardly have dreamed of in Spain; but the steady drift overseas of men of courage and ability was a serious loss to Spain. The silver of the Indies, the most valued prize of empire, which paid the armies of Italy and Flanders, in the end created more problems than it solved. The great increase in the amount of silver in circulation in Spain, and in due course throughout Europe, the consequent rise in commodity prices, and the upsetting of the established bimetallic ratio, together caused great confusion and great hardship. Since the rigidity of the Castilian economy made it impossible for industry and agriculture to respond adequately to the stimulus of rising prices,[1] the result was to place Spain at a serious disadvantage in international trade.

Of specie remittances to Spain, between a quarter and a third were Crown revenue under various heads of taxation. Until about the middle of Philip II's reign this Indies revenue was not a major item in the total receipts of the Crown, not more than about 10 per cent in most years. In the last two decades of the sixteenth century it mounted rapidly, and in one year—1585—reached 25 per cent. Moreover, the income which private individuals drew from the Indies helped to increase the yield of taxation in Spain. The Indies revenue, therefore, though much smaller than most contemporaries, Spanish and foreign, supposed, was important enough to affect royal policy considerably, and to produce effects more insidious than monetary inflation alone. A nation cannot live, or fancy itself to be living, by the efforts of subjects overseas, without some demoralisation of its public life at home. As early as 1524 the cortes of Castile had protested against the proposal to sell the Moluccas to Portugal, on the ground that the possession of the islands secured to the emperor a steady income, independent of taxation. The deputies were prepared to relinquish their only political bargaining counter—the control of financial supply—in order to relieve the immediate burden of taxes. According to the economic theories of the time the argument was reasonable; but it augured ill for the constitutional future of Spain. The possession of the Indies encouraged Philip II more and more to ignore unwelcome advice from the cortes, from the nobility and from public opinion generally, in

[1] Cf. above, p. 49.

Castile; and public opinion grudgingly acquiesced in the growth of absolutist practices born of successful imperialism. Bureaucratic absolutism spread, as it were by contagion, from the Indies to Castile, where it was naturally more directly felt, more burdensome, less tempered by distance and procrastination. The possession of the Indies also helped to make permanent the preponderance of Castile—the most warlike, the least productive, in many ways the most backward of the Iberian kingdoms—over the rest of the peninsula. Finally, exaggerated estimates of the value of the Indies intensified the fear and hostility which Habsburg policy provoked in many parts of Europe, while encouraging the Spanish Crown to pursue an international policy which it could not afford to maintain, and which was to lead it to impoverishment and defeat.

CHAPTER XX

EUROPE AND THE EAST

FIRST among Europeans to reach the East by sea were the Portuguese. Opening the new route round the Cape in 1498, they quickly showed their strength in the Arabian Sea and the lands near it. By 1509 they had already vanquished the fleets of their chief enemies at Diu, plundered much merchant shipping and sacked a number of coastal towns. In the next decade their influence grew wider and more firmly rooted. Afonso de Albuquerque, governor of the Portuguese in the East from 1509 to 1515, revolutionised the position of the Portuguese in the East, while, simultaneously, his king's trade and government in Asia approached a fairly settled form. The period from 1509 to about 1520 was a crucial phase in the history of the Portuguese in the East, for it saw the king's ambition spread and many of his institutions in Asia take permanent shape. After 1520 the king's authority got slowly weaker, but private Portuguese trade went on and flourished, especially in the second half of the sixteenth century. In 1580 the king had the burdens of government and private merchants most of the profit from trade, a sure sign that overseas enterprise had failed to fulfil the hopes which members of the royal family of Portugal had put in it since the early part of the fifteenth century.

Portuguese interest in the East began with the impetus of a belated crusade and developed from the desire of Prince Henry 'the Navigator' for discoveries beyond Cape Bojador, on the coast of Rio de Oro. As governor of the military Order of Christ, the prince sent out his first explorers of the African coast in 1421. About thirty-five years later the pope granted the Order of Christ spiritual jurisdiction and freedom to trade 'as far as the Indians'. From that time, if not before, the Portuguese were probably concerned with the idea of a sea route to India. They did not find it swiftly: not till 1488 did a Portuguese vessel pass east of the Cape of Good Hope. Shortly afterwards King John II seems to have received news of ports of western India and south-eastern Africa. It now became almost certain that men could reach Asia by sea. But no Portuguese tried to do so until 1497 when Vasco da Gama set out on his first major voyage, in command of a royal fleet.

From the start Portuguese actions in Asia were those of a branch of government—a point of much importance. Manuel I (1495–1521), under whom Gama sailed, followed the same policy as John II (1481–95) and regarded Portuguese activity in West Africa and beyond as the business of royal officials. He did not normally license adventurers, despatch them to Asia with encouragement and advice, and then hope for a moderate

591

percentage of any profit they might chance to make. With a few exceptions, the king alone sent expeditions to the East: he financed them from royal revenues or loans and tried to take the lion's share of profits on trade between Asia and Europe. He also appointed the commanders of expeditions, gave them detailed orders and laid down who might go with them. The law always forbade departures for Asia without royal licence and few Portuguese of the sixteenth century began life in the East as private adventurers. They generally went there as military or civil servants of the Crown, or else as clergy: they were invariably paid by the king and sometimes highly conscious of their dignity as his servants. At the outset these arrangements gave added force to Portuguese actions in Asia. Above all, they put control of policy into royal hands.

King Manuel seems to have had two chief aims in the East. He wanted a share in the trade that flowed from Asia to Europe and he wished to strike a blow at the Muslims, his enemies 'as if by direct succession'. Trade and war went together. War could not be waged without profits from trade because the resources of Portugal were too small: at the same time, war with Muslims in the East meant an attack on the Arabs who had a strong grip on the commerce between India and the Near East. But when the Portuguese first reached Asia they doubted their power to act alone and hoped to find an ally. They sometimes identified him with 'Prester-John', the Christian 'priest-king' of Ethiopia. The help of his soldiers was to make up for their small numbers.

Local conditions favoured the Portuguese when they arrived in Asia. There were then few strong navies in eastern waters. This was significant because Portuguese power in Asia was ultimately maritime. For most of the sixteenth century the Portuguese in Asia were not interested in large territorial dominion, if only because they had not the means to acquire it. They were concerned with the coasts and the sea: in both places their strength depended on their fleets. In the early years of the sixteenth century only three Asian countries challenged them at sea with any chance of winning a decisive victory. These were the Mamluk empire of Egypt and Syria, the Indian sultanate of the Gujarat and the Javanese state of Japara. Each of these states had large vessels which mounted artillery: Portuguese guns were only slightly better than those of the Egyptians and Gujaratis. In the Far East the Chinese occasionally sent out a fleet which could repulse a fair-sized Portuguese squadron and drive it from the shores of Kwangtung, Fukien or Chekiang. Yet in the reign of Cheng-te (1506–22) foreigners generally received a friendly reception near Canton, the city most involved in trade to the south and west. In the Malay Archipelago the sultanate of Malacca and other states could form large fleets of light craft. Their nuisance value was great, but they needed overwhelming numbers to face the Portuguese on the open sea with any hope of success. The same was true of the forces of Calicut, a small state on the Malabar Coast of India. As for the rest of Asia, the large states—Siam, Bengal, the Hindu Vijayanagar empire in South India, the sultanate of Delhi, and Persia—were essentially land empires whose rulers had little interest in naval matters. And at this time Japan was passing through an age of civil wars: its naval activity was mere piracy on and near the coast of China. Most other countries in the East did not have big navies. In these circumstances Portuguese fleets soon wielded great power in parts of the Indian Ocean, though they could not maintain it in many places at the same time.

The nature of eastern commerce also helped the Portuguese. In the sixteenth century the trade of Asia often ran in narrow channels. This tendency increased when valuable products grew only in small areas. For instance, pepper vines grew principally in Malabar, northern and western Sumatra, Kedah and western Java. About 1500 it seems that pepper from the last three places went mostly to China, Siam, Pegu and Bengal. It follows that Malabar then virtually controlled the highly profitable exports of pepper to Europe and the Near East. For the purposes of international trade, ginger was another product found primarily in Malabar, while the best cinnamon came from the nearby island of Ceylon. The so-called finer spices—cloves, nutmegs and mace—throve in an even more restricted area. Cloves grew only in the Moluccas, and nutmeg and mace, which come from the same plant, could be gathered only in and near the tiny Banda Islands, a little to the south of the Moluccas. To reach India, most goods from the Malay Archipelago, together with Chinese exports like brocades, porcelains and musk, had to pass through the Malacca or Sunda Straits, both of which are narrow and easy to blockade. At the end of the fifteenth century a large part of the westward bound trade of China and the Archipelago apparently passed through the port of Malacca. Chinese goods came to India in this way because of the difficulties and expense of transport by land and also because of the power of Malacca and its convenience as a place to pick up exports from the Archipelago, India or the Levant. Further west, trade between India and the Near East went mainly through the narrow waters at the mouth of the Red Sea or the Persian Gulf. Trade suffered yet another limitation, for throughout Asia seasonal winds confined navigation to certain times of the year.

In 1500 much overseas commerce of the countries of Asia lay in the hands of communities of foreign merchants. Arabs predominated in trade to places on the shores of the Arabian Sea. In East Africa they ruled independent cities: on the west coast of India they had strong settlements and influence from Malabar to the Gujarat. Foreign traders were also powerful at Malacca, where Javanese, Tamils and Gujaratis all had important colonies. In some ports most foreigners opposed the Portuguese, who won influence only with the support of a local ruler:

this was what happened in Malabar. In Malacca the situation was partly reversed: some merchants were friendly, others and the ruler were hostile.

These things—the production of certain goods only in small areas, the narrowness of various important channels of trade and the amity of some Asian rulers and merchants—aided the Portuguese considerably. Without such assistance they could never have intervened successfully in eastern trade, for too many markets were specialised and easily upset, or else under a Muslim ascendancy. Given this assistance and Portuguese sea power as well, the position was at least promising. The Portuguese soon found that local rivalries helped as well as embarrassed them. More important, they quickly saw that their fleets could not merely hamper eastern commerce, but seek to deflect it from its course. Where prized crops grew only in small regions, they might think of monopolising them; where trade ran in narrow channels, they might stop it or levy a toll on it. Conditions encouraged the Portuguese to make bold plans. The danger was that they would aim too high. Men were soon at hand with schemes for making new conquests or seizing rich trades: the government was continually tempted to let its ambition outrun its resources. Kings and governors had to bear in mind the limitations of Portuguese power: fortune sometimes gave the Portuguese more chances than they could profitably use.

Despite these advantages the Portuguese did not at once leap into power in the East, nor yet into prominence. Vasco da Gama's expedition was essentially a reconnaissance. He commanded a small fleet of four vessels and about 170 men; he had instructions to deliver letters of credence to the princes that he met, and he may have been told to inform each one that was important and a Christian that the king of Portugal 'was his brother and friend'. He left Lisbon in July 1497. Eight months later he reached Mozambique, one of the East African ports under Arab rule. There he had an unfriendly reception which was repeated farther up the coast at Mombasa, another Arab settlement. Only at Malindi, a rival city of Mombasa, was he well entertained. Thence he crossed the Arabian Sea to Malabar where he anchored off Calicut on 20 May 1498. Gama stayed over three months in Calicut, trying to establish cordial relations with the ruler and to get a cargo of local products. He had little success. Lack of suitable goods for exchange and the antagonism of the powerful colony of Arab merchants prevented him from getting much cargo: the Arabs even helped to cause strained relations between Gama and the samuri,[1] the ruler of Calicut. The Portuguese left Calicut in August 1498 and got back to their own country in June 1499. Besides samples of Eastern goods, they brought back the impression that the Hindu inhabitants of Malabar were Christians of an heretical type.

---

[1] The title samuri derived from Malayalam *tāmāturi* or *tamūri*, meaning sea king. The normal Portuguese version of the title is Samorim.

In the light of this news Manuel I thought that he could seek the samuri's help against the Muslims, to which end he prepared a second expedition. It was far larger than the first, for it comprised thirteen vessels and 1500 men. The commander, Pedro Álvares Cabral, was ordered to establish trading relations and a business agency—a factory— at Calicut, and to land priests for the better instruction of the ruler and people in the Christian faith. After loading a return cargo, Cabral was to explain the attitude of the Portuguese to the Muslims and to give warning that he was bound to attack Muslim vessels on the high seas: he was to go on to urge the samuri to drive the Arabs from Calicut, 'because in this he would comply with his duty as a Christian king, if he would expel them from his country and not allow them to come there nor to trade in it'. Cabral left Lisbon in March 1500 and reached Calicut in September of the same year, but with only six ships. He soon found that the samuri was not a Christian: with this discovery went the collapse of Portuguese hopes of receiving particularly favourable treatment. Cabral got permission to establish a factory, but the Arabs hampered its trade. An attempt to check this obstruction led to a riot in which forty-eight Portuguese were killed and the factory destroyed. Cabral retaliated by burning some vessels and bombarding the town. He then went to Cochin, a rival town of Calicut farther down the coast, whither he had previously been invited. There he set up a factory and obtained a small cargo of ginger and pepper. In January 1501 he sailed for home.

King Manuel's plans had failed. The effort to win an ally in India had come to nothing because it had been based on a false assumption. The attempt to trade had won small success, chiefly owing to the opposition of the Arabs, who had no wish to see their prosperity impaired by their religious adversaries. From 1501 to 1505 the Portuguese in the East were mainly employed in trying to establish themselves at Cochin and Canna- nore, in the teeth of resistance from Arab merchants and their Hindu allies at Calicut. During this time there was little Portuguese expansion farther afield.

In 1502 Manuel sent Vasco da Gama to India to exact reparation for the losses suffered in 1500. Gama confirmed the friendship with Cochin and the enmity with Calicut. In many ways this was unavoidable. Once Calicut became unsafe for the Portuguese, it was natural that they should accept an invitation to Cochin and try to win the rajah's good will. Friendship with the Portuguese tended to strengthen Cochin and thereby roused the hostility of Calicut. Consequently, Cochin had to expect an attack by the samuri after Gama left for Portugal. The rajah of Cochin was ill placed to meet this attack because his state was the weaker power: the only way he could save himself was by calling in Portuguese help. The upshot was that Cochin came to depend on the support of the Portuguese: between 1503 and 1505 it declined in status from a friend to a subordinate.

By the beginning of 1505 Cochin had become a dependent whose defence preoccupied commanders of Portuguese fleets and placed a financial burden on the Portuguese government. Yet the Portuguese had to protect Cochin, for it was their only foothold in the East. If Gama's voyage led to difficulties, it also pointed to their solution. The weakness of Cochin enabled Gama to fix the prices at which he bought pepper there. In 1504 the Crown went a step further: the commander of the fleet going to India in that year was ordered to prevent any vessel leaving Cochin while the Portuguese fleet was in harbour and so to attempt a monopoly. It was possible to turn the dependence of Cochin to some profit. At the same time, the enmity of the samuri was not very terrible. Gama's second voyage affirmed the superiority of a few well-gunned Portuguese vessels over a mass of lightly armed Malabari craft. Above all, Gama's second expedition gave the Portuguese their first large cargo of spices. It made it possible to think that, if the success could be repeated, the money gained from sales of spices in Europe could finance an ambitious scheme of expansion in the East, carried out by the Portuguese alone.

Even before Gama's return the Crown had not confined its attention to Malabar. In 1502 and 1503 Manuel sent small fleets to cruise at the mouth of the Red Sea, with orders to attack Muslim vessels. In 1505 he adopted a much bolder policy. In March of that year he sent Dom Francisco de Almeida to be his viceroy and permanent representative in the East. Almeida had far-reaching instructions. First, he was to establish forts at Kilwa and Anjadiva. Kilwa was a hostile Muslim city on the East African coast and Anjadiva an island off the west coast of India where Portuguese vessels usually called for water on their way to and from the East. Next, Almeida was to start other forts at Cannanore and Cochin.[1] His third task was to sail to the mouth of the Red Sea and begin a fortress in a suitable place, 'so that no more spices can pass to the land of the Soldam (Egypt) and all those of India may lose the notion of being able to trade with anyone but us, and also because it is near Prester John there'. Returning from the Red Sea to Malabar, Almeida was to commence a fort at Quilon (Kollam), a pepper exporting centre which lay to the south of Cochin: the Portuguese had visited it for the first time in 1503. The viceroy was to supervise the loading of cargoes of pepper for Portugal and to deal with Calicut, making peace only if the rajah of Cochin approved and the samuri consented to expel the 'Mecca Muslims', that is, the Arabs. If possible, Almeida was to send vessels to Ormuz and up the Indian coast to Dabul, Chaul and the Gujarat: here the Portuguese were to attack all Muslim shipping: the Muslim rulers of these places might obtain peace only if they agreed to pay tribute and let Portuguese vessels enter their ports to buy supplies for the fortresses. Finally, the king urged the viceroy to send expeditions of discovery to Ceylon, Pegu,

[1] The Portuguese had already built a wooden fort at Cochin in 1503.

Malacca and other places. To carry out these projects Almeida was to have a fleet of a dozen medium-sized vessels and 1500 men-at-arms.

Almeida's instructions marked the beginning of an ambitious and rapid expansion which lasted in full force until Manuel's death in 1521 and gradually petered out in the following decade. In 1505 the Portuguese started an attempt to stifle or check a good part of the seaborne trade of the Muslims in the East: simultaneously, they sought to monopolise the carriage of pepper and ginger to Europe and to increase their power in various regions between East Africa and the Moluccas.[1]

Almeida could not carry out all the plans thrust upon him, but he did achieve a good deal. In 1505 he founded fortresses at Kilwa, Mombasa, Anjadiva, Cannanore and Cochin. In 1506 a fleet which was meant to attack Muslim shipping got off course and paid the first Portuguese visit to Ceylon. In the same year the samuri received a crushing defeat at sea and the Portuguese harried Muslim vessels off the Malabar Coast: in 1507 they carried the campaign north to Dabul and Chaul. In 1506, in response to a reminder from the king who was anxious to forestall a threatened Spanish approach from America, Almeida despatched men to Malacca, but they failed to get beyond the Coromandel Coast. The Viceroy did not establish a fort at the mouth of the Red Sea, but that did not matter. In 1506 the king sent out a fleet to capture the Muslim fort on the island of Sokotra, which he had now chosen as the site for a Portuguese base near the Red Sea, and the task was accomplished in 1507. Most of the vessels went on to India, but a small squadron remained to blockade the entrance of the Red Sea. Its commander, Afonso de Albuquerque, disobeyed his orders and went to Ormuz (at the mouth of the Persian Gulf) which he made tributary to the king of Portugal in October 1507. He began to build a fort there but could not complete it because of local resistance and the desertion of some Portuguese. Meanwhile, other Portuguese expeditions had started forts at Sofala, the southernmost port in East Africa, in 1505, and at Mozambique in 1507.

All this made up considerable and varied activity, but Almeida was soon to reap a whirlwind. Before 1505 Portuguese attacks on Muslims were confined mostly to vessels which plied between Malabar and the Red Sea, and Portuguese successes had been the temporary and partial achievements of visiting fleets. From the time Almeida reached India, Portuguese attacks became more generalised and effective. Muslim states now began to stiffen their attitude to the newcomers. For some time there had been talk of efforts by the samuri to make an alliance with Egypt and the Gujarat, and for some time there had been rumours of an Egyptian fleet coming to annihilate the Portuguese in India. With the growth of Portuguese activities between 1505 and 1507 both the alliance

[1] Cf. also above, pp. 520, 530.

and the fleet became a reality. Towards the end of 1507 an Egyptian fleet reached Diu, in the Gujarat. In March the following year the Egyptians and Gujaratis caught a Portuguese fleet at Chaul and defeated it. The reverse was serious. The Portuguese had already run into other difficulties. Attacks provoked by the Muslim ruler of Goa had partly caused the abandonment of Anjadiva in 1506. In the same year there was a rising against the Portuguese at Sofala; another occurred at Cannanore in 1507. Luckily for the Portuguese, the Muslims did not pursue their victory at Chaul and sail south to attack Cochin. The Portuguese had time to re-gather strength, and in February 1509 the viceroy defeated the hostile fleets at Diu. The battle gave the Portuguese temporary naval supremacy in the Arabian Sea.

A few months later Afonso de Albuquerque became governor of the Portuguese in India, retaining authority until his death in December 1515. When he took office he found the Portuguese feeble on land and strong but misguided at sea. Some fortresses were badly sited, others hampered by local politics, nor had the Portuguese always used their fleets wisely. Albuquerque soon changed matters. A vigorous leader, he built on the power conferred by the battle of Diu. When he died he left behind the beginnings of a maritime empire, with good naval bases, squadrons to command trade routes and a fairly consistent policy towards Asian merchants. Albuquerque impressed his ideas on many aspects of Por-tuguese activities in the East. He scored such notable triumphs that a contemporary wrote: 'Mohammed is cornered and cannot go farther and flees as much as he can...and the truth is that Mohammed will be destroyed and destroyed he cannot help but be.'

One of the keys to Albuquerque's success was his common sense. He related his policy closely to the strength and interests of the Portuguese. He therefore approved the king's wish to monopolise the carriage of pepper and ginger from Asia to Europe and supported the attempt to stifle trade between Malabar and the Red Sea. Nor was he less anxious than Manuel to build up Portuguese commerce in Asia. But he distin-guished better than his master between increasing trade and seizing political power. Thus, he rarely imposed tribute unless, at the same time, he gained permanent authority to collect it and exact other benefits. To do otherwise was to invite a refusal to pay or else requests for aid against local rivals of the tributary state. Albuquerque generally sought to with-draw from entanglements in Asian politics except when a clear advantage accompanied his intervention. He also wished to change the policy towards Muslim shipping. He saw that the indiscriminate attacks of Almeida's time had caused widespread resentment and brought only small sums into the royal exchequer. Even if rich prizes were made, it was hard to stop officials and soldiers defrauding the Crown of its just due. Above all, Albuquerque realised that general Muslim hostility, backed by the sea power of Egypt and the Gujarat, might ruin the Portuguese in the East. The coalition of 1507-9 had not derived from a passing political foible: it had been the reaction of strong and enduring forces which the Portuguese had antagonised.

Albuquerque had little hope of appeasing the Muslims; he therefore strove to weaken the coalition by isolating its members from one another. To this end he wanted fortresses in strategic places: Aden, Ormuz, Diu and Goa were the ones he had in mind; later he added Massawa'. At Goa and at some if not all the other cities he wished to make his countrymen the rulers. He thought that the Portuguese could uphold their claims in Asia only if they had bases that were entirely in their own hands: they would then be free from interference and restraint. Each fortress was to guard a port from which Portuguese vessels could sail out and act against their opponents. Albuquerque was anxious to prevent a second sally into the Arabian Sea by the Egyptian fleet, which he considered the hope and comfort of the enemies of the Portuguese in India. Once the fortresses were built and the Portuguese position in India secure, the way would lie open for an advance up the Red Sea and an attack on Jiddah and, perhaps, on Mecca as well.

Albuquerque's plan involved great military exertions and heavy expenses. To meet the latter he hoped to resolve the old crusading dilemma about trade with the infidels. Commerce was as essential to the Portuguese government in Asia as it had been to the kingdom of Jerusalem. But it was impossible to trade only with Hindus, as Manuel I suggested. 'The Hindus and these native Christians', wrote Albuquerque, with some exaggeration, 'have little capital to destroy the trade and companies of the Moors quickly, for the Moors are rich men with much capital and they trade in a big way and with a large number of vessels.' Trade in the East meant doing some business with Muslims whose commerce was too vast and deep-rooted to be annihilated by the Portuguese. Albuquerque tried to answer this problem by crushing part of Muslim trade and regulating much of what remained. The fortresses he wished to build were not to be mere naval bases. They would lie at important centres of trade whose domination, together with that of Malacca, was to make the Portuguese controllers of some of the chief commerce of Asia. All trade to the Red Sea was to end, but it might continue with other places under licence. In addition, Albuquerque planned to enlarge the king's trade in the East.

In his first year of power Albuquerque seized Goa which he intended to make the central base of the Portuguese in Asia. Malacca followed in 1511. In the same year the Portuguese abandoned the fort at Sokotra: Albuquerque considered the island unsuitable for any useful purpose. In 1513 the governor attacked Aden without success, but his subsequent entrance into the Red Sea was said to have made a strong impression in the East.[1] His attempts to get a fortress at Diu by negotiation failed, but he did manage to end the war with Calicut. In 1513 a new samuri, who had poisoned his predecessor at Albuquerque's instigation, granted the Portuguese a site for a fortress at Calicut and the right of preemption on all pepper. In 1515 Albuquerque revisited Ormuz where he put Portuguese authority on a firm footing. He planned to go to the Red Sea in 1516, but was prevented by his dismissal and death. He had established his country's power from Malaya to the Persian Gulf. By 1515 the Portuguese had considerable political authority on the west coast of India and near the cities of Malacca and Ormuz. They had forts in key positions, and their fleets had a strong influence on the course of trade. On the other hand, he failed to make the Portuguese enterprise financially self-supporting and continually complained of shortages of men, money and materials. Yet the king's trade certainly advanced while he was governor.

Albuquerque was not above error. He probably overestimated the wealth of the Malay Archipelago, and his policy in the Far East may have encouraged too many of his countrymen to go there. He gave trade a yet more important place in Portuguese affairs and may thereby have caused men to think less of war with Muslims. He may also have laid too much stress on the need for forts which Almeida had thought both costly and unnecessary. 'The greater number of fortresses you hold,' the viceroy had written to the king, 'the weaker will be your power. Let all your force be on the sea, for if we should not be powerful at sea everything will at once be against us.' The truth seems to be that Almeida was obsessed by the disaster that would follow a loss of sea power. Albuquerque looked to bases to enable fleets to act more effectively. He may have hoped for too much from the fortresses, but he was generally careful to adjust his policies to the needs and capacity of the few thousand men and few dozen ships that represented Portugal in the East. Despite mistakes, he vastly improved the Portuguese position in Asia. After his death his successors spent much time in trying to consolidate the gains—political and commercial—that he had made.

While Albuquerque was governor the king's trade and administration in Asia became more organised. By 1515 royal trade had already fallen into a routine. The Crown claimed a monopoly of certain items of Asian commerce. The India Ordinances of 1520 defined them as pepper, ginger, cinnamon, cloves, nutmeg, mace, lac, silk and crude borax. No one— Christian, Muslim, Hindu or other—was to trade in these goods without royal permission. Most royal officials were forbidden to do any trade on their own account. These rules were not always observed; both Portuguese and Asians broke them. In the early days it was particularly awkward to enforce the law against trade by Portuguese officials, for many of them were paid partly in kind until the last years of Manuel I. Even after pay-

[1] Cf. above, p. 520.

ment in kind had officially died out, the Crown could not stop its officers trading. Their salaries were frequently poor and sometimes inadequate. Corruption sapped the king's revenue and made it impossible for him to pay his servants well: low pay fostered yet more corruption and a greater tendency to private trade. By the middle of the century private trade seems to have been fairly general among Portuguese officials. Asian merchants obeyed the law when they had no choice: at other times they often seem to have ignored it or bribed their way round it. The Portuguese government could never make its monopolies absolute. By 1550 Asian traders had broken them all, and spices, including pepper, again travelled up the Red Sea. Albuquerque's scheme for licensing Asian shipping never became universal. Scattered Portuguese patrols could not watch over anything like all the seaborne commerce of the East. Strong Portuguese control usually existed only on parts of the west coast of India and near Ormuz; even there smuggling was possible.

The king's trade to Asia was partly organised from the India House at Lisbon which supervised much of Portuguese administration in the East. Every year vessels sailed from Lisbon to Malabar to load spices for the king. The Crown normally chartered ships for the voyage; they were supposed to be distinct from fighting vessels and the India Ordinances laid down that they should take no prizes nor deviate from the course their captains were told to follow. On the outward voyage vessels carried bullion and goods like copper to pay for the spices; they also took arms and stores for the Portuguese. The bullion might come from merchants who wished to secure part of the return cargo in Europe. In the East royal officials usually carried on all the king's trade in the goods he had monopolised. The Crown long bought pepper at Cochin at the price fixed by Gama in 1502: when this fell below the market rate pepper was sometimes hard to get. The cargo sent home varied in size from year to year, but about 30,000 quintals[1] between all vessels seems to have been thought a fairly good load. Records are very fragmentary, but nearly all the cargo seems to have been pepper, especially in the early years. The government in India later sent royal trading vessels to the Moluccas and other places, but it is doubtful if the practice largely increased Portuguese imports of the finer spices. Once cargoes reached Lisbon the Crown generally sold them to merchants, but Manuel I sent some to Antwerp on his own account.

Developments in Portuguese government in the East were no less important than those in trade. The structure of administration was becoming more rigid. Men who served in Asia had their names entered on *matricula* rolls, together with the date of their arrival in the East and the rate of pay they were entitled to. If a soldier were fined or an official's

---

[1] A quintal weighed 128 *arrateis*. An *arratel* of the new weight contained 16 ounces and was equal to the English pound.

accounts found out of order, a note was inserted in the registers, so that the government might retain any money still due to him. Men as a rule had credit balances, for the government soon fell behind in the payment of its servants in the East. Arrears of pay could press hard on a Portuguese man-at-arms, for the Crown seems usually to have given him neither free clothes, weapons nor accommodation. He often had to buy his weapons, but if he purchased them from the government he could have the cost deducted from his pay. If his pay was heavily in arrears, he virtually gave nothing for his weapons.

When men were not paid one of five things tended to happen. A man could sell his pay claim, at a discount, to someone with ready cash. Though illegal, this was always being done. From quite early in the sixteenth century people bought up soldiers' pay and used their own or others' influence to get themselves paid in full by the government. Second, a soldier could try to find a powerful patron to protect him. Portuguese soldiers in the East were not grouped in regular companies or battalions, but were merely attached or attached themselves to individual captains; in time of war a captain would often keep fairly open hospitality to attract the best men into his service. Third, if he could not find a patron, a soldier could become a beggar. Or, fourth, he could sell his weapons. And, finally, he could desert and become an adventurer. Of these five things all but the second—attachment to a patron—were illegal or dangerous to Portuguese power. Partly to remove these temptations, Albuquerque encouraged his soldiers to marry Indian women. He gave land to married settlers (*casados*) and hoped that they and their children would be able to maintain themselves by farming or skill in some craft. In this way the government would have a reserve of men whom it need not pay. The system did not work out as Albuquerque planned. Some places never attracted many settlers: in others the *casados* clamoured for privileges which cost the Crown money.

Albuquerque tried to reform the administration. He tightened the system of accounting and acted vigorously against private trade, but never managed to stamp out corruption. After his death it grew worse, while methods of government became more elaborate in an effort to check it. Representatives of the Crown never found it easy to control men scattered here and there on the coasts and islands of Asia. Officials at outposts were particularly prone to disobedience and sometimes disregarded the governor's orders. Each fortress had its captain or governor who often ruled the fort and the adjacent town. He directed affairs through two or three types of officials. Military and naval officers kept discipline in the garrison and led warlike expeditions; the factor and his underlings carried on the king's trade, collected taxes and disbursed money to cover expenses; in places where the Portuguese had direct authority over the town, local notables sometimes had charge of most of the government of Asians. In the early days the Portuguese showed little interest in their Asian subjects unless they turned Christian. King Manuel laid down that all Christians —Asian and Portuguese—should receive equal treatment, but officials in the East frequently ignored this order. There were many complaints of the arrogance of the Portuguese, who, it was said, did not mix socially with Asians and maintained an effective colour bar. Yet even in the first half of the century this failing was not universal. When at war with Asians the Portuguese were sometimes cruel: it is fair to add that their enemies and friends sometimes rivalled or exceeded them in brutality.

Portuguese in the East tended to be unruly. Each fortress had a Portuguese judge (*ouvidor*) to deal with crime among his countrymen: his bailiff and peons arrested offenders. Gentlemen (*fidalgos*), knights, judges, doctors of law or medicine could not be arrested either in Portugal or the East unless they had committed a crime for which the penalty was death. In other cases they could only be made to give a bond to restrict their movements: in the East this generally meant a form of house arrest. Fortress judges had complete jurisdiction over slaves and ordinary soldiers: other people could appeal to the governor in India in criminal cases. Civil suits could be carried to the governor when they concerned large sums of money. At first, the chief justice in India (*ouvidor-geral da Índia*) disposed of these appeals; not till 1544 did the Crown set up a high court (*Relação*) and chancery for India.

In Goa and Cochin Portuguese settlers soon obtained the right to elect municipal councils: other communities eventually gained the same privilege. In the second half of the century these councils (*senados da câmara*) occasionally acquired considerable influence. They watched over local trade and public works, including hospitals. The State recognised a responsibility towards its sick servants: in nearly every fortress it started and financed, but did not always administer, a hospital for Portuguese. Private charity supplemented this care. By 1520 Portuguese Asia had its first House of Mercy (*Casa da Misericordia*); half a century later it had nearly twenty scattered among important colonies from China to Ormuz. Run by brotherhoods of affluent and literate men and supported by gifts and legacies, Houses of Mercy aided the needy, ran some royal hospitals, and founded others of their own. They also kept an eye on the possessions of Portuguese who died. Strictly, it was the job of a royal official (*provedor das fazendas dos defuntos*) to sequester and then sell such goods. The price they fetched was supposed to be credited to the dead man's heirs in Portugal or elsewhere, with allowances to pay off his debts and reward the *provedor* for his services. The vigilance of Houses of Mercy helped to check fraud and loss. In the early days the State itself undertook work of charity: it distributed alms to 'poor Christians of the country and the children of necessitous Portuguese'.

Portuguese Asia had no regular civil service, with a neat hierarchy and ingrained respect for routine. The king granted office as a mark of favour: men obtained it on his judgment of their merits, as a reward for past efforts or as a recognition of promise for the future. They were appointed as individuals rather than as people taking normal steps in a *cursus honorum*. Their triumphs and failures in the East were primarily personal. Portuguese administration in Asia stressed the individual rather than the system. Its co-ordination was weak and it lacked *esprit de corps*. Fortresses were often troubled by disputes between officials. Such quarrels spelt danger in the years just after Albuquerque's death. He left his successors two immediate legacies, but the Portuguese could attain neither without discipline and resolute effort. One was the desire for a fortress at Aden and an advance up the Red Sea, the other an interest in expansion in the Far East. In 1516 the first seemed important. A new Egyptian fleet had assembled: though in the end it achieved nothing, it appeared threatening for a time. The Portuguese did not do much better. Two of their governors led futile expeditions into the Red Sea in 1517 and 1520. Small Portuguese fleets sailed to blockade the entrance to the Red Sea in 1516 and 1518: the first never reached its destination, the second did little.

The Portuguese had more success in the Far East. The years from 1512 to 1520 were the heyday of their expansion in south-east Asia. Albuquerque had hoped that trade there would help finance wars west of Ceylon. After he conquered Malacca he took steps to revive its commerce. Lesser men backed his efforts vigorously: vessels soon left Malacca to trade with Bengal, Pegu, Sumatra, Kedah, Java, the Moluccas, the Bandas, Pahang, Patani, Siam and China. In 1519 the Portuguese even tried to find a mythical island of gold, said to lie south-west of Sumatra. Most of these Portuguese voyagers were fairly peaceful, but they sometimes attacked Muslim shipping. News or rumours of this habit won them a bad reception in Bengal in 1518 and in Pegu in 1521.

The expansion may have been too swift: it was certainly hard to govern. There were complaints of overstocked markets and a fall in the price of goods that the Portuguese wished to sell. Just as serious was the cry that most profits from trade were going to private men. Once or twice, Crown and governors made feeble attempts to assert the royal monopoly of trade in spices in the Malay Archipelago, but they dared not act strongly for fear of ruining merchants at Malacca. Military dangers also confronted the Portuguese in that city: in 1513 they had to beat off an attack by a large Javanese fleet from Japara, and from 1512 to 1526 they were frequently harassed by followers of the ex-sultan of Malacca. Malay plots, and deaths and dissensions among Portuguese officials, added other trouble. After 1520 misfortunes multiplied and Portuguese expansion came gradually to a halt. It received a big check from the growth of Spanish interest in the Spice Islands—the Moluccas. Spain claimed that the line of demarcation fixed by the Treaty of Tordesillas ran right round the world, with the Moluccas falling in the area allotted to herself. Avoiding an open challenge to Portuguese authority, her kings did not send vessels to Asia by the Cape route but preferred to look for a strait which would lead through the New World to the eastern seas. From the days of Columbus men had sought this passage without success. In 1518 Manuel learned that the king of Castile, soon to be the Emperor Charles V, was preparing a fleet which was to go to the Spice Islands by the yet undiscovered westward route under the command of Ferdinand Magellan. The Portuguese government took alarm. Magellan was a Portuguese who had recently entered Spanish service: he had spent some years in the East and been present at the capture of Malacca in 1511. If he failed to find a new route, he might go by the old one which he had already used. Thus the king took up the challenge from Spain. At the same time he showed much ambition to increase his power in Asia where he was very aggressive in the last years of his reign. Between 1519 and 1521 he ordered seven new fortresses to be built in the East: China, the Moluccas, Sumatra, the Maldives and Madagascar were to have one each, as were the north Indian ports of Chaul and Diu. Two fortresses—those in China and the Moluccas—were clearly intended as bastions against Spanish encroachment. Magellan's voyage has already been described;[1] here we may note that a Portuguese expedition, arriving at Tidore after the Spanish vessels had left, seized the men left behind and confiscated their goods. In June 1522 the Portuguese began to build a fortress at Ternate, another island in the Moluccas.

The Spaniards had failed to hold their own in the Spice Islands, but the Portuguese feared that new Spanish expeditions would sail to the East. In 1524 representatives from both sides met between Badajoz and Elvas to decide the questions of the possession and ownership of the Moluccas; the discussions soon turned into wrangles and failed to settle either matter. Anticipating this conclusion, the new king of Portugal, John III, gave revealing orders to Vasco da Gama who sailed for India in April 1524 to become viceroy. Ever since he had ascended the throne in 1521, John III had adopted a more cautious policy than Manuel I, and his wariness grew in face of the continued danger from Spain. The viceroy received orders to demolish four fortresses in India, Ceylon and Sumatra, but was told to build one at Sunda, that is, in western Java. These orders are a sign of the financial state of the Portuguese enterprise in the East. It is doubtful if the Crown's annual receipts from the sale of cloves, nutmegs and mace in Europe before 1524 ever approached, at most, one quarter of the money obtained from sales of pepper at Lisbon and Antwerp. True, royal agents sold the finer spices in Asia, but so they sold pepper. Despite the spread of Portuguese activities in south-east Asia from 1511 to 1520, it is likely that the financial basis of Portuguese power in the East still lay where

[1] Above, pp. 568f.

Gama had put it in 1502—on pepper. It even appears that the *Estado da India*—a name which the Portuguese used as a general description for their conquests in Asia—depended heavily on the Crown's trade in pepper from East to West and the stability of pepper prices in Europe. The upset of either would probably have thrown the Portuguese government in Asia into difficulties. The home country, with its small resources, could then have given little help. The importance of pepper apparently accounted for the instruction to build a fort at Sunda—a pepper-producing area which the Spaniards might well visit—at a time when other fortresses were to be given up. In 1525 the king probably sent the governor orders which again stressed the importance of Sunda. The Crown was as keen as ever to prevent competition for supplies of pepper, but now seems to have been ready to give up its open monopoly of the finer spices of the Moluccas. The orders of 1525 were drafted in the knowledge that another Castilian fleet was about to leave for the East. It sailed in July 1525, but only one of its seven vessels reached the Moluccas—the flagship, which arrived off the island of Geilolo in October 1526. The crew of this one vessel, reinforced from the New World in 1528 and helped by the sultan of Tidore, caused much trouble until it capitulated to the Portuguese in October 1529. Five months previously the emperor had sacrificed his claims in the treaty of Zaragoza.[1]

Meanwhile, the Portuguese had suffered defeats in China and near Malacca. In 1521 the Chinese broke off relations with the Portuguese; in the following year they repulsed a small fleet whose commander had come from Portugal with orders to start a fortress near Canton. In 1521 the Portuguese failed to capture Acheh[2] and Bintan: the first was the capital of a rising sultanate in North Sumatra, the second the island stronghold of the ex-sultan of Malacca, lying south-east of the Singapore Strait. The Portuguese founded a fort at Pasai, in North Sumatra, in 1521, but abandoned it in 1524. In the next year Malays from Bintan besieged Malacca. Not till 1526 did the situation in Malayan waters improve, with the ejection of the ex-sultan of Malacca from Bintan. But Acheh was now a threat to the Portuguese at Malacca, while three attempts to found a fortress at Sundra misfired between 1526 and 1529.

West of Ceylon the chief Portuguese troubles were revolts in Ormuz and wars with the Gujarat and on the Malabar Coast. Plans for fortresses in the Maldives and Madagascar had soon collapsed; elsewhere, the fort at Colombo was given up in 1524, after six years' occupation; the fort at Calicut met the same fate in 1525. As a crowning evil, 1527 was a year of bitter disputes over the succession to the governorship. Yet the 1520's were not wholly bleak. Afonso Mexia, the financial superintendent of Portuguese India from 1524 to 1531, improved methods of administration,

---

[1] Cf. above, p. 569.
[2] Often written as Achin on English maps.

and Lopo Vaz de Sampayo, unchallenged governor from 1527 to 1529, built up a strong navy. Between 1523 and 1528 the Portuguese managed to send four fleets to blockade the entrance to the Red Sea. They also gained success in war against the naval forces of Diu, culminating in a crushing defeat of the Gujaratis in 1529.

By that time the Portuguese in the East had passed out of their age of gold. As an enterprise of State, Portuguese Asia had begun to contract: the vision of its rulers had narrowed. In a long governorship of nine years (1529–38) Nuño da Cunha fixed most of his attention on the west coast of India, where he won small gains at heavy cost. He entangled the Portuguese more deeply in local affairs and his policy was less coordinated than Albuquerque's. Yet he awoke no sense of great decline: if the age of bronze had arrived, some people still mistook it for gold. Cunha sailed for India in 1528. Three thousand men-at-arms went with him: never before, said the chronicler Castanheda, had such a brilliant company gone to Asia under the Portuguese flag. He reached India in 1529 and soon began vigorous war on the Malabar Coast. In 1531 he started a fortress at Chaliyam, six miles from Calicut. At first, he did not neglect the Red Sea: fleets sailed to blockade its entrance in every year from 1531 to 1534. He had orders to build a fortress at Diu, a task which preoccupied him for most of his term of office. In 1531 he led to Diu the most powerful armada the Portuguese had ever gathered in India: it is said to have mustered over 100 vessels with eight thousand men, three thousand of them Portuguese. This force failed to do more than bombard the city and harass the nearby coast. The Portuguese again raided the coast of the Gujarat in 1532 and 1533. The sultanate was then in sore straits, for it was at war with both the Portuguese and the newly established Mogul empire of northern India. In 1533 the sultan tried to buy off the Portuguese by giving them land for a fortress at Bassein, on the east side of the gulf of Cambay. Less than two years later Cunha pressed his advantage further and extorted a treaty which gave him a site for a fortress at Diu.

Disputes between the Gujaratis and Portuguese did not end after the Portuguese got their long coveted foothold at Diu. Each side distrusted the other. In 1537 the sultan was killed in a scuffle with Portuguese in the harbour of Diu. Cunha then tried to support one of the two claimants to the throne. With the defeat of the governor's candidate by his rival, the Portuguese position at Diu became critical. A truce with the new sultan eased the tension for only a short time. In June 1538 the Gujaratis laid siege to Diu; during the past year the Portuguese had occupied the city as well as their fort. By August only the fort remained to them. Worse was to come. The Gujaratis had previously sought help from the Ottoman empire, which had conquered Egypt and Syria in 1516–17. The Turks, who had a strong navy, were ready to act, and on 4 September 1538 a large

Turkish fleet anchored in the port of Diu.[1] The peril of 1508 had revived. Powerful enemies had coalesced. The arrival of the Turks in India showed how mistakenly the Portuguese had followed out Albuquerque's plans. The great governor had insisted on fortresses at Aden and Diu, but he had put Aden first and he had stressed the need for naval operations in the Red Sea. In the 1530's Crown and governor were apparently obsessed with the idea of a fortress at Diu. They became blind to the importance of the Red Sea: between 1535 and 1538 Cunha did not send a single fleet there. In September 1538 it seemed that his neglect would reap a terrible reward. Luckily for the Portuguese, dissensions among their enemies caused the departure of the Turkish fleet in November 1538. Diu still held out, and in 1539 a newly arrived Portuguese viceroy obtained peace with the Gujarat. The Portuguese now turned their attention to the Red Sea where they planned to attack the Turkish fleet; they also hoped to capture Aden. An expedition did sail to the Red Sea in 1541; some of its members reached Suez, but they found the defences too strong for an assault on the beached galleys of the Turks.

The 1530's saw crises east of Ceylon, but none proved insurmountable. Malacca passed through wars with Johore and Acheh between 1534 and 1537, but survived them without much harm. In the Moluccas the Portuguese experienced worse troubles, especially while the avaricious Tristão de Ataíde was captain of the fortress at Ternate. During his time (1533–6) most of the islands of the Moluccas rose against the Portuguese who were nearly driven out. Ataíde's successor, António Galvão, had to quell the rising. He did rather more besides. In the four years that he stayed in Ternate he so won the affection of the people that they are said to have called him the father of their country. In Bengal the Portuguese met with hostility in 1533: the ruler only became friendly when he was hard pressed by enemies. Despite disturbances in south-east Asia and India, private Portuguese commerce probably increased in many parts of the eastern seas during this decade. The State might suffer, but some private men prospered.

The great problem of Portuguese Asia was still finance. Though Albuquerque had meant to provide the government with ample revenue, he had never succeeded: some of his plans were never carried out, while others proved too sanguine. But at least he saw that the *Estado da India* must raise enough money to support itself. After his death the Portuguese government did not always give sufficient thought to this question. In the 1530's it spent heavily on fleets and armies which it used for un-remunerative schemes, thus increasing its needs without attempting to satisfy them. Corruption among officials made matters worse. The kings of Portugal never received all their rightful Asian revenue in the sixteenth century and they frequently paid in excess for goods and services. John III

[1] Cf. also above, p. 521.

tried to check the misdeeds of his servants, but it was hard to control men who were far from Portugal and subject to strong temptations. Few reforms seem to have won permanent success and, since before 1520, tale-bearers said that abuses in Asia were getting worse. Consequently, the extra expenses of the 1530's forced the king to borrow large sums which he could ill repay. He got deeply into debt: in 1544 he owed nearly two million cruzados, an enormous sum. For the rest of the century poverty oppressed the Portuguese government in Asia and its weakness gradually became apparent to all. Until Cunha relinquished office the decline of Portuguese power in the East was more real than observed: thereafter, the government's severe shortage of money revealed the truth. Lack of men was also becoming acute. Desertion from the king's service seems to have grown after 1530: it was probably given a fillip by the outbreak of wars in Pegu and Siam, where a number of Portuguese served as mercenaries. In addition, it may be fair to point to a spiritual decline. The Portuguese could still fight well, but they seem to have lost much of the zest of their early days in the East. Few now spoke of destroying Muhammad. In part, a less warlike attitude was natural as the Portuguese came to have more commercial and other contacts with the Muslims.

In the 1540's two governors tried to improve the financial position. Martim Afonso de Sousa (1542–5) gained money for the king by debasing the coinage at Goa and by sending Simão Botelho to reform the customs collection at Malacca. Outside Portuguese possessions, the governor meddled in the politics of Bijapur, the Indian state nearest Goa, to the profit of himself and the Crown. Sousa's successor was Dom João de Castro who hoped to cut down expenses. He failed to do so because of renewed war with the Gujarat. Neither Sousa nor Castro found the answer to the financial difficulties of the Portuguese, and when Castro died in 1548 the king still had costly entanglements in India and large debts at home. In 1552 he owed nearly three million cruzados.

Two things probably saved the Portuguese enterprise in the East from accelerated decline. One was a spiritual revival; the other was the development of private Portuguese trade in Asia.

Priests had always served with the Portuguese in the East. The Franciscans founded a convent at Goa in 1517, and in 1538 the city became the seat of a bishopric. In the early days the Church ministered chiefly to Portuguese and their families; missionary work was not one of the main activities of a clergy who sometimes failed to maintain high standards of behaviour among fidalgos or themselves. This situation changed after Francis Xavier reached India in 1542. One of the first members of the Society of Jesus, Xavier travelled about Asia for the next ten years until he died 'a poor and humble death, not unperplexed'[1] on an island off the coast of China. During his stay in the East Xavier gave the Portuguese

---

[1] J. Brodrick, *Saint Francis Xavier* (London, 1952), p. 526.

a new ideal of proselytism to replace the dying ideas of religious war; he also taught them to accept a stricter religious discipline.

Xavier and his successors achieved much. As time passed the Jesuits and members of other orders kept a closer watch on the faith and morals of the Portuguese in Asia. In 1557–8 the creation of the archbishopric of Goa with suffragan sees at Cochin and Malacca gave some help in this task; more powerful aid came from the establishment of the Inquisition at Goa in 1560. The orders paid attention to education and built many churches. With the support of the secular power, particularly in the time of a devout viceroy like Dom Constantino de Bragança (1558–61), they made many converts among the Indians near Goa. The State issued decrees which gave privileges to converts. Outside Portuguese possessions the religious won victories from Sokotra to Japan. Before 1542 few Portuguese priests in Asia showed much interest in their surroundings, but the Jesuits and other religious now learned Asian languages and made some study of Asian beliefs and doctrines. In some places they tried to convert the ruler, thinking that if he were won his subjects would follow him. Elsewhere they laboured among humble people. Xavier himself showed special concern for the poor fishermen of the Cape Comorin Coast and baptised many of them. Other Jesuits carried on the work: in 1552 the Christians there were said to number 60,000 with thirty big churches. In Ceylon the young king of Kotte became a Christian in 1557. In 1579 Akbar, the greatest of the Mogul emperors, sent to ask for some learned priests. With high but mistaken hopes three Jesuits went to his court in 1580. Little could be done in Malaya and Sumatra, but the Dominicans began a mission at Solor, in the Lesser Sunda Islands, probably in 1562. In the Moluccas Christianity suffered several ups and downs, but, though driven from many places, it was still holding out in Amboina in 1580. In China the missionaries made little progress before 1583. Japan was the scene of greater achievement, notably in the island of Kyushu. By 1580 there were eighty-five Jesuit missionaries in Japan and it was reported that the number of converts was 150,000. Five-sixths of these Christians lived in Kyushu, mostly on the lands of lords who had turned Christian. By 1583 it was estimated that there were 600,000 Christian converts throughout Asia.

While Jesuits worked with missionary zeal, private Portuguese merchants developed a rich trade between Asian ports. This commerce flourished in the second half of the sixteenth century and in 1580 was probably more prosperous than ever before. The Crown did not share in the success. It had never managed to control private trade in Asia: at most it got customs duties and frequently it got nothing. It had concentrated on the trade from Asia to Europe which expenses and Arab competition made less profitable after 1550. In the 1570's the king even farmed out his monopoly of trade by sea between the two continents.

Only one branch of private trade fell under strong royal influence—the Japan trade, which was perhaps the most profitable of all.

The Portuguese probably discovered Japan in 1543. Soon afterwards they began a trade between China and Japan which circumstances made lucrative for them. China forbade its subjects to go abroad and had, since 1480, closed its ports to Japanese. Yet she needed Japanese silver and Japan wanted Chinese silks. Smuggling could satisfy only part of these markets, leaving the Portuguese to supply the remainder at a high profit to themselves. The Portuguese strengthened their position in China after they obtained a permanent foothold at Macao in 1555. From that time their relations with the Chinese authorities gradually improved. In Japan the Portuguese made important trading contracts with Kyushu. After 1571 they sailed chiefly to the island's new port of Nagasaki; until 1590 the government of the town lay virtually in the hands of the Jesuits and the commanders of Portuguese voyages. By 1550 Portuguese commerce with Japan was already a royal monopoly. Every year the king or his viceroy in India allotted the trade to a captain-major of the voyage of China and Japan. Sometimes the Crown sold the privilege to make the journey: even if it did not do so, customs duties gave it a share of the large profits. Revenue from the voyage became a mainstay of the government, but could not prevent the decline of the *Estado da India* as a political force.

The new revenue was all the more needed because the Portuguese financial position had grown worse in Europe. The king of Portugal had relied mostly on Antwerp for loans, but its financiers were less able to lend after the monetary crisis of 1557. Even before this occurred, lack of money made Portuguese action in the East mainly defensive. In 1552 the Turks tried to capture Ormuz, but failed. In the next two years the Portuguese scored some success in two sea fights with the Turks in the Persian Gulf. But they did not counter-attack in the Red Sea, as they had done after the first siege of Diu. Between 1554 and 1580 they were much occupied with petty wars and campaigns in Ceylon and on the west coast of India. Portuguese intervention in Ceylon developed rapidly after 1539. It started as an effort to protect the friendly king of Kotte; later it was influenced by the desire to spread the Christian faith. Wars and sieges punctuated the history of Portuguese relations with the Sinhalese and by 1580 the island was yet another expensive entanglement for the Portuguese government. War in India also increased the financial burdens of the Crown: among other things it led to the foundation of new forts at Daman, Mangalore, Honavar and Basrur.

In the Malay Archipelago the Portuguese suffered many attacks. Between 1550 and 1580 Malacca had to face five onslaughts: three of them were made by Acheh, which was striving for dominance in Sumatra and the Malay Peninsula. In 1571 the home government tried to improve affairs by creating a separate governorship for Malacca: the holder of the post was probably meant to conquer Acheh. Lack of resources caused the plan to fail. In the late 1570's there were naval combats between the Portuguese and the Achinese, especially near the Singapore Strait where the Portuguese inflicted three defeats on their enemies. But the danger was scotched, not killed. In the Moluccas continual fighting and disputes led the Portuguese to evacuate the fortress at Ternate in 1574, though they still maintained footholds in Tidore and Amboina. Spanish interest in the western Pacific was another threat to them in south-east Asia. In 1542 an expedition left Mexico to found a colony in the 'Western Isles', afterwards called the Philippines. It failed. Just over twenty years later, in 1564, another expedition, which comprised four vessels and 350 men, set out from the New World under the command of Miguel López de Legazpi. The Spaniards reached the Philippines in the following year and were favourably received. They founded a settlement at Cebu and then, very slowly, started to extend their power to other islands. The Portuguese tried to expel them in 1569, but were driven off. Two years later Legazpi occupied Manila, in Luzon. Unlike Portuguese outposts in the East, Spanish establishments in the Philippines were primarily colonies of settlement, though, under an ambitious governor in the late 1570's, Spaniards thought up a madcap scheme for the conquest of China. In the same period they also tried, without much success, to gain authority at Brunei. Despite these projects, the Philippines gradually settled down into the normal Spanish colonial system. An *audiencia* was established at Manila in 1583. Any military danger to Portuguese possessions from the Philippines disappeared with the union of Portugal and Spain in 1580, news of which reached Goa in 1581. It raised no outcry there or at any other place in Asia. The *Estado da India* passed peacefully into the hands of Philip of Spain, who promised that his Portuguese and Spanish colonial dominions would remain separately organised.

Philip had gained control of the Portuguese government in the East, but that government was already past its prime. True, it preserved a certain grandeur. The number of fortresses had never been bigger; the administration was highly elaborate. Yet the State was growing weaker. It was continually in debt and usually hard pressed if it had to equip a special expedition. It could not even disguise its predicament. The poorest soldiers could see what was happening and had favourite explanations for it. According to them, all evils reduced to two: the poverty of the government and the misconduct of officials. There was some truth in this assertion, but it did not completely account for the decline. As early as Albuquerque's time there was corruption and a shortage of money. At bottom, the strength of the State had never lain in a full treasury and a pure administration. It is more likely that, at the beginning of the sixteenth century, Portuguese power in Asia rested on two bases: unity of purpose between the king and his servants, and the strength of the Portuguese fleet.

Unity was vital. The distance of India from Portugal not only made it hard for the king to control his subjects in the East: it made it almost impossible for him to compel their assistance for any long period. At the same time, fidalgos and officials often had high notions of their rights. Apart from legal privileges, they sometimes claimed the right to advise the king's military commanders. If a commander refused to heed the fidalgos' counsel, he might have to face their obstruction or even desertion. Most serious of all, fidalgos, knights and royal servants frequently thought they had a special title to the king's bounty. They tended to consider office in the East as a reward for past services. Consequently, there was always the chance that they would make the reward as large as possible, generally by interfering with trade or administration to the detriment of the king's revenue. Far away in Portugal the monarch could do little to check these misdeeds. Private men could severely hamper Portuguese government in the East; sometimes they might almost paralyse it. If the king wished to gain success in Asia, and if his government there was to flourish, private men had not only to accept his aims, but of their own free will help achieve them. In the time of Manuel I the Portuguese in the East seem to have had a broad unity of aim. On smaller matters, such as a plan for a battle or the division of spoils, they differed many times, but they generally agreed that they were in Asia to fight Muslims and seize their trade. On this large issue king, merchant, military leader and priest could all come to terms. In those early days the general aim of Portuguese enterprise in the East could embrace selfish and unselfish desires at the same moment, with little conscious contradiction. In Asia it seemed that to profit from trade was to smite the Muslim, and that to smite the Muslim was the way to profit.

Two things gave this unity practical force in the reign of King Manuel. The first was the vigour of Portuguese life; the second was the king's direction of enterprise overseas. At the beginning of the sixteenth century the energy which the Portuguese showed in Asia and Africa was paralleled by a stir of activity at home. Manueline decoration, the dramas of Gil Vicente, notable experiments in poetry, the spread of classical studies and advances in nautical science, law and administration all date from this period. And in Asia the king's control reinforced action, for Manuel at least prevented his subjects from scattering their efforts disastrously. United in spirit and under one director, the Portuguese swept round the Eastern Seas between 1500 and 1520. However, by this latter date, purpose had already started to weaken. Affairs in the East were more complex than the king had first assumed. Duty and interest did not coincide on every occasion. The Portuguese government in the East did not always profit when Muslims were killed: at the same time it needed profit, for it could not live without it. Albuquerque tried to resolve this dilemma, but his success was limited and his methods opened the way to increased corruption. After his death the State's policy grew distracted and more doubtful; correspondingly, private men became less ready to accept the king's control. By 1540 the old balance of ideals and interests had almost completely disappeared. Thoughts of religious war were in the background: most priests and laymen had ceased to regard Portuguese enterprise in the East as a crusade, except in a remote sense. In a crisis Portuguese would generally still rally to defend the fortresses of their king: Portuguese possessions could still put up a tough defence when attacked. At other times private men worked chiefly for their own good. Deprived of their close support, the Portuguese government in the East declined. In the 1570's it could only defend its possessions and try, here and there, to snatch a small advantage. Though the Portuguese had kept their vigour, it was expressed in the second half of the sixteenth century in missionary activity and widespread private trade, while the State now took second place.

Thus, by 1580, Portuguese government in Asia was weak. What authority it retained it owed largely to the second basis of its power—the fleet. The early success of the Portuguese had shown that fleets and fortresses could be used to gain control of part of the seaborne trade of Asia. In the second half of the sixteenth century fleets still gave the *Estado da India* some influence which was not seriously challenged till the Dutch arrived in the East in 1595. Even then, the next 150 years saw the working out of the lesson which the Portuguese had taught: throughout that time strength at sea was one of the major foundations of European power in Asia.

INDEX

Alberti, Leon Battista, Italian architect, 402
Albuquerque, Afonso de
  Portuguese governor in the east, 591,
    598–601, 602, 604, 608
  reduces Ormuz (1507), 597
  attitude to trade with Muslims, 599, 613–
    14
  dismissal and death (1515), 600
  concentration on sea power, 600
  attempts to reform administration, 602
Alcalá, university of, 292, 427–8
Alchemy, persistence of interest in, 403–4
Alciati, Andrea, Italian scholar, 372
Alciati, Giovanni Paolo, and Anti-Trini-
  tarianism in Poland, 206, 207
Aldrovandi, Ulissi, naturalist, 392, 407
Aldus, see Manutius, Aldus
Aleander, Girolamo, cardinal
  and Erasmus, 81, 90
  at the Diet of Worms (1521), 81–2
  and the Frankfurt Interim (1539), 176
  lectures at Paris, 418
Alençon, clandestine printing at, 213
Alençon, duchy of, united with France
  (1525), 440
Aleppo, 511, 524, 525, 531
Alexander I, king of Poland, grand duke of
  Lithuania, 186, 473, 538–9, 547
Alexander VI, Pope (Rodrigo Borgia), 252,
  539
Alexander of Ville-Dieu (Dolensis), his
  school textbooks, 416, 418, 424–5
Alexandria, the spice trade at, 531
Alexandrovskaya Sloboda, 554
Algiers
  failure of Charles V's expedition (1541),
    181, 325, 336, 351, 506, 531
  lost to Spain (1516), 324; controlled by
    Khair ad-Dīn Barbarossa, 324; under
    Turkish suzerainty, 517, 532; alliance
    of corsairs with Turks, 518, 520;
    attack on Malta (1565), 532
'Alī Beg, Turkish admiral, 531
'Alī Pasha, beglerbeg of Buda, 526
'Alī Re'īs, Turkish admiral, 530
Allstedt, Münzer at, 86–8, 111
Almaden, mercury mines at, 313
Almagro, Diego de, companion of Pizarro
  in Peru, 575, 576–7, 578
Almaza, Miguel Perez de, royal secretary
  in Spain, 447
Almeida, Francisco de, Portuguese viceroy
  in the east, 596–8
Almsgiving, see Social relief
Altdorf, 109
Altenburg, reform in, 86
Altieri, Baldassare, and Protestantism in
  Vienna, 262–3

Altomünster, 104
Alva, Fernando Alvarez de Toledo, 3rd
  duke of, 65, 329, 357
Alvarado, Pedro de, 569
  his expedition to Guatemala (1523), 567;
    in Peru, 576
Alvarez, Emmanuel, Jesuit, 425
Amadis of Gaul, 381
Amasia, 513, 516, 528, 530
Amazon, river, descended by Orellana
  (1541–2), 587
Amboina, Portuguese at, 612
Amboise, the Placards, 220
Ambrogini, Angelo, see Politian
America, Spanish
  the Spanish conquest and the beginnings
    of the ascendancy of Europe, 21
  missions of the religious orders, 298,
    565–7; plans for Camaldolese founda-
    tions, 278
  administration: the Council of the Indies,
    333, 445, 573; the encomienda system
    (q.v.), 564–5; the audiencia, 569–70,
    570–1; assertion of royal control, 571–
    4, 578–80, 590; occasional election of
    governors, 588; the New Laws, 588;
    legal theory and administration, 588–9
  agricultural economy, 581–2
  trade with Spain, 584–6; Castilian
    monopoly, 312, 584; Welsers' interests
    in Venezuela, 313; export of precious
    metals, 321–2, 333, 589; effect in
    Europe of thei ntroduction of specie,
    16; essential to Spanish dominance in
    Europe, 335; ultimately harmful to
    Spanish economy, 589–90; prohibition
    of trade between viceroyalties, 583;
    English and Portuguese interlopers,
    585–6; the slave trade, 585–6
  see also Chile; Indians; New Galicia;
    New Granada; New Spain; Peru;
    Venezuela
Amsdorf, Nicholas, bishop of Naumburg, 86
Amsterdam, 51–2, 62, 313
Anabaptism in, 127, 131
Amyot, J., his translation of Plutarch, 382
Anabaptists, 70
  rejection of civil authority, 5–6, 97, 102,
    123, 133; the Schleitheim Confession
    (1527), 125; attacked by Calvin, 114, 129;
    by Cranmer, 130; and cf. Communism;
    Law; Pacifism
  the Zwickau prophets, 84, 110, 119–20
  Münzer's relations with, 88, 128
  condemned in Confession of Augsburg
    (1530), 94, 124–5
  and Zwingli's service of 'prophesying'
    101

Brandenburg-Ansbach, George, margrave
of, 93, 429
see also Prussia, Albrecht of Brandenburg-
Ansbach, duke of
Brandenburg-Culmbach, Albert Alcibiades,
margrave of, 182, 357, 480
Brandenburg-Küstrin, John (Hans), mar-
grave of, 357
Brandenburg-Prussia
rise to power associated with Russian
and Turkish pressure, 21
peasantry, 35–6
Braniewo (Braunsberg), Lutheranism in, 201
Brantôme, Pierre de Bourdeilles, seigneur
de, 498
Brask, Hans, bishop of Linköping, 146–9
Brassó (Kronstadt), Lutheranism in, 198
Bratislava, *see* Poszony
Braunsberg, *see* Braniewo
Brazil
dye-wood trade, 61, 586
Jesuit missions, 298, 299, 586–7
Portuguese settlements, 586–7; conflict
with Spain, 587–8
agriculture and population, 587
Bremen, joins the Schmalkaldic League, 350
Brenz, Johannes (Johann Brentzen), 104
and the Reformation in Schwäbisch Hall,
86; eucharistic controversy with Oeco-
lampadius, 91, 105; in Württemberg,
166; refuses to accept the Augsburg
Interim, 183; composes Confession for
the Council of Trent, 184, 185
Brescia, 288–9
Breslau, 53, 424
Brethren of the Common Life, 167
multiplication of manuscript texts, 360
educational work, 417
Briceño, Isabella, 266
Briçonnet, Guillaume, minister of Charles
VII, 214
Briçonnet, Guillaume, bishop of Meaux
biographical summary, 214–15
his defence of traditional doctrine, 215
denounced, 216–17
his death (1534), 219
Brie, trial of heretics in, 224
Brieg, principality of, official adoption of
the Reformation, 165
Briesmann, Johannes, 159
Brittany, united with France, 440
Brno (Brünn), Ferdinand of Habsburg
summons federal parliament, 467
Broet, Paschase, 292, 299
Bromberg, *see* Bydgość
Brucioli, Antonio, 251
Brueghel, Peter the elder, Flemish painter,
403

Bruges
establishment of Portuguese spice-staple
(*c.* 1460) and transfer to Antwerp
(1499), 50, 55; commercial supremacy
passes to Antwerp, 51; Italian banking
firms move to Antwerp, 53; treatment
of foreign merchants, 55; Spanish
merchants at, 304
road communication with Cologne and
Antwerp, 53
early printing at, 362
Bruges, Treaty of (1521), 341
Brunfels, Otto, his work in botany, 407
Bruni, Leonardo, *see* Aretinus
Bruno, Giordano, 400
Brunschwig, Jerome, *de arte distillandi*, 404
Brunswick-Grubenhagen, Ernest, duke of,
joins the League of Nuremberg (1538),
354
Brunswick-Grubenhagen, Philip, duke of,
joins League of Schmalkalden (1531),
350
Brunswick-Lüneburg, Ernest, duke of, and
the Diet of Speyer (1526), 92; signs
the *Protestation* of Speyer (1529), 93;
joins League of Torgau (1526), 340;
and Schmalkalden (1531), 350
Brunswick-Lüneburg, Francis, duke of, at
Diet of Speyer (1526), 92; joins League
of Schmalkalden (1531), 350
Brunswick-Lüneberg, Otto, duke of, joins
League of Schmalkalden, 350
Brunswick-Wolfenbüttel, Henry, duke
supports resort to force, 179
joins League of Nuremberg (1538),
354
driven out by the Protestants (1542), 354
Brussels, 317, 318
Convention of (1522), 339–40
Bucer, Martin (Kuhhorn), German theologian and Reformer, 17, 181, 261
his reform in Strassburg, 86, 108–110, 112;
eucharistic views and attempts to reach
agreement, 91–2, 111–12, 161, 162, 166,
167–70; and the Tetrapolitan Confession, 95, 111, 161; takes refuge in
Ebernburg, 104; and Oecolampadius'
plan for church discipline, 106, *and cf.*
115; his *De Regno Christi* and the
'gospel of hard work', 107; attitude to
the *jus reformandi* of the magistrates
and concern for church discipline, 109;
and the Peasants' War, 109; marriage,
110; his order of baptism, 111; his views
on pastoral care and doctrine, 111, *and
cf.* 115; his missionary zeal, 111, *and cf.*
70; refusal to sign Augsburg Interim, and
exile, 112, 183; his character and repu-

657

Schmalkaldic League, 149, 168, 173
  formation (1531), 162, 163; and member-
    ship, 350
  negotiations for inclusion of Zwinglians,
    162-3, 164, 166
  negotiations with Charles V and Peace of
    Nuremberg (1532), 163-4, 176
  attitude to attendance at a general
    council, 170, 171, 172-3
  negotiations for alliance with England
    (1535), 171, 240, and cf. 238, 239
  the Frankfurt Interim (1539), 175-6
  exclusion of the duke of Cleves, 180
  refusal of support to Hermann von Wied
    in Cologne, 181
  preparations for war with Charles V,
    182-3
  revolt in Bohemia in support of (1547),
    202, 472
  appeal to, from Venetian Protestants, 263
  desertion of Philip of Hesse (1541), 354;
    and of Maurice of Saxony (1542), 355;
    Hesse rejoins (1544), 355
  restoration of duke Ulrich to Württem-
    berg (1534), 353
  its influence against imperial unity, 479
Schmalkaldic War (1546), 112, 331, 354-6,
  479-80, and see Mühlberg
Schnepf, Erhard, 166
Schoeffer, Peter, copyist and printer, 361
Schöning, Thomas, archbishop of Riga, 159
Scholasticism
  Luther and, 71, 73, 74, and cf. 72, 75
  reformers' rejection of scholastic cate-
    gories in explanation of the eucharist,
    91
  Zwingli's studies, 97, 98
  and scientific inquiry, 392
  see also Duns Scotus; Occam; Thomas
    Aquinas, St
Schools, see Education
Schwäbisch Hall, 86, 166
Schwarz, Theobald, 86, 110
Schwarzach, imperial victory (1554), 357
Schweinfurt, 111, 163-4
Schwenckfeld, Caspar, radical reformer
  and mystic, 110, 119
  relations with Anabaptists, 124, 126, 127,
    131
  Agricola's Finnish translations, 155
Schwendi, Lazarus von, 489
Schwertler (men of the sword), Anabaptists,
  respect civil authority, 123
Science
  emergence of scientific attitude, 1, 4-5,
    412-13; continued influence of human-
    ism, 17
  use of the vernacular, 383-4, 411

  persistence of classical and medieval
    ideas, 387-93 passim, 403, 406, 411-12
  instrument-making, 388, 394, 395, 402
  the influence of printing, 389-91
  artistic skill and scientific illustration,
    390-1
  application to engineering, 402
  in secondary education, 419
  biology, 406, 407
  botany, 406; herbals, 390, 392, 407-8
  chemistry: evidence of Islamic descent,
    391; practical work and observation,
    393; persistence of interest in alchemy,
    403-4; the iatrochemical school, 403,
    405-6, 411; industrial applications,
    404-5
  mechanics, 401, 402
  optics, 388, 402
  physics, 387, 389, 401-2, 412
  physiology, 406, 410-11
  zoology, 406, 407
  see also Astronomy; and (including
    Anatomy) Medicine
Scotland, 8, 362, 438, 490
Secemin, Cruciger at, 204
Sects, see Anabaptists
Secundus, Johannes, Basia, 369
Segovia, 319, 585
Seklucjan, Jan, 201, 501
Selim, I, Ottoman Sultan
  extends Ottoman power, 347; acknow-
    ledged as suzerain of Algiers, 324;
    conquest of Egypt, 510, 511, 521;
    victory at Tchaldiran (1514), 516
  see also Ottoman Turks
Seripando, Girolamo, cardinal
  and the movement for Catholic reform,
    270; reversion to orthodoxy, 272
  associated with Valdés, 266
  and Council of Trent, 266, 274
  his Platonism, 266
Servetus (Miguel Serveto y Reves), 110, 262
  his Errors of the Trinity, attack on Calvin,
    and burning (1553), 117, 129, 132, 268
  his work in medicine, 117, 411
  and Anabaptism, 124, 129, 268
  destruction of copies of his Christianismi
    Restitutio, 364
Servi, emancipation of, in Italy, 25, 48
Seven Years' War, between Sweden and
  Denmark (1563-70), 559
Seville, 352, 563, 568, 584
Seysell, Claude de, political theorist, 459, 462
Sforza, Francesco Maria, see Milan,
  Francesco, duke of
Shah Ali, Khan of Kazan Tatars, 549
Shakespeare, William, 17, 415
Shari'a, law of Islam, 532, 533